Applied Business Statistics

second edition

Applied

HOLDEN-DAY, INC. *San Francisco*

London · Dusseldorf · Singapore
Sydney · Tokyo · New Delhi · Mexico

Business Statistics

second edition

Elam E. McElroy

Associate Professor
Marquette University

APPLIED BUSINESS STATISTICS
Second Edition

500 Sansome Street, San Francisco, CA 94111

Library of Congress Catalog Card Number: 78-62068
ISBN: 0-8162-5535-0

Printed in the United States of America

234567890 809

Acquisition & Development Frederick H. Murphy
Production Supervision Michael Bass & Associates
Production Assistant Barbara Gordon
Editing Douglas Bullis
Text Design Michael Bass
Creative Graphics Lorena Laforest Bass
Cover Design Lorena Laforest Bass
Technical Illustrations Carl Brown
Layout Michael Bass
Composition Pace Publication Arts, Inc.
Printing Book Press

to Irene,
Randy, and Mark

Contents

Preface

This second edition of *Applied Business Statistics* prepared for undergraduate students of business and economics resulted from a revision, updating, and expansion of the first edition. It contains the basic statistical methods but is somewhat different from most of the textbooks in that it has a more adequate discussion of data collection and presentation which are highly important to the field of statistics. It has a somewhat broader coverage of multiple correlation than many comparable texts. It also has more extensive coverage of index numbers and time-series analysis than most business statistics books designed for the typical undergraduate student.

The relevance of statistics in business and economics is brought out through examples and exercises which have been based on both actual and life-like data and situations. As the title implies, emphasis is placed on the practical application of statistical methods rather than theory and derivation of formulas. Business and Economics students with sound backgrounds in elementary algebra should be able to handle the mathematics without difficulty.

The first nine chapters could be used for a first semester course and the last nine for second semester course. However, the instructor of a one-semester course who wishes to move faster can use the first nine chapters and Chapters 11 and 12, or 12 and 14. A one-semester accelerated course for students in economics might incorporate the first nine chapters, Chapter 12 and Chapters 14–17. Several other chapter combinations can be made to fit an instructors particular needs. Also, an instructor in a one-semester course could use all of the chapters but omit certain topics. For example, the material on correlation of grouped data in Chapter 12 and the graphic method of measuring seasonality in Chapter 17 could be omitted.

I am grateful for the assistance of numerous people in the preparation of the revised manuscript. Helpful suggestions were given by Professors James Beckett, L. B. Blackwell, John Chiu, David D. Farris, Ke. T. Hsia, Ronald S. Koot, Robert A. McLean, Gerald T. Simon, and Edwin A. Swanson. Thanks are extended to Joseph Ragonese, a graduate assistant, for checking the accuracy of many of the problems and to Dolores Rewolinski who did a superb job of typing the manuscript.

I am also indebted to the Literary Executive of the late Sir Ronald A. Fisher, F.R.S., to Dr. Frank Yates, F.R.S., and to Oliver and Boyd Ltd., Edinburgh, for permission to reprint Tables A-4 and A-5 from *Statistical Tables for Biological, Agricultural and Medical Research*. I appreciate the assistance of Michael Bass, Douglas Bullis, and Holden-Day executives and employees in the preparation of the manuscript and production of the book.

ELAM E. McELROY

Milwaukee, Wisconsin
September, 1978

1

Business Statistics – Foundations for Decisions

Business firms, government agencies, and numerous other types of organizations routinely apply theories and tested methodologies in collecting, presenting, analyzing and interpreting quantitative data. When you study these theories and methodologies you are studying "statistics." In this sense, then, statistics is a body of knowledge or a subject of study rather than just a collection of data, figures, or numerical facts.

A *statistician* is not, as many people believe, one who merely assembles numerical data. He designs experiments and analyzes their results, which hopefully lead to the accumulation of additional information upon which useful decisions may be based. To do this he uses the methodologies discussed in this book and perhaps many that are too complex to be included in a first course in statistics. Statisticians have their own particular terminology, as we are about to discover.

USES OF STATISTICS IN BUSINESS

Estimating and Projecting

Statistics, as we have defined it, is comprised of a variety of methods that enable businessmen, economists, and others to make better decisions because they help maximize the accuracy of the estimates and forecasts upon which such decisions are based. Three of the main tools of estimating and forecasting are sampling, time series analysis, and regression and correlation analysis.

Sampling. The subject of sampling encompasses the scientific methods used to select and analyze samples of universes, or populations. A *universe,* or *population,* consists of all elements or members of a well-defined group that is to be investigated; a *sample* is a subset of a universe. For example, if an analyst wishes to determine what percentage of the households in the Dallas, Texas, metropolitan area have color television sets, then the universe consists of *all* households in the Dallas metropolitan area, while a sample consists of *some* of those households. When we use a scientifically selected sample in a study, we can estimate characteristics of the universe from which the sample has been drawn and test hypotheses concerning both sample and universe values. A properly conducted sample study provides information about the universe much more quickly and cheaply than a study of the entire universe. For this reason, more and more sample data are being published by private organizations and government agencies. Many economic indicators consulted by businesses to facilitate decision-making are composed partly or entirely of sample data. Such indicators include the Consumer Price Index, the Index of

Industrial Production, Value Added by Manufacture, and series that show what part of the working force is employed or unemployed.

A businessman needs a good knowledge of sampling theory and practice so that not only will he use the right methods to conduct a sample study, but also so that he will be able to evaluate sample data from other sources to analyze and solve his problems. Sampling theory and the analysis of sample data are the subjects of chapters 8, 9, 10, and 11.

Time series analysis. Time series analysis, which is analysis of data classified by years, quarters, months, or other periodic intervals, is mainly a tool of forecasting. Analysis of time series data reveals past patterns of growth and change that often can be averaged or measured in such a way that a projection into the future can be made. Both long-range and short-range projections can be used to determine what the volume or level of business activity will be in the future. Some of the basic methods for making projections are covered in Chapters 16 and 17.

Regression and correlation analysis. Regression and correlation analysis, or analysis of the nature and closeness of the movements of two or more sets of data, are also tools of estimation and forecasting. For example, we might find that changes in retail sales and income in a given area move in such unison over a period of time that an accurate estimate of sales could be made, based on income projections.

The subject of correlation probably is not entirely foreign, for you have certainly read of the relationship between the amount of smoking people do and the rate of occurrence of certain diseases. You undoubtedly have observed too the relationships between alcohol consumption and drunkenness, food consumption and body weight, and studying and learning.

In Chapter 12 we will study the correlation analysis of two variables. Multiple correlation, which concerns the associated movements of three or more variables, is covered in Chapter 13.

Management Areas Using Statistics

Almost every part of a business organization uses statistical methods in its operations. Some of these are discussed below.

Marketing research. Suppose the marketing research department of a firm wants to find new markets for the company's products. To do this they need data on the characteristics of potential customers in the proposed market areas. Only part of the necessary data may be available from published sources, so a field survey requiring the formulation of questionnaires and the selection of a sample may be called for. The researchers would use the statistical methods for surveying, sampling, and analyzing their data.

Sales management. If the sales manager of a firm wants to estimate sales potentials in established territories in order to evaluate the performance of his salesmen, he must gather and analyze data concerning each territory. Incidentally, this might be done for the sales department by the marketing research department.

Personnel management. The personnel department of a firm uses statistical methods to keep management apprised of the makeup of the firm's work force. If, for example, the board of directors wants an estimate of the cost of a proposed pension plan, they need data on the age composition of the firm's employees. The statistical methods discussed in this text could be used by the personnel department to provide management with simple measurements indicating age composition rather than, say, a long list of the employees' ages.

Production management. Statistical methods are used in controlling the quality of products as they are being manufactured, in time and motion studies, and in inventory control. Statistical quality control operations are often supervised by an engineer with training in scientific sampling theory.

Economic analysis. Economic analyses and forecasts of general economic conditions in the nation, in specific geographic areas, and in industry aid in planning sales campaigns, inventories, production volumes, plant expansions, and employment levels. Statistical methods are used in collecting and presenting economic information and so must be used to analyze and interpret the data. The economist, in predicting general business levels, makes extensive use of time series analysis and correlation analysis.

Accounting and finance. Statistical techniques also aid in the analysis of accounting and financial records. For example, sampling techniques are useful in auditing, and time series analyses provide a tool for long-range planning.

STATISTICAL METHODS

In order to solve a problem, a businessman must have facts pertaining to the problem. These facts must be gathered in a manner that assures their accuracy and authenticity and then assembled and presented so that their general characteristics become evident. Moreover, mathematical analyses are often required to reveal the detailed characteristics and nature of assembled facts. It is important to interpret the results of these analyses correctly because decisions are based on interpretations. A general discussion of these aspects of statistics will help you to understand the more detailed discussion that follows.

Collecting Data

When gathering data we must choose the sources carefully. Published data should be selected from sources with established reputations for reliability. Data obtained directly from the files of organizations or from individuals should be solicited only from those held in high esteem by the public or by professional societies and business organizations. When information must be gathered by surveys taken by interviewers or by means of mail questionnaires, certain rules and procedures should be applied if useful information is to be obtained. When samples are selected from which to collect data, techniques based on sampling theory should be used. Chapter 2 gives a detailed discussion on many aspects of data collection, and Chapter 8 provides a somewhat comprehensive discussion of types of sample used in collecting data.

Presenting Data

Masses of unorganized figures are of little or no value. They must be assembled in systematic groups or classifications. Charts or graphs often aid in showing significant aspects of the data. Statistical tables and charts must be organized so that their intent can be easily understood by the reader. The rules or guides that have been developed for determining the general format, proper classifications, dimensions, rulings, and wordage for tables and charts are discussed in Chapter 3. When properly applied, these rules enable us to present numerical information more effectively, with the least bias.

Analyzing Data

Tables and charts showing simple classifications of data do not always reveal or describe important characteristics of the data. Therefore, we may need to compute statistical measures that *describe* these characteristics or enable us to *make inferences* about an entire body of data from which a sample has been selected. These measures may be simple ratios, percentages, or averages, or perhaps, geometric averages, standard deviations, secular trends, confidence intervals and coefficients of correlation. These are some of the statistical measures discussed in Chapters 4 through 18. When you have learned how to compute them, you will be able not only to use these tools to analyze business problems, but you will also have a foundation for learning more advanced statistical techniques.

Interpreting Data

When we interpret data, we decide what the comparisons and analyses mean and draw conclusions. Many correct interpretations require only the application of common sense. To insure a high degree of accuracy in interpreting the results of a statistical study, however, we need a sound understanding of the nature and characteristics of statistical measures. Moreover, we must understand how and why data are often misinterpreted. Reasons for misinterpretations are discussed next.

MISUSE AND MISINTERPRETATION OF NUMERICAL DATA

Your study of statistics will enable you to make effective use and proper interpretation of the data you have collected, organized, and analyzed. However, you also need to be constantly aware that numerical data can be abused, misused, and wrongly interpreted, especially by people who have no formal training in statistical methods. Inaccurate data lead to wrong interpretations, which lead to poor decisions. Just because figures are *published* does not mean that they are accurate and useful; just because information comes from a *study* does not mean that the information is truthful; and just because the information is *numerical* does not mean that it is accurate.

Errors in data, misuse of data, and wrong interpretations often result from any of the following: unscientific studies, subjective bias, noncomparable data, inappropriate calculations, incorrect charts, improper assumptions, conditional forecasts, spurious accuracy, carelessness, or *lack of knowledge*. A brief discussion of these hazards will illustrate the need for caution when using and interpreting numerical data.

Unscientific Studies

All kinds of studies are made and published to provide information to the public. Before we can accept and apply the results of any study, however, we should know how it was conducted. For example, studies often involve the use of poorly constructed questionnaires or *published* figures that are of questionable accuracy and reliability. Also, studies made from a mail survey can often be misleading because of a bias resulting from nonresponse on the part of many people who receive questionnaires; and many surveys made by mail or by interviewing respondents might be inaccurate for a variety of reasons, such as poor memories of respondents and dishonesty on the part of the interviewers or respondents. For example, a survey questionnaire sent to members of a certain professional group contained a list of book titles, some of which were fictitious, and asked the respondents to check the books they had read. When the replies were tabulated it was found that a large number of the respondents had checked titles of nonexistent books.

A thorough discussion of the survey type of study and how to conduct one is presented in Chapter 2.

Subjective Bias

Human subjectivity can affect any part of a study and can seriously mar its value. For example, a researcher's interpretation of an objective measure can bias the reader. If research reveals that government spending increased 10% in one year, one analyst might write "government spending *leaped* 10%" while another might say "government spending *rose only* 10%." Although both statements are based on the same fact, the psychological impact on a reader would differ. It is important to be alert to the influence of such subjective bias so that we can take it into account.

Noncomparable Data

When analyzing relationships, we should ascertain whether the data are comparable, that is, whether they originate from the same base and are equivalent in what they measure. Differences in definitions are a main cause for noncomparability of data. For example, the population of the Milwaukee, Wisconsin, metropolitan area increased from 871,000 in 1950 to 1,453,000 in 1976; a growth of 67%. This figure can be misleading, however, because in 1950 the Milwaukee metropolitan area was composed of Milwaukee County only, but by 1976, the metropolitan area was defined geographically as Milwaukee, Ozaukee, Waukesha, and Washington Counties. A fairer comparison for most purposes requires a constant definition. Using the 1976 four-county definition, the population of the Milwaukee metropolitan area grew from 980,000 in 1950 to 1,453,000 in 1976, an increase of only 48%. The latter comparison shows the change in the concentration of people in an area of constant size and would be more valuable for marketing and economic planning.

Another example of data that are noncomparable are university enrollments listed in a recent edition of a popular almanac. Some universities have large evening divisions with numerous part-time students and large enrollments in non-credit adult education programs. Figures for such universities are not comparable to those for a university with few or no part-time students. To make comparisons, enrollment data for each university would need to be adjusted to an equivalent, full-time student basis.

Inappropriate Comparisons

A newspaper article mentioned that a certain softball player had, at the end of the conference games, a batting average of 66⅔%, the highest average of all players in the league. The article did *not* explain that this player had batted only three times and had gotten two hits, whereas some of the other players with lower averages had been up to bat 30 to 40 times. The performance in three times at bat is not likely to represent the batting ability of any player, so the comparison was inappropriate.

Incorrect Charts

Relationships among data can be biased and distorted by improperly prepared charts. Certain rules of chart construction must be followed if an accurate graphic presentation of data is to be made. These rules, together with examples of both good and bad charts are given in Chapters 3 and 15.

Inaccurate Assumptions

Faulty assumptions are often to blame for estimates that are far from the actual value. For instance, population estimates, by age group, were made by assuming that the percentage distribution of population by age was the same for a particular city as that for the entire United States. This assumption proved approximately correct for age groups that are not highly migratory. For the 20–29 age group, however, the assumption led to a wide margin of error in the population estimate because many people in this age group had migrated from farms and small towns to the city, causing the proportion of the total population in that age bracket to be much higher than for the nation as a whole.

A retail executive once stated that there was less shoplifting in the shopping center where his store was located than in any other shopping center in the city. He said this because fewer shoplifters had been apprehended in his shopping center, assuming that there was a relationship between apprehension of shoplifters and incidences of shoplifting. Could it be, however, that the shoplifters in that particular center were slicker thieves or that the police there were less efficient in the performance of their duties?

Sometimes assumptions can never be proved true or false, but extremely careful thought should be given to the logic of the assumptions before drawing conclusions from them.

Conditional Forecasts

Most of us have heard speakers who said nothing in ten thousand well-chosen words. Some economic forecasters are experts at this. Reduced to one sentence some lengthy economic forecasts say merely that "if economic conditions don't change they will remain the same."

Economic forecasting is easy for anyone who makes forecasts conditional. For example, a forecaster might predict that "wages will increase if prices rise" without saying what will happen to prices. Another might predict that "we will have full employment and rising wages if consumer and investment spending continues to rise" without predicting the pace of consumer and investment spending. These examples, of course, are somewhat exaggerated, but the type of reasoning they illustrate is sometimes encountered.

Spurious Accuracy

You may have heard it said that "Figures never lie." Not so. The publication of a large figure can lead to wrong inferences concerning the accuracy of its measurement. An example occurred when the chamber of commerce of a large city conducted a survey of visiting convention delegates to determine how much they were spending. They concluded that delegates spent $10,202,079 during the year. This figure was the actual result of their calcuations. The publication of so precise a figure, however, attributed a degree of accuracy that was spurious. In fact, the survey was conducted in such a way that the estimate might have been off by a million dollars or more. A more acceptable, more realistic estimate would have stated that "about $10 million" was spent.

A similar situation is exemplified by the population signs posted along highways. In 1977, the population of the Village of Bayside, Wisconsin, was posted as 4,338. This, however, was the population count according to the 1970 census. The population in that village had grown considerably by 1977 and was estimated to be around 5000. Thus, we must be wary of large figures that show an exact magnitude to the last digit. They could be misleading.

Carelessness

Sometimes different, equally reasonable conclusions can be drawn from the same facts, making it difficult to determine which, if any, is right. For example, from the same set of facts a labor union might conclude that wages are too low while management might decide that they are too high. Difference conclusions such as these may result from different philosophies, leaving the way open to honest debate.

Not all interpretations can be justified or defended, however. An example of misinterpretation of data, which was probably due to carelessness, comes from a newspaper article that concluded that "an executive's pay in small and medium-sized companies did not keep up with the firms' soaring sales performance in 1976."*Giving the figures that apparently were used to draw this conclusion the article went on to say that out of 8000 companies surveyed, 68% enjoyed increased sales, but of these companies, only 57% of their executives reported an increase in salaries and 17% reported a decline. The figures compared, however, do not indicate whether increases in *total* sales in the firms outpaced increases in *total* executive pay, which would be required to substantiate the conclusion. In fact, from the figures given, it would be difficult to correlate sales to executive pay because some executives in each of the firms could have gotten pay increases, and the average executive pay increase could have been relatively larger than the average sales increase for the firms.

*From the *Milwaukee Journal,* August 19, 1969.

Lack of Knowledge

While carelessness in comparing figures, as in the previous illustration, can account for misinterpretations, lack of knowledge also can lead to misinterpretations. Because the U.S. Consumer Price Index is often referred to as "cost-of-living" index, some people think that it can be used to compare the cost-of-living in one city to that of another. Therefore, a person might conclude that in May 1976 it cost more to live in Detroit than in Chicago because in that month the consumer price indexes for those cities were *167.5* and *163.7*, respectively. Once the person understood that the Consumer Price Index measures only *changes* in consumer prices, he would realize that the only possible conclusion is that from the base period (1967 = 100) the price index rose by a greater percent in Detroit than in Chicago. Since we do not know the relative costs for Chicago and Detroit in the base period, we cannot evaluate the present relationship. Only by knowing the characteristics and meaning of the statistical measures can we compensate for a lack of knowledge of the data being compared.

THE ELECTRONIC COMPUTER

The electronic computer has resulted in more and better economic and business data for the businessman to use in analyzing his problems, enabling him to process a given amount of numerical data quicker and at lower cost than was possible before the computer age.

As statistics students, you need to become familiar with mechanical and electronic data-processing equipment. While many of you will take at least one course in data processing or computer technology, for the purposes of this course you need to learn the basics of computer capabilities and of complementary business machines in order to work intelligently and efficiently with computer programmers and analysts.

Computer Uses in Business

When the volume of work to be done is large or the calculations repetitious or routine the computer often can be used efficiently and at a reasonable cost in view of the amount of time saved.

Statistical analysis. Certain types of statistical analyses, for example, multiple correlation analysis, were not often made in the pre-computer days because calculations with mechanical desk calculators were burdensome, required a lot of time, and therefore, were costly. Today the multiple correlation analysis of a large number of variables can be performed in a short time. Also, computers are used to calculate trend projections, seasonal indexes, index numbers, and other statistical measures. The availability of "canned" programs makes it unnecessary to write a program for every statistical analysis to be made on a computer. To use some of these programs the analyst needs only to type four or five simple instructions and in a few minutes the analysis will be made and returned in printed form.

Simulation. Computers are used to develop and apply mathematical models to help the businessman solve problems. For example, a firm might develop a model that simulates its entire operation to aid in decision-making.

The computer enables the analyst to feed a lot of data into a model to test a large number of alternatives for action and get estimates of the outcome. He can also test, improve, and refine a model to make it a useful management tool.

Record keeping and clerical operations. In business, computers are used mostly for keeping records and performing clerical operations. Thus they provide executives with a constant and instant source of information for decision-making. For example, the computer can give an executive the supply of any item in the inventory at any time and also calculate the weekly pay of thousands of workers in a few minutes.

Computers enable airlines to provide instantaneously information on available seating space on any flight, thus assuring greater accuracy in making and confirming flight reservations.

Banking and other financial institutions can record deposits and withdrawals and keep up-to-the-minute records of the balances of individual checking and savings accounts.

Careless Acceptance of Computer Output

There seems to be a tendency for people to accept without question any analysis made by a computer. In other words, they feel that if the computer did the work the findings must be true. A businessman must be careful not to make this error. If biased data are fed to a computer, biased answers will be returned. An input of unreliable data will result in an output of unreliable data, or, as the current expression goes, "garbage in—garbage out."

Hand Calculators

Electronic hand calculators are becoming as common to business as pencils and paper. There is such a wide range of capabilities, qualities, and prices that the choice of a calculator is not easy. Some calculators have built-in programs to compute many of the statistical measures discussed in this book. However, these programmed calculators are of little help in learning the basic principles and concepts of statistical methods. Generally, a calculator that will perform the four arithmetic functions and compute square roots is sufficient for a first course in statistics. However, calculators with additional capabilities, such as the computations of logarithms, reciprocals, and *n*th roots, expedite the calculation of many of the statistical measures that you will study in this book.

REVIEW QUESTIONS

1. Does *statistics* mean *statistical methods?* Explain.
2. What are statistical methods?
3. What business areas use statistical methods to solve problems?
4. Why is *presentation* of data necessary?
5. Data that come from a "study" are always reliable. True or false? Explain.
6. What do we do when we *interpret* data?
7. What uses does business make of statistics in making decisions?
8. Can accurate data be misused? Explain.

9. Explain some of the ways that numerical data can be misused or misinterpreted.

10. Published data are more accurate than unpublished data. True or false? Explain.

11. In city A unemployment increased by 100% in one month. In city B unemployment increased by 50% during the same period. Therefore, economic conditions have gotten worse in city A than in city B. True or false? Explain.

12. Men have more auto accidents than women; therefore women are better drivers than men. True or false? Explain.

13. An association of business organizations has 242 member firms. In 1969, 124 of these firms responded to a survey and it was found that nine percent of all their employees were nonwhite. A year before, 153 of the member firms reported that eight percent of their employees were nonwhite. Based on these findings the association concluded that nonwhite employment was on the upswing in member firms. Could this conclusion be false? Why?

14. Why is an electronic computer useful in analyzing data?

15. What can computers do?

16. Calculations made on an electronic computer are more reliable than those made without a computer? True or false? Explain.

2

Collection of Data

Statistical methods, we learned in Chapter 1, include methods of collecting data. It is important, therefore, to have a basic knowledge of the types of classifications. Also, we should become familiar with some of the published sources of business and economic data and develop a background in the methods used to secure raw data.

CLASSIFICATIONS OF DATA

Data used by a business firm in its solution of problems are classified as external or internal and primary or secondary.

External and Internal Data

External data are those from sources outside the firm. *Internal data* come from company records relating to the company's activities.

If an economist in a firm uses figures on industrial production in the United States in an analysis, he is using external data. When he analyzes figures on the firm's production volume, inventory volume, employment, and sales he is using internal data. Both types of data are often used to analyze a firm's performance and to forecast future operations. For example, a firm may compare its own output over the past several months or years to output in the United States for the same period to see if the firm is keeping pace with national growth.

Primary Data

Data collected through mail surveys or personal interviews are called *primary data*.

Moreover, data obtained directly from the organization that originally collected them are primary data. For example, population figures for the United States obtained directly from the U.S Bureau of the Census are classified ''primary'' because that is where the data originated.

Secondary Data

Secondary data come from a source other than the one that originally compiled them.

Population data compiled by the Census Bureau, but taken from a textbook, newspaper, or a source not published by the U.S. Bureau of the Census are classified "secondary."

It is advisable, as a general rule, to use primary data in statistical analysis because they are likely to be more accurate or reliable than secondary data, which are sometimes rounded, combined, or adjusted so that the original accuracy is lost. Moreover, explanatory notes clarifying the meaning of the data are often left out of secondary sources.

SOURCES OF DATA

Sources of data are classified as published or unpublished, and published sources can be subgrouped into primary and secondary. The *Annual Survey of Manufactures*, published by the U.S. Bureau of the Census, contains only primary data because the Bureau itself gathers the data by surveying manufacturing firms. On the other hand, the *U.S. Industrial Outlook for 1977*, issued by the U.S. Business and Defense Services Administration, is a secondary source because its data is collected from other publications and organizations.

Many published sources contain *both* primary and secondary data. Perhaps one of the most widely used sources on the United States economy is the *Statistical Abstract of the United States*, published annually by the U.S. Bureau of the Census. It contains economic and business data on almost every subject you could name. These data originate from government agencies and private organizations, as well as from the Bureau itself. It is highly recommended as a source for papers in economics, finance, and marketing.

Hundreds of publications carry economic and business data, and there are books available that list the numerous sources: A large number of publications containing data on economic and business activity could be listed here, but this would be of little value unless you were to investigate each source and study its contents. The only way to discover good sources of data is to use them; therefore, only a few key sources will be named with the hope that you will investigate them, making at least a cursory examination of their contents.

Publications of Private Organizations

Many private organizations publish data that are useful in solving business problems. Three of general interest are:

1) *Survey of Buying Power*, a special annual issue of *Sales, Marketing and Management*, gives annual estimates of population, retail sales, income and buying power indexes for cities, counties, and states in the United States. Data for Canadian cities and counties are also given.
2) *Editor and Publisher Market Guide*, a publication that is issued annually, provides data on population, retail sales, income, and other market data for a large number of cities in the United States and Canada.
3) *A Guide to Consumer Markets* is published by the National Industrial Conference Board. This volume provides a variety of information, most of which is statistical data on population, employment, income, expenditures, production, distribution, and prices.

Studies by the U.S. Bureau of the Census

Numerous separate publications result from census and sample studies conducted by the U.S. Bureau of the Census, so only the general title of each study is given.

1) *U.S. Census of Population*. Publications with this main title result from the population censuses conducted every 10 years since 1790. They contain detailed information on certain characteristics of the U.S. population, such as the number of people by age, sex, race, and occupation.
2) *U.S. Census of Housing*. These reports include data on types, nature, conditions, and value of housing and are published in conjunction with the population census.
3) *U.S. Census of Manufactures*. These publications contain data on manufacturing activity in the United States that are gathered approximately every five years.
4) *U.S. Census of Business*. Separate publications are released for retail trade, wholesale trade, and service establishments. The censuses are conducted about every five years.
5) *U.S. Census of Transportation*. This census study was first released with data gathered for 1963; others are planned for about five-year intervals.
6) *U.S. Census of Agriculture*. These books are published every five years, after each new study is made.

Monthly Publications

Four popular, monthly publications that contain up-to-date monthly indicators of economic activity are:

1) *The Survey of Current Business*, published by the office of Business Economics of the United States Department of Commerce.
2) *The Federal Reserve Bulletin*, published by the Board of Governors of the Federal Reserve System.
3) *Business Conditions Digest*, published by the Bureau of the Census, United States Department of Commerce.
4) *Economic Indicators*, published by the Congressional Joint Committee on the Economic Report.

Data Directories

Because of the very large number of private and public volumes of statistical information available, a researcher finds data source directories of great value. Two such directories are:

1) *Statistics Sources*, published by the Gale Research Company, is a guide to sources of data on thousands of subjects. It cites periodicals, yearbooks, directories, and other compilations of private and government organizations.
2) *Bureau of the Census Catalog* is a quarterly directory that lists the publications of the Bureau of the Census during the past quarter, classified by subject and geographical area. A monthly supplement is available for those who need to be informed immediately about new publications.

Organizations as Sources

Information not available in published form sometimes can be obtained from the files of organizations such as chambers of commerce, trade associations, professional associations, and from government agencies at the federal, state, and local levels.

Private organizations. There are thousands of trade and professional associations from which information can be obtained. Directories listing the names and addresses of these are useful research tools.

The Board of Governors of the Federal Reserve System collects and disseminates most of the data on banking in the United States. In addition, each Federal Reserve Bank compiles data on its own district.

Organizations such as the U.S. Chamber of Commerce and the National Industrial Conference Board conduct numerous economic studies and make the findings available to their members and to the general public.

Almost every city has a chamber of commerce that keeps economic information on its city. Many trade associations have collected and maintain data about their members. An automobile dealer's association, for example, is likely to have information on automobile sales.

Government agencies. A businessman should be aware of the government agencies that he can contact for information. Thus, a general knowledge of the bureau and departmental structure of the government at each level is a valuable asset when searching for data. You should know, for example, that the Bureau of the Census in the U.S. Department of Commerce and the Bureau of Labor Statistics in the Department of Labor provide most of the general economic and business data used by businessmen and economists. In fact, every cabinet secretary heads a department that provides data on its activities, and much unpublished information can be obtained from them. The Bureau of the Census sells special tabulations and classifications of data it gathers, but does not publish in the census reports. The computer has enabled the Bureau to do more of this in recent years.

COLLECTION PROBLEMS

A problem that most researchers frequently face is that of collecting data worthy of analysis. Sometimes the only data available that relate to the subject being studied are noncomparable, sometimes the reliability of available data is questionable and sometimes no data at all are available.

Noncomparable Data

You have been warned about the dangers of using noncomparable data; therefore you should understand the necessity of collecting comparable data. However, if only noncomparable data relating to a topic of study can be found, adjustments can sometimes be made to approximate comparability. When this cannot be done, all or part of a research project may have to be abandoned.

Doubtful Reliability of Data

Sophisticated statistical analysis of data that may be unreliable is a waste of time. Often an analyst must use figures on population, sales, employment, production, and other series that have been estimated by crude methods, so the accuracy of these estimates may be unknown or unmeasurable. It is important to know the extent of the accuracy or reliability of the data in order to choose appropriate techniques and interpret the results accurately.

Nonexistent Data

Another disheartening fact occasionally confronted by a researcher is that the desired data are not available and that reliable data cannot be obtained because records have not been kept or because those who have the data will not release them. For example, there are no figures for the 1920's and 1930's that are comparable to many of the economic indicators we use today to gauge the pace of the U.S. economy. Sometimes data are available in the files of business firms, but cannot be obtained because they are confidential or because the cost of compiling them is prohibitive.

When a researcher finds that the data he needs have never been collected, he may be able to get raw data by means of a mail survey or a field study. Field studies requiring interviewers can be expensive and time consuming. Both time and money can be saved, however, if representative samples are selected and analyzed rather than an entire universe. Techniques of sampling and surveying are covered in Chapter 7.

PLANNING A SAMPLE SURVEY

A sample is a small part of a universe of objects, elements, or items. For example, we might select a sample of 100 homes from the universe of all homes in a city. In Chapter 8 we will learn about various types of samples and the importance of selecting a sample that is representative of the universe from which it is drawn.

It is also important that the information a sample provides about a universe will fulfill the purpose of the sampling study. Moreover, it is necessary to plan carefully other aspects of a study in which a sample is involved. For example, if a market or economic study requires the use of a questionnaire, the questionnaire must be constructed so that the questions will elicit accurate and meaningful answers. A poorly constructed questionnaire will bring misleading information even when a probability sample is used.

It is a waste of time to apply the analytical techniques discussed in Chapter 8 to data that are inaccurate. Therefore, if a survey involves a sample, it should be carefully planned and logically conducted. A logical sequence for planning and implementing a typical economic or marketing survey will be outlined.

[1]The steps that do not relate exclusively to samples also can be applied to universe studies (census studies).

TEN PLANNING STEPS

Step 1 The first step in planning a study is to define the problem and state the purpose of the survey.

This will be the basis of the whole study, enabling us to gather and analyze only that information necessary to fulfill the purpose of the study.

Step 2 Ascertain the conditions under which the survey will be conducted.

This involves the determination of what information is needed, when it is needed, what degree of accuracy is desired, how much money can be spent on the survey, what geographical area is to be surveyed, and the definition of terms. We need to know all of this before we can plan the size and type of sample to be selected for the study.

Step 3 Determine whether all or part of the information needed is already available.

This must be done so that time and money will not be wasted by duplicating a study that has already been made. This step might require library research, writing letters to private and government organizations, and contacting individuals who would know if such a study has already been made.

Step 4 If Step 3 does not uncover the desired information, choose the type and size of the sample, the method of selecting sample items, and the method to be used in collecting data.

These decisions will be based largely on the decisions made in Step 2. Types of samples, methods of determining sample sizes, and methods of drawing sample items are discussed in Chapter 8. Collecting data will be discussed later in this chapter.

Step 5 Prepare the questionnaire.

Because of the importance of its construction, some useful rules will be presented in a separate discussion.

Step 6 Collect the data.

At this point, interviews are conducted or the questionnaires mailed or the telephone calls made. The advantages and disadvantages of these methods of collecting data will be discussed separately.

Step 7 Edit the returned questionnaire to check whether questions have been answered and whether the answers are meaningful and logical.

Questionnaires should be edited by someone who knows the problem under consideration and the purpose of the survey. The results of this step may be the discarding of some entire questionnaires and the decision to eliminate answers to some questions.

Step 8 Tabulate and classify the information on the questionnaires.

This might be done by hand for simple surveys, but by computer for surveys with numerous questions and a large number of questionnaires.

Step 9 Analyze the information.

This will involve the computation of some statistical measures such as averages, measures of dispersion, trend projections, and coefficients of correlation.

Step 10 The final step is to interpret the findings and report them.

The report might be so comprehensive that a summary report is necessary for the general reader.

PREPARING A QUESTIONNAIRE

If a sample survey is to give useful, reliable information the questionnaire must be carefully prepared, preferably by two or three people. One might prepare the first draft and pass it to one or two other persons for review and suggested changes. The revised questionnaire should be tested under actual survey conditions, so it should be mailed to a small sample of the universe or used in interviews. Such a pilot study usually illuminates poorly worded questions and questions that will not or cannot be answered.

Rules to Follow

The best assurance that a questionnaire will elicit truthful, meaningful, and easy-to-tabulate answers is obtained by observing the following rules.

Rule 1 Use terms that can be understood. Words that have several meanings and may be interpreted in different ways by survey respondents should be avoided or clearly defined for the respondents.

The following questions will serve as examples:

1) What is your occupation?
2) How long has your chamber of commerce published its magazine?
3) What is the most important industry in your city?

At first reading, these questions seem to be clear and easy to answer. However, a careful study will reveal that they are not clear and are difficult for the thoughtful person to answer. In question 1, the term "occupation" can be interpreted in a variety of ways to give a wide choice of answers. An economics professor might give any of the following answers: economist, professor, economic analyst, teacher, college instructor, or social scientist. The controller of a business firm might answer: businessman, accountant, or office worker. Answers such as these could be wrongly interpreted by those conducting the study or, in fact, may not be subject to interpretation at all. If the purpose of the question was to find out what people actually do on their jobs or to get some idea of their wage or salary level, more accurate information could be obtained by asking a series of questions about place of work, job title, and job duties. In wage and salary surveys conducted by the U.S. Bureau of Labor Statistics, occupational titles such as secretary, accountant, and file clerk are explicitly defined on the survey forms.

Question 2, which was used in a survey of large chambers of commerce, was intended to get answers such as "10 years," "6 months," and "3½ years." However, some respondents wrote "several years" and one replied "since I went to work for the chamber." The question could have been worded to provide quantitative answers. The meaning of the word "long" is not clear, so the question might have been a check question worded thus:

How many years has your chamber of commerce published its magazine?

Check: ( ) Under 1
( ) 1–4
( ) 5–9
( ) 10 and over

Or the question might have asked what year the magazine was first published.

Question 3 is not clear because the terms "important" and "industry" have many meanings. How do we measure the importance of an industry? Is it by volume of output, number of employees, amount of capital investment, or some other indicator? Does the word ''industry'' refer to process classifications, such as manufacturing, wholesaling, retailing, construction, and service, or does it refer to product classifications, such as machinery, food, lumber, and apparel? Terms such as these must be clarified or the question worded in accordance with the purpose for asking it.

Rule 2 Avoid ambiguous questions.

If we want to find out what size milk container is the most popular among families in a survey, we should not ask,

> Do you usually buy milk in gallon, half-gallon, or quart containers?

If a line is left for a write-in answer, some people will write ''yes'' rather than one of the three possible sizes. Ambiguity can be eliminated by listing the three sizes after the question and asking the respondent to check one.

Rule 3 Be sure the question can be answered accurately.

In a survey concerning gasolines, oils, and other automotive products, a question asking for the brand of gasoline used by the respondents was followed by the question, ''What do you like most about this gasoline?'' and a line for the answer. Undoubtedly, some people write answers such as ''it keeps my engine from knocking,'' ''it gives more power,'' and ''it prevents my car's fuel line from freezing.'' But would not the most truthful answer for most people have been ''it makes my car run?'' Do many people know or recognize qualitative differences in gasolines? Answers to such questions are useless for almost any purpose.

Rule 4 Avoid the double question.

Two questions are sometimes asked in the same sentence with ''yes,'' ''no,'' and ''don't know'' listed as alternative answers for checking. If the answer to one question can be ''yes'' and the answer to the other ''no'' or ''don't know,'' the question is useless.

For example, a survey of business firms was made in a city located on Lake Michigan to help determine whether a ferry service to carry trailer trucks across Lake Michigan should be started. One of the questions on the form was

> Would you like to see the ferry service started and would you use it?
> Check: ( ) Yes ( ) No

Answering this question presented a dilemma for those businessmen who would like to see the service started because it would help other businesses, but not their own because they would not require this type of service.

Rule 5 Avoid direct, embarrassing questions.

If a bath soap manufacturer needs to learn how frequently prospective customers bathe, he is not likely to get truthful answers by asking, "How many baths do you take each week?" Such questions reduce response on mail questionnaires; in personal interviews, the interviewer might be shown the door or the person being interviewed might refuse to answer other questions that are not the least bit embarrassing. Information of this nature can be better obtained with an indirect question.

Rule 6 Word questions so that the answers can be easily tabulated and classified.

Questions that call for one-word answers and answers that are listed for checking facilitate counting and classifying. A question such as, "What are the advantages of the free enterprise system?" will induce responses that vary so widely that summarizing them would be extremely difficult, if not impossible, unless a list of advantages is provided to choose from.

It is important to remember that questions that list answers for checking should, theoretically, list all possible answers. This is not practicable in many instances; therefore, the most likely answers are listed and an "other" category is included for less likely or unusual answers. The following question illustrates this idea:

What brand of toothpaste did you buy last?
Check one: ( ) Colgate
( ) Crest
( ) Pepsodent
( ) Macleans
( ) Other ______________________
(Write in)

There are so many brands of toothpaste that a list of all of them would take up much space and probably would not enhance the results of the survey. If the name of a brand that would fall in the "other" category is desired, a space for it to be written in should be made available.

Rule 7 Avoid leading questions, which imply that there is one, and only one, answer.

Take the following question:

Are you going to XY University because you want an education?
Check: ( ) Yes ( ) No

Such a question would probably bring a preponderance of yes's. How many of the respondents would write in "I want a better education" if the question were open-end?

An open-end question would probably result in answers such as "because it's a private university," "because my father attended this university," or "because it's the only university that would admit me."

Leading questions can be effectively avoided by using the check question and listing either all answers or the most likely answers. Special care should be given, however, to the interpretation of questions asking the *reasons* people do things because the real reasons are often unknown to the respondent. It takes a high degree of knowledge and skill to get useful answers to such questions.

Rule 8 List questions in a logical order.

All questions that pertain to a particular subject should be asked before shifting to a different subject. Sometimes subjects overlap, but some systematic arrangement usually can be devised.

Rule 9 Make the questionnaire short and attractive.

The shorter the questionnaire, the greater the response. A questionaire should ask only necessary questions, and for this reason it is important to keep in mind the purpose of the survey during its construction. Making a questionnaire attractive is particularly important for mail surveys. The questions should be arranged so that they are easy to read. A good duplication process should be used so that the print is sharp and clear. Sometimes drawings and illustrations that relate to the questions will arouse the interest of the respondent.

Rule 10 Place the research organization's name and address on each questionnaire.

This rule applies chiefly to mail questionnaires. It is important because letters and self-addressed envelopes that accompany questionnaires often are misplaced or destroyed; the result is nonresponse if the surveyor's address does not appear on the questionnaire.

METHODS OF GATHERING DATA BY QUESTIONNAIRE

In sample surveys data usually are obtained from personal interviews, by mail, over the telephone, or by a combination of these methods. The method chosen depends on the purpose of the study and the conditions relating to the problem, such as the nature of the universe, the time and money available for the study, and the accuracy desired in the answers. These conditions should be considered in relation to the advantages and disadvantages of the three methods of gathering the data.

The Personal Interview

Advantages. If the individuals to be surveyed can be reached by an interviewer and if the questions are few, easy to answer, and not embarrassing, then the personal interview method results in a higher percentage of response and, therefore, better sample results than the mail questionnaire or telephone interview methods.

A second advantage is the certainty that the right person answers the question. If answers are desired from presidents of companies, the interviewer will know whether he is talking to the right person. Mail questionnaire directed to busy executives are often given to subordinates to fill out and return.

A third advantage is that the personal interviewer can judge the sincerity of the respondent as he gives his answers.

A fourth advantage is that useful information can be obtained by observation. For example, the interviewer can see the environment of the respondent, which can help him estimate economic or social status.

Disadvantages. Using personal interviewers in surveys is expensive; because of this personal interviews are not conducted as frequently as they should be. How costly the interviewers are depends on factors such as their professional training, the time needed for conducting an interview, and the geographical dispersion of those to be interviewed.

A second disadvantage of the personal interview method is the inability of the respondent to remain anonymous. This might inhibit responses to certain types of questions.

A third disadvantage is that answers that require thought, computations, and analysis usually cannot be obtained. Sometimes, however, a questionnaire that would take a lot of time to fill out can be personally delivered to the desired individual to get his cooperation and left with him to complete at his convenience.

A fourth disadvantage results from the difficulty of reaching certain people during normal interviewing hours. For example, the working housewife cannot be interviewed during the normal work day, and a medical doctor or dentist is unlikely to permit an interview on general marketing and economic subjects when it means keeping his patients waiting for their appointments.

A fifth disadvantage is that the interviewer can introduce bias in the study by suggesting a possible answer to a question when the respondent has difficulty giving one. The respondent may use the suggested answer, which may be inaccurate, to make his choice easy.

The Mail Questionnaire

Advantages. More surveys are conducted by mail than by any other method because the cost of gathering data by this method is relatively low. The direct cost per questionnaire depends on the cost of postage and the percent of returns. If 1000 questionnaires are mailed at thirteen cents each and a stamped self-addressed envelope is included with each for return, the total postage cost is $260. However, the cost per questionnaire will be more than 26 cents because all of them will not be returned. If 200 are completed and mailed back the cost for returned questionnaires is $260/200 or $1.30 each. But this still is much cheaper than personal interviews.

A second advantage is that the recipient of a mail questionnaire can fill it out at his convenience. This is especially important if the questions are time-consuming or if a person's job is of such a nature that he cannot interrupt his work to answer questions.

A third advantage is that a wide geographical area can be covered quickly. In fact, sometimes the mail questionnaire is the only method that is practical. For example, a large university desired to gather certain information from a random sample of its alumni. The sample included 12,000 alumni who were scattered all over the world. In this survey it would have been almost impossible to contact each alumnus personally; therefore, the personal interview method was not even considered.

The mail questionnaire has a fourth advantage if a survey requires time to complete. Some questionnaires may take several hours to complete. For this type of study the personal interview and telephone interview cannot be considered.

Disadvantages. Serious consideration should be given to the disadvantages of the mail survey, which can result in misleading information that, in turn, leads to wrong inferences and decisions.

One of the main disadvantages of gathering data by mail is that only a relatively small number of those receiving questionnaires return them. This may result in a nonrepresentative sample. It is likely that those returning the questionnaires have an interest in the subject being studied while those not responding are indifferent. Also, there is no way of determining the magnitude of errors in sample surveys conducted by mail when nothing is known about the universe from which the sample was drawn.

A second disadvantage of the mail questionnaire is that it is difficult for the surveyor to judge the honesty and sincerity of the answers. For example, there is no sure way of knowing whether a numerical answer given by an individual was calculated or guessed at.

A third disadvantage of the mail survey is that those doing the study cannot be sure the proper person supplied the information. For example, a business executive may ask his secretary to fill out a form which requests his opinions concerning world problems. When a mail questionnaire is given to a subordinate employee to complete, it may be filled out in a careless manner because the employee's purpose might be to please the boss rather than to cooperate in the study.

The Telephone Interview

Advantages. The telephone can be a useful instrument for conducting sample marketing and economic surveys if certain conditions exist and certain rules are observed.

One important condition is that the individuals, homes, businesses, or organizations that make up the universe have telephones. It would be impossible knowingly to draw a representative sample of households of a city from a telephone directory because all households in a city do not have telephones and some that do are not listed in the directory.

A second condition is that the questions asked will not embarrass the respondent and are easy to answer. Most people will not spend much time answering a lot of questions for a stranger on the phone and hardly anyone will answer personal questions such as, "What is your annual income?"

If these conditions exist, then one advantage of the telephone survey is that a relatively high percentage of response can be obtained. For example, a university bureau of business research in a midwest city got a 95% response to a telephone survey of a sample of housewives. In this survey the following three questions were asked:

1) Do you save trading stamps?
2) What brands of trading stamps do you save?
3) Do you patronize only those stores that issue trading stamps? (Asked only if the answer to question 1 was "yes.")

These questions were not embarrassing to most of the people called, and they could be answered quickly. Callbacks, of course, had to be made if the respondent was not at home.

A second advantage of telephoning is that it enables us to get information faster and less expensively than we could by personal interviews and faster than by mail.

The telephone also helps to get information from people before they forget the facts. For example, if a local radio station wants to estimate the percentage of people who listened to a particular program, it might telephone a sample of people while the program is on to ask whether they *are listening* rather than mail a questionnaire to ask if they *listened*. Mail questionnaire respondents might not recall whether or not they listened.

Disadvantages. The fact that everyone to be contacted may not have a phone handicaps this survey method. A second disadvantage is that some people are difficult to reach during normal surveying hours. A professor may be conducting a class, or a traveling salesman may be traveling while the survey is being conducted. A dentist or medical doctor may be irritated if he leaves a patient to answer the phone and finds that a market surveyor wants to ask questions about shoe polishes.

THE COVERING LETTER

Most mail surveys are accompanied by a letter explaining what the survey is. It is important to prepare the letter carefully because it is the sales pitch to induce the receiver to fill out the questionnaire and return it.

The letter should be written in a warm, friendly tone and should appear to the cooperative and helpful nature of people. Many people are willing to cooperate in a worthwhile undertaking if it doesn't cost them money, take too much time, or negatively affect their emotions.

The letter also should make the recipient feel that his advice is important and that his response will improve the survey. This appeal, however, should not be overdone.

Another important ingredient that should go into the covering letter is a statement of purpose of the study. No one wants to provide information unless he knows how that information will be used. If the study will help the respondent, tell him so because this will stimulate response. If it will help only the firm doing the study, be truthful and say so. If it will be beneficial to society at large, the letter should state this.

The letter should be kept to one page if possible. The longer it is, the less likely it is that a person will read it.

Sometimes a gift can be offered to induce response. For example, a copy of the resulting report may be offered to business firms that will cooperate in a survey of personnel practices and policies. Another example of the effective use of a gift comes from an actual case of a midwest marketing research firm. This firm was testing the psychological effect of pastel-colored ironing board covers on a sample of housewives in a city. The test required that the housewives use the different colored covers for two or three weeks. They were supplied with the covers and with a high quality ironing board and told that they could keep the ironing board as a reward for cooperating. This gift induced a high percentage of response from the sample.

Indiscriminate use of gifts, however, can be dangerous. Gifts may induce people to respond to a questionnaire with careless or wrong answers just to get the gift, thus nullifying the value of the survey. Because of this, the possible effect of a gift should be carefully analyzed before it is offered.

REVIEW QUESTIONS

1. Define and give examples of *external* data and *internal* data.
2. Define and give examples of *primary* and *secondary* data.
3. Why is it advisable to use primary data for statistical analysis?
4. Name three U.S. government publications that are good sources of business and economic data.
5. What problems often confront a researcher when he is gathering data?
6. Why should an analyst know the accuracy of the data he plans to analyze?

7. Consult the latest copy of the *Survey of Current Business* and list ten major categories of published economic indicators.

8. Use the latest copy of the *Statistical Abstract of the United States* to list the section headings that relate to business and economic data.

9. If your library has *Statistics Sources*, by the Gale Research Company, use it to list the names of ten publications that provide business and economic data. State briefly the types of data that each contains.

10. Review the latest annual *Catalog of United States Census Publications* and list the names of ten publications that contain business and economic data. State briefly the type of data that each contains.

11. Outline the steps that are involved in planning a sample survey.

12. List ten rules that are useful for making out questionnaires.

The following mail questionnaire was sent by a midwestern government organization to housewives in a large city. The basic purpose of the study was to gather information that would enable the organization to better advise housewives on purchasing food items and to advise manufacturers and retailers of changes needed in merchandising practices. Questions 13–23 relate to this questionnaire.

Age of person filling out this form ________
Number of children now living at home ________
How many years experience buying food ________
For a family: More than 20 years ________
5 to 20 years ________
Less than 5 years ________
Circle monthly take-home pay:
Below $300.00
300.00 to 399.00
400.00 to 499.00
500.00 or over

1. How often do you buy canned fruits or vegetables?
   a. To serve as needed on a daily basis ________
   b. A week's supply at a time ________
   c. To maintain a stocked supply ________
   d. Usually only when a store special is advertised ________

2. Below in the left hand column are numbers used when can sizes are referred to. Match the numbers in column 2 with the correct can size.

COLUMN 1		COLUMN 2
No. 3 cylinder	________	1. 16-17 oz.
No. 303	________	2. 6¾ lb.
No. 2½	________	3. 20 oz.
No. 2	________	4. 29 oz.
No. 10	________	5. 46 oz.

3. Which measurement would you prefer to see on the can?
   Can size ________ Ounces ________ Servings ________

4. Do you own a freezer? ________ How many cubic feet capacity? ________

5. Of the money you spend on fruits and vegetables, what percentage goes for each of the following:
   Fresh for eating ________%
   Fresh for canning ________%
   Frozen ________%
   Canned ________%

6. Do you purchase canned fruits and vegetables by brand name?
   a. Always buy same brand ________
   b. Strong preference for one brand ________
   c. Preference, but occasionally buy other brand ________
   d. No brand preference ________

7. Do you ever buy HIGHEST quality? ________
   For what purpose? ________
   Do you ever buy LOWEST quality? ________
   For what purpose? ________

8. What would be your advice to the young housewife starting out in homemaking concerning buying canned fruits and vegetables? How can she be sure she is buying a good quality product?

9. Where do you frequently buy canned fruits and vegetables?

A and P	____	I.G.A.	____	KOHL	____
KROGER-KRAMBO	____	NATIONAL	____	SENTRY	____
LOCAL STORE	____	INDEPENDENT	____	HALAN'S	____

10. Rate the following names for quality. (1. Top quality, 2. Good, 3. Poor)

____	Garden Fresh	____	Avondale	____	Sultana
____	Ann Page	____	Old Time	____	Iona
____	Serve U Rite	____	Kroger	____	Del Monte
____	Natco	____	Roundy's	____	Libby's

11. When you are buying canned foods, peaches for example, how important are each of the following to you? (Place X in column.)

	VERY IMPORTANT	DESIRABLE	NOT TOO IMPORTANT
Firmness	______	______	______
Flavor	______	______	______
Color	______	______	______
Low percentage of syrup or juice	______	______	______
Odor	______	______	______
Food value	______	______	______
Uniform size	______	______	______

12. What do the government grades A, B, C mean to you? ______________________

13. Would you like such letter grades on all canned fruits and vegetables?
    Yes ______ No ______
    Please state your reason why or why not.

14. When can labels show suggestions for serving canned fruits or vegetables do you make use of them?
    Yes ______ No ______

15. Rather than the serving suggestion, would you prefer to see recipes on the labels of canned fruits and vegetables?
    Yes ______ No ______

16. Some foods are sold with an official grade on the package. Do you happen to recall how each of the following foods is sold? (Place X in column.)

	PACKAGE ALWAYS SHOWS GRADE	SOMETIMES SHOWS GRADE	NEVER SHOWS GRADE	DON'T RECALL
Butter	______	______	______	______
Cheese	______	______	______	______
Canned Tuna	______	______	______	______
Hamburger	______	______	______	______
Frozen Fish	______	______	______	______
Canned Peas	______	______	______	______
Fresh Apples	______	______	______	______
Pork Loin Roast	______	______	______	______
Canned Beets	______	______	______	______
Eggs	______	______	______	______

PLEASE RETURN THIS FORM IN THE STAMPED ADDRESSED ENVELOPE BY MAY 26.

THANK YOU

13. Why does the questionnaire ask for the age of the respondent?

14. In the question asking for the number of children, what does the word *children* mean?

15. The respondent is asked to circle monthly take-home pay. What is "take-home pay"? Whose take-home pay is to be circled?

16. In Question 1, are all possible answers listed? If not, devise another answer.

17. Do you think most people could give an accurate answer to Question 5? Why?

18. In Question 7, is it clear what would be bought at highest or lowest quality? If a respondent were to write "to eat" in answer to the question "For what purpose?" would the answer be useful to the surveyor?

19. What rule does Question 9 violate?

20. Is Question 11 likely to elicit useful answers? Is a respondent who has canned peaches in mind as he answers the question likely to give the same answers as one who is thinking of canned turnip greens?

21. Could Questions 14 and 15 be answered accurately by every respondent with a yes or no? If not, why?

22. What might be the purpose of Question 16?

23. What are the good points about the questionnaire?

The letter below accompanied a questionnaire mailed to households in a metropolitan area. Evaluate the letter by answering Questions 24–27.

Dear Householder:

Have you ever felt that your opinion could be useful to the management of a corporation? We have a client who feels that your thoughts will be valuable in the conduct of his business; consequently, we are writing to request a favor.

Attached is a questionnaire asking your opinion about the television stations in Milwaukee. Its purpose is to determine your feelings and ideas about the stations rather than programs. It is not a program popularity poll. It is not necessary that you fill in every blank. You are only requested to answer as you know, feel, and think.

Your opinion may be signed or anonymous, as you choose. In order to lend more value to your efforts, the enclosed stamped envelope for returning your answer is addressed to the Muscular Dystrophy Associations, to which our client has agreed to donate a sizeable sum, based upon the number of replies. It is their way of saying "Thank You."

Thank you very much for your cooperation.

Cordially,

24. Is it a good sales piece? Do you think you would want to cooperate in the study?

25. Is it written in accordance with the general rules for constructing covering letters for mail questionnaires?

26. Does the letter say who will benefit from the survey? Should it?

27. What inducements are offered to get response to the survey?

28. Give two advantages and two disadvantages of each of three basic methods of gathering raw data.

29. If a questionnaire asks questions that are understood by the respondents, can the answers to the questions be considered reliable and useful? Explain.

30. Will a well-worded questionnaire always provide useful information? Explain.

3

Presentation of Data

When data are collected for analysis they must be organized or grouped to facilitate the analysis. Also, when data are to be released in a report, they must be presented in a form that enables the reader to understand clearly what he is reading. Most data, therefore, should be presented in accurately constructed tables and/or charts. To do this requires that the assembled data be classified first.

Data Classification

Data can be classified in one or more of the following ways: by amount, by kind, by location, and by time.

Classification by amount gives the number of observations that fall within specified quantitative groups. Table 3-8 shows a classification of employees by the *amount* of their earnings. A classification by kind is illustrated by Table 3-1a, which shows employment by *kind* of industry. A table showing data by country, state, or other geographical area, such as Table 3-3, is a classification by *location*. Any table showing data for more than one time period exemplifies a classification by *time;* Table 3-4 is an example.

Certain rules and guides for table and chart construction must be followed if tables and charts are to be understood and easily read. You will realize the necessity or reasonableness of these rules when you begin to find charts and tables in popular publications that are difficult to understand. The rules will make even more sense when you start constructing your own tables and charts.

STATISTICAL TABLES

Statistical tables are sometimes constructed for general reference, as are those in the *Statistical Abstract of the United States*. Others, such as those found in business reports, magazines, textbooks, and students' term papers, are constructed for special purposes. The general reference type of table is more complicated and requires much more instruction than is practical here. For our purposes, it is sufficient to know only the basic, more important rules.*

*Detailed explanations of the multitudinous rules for constructing a wide variety of tables can be found in the *Bureau of the Census Manual of Tabular Presentation*, published by the U.S. Bureau of the Census.

Parts of Statistical Tables and Their Functions

Obviously, the purpose of numbering a table is to facilitate referring to it. Generally, Arabic rather than Roman numerals are used because they are easier to read, especially when large numbers are necessary. The table number is placed at the top of the table. Just as the table number is a label and has a specific purpose, the other parts of a table likewise can be labeled, and specific rules can be applied to each so that they perform their proper functions. In Table 3-1a, the following parts are identified: number, title, headnote, captions, body, stub, stub head, stub items, footnote, and source note.

Number **TABLE 3-1a Number of Employees in Nonagricultural Industries, by Industry, United States, 1970 and 1975** *Title*

(Covers full and part-time employees who worked during or received pay for any part of the pay period including the 12th of the month.) *Headnote*

Stub head	*INDUSTRY*	*AVERAGE ANNUAL NUMBER EMPLOYED (In thousands)*		*Captions*
		1970	*1975*	
	TOTAL	*70,920**	*76,985*	
Stub items	Manufacturing	19,349	18,347	*Body*
	Mining	623	745	
	Contract construction	3,536	3,457	
	Transportation and public utilities	4,504	4,498	
	Trade	15,040	16,947	
	Finance	3,687	4,223	
	Service	11,621	13,995	
	Government	12,561	14,773	

*Components do not add to total due to rounding. *Footnote*

Source: U.S. Department of Commerce, Bureau of the Census, *Statistical Abstract of the United States*, 1975, p.353, and *Survey of Current Business*, November, 1976. *Source note*

The title. The title of a table should be as short and concise as possible, yet tell the reader three things: (1) what the data are, (2) to where the data refer, and (3) to when the data refer. It is many times advisable and sometimes necessary to word the title so that it will also tell how the data are classified. In Table 3-1a, the words "number of employees in nonagricultural industries" tell us what the data are. To where the data refer is given by the words "United States," and the dates 1970 and 1975 identify the time period. Also, the words "by industry" and the dates 1970 and 1975 indicate the two ways by which the data in this table are classified: by kind and by time.

The headnote. The information in parentheses following the title is called a headnote. It explains some general characteristic about the data that the reader should know in order to use and interpret the table properly. Headnotes should be stated as briefly as possible, but it is better to be wordy and clear than to forsake clarity for brevity.

The captions. Column headings, which are often called captions, identify the figures in the columns. When a single caption spreads over two or more columns, as is often done to avoid repetition, it is called a common caption or spanner.

The body. The body of the table is composed of the figures. Rules for arranging these figures will be discussed shortly.

The stub and stub head. The column on the left side of the table is called the stub, and the individual listings, which identify the contents of the rows and figures, are referred to as stub items. The heading above the stub item is called the stub head.

The footnotes. Footnotes often accompany tables, usually to point out a particular irregularity, omission, or characteristic in the table. Footnotes are usually numbered, or lettered, when there are several of them. If there are only one or two, asterisks and symbols such as the number sign (#) can be used to denote them. The word ''footnote'' should not be written at the bottom of the table.

The source note. The last (lowest) part of a statistical table is the source note. This highly important note should be included for four reasons: (1) to give proper credit to the original source; (2) to indicate the reliability of the data; (3) to enable the reader to refer to the source if he desires; and (4) to protect ourselves from blame for errors found in the table that are present in the original source.

If an agency spends hundreds or thousands of dollars gathering data and gives you access to them it is right that credit be given to the agency as the original source. If the source from which you obtain the figures is a reliable and trustworthy one, it adds authenticity to the figures. If the reader wants to check the accuracy of any figure in the table or desires to get more detailed information or related facts, he may be able to do so if the source of the table is given. Also, if an error is found in the figures, the person presenting the table must assume the blame if he gives no source for the figures, even though the error appears in the original figures.

The source note should be explicit, as illustrated in Table 3-1a. In most cases, it would not be sufficient to give the source of the data in Table 3-1a merely as the Bureau of the Census because the Bureau issues many publications other than the *Statistical Abstract,* from which these data were taken. Table 3-4 gives the name of an organization, not a publication, as the source because the figures were obtained directly from the files of the organization.

Sometimes it is proper to give two sources in a source note. If, for example, you use the figures in Table 3-1a in a term paper for an economics course you should name the textbook as your source. However, you might mention also the original source, the U.S. Bureau of the Census, to indicate to the reader that the data originated from a reliable source.

Ruling a Table

Lines drawn at proper places on a table can improve its general appearance and readability, although very simple tables may be presented adequately with no lines at all. Table 3-1a is ruled properly. Notice that the sides of the table are left open, which is a custom more than a rule. Table 3-1b is the same table improperly ruled. So many lines clutter the table and certainly do not facilitate its readability. Tables 3-2a and 3-2b have been ruled in the proper fashion. Notice that the length of the line separating the captions in each table indicates the columns to which the common caption refers. The dashed line in the last column shows the reader that 9.2 is not meant to be a total of 12.9 and 4.5, but is the percent of change between the totals in the previous two columns. The rules on Table 3-3 do little to improve its readability, but they do improve its appearance.

TABLE 3-1b Number of Employees in Nonagricultural Industries, by Industry, United States, 1970 and 1975

(Covers full and part-time employees who worked during or received pay for any part of the pay period including the 12th of the month.)

INDUSTRY	*AVERAGE ANNUAL NUMBER EMPLOYED (in thousands)*	
	1970	*1975*
TOTAL	*70,920**	*76,985*
Manufacturing	19,349	18,347
Mining	623	745
Contract construction	3,536	3,457
Transportation and public utilities	4,504	4,498
Trade	15,040	16,947
Finance	3,687	4,223
Service	11,621	13,995
Government	12,561	14,773

*Components do not add to total due to rounding.

Source: U.S. Department of Commerce, Bureau of the Census, *Statistical Abstract of the United States*, 1975, p. 353 and *Survey of Current Business*, November, 1976.

TABLE 3-2a Number of Employees in Durable and Nondurable Manufacturing Industries, United States, 1960 and 1975.

Industry	*AVERAGE ANNUAL NUMBER EMPLOYED (in Thousands)* 1960	1975	Percent change
Durable	9,459	10,679	+12.9
Nondurable	7,336	7,668	+ 4.5
Total*	16,796	18,347	+ 9.2

*Components will not add to totals due to rounding.

Source: U.S. Department of Commerce, *Business Statistics*, 1975, pp.70-72; and *Survey of Current Business*, Nov. 1976.

TABLE 3-2b Number of Employees in Durable and Nondurable Manufacturing Industries, United States, 1960 and 1975.

	AVERAGE ANNUAL NUMBER EMPLOYED (in Thousands)		
Year	Durable	Nondurable	Total*
1960	9,459	7,336	16,796
1975	10,679	7,668	18,347
Percent change	+12.9	+4.5	+9.2

*Components will not add to totals due to rounding.

Source U.S. Department of Commerce, *Business Statistics*, 1975; and *Survey of Current Business*, Nov. 1976.

Arrangement of Figures

There may be two or more ways that figures can be arranged in a table and still be easily read and understood. When this is the case, we should keep in mind that, because we read from left to right and from top to bottom, the figures nearest the upper left-hand corner will be emphasized by their position. Therefore, if we want to emphasize certain figures we should place them in the first column or first row unless the result will be an awkward over-all presentation. For example, in Table 3-4 the data on value added by manufacture could be placed in the first column if we desired to emphasize it. Moreover, if the more recent dates needed to be emphasized, the chronological order could be reversed, with the 1975 figures appearing in the top row.

If two sets of figures are to be compared, they should be placed in adjacent *columns* rather than in adjacent *rows*, because comparisons are made more easily by moving the eyes from left to right than by moving the eyes up and down. An illustration of this reasoning can be seen by comparing Tables 3-2a and 3-2b, which shows the same data, but differently arranged. If we want to compare the change in the numbers of employees in durable and nondurable industries between 1960 and 1975 the data arrangement in Table 3-2a is preferable to that in Table 3-2b.

TABLE 3-3 Value of United States Exports of Merchandise by Geographic Region, 1974.

REGION	VALUE ($000,000)
Africa	3,659
Asia	25,784
Australia and Oceania	2,697
Europe	30,070
Northern North America	19,938
Southern North America	7,549
South America	7,857
Total	97,953

Source: U.S. Department of Commerce, *Business Statistics*, 1975.

TABLE 3-4 Selected Economic Indicators for the Milwaukee Metropolitan Area, 1961-1975.

YEAR	*NUMBER EMPLOYED (000)*	*VALUE ADDED BY MFG. ($000,000)*	*RETAIL SALES ($000,000)*	*AVERAGE WEEKLY EARNINGS OF MFG. PRODUCTION WORKERS*
1961	511	$2,009	$1,624	$107
1962	516	2,248	1,665	114
1963	520	2,313	1,759	116
1964	533	2,447	1,848	121
1965	552	2,653	1,931	126
1966	572	2,929	2,029	133
1967	587	2,979	2,183	135
1968	600	3,077	2,335	141
1969	609	3,308	2,414	152
1970	613	3,374	2,438	157
1971	605	3,400	2,600	168
1972	620	3,700	2,900	184
1973	648	4,300	3,200	201
1974	624	4,900	3,350	216
1975	610	4,900	3,800	232

Source: Metropolitan Milwaukee Association of Commerce.

Although no illustration is shown, we could emphasize a single figure in a table by rendering it in italics, boldface type, or by circling or underlining it.

When time series data are presented, the years may be placed as shown in Table 3-4 or across the top as captions. In this case, the presentation would be awkward if the dates had been placed at the top and the four classifications by kind had been placed in the stub; the resulting table would be too wide and too flat to be attractive. When fewer years are shown, as in Table 3-5, the presentation is more readable with the years placed at the top. Incidentally, notice that Tables 3-4 and 3-5 have not been ruled, yet they are easy to read.

TABLE 3-5 Selected Economic Indicators for the Milwaukee Metropolitan Area, 1970 and 1975.

INDICATOR	*1970*	*1975*	*PERCENT CHANGE*
Number employed (000)	613	610	−0.5
Value added by manufacture ($000,000)	$3,374	$4,900	+45.2
Retail sales ($000,000)	$2,438	$3,800	+55.9
Average weekly earnings of production workers in manufacturing industries	$ 157	$ 232	+47.8

Source: Metropolitan Milwaukee Association of Commerce.

Another good idea when showing data for many months or years is to place the time periods in clusters as is done in Table 3-4. This makes a table easier to read.

Table Format

Tables usually look better if they are slightly wider than they are high. This cannot always be done, but we should avoid making tables extremely flat and wide or high and narrow because of the awkward appearance they make. Your own tables can be made neat and very readable by placing the title at the top, with the second line of a long title centered under the first. Third lines should also be centered.

Rounding and Identifying Figures

Notice in Table 3-4 that the data for retail sales and value added by manufacture have been rounded to the nearest millions and the figures for motor vehicle registrations have been rounded to the nearest thousand. Such rounding makes the figures easy to read, but does not impair the use of the figures for most purposes. The table would appear uninviting to many readers if the last six digits were shown for each figure on "retail sales" and "value added by manufacture," and showing them would add nothing of value to most analyses or interpretations that might be made from the data. Using ($000,000) at the top of a column of figures to indicate that the data are in millions of dollars is acceptable. However, writing (millions of dollars) is also acceptable.

The Frequency Distribution

Frequency Distribution

A frequency distribution is a table in which a mass of data have been divided into quantitative groups, called *classes*, to bring out general characteristics.

The construction of a frequency distribution table is not easy and sometimes requires a "trial-and-error" process to get the best presentation even though there are rules to facilitate the work. Raw data, such as those in Table 3-6, must be organized in a meaningful form. The natural procedure is to set up classes and then count the number of figures that fall within each group. However, the following questions arise: How many classes should there be? What should be the size of each class? With what figure should the first class start? What general distribution should the numbers have after they are

TABLE 3-6 April 1975 Earnings of 50 OS University Students Employed Part-Time (Rounded to the Nearest Dollar)

$183	$147	$102	$195	$148
219	125	174	176	130
164	138	188	130	135
58	147	78	145	147
73	169	121	142	108
203	111	131	120	118
155	98	139	117	137
164	124	147	105	124
165	150	170	160	140
80	94	85	135	160

Source: OS University.

placed in classes? These questions are not easy to answer, but the following rules might help:

1) Use not less than five nor more than fifteen classes.
2) Determine the tentative interval of the classes (the spread between the lower and higher figures) by dividing the tentative number of classes you think you need into the range (the difference between the largest and smallest observations) of the data.
3) Start the first class with a figure lower than the lowest number to be classified, but try to use a round easy-to-read figure, such as 10, 15, 20, or an integral multiple of these figures.
4) Write all classes in easy-to-read terms, provided other desired objectives can be obtained. For example, for noninteger data classes reading 10-14, 15-19, and 20-24 are easier to read than 11-16, 17-22, and 23-28.
5) Make the classes mutually exclusive, that is, write the class limits so that a value can be placed in only one class. Integer data classes written 50-75, 75-100, and 100-125 are ambiguous because it is not clear which of the classes contain the exact values 75 and 100. Classes written 50 but under 75, 75 but under 100, and 100 but under 125 are not ambiguous.
6) Try to make the intervals of all classes the same and yet obtain a unimodal (single-peaked) frequency distribution. In some cases, it would be futile to attempt this, because of the nature of the data.
7) Use open-end distributions and unequal class intervals only when there is no other way to make a reasonable presentation of the data. An open-end distribution is one that has no lower limit for the first class and/or no upper limit for the last class, such as in Table 3-10.

TABLE 3-7 April 1975 Earnings of 50 OS University Students Employed Part-Time (Rounded to the Nearest Dollar)

i = $27		*i* = $20		*i* = $25		*i* = $50	
EARNINGS	*NO. OF STUDENTS*	*EARNINGS*	*NO. OF STUDENTS*	*EARNINGS*	*NO. OF STUDENTS*	*EARNINGS*	*NO. OF STUDENTS*
$ 50– 76	2	$ 50– 69	1	$ 50– 74	2	$ 50– 99	7
77–103	6	70– 89	4	75– 99	5	100–149	27
104–130	12	90–109	5	100–124	10	150–199	14
131–157	16	110–129	8	125–149	17	200–249	2
158–184	10	130–149	16	150–174	10	Total	50
185–211	3	150–169	9	175–199	4		
212–238	1	170–189	4	200–224	2		
Total	50	190–209	2	Total	50		
		210–229	1				
		Total	50				

Table 3-7 shows four frequency distributions that were constructed from the raw data in Table 3-6. Each distribution was constructed according to one or more of the rules just given. The first step was to determine the tentative number of classes. This step is always a judgment, which becomes easier with experience. An experienced analyst would know that fifteen classes ordinarily are too many for tabulating only fifty figures. He would probably judge that six or seven classes would be sufficient to construct a good table. In this case, six classes was the tentative choice. The second step was to calculate the tentative class interval with the following formula:

$$\text{Tentative interval} = \frac{\text{Range}}{\text{Tentative no. of classes}}$$

$$= \frac{219 - 58}{6} = \$27$$

The third step was to decide on the lowest figure for the first class. Although any figure, such as $58, $57, or $53 could have been used, $50 was chosen because it is easy to read. The fourth step was to count the number of students that had earnings in each class. This was done with a tally sheet. The tally sheet for the $27 interval is shown below.

Tally Sheet for Counting Students in Earning Groups with Intervals of $27

MONTHLY EARNINGS	*NO. OF STUDENTS*
$ 50— 76	//
$ 77—103	~~////~~ /
$104—130	~~////~~ ~~////~~ //
$131—157	~~////~~ ~~////~~ ~~////~~ /
$158—184	~~////~~ ~~////~~
$185—211	///
$212—238	/

The first distribution in Table 3-7 shows a tabulation of the earnings data where the interval for each class is exactly $27. (The interval may appear to be $26, but this discrepancy will be explained later.) Because the first class started with $50, the distribution has seven rather than the six classes that was expected. If the first class had started with $58 there would have been six classes. This distribution with an interval of $27 is *unimodal*, meaning that the data reach a peak only once. An example of a trimodal distribution is shown in Table 3-8. The three high points, or peaks are 7, 11, 18. Bimodal (double-peaked) and trimodal characteristics can sometimes be eliminated by reducing the number of classes and/or changing the starting figure for the first class.

TABLE 3-8 Average Weekly Earnings of Class A Computer Operators in Large Manufacturing Establishments, in the Milwaukee Metropolitan Area, April, 1975.

WEEKLY EARNINGS (DOLLARS)		*NO. OF OPERATORS*
$140 but under $160		7
$160 but under $180		5
$180 but under $200		11
$200 but under $220		7
$220 but under $240		18
$260 but under $280		3
$280 but under $300		1
	Total	55

Source: U.S. Department of Labor, Bureau of Labor Statistics, *Area Wage Survey*, Milwaukee, Wisconsin Metropolitan Area, April 1975.

Since $27 was only a tentative class interval and because it is an odd number, it would be wise to construct distribution with a $25 interval because numbers that come in 5's, 10's are comfortable to handle in the thinking process. The third distribution in Table 3-7 shows the earnings with a $25 interval. A smooth unimodal distribution of seven classes is obtained with this interval, and by using $50 as the starting point, the entire distribution is made easier to read than the one with an interval of $27.

So that you can see the results of using different intervals, distributions with intervals of $20 and $50 are also shown in Table 3-7. The $20 interval would produce a table that would show too many details for some purposes. The $50 interval, on the other hand, would result in a table with too much summarization for some purposes. For particular purposes, any of the four distributions might be satisfactory; but for general purposes, the class interval of $25 produces the best frequency distribution, because its classes are easy to read, it is unimodal, and the over-all distribution shows a smooth gradation of numbers from the first frequency to the peak and from the peak to the last frequency.

On some occasions frequency distributions may show more than one peak. Bimodal (double-peaked) and trimodal (triple-peaked) characteristics can sometimes be eliminated by reducing the number of classes and/or changing the starting figure for each class. However, sometimes nothing can be done. Chart 3-2, made from Table 3-8 exemplifies frequency distributions which often result from following the rules for their construction.

Writing class limits. Class limits, which are the smallest and largest values that can be placed in a class, may be written several ways, any of which may or may not be right for a set of data. They should be written so that they do not indicate a higher degree of accuracy than that of the data to be classified. For example, classes written $50 but under $75, $75 but under $100, $100 but under $125, $125 but under $150, and so on, could result in faulty tabulation for figures rounded to the nearest dollar. To illustrate: The $125 figure in Table 3-6 would be placed in the class $125 but under $150. However, this figure ($125) actually may have been less than $125 before it was rounded, even as low as $124.50. If this is the case, then the figure should be in the class reading $100 but under $125.

The class limits in Table 3-9. are correct for the data in Table 3-6 because they prohibit a false classification of any figure regardless of its value before it was rounded.

TABLE 3-9 April 1975 Earnings of 50 OS University Students Employed Part-Time

EARNINGS	*NO. OF STUDENTS*
$ 50– 74	2
75– 99	5
100–124	10
125–149	17
150–174	10
175–199	4
200–224	2
Total	50

Source: OS University

The number of options for writing class limits depends upon whether the data are continuous or discrete. Data that are rounded are usually *continuous data*. For continuous data the degree or fineness to which a measurement can be made is infinite. The opposite, *discrete data*, are those for which the magnitude of measurement is finite or limited. The weight distribution of 100 students would illustrate continuous data because, theoretically, there is no limit to the fineness of the measurement. Although weights are usually rounded to the nearest ounce or pound, measurements can be made to the millionth of a pound. An example of discrete data would be a distribution showing the number of families in an area by the size of the family. Families might have one, two, three, or more persons but no family has two and one tenth persons nor do we talk about millionth of a person. As you can see, the options for stating class limits for family sizes are more limited than those for stating class limits for students' weights: that is, each class must start with a whole person and end with a whole person.

Another example of discrete data is the following distribution of the number of shoes sold, by size:

SIZE	*NO. OF SHOES SOLD*
6½ to 7½	3
8 to 9	12
9½ to 10½	15
11 to 12	10
12½ to 13½	2
Total	42

Here, the real class limits are those stated, because no shoe is measured more precisely than to a half-size.

Dollars and cents figures are sometimes continuous data and sometimes discrete. The arithmetic mean* weekly earnings of each of a group of salesmen for a year could be measured to any fraction of a cent, so the data would be continuous. However, earnings of each salesman in a particular week would be discrete data because the penny would be the measurement limit to which the earnings figures could be stated for each salesman.

Written class limits versus real class limits. Certain statistical calculations from frequency distributions require what are termed *real* class limits. The *stated* or written limits are not often the real limits; stated class limits are rounded from real class limits, which must be determined by the analyst. An examination will show that the class limits in Table 3-9 are not the real class limits. The real class limits for the individual classes are $49.50–74.50, $74.50–99.50, $99.50–124.50, etc.† For example, the lowest figure, in dollars and cents, that would fall in the first class of $50–74 would be $49.50 and the highest would be $74.50, because any figure as low as $49.50 would have been rounded to $50 and any figure as high as $74.50 would have been rounded to $74.

When determining real classes from stated classes, we should give thought to the way the data are rounded. Consider, for illustration, the following age distribution of 30 employees:

*The arithmetic mean is the commonly used average that is computed by dividing the sum of the values by the number of values. It is fully discussed in Chapter 4.

†Technically, the original earnings figures that make up this distribution might have been discrete. However, it is convenient and practical to treat the distribution as having been constructed from continuous data. A more precise statement of the real class limits for the distribution as a continuous one is $49.500 . . . 00–$74.499 . . . 99, $74.500 . . . 00–$99.499 . . . 99, etc. Treated as though constructed from discrete data, the real class limits are $49.51–74.50, $74.51–99.50, etc.

AGE	NO. OF EMPLOYEES
18–22	3
23–27	7
28–32	10
33–38	6
39–43	4
Total	30

If the age figures in this distribution were rounded to the nearest year, then the real limits would be 17.50–22.50, 22.50–27.50, etc. However, if the ages were rounded to the last birthday, as is sometimes done, the real age limits would be 18–23, 23–28, etc. The purpose for recording the age data might give the analyst a clue as to which rounding system was used if he does not already know. When there is doubt as to which rounding system was used for any set of data, it is probably wise to assume that the data were rounded to the *nearest* whole unit because that is the most common rounding system.

Unequal class intervals and open-end distributions. Although a general rule is to construct frequency distributions with equal class intervals and closed-end distributions, it is sometimes impractical to do so. A good example of the type of data that would require unequal class intervals and an open-end distribution would be family income for a given geographical area. A frequency distribution of family income in the Milwaukee, Wisconsin, metropolitan area is presented in Table 3-10. The first class of this income distribution has an interval of $3,000*. If every Milwaukee family were included in a closed-end distribution with intervals of $3,000, 100 classes would be needed if the highest family income in 1975 had been $300,000. Such a table would be multimodal, unwieldy, and unattractive and would have little use in economic analysis. In order to present the table with a reasonable number of classes, the class intervals were chosen to bring out the "natural" concentrations of incomes of families in the Milwaukee metropolitan area. Note that the first and last classes have open ends. An open-end class is one for which the lower or upper limits cannot be determined. Also, the midpoints of open-end classes cannot be determined. (Midpoints are discussed in Chapter 4.)

TABLE 3-10 1975 Family Incomes in the Milwaukee Metropolitan Area.

INCOMES	PERCENT OF FAMILIES
Under $3,000	5
$3,000–4,999	6
$5,000–7,999	10
$8,000–9,999	9
$10,000–14,999	32
$15,000–24,999	30
$25,000 and over	8
Total	100

Source: The *Milwaukee Journal Consumer Analysis*, 1975

*It is possible that some family had no income. However, in open-end classes such as this we cannot always assume that the lower limit is zero.

STATISTICAL CHARTS

If a picture is worth a thousand words, then surely a properly constructed chart will attract more attention than a properly constructed table. Charts are used as analytical devices as well as for presenting the results of an analysis. A properly constructed chart shows basic characteristics and general relationships among quantitative measurements without distortion or bias. To avoid distortion, the chartmaker should be familiar with some fundamental rules for chartmaking. Some apply to all types of charts while others apply only to particular types.

There are eight basic types of charts, some of which have several variations. These basic types are:

1) The frequency polygon
2) The frequency histogram
3) The bar chart
4. The pictograph
5) The circle chart
6) The statistical map
7) The scatter diagram
8) The time series line chart.

Rules for constructing the first six will be discussed in this chapter. The scatter diagram is discussed in Chapter 12; the time series line chart is explained in Chapter 15.

Each type of chart has rules unique to that type. However, all charts should have titles that tell what the data are, to where the data refer and to what time periods the data relate. Moreover, all require source notes and some should have footnotes.

The Polygon and Histogram

The shape of frequency distribution may be pictured in a line chart called a polygon, or in a chart with a series of adjacent rectangles called a histogram. These charts should ordinarily be slightly wider than high. Further, the vertical scale number should start with zero, letting the vertical distances on the scale represent equal absolute amounts.

The vertical axis is scaled for plotting frequencies and the horizontal axis presents the real class limits of the frequency distribution. The data in Table 3-9 will be used to demonstrate the construction of both types of charts. Table 3-9 is a repeat of the frequency distribution in Table 3-7 that has a class interval of $25.

The polygon. Chart 3-1 is a polygon. The vertical scale numbers are easy to read and reach a value of 20, which is higher than the largest frequency, 17, so that the line will not go to the top of the chart. The values on the horizontal axis are the real limits of the monthly earnings. Extra classes are added at both ends of the distribution.

Chart 3-1 April earnings of 50 OS University students employed part-time.

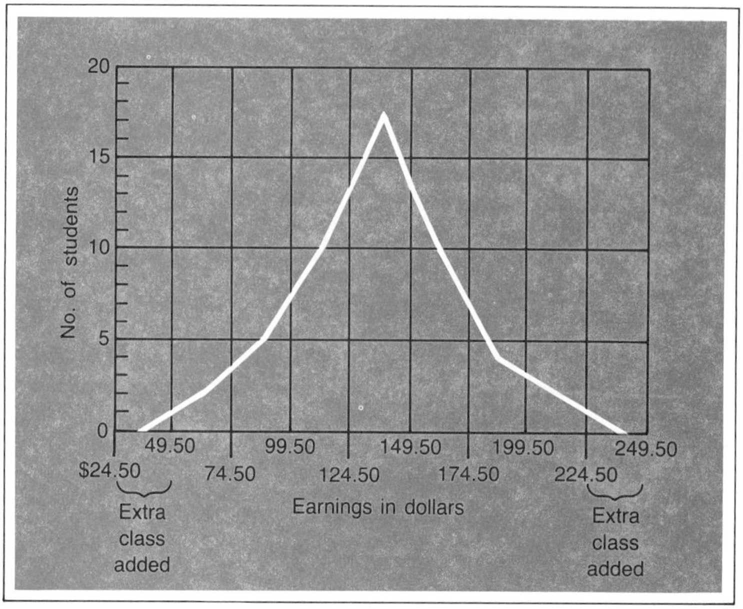

Source of data: Table 3-9.

Use of real class limits, that is $24.50, $49.50, rather than $25, $50, etc., is technically correct. In actual practice, however, an analyst might use the stated limits of this distribution because the convenience in charting and reading might outweigh the importance of $.50 errors in each class limit.

After the real class limits have been written, the frequencies are plotted to the midpoints of the classes. A class is represented by the space between two class limits. The midpoint of a class, therefore, is represented by the middle of space. The plotted points are connected with straight, not curved lines.

Two extra classes with zero frequencies are often added to a polygon chart, one at each end of the distribution, when sample data are being plotted. This is done to indicate the likelihood that the universe from which the sample was drawn had a few values that were smaller, and a few that were larger than those revealed by the sample. It is reasonable to believe, for example, that if the data in Table 3-9 come from a sample of a very large number of students, a few students earned less and $49.50 and a few earned more than $224.50. This likelihood is revealed by bringing the polygon line in Chart 3-1 down to the base (0) at the midpoints of the two added classes. Doing this also reveals more completely the over-all shape of the distribution of the universe from which the sample was drawn.

Chart 3-2 is another polygon. Charted from the data in Table 3-8, this chart pictures a trimodal distribution and illustrates a situation in which the real and stated limits are the same.

Chart 3-2 Average weekly earnings of Class A computer operators in large manufacturing establishments in the Milwaukee metropolitan area, April, 1975.

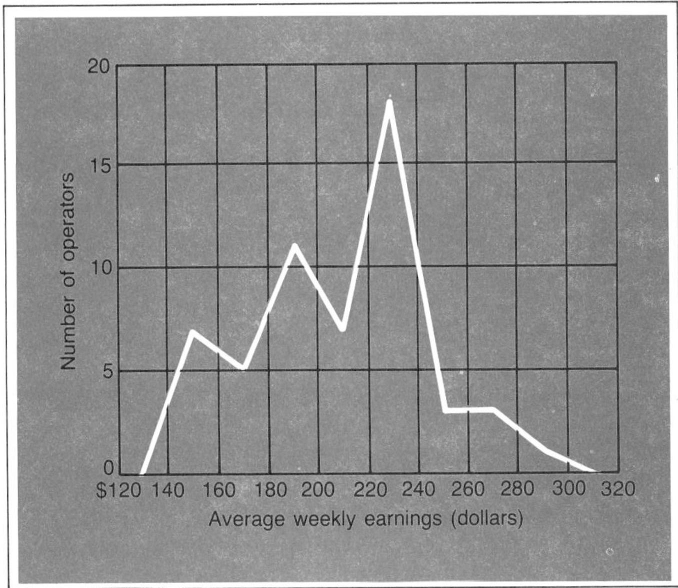

Source of data: Table 3-8.

An analyst usually tries to avoid a bimodal or multimodal (multi-peaked) shape when constructing a frequency distribution from raw data. However, in some cases, as was previously pointed out, the "natural" shape of the data might be bimodal or multimodal. If the data are multimodal in nature, then we would want this revealed in our presentation.

The class limits written on the horizontal axis in chart 3-2 are in even dollars, as given in Table 3-8, because the stated limits and real limits of the classes in the table are the same.

The histogram. Histograms, which are charts with adjacent rectangles, are exemplified by Charts 3-3 and 3-4. After the frequencies have been plotted to the midpoints of the classes, the rectangles are drawn as depicted. The adjacency of the rectangles suggests continuity and flow of frequency values from one class to another. If these rectangles were separated into bars, the spaces between the bars would wrongly suggest discontinuity, so ordinarily we avoid using bar charts for frequency distributions of continuous data.

The polygon has certain advantages over the histogram as a tool for presenting frequency distributions, as you can see by comparing Chart 3-1 with 3-3 and Chart 3-2 with 3-4. First, the polygons show the overall shape of the distributions better by the unbroken lines than do the vertical lines of the rectangles on the histograms. Secondly, the slopes of the lines from midpoint to midpoint on the polygons suggest a graduation of values within classes, which is normally the case, whereas the flat tops of the rectangles in the histograms suggest that all values in a class are the same, which is not normally the

Chart 3-3 April 1975 earnings of 50 OS University students employed part-time.

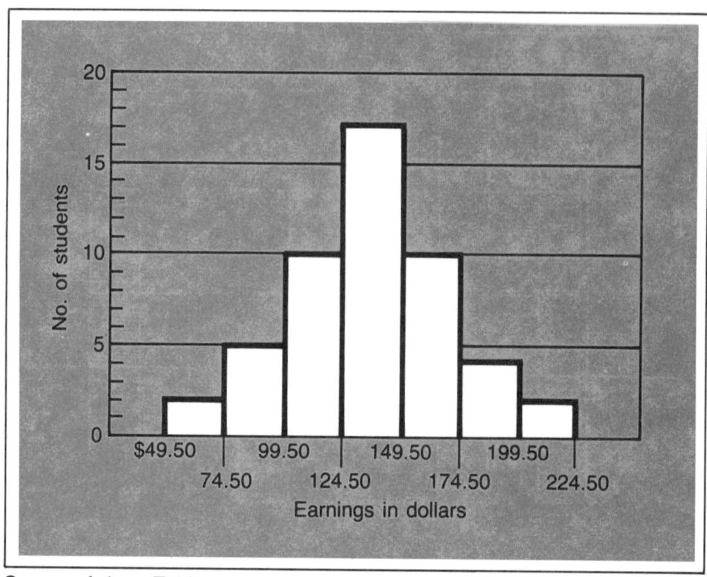

Source of data: Table 3-9.

Chart 3-4 Average weekly earnings of Class A computer operators in large manufacturing establishment, in the Milwaukee metropolitan area, April, 1975 .

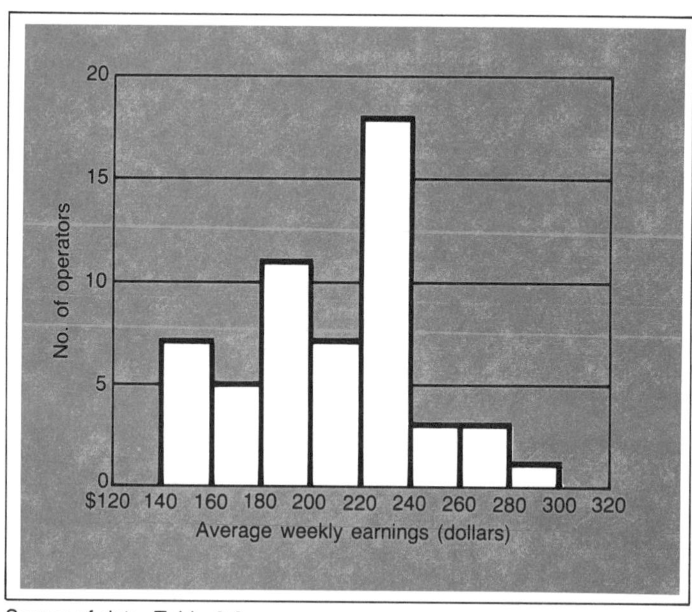

Source of data: Table 3-8.

Chart 3-5 Distribution of final exam grades of two sections of elementary statistics, spring 1975 (50 students in each section).

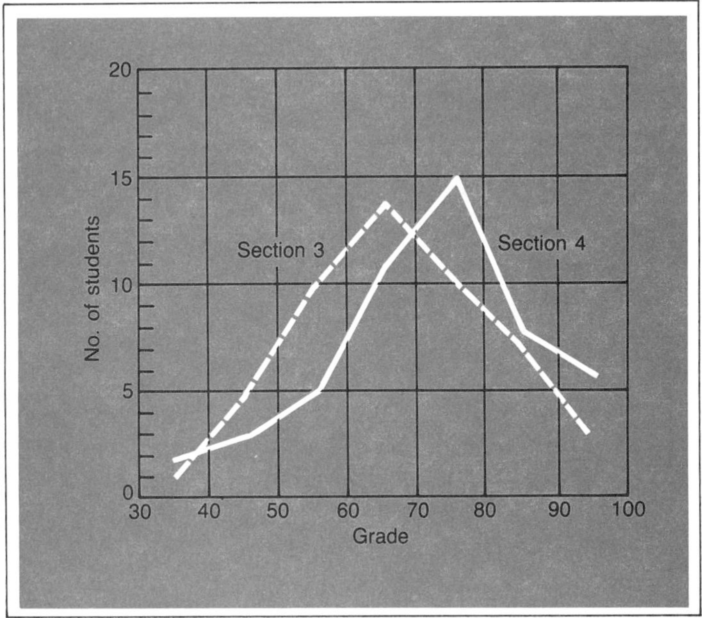

Source of data: Hypothetical.

case. Thirdly, one polygon can be used to compare two or three distributions, as demonstrated by Chart 3-5 but a histogram can be used to chart only one distribution.

TABLE 3-11 Distribution of Midterm Grades of Two Sections of Elementary Statistics, Spring 1976

	NUMBER OF STUDENTS		*PERCENT OF STUDENTS*	
GRADE	*SEC. 1*	*SEC. 2*	*SEC. 1*	*SEC. 2*
30 but under 40	2	1	4.0	3.3
40 but under 50	5	3	10.0	10.0
50 but under 60	7	4	14.0	13.3
60 but under 70	13	12	26.0	40.0
70 but under 80	15	5	30.0	16.7
80 but under 90	5	3	10.0	10.0
90 but under 100	3	2	6.0	6.7
Total	50	30	100.0	100.0

Source: Hypothetical.

Chart 3-6. Percentage distribution of midterm grades of two sections of elementary statistics, spring 1976.

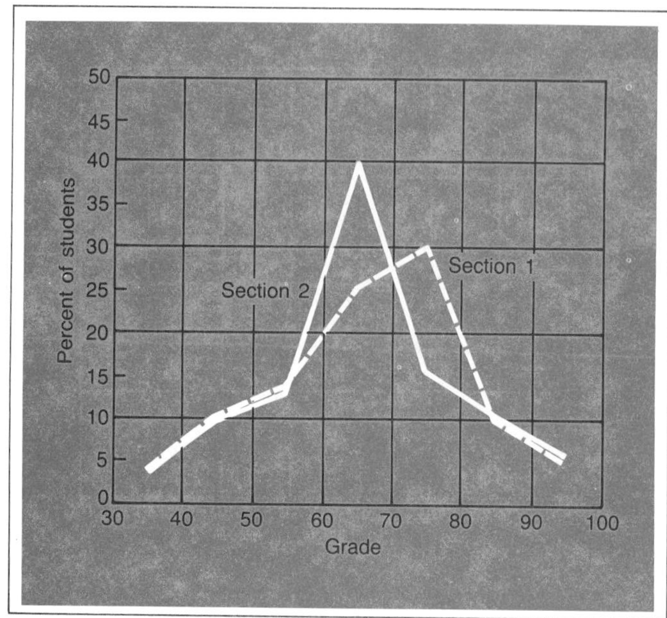

Source of data: Table 3-11.

If the absolute frequencies of two or more distributions are to be compared on the same grid, the totals of the distributions should be the same, or very nearly so, and the class intervals and units in which the classes are measured also should be the same. When the totals differ, comparison in absolute terms becomes difficult. If we want to compare, for example, the grade distributions of two statistics sections, one with 50 students and the other with 30 students, we should use percentage frequencies to make the comparison meaningful. Table 3-11 shows such a distribution and Chart 3-6, a polygon, properly pictures the percentage frequencies.

When two or three distributions are shown on the same grid, comparisons of the dispersion and skewness are often made. Measures of dispersion and skewness are discussed in Chapter 5.

The Bar Chart — Rules for Construction

The bar chart usually does a good job of picturing relationships among data that are classified by geographical area, by kind, or short periods of time. The most widely used types of bar charts are the simple, the component-parts, and the cluster charts. Bar charts are constructed in reference to two perpendicular lines called *axes*.

Quadrant 2	Quadrant 1
Quadrant 3	Quadrant 4

The intersecting horizontal and vertical axes divide the plane into four sections called *quadrants*. Most data are plotted in the first quadrant. Occasionally, negative values require plotting in quadrants 2 and 4, but the third quadrant is rarely used. The following rules help to make bar charts that can be easily interpreted.

Bar Charts, Rules

1) Make the chart slightly wider than it is high.
2) Start the scale values with zero and write them in 5's or 10's or integral multiples of 5's and 10's.
3) Make the width of the space between the bars less than the width of the bars and leave spaces between the margins of the chart and the first and last bars.
4) Shade or cross hatch the bars.

Chart 3-7 Employees in nonagricultural establishments, United States, 1955, 1965, and 1975.

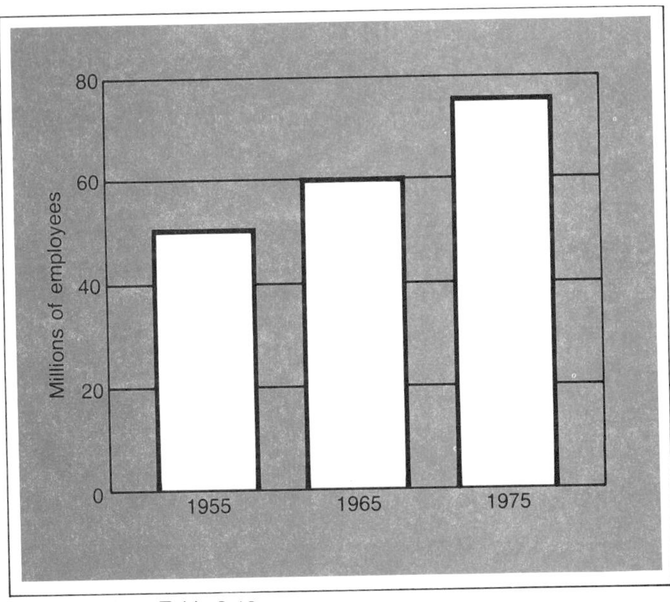

Source of data: Table 3-12.

The simple bar chart. Chart 3-7 is a simple bar chart of employment data from Table 3-12 for selected years. This is a *vertical bar chart*. Vertical bars are usually constructed for data classified quantitatively or by time. Classification by geographical area or by kind is more easily shown in horizontal bar charts because of the wording necessary to identify each bar. Chart 3-8 is a horizontal bar chart of the 1975 data from Table 3-12. It would have looked somewhat awkward to have written "wholesale and retail trade" below a narrow bar; therefore, a horizontal bar chart seems best for that classification of data. Sometimes the choice of a vertical or horizontal bar chart may be arbitrary. If identification of bars requires single, short words, there is no reason why either type could not be used.

The component-parts bar chart. This type of chart is similar to the component-parts line chart. Each bar is divided into the components that make up the total, which is represented by the total length of the bar. Chart 3-9 also was constructed from the data in Table 3-12. In fact, Chart 3-9 is the same as Chart 3-7 except that each bar is divided into four components.

TABLE 3-12 Employees in Nonagricultural Establishments, by Industry, United States, 1950—1975

	THOUSANDS OF EMPLOYEES				
Year	Total*	Manufacturing	Wholesale and retail trade	Government	Other†
1950	45,222	15,241	9,386	6,026	14,569
1955	50,675	16,882	10,535	6,914	16,344
1960	54,203	16,796	11,391	8,353	17,663
1965	60,444	17,984	12,588	10,051	19,821
1970	70,920	19,341	15,040	12,561	23,978
1975	76,985	18,347	16,947	14,773	26,918

	PERCENT OF EMPLOYEES				
Year	Total*	Manufacturing	Wholesale and retail trade	Government	Other†
1950	100.0	33.7	20.8	13.3	32.2
1955	100.0	33.3	20.8	13.6	32.3
1960	100.0	31.0	21.0	15.4	32.6
1965	100.0	29.8	20.8	16.6	32.8
1970	100.0	27.3	21.2	17.7	33.8
1975	100.0	23.8	22.0	19.2	35.0

*Components may not add to totals due to rounding

†Includes mining, contract construction, transportation, public utilities, finance, insurance, real estate, service and miscellaneous industries.

Source: U.S. Department of Commerce, Bureau of the Census, *Statistical Abstract of the United States*, 1966, p. 221, 1975, p. 353; and *Survey of Current Business*, November, 1976.

Chart 3-8 Employees in nonagricultural establishments, by industry, United States, 1975.

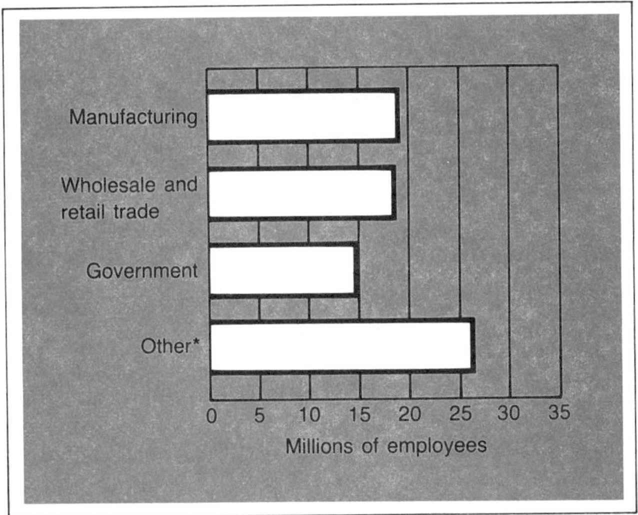

* Includes mining, contract construction, transportation, public utilities, finance, insurance, real estate, service and miscellaneous.

Source of data: Table 3-12.

Chart 3-9 Employees in nonagricultural establishments, by industry, United States, 1955, 1965, and 1975.

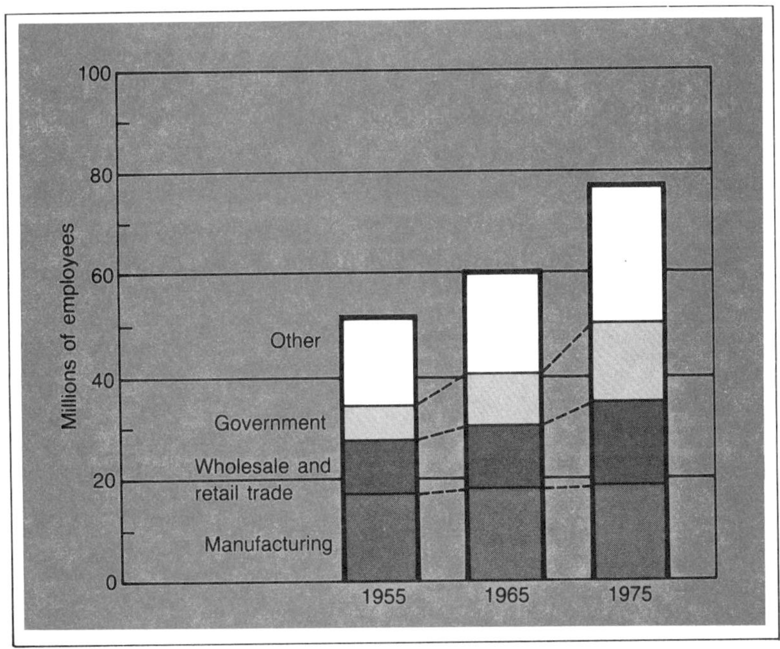

Source of data: Table 3-12.

The cluster bar chart. One frequently sees groups, or clusters, of bars that picture data related to the same time. Chart 3-10 is a good illustration of a cluster bar chart. This chart also demonstrates the effective use of separate legends to identify each bar.

Although Chart 3-10 is acceptable, it is close to being an example of a chart with too many different bars. The purpose of a chart—to reveal meaningful relationships quickly and attractively—is not fulfilled by showing too many relationships. Sometimes it is more effective to present several charts than to show too much on one.

Chart 3-10 Per-capita pieces of mail handled by the U. S. Postal Service, by type, 1960, 1970, and 1975.

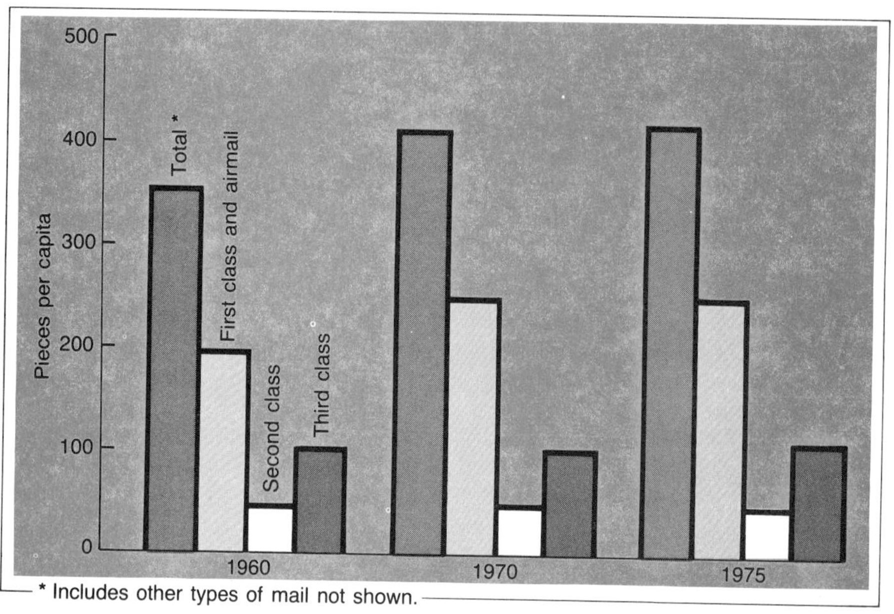

Source of Data: U.S. Department of Commerce, Bureau of the Census, *Statistical Abstract of the United States*, p. 531.

The Pictograph

A properly constructed pictograph is really a bar chart in which each bar is rendered by a series of small pictures. In fact, we could call a pictograph a pictorial bar chart. These attractive charts are effective if the following rules are followed.

Pictograph, Rules

1) Use pictures that depict the units, phenomena, or objects measured.
2) Make all of the pictures the same size.
3) Make each picture represent a large, round, even quantity.

Chart 3-11 has been constructed according to the above rules. In this chart, a *large number* of symbols are used to show increasing magnitudes. This is advisable. Using *larger* symbols is difficult, and it is difficult to construct differently sized symbols so that their sizes will be proportional to the magnitudes of the figures being compared. Chart 3-12 does not reveal the growth in the male population in the United States as well as Chart 3-11.

Chart 3-11 Male population in the United States, 1930, 1960, and 1990 (projection).

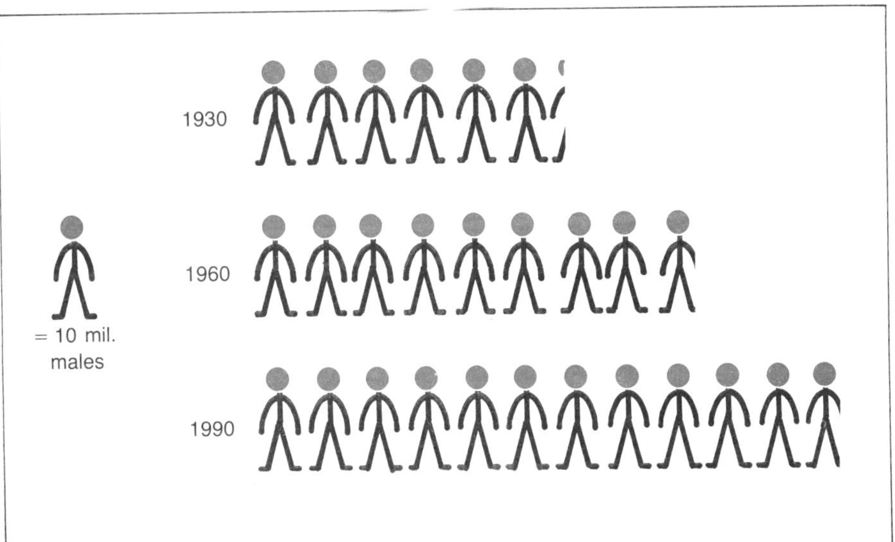

Source of data: U.S. Department of Commerce, *Statistical Abstract of the United States*, 1966, p. 2, and 1975, p. 6.

Chart 3-12 Male population in the United States, 1930, 1960, and 1990 (projection).

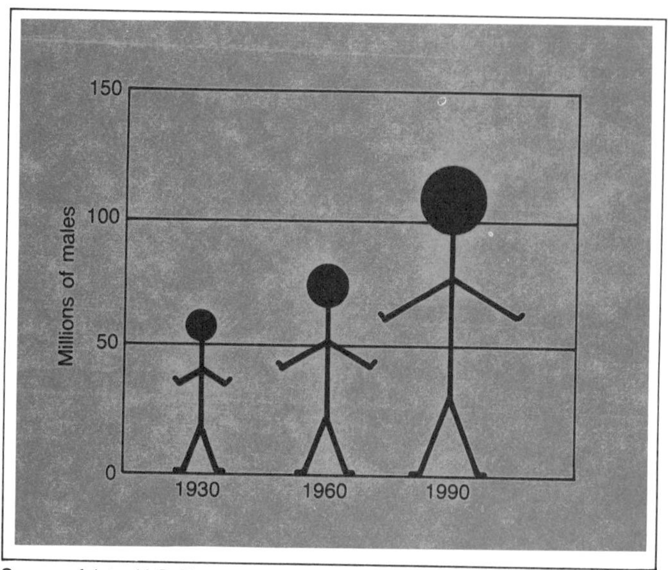

Source of data: U.S. Department of Commerce, *Statistical Abstract of the United States*, 1966, p. 2, and 1975, p. 6.

The Circle or Pie Chart

The percentage distribution of components of a total can be effectively revealed for comparison with the use of circles. Segments of the circles, which resemble pie slices, represent the components. Although components can nearly always be compared on a component-parts bar chart, the circle chart provides variety in a report where several charts are needed. Chart 3-13 exemplifies a properly constructed and effective circle chart.

In this type of chart each circle represents 100%; therefore, when two or more circles are used, all of the circles should have the same diameter because it is extremely difficult for a reader to relate changes in areas of circles to changes in the magnitudes of totals. Also, too many circles should not be used. The author feels that four is the maximum that can be used without creating difficulty for the reader.

Segments (pie slices) of the circle chart are measured with a protractor. Since there are 360° in a circle and since each circle represents 100 %, 3.6° represents 1 %. On the circle for the United States in Chart 3-13, for example, $9 \times 3.6° = 32.4°$ is marked off to represent "electrical, electronic equipment."

When drawing in segments we should be consistent with starting point and order.

Chart 3-13 Percent distribution of value added by manufacture, by industry group, 1972, in the Milwaukee Metropolitan Area and the United States.

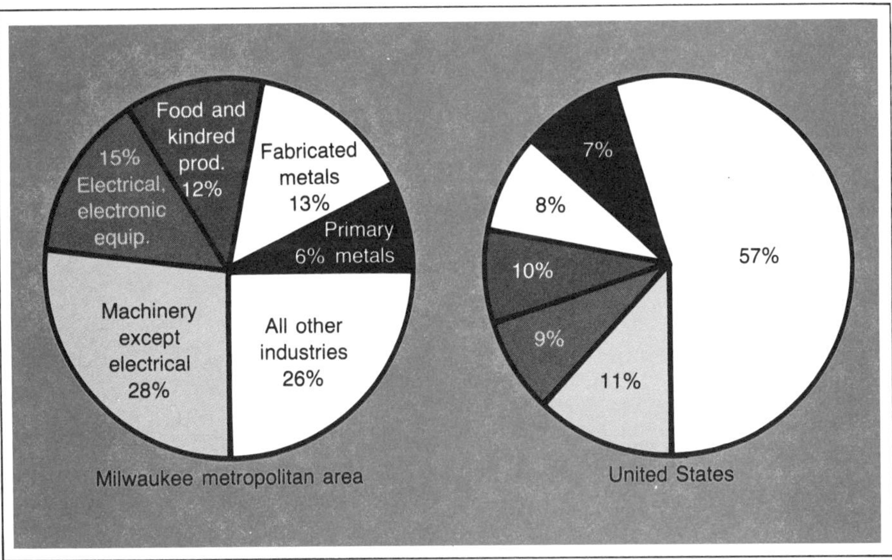

Source of data: U.S. Bureau of the Census, *Census of manufacturers.* 1972.

The layout on both circles in Chart 3-13 started at six o'clock with "machinery, except electrical," and the order of the layout of the other components is the same in both charts.

On this chart, the percentage represented by each component is shown. This is frequently done, but is not always necessary. Notice also that the segments are labeled only in the first circle, which serves as a legend for the second. The use of a separate legend to identify the segments is permissible, but not advisable when it can be done as illustrated, because the eye must shift from the legends to the circles and the reader must remember the legend identifications.

Statistical Maps

There are several types of statistical maps that display numerical relationships attractively and effectively. One of the most commonly used styles is shown in Chart 3-14. This is called a *cross-hatched map*. Cross-hatched maps are often used for quantitative measurements that fall into frequency distribution classes. A separate legend identifies the quantitative classes represented by cross-hatched designs. Separate legends, as shown at the bottom and leftside of the map, are a necessity on these maps.

Chart 3-14 Life insurance in force in the United States by state, 1972.

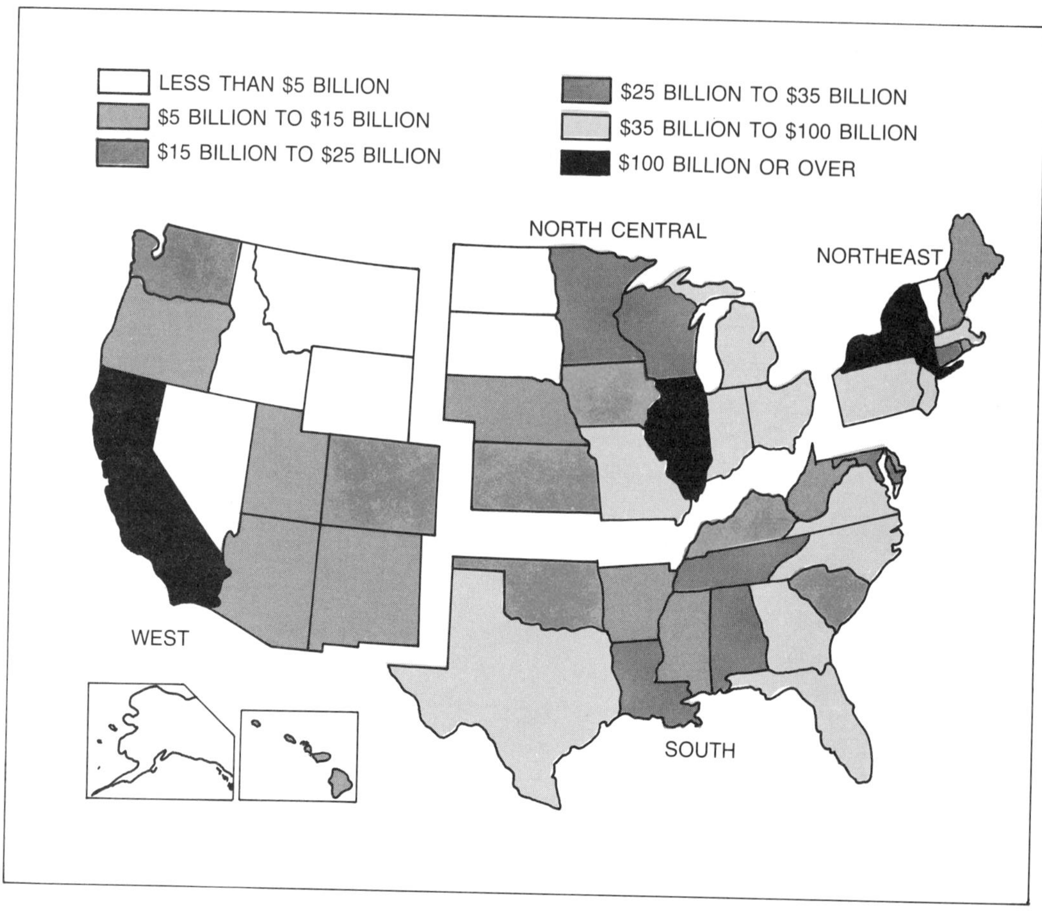

Source: *Life Insurance Fact Book*, 1973.

Another type of map frequently seen is a *dot map*, in which dots are used to represent numerical magnitudes. For example, we might show the geographical distribution of cattle in Texas, by county, by letting one dot represent 100,000 head of cattle. A county with a million head would have 10 dots within its boundaries.

Charting Aids

You do not have to be an artist to construct attractive charts. Tools for lettering, available in many artist's supply houses, make it possible, with just a little practice, to print professional-looking headings, scale values, etc.

Also, perfectly good charts can be constructed without the use of ink. Narrow tapes of various widths and colors are available for marking grid lines and lines that depict fluctuations in data.

Cross-hatched charts can be prepared with commercial cross-hatched paper, which comes in dozens of designs. It is sold in large sheets, about the size of legal stationery, and is slightly adhesive on one side so that the design will stick to the chart. Symbols for making pictographs are also available on adhesive sheets.

Colors may enhance the appearance of a chart if they are carefully chosen. Subdued tones should usually be used. Bright colors tend to distract the reader from the relationships revealed in the chart. Chart 3-14 exemplifies an effective use of color.

REVIEW QUESTIONS

1. Name and give the function of each part of a statistical table.
2. How can figures in a table be emphasized?
3. Discuss the ruling of a table.
4. Give five good rules for constructing tables, other than those special rules relating to frequency distributions.
5. What special rules should be considered when constructing a frequency distribution?
6. Give five general rules for constructing charts.
7. What special rules apply to the drawing of pictographs and circle charts?
8. Why should the numerical scale of a chart begin with 0? Are there any exceptions?
9. Discuss the advantages of the polygon over the histogram.

PROBLEMS

Instructions: Type statistical tables if possible. Construct all charts on commercial chart paper, using a ballpoint pen to draw necessary lines.

1. Using Exercise Table 3-1 below, set up a table showing only the data for 1970 and 1975, and percentage change in the number of each type of construction between those two years.

EXERCISE TABLE 3-1 Value of New Private Construction in the United States By Type, 1970–75. (Billions of Dollars.)

YEAR	*TOTAL*[1]	*RESIDENTIAL*	*INDUSTRIAL*	*COMMERCIAL*	*OTHER BUILDINGS*[2]	*PUBLIC UTILITIES AND OTHER*
1970	66.8	31.9	6.5	9.8	5.1	13.5
1971	80.1	43.3	5.4	11.6	5.4	14.3
1972	93.9	54.3	4.7	13.5	5.9	15.6
1973	103.4	57.6	6.2	15.5	5.9	18.2
1974	97.1	47.0	7.9	16.0	5.8	20.4
1975	89.9	42.9	7.8	12.8	5.6	20.8

[1]Components may not add to totals due to rounding.

[2]Includes religious, educational, hospital, institutional, and other buildings.

Source: *Federal Reserve Bulletin*, April 1976, p.A51.

2. From the information on page 79 of *Business Statistics*, 1975, published by the U.S. Department of Commerce, construct a table showing only the data for 1964 and 1974, the percentage change for each type of industry, and the total for all industries.
3. A table in the April, 1976 *Federal Reserve Bulletin* (page 46) reveals that total installment credit outstanding in the United States grew from $148,278 million in 1973 to $161,819 million in 1975. The largest holders of this installment credit, commercial banks, had an increase from $71,871 million in 1973 to $75,710 in 1975. Other holders of installment credit had the following respective 1973 and 1975 volumes: finance companies, $37,243 and $38,932 million; credit unions, $19,609 and $25,354 million; retailers, $16,395 and $18,328 million, and others, $3,155 and $3,495 million. Construct a table from this information and show the percentage increase in each category.
4. Construct two different frequency distributions from Exercise Table 3-2 below. Use a different class interval for each table, but try to use equal class intervals in each table and still get a unimodal distribution. (In Exercise Table 3-2 the word ''average'' refers to the arithmetic mean.)

EXERCISE TABLE 3-2 Average Hourly Earnings of Production Workers in Manufacturing Industries, by State, 1974.

STATE	*AVERAGE HOURLY EARNINGS*	*STATE*	*AVERAGE HOURLY EARNINGS*
Maine	3.51	North Carolina	3.28
New Hampshire	3.64	South Carolina	3.32
Vermont	3.78	Georgia	3.54
Massachusetts	4.16	Florida	3.74
Rhode Island	3.62	Kentucky	4.30
Connecticut	4.42	Tennessee	3.62
New York	4.53	Alabama	3.76
New Jersey	4.57	Mississippi	3.18

STATE	AVERAGE HOURLY EARNINGS	STATE	AVERAGE HOURLY EARNINGS
Pennsylvania	4.57	Arkansas	3.30
Ohio	5.12	Louisiana	4.40
Indiana	5.04	Oklahoma	3.97
Illinois	4.91	Texas	4.08
Michigan	5.62	Montana	4.95
Wisconsin	4.81	Idaho	4.39
Minnesota	4.66	Wyoming	4.85
Iowa	4.91	Colorado	4.16
Missouri	4.37	New Mexico	3.33
North Dakota	3.83	Arizona	4.40
South Dakota	3.79	Utah	3.92
Nebraska	4.06	Nevada	4.89
Kansas	4.24	Washington	5.23
Delaware	4.58	Oregon	5.02
Maryland	4.62	California	4.73
Virginia	3.65	Alaska	6.83
West Virginia	4.53	Hawaii	4.25

Source: U.S. Department of Commerce, Bureau of the Census, *Statistical Abstract of the United States*, 1974, p.367.

5. Using the information in Exercise Table 3-3, set up another table showing only the percent increase in each type of insurance in force, and the percent increase in the total between 1970 and 1975.

EXERCISE TABLE 3-3 Amount of Life Insurance in Force, in the United States, 1969–1975. (Billions of Dollars.)

YEAR	ORDINARY	GROUP	INDUSTRIAL	CREDIT	TOTAL*
1969	682	489	39	75	1,285
1970	735	551	39	77	1,402
1971	792	590	39	82	1,503
1972	854	641	40	93	1,628
1973	928	708	41	101	1,778
1974	1,009	827	39	110	1,985
1975	1,083	904	39	112	2,140

*Components may not add to totals due to rounding.

Source: Institute of Life Insurance, *Life Insurance Fact Book*, 1976, p.21.

6. From Table 433 of the 1976 *Statistical Abstract of the United States* (p. 268), construct a frequency distribution showing the total amount of direct general expenditure of state and local governments for the fifty states in 1974.

7. From Exercise Table 3-4 compute the percent of total tax revenue collected by each type of government for each of the years and show this information in another simple table.

EXERCISE TABLE 3-4 Tax Revenue, by Level of Government, United States, Selected Years. (Billions of Dollars.)

LEVEL OF GOVERNMENT	1950	1955	1960	1965	1970
Federal	$35.2	$57.6	$77.0	$93.7	$146.1
State	7.9	11.6	18.0	26.1	48.0
Local	8.0	11.9	18.1	25.5	38.8
Total	51.1	81.1	113.1	145.3	232.9

Source: U.S. Department of Commerce, Bureau of the Census, *Statistical Abstract of the United States*, 1966 and 1975.

8. Picture all of the information in Exercise Table 3-4 as a component-parts bar chart.
9. Using the percentages of total for each of the years computed in Problem 7, draw a component-parts bar chart.
10. Make a circle chart of the percentages of total computed for 1950 and 1970 in Problem 7.
11. Chart one of the frequency distributions constructed in Problem 4 as a histogram. Chart the other distributions as a polygon.

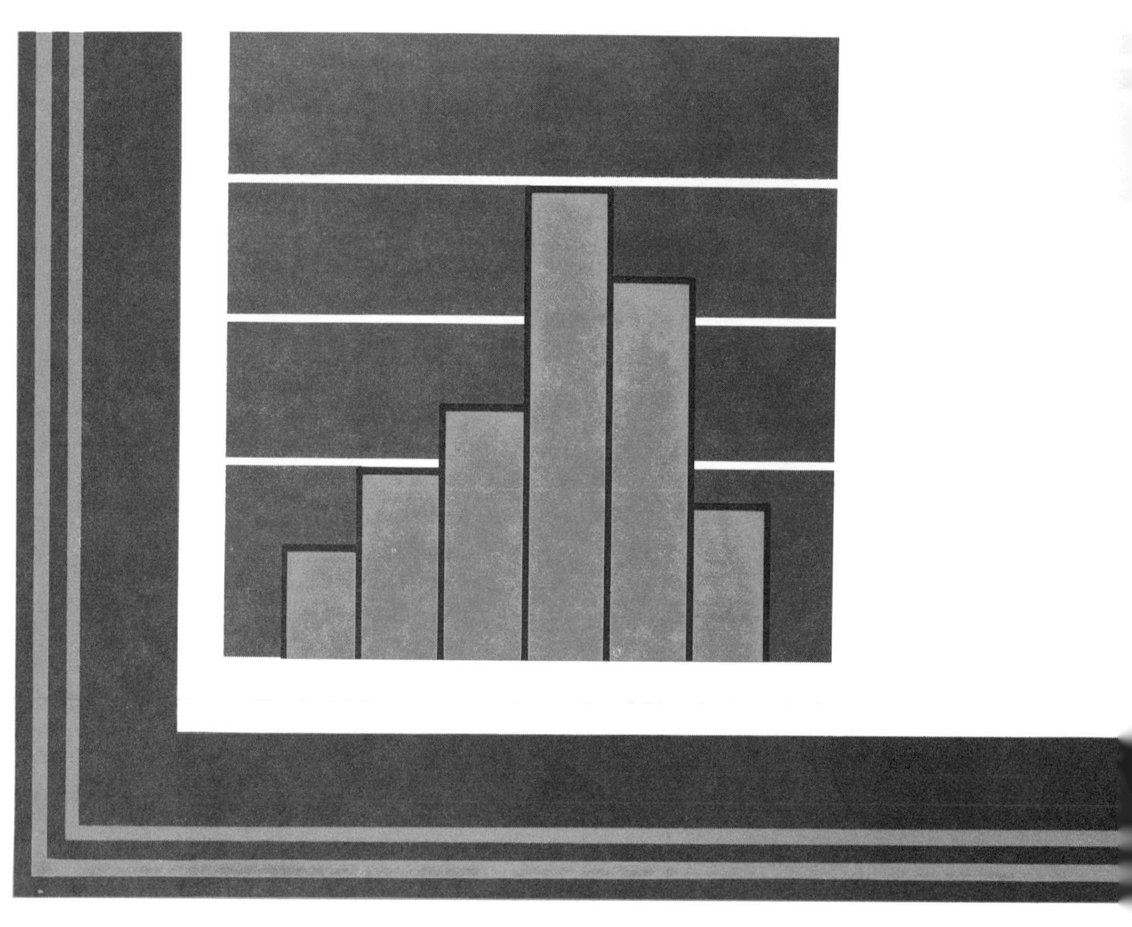

4

Averages

When an analyst describes the characteristics of a large group of numbers he tries to do it in a simple way that is clear and useful to himself and to others. For example, if he wants to describe the general or typical magnitude of a group of figures, he usually computes a single figure called an *average*.

Most of you are familiar with the concept of averages, at least in a nebulous sort of way, because teachers give class averages for grades on examinations and other work. However, most people do not realize that there are several types of averages and that these averages have special names, unique characteristics, and special uses. Regardless of which average is used, the basic purpose of an average is to measure, with one figure, the general magnitude of a group of numbers.

TYPES OF AVERAGES

There are five types of averages in general use and three of these are used more frequently than the others. These are the *arithmetic mean*, the *median*, and the *mode*. The *geometric mean* and the *harmonic mean* are used less frequently, but they are important enough to discuss.

The calculation of each of these averages from ungrouped data and the estimation of the mean, median, and mode from frequency distributions will be demonstrated. Their definitions, characteristics, and uses will be emphasized because no statistical measure is of value to anyone if he does not know how and when to use it and what it means.

AVERAGES OF UNGROUPED DATA

The Arithmetic Mean

Arithmetic Mean

The most widely used average, the arithmetic mean is defined as the sum of a set of numbers divided by the number of numbers in the set.

For example, the arithmetic mean age of five children of a family whose ages are 5, 12, 16, 18, and 24 years is:

$$\frac{5 + 12 + 16 + 18 + 24}{5} = \frac{75}{5} = 15 \text{ years}$$

This average might be used to represent the age of all five children, but note that no child in the family is the average age. Note also that the average would be more representative of the ages of the five children if they were 13, 14, 15, 16, and 17 years old. In other words, an arithmetic mean effectively describes the general magnitude of a group of figures only if the figures are somewhat homogeneous.

A general formula for computing the arithmetic mean of a list of numbers can be written

$$\overline{X} = \frac{\Sigma X}{N}$$

where $\overline{X}$ is the symbol for the arithmetic mean of the values labeled X. The Greek symbol Σ (a capital sigma) represents the summing of the values, and N stands for the number of values being averaged. Calculations and substitutions in this formula for the five ages given above are:

	X
	5
	12
	16
	18
	24
Total =	75

$$\overline{X} = \frac{\Sigma X}{N} = \frac{75}{5} = 15$$

The symbols in this formula are more or less standard among statisticians. Sometimes, however, we might label figures Y or Z. If so, the formula becomes

$$\overline{Y} = \frac{\Sigma Y}{N} \text{ or } \overline{Z} = \frac{\Sigma Z}{N}$$

The symbol Σ is used almost universally as a summation symbol.

Arithmetic Mean

The arithmetic mean normally should be used only if the figures are being averaged are quite uniform in magnitude.

For example, suppose there are six families on the block where your family lives and their respective annual incomes are $9,500, $10,400, $10,800, $11,300, $12,000, and

$150,000. The arithmetic mean of these incomes is $34,000, which is highly unrepresentative of the general income level on the block. In a case such as this, it might be better, for most purposes, to compute a modified arithmetic mean by eliminating the family income of $150,000 and then computing the arithmetic mean of the other five. A *modified arithmetic mean* is one that is computed with figures that remain after atypical (extremely high and/or low) figures have been removed. Its practical use is illustrated in Chapter 14.

Many marketing researchers and sales managers prefer some other average to represent the income levels of families in specific geographical areas because the arithmetic mean is easily biased upward by a few, relatively wealthy families. Of course, downward biases also can result from extremely low figures. Such biases are due to an important characteristic of the arithmetic mean.

Arithmetic Mean

The magnitude of every figure in the calculation affects the magnitude of arithmetic mean.

The arithmetic mean is subject to algebraic manipulation, so it is very useful in certain types of analyses, particularly in sampling.

Arithmetic Mean

The arithmetic mean multiplied by the number of figures from which it was calculated equals the sum of the figures.

To illustrate, if all we know about the families on your block is that the arithmetic mean income is $34,000 annually and that six families live on the block, then we can multiply $34,000 by six to get the total annual family income in the block, $204,000; that is, if $\overline{X} = \Sigma X/N$, then $\Sigma X = \overline{X}N$.

Arithmetic Mean

An advantage of the arithmetic mean over other averages is that it can be computed even if only the total of the figures and the number of figures is known.

To exemplify: The 1975 *Statistical Abstract of the United States* shows that in 1974, 20,046,000 manufacturing employees in the United States earned a total of $211.2 billion; therefore, dividing the number of employees into the total earnings gives the arithmetic mean earnings of each employee as $10,536.

The weighted arithmetic mean. Occasionally, when the arithmetic mean of certain data is desired the nature of the data is such that weighting also is required. A simple illustration will make this clear. Assume that a student receives the following grades during a semester: English, B; Math, A; Chemistry, A; History, C; and Speech, C. Assume also that the quality points for each grade are: A, 4; B, 3; C,2; and D, 1. If the student desires to compute his quality point average for the semester, he can take the sum of the quality points for each course, 3 + 4 + 4 + 2 + 2, divide it by 5, the number of courses he took, and get the arithmetic mean of 3 quality points. This unweighted arithmetic mean would be correct if each course carried the same number of credit hours.* If, as is usually the case, the number of credit hours differed, then the quality points would need to be weighted. If English was a 3-hour course,math a 4-hour, Chemistry a 5-hour, History a 3-hour, and Speech a 2-hour course, the weighted arithmetic mean would be calculated as illustrated in Table 4-1. There, each grade is "weighted" by multiplying by its number of hours; these products wX are added, and the sum is divided by the total number of hours, or "weights." $\overline{X}_w$ is the symbol for the weighted arithmetic mean; the numerator ΣwX is the sum of the weighted values; and the denominator Σw is the sum of the weights. The result, 3.24, is the weighted and more correct average of quality points per credit hour.

TABLE 4-1 Calculation of the Weighted Arithmetic Mean of the Grade Quality Points Earned in Five Courses

COURSE	*GRADE*	*QUALITY POINTS (X)*	*CREDIT HOURS (w)*	*WEIGHTED QUALITY POINTS (wX)*
English	B	3	3	9
Math	A	4	4	16
Chemistry	A	4	5	20
History	C	2	3	6
Speech	C	2	2	4
Total		15	17	55

$$\overline{X}_w = \frac{\Sigma wX}{\Sigma w} = \frac{55}{17} = 3.24$$

*An unweighted arithmetic mean is in reality a weighted mean with equal weights given to each value. Some analysts call it the *simple* arithmetic mean.

TABLE 4-2. Calculation of the Weighted Arithmetic Mean of the April 1975 Weekly Earnings of Drafters in the Milwaukee Metropolitan Area

CLASS OF DRAFTERS	*APRIL 1975 WEEKLY EARNINGS* (X)	*NO. OF DRAFTERS* (w)	*WEIGHTED EARNINGS* (wX)
A	$ 231.50	474	$109,731.00
B	201.00	304	61,104.00
C	161.00	225	36,225.00
Tracers	133.50	66	8,811.00
Total	$ 727.00	1,069	$215,871.00

$$\overline{X}_w = \frac{\Sigma wX}{\Sigma w} = \frac{215{,}871.00}{1{,}069} = \$201.94$$

Another example using the weighted arithmetic mean may be helpful. The U.S. Bureau of Labor Statistics reports arithmetic mean weekly earnings of four classes of draftsmen in the Milwaukee, Wisconsin, metropolitan area as follows: class A, $231.50; class B, $201.00; class C, $161.00; and tracers, $133.50. To get the arithmetic mean weekly earnings for all four classes requires the calculation of the weighted arithmetic mean because the number of employees in each class differs. The necessary calculations are shown in Table 4-2. The result, $201.94 is the correct arithmetic mean weekly earnings because it is found by dividing the total earnings in a week by the total number of workers. The unweighted arithmetic mean

$$\frac{\Sigma X}{N} = \frac{727.00}{4} = \$181.75$$

is unrealistic. This illustration should be a warning to always ask yourself if the data to be averaged should be weighted first in order to avoid serious mistakes.

The Median

Median

The median is defined as the middle number of an ordered group of numbers or that number in a group that has 50% of the numbers equal to or smaller than it and 50% of the numbers equal to or larger than it.

The median of the figures 7, 8, 11, 13, and 19 is 11. This figure divides the list into two equal groups.

The median is always one of the listed figures when there is an odd number of them. When there is an even number of figures, however, the median is determined by taking the arithmetic mean of the two central numbers in the arrayed list. For the numbers 7, 8, 11, 13, 19, and 20, the median is

$$\frac{11 + 13}{2} = 12$$

Three of the figures are smaller than 12 and three are larger. This method of determining the median of an even number of figures has general acceptance among analysts, statisticians, and mathematicians.

Median

Once the median has been determined, the magnitudes of the figures on both sides of it have no influence on its magnitude, and changing the values of the figures does not change the value of the median unless another figure replaces it as the center figure.

For the six numbers 7, 8, 11, 13, 19, and 20, the median will still be 12 if the number 20 is changed to 200, 20,000, or any other number larger than 13. However, the arithmetic mean of the six numbers is

$$\frac{7 + 8 + 11 + 13 + 19 + 20}{6} = \frac{78}{6} = 13$$

But when the 20 changes to 200 or some other number the mean is no longer 13. Because the median is not affected by the extreme values we often see mention of median family incomes, median monthly rents and medians of other data where a few unusually high figures would distort the typicalness of an arithmetic mean.

A shortcoming of the median is that it cannot be used to estimate the total of a group of figures as can the arithmetic mean, unless, of course, it is equal to the arithmetic mean.

Median

The median cannot be treated algebraically like the arithmetic mean, but it is the only average that can be reliably estimated for an open-end frequency distribution and it is a useful average for highly skewed data.

The Mode

Mode

The mode of a group of figures is the figure that appears most often. (The mode of the numbers 5, 10, 10, 19, 20, and 25 is 10.) Like the median, its value is not affected by the magnitudes of the other figures once it is determined and it cannot be treated algebraically.

We must be careful in choosing the mode as an average to represent a group of figures, as the following example will illustrate. Suppose that in a group of 12 people there are 10 adults, each a different age, and two children both aged three. In this case, three years is the modal age of the group, but it certainly does not represent the ages of all 12 people. On the other hand, a list of the ages of 300 college freshmen might reveal that 250 are 18 years of age, which would be the mode and which also would be a very good average to use for the ages of those freshmen. These illustrations point out an important guideline for using the mode.

Mode

The mode should be used as an average only when it is a highly predominate figure in the group.

The mode can be the only average that applies in a given situation. This fact was well illustrated to the author when he asked a neighbor at a luncheon what business he was in. The man replied, "I manufacture windows." When asked what size window he manufactured, he answered, "The average size." This manufacturer may have never heard of the term "mode," but it is likely that that was the average he was talking about; that is, he manufactured the size window used more often than other sizes. The arithmetic mean size or median size might not fit any window frame. You can see, therefore, that at times the mode is the natural or only average to use.

A characteristic of the mode is that its value is not affected by the magnitude of the other figures once it is determined. For example, the mode of the numbers 6, 10, 7, 7, 7, 10, and 12 is 7, and the mode of the numbers 6, 10, 7, 7, 7, 10, and 1000 is also 7. It is left to you to determine the differences in the arithmetic means of these two groups of numbers.

The Geometric Mean

Geometric Mean

The geometric mean is defined as the Nth root of the product of N values. Therefore, all of the values being averaged directly affect its magnitude.

Letting G stand for geometric mean, N the number of values, and X a value, the general formula for this measure can be written

$$G = \sqrt[N]{X_1 \cdot X_2 \cdot X_3 \cdots X_N}$$

A calculation of the geometric mean of three values, 10, 15, and 20 is

$$G = \sqrt[3]{10 \times 15 \times 20} = \sqrt[3]{3000} = 14.42$$

This is less than the arithmetic mean of the values, which is 15.

Geometric Mean

The geometric mean will always be less than the arithmetic mean of the same numbers, unless the numbers are all the same, because the geometric mean gives less weight to the larger values than does the arithmetic mean. Moreover, the geometric mean is zero if any value in the series is zero, and it may be imaginary if negative values are used.

The geometric mean is used primarily to obtain the average rates of change in values over periods of time. Consider the data in Table 4-3, which shows a family's income in each year 1972 through 1975 as a percent of the previous year's income. If we want the average annual *rate of change* in the family's income for the entire period, we must compute $G - 1$ because G will give the average annual *ratio of change*. Since the ratios in the table are the X values,

$$G = \sqrt[4]{1.05 \times 1.17 \times 1.33 \times 1.25}$$

It will be expedient to calculate the fourth root of the product of these four ratios with logarithms;* therefore

$$\log G = \log \sqrt[4]{1.05 \times 1.17 \times 1.33 \times 1.25}$$

$$= \frac{\log 1.05 + \log 1.17 + \log 1.33 + \log 1.25}{4}$$

$$= \frac{0.0212 + 0.0682 + 0.1239 + 0.0969}{4}$$

$$= \frac{0.3102}{4} = 0.07755$$

$$G = 1.196$$

which is the average annual ratio of increase in the family's income. Therefore

$$G - 1 = 1.196 - 1 = 0.196 = 19.6\%$$

which is the average annual percentage *increase* in the family's income between 1972 and 1975.

There is a quicker way to calculate an average rate of change in data classified by time when the values used to compute the individual ratios of change from one period to another are available. The retail sales data in Table 4-4 will help to demonstrate this method.

If we let S_0, S_1, S_2, S_3, S_4, and S_5 be the values of sales in 1970, 1971, 1972, 1973, 1974, and 1975, respectively, then

$$X_1 = \frac{S_1}{S_0}, X_2 = \frac{S_2}{S_1}, X_3 = \frac{S_3}{S_2}, X_4 = \frac{S_4}{S_3}, X_5 = \frac{S_5}{S_4}$$

and

$$G = \sqrt[5]{\frac{S_1}{S_0} \times \frac{S_2}{S_1} \times \frac{S_3}{S_2} \times \frac{S_4}{S_3} \times \frac{S_5}{S_4}} = \sqrt[5]{\frac{S_5}{S_0}}$$

Substituting the sales for 1970 and 1975

$$G = \sqrt[5]{\frac{585}{381}} = \sqrt[5]{1.535}$$

$$\log G = \log \sqrt[5]{1.535} = \frac{\log 1.535}{5} = \frac{0.1861}{5} = 0.0372$$

*Calculations with logarithms is reviewed in Appendix C.

$$G = 1.090$$

$$G - 1 = 1.090 - 1 = 0.090 = 9.0\%$$

which is the average annual rate of increase for the entire period.

Below Table 4-4 the geometric mean is calculated using all five annual ratios of change, and the answer is the same as that obtained in the preceding calculations. The difference between the sum of the logarithms of the five ratios shown in the table, 0.1855, and the logarithm of 1.535, which is 0.1861, is due to rounding of the ratios.

TABLE 4-3. Income of a Family as Ratios of Preceding Years, 1972—1975.

YEAR	*INCOME AS A RATIO OF PRECEDING YEAR (X)*
1972	1.05
1973	1.17
1974	1.33
1975	1.25

TABLE 4-4. Calculation of the Geometric Mean of Annual Ratios of Change in Retail Sales in the United States, 1970—1975.

YEAR	*RETAIL SALES IN THE U.S. (BILLIONS) (S)*	*RATIO OF SALES TO PRECEDING YEAR'S SALES (X)*	*LOG OF THE RATIOS (log X)*
1970	$381	—	—
1971	410	1.076	0.0318
1972	449	1.095	0.0394
1973	505	1.124	0.0508
1974	538	1.065	0.0273
1975	585	1.087	0.0362
Total	—	—	0.1855

$$G = \sqrt[5]{X_1 \cdot X_2 \cdot X_3 \cdot X_4 \cdot X_5}$$

$$\log G = \frac{\log X_1 + \log X_2 + \log X_3 + \log X_4 + \log X_5}{5}$$

$$\log G = \frac{0.1855}{5} = 0.0371$$

$$G = 1.090 = 109.0\%$$

Since the calculation of the average ratio of change over a time span requires only the values for the beginning and ending periods, which can be called P_0 and P_n, we can compute the average rate of change for the years, months, or other time intervals between P_0 and P_n without knowing the values for the intervening time periods. For example, the population of Wisconsin was 3,952,000 on April 1, 1960, and 4,418,000 on April 1, 1970. Computing the average annual ratio of increase

$$G = \sqrt[N]{\frac{P_n}{P_0}} = \sqrt[10]{\frac{4{,}418{,}000}{3{,}952{,}000}} = \sqrt[10]{1.118}$$

$$\log G = \frac{\log 1.118}{10} = \frac{0.0484}{10} = 0.0048$$

$$G = 1.011$$

$$G - 1 = 1.011 - 1 = 0.011 = 1.1\%$$

We could also compute the average monthly rate of growth in Wisconsin's population for the decade by computing

$$G - 1 = \sqrt[120]{1.118} - 1 = 1.00093 - 1 = 0.00093 = 0.093\% \text{ per month}$$

because there are 120 months between April 1, 1960 and April 1, 1970.

The Harmonic Mean

Harmonic Mean

The harmonic mean is the reciprocal of the arithmetic mean of the reciprocals of the numbers being averaged; therefore, each figure being averaged directly affects its magnitude. The harmonic mean of a set of ratios equals the *weighted* arithmetic mean of the ratios if the numerators from which the ratios were computed are the same.

Written as a statistical formula the harmonic mean may be defined as

$$H = \frac{1}{\frac{\Sigma \frac{1}{X}}{N}}$$

where H is the symbol for the harmonic mean, X is a number in the series, and N represents the number of numbers. With the use of simple algebra the formula can be converted to read

$$H = \frac{N}{\Sigma \frac{1}{X}}$$

which makes it more convenient to use. The calculation of the harmonic mean of the numbers 5, 10, and 20 is:

$$H = \frac{3}{\frac{1}{5} + \frac{1}{10} + \frac{1}{20}} = \frac{3}{\frac{4}{20} + \frac{2}{20} + \frac{1}{20}} = \frac{3}{\frac{7}{20}} = \frac{60}{7} = 8.57$$

Incidentally, the arithmetic and geometric means of these three numbers, 11.7 and 10.0, respectively, are larger than the harmonic mean because the harmonic mean gives less weight to the larger values and more weight to the smaller values than do the arithmetic and geometric means. This characteristic always results in a harmonic mean that is smaller than the other two unless the numbers being averaged are the same. For example, the arithmetic mean, the geometric mean, and the harmonic mean of 10, 10, and 10 are all equal to 10. Moreover, the harmonic mean cannot be determined if any of the values are zero because zero does not have a reciprocal.

Use of the harmonic mean. Table 4-5 illustrates three conditions for which the harmonic mean has been calculated. Since the harmonic mean is used most frequently for averaging rates, wage rates are considered in the table, which shows the hourly wage in three factories. In factories A, B, and C, the respective hourly wage of production workers is $4.00, $5.00, and $8.00. If we need to know the average hourly wage of the production workers in all three plants, is the harmonic mean the *best* average to use for each example? The answer depends upon the conditions that exist for a particular example. The weighted arithmetic mean would always be the correct one, but its computation would require the hours worked at each rate. If the hours worked at each rate are equal, as in Example 1, the unweighted arithmetic mean would be correct because it gives the same answer as the weighted arithmetic mean. The harmonic mean is not appropriate because it should be used only when the numerators of the fractions from which the wage rates were computed are the same. Such a condition exists in Example 2 of Table 4-5. The hourly wage rate for a group of workers can be computed by dividing the total number of hours worked into the total earnings of the workers. In Example 2, it is assumed that the total earnings in each of the three factories was the same—$40,000—but that the hours worked differed. Under these conditions, the harmonic mean, $5.217, is the same as the weighted arithmetic mean, which is always appropriate; therefore, the harmonic mean correctly measures the average hourly wage for the three plants in Example 2. The unweighted arithmetic mean under these conditions would not be appropriate.

Example 3 of Table 4-5 shows that neither the unweighted arithmetic mean nor the harmonic mean would be a correct measure of the average if both the hours worked and

TABLE 4-5. Determination of the Average Hourly Wage of Production Workers in Three Factories Using the Harmonic Mean.

FACTORY	HOURLY WAGE (X)	RECIPROCAL $\left(\frac{1}{X}\right)$	EXAMPLE 1[1] HOURS WORKED (w)	EXAMPLE 1[1] TOTAL EARNINGS (wX)	EXAMPLE 2[2] HOURS WORKED (w)	EXAMPLE 2[2] TOTAL EARNINGS (wX)	EXAMPLE 3[3] HOURS WORKED (w)	EXAMPLE 3[3] TOTAL EARNINGS (wX)
A	$ 4.00	0.250	10,000	$ 40,000	10,000	$ 40,000	10,000	$ 40,000
B	5.00	0.200	10,000	50,000	8,000	40,000	12,000	60,000
C	8.00	0.125	10,000	80,000	5,000	40,000	11,000	88,000
	$17.00	0.575	30,000	$170,000	23,000	$120,000	33,000	$188,000

$$\overline{X} = \frac{\Sigma X}{N} = \frac{17.00}{3} = \$5.667 \qquad \overline{X}_w = \frac{\Sigma wX}{\Sigma w} = \frac{170{,}000}{30{,}000} = \$5.667$$

$$\overline{X}_w = \frac{\Sigma wX}{\Sigma w} = \frac{120{,}000}{23{,}000} = \$5.217 \qquad \overline{X}_w = \frac{\Sigma wX}{\Sigma w} = \frac{188{,}000}{33{,}000} = \$5.697$$

$$H = \frac{N}{\Sigma \frac{1}{X}} = \frac{3}{0.575} = \$5.217$$

[1]Under these conditions the harmonic mean would be inappropriate. The unweighted mean would be appropriate because it is the same as the weighted arithmetic mean.

[2]Under these conditions the harmonic mean would be appropriate because it is the same as the weighted arithmetic mean. The unweighted arithmetic mean would be inappropriate.

[3]Under these conditions both the harmonic mean and the unweighted arithmetic mean would be inappropriate because neither is the same as the weighted arithmetic mean.

Source: Hypothetical.

the total earnings differ in the three plants. The weighted arithmetic mean provides a valid average in that case.

Another look at Example 2 shows that the proportionate relationship of the weights (the hours worked) is inverse to the proportionate relationship of the hourly earnings figures. In other words, 10,000 hours is to 8,000 hours as $5.00 is to $4.00, and 8,000 hours is to 5,000 hours as $8.00 is to $5.00. This inverse relationship between the rates being averaged and the weights should exist, or nearly so, if the harmonic mean is to be useful.

ESTIMATING AVERAGES FROM GROUPED DATA

Often an average of a frequency distribution must be computed because the individual figures from which the distribution was constructed are not available. The computed average is an *estimate* of the average that we would calculate from the original, ungrouped figures. Methods of computing the arithmetic mean, median, and mode from a frequency distribution will be illustrated, but since the geometric and harmonic means are rarely computed from a frequency distribution, the computation of these two averages has been omitted.

The Arithmetic Mean

The calculation of the arithmetic mean from a frequency distribution, which can be done only with a closed-end distribution, involves the concept of the weighted arithmetic mean. One method of calculation, which we shall call the *weighted midpoint method*, requires the direct weighting of the midpoints of the classes with the frequencies. Another method, the *weighted deviation method*, indirectly weights the midpoints of the classes with the frequencies.

Weighted midpoint method. This method can be applied only to closed-end frequency distributions, but the class intervals may be unequal. The formula for computing the arithmetic mean by this method is

$$\overline{X} = \frac{\Sigma fm}{N}$$

where f represents the frequencies, m the midpoints of the classes, and N the total number of frequencies. Table 4-6 shows the calculations for estimating the arithmetic mean of the earnings of 50 university students that appeared in a frequency distribution in Table 3-9. In order to make these calculations, we must determine the midpoint of each class by adding the class lower limit to the class upper limit and dividing by 2. A midpoint, m, is an estimate of the arithmetic mean of the frequencies of a class. For example, the first midpoint, 62, is an assumed estimate of the arithmetic mean of the earnings of the two students in that class. Thus $2 \times 62 = 124$, an estimate of the total monthly earnings of the two students. All of the fm values in the table are, therefore, estimated totals of the frequencies that fall in the classes, and the total of the fm values, \$6,800, is an estimate of the total of the figures from which the distribution was constructed. Substituting in the formula,

$$\overline{X} = \frac{6{,}800}{50} = \$136.00$$

which is an *estimate* of the arithmetic mean of the 50 original earnings figures shown in Table 3-6. The actual mean of those figures is \$137.48. The difference between the estimated and actual mean, \$1.48, results from assuming that the midpoints of the classes are the arithmetic means of the frequencies that fall within those classes. While such errors cannot be avoided, an estimate of an arithmetic mean computed from a frequency distribution is usually close enough to the actual arithmetic mean to be useful.

TABLE 4-6. Computation of the Arithmetic Mean of the April 1975 Earnings of 50 OS University Students Employed Part-Time (Weighted Midpoint Method).

EARNINGS	*NUMBER OF STUDENTS (f)*	*CLASS MIDPOINT (m)*	*WEIGHTED MIDPOINT (fm)*
$ 50– 74	2	62	$ 124
75– 99	5	87	435
100–124	10	112	1120
125–149	17	137	2329
150–174	10	162	1620
175–199	4	187	748
200–224	2	212	424
Total	50		$6800

$$\overline{X} = \frac{\Sigma fm}{N} = \frac{6800}{50} = \$136.00$$

Source: Table 3-9.

Weighted deviation method. The computation of an arithmetic mean by the weighted deviation method involves a priciple that can be illustrated with four simple numbers: 5, 10, 15, and 20. The arithmetic mean of these numbers is $\Sigma X/N = 50/4 = 12.5$. This figure can be obtained a different way: We can assume that some number, say 10, is the arithmetic mean and then add an adjustment factor to correct the error in that assumption. The adjustment factor is the arithmetic mean of the deviations, d, of the numbers from $\overline{X}_a$, the assumed arithmetic mean. Table 4-7 displays the necessary calculations.

TABLE 4-7. Calculation of an Arithmetic Mean by the Deviation Method

NUMBER (X)	*DEVIATION FROM ASSUMED MEAN OF 10 (d)*
5	−5
10	0
15	+5
20	+10
Total	+10

$$\overline{X} = \overline{X}_a + \frac{\Sigma d}{N}$$

$$= 10 + \frac{10}{4}$$

$$= 10 + 2.5 = 12.5$$

When we add the adjustment factor, $\Sigma d/N$, to $\overline{X}_a$, the assumed arithmetic mean, the resulting sum is the arithmetic mean; therefore, the entire formula is

$$\overline{X} = \overline{X}_a + \frac{\Sigma d}{N}$$

and substitutions from Table 4-7 show that

$$\overline{X} = 10 + \frac{10}{4} = 10 + 2.5 = 12.5$$

Using a number other than 10, repeat the preceding calculations to prove to yourself that it makes no difference what number you choose for the assumed mean.

It would be ridiculous to compute the arithmetic mean of a group of numbers such as those in Table 4-7 by this method because it would take longer than it would to add the figures and divide the sum by the number of figures. Applied to a frequency distribution, however, the weighted deviation method shortens the computation time and gives the same estimate that the weighted midpoint method gives.

Since the individual numbers used to construct a frequency distribution are not known, the deviations equal the differences between the assumed mean and the midpoints of the classes. Moreover, the deviations, d, must be weighted by the frequencies, f, to get their estimated totals. The assumed arithmetic mean, $\overline{X}_a$, is one of the class midpoints, so the formula is

$$\overline{X} = \overline{X}_a + \frac{\Sigma fd}{N}$$

To illustrate this formula we will use the distribution of the earnings of the 50 university students and assume that \$137, the midpoint of the class \$125–149, is the arithmetic mean. The differences between this assumed mean and each of the midpoints of the other classes appear in Table 4-8. These deviations represent the arithmetic means of the deviations of the individual class values from the assumed arithmetic mean of the frequency distribution. For instance, the deviation −25 is assumed to be the arithmetic mean of the differences between the 10 earnings figures in the class \$100–124 and the assumed distribution arithmetic mean, \$137. If we multiply 10 by −25, then we have an estimate of the total of all deviations in that class. The "*fd*" column results if we perform the same calculations for each class. The arithmetic mean of this column, $\Sigma fd/N$, is computed and added to $\overline{X}_a$, the assumed arithmetic mean, to get the estimated arithmetic mean, $\overline{X}$. Substitutions in the formula show that

$$\overline{X} = 137 + \frac{-50}{50} = \$136$$

which is, as it should be, the same answer obtained by the weighted midpoint method.

Weighted deviation method using a shortcut. The computations for the weighted deviation method can be shortened by expressing the deviations shown in the "*d*" column of Table 4-8 in class interval units and putting the class interval units back in with a single multiplication. The formula for this method is

$$\overline{X} = \overline{X}_a + \frac{\Sigma fd'}{N} i$$

TABLE 4-8. Computation of the Arithmetic Mean of the April 1975 Earnings of 50 OS University Students Employed Part-Time (Weighted Deviation Method).

EARNINGS	NUMBER OF STUDENTS (f)	DEVIATION OF CLASS MIDPOINTS FROM ASSUMED ARITHMETIC MEAN (d)	WEIGHTED DEVIATION (fd)
\$ 50– 74	2	−75	−150
75– 99	5	−50	−250
100–124	10	−25	−250
125–149	17	0	0
150–174	10	25	250
175–199	4	50	200
200–224	2	75	150
Total	50		−50

$$\overline{X} = \overline{X}_a + \frac{\Sigma fd}{N} = 137 + \frac{-50}{50} = 137 - 1 = \$136$$

The use of this method, which is advisable only when the intervals for all the classes are equal, is illustrated in Table 4-9. The d' values represent the number of class intervals ($i = \$25$) separating \$137 (the assumed mean) and the midpoints of the other classes. For example, the midpoint of the class \$100–124 is \$112. Subtracting \$137 from \$112 we get \$−25, which is −1 class interval. Also, subtracting \$137 from \$87, the midpoint of the class \$75–99, gives \$−50, or −2 class intervals. (Actually, the d' values in Table 4-9 are equal to the d values in Table 4-8 divided by 25.)

As the table shows, the d' values then are weighted by f, the frequencies. These products (fd') are summed and multiplied by i (the common class interval) and divided by N to get the correction factor,

$$\frac{\Sigma fd'}{N} i$$

This correction factor is then added to the assumed arithmetic mean, $\overline{X}_a$. Substitutions show that

$$\overline{X} = 137 + \frac{-2}{50}\, 25 = 137 - 1 = \$136$$

which is the same as that previously calculated.

The relationship between the weighted midpoint and weighted deviation methods might be clearer if you can see their calculations in one master work table, such as Table 4-10, which is based on data from Table 3-11. The formulas, substitutions in the formulas, and the results are shown below the work table. The answer would have been the same. For this illustration, 75 (the midpoint of the fifth class) was chosen as the assumed mean for the weighted deviation method. However, any of the other midpoints could have been used and, of course, the answer would have been the same.

TABLE 4-9. Computation of the Arithmetic Mean of the April 1975 Earnings of 50 OS University Students Employed Part-Time (Weighted Deviation Method using a Shortcut)

EARNINGS	NUMBER OF STUDENTS (*f*)	DEVIATION OF CLASS MIDPOINTS OF ASSUMED ARITHMETIC MEAN IN CLASS INTERVAL UNITS (*d'*)	WEIGHTED DEVIATIONS (*fd'*)
$ 50– 74	2	−3	−6
75– 99	5	−2	−10
100–124	10	−1	−10
125–149	17	0	0
150–174	10	1	10
175–199	4	2	8
200–224	2	3	6
Total	50		−2

$$\overline{X} = \overline{X}_a + \frac{\Sigma fd'}{N} i = 137 + \frac{-2}{50} 25 = 137 + \frac{-50}{50}$$

$$137 - 1 = \$136$$

TABLE 4-10. Computation of the Arithmetic Mean of the Midterm Grades of 50 Students Taking Elementary Statistics (by the Weighted Midpoint and Weighted Deviation Methods)

	WEIGHTED MIDPOINT METHOD			WEIGHTED DEVIATION METHOD		WEIGHTED DEVIATION METHOD (SHORTCUT)	
GRADE	*f*	*m*	*fm*	*d*	*fd*	*d'*	*fd'*
30 but under 40	2	35	70	−40	−80	−4	−8
40 but under 50	5	45	225	−30	−150	−3	−15
50 but under 60	7	55	385	−20	−140	−2	−14
60 but under 70	13	65	845	−10	−130	−1	−13
70 but under 80	15	75	1125	0	0	0	0
80 but under 90	5	85	425	10	50	1	5
90 but under 100	3	95	285	20	60	2	6
Total	50		3360		−390		−39

$$\overline{X} = \frac{\Sigma fm}{N} = \frac{3360}{50} = 67.2$$

$$\overline{X} = \overline{X}_a + \frac{\Sigma fd}{N} = 75 + \frac{-390}{50} = 75 - 7.8 = 67.2$$

$$\overline{X} = \overline{X}_a + \frac{\Sigma fd'}{N} i = 75 + \frac{-39}{50} 10 = 75 + \frac{-390}{50} = 75 - 7.8 = 67.2$$

The Median

To compute the median of a frequency distribution we must estimate it by interpolating into the class that contains the middle frequency. A generally accepted estimate of the median is made by determining the real lower limit of the median class and adding to it the interpolated value; the median class is found by dividing two into the total of the frequencies and then finding the class that contains this number.

Shown in Table 4-11 are the classes and frequencies from Table 4-6, with certain values in the median formula identified. The sum of the frequencies divided by two is $50/2 = 25$. The class containing the 25th frequency is the class $125–149. This median class is found by cumulating the frequencies, starting with the first class, until the cumulation reaches $N/2$ (in this case, 25) or a larger number. Note that the first three classes contain the first 17 frequencies and that the $125–149 class contains the 18th through the 34th. In other words, the 25th frequency is one of the 17 that fall in the class $125–149. Therefore, the value of the 25th frequency, the median, is somewhere between $124.50 and $149.50, the real limits of the median class.

TABLE 4-11 Values Needed to Calculate the Median of the April 1975 Earnings of 50 OS University Students Employed Part-Time.

	EARNINGS	NUMBER OF STUDENTS (f)	
	$ 50– 74	2	$F_{me} = 17$ (first three classes)
	75– 99	5	
	100–124	10	
Median class	125–149	17	f_{me}
	150–174	10	
	175–199	4	
	200–224	2	
	Total	50	N

$$M_e = L_{me} + \frac{N/2 - F_{me}}{f_{me}} i_{me}$$

$$= 124.50 + \frac{25 - 17}{17}(25) = \$136.26$$

All the calculations needed for the median are expressed in the formula

$$M_e = L_{me} + \frac{N/2 - F_{me}}{f_{me}} i_{me}$$

where M_e is the symbol for the median
L_{me} is the real lower limit of the median class
N is the total of the frequencies

F_{me} is the cumulation of frequencies to the median class
f_{me} is the frequency of the median class
i_{me} is the interval of the median class

The median from the distribution above is gotten by substituting in the formula:

$$M_e = 124.50 + \frac{25 - 17}{17}(25)$$

$$= 124.50 + \frac{200}{17} = 124.50 + 11.76$$

$$= \$136.26$$

Thus, by adding an interpolated value,

$$\frac{N/2 - F_{me}}{f_{me}} i_{me},$$

to $124.50, we can estimate that one half the students earned $136.26 or less and the other half earned that much or more.

Charting the median. A graphic estimate of the median may clarify its meaning. A graphic estimate is made from an *ogive chart*, which is a chart of a cumulative frequency distribution. To construct a cumulative frequency distribution of the data in Table 4-11, the frequencies are cumulated on a "less than" and an "as much or more than" basis. This is done by counting the number of students that earned less than the amounts of each real class limit and the number that earned as much or more than each real class limit.

Because the classes in the table are set up for earnings rounded to the nearest dollar, the real class limits are $49.50–74.50, $74.50–99.50, and so on. The real limits for all the classes are listed in Table 4-12 together with the cumulated frequencies. To get the

TABLE 4-12. Number of OS University Students Earning Less Than, or As Much As, or More Than Stated Earnings, April 1975.

EARNINGS	*NUMBER EARNING LESS*	*NUMBER EARNING AS MUCH OR MORE*
$ 49.50	0	50
74.50	2	48
99.50	7	43
124.50	17	33
149.50	34	16
174.50	44	6
199.50	48	2
224.50	50	0

Source: Table 4-11.

frequencies in the "less than" column, the frequencies in Table 4-11 were cumulated starting from the top. The "as much or more than" column was obtained by cumulating the same frequencies from the bottom. In other words, all we have to do is answer two questions: How many frequencies are smaller in value than each class limit? How many frequencies are greater in value than each class limit?

The curves formed by the frequencies in Table 4-12 are shown in Chart 4-1. The curves, called *ogives*, intersect at the halfway point, $N/2$. If a perpendicular is dropped from their point of intersection to the horizontal axis, the value of the median can be read on that scale. This reading should correspond to the value obtained with the median formula.

Skewed distributions. The median becomes important when quite homogeneous data with a few extremely large or small values are being analyzed, as we noted when discussing the median of ungrouped data. When data with extreme values are grouped, they are usually shown in an open-end frequency distribution such as the one in Table 4-13.

Chart 4-1. Number of OS University students earning less than, or as much as, or more than stated earnings, April 1975.

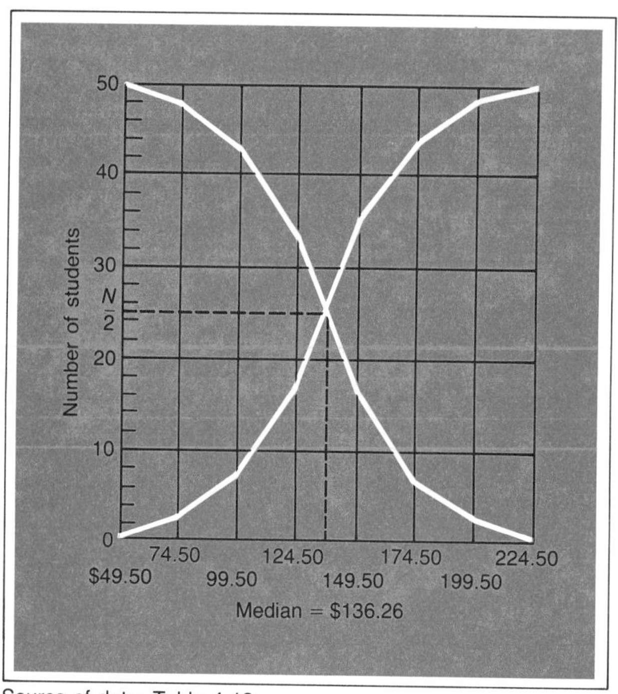

Source of data: Table 4-12.

TABLE 4-13. Percentage Distribution of Families by Income Group in the United States, 1974.

INCOME	PERCENT OF FAMILIES
Under $3,000	5
$ 3,000 but under $ 5,000	8
5,000 but under 7,000	9
7,000 but under 10,000	14
10,000 but under 15,000	24
15,000 but under 25,000	28
25,000 and over	12
Total	100

Source: U.S. Department of Commerce, Bureau of the Census.

The calculation of the median of the income distribution in Table 4-13 is

$$\begin{aligned} M_e &= L_{me} + \frac{N/2 - F_{me}}{f_{me}} i_{me} \\ &= 10{,}000 + \frac{100/2 - 36}{24}(5000) \\ &= 10{,}000 + \frac{14}{24}(5000) \\ &= 10{,}000 + 2{,}917 = \$12{,}917 \end{aligned}$$

(The arithmetic mean cannot be computed from this frequency distribution because the midpoints of the open-end classes cannot be determined.)

The median of the grade distributions shown in Table 4-10 is calculated thus:

$$\begin{aligned} M_e &= L_{me} + \frac{N/2 - F_{me}}{f_{me}} i_{me} \\ &= 60 + \frac{50/2 - 14}{13}(10) \\ &= 60 + \frac{11}{13}(10) \\ &= 60 + \frac{110}{13} = 60 + 8.5 = 68.5 \end{aligned}$$

So one half the class had grades of 68.5 or less and one half had grades of 68.5 or more. This median is larger than the arithmetic mean, which was shown to be 67.2, because the distribution is skewed to the left; that is, if we were to chart the distribution, the resulting curve would tail off to the left. Skewness, which refers to departure from symmetry, and its measurement are discussed in Chapter 5.

The Mode

If a mode is computed from a frequency distribution, it must be redefined as *that figure around which the other figures cluster*. The strict definition of the mode does not apply because there may have been no figure in the ungrouped list from which the distribution was constructed that appeared more than once. Also, the mode, according to the strict definition, could fall in any class with two or more frequencies and we have no way of knowing which class it was in. Furthermore, if the mode did not fall in the class with the highest frequency, it would be of little value, because to be useful, a mode must be a highly predominant figure. A count of the figure in Table 3-6 will reveal that $147 appears four times, more often than any other figure, and is, therefore, the mode according to its strict definition. However, we would not want to use that figure as an average of all fifty numbers.

To find the figure around which other figures cluster in a frequency distribution, which we will call the mode, we will use the formula:

$$M_o = L_{mo} + \frac{d_1}{d_1 + d_2} i_{mo}$$

where M_o is the symbol for the mode
L_{mo} is the lower limit of the modal class (the class with the highest frequency
d_1 is the difference between the frequencies of the modal class and preceding class
d_2 is the difference between the frequencies of the modal class and the following class
i_{mo} is the interval which is common to the modal class and the two adjacent classes

The part of the formula

$$\frac{d_1}{d_1 + d_2}$$

is a ratio that pulls the concentration point away from the center of the modal class. The direction in which it is pulled depends on the direction that the distribution is skewed or departs from symmetry. The mode formula and calculations are shown below Table 4-14. The mode in this distribution is the midpoint of the modal class. This is always the case when d_1 and d_2 are equal.

However, substitution in the modal formula for the mid-term grade distribution in Table 4-10 gives

$$M_o = 70 + \frac{2}{2 + 10} 10 = 70 + \frac{20}{12} = 71.7$$

A mode for the family income distribution in Table 4-13 cannot be computed with this formula because the interval of the modal class ($7,000 but under $10,000) is not the

TABLE 4-14. Values Needed to Calculate the Model of the April 1975 Earnings of 50 OS University Students Employed Part-Time.

	EARNINGS	NUMBER OF STUDENTS	
	\$ 50– 74	2	
	75– 99	5	
	100–124	10	$d1 = 17 - 10 = 7$
Modal class	125–149	17	
	150–174	10	$d2 = 17 - 10 = 7$
	175–199	4	
	200–224	2	
	Total	50	

$$Mo = Lmo - \frac{d1}{d1 + d2} imo$$

$$= 124.50 + \frac{7}{7 + 7}(25)$$

$$= 124.50 + 12.50 = \$137.00$$

same as those for the classes immediately preceding and following the modal class. The intervals of the three classes involved in the calculation of the mode of a frequency distribution must be of equal size.

Charting the mode. A graphic estimate of the mode of a distribution can be made from a histogram, which will give the same answer as the formula if the drawing is done accurately. Chart 4-2 shows a histogram of the grade distribution in Table 4-10. If diagonal lines are drawn through the modal rectangle as pictured, a perpendicular dropped to the horizontal axis from their point of intersection fixes the mode on the scale. Note that the relatively high rectangle to the left of the modal rectangle pulls the point of intersection of the two diagonal lines to the left of center. The modal formula does the same thing mathematically. Had the rectangle to the right of the modal rectangle been higher than that to the left, the point of intersection would have been pulled to the right.

Relationship of the Arithmetic Mean, Median, and Mode

In the midterm grade distribution of the statistics students, the mode, 71.7, was larger than the median, 68.5, which was larger than the arithmetic mean, 67.2. The magnitudes of these three averages reveal that the grade distribution is not symmetrical and tails off to the left as depicted in Chart 4-3. Chart 4-4 pictures symmetrical and skewed distributions and the general relationships found among the arithmetic mean, the median, and the mode.

Chart 4-2. Midterm grade distribution of 50 students of elementary statistics, Section 1.

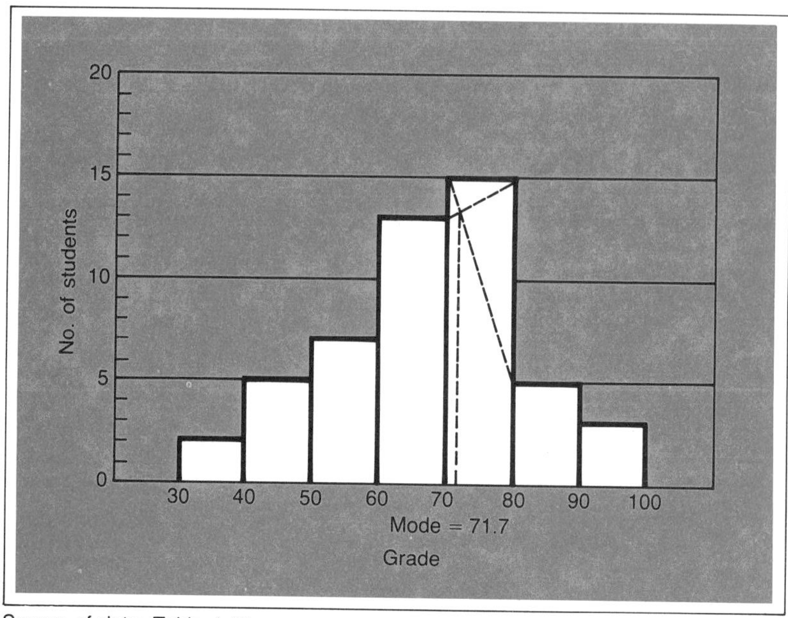

Source of data: Table 4-10.

Chart 4-3. Midterm grade distribution of 50 students of elementary statistics, Section 1.

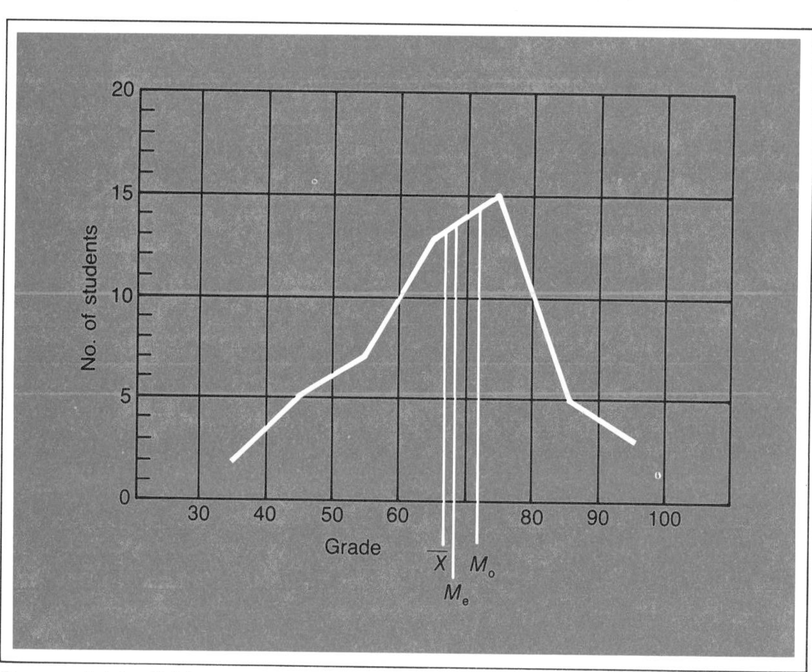

Source of data: Table 4-10.

Chart 4-4. The general relationship of the arithmetic mean, median, and mode in symmetrical and skewed distributions.

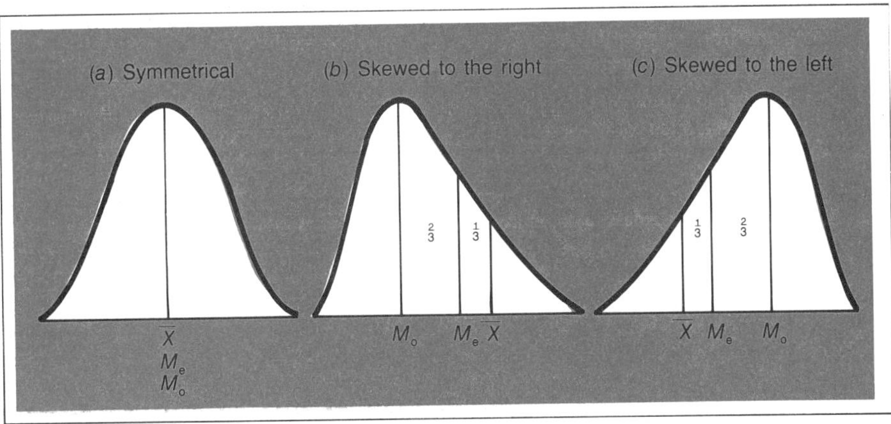

If a distribution is symmetrical, as in Chart 4-4*a*, the three averages are equal in value. If a distribution is skewed to the right, the arithmetic mean is biased upward due to the few extremely large values to the right (Chart 4-4*b*). When a distribution is skewed to the left, the arithmetic mean is the smallest and the mode is the largest (Chart 4-4*c*). Moreover, in most skewed distributions, we find that the difference between the arithmetic mean and the median is about one third of the difference between the arithmetic mean and the mode. In fact, this relationship is used to compute a coefficient of skewness, which is discussed in the next chapter.

This ⅓ relationship does not hold precisely for every skewed distribution. For example, in the midterm grade distribution, the mode minus the arithmetic mean is $71.7 - 67.2 = 4.5$ and the median minus the arithmetic mean is $68.5 - 67.2 = 1.3$; and $1.3/4.5 = 0.29$. This is close enough to ⅓ to be used to measure the degree of skewness of the curve, as we will see.

REVIEW QUESTIONS

1. Define an average.
2. Define: arithmetic mean, median, mode, geometric mean, and harmonic mean.
3. Give a chief characteristic of each of the five averages listed in Question 2.
4. Under what general condition is each of the five averages the most appropriate to use for a given group of figures?

5. Why can't the arithmetic mean be computed from an open-end frequency distribution?

6. Why isn't an average computed from a frequency distribution exactly the same as that computed from original figures used to construct the distribution?

7. When computed from the same data, which of the following averages will be the largest, second largest, and the smallest: arithmetic mean, geometric mean, and harmonic mean? Why?

8. Why is the median usually a better average for a highly skewed frequency distribution than the arithmetic mean?

9. In order to use the formula for the mode,

$$M_o = L_{mo} + \frac{d_1}{d_1 + d_2} i_{mo}$$

why must the interval of the modal class and the two adjacent classes be the same?

10. Which average is the largest, second largest, and smallest computed from a frequency distribution that is skewed to the right: the arithmetic mean, the median, the mode?

11. If your company president asked you to plan an evening of entertainment for the sons of the company's employees and told you that the average age of the sons was 14, what more would you want to know about the ages before you started planning?

12. A man who stated that he manufactured lids for glass jars was asked what size lids he manufactured. He replied, "the typical size." To which average was he referring?

13. Could a man six feet tall drown crossing a river with an average depth of two feet?

14. A U.S. Department of Commerce report gives the normal monthly average temperature for the years 1931–1960 as 51.1° in Seattle, Washington, and 51.1° in Omaha, Nebraska. If you were planning to take a job in one of these two cities, would this information be of use to you? Could this information be misleading? How? Which average do you think was used for these temperatures?

15. In 1967, the arithmetic mean buying income of families in the Milwaukee metropolitan area was $9900. The median family income was $8200. If you were planning a large sales campaign in Milwaukee for a product that would be purchased by families in the middle and upper-middle income groups, which of the two averages would be more useful? Why?

16. The arithmetic mean of each of the three sets of data in Exercise Table 4-1 is 10. For which set does the arithmetic mean do the poorest job of representing the data? Why?

EXERCISE TABLE 4-1. Three Sets of Data, Each with an Arithmetic Mean of 10.

SET A	*SET B*	*SET C*
10	2	8
10	4	9
10	10	10
10	14	11
10	20	12

PROBLEMS

1. Compute the arithmetic mean, median, and mode of the ages in Exercise Table 4-2, and determine which average best describes the age of the sales force?

EXERCISE TABLE 4-2. Ages of 12 Salesmen Employed by a Wholesale Establishment, 1975.

25	30	33	60
26	30	34	63
28	30	35	65

2. Exercise Table 4-3 gives the total tax revenue collected in the United States by all levels of government for four years. Compute the average annual rate of increase in tax revenue for the four-year period.

EXERCISE TABLE 4-3. Total Tax Revenue Collected in the United States by All Levels of Government, 1970—1973.

YEAR	*TAX REVENUE (BILLIONS OF DOLLARS)*
1970	$233
1971	232
1972	263
1973	287

3. Between 1974 and 1975, Harry's income increased 15%; between 1975 and 1976, it increased 2%, and between 1976 and 1977, his income jumped 28%. What was his average annual increase in income between 1974 and 1977?

4. From the data in Exercise Table 4-4 compute arithmetic mean, median, and mode. Chart the distribution as a polygon, locate the three averages on the horizontal axis, and construct ordinates at those points to show the relationship of the three averages.

EXERCISE TABLE 4-4. Annual Salaries of 40 Manufacturing Executives, 1975

SALARY	*NUMBER OF EXECUTIVES*
$10,000 but under $15,000	5
$15,000 but under $20,000	7
$20,000 but under $25,000	14
$25,000 but under $30,000	10
$30,000 but under $35,000	4
Total	40

5. Compute the median from the data in Exercise Table 4-5. Is the median the best average in this case? Can any other averages be computed? Would the mode be a useful average of these data? Why?

EXERCISE TABLE 4-5. Age Distribution of Male Heads of Households in the Milwaukee Metropolitan Area, 1975.

AGE (NEAREST BIRTHDAY)	*NUMBER OF HEADS (000)*
18 to 24	22.6
25 to 34	85.7
35 to 49	126.3
50 to 64	112.8
65 and over	45.1
Total	392.5

Source: *Milwaukee Journal Consumer Analysis,* 1975.

6. A truck driver made three different deliveries to a city 1000 miles from his home city. On the first trip he averaged 43 miles per hour. On the second he averaged 37 and on the third 48. Compute the arithmetic mean and the harmonic mean of these three averages. Which average best answers the question: What was the driver's average speed on all three trips?

5

Variation, Skewness, and Kurtosis

In Chapter 4, we discovered how an average is used to represent or describe the general magnitude of a group of figures. We learned that the more homogeneous a group of figures is, the better an arithmetic mean represents their magnitude. For example, we know that if all the figures in a group are the same, the arithmetic mean provides perfect representation. Also, by comparing two groups of data, one more varied than the other, we saw that the arithmetic mean of the more varied group was not as typical as the arithmetic mean of the less varied group. This observation was made without performing a particular calculation because only a few figures appeared in each group and only two groups were considered. Had we had many groups containing numerous values, however, accurate comparisons by observation would have been difficult or impossible. Under such conditions, it would have been necessary to compute a measure of variation for each group and then compare those measures.

In Chapter 4 we also learned that data distributions that depart from symmetry are skewed; that is, they have some extremely large or extremely small values. An absolute measure of skewness can be obtained by taking differences between the arithmetic mean, median, and mode, but such measures have limited value. An analyst is more interested in measuring the *degree* of skewness of one or more distributions by computing a coefficient of skewness.

Sometimes it is desirable to measure the *degree* to which a frequency curve is flattened or peaked so we will know how concentrated the values are at its high point. This measure, which is one of kurtosis, will be briefly discussed in this chapter. First, however, we will learn about computations of measures of dispersion from ungrouped data and then go on to their estimation from grouped data and computations of measures of skewness and kurtosis.

MEASURES OF VARIATION

Variation

The term "variation" means dispersion, scatter or spread. A measure of variation sums up in one figure the amount, or degree, of scatter of the values of the group so that we can determine how well an average represents the data from which it was computed.

This measurement is usually made of the variation of the values from their arithmetic mean, but sometimes variation around the median is measured. Sometimes, however, we measure variation to compare the scatter of two or more sets of data without having a direct interest in averages of the data.

The Range

Range

The simplest measure of variation is the *range*, which is the difference between the lowest and highest figures in a group. In a frequency distribution, the range is the difference between the lower limit of the smallest class and the upper limit of the largest class.

This measure has limited value because it reveals nothing about the variation of the figures between the two extremes. For example, a teacher may report to a class that the grades on an examination ranged from 33 to 97. This information tells each student only whether his grade was the highest or lowest. It does not enable the student with a grade of 76 to determine how well he did in comparison to the entire class. All other grades between 33 and 97 could have been in the 60's, or 80's, or evenly graduated from 33 to 97.

Using the range may lead to wrong inferences if we *assume* that the figures between the two extremes are more or less evenly graduated when they are not. Therefore, we should not ordinarily rely on the range as a measure of scatter unless there is a somewhat gradual progression from the low figure to the high figure.

Quartiles and the Middle Range

Middle Range

Quartiles are numbers that divide an array of numbers into four equal parts so that one quarter of them are smaller than the first quartile and one quarter are larger than the third quartile. Therefore, one half of the figures lie between the first and third quartiles. The *middle range*, sometimes called the interquartile range, measures the interval from the first quartile to the third quartile and so includes the middle half of the figures from which it is computed.

A quartile sometimes has the same value as one of the figures being analyzed and sometimes it falls between two of the figures. To illustrate this point, we will first consider the median, which is the second quartile. In the arrayed list A in Table 5-1, the middle figure, the median, is 23. In list B there is no middle number, so the median is halfway between the two central figures, namely, the arithmetic mean of 23 and 28.

TABLE 5-1. Location of Quartile Positions in Arrayed Numbers.

A (11 NUMBERS)		*B (12 NUMBERS)*		*C (10 NUMBERS)*	
10		10		20	
12		12		23	
15		15		27	First quartile = 27
19			First quartile = 17	29	
22		19		35	
23	Median = 23	22			Median = 36
	(Second quartile)	23			(Second quartile)
28			Median = 25.5	37	
30			(Second quartile)	41	
35		28		48	Third quartile = 48
42		30		53	
50		35		59	
			Third quartile = 37.5		
		40			
		50			
		56			

Notice that there are 11 figures in list A and that the middle figure is the sixth in the array. We can find its location by computing

$$\frac{N}{2} = \frac{1}{2}$$

which is a general formula for locating the median figure. In this case,

$$\frac{N}{2} + \frac{1}{2} = \frac{11}{2} + \frac{1}{2} = 5\frac{1}{2} + \frac{1}{2} = 6$$

so the median is the sixth figure. The location formula can be used also for an even number of arrayed figures. For list B, which has 12 numbers,

$$\frac{N}{2} + \frac{1}{2} = \frac{12}{2} + \frac{1}{2} = 6\frac{1}{2}$$

which means that the median is the value halfway between the sixth and seventh figures.

Similar formulas can be used to locate the first and third quartiles. In the list of 10 numbers shown in column C of Table 5-1, the value of the first quartile is located at

$$\frac{N}{4} + \frac{1}{2} = \frac{10}{4} + \frac{1}{2} = 3.$$

Therefore, the first quartile is 17, the third figure from the top. The third quartile value is 48, the value of the eighth figure, because

$$\frac{3N}{4} + \frac{1}{2} = \frac{30}{4} + \frac{1}{2} = 8$$

In list B of Table 5-1,

$$\frac{N}{4} + \frac{1}{2} = \frac{12}{4} + \frac{1}{2} = 3\frac{1}{2}$$

Therefore, the first quartile value is halfway between 15 and 19, or 17. Moreover,

$$\frac{3N}{4} + \frac{1}{2} = \frac{36}{4} + \frac{1}{2} = 9\frac{1}{2}$$

which means that the third quartile is halfway between 35 and 40, the ninth and tenth figures; it is 37.5. The middle range is, therefore, from 17 to 37.5. You should now be able to determine the values of the first and third quartiles of list A.

If a quartile is one of the numbers in a finite list, that number is considered to fall as much in one quarter as another. For example, in list C of Table 5-1 the first quartile, 17, is considered to belong as much in the first quarter as the second.

The middle range is often helpful for decision-making. Its value is recognized by the U.S. Bureau of Labor Statistics in that bureau's presentation of middle ranges for earnings of numerous occupational classifications in its annual *Area Wage Survey* for many U.S. metropolitan areas.

If you had just started a business in a metropolitan area and you were planning to hire a female secretary, you would need to know how much to pay her. Perhaps the only way to decide would be to find out what the prevailing pay rate was in the particular area. An "average" earnings figure would be helpful, but more so if the dispersion of secretaries' wages was also known. For instance, the arithmetic mean weekly earnings of secretaries in the Milwaukee, Wisconsin, metropolitan area was $116.00 in April 1968. How representative is this average for the earnings of all secretaries in the area? You have no way of knowing unless the individual earnings figures are available or unless the spread or dispersion of the data has been measured. According to the Bureau of Labor Statistics, which published the average, the middle range was from $101.00 to $128.50 per week. This additional information provides a more meaningful guide in deciding what to pay a newly hired secretary. You probably would not want to pay below $101.00 or above $128.50 per week to a secretary with normal talents if you know that the middle 50% of secretaries have earnings in that interval.

One fault with the middle range is that we can never be certain how the figures in that range are distributed. It might be wise to use the middle range as a measure of dispersion when there is a more or less even gradation of values in the range. Also the middle range reveals nothing about the scatter of values in the first and last quarters.

The Quartile Deviation

The limits of the middle range are sometimes used to compute what is commonly called the *quartile deviation*. It is computed by dividing the middle range by two.

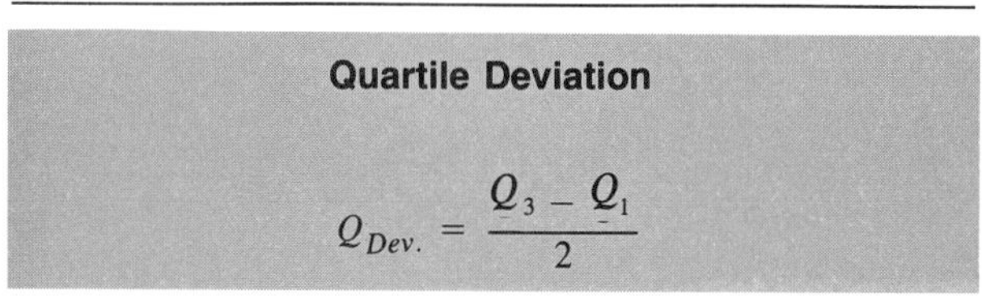

Quartile Deviation

$$Q_{Dev.} = \frac{Q_3 - Q_1}{2}$$

$Q_{\text{Dev.}}$ is the symbol for the quartile deviation, Q_3 is the third quartile and Q_1 is the first quartile. This measure by itself is useless, but when it is added to and subtracted from the arithmetic mean or median it gives an indication of skewness. It gives the same values as the first and third quartiles if the distribution is an arithmetic progression or if it is symmetrical. In symbolic terms, for a symmetrical distribution,

$$\overline{X} \pm Q_{\text{Dev.}} \text{ includes 50\% of the values}$$

and

$$M_e \pm Q_{\text{Dev.}} \text{ includes 50\% of the values.}$$

For a skewed distribution or a list of numbers such as list B of Table 5-1, the middle range is only approximate. For that list

$$Q_{Dev.} = \frac{Q_3 - Q_1}{2} = \frac{37.5 - 17}{2} = \frac{20.5}{2} = 10.2$$

The arithmetic mean of the values is 28.3. Therefore,

$$\overline{X} \pm Q_{\text{Dev.}} = 28.3 \pm 10.2 = 18.1 \text{ to } 38.5$$

which is close to the Q_1 to Q_3 values, 17 to 37.5, but shows some skewness. For the same list

$$M_e \pm Q_{\text{Dev.}} = 25.5 \pm 10.2 = 15.3 \text{ to } 35.7$$

which is reasonably close to the actual middle range.

An advantage of the middle range and quartile deviation is that they can be computed from open-end distributions, whereas the mean deviation and standard deviation cannot.

The Mean Deviation

Mean Deviation

The mean deviation, sometimes called the *average deviation*, is the arithmetic mean (average) of the absolute differences between the arithmetic mean of the values and the individual values;[1] it can be computed also by taking deviations around the median.

Stated as a formula the mean deviation is:

$$\text{M.D.} = \frac{\Sigma|X - \overline{X}|}{N} = \frac{\Sigma|x|}{N}$$

where M.D. is the symbol for the mean deviation, $|x|$ represents the absolute[2] deviation of a value from the arithmetic mean, and N is the number of deviations. The arithmetic mean of the numbers 10, 15, 20, 25, and 30 is 20. The calculation of the mean deviation is shown in Table 5-2. The mean deviation is 6, that is, the average amount of deviation of the individual values from their mean.

Table 5-2. Calculation of the Mean Deviation of a List of Numbers.

	X	$\|x\|$ $\|X - \overline{X}\|$
	10	10
	15	5
	20	0
	25	5
	30	10
Total	100	30

$$\overline{X} = \frac{\Sigma X}{N} = \frac{100}{5} = 20$$

$$\text{M.D.} = \frac{\Sigma|x|}{N} = \frac{30}{5} = 6$$

[1]The arithmetic mean of the algebraic differences, $\Sigma x/N$, is equal to zero. This is known as the first moment about the arithmetic mean. Moments will be used later in this chapter in the calculations of coefficients of skewness and kurtosis.

[2]The vertical bars stand for *absolute value*. Generally, $|a| = a$ if a is positive, $|a| = -a$ if a is negative, and $|0| = 0$.

Sometimes a mean deviation is computed around the median. However, in a group of numbers that forms a straight line or a symmetrical distribution, the results would be identical.

The concept of the mean deviation seems to be readily understood by most people. It is not used as widely and as often, however, as the standard deviation.

The Standard Deviation—Long Method

Because of its application to normal curve theory in the analysis of sample data (see Chapters 8 and 9,) the standard deviation is the most widely used and, in general, most important measure of variation.

Standard Deviation

The standard deviation is the square root of the arithmetic mean of the squared deviations of the values from their arithmetic mean. It is larger than the mean deviation when computed from the same data, but like the mean deviation, it cannot be computed for an open-end frequency distribution.

If we wish to compute the standard deviation of the five numbers in Table 5-2, all we need to do is to square the deviations, x, sum the squared deviations, x^2, divide by the number of deviations, N, and take the square root of the quotient. The entire formula is

$$\sigma = \sqrt{\frac{\Sigma x^2}{N}}$$

All the necessary calculations are given in Table 5-3, where a standard deviation of 7.1 is revealed.

The small Greek letter sigma, σ, is the symbol for the standard deviation.* In this formula the absolute value of x need not be taken because negative deviations become positive when squared.

The Standard Deviation—Short Method

A quicker way to compute the standard deviation of a list of numbers is to take deviations around an assumed arithmetic mean of 0 and apply a correction factor to compensate for the wrong assumption. The formula is:

$$\sigma = \sqrt{\frac{\Sigma X^2}{N} - \left(\frac{\Sigma X}{N}\right)^2}$$

*σ^2, the square of the standard deviation, is called the *variance*.

In this formula X represents the deviation of each of the numbers from an assumed arithmetic mean of 0, thereby allowing each number to retain its original value. The expression $\Sigma X^2/N$ is the arithmetic mean of the squared values, and $(\Sigma X/N)^2$ is the correction factor. The calculation of the standard deviation for the five numbers in Table 5-3 is demonstrated again in Table 5-4. The result, 7.1, is the same as that obtained previously.

The short formula should ordinarily be used because it eliminates the calculations of the deviations required by the long method.

The standard deviation computed for the five numbers, 7.1, was larger than the mean deviation computed for the same numbers, 6, because the standard deviation gives more weight to the larger numbers by squaring them.

Table 5-3. Calculation of the Standard Deviation of a List of Numbers by the Long Method.

	X	x $(X - \overline{X})$	x^2
	10	−10	100
	15	−5	25
	20	0	0
	25	5	25
	30	10	100
Total	50	0	250

$$\overline{X} = \frac{\Sigma X}{N} = \frac{100}{5} = 20$$

$$\sigma = \sqrt{\frac{\Sigma x^2}{N}} = \sqrt{\frac{250}{5}} = \sqrt{50} = 7.1$$

TABLE 5-4. Calculation of the Standard Deviation from a List of Numbers by the Short Method.

	X	X^2
	10	100
	15	225
	20	400
	25	625
	30	900
Total	100	2250

$$\sigma = \sqrt{\frac{\Sigma X^2}{N} - \left(\frac{\Sigma X}{N}\right)^2} = \sqrt{\frac{2250}{5} - \left(\frac{100}{5}\right)^2} = \sqrt{450 - (20)^2} = \sqrt{450 - 400}$$

$$= \sqrt{50} = 7.1$$

TABLE 5-5. Calculation of the Values Needed to Compute the Standard Deviation of the April 1975 Earnings of 50 OS University Students.

	X	X^2	X	$X+$	X	X^2	X	X^2	X	X^2
	183	33,489	147	21,609	102	10,404	195	38,025	148	21,904
	219	47,961	125	15,625	174	30,276	176	30,976	130	16'900
	164	26,896	138	19,044	188	35,344	130	16,900	135	18,225
	58	3,364	147	21,609	78	6,084	145	21,025	147	21,609
	73	5,329	169	28,561	121	14,641	142	20,164	108	11,664
	203	41,209	111	12,321	131	17,161	120	14,400	118	13,924
	155	24,025	98	9,604	139	19,321	117	18,689	137	18,769
	164	26,896	124	15,376	147	21,609	105	11,025	124	15,376
	165	27,225	150	22,500	170	28,900	160	25,600	140	19,600
	80	6,400	94	8,836	85	7,225	135	18,225	160	25,600
Total	1,464	242,749	1,303	175,085	1,335	190,965	1,425	210,029	1,347	183,571

$\Sigma x = 1{,}464 + 1{,}303 + 1{,}335 + 1{,}425 + 1{,}347 = 6{,}874$

$\Sigma x^2 = 242{,}794 = 175{,}085 + 190{,}965 + 210{,}029 + 183{,}571 = 1{,}002{,}444$

It might be interesting to see the calculation of the standard deviation of the earnings of fifty OS University students given in Table 3-6. Table 5-5 provides the necessary information.

The sum of the X values is 6,874 and the sum of the X^2 values is 1,002,444. Therefore:

$$\sigma = \sqrt{\frac{\Sigma X^2}{N} - \left(\frac{\Sigma X}{N}\right)^2} = \sqrt{\frac{1{,}002{,}444}{50} - \left(\frac{6{,}874}{50}\right)^2}$$

$$= \sqrt{20{,}048.88 - (137.48)^2} = \sqrt{20{,}048.88 = 18{,}900.75}$$

$$= \sqrt{1{,}148.13} = \$33.88$$

The Coefficient of Variation

To compare the variations of two or more series of numbers, we can compare their measures of absolute variation, such as their standard deviations, if the arithmetic means of the series are all the same. When the arithmetic means of the series differ, however, a measure of relative dispersion is needed before we can compare them. For example, assume that a firm has a manufacturing plant, A, in the South and another, B, in the North. Assume further that the turnover rate of secretaries in plant B is somewhat higher than in plant A and that it has been suggested by an analyst that there is a wider variation in the secretaries' weekly salaries in plant B, which may be the cause of discontent and, therefore, the higher turnover rate. To back up his statement, the analyst says that his calculation of the standard deviations of the secretaries' weekly salaries are $30 in plant B and $25 in plant A. Unfortunately, the analyst did not take into account the fact that the general salary level in plant B, in the North, is higher than in plant A, in the South. If we assume the arithmetic means of the weekly salaries in plant B and plant A are $225 and $175, respectively, we find by computing the coefficients of variation that, relative to their means, the salary variation is greater in plant A.

Coefficient of Variation

The most widely used method of computing coefficients of variation, is to divide the standard deviations by the arithmetic means.

The formula is

$$V = \frac{\sigma}{X}$$

where V is the coefficient of variation. For the preceding example,

$$\text{Plant A (South)} \qquad V = \frac{25}{175} = 0.1428$$

$$\text{Plant B (North)} \qquad V = \frac{30}{225} = 0.1333$$

According to these computations, the theory that a wider variation of salaries in plant B is a cause for a higher turnover of secretaries is less plausible.

While the preceding coefficient-of-variation formula is probably used more often than any other, another method is to divide the mean deviation by the arithmetic mean. Still another formula

$$\frac{Q_3 - Q_1}{Q_3 + Q_1}$$

which uses the quartiles, and facilitates comparing variations of open-end frequency distributions. It will be discussed in more detail later.

A coefficient of variation is especially valuable for comparing variations in two or more series that are expressed in different units. We could, for example, compare variation in the heights of a group of people with variation in their weights.

Furthermore, it was mentioned previously that the more homogeneous a group of figures, the better an arithmetic mean serves as an average of the group. In the illustration concerning secretaries' salaries, the arithmetic mean salary of $225 for plant B is more representative of that plant's salary level than plant A's $175 is of its salary level.

MEASURING VARIATION IN FREQUENCY DISTRIBUTIONS

All of the measures of variation previously mentioned can be computed from frequency distributions. The calaculations from a frequency distribution, however, result in *estimates* of the measures that would be obtained by working with the original figures; in most cases, though, the estimates are close, and since frequency distributions are often all we have available for analyzing, we need to rely on them.

The Range

The only way to measure the range from a frequency distribution is to find the difference between the real lower limit of the first class and the real upper limit of the last class. The range for the distribution of the earnings of the OS University students, repeated in Table 5-6, is $49.50 to $224.50.

TABLE 5-6. Location of Classes Containing the First and Second Quartiles of the April 1975 Earnings of 50 OS University Students Employed Part-Time.

	EARNINGS	*NUMBER OF STUDENTS*		
	$ 50– 74	2	$F_{q1} = 7$	$F_3=34$
	75– 99	5		
Q_1 Class {	100–124	10		
	125–149	17		
Q_3 Class {	150–174	10		
	175–199	4		
	200–224	2		
	Total	50		

Quartiles and the Middle Range

The middle range is especially valuable because it can be computed for an open-end frequency distribution.* The procedure for computing the first and third quartiles is identical to that for computing the median, which, we have learned, is the second quartile. The formulas provide for an interpolation between class limits to give estimates for the quartiles. The formula for the first quartile is:

$$Q_1 = L_{q1} + \frac{(N/4) - F_{q1}}{f_{q1}} i_{q1}$$

where Q_1 stands for the first quartile, L_{q1} is the lower limit of the class that contains Q_1, N is the total of the frequencies, F_{q1} is the sum of the frequencies preceding the first quartile's class, f_{q1} is the frequency of the first quartile's class, and i_{q1} is the interval of the first quartile's class. Substitutions in this formula from Table 5-6 give:

$$\begin{aligned} Q_1 &= 99.50 + \frac{(50/4) - 7}{10}(25) \\ &= 99.50 + \frac{12.5 - 7}{10}(25) \\ &= 99.50 + \frac{5.5 \times 25}{10} \\ &= 99.50 + 13.75 = \$113.25 \end{aligned}$$

The calculation

$$\frac{N}{4} = \frac{50}{4} = 12.5$$

is done first because we want to find the frequency (the 12.5th) that is one quarter of the way down from the first. The 12.5th frequency lies in the class \$100–124, which has a real lower limit of \$99.50. This, then, is the class that contains the first quartile. The sum of the frequencies preceding the first quartile class, F_{q1}, is $2 + 5 = 7$. The frequency of the class, f_{q1} is 10, and the class interval is \$25.

The computation of the third quartile is similar. The formula is

$$Q_3 = L_{q3} + \frac{(3N/4) - F_{q3}}{f_{q3}} i_{q3}$$

where Q_3 symbolizes the third quartile. The other symbols have the following representations: L_{q3} is the real lower limit of the class containing the third quartile (i.e., the class that has the frequency that is ¾ of the way down, determined by $3N/4$); F_{q3} is the sum of the frequencies preceding the third quartile's class; f_{q3} is the frequency of the third quartile's class; and i_{q3} is the interval of the third quartile's class. Substitutions in the formula for the earnings distribution in Table 5-6 give:

$$\begin{aligned} Q_3 &= 149.50 + \frac{37.5 - 34}{10}(25) \\ &= 149.50 + \frac{3.5 \times 25}{10} \\ &= 149.50 + 8.75 = \$158.25 \end{aligned}$$

*This is not true, however, if the first or third quartile value falls in an open-end class, because in such a case, Q_1 or Q_3 could not be computed.

The middle range of the earnings is, therefore, \$113.25 to \$158.25. This, then is the estimated interval of earnings for about 25 of the 50 students.

In addition to the fact that the middle range can usually be computed for a distribution with an open end, it is also important to know that the computation can be made for a distribution with unequal class intervals, such as the one in Table 5-7, which is open-ended. Calculations for the first quartile for this distribution are:

Table 5-7. Distribution of Savings Associations in the United States by Asset Size, December 31, 1975.

ASSET SIZE (MILLIONS)	*NUMBER OF ASSOCIATIONS*
Under \$1	426
\$ 1 and under \$ 5	489
5 and under 10	503
10 and under 25	1,164
25 and under 50	1,019
50 and under 100	661
100 and under 150	261
150 and under 200	139
200 and under 300	116
300 and over	185
Total	4,964

Source: United States Savings and Loan League, *Savings and Loan Fact Book*, 1976, p.53.

$$
\begin{aligned}
Q_1 &= L_{q1} + \frac{(N/4) - F_{q1}}{f_{q1}} i_{q1} \\
&= 5 + \frac{1{,}241.00 - 915}{503}(5) \\
&= 5 + \frac{326.00 \times 5}{503} \\
&= 5 + \frac{1{,}630}{503} \\
&= 5 + 3.24 = \$8.24 \text{ million}
\end{aligned}
$$

Computations for the third quartile are:

$$
\begin{aligned}
Q_3 &= L_{q3} + \frac{(3N/4) - F_{q3}}{f_{q3}} i_{q3} \\
&= 50 + \frac{3{,}723.00 - 3{,}601}{661}(50)
\end{aligned}
$$

$$= 50 + \frac{122 \times 50}{661}$$

$$= 50 + 9.23 = \$59.23 \text{ million}$$

Thus the middle range, the Q_1 to Q_3 interval, which contains about 50% of the savings associations, is $8.24 to $59.23 million.

To get an estimate of the actual percentage of associations in the middle range, additional calculations are necessary. It is obvious that the 2,183 associations in the $10 to $50 interval are in the middle range. Interpolations must be made, however, to determine how many of the associations in the "$5 and under $10" and the "$50 and under $100" classes are in the interval.

To interpolate, we first go backward in the $5 to $10 class to the $8.24 point and estimate by interpolation how many of the 503 associations have assets between $8.24 and $10 million:

$$\frac{\text{Upper class limit} - Q_1}{\text{class interval}} \times \text{class frequency} = \frac{10 - 8.24}{5}(503)$$

$$= \frac{1.76}{5}(503)$$

$$= 177 \text{ associations}$$

Next we go forward to $50.00 and estimate how many of the 661 association in the $50 and $100 class have assets between $50 and $59.23:

$$\frac{Q_3 - \text{lower class limit}}{\text{class interval}} \times \text{class frequency} = \frac{59.23 - 50}{50}(661)$$

$$= \frac{9.23}{50}(661)$$

$$= 122 \text{ associations}$$

Now we have 2183 + 177 + 122 = 2482 associations with assets in the middle range of $8.24 to $59.23 million. This is 50% of the total, 4964.

The Quartile Deviation

The quartile deviation for the distribution of earnings from the OS University students (see Table 5-6) is:

$$\frac{Q_3 - Q_1}{2} = \frac{158.25 - 113.25}{2} = \frac{45}{2} = \$22.50$$

The arithmetic mean of these earnings computed from the distribution in Chapter 4 is $136.00. The interval $\overline{X} \pm Q_{\text{Dev.}}$, therefore, is 136.00 ± 22.50 = $113.50 to $158.50, which would be the middle range in a symmetrical distribution. Notice that these two figures are very close to the Q_1 and Q_3 of \$113.25 and \$158.25 computed previously.

The $\bar{X} \pm Q_{\text{Dev.}}$ for the distribution of savings associations cannot be determined because the arithmetic mean cannot be calculated.

The Mean Deviation

In order to compute the mean deviation for a frequency distribution, we must be able to determine the *midpoints* of all the classes. Thus, the mean deviation can be found only for a closed-end distribution. In this computation, we assume that the difference between the arithmetic mean of the distribution and the midpoint of a given class is the arithmetic mean of the differences between the values in that class and the arithmetic mean of the frequency distribution. In Table 5-8, for example, the difference between $\bar{X}$, \$136 (computed in Chapter 4), and \$62, the midpoint of the first class, is 74. This is an estimate of the arithmetic mean of the differences between the two individual figures in that class and the arithmetic mean of all 50 figures. Therefore, $2 \times 74 = 148$ is an estimated total of the two deviations.

The $f|D|$ column contains estimates of the totals of the deviations for the classes. The sum of these totals gives the estimated total for all classes, $\Sigma f|D|$, or 1,266. When this is divided by N we have the mean deviation, \$25.32, which is the arithmetic mean of the differences between each student's earnings and the arithmetic mean earnings of \$136.00.

The Standard Deviation—Long Method

Finding the standard deviation of values in a frequency distribution, like the mean deviation, requires weighting by frequencies. In Table 5-8, the deviations, $|D|$, multiplied by the weighted deviations, $f|D|$, give the fD^2 values that are needed in the standard deviation formula

$$\sigma = \sqrt{\frac{\Sigma fD^2}{N}}$$

Applying this formula in Table 5-8 gives a standard deviation of \$33.90. Because it requires the calculation of the arithmetic mean and differences between the arithmetic mean and the midpoints, this method is sometimes called the "long method." It should be used when the frequency distribution has unequal class intervals.

The Standard Deviation—Shortcut Calculation

A quicker way to compute the standard deviation of a distribution when its class intervals are equal is to use the deviation values that were used in the shortcut method for finding

TABLE 5-8. Computation of the Mean and Standard Deviations of the April 1975 Earnings of 50 OS University Students Employed Part-Time.

EARNINGS	NUMBER OF STUDENTS (f)	CLASS MIDPOINTS	DEVIATION OF CLASS MIDPOINTS FROM $\bar{X}$ ($\lvert D \rvert$)	$f\lvert D \rvert$	fD^2
$ 50– 74	2	62	74	148	10,952
75– 99	5	87	49	245	12,005
100–124	10	112	24	40	5,760
125–149	17	137	1	17	17
150–174	10	162	26	260	6,760
175–199	4	187	51	204	10,404
200–224	2	212	76	152	11,552
Total	50			1,266	57,450

$$\bar{X} = 136.00$$

$$\text{M.D.} = \frac{\Sigma f|D|}{N} = \frac{1{,}266}{50} = \$25.32$$

$$\sigma = \sqrt{\frac{\Sigma fD^2}{N}} = \sqrt{\frac{57{,}450}{50}} = \sqrt{1{,}149} = \$33.90$$

the arithmetic mean. These are the values between the midpoints of the classes and the midpoint of one of the classes that is assumed to be the arithmetic mean. Table 5-9 illustrates this shortcut method. The formula is:

$$\sigma = i\sqrt{\frac{\Sigma f(d')^2}{N} - \left(\frac{\Sigma f d'}{N}\right)^2}$$

As in the shortcut formula for the arithmetic mean, d' represents the number of class intervals between the midpoints of the classes and the midpoint of the class assumed to be the arithmetic mean. As in other formulas, f represents the individual frequencies, N the total frequency, and i the common class interval. The last part of the formula, $(\Sigma fd'/N)^2$, corrects for the error in the assumed mean.

Substitutions in the formula are shown below Table 5-9 and, as it should be, the result, $33.90, is the same as that obtained by the long method in Table 5-8. Note that this estimated standard deviation calculated from the frequency distribution is very close to the standard deviation of $33.88 computed from the ungrouped data shown in Table 5-5.

The percentage of frequencies that fall within the interval $\bar{X} \pm \sigma$ can be estimted by making two interpolations. The interval $\bar{X} \pm \sigma$ for the values in Table 5-9 is $136.00 ± $33.90, or $102.10 to $169.90. It is obvious that the 17 students in the class $125–149 are in this interval, but interpolations into the classes $100–124 and $150–174 are required to determine how many of the frequencies in those classes fall in the interval. Letting f represent the frequency of the class interval for an interpolation, we have

\$124.50	(Upper real class limit)
−\$102.10	(Lower interval limit)
\$ 22.40	(Difference)

$$\frac{\text{Difference}}{\text{Class interval}}f = \frac{20.40}{25.00}(10) = 9 \text{ students}$$

and

\$169.90	(Upper interval limit)
−\$149.50	(Lower real class limit)
\$ 20.40	(Difference)

$$\frac{\text{Difference}}{\text{Class interval}}f = \frac{20.40}{25.00}(10) = 8 \text{ students}$$

Therefore, 17 + 9 + 8 = 34 students are estimated to fall in the interval. This is 68% of the 50 students.*

TABLE 5-9. Calculation of the Standard Deviation of the April 1975 Earnings of 50 OS University Students Employed Part-Time.

EARNINGS	*NUMBER OF STUDENTS* (f)	*DEVIATION OF CLASS MIDPOINTS FROM ASSUMED ARITHMETIC MEAN IN CLASS INTERVAL UNITS* (d')	*WEIGHTED DEVIATION* (fd')	*WEIGHTED SQUARED DEVIATION* $f(d')^2$
\$ 50– 74	2	−3	−6	18
75– 99	5	−2	−10	20
100–124	10	−1	−10	10
125–149	17	0	0	0
150–174	10	1	10	10
175–199	4	2	8	16
200–224	2	3	6	18
Total	50		−2	92

$\overline{X}_a$ = \$237 (Midpoint of \$125–149)

$$\sigma = i\sqrt{\frac{\Sigma f(d')^2}{N} - \left(\frac{\Sigma fd'}{N}\right)^2} = 25\sqrt{\frac{92}{50} - \left(\frac{-2}{50}\right)^2}$$

$$= 25\sqrt{1.8400 - 0.0016}$$

$$= 25\sqrt{1.8384} = 25 \times 1.3559 = \$33.90$$

*Chapter 6 introduces the *normal distribution* and shows that for such a distribution $\overline{X} \pm \sigma$ includes 68.27% of the frequencies.

The Coefficient of Variation

The formula for the coefficient of variation is the same for ungrouped data and frequency distributions:

$$V = \frac{\sigma}{\overline{X}}$$

However, we have seen that the formulas for the arithmetic mean and standard deviation differ, so that to compare the coefficients of variation of two frequency distributions we should use the shortcut formulas for the arithmetic mean and standard deviation if the data lend themselves to such use. Table 5-10 shows the calculations from earnings distributions of Class A and Class B computer operators. In each distribution there is a uniform class interval; therefore, the shortcut methods have been used. The coefficient of variation for the distribution of Class A operators, 0.167, is larger than that for Class B, 0.151, which means that the Class B earnings are more homogeneous and that the arithmetic mean of $184.77 is a bit more representative of the Class B operators' earnings than is the $208.18 arithmetic mean of the earnings of Class A operators.

TABLE 5-10. Calculation of Coefficients of Variation of Weekly Earnings of Class A and Class B Computer Operators in Large Establishments in the Milwaukee, Wisconsin, Metropolitan Area, April 1975.

CLASS A OPERATORS					*CLASS B OPERATORS*				
Earnings	f	d'	fd'	$f(d')^2$	Earnings	f	d'	fd'	$f(d')^2$
$140 but under $160	7	−4	−28	112	$120 but under $140	2	−2	−4	8
$160 but under $180	5	−3	−15	45	$140 but under $160	16	−1	−16	16
$180 but under $200	11	−2	−22	44	$160 but under $180	37	0	0	0
$200 but under $220	7	−1	−7	7	$180 but under $200	24	1	24	24
$220 but under $240	18	0	0	0	$200 but under $220	14	2	28	56
$240 but under $260	3	1	3	3	$220 but under $240	10	3	30	90
$260 but under $280	3	2	6	12	$240 but under $260	3	4	12	48
$280 but under $300	1	3	3	9	$260 but under $280	1	5	5	25
Total	55		−60	232		107		79	267

$$\overline{X} = 230 + \frac{-60}{55}20 = \$208.18 \qquad \overline{X} = \overline{X}_a + \frac{\Sigma fd'}{N}i \qquad \overline{X} = 170 + \frac{79}{107}20 = \$184.77$$

$$\sigma = 20\sqrt{\frac{232}{55} - \left(\frac{-60}{55}\right)^2} \qquad \sigma = i\sqrt{\frac{\Sigma F(d')^2}{N} - \left(\frac{\Sigma fd'}{N}\right)^2} \qquad \sigma = 20\sqrt{\frac{267}{107} + \left(\frac{79}{107}\right)^2}$$

$$= 20 \quad 3.028 = \$34.80 \qquad\qquad = 20\sqrt{1.9502} = \$27.93$$

$$V = \frac{34.80}{208.18} = 0.167 \qquad V = \frac{\sigma}{\overline{X}} \qquad V = \frac{27.93}{184.77} = 0.151$$

If we want a measure of relative dispersion for an open-end frequency distribution, we cannot use these based on the arithmetic mean and standard deviaiton, because these values cannot be computed for an open-end distribution. Instead, we calculate a coefficient based on the quartiles:

$$V = \frac{Q_3 - Q_1}{Q_3 + Q_1}$$

Substituting in this formula the values computed for the open-end distribution in Table 5-7 gives

$$V = \frac{22.52 - 2.37}{22.52 + 2.37} = \frac{20.15}{24.89} = 0.81$$

This measure relates only to the variation of the middle 50% of the data.

MEASURES OF SKEWNESS

In Chapter 4 we defined a skewed distribution as one that departs from symmetry.

Skewness

In a distribution that is skewed to the right, the arithmetic mean is larger than the mode, and in a distribution skewed to the left, the arithmetic mean is smaller than the mode. The *degree* of the skewness of a distribution may be measured by computing a *coefficient of skewness*. A positive coefficient of skewness indicates that a distribution is skewed to the right, while a distribution having a negative coefficient of skewness is skewed to the left.

The Pearsonian Coefficient of Skewness

A measure of the degree to which a distribution is skewed is the so-called Pearsonian coefficient. Its formula, based on the arithmetic mean–mode relationship, is

$$\text{Sk} = \frac{\overline{X} - M_o}{\sigma}$$

If this formula gives a positive result, the distribution is skewed to the right. If the result is negative, the distribution is skewed to the left. This is a rough measure, but it is adequate for many purposes.

Another formula for getting approximately the same measure of the degree of skewness, also proposed by the statistician Karl Pearson, is

$$\text{Sk} = \frac{3(\overline{X} - M_e)}{\sigma}$$

This formula is based on a general relationship of the arithmetic mean, median, and mode in skewed distributions, as pictured in Charts 4-2 and 4-3. Chart 4-3 indicates that the difference between the arithmetic mean and median is about one third of the difference between the arithmetic mean and the mode. This is true, at least approximately, for slightly skewed, unimodal frequency distributions.

The way to compare the skewness of the two distributions is to determine a coefficient of skewness for each. For example, the two distributions in Table 5-10 are both skewed, but we cannot tell by looking at them which is more skewed. But by computing the medians for both distributions and substituting with the arithmetic means and standard deviations calculated in Table 5-10 to find the coefficient of skewness, we can make a meaningful comparison. The median for the distribution of Class A operators is:

$$M_e = L_{me} + \frac{(N/2) - F_{me}}{f_{me}} i_{me} = 200 + \frac{27.5 - 23}{7}(20) = \$212.86$$

The median for the distribution of Class B operators is:

$$M_e = L_{me} + \frac{(N/2) - F_{me}}{f_{me}} i_{me} = 160 + \frac{53.5 - 18}{37}(20) = \$179.19$$

The coefficient of skewness for the Class A operator's earnings is:

$$\text{Sk} = \frac{3(\overline{X} - M_e)}{\sigma} = \frac{3(208.18 - 212.86)}{34.80} = -0.403$$

For the distribution of the earnings of the Class B operators:

$$\text{Sk} = \frac{3(X - M_e)}{\sigma} = \frac{3(184.77 - 179.19)}{27.93} = +0.599$$

On the basis of these calculations, we can say that the earnings of the Class B operators are more highly skewed than those of the Class A operators. Also, the two distributions are skewed in opposite directions.

A Coefficient of Skewness Based on Quartiles

Another formula for measuring the degree of skewness of a distribution involves quartiles:

$$\text{Sk} = \frac{Q_3 + Q_1 - 2Q_2}{Q_3 - Q_1}$$

This formula assumes that Q_3 and Q_1 are equally separated from the median in a symmetric curve, that is, $Q_3 - Q_2 = Q_2 - Q_1$ or $Q_3 + Q_1 - 2Q_2 = 0$. A skewed curve does not have this equality of separation, and skewness will be revealed if Q_3 is farther from Q_2 than is Q_1, or if Q_1 is farther from Q_2 than is Q_3. Dividing $Q_3 + Q_1 - 2Q_2$ by $Q_3 - Q_1$ makes the measure a relative one and, therefore, useful for comparing the degrees of skewness of two or more frequency distributions. This skewness formula based on quartiles can be used for open-end frequency distributions whereas the one based on the arithmetic mean, median and mode cannot.

A Coefficient of Skewness Based on the Third Moment

A more precise measure of skewness than that based on the difference between the arithmetic mean and the mode or the arithmetic mean and the median is based on the *third moment* about the arithmetic mean. The first moment about the arithmetic mean is the mean of the deviations of the values from their arithmetic mean (it is always equal to zero). The second moment about the arithmetic mean is the arithmetic mean of the deviations after they have been squared. As a formula, is written

$$M_2 = \frac{\Sigma x^2}{N}$$

This is called the variance; we have already seen that the standard deviation is the square root of the variance. The third moment about the mean is the mean of the cube of the deviations from their arithmetic mean. The formula is

$$M_3 = \frac{\Sigma x^3}{N}$$

This computation gives an absolute measure of skewness. Since each x^3 retains its original plus or minus sign, for a symmetrical distribution, Σx^3 would be zero and, therefore, M_3 would be zero. If there is a skewness toward the larger values, however, M_3 will be positive. A negative M_3 will result from skewness toward the smaller values.

A measure of the relative skewness using the third and second moments may be computed with the following formula:

$$\text{Sk} = \frac{M_3{}^2}{M_2{}^3}$$

Table 5-11 shows the values necessary to compute M_2 and M_3. Substituting from the table,

$$M_2 = \frac{\Sigma x^2}{N} = \frac{160}{5} = 32$$

and

$$M_3 = \frac{\Sigma x^3}{N} = \frac{720}{5} = 144$$

Therefore,

$$\text{Sk} = \frac{(144)^2}{(32)^3} = \frac{20{,}736}{32{,}768} = 0.63$$

Five simple figures were used in this calculation to illustrate the concept of moments and the measure of relative skewness based on them. If many values are to be analyzed for skewness, the computations become laborious, and if a computer is not available, grouping the data before making any calculations saves time.

The second and third moments can be estimated from a frequency distribution by using deviations of class midpoints from the arithmetic mean of the distribution. The formula is:

$$M_2 = \frac{\Sigma f D^2}{N}$$

$$M_3 = \frac{\Sigma f D^3}{N}$$

TABLE 5-11. Calculation of Values Needed to Compute a Coefficient of Skewness of a List of Values.

	X	x $(X - \bar{X})$	x^2	x^3
	2	−6	36	−216
	4	−4	16	−64
	6	−2	4	−8
	10	+2	4	+8
	18	+10	100	+1000
Total	40	0	160	720

$$\bar{X} = \frac{\Sigma X}{N} = \frac{40}{5} = 8$$

TABLE 5-12. Calculation of Values Needed to Compute Coefficients of Skewness and Kurtosis of Weekly Earnings of Class B Computer Operators in the Milwaukee, Wisconsin, Metropolitan Area, April, 1975.

EARNINGS	f	d'	fd'	$f(d')^2$	$f(d')^3$	$f(d')^4$
\$140 but under \$160	2	−2	−4	−8	−16	32
\$160 but under \$180	16	−1	−16	16	−16	16
\$180 but under \$200	37	0	0	0	0	0
\$200 but under \$220	24	1	24	24	24	24
\$220 but under \$240	14	2	28	56	112	224
\$240 but under \$260	10	3	30	90	270	810
\$260 but under \$280	3	4	12	48	192	768
\$280 but under \$300	1	5	5	25	125	625
	107		79	267	691	2,499

When the deviations of the midpoints of the classes are taken around an assumed mean and are expressed in class interval units the formulas become:

$$M_2 = \frac{\Sigma f(d')^2}{N} - \left(\frac{\Sigma fd'}{N}\right)^2$$

$$M_3 = \frac{\Sigma f(d')^3}{N} - \frac{3\Sigma fd'}{N}\frac{\Sigma f(d')^2}{N} + 2\left(\frac{\Sigma fd'}{N}\right)^3$$

Table 5-12 shows how to measure the degree of skewness of the weekly earnings of class B file clerks with these formulas. Substituting,

$$M_2 = \frac{267}{107} - \left(\frac{79}{107}\right)^2 = 1.9502$$

$$M_3 = \frac{691}{107} - 3\left(\frac{79}{107}\right)\left(\frac{267}{107}\right) + 2\left(\frac{79}{107}\right)^3 = 1.7358$$

The coefficient of skewness is

$$\frac{M_3{}^2}{M_2{}^3} = \frac{(1.7358)^2}{(1.9502)^3} = 0.4062$$

MEASURES OF KURTOSIS

Kurtosis means *peakedness*. A curve that is rather flat is *platykurtic*, a highly peaked curve is *leptokurtic*, and a curve with a shape somewhat between these two is *mesokurtic*. Chart 5-1 illustrates these types of kurtosis. A measurement of the *degree* of peakedness is a *coefficient of kurtosis*. The formula for this coefficient, which is based on the fourth moment, is

$$\text{Kur} = \frac{M_4}{M_2{}^2}$$

where

$$M_4 = \frac{\Sigma f(d')^4}{N} - 4\frac{\Sigma fd'}{N}\frac{\Sigma f(d')^3}{N} + 6\left(\frac{\Sigma fd'}{N}\right)^2\frac{\Sigma f(d')^2}{N} - 3\left(\frac{\Sigma fd'}{N}\right)^4$$

For the weekly earnings of class B file clerks,

$$M_4 = \frac{2499}{107} - 4\left(\frac{79}{107}\right)\left(\frac{691}{107}\right) + 6\left(\frac{79}{107}\right)^2\left(\frac{267}{107}\right) - 3\left(\frac{79}{107}\right)^4 = 11.5530$$

Chart 5-1. Types of kurtosis.

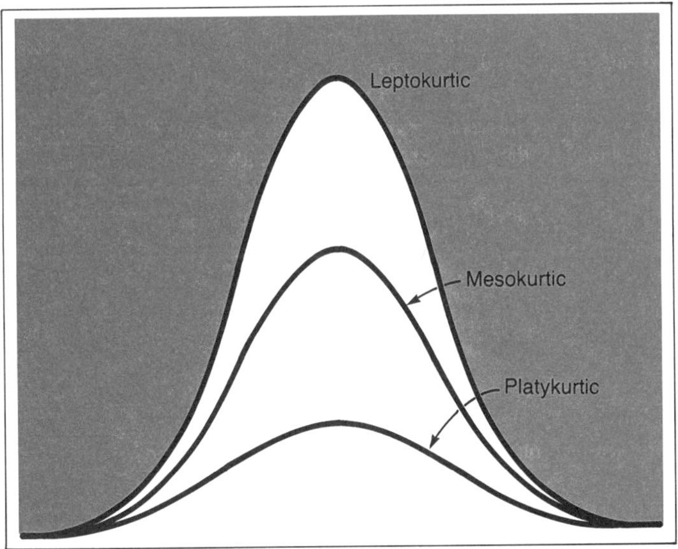

so

$$\text{Kur} = \frac{M_4}{M_2^2} = \frac{11.5530}{(1.9502)^2} = 3.0376$$

It should be pointed out that a coefficient of kurtosis is of little value unless it is compared to the coefficient of kurtosis of another curve. When such a comparison is made the distribution with the highest coefficient is the one that is more peaked.

REVIEW QUESTIONS

1. What is a measure of dispersion? Why is it computed?
2. Differentiate the following measures of dispersion: range, quartile deviation, mean deviation, standard deviation.
3. Which of the measures of dispersion listed in Question 2 can be computed for an open-end frequency distribution? Which cannot? Why?
4. Why is a measurement of dispersion computed for a frequency distribution not equal to that computed for the original figures from which the distribution was constructed?

5. When computed from the same data which will be larger, the mean deviation or the standard deviation? Why?

6. Which measure of dispersion is most widely used?

7. How can we compare the variations of two or more distributions if the arithmetic means of the distributions are the same? If they are different?

8. Why can a standard deviation be computed faster using

$$\sigma = \sqrt{\frac{\Sigma X^2}{N} - \left(\frac{\Sigma X}{N}\right)^2}$$

$$\sigma = \sqrt{\frac{\Sigma x^2}{N}}$$

9. What are measures of relative dispersion? How are they used?

10. What is a coefficient of variation?

11. Describe a skewed distribution.

12. From smallest to largest, what is the order of size of the arithmetic mean, median, and mode in a distribution that is: (a) symmetrical, (b) skewed to the right, (c) skewed to the left? Why?

13. For what are coefficients of skewness used?

14. What does kurtosis mean?

15. Define mesokurtic, platykurtic, and leptokurtic.

PROBLEMS

1. For the list of figures in Exercist Table 5-1, determine the range and the middle range, and compute the mean deviation and standard deviation. Use both the short method and long method for the standard deviations. Both methods should give the same answers.
2. The arithmetic mean of 5, 10, 15, 20, and 25 is 15. The arithmetic mean of 6, 9, 14, 21, and 25 is also 15. Compute the proper measure of dispersion to determine which of the two lists of numbers is more varied.
3. Calculate coefficients of variations for the number of points scored by basketball players A and B listed in Exercise Table 5-2, and determine which player was more consistent in his scoring. Do you think a basketball coach should be interested in the consistency of a player's scoring? Why?

EXERCISE TABLE 5-1. Number of Blocks Traveled by a Deliveryman to Deliver Products to 20 Customers.

6	8	28	33
17	18	23	29
8	9	19	14
19	16	25	30
13	20	21	27

Source: Hypothetical data.

4. *The National Survey of Professional, Administrative, Technical and Clerical Pay*, June 1967, published by the U.S. Bureau of Labor Statistics shows that 6455 top-grade accounts (accountants V) in the United States received an arithmetic mean monthly salary of $1066, a median monthly salary of $1050, and that the middle range of their monthly salaries was $955 to $1174. Using this information answer the following questions.
   (a) Which direction is the salary distribution skewed?
   (b) Can we estimate the mode of the monthly salaries? If so, what is it?
   (c) What are the values of the first and second quartiles?
   (d) If you were planning to hire a top-grade accountant, how would these date be helpful to you?

EXERCISE TABLE 5-2. Calculation of the Coefficient of Variation of Points Scored by Two Basketball Players in Ten Practice Games.

PLAYER A		PLAYER B	
X	X^2	X	X^2
13	169	26	676
17	289	20	400
10	100	18	324
14	196	28	784
8	64	25	625
15	225	14	196
11	121	18	324
13	169	26	176
12	144	16	256
7	49	19	361
120	1526	210	4622

5. Using the data in Exercise Table 5-3, determine which grade of keypunch operator has a more homogeneous salary structure. Also determine which salary distribution has the highest degree of skewness.

6. Using the data in Exercise Table 5-3, compute the interquartile ranges for keypunch operators I and II.

EXERCISE TABLE 5-3. Percent Distribution of Class I and Class II Keypunch Operators by Monthly Salary Classes, United States, March 1975.

MONTHLY SALARY	PERCENT OF TOTAL	
	OPERATORS CLASS I	OPERATORS CLASS II
$ 300 but under $ 400	1.8	0
400 but under 500	24.2	4.5
500 but under 600	35.9	24.0
600 but under 700	19.2	34.6
700 but under 800	9.5	18.6
800 but under 900	5.2	9.8
900 but under 1,000	2.5	6.5
1,000 but under 1,100	1.7	1.0
1,100 but under 1,200	0	1.1
Total	100.0	100.0

Source: U.S. Department of Labor, Bureau of Labor Statistics, *National Survey of Professional, Administrative, Technical and Clerical Pay*, March, 1975.

7. Exercise Table 5-4 shows how many miles a taxicab driver traveled in 50 trips to deliver customers from Union Station to their destinations. Compute the middle range for the number of miles traveled on these 50 trips.

EXERCISE TABLE 5-4. Distribution of 50 Taxicap Trips to Union Station by Miles Traveled to Deliver Passengers.

MILES TRAVELED	NUMBER OF TRIPS
Under 1	4
2 but under 3	7
3 but under 4	9
4 but under 5	15
5 but under 10	9
10 and over	6
Total	50

Source: Hypothetical data.

8. Exercise Table 5-5 shows the actual ages of 20 office employees. Exercise Table 5-6 is a frequency distribution of the ages of the same twenty employees. For the data in each table compute: the mean, quartile deviation, mean deviation, standard deviation, and coefficient of variation, $\sigma/\overline{X}$. Do the answers for each measure computed from the two tables differ? If so, why? If so, which answer is more accurate?

9. From the data in Exercise Table 5-6 compute coefficients of skewness using the Pearsonian formula and the formula based on quartiles. Do the answers differ? If so, why?

10. Calculate a coefficient of skewness based on the third moment for the numbers 2, 5, 7, 9, 12, and 20.

EXERCISE TABLE 5-5. Ages of 20 Office Employees (to Nearest Birthday).

27	22
19	28
32	18
29	47
43	36
39	51
53	49
33	39
42	62
40	44

Source: Hypothetical.

11. Compute coefficients of skewness and kurtosis, based on moments, for the data in Exercise Table 5-6.

12. Measure the degrees of skewness and peakedness of the distribution in Exercise Table 4-4, using the formulas based on moments.

EXERCISE TABLE 5-6. Distribution of 20 Office Employees by Age Group.

AGE	*NUMBER OF EMPLOYEES*
15–24	3
25–34	5
35–44	7
45–54	4
55–64	1
Total	20

Source: Exercise Table 5-5.

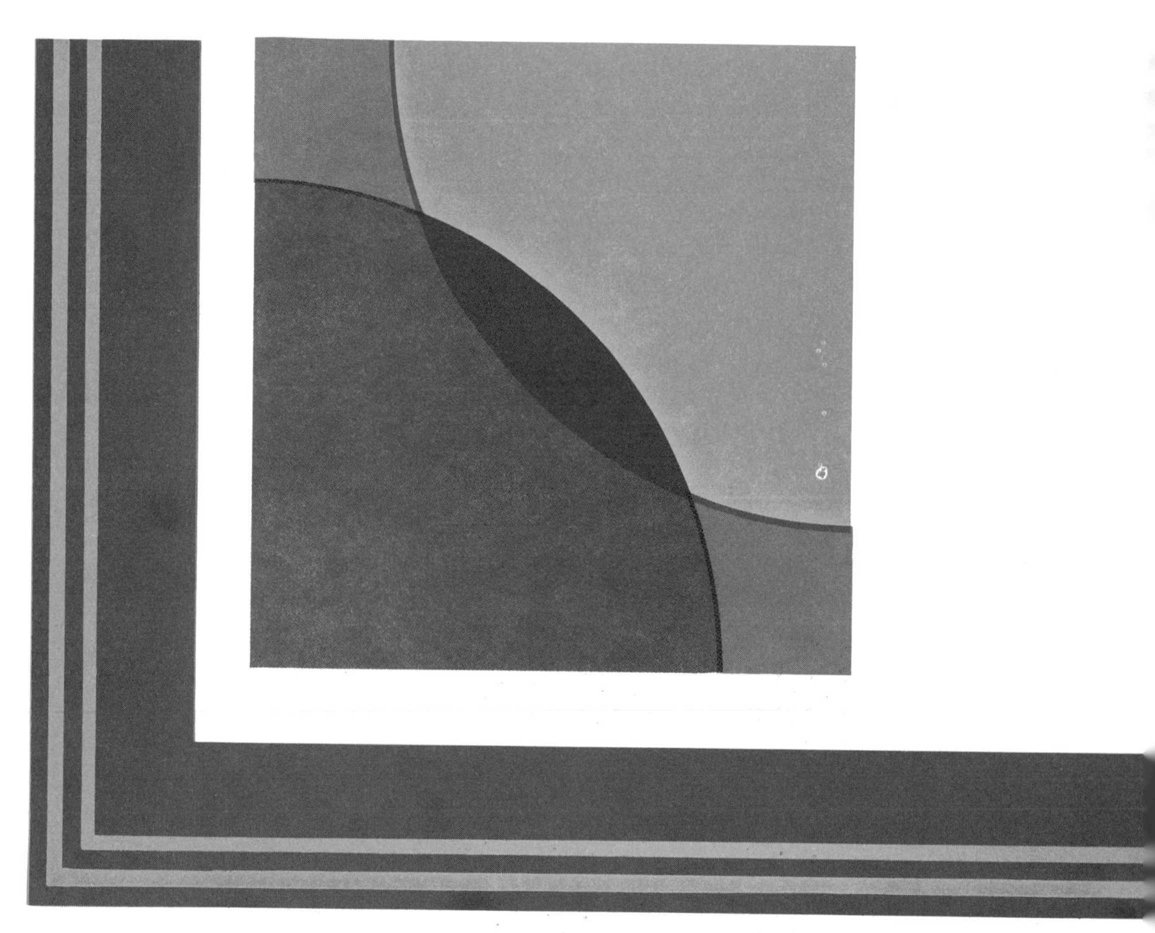

6

Basic Probability

Most decisions we make in every walk of life are based consciously or subconsciously, on probabilities. These probabilities result from our own experiences or the knowledge of other people's experiences. Often, these probabilities are not mathematically measured or used in a formal way. However, management problem-solving in a business enterprise can be facilitated and improved if the decision-maker has a basic knowledge of probability concepts and uses them in a formal way. In this chapter we will be concerned with the fundamentals of probability theory and probability calculations. This will prepare you for the study of probability distributions in Chapter 7, which are the foundations for understanding sampling theory and applications.

PROBABILITY CONCEPTS

Probability

Probability is often defined as the likelihood of the occurrence of an event or as the relative number of times an event can occur in an infinite number of tries. Based on relative frequencies, it is expressed in quantitative form as a decimal fraction or a common fraction.

An event must be the result of random action or process. When an event or phenomenon occurs x out of n times, the relative frequency of its occurrence is expressed as x/n. If we let y represent the number of times the event or phenomenon does not occur, the relative frequency of failure to occur is y/n; therefore, $x + y = n$ and

$$\frac{x}{n} + \frac{y}{n} = 1$$

One of the most common illustrations of probability relates to the flipping of a well-balanced coin. The relative frequency that a coin lands with the head side up is $x/n = 1/2$ and the relative frequency of a tail is also $1/2$. Therefore, we can say that the probability of a head appearing is $1/2$, the probability of a tail is $1/2$, and the probability of one or the other appearing $1/2 + 1/2 = 1$, or certainty. The probability of neither appearing is zero. In other words, if you were to flip a balanced coin a million times you could expect to get heads five hundred thousand times and tails five hundred thousand times.

Because there is only one ace of spaces in a deck of 52 cards, the relative frequency of its appearance is $x/n = 1/52$, and therefore, the probability of getting it in one draw from a well-shuffled deck of cards is 1/52. The probability of not drawing an ace of spades is

$$\frac{y}{n} = \frac{51}{52}$$

so

$$\frac{x}{n} + \frac{y}{n} = \frac{1}{52} + \frac{51}{52} = 1$$

To illustrate further: If there are 3,000 females and 7,000 males in a group of people, the probability of choosing a female from a selection of one person by a random process (one that will give each person an equal chance of being chosen) would be

$$\frac{3{,}000}{10{,}000} = 0.3$$

The probability of choosing a male (not getting a female) would be

$$\frac{7{,}000}{10{,}000} = 0.7$$

and the sum of these probabilities is $0.3 + 0.7 = 1$.

In these illustrations the probabilities are based on known relative frequencies and are called *a priori* probabilities. Sometimes, experiments have to be made to estimate relative frequencies before probabilities can be determined. These probabilities are called either empirical or *a posteriori* probabilities. To determine the probability that a particular baseball player will get a hit when he comes to bat, we would use his batting average as the relative frequency x/n. If a player's average is 0.327, then the best estimate of the probability that he will get a hit the next time he is at bat is 0.327. Another example: A light bulb manufacturer may inspect thousands of bulbs produced and classify 10% of them "defective." Based on this study, he might establish that 0.10 is the probability tha any bulb manufactured under the same conditions would be defective.

Probability Rules

When the occurrence of one event precludes the occurrence of the others, the events are said to be *mutually exclusive*. For example, if a die is tossed, the appearance of one number precludes the appearance of any other. Events are *independent* when the occurence of one does not affect the occurrence of any other. An example: When a pair of dice are tossed, the number appearing on one die is not affected by the number appearing on the other. Two important special rules for calculating probabilities are the *addition rule for mutually exclusive events* and the *multiplication rule for independent events*.

The Special Addition Rule

The probability of the occurrence of one or the other of two events that are mutually exclusive is the sum of the two individual probabilities.

For example, the probability of getting a five spot on the roll of a die is 1/6 and the probability of getting a six spot is 1/6; therefore, the probability of getting either a five spot or a six spot is 1/6 + 1/6 or 1/3. This rule can be expanded to more than two events, so the probability of rolling a three, four, or five spot is 1/6 + 1/6 + 1/6 or 1/2. The probability of drawing any one of the four jacks in a deck of cards is

$$\frac{1}{52} + \frac{1}{52} + \frac{1}{52} + \frac{1}{52} = \frac{4}{52} = \frac{1}{13}$$

The probability of not drawing a jack is

$$1 - \frac{1}{13} = \frac{12}{13}$$

because the sum of the probabilities of drawing each of the 52 cards is 1 or certainty.

The Special Multiplication Rule

The probability that two independent events will occur at the same time is the product of the probabilities of the events.

The probability of a five spot appearing in one throw of a die is 1/6; therefore, the probability of two five spots appearing in a throw of two dice is $1/6 \times 1/6 = 1/36$. Similarly, the probability of getting a five spot on each of three successive rolls of a die is $1/6 \times 1/6 \times 1/6 = 1/216$.

Sometimes probabilities must be computed with both the addition and multiplication rules. Suppose that we want to know the probability of obtaining a total of 4 with one toss of two dice. This can be determined three ways. Calling one die A and the other die B, we could get the following combinations, each of which adds to four.

DIE A	*DIE B*	*TOTAL*
1	3	4
3	1	4
2	2	4

The probability that die A will turn up 1 is 1/6 and the probability that die B will turn up 3 is 1/6; therefore, the probability that both will turn up at the same time is 1/6 × 1/6 = 1/36. The probability that die A will turn up 3 is 1/6 and the probability that die B will turn up 1 is 1/6; therefore, the probability that both will turn up simultaneously is 1/6 × 1/6 = 1/36. Similarly, the probability of the appearance of 2 on each is 1/6 × 1/6 = 1/36. The probability of rolling a four is the sum of these three products, or 1/36 + 1/36 + 1/36 = 3/36 = 1/12.

An illustration of the relationship between probabilities and relative frequencies can be made with the figures in Table 6-1, which shows the 36 possible outcomes from a throw of a pair of dice. Since there are 36 possible outcomes and the number 4 appears in the diagram three times, 3/36 = 1/12 is the relative frequency of a 4. It is also the probability of throwing a 4 with one roll of a pair of dice as calculated by the addition and multiplication rules.

TABLE 6-1. Thirty-Six Possible Outcomes from a Throw of a Pair of Dice.

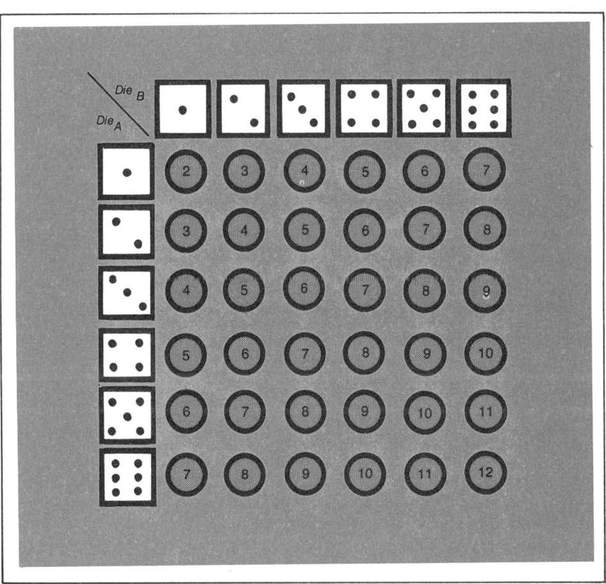

The individual probabilities of the possible outcomes for a throw of two dice are listed in Table 6-2, which may be called a *probability distribution* because the probability for each number in the list is positive and less than or equal to 1 and the sum of the probabilities is 1. Probability distributions will be discussed in Chapter 7.

TABLE 6-2. Probabilities of Obtaining Possible Numbers from a Throw of Two Dice.

POSSIBLE NUMBER	*PROBABILITY OF GETTING POSSIBLE NUMBER*
2	1/36
3	2/36
4	3/36
5	4/36
6	5/36
7	6/36
8	5/36
9	4/36
10	3/36
11	2/36
12	1/36
Total	36/36

Sample Space and Sample Points

The terms *sample space* and *sample points* are frequently used in a discussion of probability.

Sample Space and Point

The set of all the possible outcomes for an experiment is a *sample space*. An individual outcome from the experiment is called a *sample point*.

For example, the 36 shaded circles in Table 6-1 constitute a sample space and each circle is a sample point representing the way a certain sum can appear with one toss of a pair of dice. The sums are given in the points. By counting the number of points in given subsets of points and expressing these numbers as fractions of the 36 points the probabilities shown in Table 6-2 were found. For example the three points numbered 4 represent the different ways that a sum of four can be obtained by a single toss of a pair of dice. Therefore the probability of getting a 4 is 3/36.

The concept of a sample space and points can also be illustrated with a coin-tossing experiment. For example, if a coin is tossed three times the possible outcomes are:

HHH HHT HTH HTT THH THT TTH TTT

Each possible outcome, which is a *simple event*, is a sample point, and all eight of the possible outcomes is the sample space. By combining the points HHT, HTH and

THH , we can calculate the probability that two heads and one tail would appear if a coin were tossed three times. The probability is 3/8.

COUNTING TECHNIQUES FOR DETERMINING PROBABILITIES

In order to determine relative frequencies, and therefore probabilities, the universe of possible events (n) that can happen under a given process must be counted. Once this has been done, subsets of events can be counted and probabilities of specific subsets occurring can be calculated.

Enumeration Tables

Table 6-3 illustrates one tool of counting, the *enumeration table*, which lists all of the possible events from which all possible subsets of events can be ascertained. The following problem will give an additional illustration of the use of the enumeration table as a tool for determining probabilities.

TABLE 6-3. Color Size and Material Combinations of Boxes.

COLOR	*SIZE*	*MATERIAL*
Red	Large	Wood
Red	Large	Cardboard
Red	Small	Wood
Red	Small	Cardboard
Blue	Large	Wood
Blue	Large	Cardboard
Blue	Small	Wood
Blue	Small	Cardboard

Two different-sized boxes (large and small) are used in the packaging of a particular product. Each of the two boxes comes in two colors (red and blue) and is made from two materials (wood and cardboard). If each size-color-material combination is used in equal numbers what is the probability that a boxed product, selected at random, will be red and small?

To help answer this question we use Table 6-3, which lists all possible color-size-material combinations. The table shows eight possible combinations, with

TABLE 6-4. Possible Display Arrangements for a Radio, Television, and Record Player.

Radio	Television	Record Player
Radio	Record Player	Television
Television	Radio	Record Player
Television	Record Player	Radio
Record Player	Television	Radio
Record Player	Radio	Television

two of them being both red and small. Therefore, the probability that a randomly selected package will be red and small is $2/8 = 1/4 = 0.25$.

Another example of the use of the enumeration table in a business situation is that of a retail clerk who is asked to display a radio, television, and record player in a row on a shelf. How many different displays can be made? If each possible display (arrangement) is equally likely to be made by the clerk, what is the probability that the radio will be displayed first (to the left of the other two)? Table 6-4 shows the six different displays (arrangements) possible. In two of these the radio is first, therefore the probability that the radio will be first in a randomly chosen display is $2/6 = 1/3$.

The Tree Diagram

Another useful counting tool is the *tree diagram*. It may be used for counting more complicated classifications than those shown in the previous illustration. The "tree" is a set of short straight lines connected in a manner that makes them resemble upside-down trees. The straight lines are connected to form a branch that shows one possible arrangement or combination of elements or events that comprise a logical possibility. The number of logical possibilities are determined by counting the ends of the branches. Tree 6-1 shows the number of ways that the radio, television and record player could be arranged on a shelf from left to right. The top three lines show that any one appliance could be displayed first. The next set of lines shows that either of the two remaining appliances could be displayed second, after the first has been determined. The last set of lines shows what appliance must be displayed last after the first two have been determined. The same probability calculations can be made from this tree that can be made from the enumerations in, Table 6-4.

To again illustrate the use of the tree, suppose that a professor gave a "quickie" test consisting of four true-false questions and that we wish to calculate the probabilities that an unprepared student who guesses at each answer will guess 1, 2, 3, or 4 answers correctly. Using C to represent a correct guess and a $\tilde{C}$ to represent a wrong guess, and using subscript p's for the number of ways that the four guesses could result in correct and incorrect answers, Tree 6-2 shows that there are 16 possible outcomes. A study of the branch that ends with p_1 shows four correct answers. Therefore the probability is 1/16

TREE 6-1. Ways in Which a Radio, Television, and Record Player can be Arranged on a Shelf.

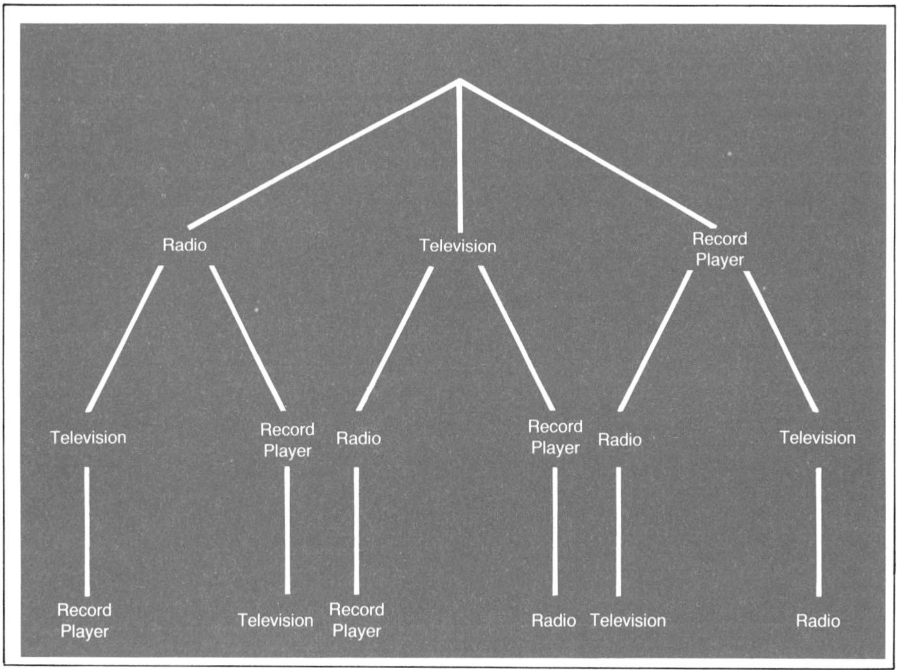

that all four questions would be answered correctly; p_2, p_3, p_5, and p_9 reveal the four ways that three answers could be guessed correctly, thus making the probability 4/16 that the unprepared student would get three correct answers. After counting the other p values, one will find that the probability of guessing 2, 1, and 0 answers correctly is 6/16, 4/16, and 1/16 respectively.

The Multiplication Rule

In a previous discussion of probabilities it was stated that the probability of two independent events occurring at the same time could be calculated by multiplying the probabilities of the two events. This same rule can be used for counting the number of possible events.

TREE 6-2. Ways that Four True-False Questions Can be Guessed Correctly (C) and Incorrectly ($\tilde{C}$).

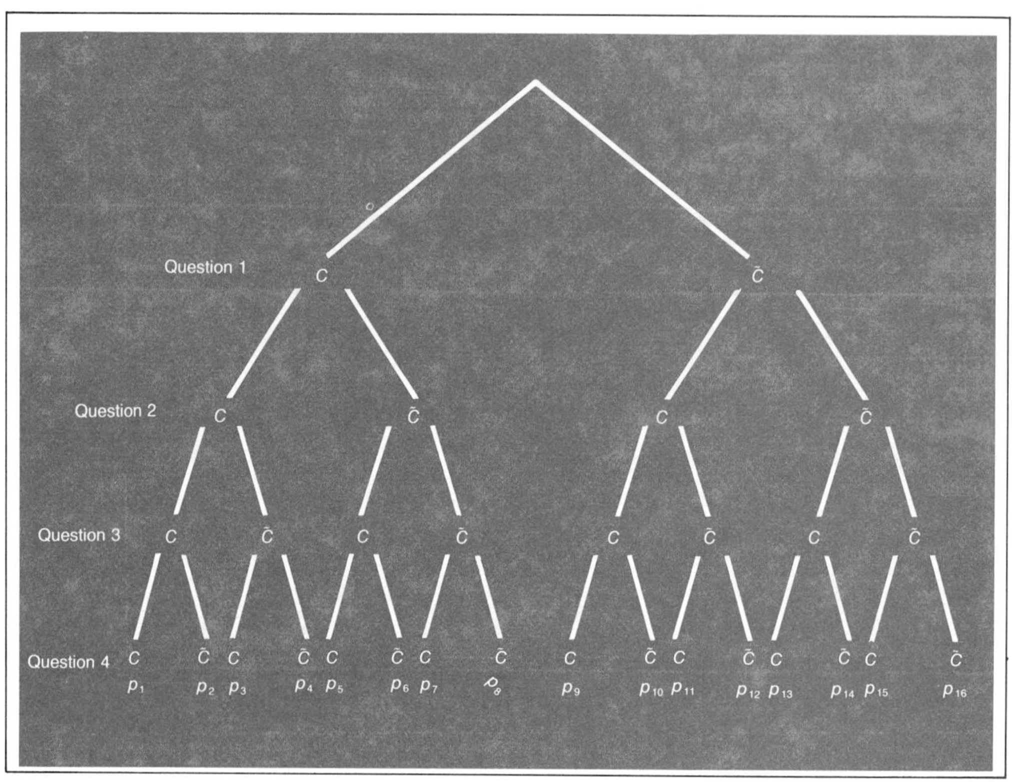

Multiplication Rule

The multiplication rule in simple form says that if one event can occur n_1 ways and for each of these n_1 ways another event can occur n_2 ways, then both can occur $n_1 \times n_2$ ways.

For example, if a president is to be chosen from four candidates and a vice-president is to be chosen from the three remaining candidates, then the number of ways a president and vice-president can be chosen is $4 \times 3 = 12$.

The multiplication rule applies to more than two events. To exemplify this, let us count the number of ways that a radio, television, and record player can be displayed in a row on a shelf. The calculation is $n_1 \times n_2 \times n_3 = 3 \times 2 \times 1 = 6$ ways, because any of the three appliances could be in the first position, and after it has been chosen any of the remaining two could be in second position, leaving only one to be in the third position. This count was shown in Tree 6-1.

The multiplication principle for counting independent events is incorporated in two other counting devices. These are the *permutation* and *combination* principles.

Permutation Principle

Counting is sometimes facilitated by making use of the *permutation principle.* Permutations are arrangements. Arrangements of events can often be shown and counted by the use of the enumeration tables and tree diagrams when the events are few in number. However, these tools would be impractical when the events become numerous. For example in Tree 6-1 we see six possible ways that the radio, television, and record player can be arranged on a shelf, but imagine the size of the tree required to depict the ways of arrangeing ten different appliances in a row on a shelf. The tree would have 3,628,800 end branches. This number was calculated by using the permutation formula for counting the number of permutations (arrangements) of n items taking n at a time. The formula may be written:

$${}_nP_n = n!$$

The ! is the factorial symbol. Thus for $n=10$ ${}_{10}P_{10}=10!=10\times9\times8\times7\times6\times5\times4\times3\times2\times1 = 3{,}628{,}800$. A count of the ways for arranging the radio, television, and record player on a shelf would be ${}_3P_3 = 3! = 3\times2\times1 = 6$.

Sometimes we wish to count the number of ways that r events out of n events can occur.) The formula for doing this may be written

$${}_nP_r = n!/(n-r)!$$

For example, the number of ways that the three letters A, B, and C can be arranged using two letters at a time is

$${}_3P_2 = 3!/(3-2)! = 3!/1! = (3\times2\times1)/1 = 6$$

These different arrangements are AB, BA, BC, CB, AC, CA. To give another example, an auto dealer carries ten different models, but can display only five at a time in his showroom. The number of different displays that are possible (each possible arrangement of five models constitutes a different display) is:

$${}_{10}P_5 = 10!/(10-5)! = 10!/5! = 10\times9\times8\times7\times6 = 30{,}240$$

How can the permutation principle be used for calculating probabilities? A simple illustration can be made with the use of two arrangements shown for the three letters A, B, and C, using two at a time, if we ask the question, "What is the probability that the letter A will be in one of the six possible arrangements if each arrangement is equally likely to occur?'' The answer is $4/6 = 2/3$, because four of the six possible arrangements includes the letter A.

A more business-like illustration can be made by using the following problem. Four ships, A, B, C, and D, are at a dock waiting to be loaded. If any sequence for loading them is equally likely, what is (1) The probability that the sequence will be that listed above? (2) That ship B will be loaded first? (3) That ship B will be loaded first and ship C second?

To answer all three of these questions, all possible sequences (permutations) of loading the four ships must be computed. The computation is,

$$_nP_n = n! = 4! = 24$$

Then the frequency of the order asked for in each question must be calculated and expressed as a fraction or percent of the 24.

For question (1) the order $ABCD$ is only one of the 24, therefore the probability is 1/24 that the order as listed would be the loading order. For question (2) the ways that ship B can be loaded first is calculated as follows:

$$1 \times n! = 1 \times 3! = 6$$

becuase after B is given first place, then there are 3! possible sequences for the loading of the remaining three ships. Therefore, the probability that B will be first is,

$$6/24 = 1/4$$

For question (3), the ways that ship B can be first and ship C be second is $1 \times 2! = 2$, because ships B and C together are placed first in the sequence, which leaves 2! sequences for ships A and D. The probability that this will occur is

$$2/24 = 1/12$$

Table 6-5 presents the twenty-four possible sequences (arrangements) so that you can verify the answers to (1), (2), and (3) by counting the sequences. The numbers next to the arrangements indicate the sequences called for in the three problems.

Combination Principle

The combination-counting formula is useful for calculating probabilities when the orders (arrangements) of items or events appearing together is not to be considered. In fact, a combination of items may be defined as merely a group of items without regard to their order. For example, $ABCD$ and $ACDB$ are the same combination of the four letters. In fact, there can be only one combination of the four letters $ABCD$. Suppose, however, we want to count the different combinations of the four letters that are possible if we take only three at a time. This count can be made with the formula

$$_nC_r = n!/r!(n-r)!$$

TABLE 6-5. Possible Sequence for Loading Four Ships.*

$ABCD$ (1)	$CABD$
$ABDC$	$CADB$
$ACBD$	$CBAD$
$ACDB$	$CBDA$
$ADBC$	$CDAB$
$ADCB$	$CDBA$
$BACD$ (2)	$DABC$
$BADC$ (2)	$DACB$
$BCAD$ (2) (3)	$DBAC$
$BCDA$ (2) (3)	$DBCA$
$BDAC$ (2)	$DCAB$
$BDCA$ (2)	$DCBA$

*The numbers in parenthesis refer to the numbers of the question asked in the text.

where ${}_nC_r$ is the symbol for the combination of n items taken r at a time, n is the total number of items and r is the number to be combined out of the n items. For this illustration $n = 4$ and $r = 3$, therefore,

$${}_4C_3 = 4!/3!(4-3)! = 4!/3!1! = 4$$

The possible combinations are ABC, ABD, ACD, and BCD.

The following probability problem can be solved by using the combination formula to count the required combinations.

There are seven men and three women on a board of directors. A random selection of a committee of three members is to be made. What is the probability that the committe will consist of (1) three women and no men, (2) two women and one man, (3) one woman and two men, and (4) no women and three men?

To solve this problem we must first determine the different number of three-person committees (combinations of 3) that are possible from ten persons, the calculation is

$${}_{10}C_3 = 10!/3!(10-3)! = 10!/3!7! = 10 \times 9 \times 8/3! = 10 \times 9 \times 8/6 = 120$$

Next, the number of committees of the different sex mixes called for must be determined and then these must be expressed as fractions of the 120 total possible committees. For (1), the count is made by multiplying the number of committees of three women that can be selected from the three women that are available by the number of men we want on the committee—NONE—that can be selected from the seven men available. The calculation is

$${}_3C_3 \times {}_7C_0 = 3!/3!(3-3)! \times 7!/0!(7-0)! = 1 \times 1 = 1$$

Therefore the probability is 1/120 that the committee will be composed of three women and no men. For (2), the count of the number of two women–one man committees is made by multiplying the number of combinations of two women that are possible out of three women by the number of combinations of one man that are possible out of seven men:

$$ {}_3C_2 \times {}_7C_1 = 3!/2!(3-2)! \times 7!/1!(7-1)! = 3 \times 7 = 21 $$

Therefore the probability of selecting a two women–one man committee is

$$ 21/120 = 7/40 $$

For (3), the count of the number of different one woman–two man committees is

$$ {}_3C_1 \times {}_7C_2 = 3!/1!(3-1)! \times 7!/2!(7-2)! = 3 \times 21 = 63 $$

and the probability of selecting such a committee is 63/120 or 21/40. For (4), the count of the number of different zero women–three man committees possible is:

$$ {}_3C_0 \times {}_7C_3 = 3!/0!(3-0)! \times 7!/3!(7-3)! = 1 \times 35 $$

and the probability of selecting such a committee is 35/120 = 7/24. In the preceding problem the probability of selecting each possible mix of woman–man committees of three was ascertained. There were four, and these four probabilities should add to 1, since each is a mutually exclusive event. Thus

$$ 1/120 + 21/120 + 63/120 + 35/120 = 120/120 = 1 $$

Venn Diagrams

Another useful counting aid is the Venn diagram. The diagram is usually depicted as a rectangle with two or three circles within. The rectangle represents the items in the universe set and the circles represent subsets of the items in the universe we will call *sets*. Separated circles represent disjoint sets which are sets with no common element. Intersecting circles show conjoint sets; which are sets with a common element. The Venn diagrams in Chart 6-1 illustrate these types.

Subsets and Their Intersection

The letters A, B, and C are used to depict sets of items. The symbol ~ means *not*, so $\tilde{A}$ means *not* A, or, that no items in the set of A are included. $\tilde{B}$ and $\tilde{C}$ have analogous meanings. In diagram (b) the shaded section is called the *intersection* of A and B. Using the symbol $\cap$ as the *and* (intersection) symbol it is identified as $A \cap B$. This is an indication that some items making up A and some of the items making up B are the same. There is no intersection of A and B in diagram (a). Other sets are depicted with the negative and positive letters. For example, $\tilde{A} \cap B$ means items that are B but not A, and $\tilde{A} \cap \tilde{B}$ means items that are not A and not B (neither A nor B). In diagram (d) there is no intersection, but in (e) there are several. The shaded area in (e) shows the intersection of all three circles, which is identified as $A \cap B \cap C$. Some other intersections shown are $A \cap B \cap \tilde{C}$, $A \cap \tilde{B} \cap C$, *and* $\tilde{A} \cap B \cap C$.

Chart 6-1. Examples of Venn diagrams.

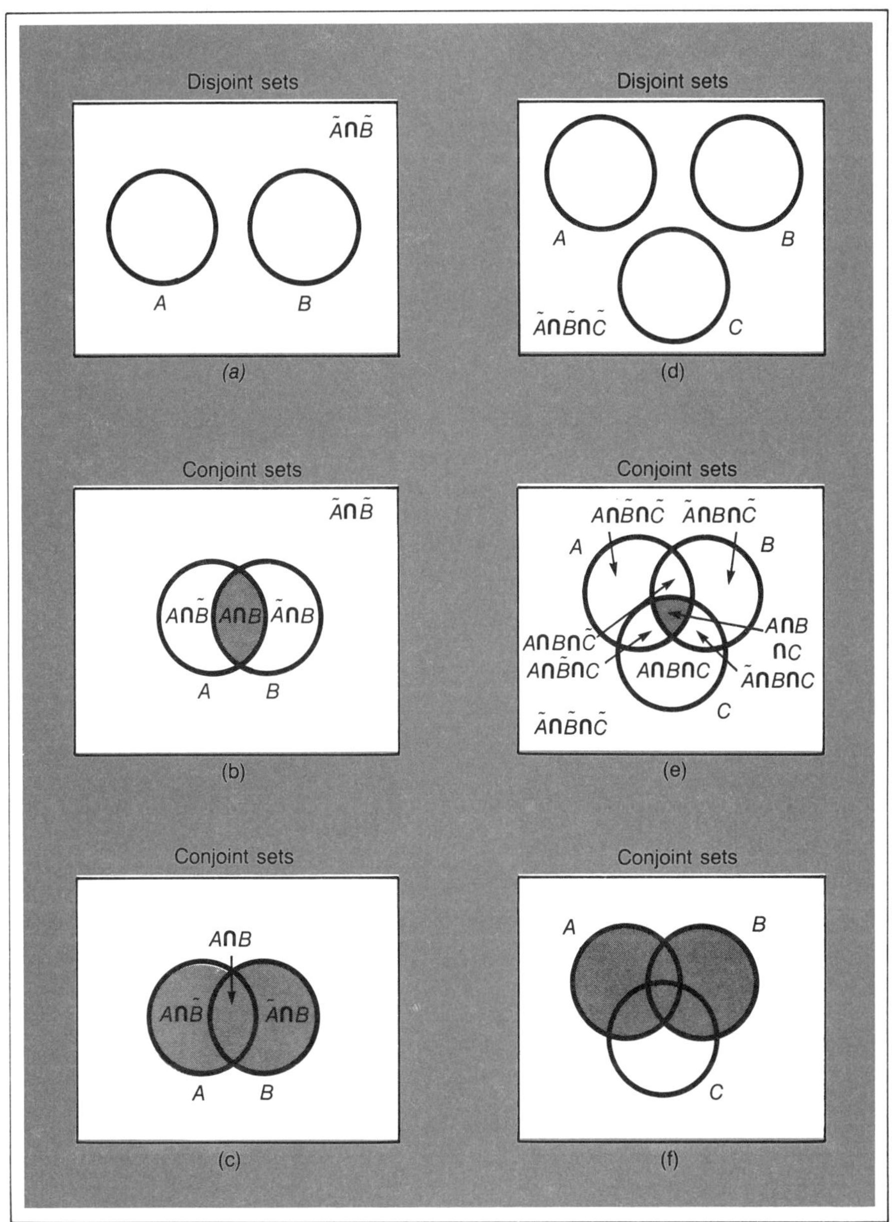

Sets and Their Union

Not only can there be an intersection of sets but there can also be a union. The *union* of sets A and B may be written as $A \cup B$, where the symbol $\cup$ represents the word "or." In other words, $A \cup B$ means all the items in set A or set B or in both A and B. The shaded areas of diagrams (c) and (f) in Chart 6-1 show the union of A and B for conjoint sets. Note from diagram (c) that

$$A \cup B = A + B - A \cap B$$

since when counting A, the elements in $A \cap B$ were counted and were counted again when counting B; therefore the second counting must be subtracted out. The two-circle Venn diagram, Chart 6-2 can be used to count items in a set, for example, in the following problem: Twenty of the 50 businessmen at a meeting are members of the Chamber of Commerce, 12 are members of the Better Business Bureau, and 22 are members of neither organization. How many are members of (1) both organizations, (2) the Chamber of Commerce only, (3) the Better Business Bureau only? Letting A represent the set of Chamber of Commerce members and B the set of Better Business Bureau members, we make a diagram that shows the three sets for which we wish to count the number of businessmen, $A \cap \tilde{B}$, $A \cap B$, and $\tilde{A} \cap B$.

The number of men in the set $\tilde{A}$ and $\tilde{B}$, is known (22) and shown. The diagram also shows the numbers in the other sets that were calculated using N to denote the number in each set, the number of men in set $A \cap B$ was obtained by substituting in the formula

$$N(A \cup B) = N(A) + N(B) - N(A \cap B)$$

Chart 6-2. Subsets of businessmen attending a meeting $N(u) = 50$.

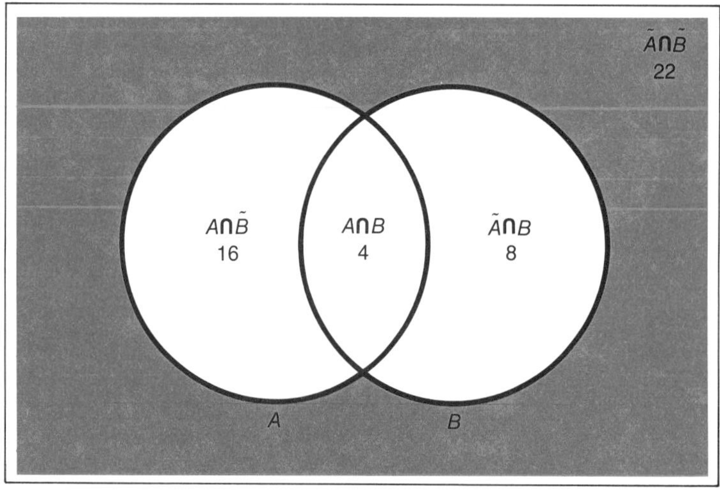

but before this could be done, $N(A \cup B)$ had to be determined by subtracting 22 from 50, the universe. Thus $N(A \cup B) = 28$. Therefore,

$$\begin{aligned} 28 &= 20 + 12 - N(A \cap B) \\ &= 32 - N(A \cap B) \\ N(A \cap B) &= 4 \end{aligned}$$

since $N(A \cap B) = 4$, then $N(A \cap \tilde{B}) = 20 - 4 = 16$, the number who are members of the Chamber of Commerce only, and $N(\tilde{A} \cup B) = 12 - 4 = 8$, the number who are members of the Better Business Bureau only. $N(u)$, the number of men in the universe is 50 and is the sum of the members in the four partitions, as it should be.

PROBABILITY—SIMPLE AND JOINT

The counting of items in sets is a prelude to calculating the probabilities of events.

Probability

If an event concerns only one characteristic it is called a *simple probability*. If the event concerns two or more combined characteristics it is called a *joint probability*.

For example, if the random selection of a businessman at the meeting is made the result may be that he is a member of the Chamber of Commerce. The calculation of $P(A)$, the probability that he will be is

$$\begin{aligned} P(A) &= N(A)/N(u) \\ &= 20/50 = 2/5 \end{aligned}$$

which is a simple probability. However, he may be a member of both the Chamber of Commerce and the Better Business Bureau. The calculation of the probability that he will be is

$$P(A \cap B) = N(A \cap B)/N(u) = 4/50 = 2/25$$

which is a joint probability. Calculations of other joint probabilities are:

$$P(A \cap \tilde{B}) = N(A \cap \tilde{B})/N(u) = 16/50 = 8/25$$

which is the probability that he would be a member of the Chamber of Commerce only.

$$P(\tilde{A} \cap B) = N(\tilde{A} \cap B)/N(u) = 8/50 = 4/25$$

which is the probability that he would be a member of the Better Business Bureau only.

$$P(\tilde{A} \cap \tilde{B}) = N(\tilde{A} \cap \tilde{B})/N(u) = 22/50 = 11/25$$

which is the probability that he could be a member of neither organization.

The following problem will illustrate the use of a three-circle Venn diagram as an aid in counting and determining probabilities.

A survey of 100 businesses that failed showed that 20 failed because of the inexperience of management, lack of money, and inadequate labor supply; none failed for only one of those reasons, 40 failed due to inexperienced management and an inadequate labor supply, 50 failed because of lack of money and an inadequate labor supply, and 30 failed due to inexperienced management and lack of money. How many of the 100 businesses failed for reasons other than the three mentioned? Chart 6-3 shows that I, M, and L represent inexperienced management, lack of money, and inadequate labor supply, respectively.

Chart 6-3. Venn diagram of reasons for business failures.

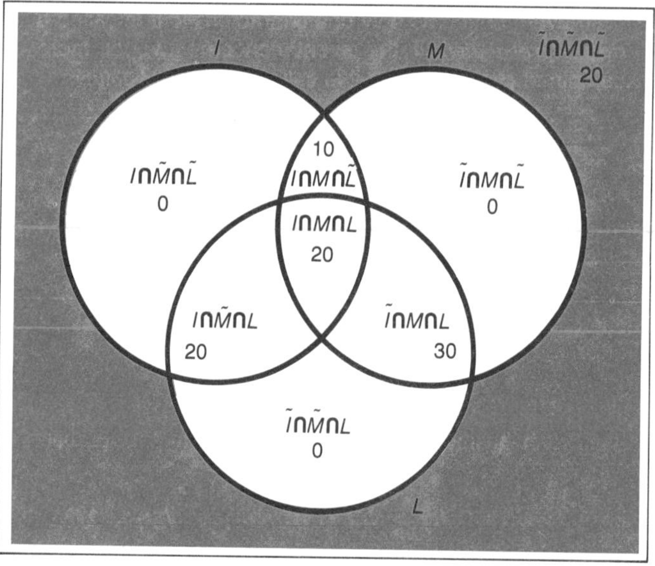

To solve this problem the numbers in the sets given directly by the problem are filled in first, therefore the number 20 is placed in the intersection of the three circles, $I \cap M \cap L$, and 0 is placed in each of the three areas that represent one reason only. Next, since 30 failed due to $I \cap M$ then $N(I \cap M) - N(I \cap M \cap L) = 30 - 20 = 10$ that failed due to $I \cap M \cap \tilde{L}$. Next, since 40 failed due to $I \cap L$ then $N(I \cap L) - N(I \cap M \cap L) = 40 - 20 = 20$ that failed due to $I \cap \tilde{M} \cap L$, and since 50 failed due to $M \cap L$, then $N(M \cap L) - N(I \cap M \cap L) = 50 - 20 = 30$ that failed due to $\tilde{I} \cap M \cap L$. The sum of these partitions inside the circles is 80. Therefore, $100 - 80 = 20$, which is the number of businesses that failed for other than the three reasons $(\tilde{I} \cap \tilde{M} \cap \tilde{L})$. This number is placed outside the circles. Now that the number of businesses in all the sets have been counted, probabilities can be calculated. For example the calculation of the probability that a business selected at random from the 100 would have failed due to reasons other than inexperienced management, lack of money, and an inadequate labor supply is

$$P(\tilde{I} \cap \tilde{M} \cap \tilde{L}) = N(\tilde{I} \cap \tilde{M} \cap \tilde{L})/N(u) = 20/100 = 1/5 = 0.2.$$

DIRECT PROBABILITY ANALYSIS

Venn diagrams are also useful in probability analyses when the probabilities of the various sets are given. When this is done the probability of the universe $P(u)$ is equal to 1 and the sum of the probabilities of the mutually exclusive sets making up the universe is equal to 1. The following problem will provide an illustration, and Chart 6-4 will help you understand the solution.

The probability that a randomly selected student in a large college is enrolled in liberal arts is 0.6. The probability that the randomly selected student is male is 0.7. The probability that the student is female and not in liberal arts is 0.1. What is the probability that the student is male and enrolled in liberal arts?

Let $P(L)$ stand for the probability that the student is in liberal arts and $P(M)$ for the probability that he is male, therefore $P(u) = 1$, $P(L) = 0.6$, $P(M) = 0.7$, $P(\tilde{L} \cap \tilde{M}) = 0.1$. Then $P(u) - P(\tilde{L} \cap \tilde{M}) = P(L \cup M) = 1 - 0.1 = 0.9$, and since $P(L \cup M) = P(L) + P(M) - P(L \cap M)$ then $0.9 = 0.6 + 0.7 - P(L \cap M)$ and $P(L \cap M) = 0.4$ which is the probability that the student would be enrolled in liberal arts and is male, and $P(L \cap \tilde{M}) = P(L) - P(L \cap M) = 0.6 - 0.4 = 0.2$, which is the probability that the student is in liberal arts and is female, and finally, $P(\tilde{L} \cap M) = P(M) - P(L \cap M) = 0.7 - 0.4 = 0.3$, which is the probability that the student is not enrolled in liberal arts but is male.

Chart 6-4. Venn diagram of probabilities of student's enrollment $P(u) = 1.0$.

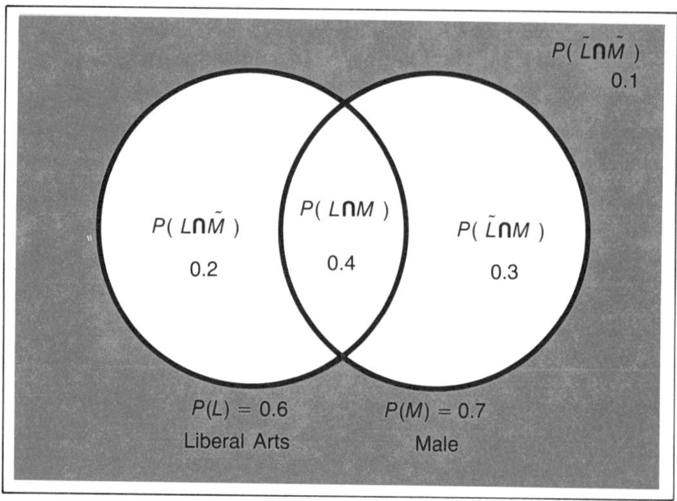

Conditional Probability

Up to this point the discussion has concerned the calculation of simple and joint probabilities. We will now consider another type known as *conditional probability*.

Conditional Probability

Conditional probability is a probability assigned to an event when a given set of circumstances is known.

Consider the previous probability problem concerning students in the liberal arts college. Now refer to Chart 6-4 and assume that we wish to know what the probability is that a randomly selected student will be enrolled in liberal arts given that he is male. The calculation would be

$$P(L\backslash M) = P(L \cap M)/P(M) = 0.4/0.7 = 4/7$$

where "$L\backslash M$" means, "L given M."

The calculation of the probability that a randomly selected student would be male given that he is enrolled in liberal arts is

$$P(M\backslash L) = P(L \cap M)/P(L) = 0.4/0.6 = 2/3$$

Now notice that the respective algebraic solution for $P(L \cap M)$ in the above two formulas shows that $P(L \cap M) = P(M)P(L\backslash M)$ and that $P(L \cap M) = P(L)P(M\backslash L)$, therefore,

$$P(M)P(L\backslash M) = P(L)P(M\backslash L)$$

and

$$P(L\backslash M) = P(L)P(M\backslash L)/P(M)$$

and

$$P(M\backslash L) = P(M)P(L\backslash M)/P(L)$$

which are simple statements from a larger body of generalizations about conditional probability known as *Bayes' theorem*. The theorem was formulated over 200 years ago by Rev. Thomas Bayes, who was also a mathematician.

Substituting in these formulas

$$P(L\backslash M) = (0.6 \times 2/3)/0.7 = 0.4/0.7 = 4/7$$

$$P(M\backslash L) = (0.7 \times 0.4/0.7)/0.6 = 0.4/0.6 = 2/3$$

which are the same answers previously calculated. An analysis of the various probabilities will also show that

$$\begin{aligned} P(L\backslash M) &= \left[P(L)P(M\backslash L)\right] / \left[P(L)P(M\backslash L) + P(\tilde{L})P(M\backslash \tilde{L})\right] \\ &= (0.6 \times 2/3)/(0.6 \times 2/3) + (0.4 \times 3/4) \\ &= 0.4/(0.4 + 0.3) = 0.4/0.7 = 4/7 \end{aligned}$$

and

$$\begin{aligned} P(M\backslash L) &= \left[P(M)P(L\backslash M)\right]/\left[P(M)P(L\backslash M) + P(\tilde{M})P(L\backslash \tilde{M})\right] \\ &= (0.7 + 4/7)/(0.7 \times 4/7) + (0.3 \times 2/3) \\ &= 0.4/(0.4 + 0.2) = 0.4/0.6 = 2/3 \end{aligned}$$

Probabilities of the type L and M are called *a priori* probabilities because they do not require further information. Probabilities of the type $L\backslash M$ and $M\backslash L$ are called *a posteriori* probabilities because they are based on the observance of a particular previous outcome.

The Use of Bayes' Formula

As an example of the use of Bayes' formula consider the following problem. In a certain community 30% of the men earn $10,000 or more. Let E represent men with such earnings and let $\tilde{E}$ represent men earning less than $10,000. Then $P(E) = 0.3$ and $P(\tilde{E}) =$ 0.7 for a randomly selected man.

A random sample of men in the community has been selected and each man in the

Chart 6-5. Venn diagram of probabilities of telling or not telling the truth about earnings. $P(u)$ = 1.0.

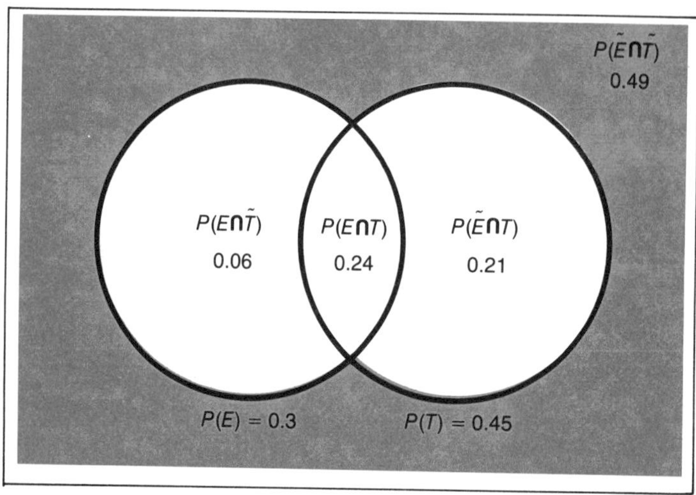

sample is to be asked if his earnings are \$10,000 or more. Some men will tell the truth (T) and some will not tell the truth ($\tilde{T}$). The following conditional probabilities that a person will or will not tell the truth about his earnings:

$$P(T\backslash E) = 0.8 \qquad P(T\backslash \tilde{E}) = 0.3$$

$$P(\tilde{T}\backslash E) = 0.2 \qquad P(\tilde{T}\backslash \tilde{E}) = 0.7$$

What is the probability that a man *does* earn \$10,000 or more when he responds that he does not? This also can be calculated with Bayes' formula. Let $P(E\backslash\tilde{T})$ represent our desired answer, then

$$\begin{aligned} P(E\backslash\tilde{T}) &= \left[P(E)P(\tilde{T}\backslash E)\right]/\left[P(E)P(\tilde{T}\backslash E) + P(\tilde{E})P(\tilde{T}\backslash\tilde{E})\right] \\ &= (0.3 \times 0.2)/(0.3 \times 0.2) + (0.7 \times 0.7) \\ &= 0.06/(0.06 + 0.49) = 0.11 \end{aligned}$$

By looking at Chart 6-5 and making the following calculations we can visualize and substantiate that 0.11 is correct:

$$P(E \cap T) = P(E)P(T\backslash E) = 0.3 \times 0.8 = 0.24$$

$$P(\tilde{E} \cap T) = P(\tilde{E})P(T\backslash\tilde{E}) = 0.7 \times 0.3 = 0.21$$

Therefore

$$P(E \cap \tilde{T}) = P(E) - P(E \cap T) = 0.3 - 0.24 = 0.06$$

and

$$P(\tilde{E} \cap \tilde{T}) = P(\tilde{E}) - P(\tilde{E} \cap T) = 0.7 - 0.21 = 0.49$$

and

$$P(E \backslash \tilde{T}) = P(E \cap \tilde{T})/P(\tilde{T}) = 0.06/(0.06 + 0.49)$$
$$= 0.06/0.55 = 0.11$$

REVIEW QUESTIONS

1. Define probability.
2. Distinguish between *a priori* and *a posteriori* probabilities.
3. What is the probability that your statistics instructor will meet with his next class? Is this an *a priori* probability or an *a posterior* probability?
4. What are the two important special rules for calculating probabilities?
5. What is the difference between a permutation and a combination?
6. In respect to set theory, explain what is meant by (1) intersection, and (b) union.
7. What is joint probability?
8. What is conditional probability?

PROBLEMS

1. If the probability of a student making an A in statistics is 0.1 and the probability of his making a B is 0.2, what is the probability of his making either an A or a B? What is the probability that he will pass or fail the course?

2. If a student has a 0.1 probability of making an A in statistics and a probability of 0.5 of making an A in accounting, what is the probability that he will make A in both?

3. A salesman has called on a particular customer 1,000 times and has made sales on 750 of those calls. What is the probability that he will make a sale on the next call?

4. A salesman figures that on his next call the probability of selling a mowing machine to the X Company is 0.7 and the probability of selling a tractor is 0.8. Assuming that the probability of selling a mowing machine is independent of the probability of selling a tractor, what is the probability that he will sell both to the company?

5. A company manufactures two different sized tops, large and small. Some are made of wood and some of plastic. Three different colors are used, red, white, and blue. Prepare an enumeration table which shows all possible size-type-color combinations of tops that are made. If an equal number of each combination is available for purchase and you make a random choice of a top, what is the probability that you will buy a large, blue top?

6. In planning his college study program, a high school senior must decide whether to attend M. U., P. U., or O. U., and whether to enter business administration and choose a major in accounting or finance, or enter liberal arts and choose a major in math or physics. Draw a tree that will show all of his possible complete choices (logical possibilities). (a) How many choices does he have? (b) If each choice is equally likely, what is the probability that he will attend O. U. and major in finance?

7. Before placing a new product on the market a company must decide (a) whether its price will be $4, $5, or $6, (b) whether it will be boxed, and if so, whether the box will be wood or cardboard, and (c) whether to guarantee the product. Construct a tree diagram that will show all possible complete decisions (logical possibilities). If each decision is equally likely to be made, what is the probability that the product will be guaranteed and sold in a cardboard box?

8. On a Wednesday a merchant decides to drastically reduce the price of two obsolete calculating machines. Any left unsold at the end of the fourth day (Saturday) will be given away. Construct a tree diagram to show the possible ways that the sales and/or give-aways can be made. If each possibility is equally likely to be made, what is the probability that both machines will be sold by the end of the fourth day?

9. A candy machine displays five different candy bars in a row. (a) How many different displays (arrangements) are possible? (b) If the names of the bars are *Choco, Hony, Nuty, Peco,* and *Taffy,* and upon loading the machine the choice of display is made by a random process, what is the probability (c) that the arrangement of the bars will be that listed above (d) that the arrangement will show *Choco* first and *Hony* second, and (e) that the arrangement will show *Choco* and *Hony* next to each other?

10. Two different shotguns and three different rifles are to be displayed in a row on a shelf. How many different displays are possible if the shotguns are to be together and the rifles are to be together?

11. A committee of three persons is to be randomly selected from a group consisting of five men and four women. What is the probability that the committee will have (1) two men and one woman, (b) three women, (c) no women, and (d) two women and one man?

12. You plan to buy a combination of two stocks and two bonds from a list of three stocks (A, B, and C), and four bonds (W, X, Y, and Z). What is the probability that the combination chosen will be stocks A and B and bonds Y and Z?

13. Females comprise 20% of a group attending a convention. Fifty percent of these are college graduates. Seventy-five percent of the males attending are college graduates. Prepare a two-circle Venn diagram showing the percent of conventioners in each of the four classifications, and calculate the probability that a randomly selected conventioner would be (a) male, and (b) a male given that the conventioner is a college graduate.

14. The probability that a business administration freshman is taking neither History nor English is 0.4, the probability that he is taking History is 0.5 and the probability that he is taking English is 0.2. Construct a Venn diagram showing four probability sets and determine the probability that the freshman is taking English but not History.

15. One-thousand factory employees were surveyed and the following facts were found: 440 drink beer, 290 drink tea and beer, and 100 drink tea but neither coffee nor beer. It was also found that 280 drink none of the three beverages, that 300 drink coffee, with 180 drinking coffee but neither tea nor beer, and one-third of the employees who drink coffee also drink tea and beer. Moreover, 20 of the coffee-drinking employees drink beer but not tea. Construct a three-circle Venn diagram showing the percent of employees in each of the subsets, and calculate the probability that a randomly chosen employee would (a) drink neither beverage, and (b) drink only two of the three beverages.

16. If 30% of the households in a city have electric dryers and 40% have electric stoves, and if 25% of those that have electric stoves also have electric dryers, what is the probability that a household selected by a random process will have an electric stove, given that it has an electric dryer?

17. The probability of A is 0.4, the probability of B is 0.5, and the probability of A and B is 0.3. What is the probability of (a) $\tilde{A}$ and $\tilde{B}$, (b) B given A, and (c) A given B?

7

Probability Distributions

In Chapter 6 we discussed basic probability theory and concepts, and illustrated their applications. In this chapter we will discuss the nature and some uses of probability distributions.

Probability Distribution

A probability distribution is a distribution of the probabilities of all the possible mutually exclusive events that can occur by a random process.

You have already been exposed to these distributions, for example, the distribution of all possible numbers that can result from the toss of a pair of dice (Table 6-1). In this section we will be concerned with only three probability distributions that have wide application in business problem-solving. These are the *binomial distribution*, the *normal distribution*, and the *Poisson distribution*.

RANDOM VARIABLES

In a discussion of probability distribution it is important to understand the term *random variable*.

Variable

A variable is a characteristic that differs or a factor that is subject to change.

Shoe size is a variable because shoe sizes differ. The weight of a person is a variable because it changes. The *result of* a toss of a pair of dice is a variable because it can change from one toss to another. However, the outcome from a toss of a pair of dice is a *random variable* because it is due to a chance process, and all of the outcomes that are possible make up the values of the random variable.

Discrete and Continuous Variables

When only a limited number of values result from a chance process, such as those from tossing dice, it is a *discrete random variable*. When the random variable can have any value within a range of values it is called a *continuous random variable*.

For example, weight would be a continuous random variable if we were to choose a random sample of people from a large number of people to ascertain their mean weight.

The binomial and Poisson probability distributions discussed in this chapter are discrete random variables. The normal distribution is a continuous random variable.

THE BINOMIAL PROBABILITY DISTRIBUTION

From the binomial expansion we can determine probabilities of multiple events to occur when the individual events are independent and can be placed into two categories (success–failure), such as heads–tails, up–down, smoke–don't smoke, and when the probability of an event remains constant throughout the experiment. Expansion of the binomial formula $(p + q)^n$ results in a binomial probability distribution if $p + q = 1$. The general formula for expanding a binomial is:*

$$(p + q)^n = p^n + np^{n-1}q + \frac{n(n-1)}{(1 \times 2)} p^{n-2}q^2 + \cdots + q^n$$

Expanding the binomial for $n = 3$ and $n = 4$ gives

$$(p + q)^3 = p^3 + 3p^2q + 3pq^2 + q^3$$

$$(p + q)^4 = p^4 + 4p^3q + 6p^2q^2 + 4pq^3 + q^4$$

Assume that four fair coins are tossed. The probabilities of getting the various combinations of heads and tails are obtained by letting p represent the probability of a head (success) on a single trial and q the probability of a tail (no head or failure) on a

*The steps in expanding a binomial are explained in Appendix B.

single trial. We use the expansion for $n = 4$ because there are four coins (the same would apply if there were four tosses of one coin):

$$(p + q)^n = \left(\frac{1}{2} + \frac{1}{2}\right)^4 = \left(\frac{1}{2}\right)^4 + 4\left(\frac{1}{2}\right)^3\left(\frac{1}{2}\right) + 6\left(\frac{1}{2}\right)^2\left(\frac{1}{2}\right)^2 + 4\left(\frac{1}{2}\right)\left(\frac{1}{2}\right)^3 + \left(\frac{1}{2}\right)^4$$

$$= \frac{1}{16} + \frac{4}{16} + \frac{6}{16} + \frac{4}{16} + \frac{1}{16} = 1$$

The sum is 1, so we have a probability distribution. From the leftmost term, we know that the probability of all four coins turning up heads (four successes) is 1/16. The other probabilities are, in order: three heads and one tail, 4/16; two heads and two tails, 6/16; one head and three tails, 4/16; and four tails, 1/16.

As another example, suppose that 25% of the households in an area have color television sets, and we want to know the probabilities of choosing 3, 2, 1, and 0 households with color television sets in a random sample of three households. Using the binomial expansion with $n = 3$, $p = 25\% = 1/4$, and $q = 1 - p = 3/4$,

$$\left(\frac{1}{4}\right) + \left(\frac{3}{4}\right)^3 = \left(\frac{1}{4}\right)^3 + 3\left(\frac{1}{4}\right)^2\left(\frac{3}{4}\right) + 3\left(\frac{1}{4}\right)\left(\frac{3}{4}\right)^2 + \left(\frac{3}{4}\right)^3$$

$$= \frac{1}{64} + \frac{9}{64} + \frac{27}{64} + \frac{27}{64}$$

which, from the left, are the respective probabilities of choosing three houses with color TV, two houses with color TV, one house with color TV, and no house with color TV in a sample of three households. The sum of these terms (probabilities) is, of course, 1.

The General Binomial Distribution Formula

We can also compute any term of a binomial without expanding the binomial. The formula is:

$$P(r) = \frac{n!}{r!(n - r)!} p^r q^{n-r}$$

where r, the number of successes, is the random variable and n is the number of tries. $P(r)$ is the probability of r successes out of n tries. The probability p must be given, of course, and q is always $1 - p$. Using this formula we could compute the probability of choosing two houses with color TV out of a sample of three, without going through the calculations of the other probabilities. Where $r = 2$ successes, $p = 1/4$, and $n = 3$

$$P(2) = \frac{3!}{2!(3 - 2)!}\left(\frac{1}{4}\right)^2\left(\frac{3}{4}\right)^{3-2}$$

$$= 3\left(\frac{1}{4}\right)^2\left(\frac{3}{4}\right) = \frac{9}{64}$$

which is the value that was obtained by expanding the binomial.

The Binomial Table

One can often determine the probabilities of given terms of a binomial without expanding it or without direct use of the general binomial distribution formula. This is accomplished by reading the desired probabilities from a table which shows the probabilities of the terms of binomials for a number of p, n, and r values. Table A-8 in Appendix E is such a table. Its use will be demonstrated with the following problem.

If 20% of the students at a university are graduate students and a random sample of 10 students is selected, what is the probability that (a) 5 will be graduate students? (b) 5 or more will be graduate students? (c) 2 or fewer will be graduate students?

The answer to (a) is found in the 0.2 column of Table A-8 where $n = 10$ and $r = 5$. The probability reading is 0.026. The answer to (b) is 0.033, the sum of the probabilities for r's of 5, 6, 7, 8, 9, and 10 for an n of 10, $(0.026 + 0.006 + 0.001 + 0.000 + 0.000 + 0.000 = 0.033)$. The answer to (c) is 0.677, the sum of the probabilities of the r's of 2, 1, and 0 for an n of 10, which are 0.302, 0.268, and 0.107, respectively.

The Arithmetic Mean and Standard Deviation of a Binomial Distribution

The methods used in Chapter 5 to compute the mean and standard deviation for a frequency distribution can be used to compute these measures for a binomial distribution. For our purposes here the formulas may be expressed as

$$\bar{r} = \Sigma[P(r)r]/\Sigma P(r) \qquad \text{and} \qquad \sigma_r = \sqrt{\Sigma[P(r)(r-\bar{r})^2]/\Sigma P(r)}$$

where $\bar{r}$ is the mean of the r values and σ_r is the standard deviation of the r values. Since $\Sigma P(r) = 1$, the formulas become

$$\bar{r} = \Sigma[P(r)r] \qquad \text{and} \qquad \sigma_r = \sqrt{\Sigma[p(r)(r-\bar{r})^2]}$$

Table 7-1 shows the computation of the arithmetic mean and the standard deviation of the expanded binomial $(1/2 + 1/2)^4$, which gives the probabilities of getting 4, 3, 2, 1, and 0 heads from 4 flips of a coin. These measures may also be calculated from the formulas

$$\bar{r} = np \qquad \text{and} \qquad \sigma_r = \sqrt{npq}$$

Substituting

$$\bar{r} = 4 \times 1/2 = 2 \qquad \text{and} \qquad \sigma_r = \sqrt{4 \times 1/2 \times 1/2} = \sqrt{4/4} = 1$$

These formulas are usually more practical to use. The formula for σ_r will be used in modified form in Chapter 8.

The Nature of the Binomial Distribution

The binomial distribution is a discrete probability distribution because it describes a discrete variable. A discrete variable, as defined in Chapter 3, is one that can take on

TABLE 7-1. Computation of the Arithmetic Mean and Standard Deviation of the Expanded Binomial $(1/2 + 1/2)^4$.

NO. OF HEADS r	$P(r)$	$P(r)r$	$r-\bar{r}$	$(r-\bar{r})^2$	$P(r)(r-\bar{r})^2$
4	1/16	4/16	2	4	4/16
3	4/16	12/16	1	1	4/16
2	6/16	12/16	0	0	0
1	4/16	4/16	−1	1	4/16
0	1/16	1/16	−2	4	4/16
Total	16/16	32/16	–	–	16/16

$$\bar{r} = \Sigma P(r)\, r = 32/16 = 2$$

$$\sigma_r = \sqrt{\Sigma P(r)(r-\bar{r})^2} = \sqrt{16/16} = 1$$

random values of limited magnitudes, such as variables showing sizes of shoes, sizes of families, and the ways that an ace can be drawn from a deck of cards.

If p in the binomial formula $(p + q)^n$ is ½, then the expanded binomial forms a symmetrical probability distribution. If p is not equal to ½, expansion results in a skewed distribution, but as n increases, the shape of the expanded binomial approaches symmetry.

If p is ½ and n is indefinitely large, the form of the distribution approaches that of a normal distribution, to be discussed next. In fact, if p is not equal to ½, but is reasonably large, the expanded binomial for an indefinitely large n also approaches the shape of the normal distribution.

THE NORMAL DISTRIBUTION

Normal Distribution

A normal distribution is a symmetrical distribution for a continuous random variable. A continuous variable, you will recall, is one that can take on any value within a range of values, such as weights, heights, and time.

The equation for a normal distribution is

$$Y_c = \frac{N}{\sigma\sqrt{2\pi}} e^{-x^2/2\sigma^2}$$

where Y_c is the height of any ordinate, N is the total frequency, σ is the standard deviation of the given distribution, the constant π is 3.14159, the constant e (the base of the Naperian system of logarithms) is 2.71828, and x is the distance between any ordinate and the ordinate at the arithmetic mean. Since $x = 0$ for the ordinate at the mean

$$e^{-x^2/2\sigma^2} = e^{-0^2/2\sigma^2} = 1$$

and the formula for the maximum ordinate, which is at the arithmetic mean, becomes

$$Y_0 = \frac{N}{\sigma\sqrt{2\pi}}$$

To illustrate, assume that $N = 100{,}000$ and $\sigma = 100$. The height of the maximum ordinate is

$$Y_0 = \frac{10{,}000}{100\sqrt{2 \times 3.14159}} = 100 \times \frac{1}{\sqrt{6.28318}}$$

$$= 100\frac{1}{2.5066} = 39.894$$

Ordinates at various distances, x, from the maximum ordinate can be computed by

$$Y_c = Y_0 e^{-x^2/2\sigma^2} = Y_0 2.71828^{-x^2/2\sigma^2}$$

For the distribution with $N = 10{,}000$ and $\sigma = 100$, the height of the ordinate at $x = 1\sigma$ is

$$Y_\sigma = 39.894 = 2.71828^{-(100)^2/2(100)^2}$$

$$= 39.894 \times 2.71828^{-1/2}$$

$$= 39.894 \times \frac{1}{\sqrt{2.71828}}$$

$$39.894 \times 0.60653 = 24.196$$

at $x = 2\sigma$ the ordinate height is

$$Y_{2\sigma} = 39.894 \times 2.71828^{-(200)^2/2(100)^2}$$

$$= 39.894 \times 2.71828^{-2}$$

$$= 39.894 \times \frac{1}{2.71828^2}$$

$$= 39.894 \times 0.13534 = 5.399$$

Note that

$$2.71828^{-x^2/2\sigma^2}$$

Chart 7-1. Normal curve showing relative heights of ordinates at selected points.

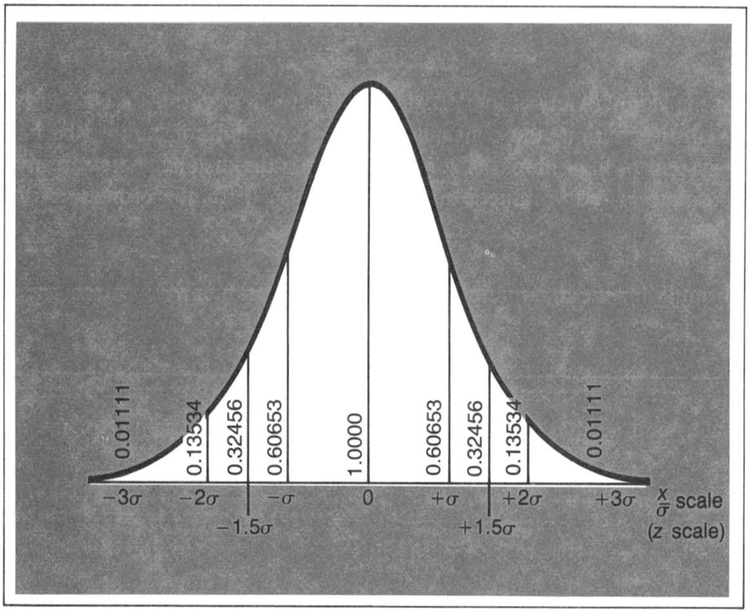

gives the height of an ordinate at any x value relative to the arithmetic mean. Thus an ordinate erected at 1σ from the mean is 0.60653 as high as the ordinate at the mean. An ordinate at 2σ from the mean is 0.13534 of the height of the ordinate at the mean. The proportionate heights of ordinates for a large number of x/σ values, which are also called z, are listed in Table A-2 in Appendix E.

The expression x/σ—or z—indicates the number of standard deviations between an X value and $\bar{X}$. Chart 7-1 shows relative heights of ordinates for a *normal curve* at 1, 1.5, 2, and 3 standard deviations from the maximum ordinate, which is at the mean. The height of the ordinate at the mean is taken as 1, and the x/σ value at the ordinate is 0 because $X - \bar{X} = 0$ at that point.

Normal Curve

A normal curve is a symmetrical, bell-shaped curve in which a certain relationship exists between the height of an ordinate erected at the mean and the heights ordinates erected at other places on the horizontal axis.

If a curve incorporates these relationships and those shown in Table A-2, it is a normal curve. These proportionate heights of ordinates are useful in certain types of sampling

Chart 7-2. Normal distribution for $N = 2507, \overline{X} = \$30$, and $\sigma = \$5$.

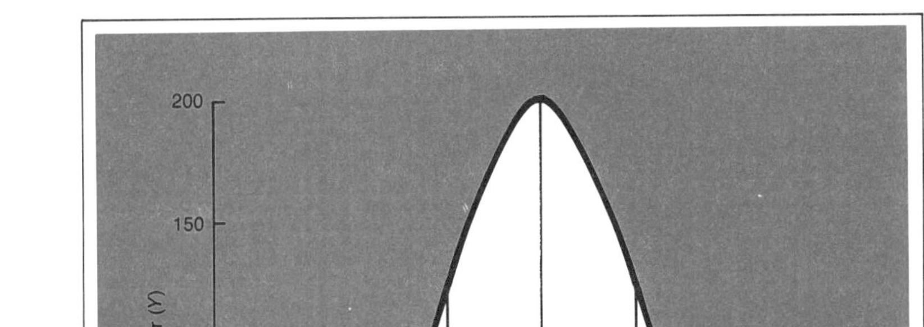

analysis, particularly in fitting a normal curve to a given curve to determine if it departs significantly from the normal curve.

The curve for any normal distribution can be drawn if the values of $N, \overline{X}$, and σ are known. Chart 7-2 shows a normal curve constructed for $N = 2507, \overline{X} = \$30$, and $\sigma = \$5$. To draw this curve, Y_o, the ordinate at the mean, was computed with the normal equation and found to be 200. Other ordinate values were computed by multiplying 200 by the relative heights found in Table A-2. For example, at one standard deviation from the mean ($x/\sigma = 1$), the relative height of the ordinate is 0.60653. Since $200 \times 0.60653 = 121$, this value is plotted on the Y scale, at $\overline{X} - \sigma$ and $\overline{X} + \sigma$, which are \$25 and \$35, respectively, on the X scale.

Theoretically, the normal curve is asymptotic to the base at both ends; therefore, theoretically, the x/σ values approach infinity. However, the curve nearly touches the base (abscissa) at $\pm 3\sigma$ from the mean.

In order to make the normal curve a probability distribution the area under the curve is equated to 1. Now the sum of all the areas between the ordinates is equal to 1. The equation for the normal distribution having unit area is

$$Y_c = \frac{1}{\sigma\sqrt{2\pi}} e^{-x^2/2\sigma^2}$$

Areas Under the Normal Curve

When ordinates are erected as in Chart 7-2, they cut off portions of the total area under the normal curve. These have been calculated using the equation for the normal curve and tabulated. A table showing the proportions is called a table of areas of the normal curve (see Table A-3, Appendix E). This table gives the proportion of the total area between the maximum ordinate (the ordinate at the mean) and ordinates at several standard deviations from the mean. Some of these area proportions are shown in Chart 7-3.

Part (a) of the chart shows that the area between the ordinate at the mean and the ordinate at one standard deviation away from the mean in either direction is 0.3413 of the total area under the curve (which has been equated to a value of 1.0000). In other words, that segment of the curve covers 34.13% of the total area under the curve. Doubling this figure, we see that 68.26% of the total area under the curve is found between ordinates erected at $\overline{X} + \sigma$ and $\overline{X} - \sigma$. This area is shaded in part (a).

Chart 7-3b shows that the area between ordinates at $\overline{X}$ and $\overline{X} + 1.96\sigma$ makes up 47.50% of the total area under the curve and that ordinates at $\overline{X}$ and $\overline{X} - 1.96\sigma$ also

Chart 7-3. Areas of the normal curve between frequently used distances from the mean.

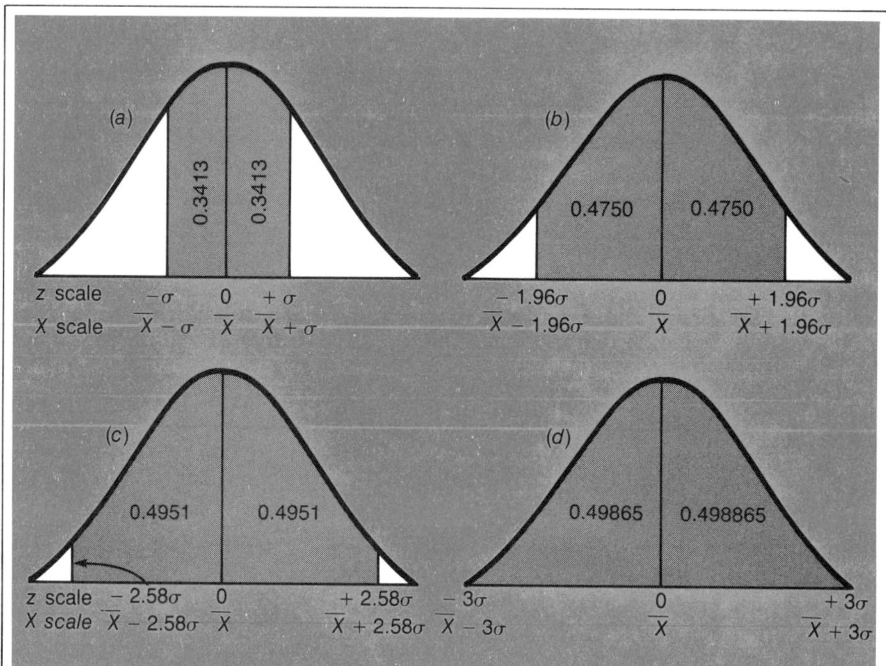

Chart 7-4. Areas of the normal curve between selected distances from the mean.

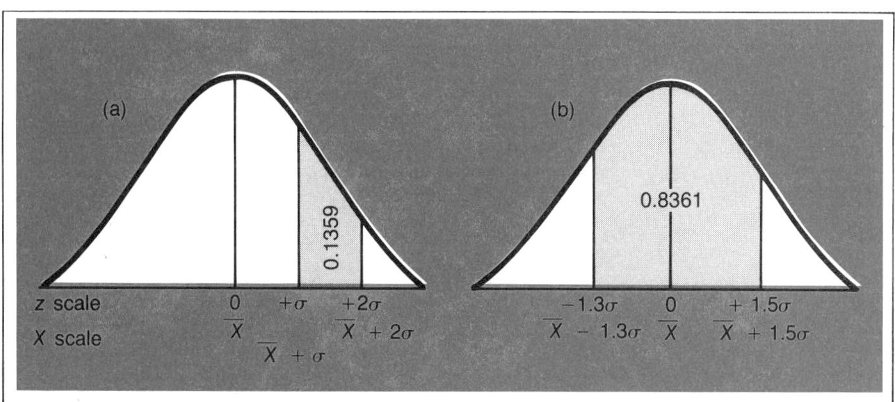

delineate 47.50% of the total area. Therefore, ordinates drawn at $\overline{X} \pm 1.96\sigma$ will include 95.00% of the total area, which is shaded. Parts (c) and (d) show the proportions of the total area under the curve that are found between ordinates at $\overline{X}$ and at 2.58σ and 3σ from the mean. Ordinates at $\overline{X} \pm 2.58\sigma$ include 99.02% of the total area and ordinates at $\overline{X} \pm 3\sigma$ include 99.73% of the total area. Using the table of areas in Appendix E, we can determine the proportion of the total area between ordinates at the mean and ordinates at $\pm 4\sigma$. It is a rare situation, however, in which area proportions for values more than three standard deviations are required. Theoretically, the areas between any $\overline{X} \pm n\sigma$ can be determined because the normal curve is asymptotic to the base.

Also, we can use a table of areas to determine the percentage of the area enclosed by *any* two ordinates. Chart 7-4 illustrates this fact. The shaded area in part (a) makes up 13.59% of the total. This is derived by subtracting the readings from the table of areas where $z = x/\sigma = 1$ and $z = x/\sigma = 2$, which are 0.3413 and 0.4772, respectively. The shaded area in (b), which is set off by ordinates drawn at $\overline{X} - 1.3\sigma$ and $\overline{X} + 1.5\sigma$, contains 83.64% of the area under the curve. This was determined by adding 0.4332 and 0.4032, the readings from the table where $z = x/\sigma$ equals 1.5 and 1.3, respectively.

Practical Use of Areas of the Normal Curve

The total area under the normal curve represents all of the frequencies that form the curve. Moreover, the proportion of the total area that lies between ordinates erected at any two values of the X-scale represents the proportion of all the frequencies with values between the two ordinates. Therefore, we can determine the probability that a single value will fall between any two values on the X-scale. To illustrate how this is done let us assume that the grades made by thousands of students on a nationwide proficiency test

Chart 7-5. Proportion of students making grades between 60 and 80 ($\overline{X} = 70$ and $\sigma = 15$).

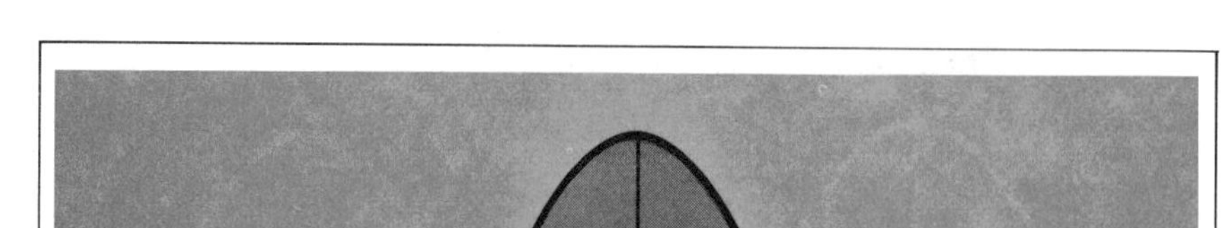

are normally distributed, the mean grade is 70 and the standard deviation of the grades is 15. Now assume that one of the students who took the test is selected at random. Determine the probability that he made a grade: (1) between 60 and 80, (2) 80 and 90, (3) 65 or less, and (4) 95 or more. To determine these probabilities we must find the proportion of the students that made grades in the given intervals. For the interval 60 to 80 the following calculations must be made:

$$z = x/\sigma = (X - \overline{X})/\sigma = (60 - 70)/15 = -10/15 = -0.67$$

$$z = x/\sigma = (X - \overline{X})/\sigma = (80 - 70)/15 = 10/15 = +0.67$$

The area reading from the table of areas (Table A3, Appendix E), for a z of 0.67 is 0.2486, thus 0.2486 + 0.2486 = 0.4972 which means that 49.72% of the students made grades between 60 and 80.

This is pictured in Chart 7-5 which shows both the z-scale values and the $\overline{X}$-scale values.

For the interval 80 to 90 we calculate,

$$z = (X - \overline{X})/\sigma = (80 - 70)/15 = 0.67$$

and

$$z = (X - \overline{X})/\sigma = (90 - 70)/15 = 20/15 = 1.33.$$

The area reading for a z of 1.33 is 0.4082 and the area reading for a z of 0.67 is 0.2486. Therefore, the area between 80 and 90 = 0.4082 − 0.2486 = 0.1596, which is the probability that the student made a grade between 80 and 90.

This is shown on Chart 7-6.

Chart 7-6. Proportion of students making grades between 80 and 90 (X = 70 and σ = 15).

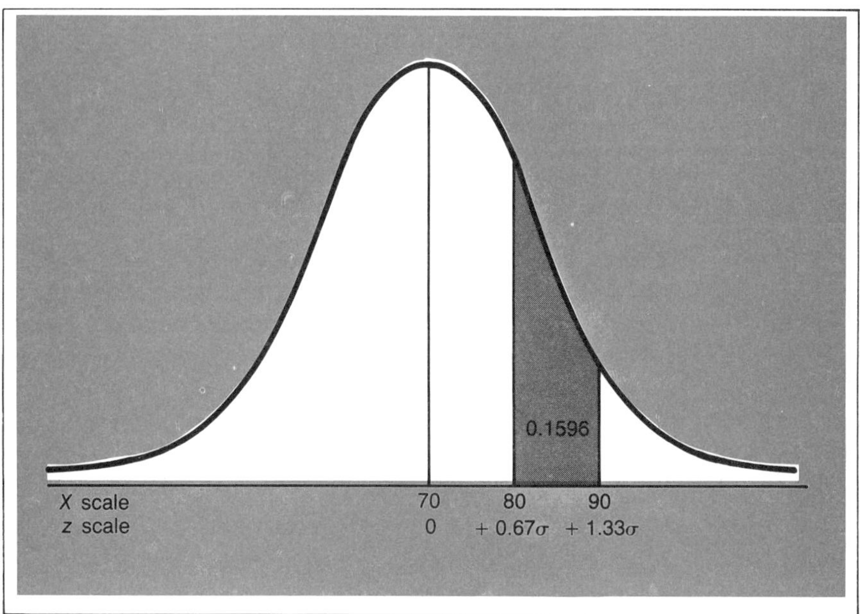

Chart 7-7. Proportions of students making grades 65 or less and 95 or more ($\overline{X}$ = 70 and σ = 15).

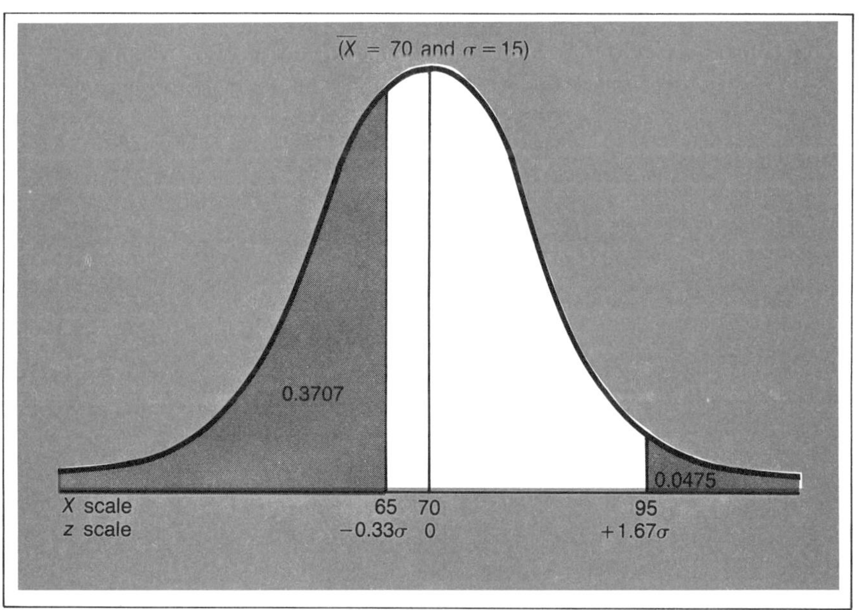

The respective z values needed for intervals of 65 or less and 95 or more are

$$z = (65 - 70)/15 = -5/15 = -0.33$$

$$z = (95 - 70)/15 = 25/15 = 1.67$$

The area reading for $z = 0.33$ is 0.1293, therefore, $0.5000 - 0.1293 = 0.3707$, which is the probability that the student made a grade of 65 or under. The area reading for $z = 1.67$ is 0.4525, therefore $0.5000 - 0.4525 = 0.0475$, which is the probability that the student made a grade of 95 or over. This may be seen in Chart 7-7.

THE POISSON DISTRIBUTION

It was stated earlier that if the binomial $(p + q)^n$ were expanded for a large n, the resulting probability distribution would approach that of the normal curve, even if p were not equal to ½, but were reasonably large. But what would the shape of the distribution be if p were very small, say 0.001?

It would be a positively skewed discrete distribution that would approach that of the *Poisson distribution*, named after Simeon D. Poisson who first described it in the early 1800s.

To help you understand the relationship between a highly skewed binomial distribution and the Poisson distribution, Table 7-2 presents the probabilities of the

TABLE 7-2. Comparison of the Probabilities of a Skewed Binomial Distribution and a Poisson Distribution.

r EVENTS	*P(r)* EXPANDED BINOMIAL $(1 + 0.9)^{10}$	*P(r)* POISSON DISTRIBUTION $m = 1$
0	0.3487	0.3679
1	0.3874	0.3679
2	0.1937	0.1839
3	0.0574	0.0613
4	0.0112	0.0153
5	0.0015	0.0031
6	0.0001	0.0005
7	0.0000	0.0001
8	0.0000	0.0000
9	0.0000	0.0000
10	0.0000	0.0000

expanded binomial $(0.1 + 0.9)^{10}$ and also the probabilities of the Poisson distribution with a mean of 1, which is the mean of the binomial, ($np = 10 \times 0.1 = 1$). It can be seen that the probabilities for the corresponding r events are rather close. Moreover, the if p were smaller and n larger, the corresponding probabilities of the two distributions would be closer.

Uses of the Poisson Distribution

The Poisson distribution can be used to measure the probability of a given number of typographical errors occurring in a page of a manuscript. It can also be used to determine probabilities of over capacity in traffic flows, telephone calls, and waiting lines. It would be the logical distribution to use to calculate the probability of a given number of house fires in a large city in a given time span.

Mean of the Poisson Distribution

When one uses the Poisson distribution, he either knows or must calculate the mean number of random events that occur within a given space or time interval.

The formula for this distribution may be written

$$P(r) = (e^{-m}m^r)/r!$$

where r, the random variable, is the number of events and $P(r)$ is the probability of r events per unit of measurement, e is 2.71828, the base of the Naperian system of logarithms, and m is the mean number of events in the given time or space. Moreover, since q is close to 1, pq is close to p and m is equal to the variance, that is, $npq = np = m$.

The following problem will illustrate the practical use of the Poisson distribution for calculating the probabilities of events.

In a large city the mean number of house fires a day is 6.5. Since there are 237,000 houses in the city this means that p, the average proportion of homes that will catch fire on a given day is

$$6.5/237{,}000 = 0.0000274.$$

Since p is very small, it is reasonable to use the Poisson distribution to find the probability of r houses catching fire on the given day. For example, if we wish to know the probability that no house will catch fire the calculation is

$$P(0) = (2.71828)^{-6.5}(6.5)^0/0! = 1/(2.71828)^{6.5} \times 1$$

and

$$\begin{aligned} \log P(0) &= \log\left[1/(2.71828)^{6.5}\right] \\ &= \log 1 - 6.5 \log 2.71828 \\ &= (10.000000-10) - 6.5(0.4343) \\ &= 10.000000-10 - 2.82295 \\ &= 7.1771 - 10 \\ P(0) &= 0.0015 \end{aligned}$$

The calculation for the probability of five houses burning is

$$\begin{aligned} P(5) &= 2.71828^{-6.5}\ (6.5)^5/5! \\ &= 0.0015\ (11602.90/120) = 17.404/120 = 0.1450 \end{aligned}$$

By the same process, the probability of any number of houses catching fire could be calculated, but that would not be necessary, since the probabilities can be read from Table A-9 in Appendix E, which lists the Poisson probabilities for a large number of m and r values. For example, the two probabilities calculated above can be found in the table where $m = 6.5$ and $r = 0$ and $r = 5$. Moreover, if we want to know the probability of 10 houses catching fire in one day this can be read where $m = 6.5$ and $r = 10$. Thus, $P(10) = 0.056$. If we want to know the probability of 10 or more houses catching fire we must add the probabilities for all of the r's of 10 and larger that are given in the table. These probabilities and their sum are $0.056 + 0.033 + 0.018 + 0.009 + 0.004 + 0.002 + 0.001 = 0.123$.

The following problem will make exclusive use of the table for its solution. The mean number of students in a large high school approaching a water fountain in a one-minute period is 0.5. Assuming the probabilities of the number of students doing this follows the Poisson distribution, what are the probabilities that 0, 1, 2, 3, and 4 students will approach the water fountain in a given one-minute period? The respective probabilities read from Table A-9 are 0.607, 0.303, 0.076, 0.013 and 0.002. The probabilities for five or more are not given because they are less than 0.001.

REVIEW QUESTIONS

1. What is a probability distribution?
2. What is a binomial distribution?
3. What is a normal distribution?
4. How is the binomial distribution related to the normal distribution?

5. Of what use is the area between two ordinates of the normal curve?

6. Describe the Poisson distribution.

7. How does one know whether to use the binomial distribution or the Poisson distribution to calculate a probability?

PROBLEMS

1. Ten percent of 10,000 manufactured items are defective. Compute the probability that 3 out of 5 items selected at random will be defective. Use the formula

$$P(r) = \frac{n!}{r!(n-r)!} p^r q^{n-r}$$

2. Twenty percent of a large number of people are known to be immigrants. If four people are drawn at random, what is the probability that three will be immigrants?
3. If the probability is 0.3 that Jones will get a strike on each roll of his bowling ball, what is the probability that he will get 10 strikes in succession? That he will get no strikes in 10 successive rolls?
4. Expand the binomial $(0.3 + 0.7)^6$.
5. If 60% of all the television viewers in a given universe are watching a certain program, what is the probability that three or more of those selected in a random sample of five will be watching the program?
6. There are 25 red marbles and 75 white marbles in a container. A random process is used to draw a sample of five marbles. Expand the binomial to determine the probabilities of choosing the following combinations of marbles: (a) 5 red, (b) 4 red and 1 white, (c) 3 red and 2 white, (d) 2 red and 3 white, (e) 1 red and 4 white, and (f) 5 white. (Their sum should be 1.)
7. Based on information in Problem 6, calculate the probability of finding 3 red and 2 white marbles in a random sample of 5 with the formula

$$P(r) = \frac{n!}{r!(n-r)!} p^r q^{n-r}$$

Compare this answer with the one obtained in Problem 6 with the expanded binomial. They should be the same.

8. If 60% of the students in a university smoke cigarettes, what is the probability that only 2 of 5 students selected by a random process will be smokers? What is the probability that none will be smokers?
9. Assume that 30% of the employees of a large firm are female. If a committee of five employees is selected from all of the employees in the firm in such a manner that each employee has an equal chance of being chosen, what is the probability of getting a committee consisting of four females and one male?
10. A box contains 10 red, 15 white, and 20 blue balls. These are mixed thoroughly, and then one is drawn from the box in a manner that gives each ball the same chance of being chosen. What is the probability that the ball will either be white or blue?

11. Compute the value of the maximum ordinate at the mean of a normal distribution with $N =$ 800 and $\sigma = \$40$ using the equation

$$Y_o = \frac{N}{\sigma \sqrt{2\pi}}$$

Also, compute the value of the ordinate at 1.5σ from the mean with the equation

$$Y_o = Y_o e^{-x^2/2\sigma^2}$$

12. If the mean of the normal distribution in Problem 11 is \$200, what is the value of the ordinate at \$220?

13. From Table A-2 in Appendix E, read the relative heights of ordinates of the normal distribution at the following standard deviation distances from the ordinate at the mean: 0.5, 1.2, 1.8, 2.7, and 3.0

14. If the height of the ordinate at the mean of a normal distribution is 80 units, how high are the ordinates at the following standard deviation distances from the mean: 1, 1.5, 2, 2.5, and 3.0?

15. The mean and standard deviation of a normal distribution are \$1000 and \$150, respectively. What proportion of the curve is above \$1150? Above \$1300? Below \$925? Between \$800 and \$1200?

16. A normal distribution has a mean of \$500 and a standard deviation of \$60. What proportion of the curve is between \$440 and \$560? Between \$410 and \$590? Between \$560 and \$620?

17. What percent of the area of a normal curve is between the ordinates erected at the following X values: $\overline{X} \pm \sigma$, $\overline{X} \pm 1.96\sigma$, $\overline{X} \pm 1.96\sigma$, $\overline{X} \pm 2.58\sigma$, $\overline{X} \pm 1.3\sigma$?

18. What percent of the area of a normal curve is outside the following intervals:

(a) $\overline{X} + \sigma, \overline{X} - \sigma$

(b) $\overline{X} + 1.96\sigma, \overline{X} - 1.96\sigma$

(c) $\overline{X} \pm 1.96\sigma$

(d) $\overline{X} - 2.58\sigma, \overline{X} + 2.58\sigma$

(e) $\overline{X} \pm 2.58\sigma$

(f) $\overline{X} + 3\sigma, \overline{X} - 3\sigma$

(g) $\overline{X} - 1.645\sigma, \overline{X} + 1.645\sigma$

(h) $\overline{X} \pm 1.645\sigma$

(i) $\overline{X} + 2.33\sigma, \overline{X} - 2.33\sigma$

(j) $\overline{X} \pm 2.33\sigma$

19. Cars arriving at a certain intersection average one a minute. Assuming that arrivals are independent and random, what is the probability of three arrivals in a one-minute period?

20. At an airline registration desk in a large city, telephone calls average about one every three minutes. Assuming that the calls are independent and come at random, what is the probability that (a) two calls will come in a given three-minute period, and (b) two or more calls will come in a given three-minute period?

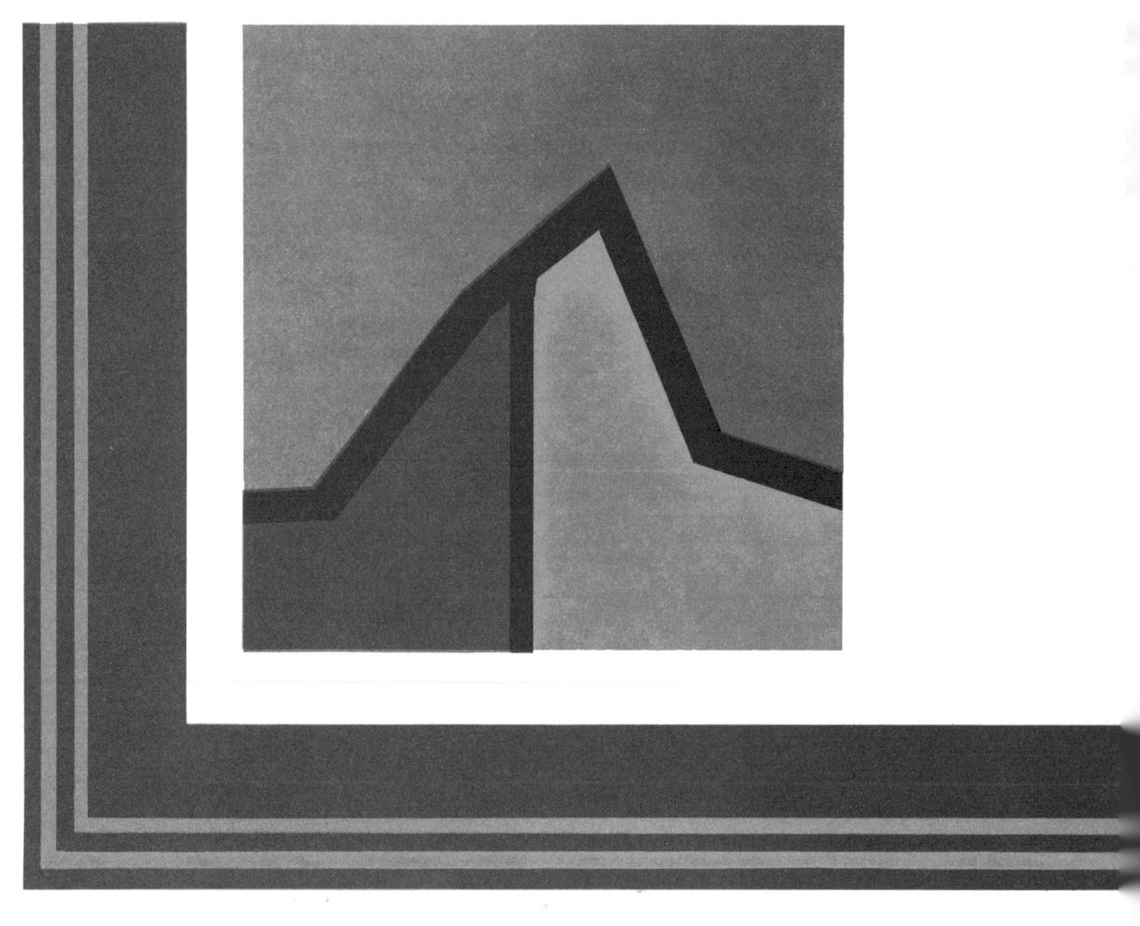

8

Sampling Theory and Confidence Intervals

The concept of sampling is simple. Like the cook who tastes a spoonful of soup to determine the flavor of the whole pot, the marketing or economic researcher samples a small part of some whole to determine the characteristics of the whole. More precisely, a sample is defined as a subset of a universe or population, which we said in Chapter 1 is a well-defined group of objects such as all of the households in a city, all the beets of a farmer's field or all the bricks manufactured by a certain process.

Business and government alike use samples extensively to gather information from which to make inferences about universes in order to solve business and economic problems. Therefore, it is important that samples be selected so that they will represent the universes from which they are drawn.

ADVANTAGES OF STUDYING SAMPLES

We study samples, rather than the entire universes from which they are drawn, for one or more of the following reasons: to save time and money, to avoid injury to or destruction of the entire universe, and because it may be the only practical way to get information about a universe.

The time it takes to analyze a 10% sample of a universe may be only one tenth the time it would take to analyze the universe. Saving time saves money and makes a report available more quickly.

Sometimes tests of manufactured items injure or destroy the product. Such testing makes sampling mandatory. For example, a battery manufacturer may want to test the durability of a certain battery under conditions of normal use. Such a test may require that the test batteries be used until they are dead. Naturally, in a case such as this, only a small sample is used in order to limit destruction.

On occasion, it may be impractical or impossible to study an entire universe because of its size or nature. For example, political pollers cannot contact every voter because there are too many and because of the transient nature of people. Moreover, the expense of studying large universes makes it impractical. Because it takes millions of dollars to conduct a census of manufactures in the United States, one is done only approximately every five years. In other years, sample surveys of manufactures are made to obtain data on their operations.

The advantages of studying samples will not be realized in many types of studies unless the procedures discussed in Chapter 2 are used for preparing the questionnaires, collecting the data and selecting the samples. It is advisable to use probability samples for reasons you will learn.

TYPES OF SAMPLES

Probability Samples

If we want to know how well our sample represents the universe from which it is drawn, then we should use a probability sample.

Probability Sample

A probability sample is one for which the probability of selecting any item in the universe is known before the selection takes place.

Two basic types of probability samples are the simple random sample and the stratified random sample.

Simple Random Sample

A simple random sample is one that is selected from a universe in such a manner that each item in the universe has an equal chance of being included in the sample.

For example, if a simple random sample of 1,000 students is to be selected from a university with 10,000 students, then each student should have a probability of 1/10 of being included in the sample.

Stratified Random Sample

A stratified random sample is one for which a heterogeneous universe is divided into homogeneous groups (strata) with a simple random sample being drawn from each group. A stratified random sample may be proportional or disproportionate.

A *proportional stratified sample* is one that has the same percentage representation of items in each group as that found in each universe group. For example, if we desired to determine the average weight of the 10,000 students in a university by weighing a representative sample of 100 students we might assure a more representative average by stratifying the universe by sex, because the general weight levels of males and females differ. In such a case, we would want to have the same percentage of females represented in the sample as exists in the student body. Therefore, if there are 3,000 female students (out of 10,000 total) we would include in our 100-student sample a simple random sample of 30 females and a simple random sample of 70 of the 7,000 males. These two samples would comprise a proportional stratified sample.

Any stratified sample that is not proportional is disproportionate. If, in the previous example, the stratified sample of 100 students was made up of 20 females and 80 males, then there would be a disproportionate representation of the universe.

A proper selection of a disproportionate stratified sample gives heavy consideration to the variation of items in the strata and the costs of including sample items from the various strata. A discussion of techniques for selecting this type of sample is beyond the scope of this book.

Cluster Sample

To get a cluster sample, a specified geographical area, such as a metropolitan area, county, or city, is divided into somewhat homogeneous, smaller geographical areas, and probability samples of these smaller areas are selected for interviews with households.

This unique type of stratified sample is often referred to as an area sample because it involves samples that are determined geographically.

A cluster (area) sample might be the only feasible way of getting a representative sample of households from a particular area because it is difficult to find directories that list the addresses of all households in an area. Such a list would be necessary for the selection of a good random sample of the area. Even if a directory of an area were available, however, it might be much cheaper to use a cluster sample because of the ease of interviewing. A random sample of households from a city directory would scatter the sample households all over the city and would require much travel time from one sample household to another. This travel time can be eliminated by the cluster sample.

If there are 300 census tracts in a city, a sample of census tracts can be drawn and each household in a sample census tract can be interviewed. This kind of door-to-door interviewing requires no automobile nor public transportation to go from one house to another.

Nonprobability Samples

Two commonly used types of nonprobability samples are the *quota sample* and the *judgment sample*.

A quota sample. To get a quota sample each interviewer is told to interview a certain number of people in an area, but the selection of those to be interviewed is left up to him. By using this method, an analyst gives up an element of control necessary for mathematical evaluation and cannot apply probability laws to the results.

Interviewers for quota sample studies will get their interviews the easiest way. If a statistics instructor were to try to determine what percentage of a university's student body smokes cigarettes by asking each of his students to interview five students in the university without telling them who to interview, a bad sample would probably result. Why? Because each student in the university would not be given a chance to be included. All the interviews might be made in the school of commerce, or student union, and they also might be made on the day of assignment, say Monday, so that students that don't have Monday classes would not have a chance to be included.

The judgment sample. For a judgment sample, the person conducting the study must judge what items constitute a representative sample. If a wage analyst wanted to know how much manufacturing firms in a metropolitan area pay new college graduates with business administration majors, he might pick five firms that he judged to be typical of all firms and get the data from them. Samples selected by this method might be good ones, but there is no way of measuring how representative or reliable they are, as can be done with probability samples. For this reason, they should be avoided.

SELECTION OF SAMPLE ITEMS

Drawing-from-a-Container Method

Any method that gives each item in a universe an equal chance of being included in the sample is a good method for selecting a simple random sample. If a universe consists of 10,000 business firms, a random sample of these firms could be selected by writing the name and address of each firm on a small card, placing the cards in a container, and drawing the desired number of cards for the sample from the container. Theoretically, after a card has been drawn and the name and address recorded, it should be replaced, and all the cards should be remixed before the next drawing. This drawing, replacement, and remixing pattern should be followed for each card selected so that the probability of any card being drawn would be 1 in 10,000. If the first card drawn was not replaced, the selection probability of the second card would be 1 in 1,999, and if the first and second cards were not replaced, the probability of a card being selected on the third drawing would be 1 in 9,998. If no drawn cards were replaced, the 100th drawing would give a probability of 1 in 9,900 for each remaining card. In actual practice, few researchers bother to replace any of the cards after drawing them because it would be too time-consuming and would make little difference in the sample results. It can be reasoned that the differences between the probabilities for each draw would be too insignificant to make any difference in the final outcome.

The principle of drawing items from a container to get a random sample is a good one, but it is usually impractical because of the time it would take to prepare the cards. Moreover, in practice this method could prove faulty because of the difficulty of thoroughly mixing the cards.

Random Number Method

A method of choosing a random sample that permits us to observe the chance principle involved in drawing cards from a container, yet eliminates the bias that results from an imperfect mix of the cards is the random number method. This method makes use of a table of random numbers.

Random Number

A random number is one that is chosen completely randomly, by chance selection. The choice of any number does not depend on the choice of previous numbers. Such numbers are listed in a table of random numbers, where one number has just as much chance of appearing in a particular location as any other number

In a large table of such numbers, say one million, one number will appear just about as often as any other number. For example, if there are ten thousand 10's, there will be close to ten thousand 20's, and any single digit 0 through 9 will appear about one tenth of the time.

Most tables of random numbers are constructed by computer. However, the principle of their construction is the same as that involved in putting ten balls numbered 0 through 9 in a container, drawing balls at random (with replacement) one at a time, and recording the results. Table 8-1 illustrates the random number principle. Tables A-7, Appendix E, gives more random numbers.

Using random numbers. Assume that Table 8-2 represents a census tract map of city X with its census tracts numbered. If we desire to draw a random sample of 10 of these

TABLE 8-1. A Page of Random Numbers.

0711	5289	6001	1290	7292	8583
5126	9919	5000	4965	0012	4978
9069	4818	4707	9526	4234	3761
1261	2770	4032	6803	0835	7630
5289	5990	1279	7269	8548	5810
7211	0375	7587	7963	5550	3513
5863	0084	5147	6032	1980	8012
4003	0008	4011	4019	8030	2050
6556	0900	7456	8356	5812	4169
2418	0700	3117	3818	6935	0754
3733	9518	3251	2770	6022	8792
0449	2477	2926	5403	8330	3733
1519	5177	6697	1875	8572	0447
6444	4400	0845	5246	6092	1388
1167	0136	7300	3630	0745	4185
2933	5437	8371	3808	2180	5988
8812	5297	4109	9406	3516	2923
0968	6133	7102	3236	0338	3574
0293	9184	9477	8661	8139	6800
5099	3520	8619	2139	0759	2899
7952	3693	1545	5339	6984	2323
3512	6084	9597	5682	5279	0961
4090	4736	8826	3562	2389	5952
9562	6489	6051	2541	8593	1135
2052	3511	5564	0076	4640	3716
6999	3778	0777	4555	5333	9889
5778	1223	7002	8226	5228	3454
3776	6733	0509	7242	7752	4994
8720	6951	5671	2622	8293	0916
8800	8263	7064	5328	2392	7721
9952	3203	3156	6359	9516	5876
4590	2520	7111	9631	6743	6375
4720	6827	1547	8375	9923	8299
6010	7276	3287	0564	3851	4415
4585	8219	2804	1023	3827	4851

Source: From a table of random numbers generated on a Marquette University computer.

tracts using the table of random numbers, we must decide on a pattern of selection. We might use the last two digits of each four digit number in Table 8-1 and start with the first number in the left hand column. We might further decide to take the columns in a serpentine fashion; that is, after reaching the bottom of the first column, we would start at the bottom of the second and go up, and after reaching the top of the second column, we would start from the top of the third column and work down, and so on until the desired sample size is obtained. Ten census tracts drawn for the sample with this pattern are circled.

With a table of random numbers, any planned pattern of selection will work. We could, for example, take every *n*th number and select numbers from horizontal or diagonal rows rather than vertical columns.

Numbers that are larger than needed (in the foregoing illustration any two digit number larger than 50) are ignored. If a number appears again after it has been selected, it too is ignored.

Sometimes, for convenience, a sampler is tempted to select a sample from a directory listing the universe items (usually names and addresses) by taking every *n*th item. With this method, which is sometimes called a "systematic" method, it is best to choose the starting number by chance rather than use an arbitrary starting point.

For example, if every tenth name is to be taken from an alphabetical list and the analyst arbitrarily starts with number 1, then he must take number 11, 21, 31, and so on. Thus, he does not give the names with the numbers in between a chance of being selected; that is, numbers 2, 3, 4, etc. and 12, 13, 14, etc. have no chance of being included and, therefore, a random selection cannot be made. However, if a table of random numbers or the drawing-from-a-hat technique is used to pick the starting number, then each number in the universe has an equal chance of being included.

ANALYSIS OF SAMPLE DATA

A sample survey conducted in April 1975 by the U.S. Bureau of Labor Statistics in Milwaukee, Wisconsin, revealed that 219 order clerks had mean earnings of $150.50 per week. This figure would not have been obtained if the earnings of all order clerks in Milwaukee had been averaged. How far is this sample mean from the actual mean?* We could never tell with certainty, but if the sample is a probability sample and if the standard deviation of the weekly earnings of the 219 clerks is known, we can, using sampling theory, determine with specified degrees of confidence maximum amounts that the sample mean might differ from the mean of the universe. For an analysis of this type we need probability laws relating to a normal distribution.

*The term "mean" in this chapter refers to the arithmetic mean.

TABLE 8-2. Census Tract Map, City X.

1	2	(3)	4	5
10	9	8	7	6
(11)	(12)	13	14	15
(20)	(19)	(18)	17	16
21	22	23	24	25
30	29	28	27	(26)
31	32	(33)	34	35
40	39	38	37	36
41	42	43	(44)	45
50	(49)	48	47	46

Normally Distributed Data

Statistical data are normally distributed if, when plotted as a distribution, they form a normal curve. Measurements of physical differences occurring in nature, such as weights and heights of a group of people who have other homogeneous characteristics, are sometimes normally distributed, or approximately so. Many business and economic measures from large universes are nearly normally distributed. For example, wage distributions of certain occupations and distribution of grades on an exam that is taken by a large number of students often approximate the normal distribution.

Other types of data that, theoretically, are normally distributed are the arithmetic means and percentages computed from all possible random samples of the same size that are drawn from the same infintely large, normally distributed universe. Also, the differences between such sample means and differences between such sample percentages, when paired in every way possible, theoretically will follow a normal curve. Thus normal curve theory is frequently used to analyze sample data and make inferences about the universes from which samples are drawn. In practice, the normal curve is often used to analyze sample means and percentages when the samples consist of

30 or more items and when the universes from which the samples are drawn are known or believed to approximate the normal curve.*

Small samples from normally distributed universes should sometimes be analyzed using the *Student t-distribution*, which forms a curve that is flatter than the normal curve; the smaller the sample, the flatter the curve.†

Random errors. Sampling distributions take certain shapes because of the nature of the universe and *random errors of sampling*. These errors, sometimes called chance errors, result from the process of selection of items that make up random samples. The term "error" refers to the chance differences between sample indicators and universe indicators or between indicators for different samples. For example, if the mean of a universe is 20 and the mean of a random sample from the universe is 18, the difference, 2 is due to random errors. A second sample of the same size from the same universe might have a mean of 17, and the difference between the two sample means is also due to random errors.

Because random selection of sample items for a large number of samples of the same size would result in different combinations of items for each sample, the means and certain other values computed from each of the samples would differ in such a way as to form a normal curve.

Random errors cannot be prevented, but fortunately, we know enough about their nature to cope with them and measure them if we have the necessary information about the universe and sample.

Probabilities Related to the Normal Curve

Conclusions resulting from an analysis of sample data are drawn not with certainty, but with probabilities of certainty. For example, based on a sample study, an analyst can determine with a specified degree of confidence that a universe mean will be within a certain interval, but he cannot state with certainty the exact value of the universe mean.

Normal Curve Probabilities

Normal curve probabilities are based on the simple principle that frequency of occurrence determines probability of occurrence.

*Some analysts use the normal curve as the base for analysis only when the sample size is 100 items or more. Theoretically, this provides a more accurate sampling analysis. However, when dealing with real-life data, samples of smaller sizes, as few as 30 items, can be analyzed in relation to the normal curve without sacrificing confidence in the conclusions based on the results of the analysis.

†This distribution, more often called only the *t-distribution,* was developed by W. S. Gosset, who published his works under the name "Student."

Determining probabilities for the occurrence of a sample value in a normally distributed universe is analogous to determining the probability of drawing at random a white ball from a container of, say, 25 white and 75 red balls after they have been thoroughly mixed. One fourth of the balls in the container are white, so the probability that in a single random draw a ball will be white is 1/4 or 0.25. Also, because a "snake eye" (one spot) appears on only one of six sides of a die, the probability of a "snake eye" appearing on one throw of a die is 1/6. These same concepts can be applied to the normal curve because areas under the normal curve represent the frequencies that form the curve, and the frequencies determine the probabilities.

Chart 7-3a shows that the area set off by the ordinates erected at $\overline{X} \pm \sigma$ makes up 68.26%of the total area. Since this area represents the frequency of occurrence, the probability of a single value falling in this area, and therefore, in the $\overline{X} \pm \sigma$ interval, is 0.6826. Similarly, the probability of a single value falling in the interval $\overline{X} \pm 1.96\,\sigma$ is 0.95. Therefore, all we need to do to determine the probability of a single value falling within any given section of the normal curve is to determine the percent of the total area that the section covers.

ANALYSIS OF SAMPLE MEANS

The Normal Curve of Sample Means

Normal curve probabilities enable an analyst to make inferences about a universe mean when he has the mean of a large random sample and the standard deviation of either the universe or the random sample. This is possible because, as was previously stated, the means of a large number of large samples from the same large universe will be normally distributed. Moreover, as depicted in Chart 8-1, they will be distributed around $\overline{X}_u$, the universe mean—half of them less than and half of them greater than the universe mean. The probability that the mean of a sample of the given size would be smaller than $\overline{X}_u$ is 0.5. The probability that it would be larger is also 0.5.

To help a class of students grasp the concept of a normal distribution of sample means an instructor selected 30 random samples of 50 numbers each from a universe of 600 numbers ranging from 25 to 59. These numbers formed the summetrical frequency distribution shown in Chart 8-2. The means computed from these samples are listed in Table 8-3, and a frequency distribution of the sample means is presented in Table 8-4 and Chart 8-3. The distribution of neither the universe nor sample means is normal, but if the universe was normal and large and all possible samples of 50 numbers were drawn from it, the means of the samples would form a normal curve. Moreover, the mean of the sample means, $\overline{X}_{\bar{x}}$, would be equal to the universe mean. In this experiment, the mean of the sample means is 42.2 and the universe mean is 42.0, which indicates that sampling theory works.

Chart 8-1. Normal curve of sample means.

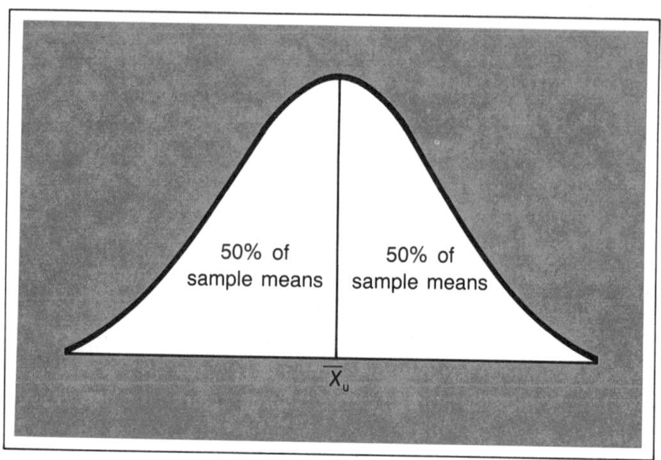

TABLE 8-3. Means Computed from 30 Random Samples of 50 Numbers Each from the Symmetrical Population of 600 Numbers Shown in Chart 8-2.

38.5	42.7	42.3	40.4	42.3	44.1
39.7	43.1	44.7	41.9	40.9	41.7
43.7	43.3	43.8	42.5	41.6	41.8
42.2	40.4	42.6	42.2	42.6	42.0
42.1	41.9	41.8	45.0	43.4	41.7

TABLE 8-4. Frequency Distribution of the Means of 30 Random Samples.

VALUE OF MEANS	*NO. OF MEANS*
38.0–38.9	1
39.0–39.9	1
40.0–40.9	3
41.0–41.9	7
42.0–42.9	10
43.0–43.9	5
44.0–44.9	2
45.0–45.9	1
Total	30
Mean	42.2

Chart 8-2. Frequency distribution of 600 numbers

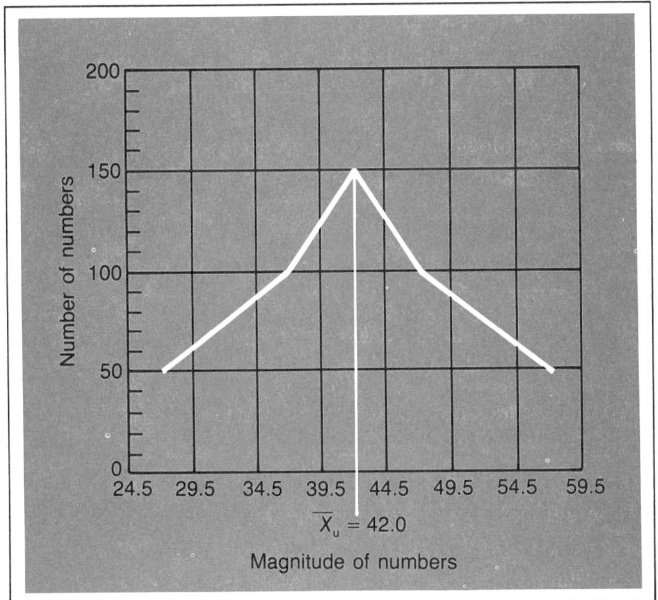

Chart 8-3 Frequency distribution of the means of 30 random samples.

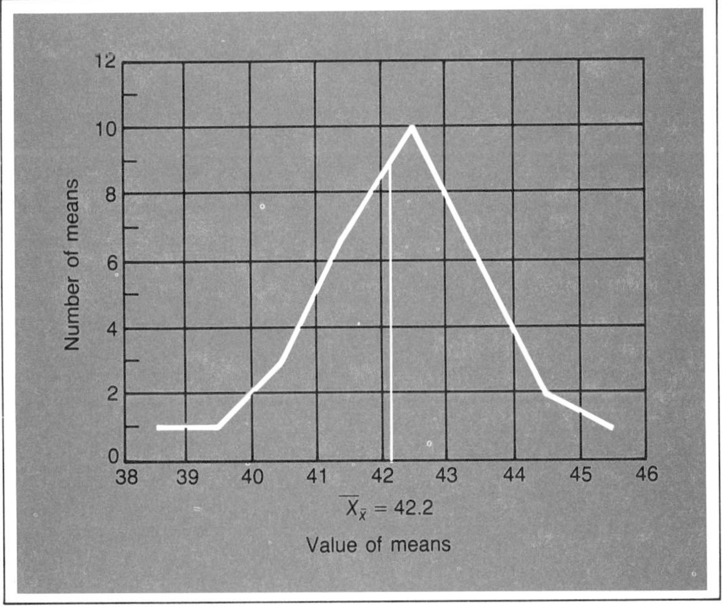

The Standard Error of the Mean

The standard deviation of the distribution of the 30 sample means $\sigma_{\bar{x}}$, was computed from the frequency distribution (Chart 8-3) and found to be 1.4; the interval $\bar{X} \pm \sigma_{\bar{x}} = 42.2 \pm 1.4 = 40.8$ to 43.6 includes 70% of the means. In a like manner, if an analyst had a large number of means of samples of the same size from the same universe, he could compute the standard deviation of the means and set up various standard deviation intervals. Four widely used intervals that he could establish are shaded in Chart 8-4.

> **Standard Error Of The Mean**
>
> The standard deviation of the sample mean distribution, $\sigma_{\bar{x}}$, is called the *standard error of the mean.*

We know that the interval $\bar{X}_u \pm 1.96\sigma_{\bar{x}}$ will include 95% of the means of the random samples that form the normal curve; therefore the probability of the mean of one of the samples falling within that interval is 0.95. Chart 8-4*c* and *d* reveal that the intervals $\bar{X}_u \pm 2.58\sigma_{\bar{x}}$ and $\bar{X}_u \pm 3\sigma_{\bar{x}}$ contain 99% and 99.73% of the sample means, respectively. Therefore, the probability of a single mean falling with $\bar{X}_u \pm 2.58\sigma_{\bar{x}}$ is 0.99 and within $\bar{X}_u \pm 3\sigma_{\bar{x}}$ is 0.9973. Probabilities of means falling in the unshaded tails of the distribution in Chart 8-4 also can be easily stated. Chart 8-4*b* shows that each of the two tails contains 2.5% of the means; therefore, the chance that a single sample mean will be smaller than $\bar{X}_u - 1.96\sigma_{\bar{x}}$ is 0.025 and the chance that it will be larger than $\bar{X}_u + 1.96\sigma_{\bar{x}}$ also is 0.025. The probability of a mean falling in one or the other of the tails is 0.05.

Using the Standard Error of the Mean

The standard error of the mean enables us to measure the difference between the mean of a random sample and the mean of the universe from which the sample was drawn. This in turn enables us to determine if it is reasonable to assume that a given sample mean is the mean of a random sample from a specified universe, provided the mean and standard deviation of the universe are known. For example, assume that a census (complete enumeration) showed that the arithmetic mean weekly earnings of stenographers in a city was \$150 and the standard deviation of their earnings was \$25. Assume further that six months after the census study was made a research agency selected a random sample of 625 stenographers in that city and found their mean weekly earnings to be \$155. A proper question would be: Do the stenographers earn a higher mean wage now than they did when the census was taken? This question cannot be answered with an unqualified yes or no, but we can establish certain degrees of confidence in a yes or no answer by determining an interval in which the mean of a random sample of 625 would fall, with

Chart 8-4. Percentages of sample means found between and beyond ordinates of a normal curve of sample means.

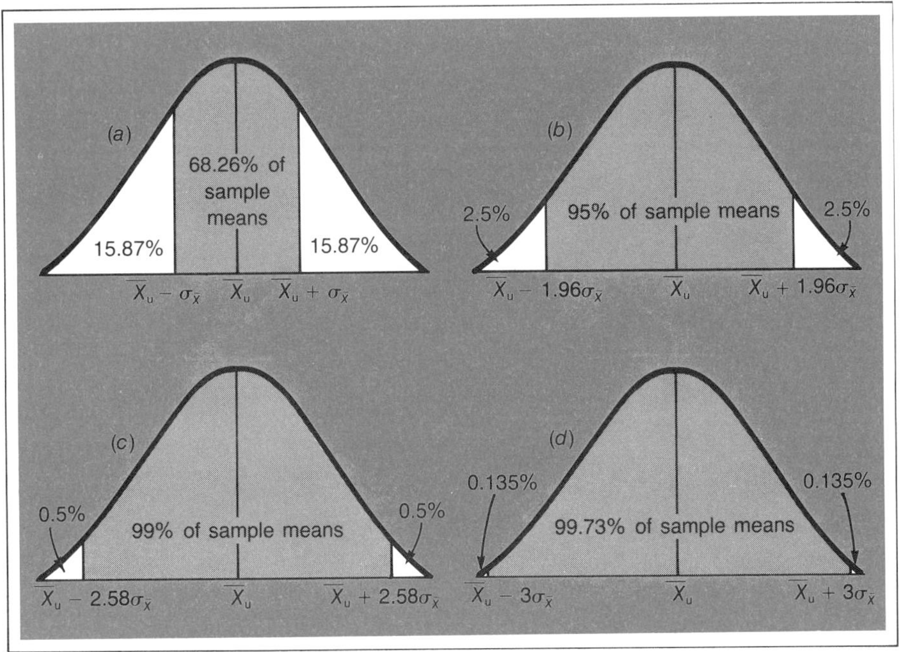

known probability, if it were drawn from a universe with a mean of 150 and a standard deviation of 25.

To do this we would need to compute the standard deviation of the normal distribution of sample means from all possible samples composed of 625 stenographers (the standard error of the mean). Those means could never be available, but the formula

$$\sigma_{\bar{x}} = \frac{\sigma_u}{\sqrt{N}}$$

will give the same answers as the general standard deviation formula

$$\sigma = \frac{\Sigma x^2}{N} \quad \text{where} \quad x^2 = (\overline{X}_s - \overline{X}_u)^2$$

and enables us to calculate the standard error of the mean when we know the standard deviation of the universe, σ_u, and the size of the sample, N. For the current problem,

$$\sigma_{\bar{x}} = \frac{\sigma_u}{\sqrt{N}} = \frac{25}{\sqrt{625}} = \frac{25}{25} = 1$$

Chart 8-5. Normal distribution of the means of all possible samples of 625 stenographers in city *X*.

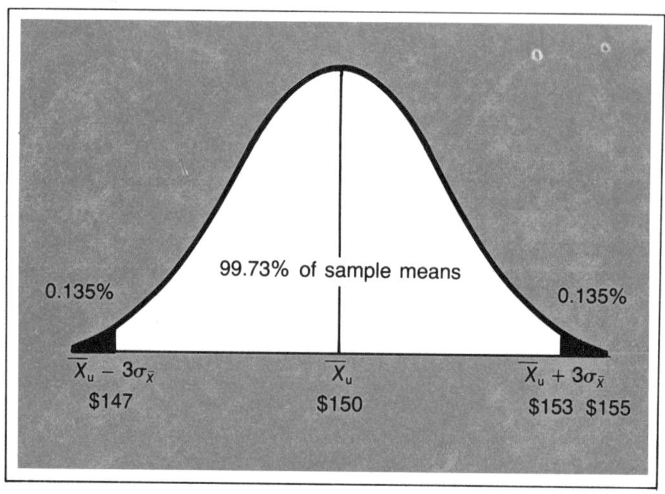

Substituting in the interval $\overline{X}_u \pm 3\sigma_{\bar{x}}$ gives

$$150 \pm 3\ (1) = 150 \pm 3 = 147 \text{ to } 153$$

The probability is 0.9973 that the mean of a random sample of 625 from a universe with a mean of 100 would fall in this interval, as Chart 8-5 illustrates. Therefore, it is almost certain that the mean of a random sample of 625 stenographers from the universe would be within $3 of the universe mean. In this case, we would conclude with a certainty of at least 0.9973 that the difference of $5.00 between the two means is too large to attribute to random errors of sampling and that the mean earnings of stenographers in the city had changed.

THE FINITE CORRECTION FACTOR

The preceding example concerned a large sample from a very large universe (theoretically, an infite universe). However, if the sample had been from a finite universe that was so small that the sample made up 10% or more of the universe, the standard error formula

$$\sigma_{\bar{x}} = \frac{\sigma_u}{\sqrt{N}}\sqrt{\frac{M - N}{M - 1}}$$

would be used by most analysts because it will give a more accurate estimate. In this formula,

$$\sqrt{\frac{M - N}{M - 1}}$$

where M is the size of the universe, it is called the *finite population correction factor*.*

*Proof that the formula gives the standard error of the mean is as follows. If a universe is made up of the numbers, 2, 4, 6, and 8, then the standard deviation of the universe equals

$$\begin{aligned}
\sigma_u &= \sqrt{\frac{\Sigma(X - \bar{X}_u)^2}{N}} \\
&= \sqrt{\frac{(2-5)^2 + (4+5)^2 + (6-5)^2 + (8-5)^2}{4}} \\
&= \sqrt{\frac{20}{4}} = \sqrt{5} = 2.2361
\end{aligned}$$

For a sample of 2 numbers

$$\begin{aligned}
\sigma_{\bar{x}} &= \frac{\sigma_u}{\sqrt{N}}\sqrt{\frac{M - N}{M - 1}} \\
&= \frac{2.2361}{\sqrt{2}}\sqrt{\frac{4 - 2}{4 - 1}} \\
&= \sqrt{\frac{10}{6}} \\
&= 1.291
\end{aligned}$$

This is equal to the standard deviation of the means of all possible samples of two numbers that can be selected from the universe. These possible samples and the calculation of the standard deviation of their means are as follows.

SAMPLES OF TWO NUMBERS	*SAMPLE MEANS*
	$\bar{X}_s$
2 and 4	3
2 and 6	4
2 and 8	5
4 and 6	5
4 and 8	6
6 and 8	7
Total	30
mean $(\bar{X}_u)$	5

$$\begin{aligned}
\sigma_{\bar{x}} &= \sqrt{\frac{\Sigma(\bar{X}_s - \bar{X}_u)^2}{N}} \\
&= \sqrt{\frac{(3-5)^2 + (4-5)^2 + (5-5)^2 + (5-5)^2 + (6-5)^2 + (7-5)^2}{6}} \\
&= \sqrt{\frac{10}{6}} = 1.291
\end{aligned}$$

To give an example of its use, suppose that the city from which our sample was selected had only 2000 stenographers, then the standard error of the mean would be

$$\sigma_{\bar{x}} = \frac{25}{\sqrt{625}} \sqrt{\frac{2000 - 625}{1999}} = 1 \sqrt{0.6827} = 1 \times 0.829 = \$0.83$$

and in this case the 0.9973 probability interval for a sample mean is

$$\$150 \pm 3(0.83) = \$150 \pm \$2.49 = \$147.51 \text{ to } \$152.49.$$

The finite correction factor in the formula takes into account the principle that the larger the sample in proportion to the universe the closer the sample mean is to the universe mean, and when applied will always result in reducing the size of the standard error.

Confidence Intervals for Universe Means—Large Samples

Usually, the mean or the standard deviation of the universe that has been sampled is not known. The mean of a random sample is a point estimate (best single estimate) of the universe mean, but it is almost never the same as the universe mean because of random errors of sample. However, for a random sample, we can, based on the sample findings, determine intervals in which we can say, with certain degrees of confidence, that the universe mean will fall. This is done by making use of the probabilities of the various separations that can occur between a universe mean and the mean of a random sample. The reasoning for the development of a confidence interval might go like this. The probability of a random sample being three standard errors or less away from the universe mean (within the interval $\overline{X}_u \pm 3\sigma_{\bar{x}}$) is 0.9973. Therefore, the chances should be 99.73 to 100 that the universe mean is separated from any random sample mean by the three standard errors or less, and we should be 99.73% confident that the mean of the universe from which the sample was drawn would fall within $\overline{X}_s \pm 3\sigma_{\bar{x}}$. The same type of reasoning should lead us to say that we are 95% confident that the interval $\overline{X}_s \pm 1.96\sigma_{\bar{x}}$ will contain the universe mean. These intervals and the interval $\overline{X}_s \pm 2.58\sigma_{\bar{x}}$ are commonly used confidence intervals.

We do not use the term probability in relation to the occurrence of the universe mean in a confidence interval because there is no distribution of universe means around a sample mean. However, we can have a certain degree of confidence in the truth of a statement that the universe mean falls within a given interval. For example, if in each of 10,000 different random sample studies an interval of $\overline{X}_s \pm 3\sigma_{\bar{x}}$ was established and a statement was made each time that the interval contained the universe mean, the statements would be right about 9,973 times and wrong about 27 times.

Application of Confidence Intervals—Infinite (or Relatively Large) Universes

Suppose a large firm that employs many typists is considering relocating in another city. It would like to know what mean weekly wage it must pay typists in the city, so an analyst selects a random sample of 100 typists in the city and calculates the mean salary, which amounts to \$140 per week. This figure, however, differs from the true mean (universe mean) because of random errors of sampling. Whether it is larger or smaller than the true mean cannot be determined, but the analyst can establish, with a specified degree of confidence, the magnitude of the error. To do this, he must know the standard error or the mean, found by computing $\sigma_u / \sqrt{N}$ when σ_u (the standard deviation of the universe) is known. If σ_u is not known, the standard deviation of the sample is used to estimate the standard error of the mean. The formula is

$$\sigma_{\bar{x}} = \frac{\sigma_s}{\sqrt{N - 1}}$$

where σ_s is the standard deviation of the sample and N is the size of the sample. The -1 is an adjustment for the fact that the standard deviation of a random sample has a tendency to be smaller than the standard deviation of the universe from which it was drawn, because a *degree of freedom* is lost in the calculation of the standard deviation of the sample. The number of degrees of freedom in the computation of the standard deviation of the sample is equal to the number of deviations of the sample values from their mean minus one. This is true because in the computations all of the deviations are free to vary except one that has an automatically determined value such that the sum of the deviations will be zero. In the analysis of large samples, however, the minus one is usually ignored because it does not significantly affect the final answer.

Suppose that the standard deviation of the weekly wages of the sample of 100 typists was calculated to be \$12; then

$$\sigma_{\bar{x}} = \frac{12}{\sqrt{100 - 1}} = \frac{12}{\sqrt{99}} = \frac{12}{10} = \$1.20$$

Therefore, the analyst is 68.26% certain that the universe mean and the sample mean differ by \$1.20 or less; that is, he can be 68.26% confident that he is telling the truth when he says that the universe mean is within the interval $\overline{X}_s \pm \sigma_{\bar{x}}$, which is \$140 ± \$1.20 or \$138.80 to \$141.20. The interval $\overline{X}_s \pm 1.96\sigma_{\bar{x}}$ is \$140 ± 1.96(1.20), which is \$137.65 to \$142.95. A statement that the mean weekly wage of all typists is in this interval has 95 chances out of 100 of being so. If the analyst were to say the true mean is \$142.65 or more, he would be 2.5% confident of telling the truth; likewise, he would be 2.5% confident of telling the truth if he said the true mean was \$137.65 or less. These intervals are pictured in Chart 8-6.

The 0.9973 confidence interval, $X_s \pm 3\sigma_{\bar{x}}$, gives practical limits to the values for the true mean. This interval, 140 ± 3 (1.20), is \$136.40 to \$143.60. The company can be almost certain (actually 99.73% certain), therefore, that the mean weekly wage of typists is between these two figures.

The intervals $\overline{X}_s \pm 1.96\sigma_{\bar{x}}$ and $\overline{X}_s \pm 3\sigma_{\bar{x}}$ used in the foregoing illustrations are the 0.95 and 0.9973 confidence intervals, respectively. They are commonly used, but the 0.99 confidence interval, $\overline{X} \pm 2.58\sigma_{\bar{x}}$ is frequently used also.

Another problem may help illustrate the practical use of confidence intervals. A large firm that is going out of business offers to sell its entire inventory of 50,000 items to another firm for \$750,000, which, the seller says, is the total cost of the items. The

Chart 8-6. Ninety-five percent confidence interval for typist's true earnings.

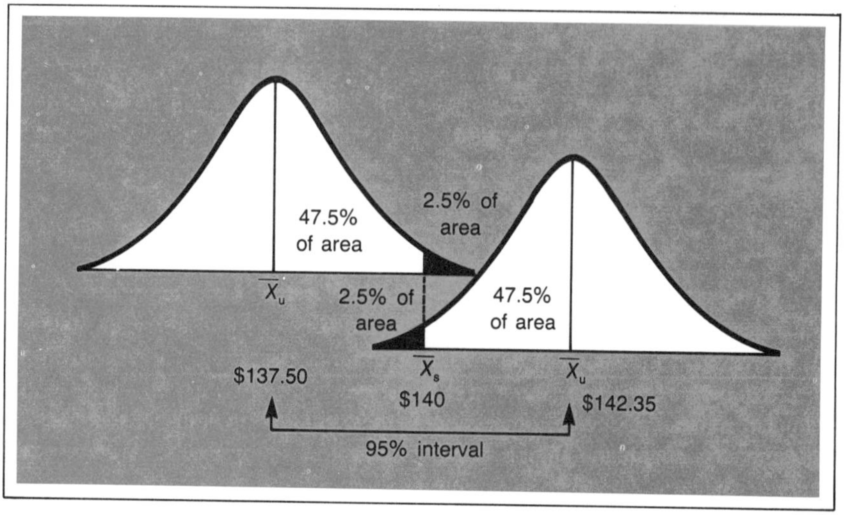

potential buyer is permitted to sample the items and he finds from his random sample of 225 items that the mean and standard deviation of the costs of the items are $13.80 and $4.50, respectively. Further calculation shows that

$$\sigma_{\bar{x}} = \frac{\sigma_s}{\sqrt{N-1}} = \frac{4.50}{\sqrt{224}} = \frac{4.50}{15} = \$0.30$$

and that

$$\overline{X}_s \pm 3\sigma_{\bar{x}} = 13.80 \pm 0.90 = 12.90 \text{ to } \$14.70$$

The buyer can be 0.9973 confident that this interval will contain the mean cost of the 50,000 items. If so, the 0.9973 interval for the true total cost of the inventory was 50,000 ($12.90 to $14.70) or $645,000 to $735,000. Therefore, it is extremely unlikely that the company's $750,000 total cost figure is accurate, and the buyer will probably request a new offer from the seller. There is, however, a very small chance that $750,000 or more was the true total cost. By computing

$$z = \frac{\overline{X}_s - \overline{X}_h}{\sigma_{\bar{x}}}$$

where $\overline{X}_s$ is the sample mean and $\overline{X}_h$ is the hypothetical true mean, the likelihood that the true total could be $750,000 or more can be determined. In this case, $\overline{X}_h$ is

$$\frac{750{,}000}{50{,}000} = \$15.00$$

and

$$z = \frac{13.80 - 15.00}{0.30} = \frac{1.20}{0.30} = 4$$

This means that four standard errors of the mean separate the sample mean and universe mean (as well as the sample total and universe total). A glance at Table A-3 (Appendix E) shows that a difference of four or more standard errors can occur 3 times out of 100,000. $(0.5 - 0.4999683 = 0.0000317.)$

Application of Confidence Intervals—Finite Universe

If the sample of 225 inventory items had come from a universe of only 1,000 items the confidence interval would have been calculated the same way. However, the standard error of the mean would have been estimated with the formula for a finite universe. The calculations are:

$$\sigma_{\bar{x}} = \frac{\sigma_s}{\sqrt{N - 1}}\sqrt{\frac{M - N}{M - 1}} = \frac{4.50}{\sqrt{224}}\sqrt{\frac{1000 - 225}{999}} = 0.30\sqrt{0.775} = 0.26$$

and the 0.9973 confidence interval for the universe mean would be $13.80 \pm 0.26(3)$. $13.80 \pm 0.78 =$ \$13.02 to \$14.58, which is a smaller interval than that calculated for the universe of 50,000 items.

Predetermining the Size of a Random Sample—Infinite Universe

The larger the sample the more costly it is; therefore, a sample should be only large enough to achieve the accuracy desired in the sample measure to be computed. The size of the sample needed to get a desired accuracy in a sample mean can be calculated with the formula for the standard error of the mean if a maximum value for the standard deviation of the universe can be assigned. If, for example, a large electronics firm needs to determine by a random sample the mean annual salary of electronics engineers in the United States and be 99% confident that the sample mean is within \$500 of the true mean, it can determine the number of engineers needed in the sample by estimating a maximum value for σ_u. Suppose that the company, based on a general knowledge of engineers salaries, feels that \$5000 is the maximum standard deviation that could reasonably be expected in the universe. Since 99% confidence that the sample mean will be within $\pm$ \$500 is desired, the mean is expected to fall within $\pm 2.58\sigma_{\bar{x}}$. Therefore $2.58\sigma_{\bar{x}} = 500$ and $\sigma_{\bar{x}} = 500/2.58$. Since $\sigma_{\bar{x}}$ also is $\sigma_u/\sqrt{N}$, we write

$$\sigma_{\bar{x}} = \frac{\sigma_u}{\sqrt{N}} = \frac{500}{2.58}$$

and

$$\frac{5000}{\sqrt{N}} = \frac{500}{2.58}$$

so

$$\sqrt{N} = \frac{5000 \times 2.58}{500} = 25.8$$

and

$$N = 666$$

Therefore, 666 engineers is the size of the sample needed to give the company the desired accuracy with the specified degree of confidence.

Predetermining the Size of a Random Sample—Finite Universe

Suppose that the electronics firm in the preceeding example wanted to determine the mean annual salary of electronics engineers in a city with only 1,000 engineers and desired 99% confidence that the sample mean would be within $500 of the universe mean. The calculation of the sample size needed would be

$$\sigma_{\bar{x}} = \frac{\sigma_u}{\sqrt{N}} \sqrt{\frac{M - N}{M - 1}}$$

so

$$\frac{500}{2.58} = \frac{5000}{\sqrt{N}} \sqrt{\frac{1000 - N}{999}}$$

and

$$\frac{250{,}000}{6.6564} = \frac{25{,}000{,}000}{N} \times \frac{1000 - N}{999}$$

and

$$\frac{25}{6.6564} = \frac{2500}{N} \times \frac{1000 - N}{999} = \frac{2{,}500{,}000 - 2500N}{999N}$$

which results in

$$24{,}975N = 16{,}641{,}000 - 16{,}641N$$

thus

$$N = 400$$

We see that a sample of 400 engineers would be large enough to give the required sampling precision.

Confidence Intervals for Universe Means—Small Samples

An analysis of means of small samples may or may not require the use of the normal distribution. Arithmetic means of all possible samples of the same size that could be drawn from the same normally distributed universe will be normally distributed. Therefore, if we know the mean and standard deviation of the universe we could use the normal distribution to determine the probability that a given sample mean would fall within a specified probability interval, just as we did with the large samples. However, if the standard deviation of the universe is not known and we wish to establish a confidence interval for the universe mean we would need to use the *Student's t distribution,* which is flatter and wider than the normal distribution. The exact form of the distribution depends upon the size of the sample. The *t* distribution is the distribution of x/σ for small samples when

$$\sigma_{\bar{x}} = \frac{\sigma_s}{\sqrt{N - 1}}$$

In this formula one can see that as N becomes smaller the dispersion of the sample means, measured by $\sigma_{\bar{x}}$, becomes larger.

Since that distribution is a family of distributions which is too large to present in one table, selected values of the *t* distribution are presented in special tables that give significance ratios at various levels of significance. Table A-4 in Appendix E gives the ratios for 1 to 30 degrees of freedom at widely used levels of significance. The significance ratios can be used for confidence intervals because, you will remember, a significance level is the complement of a confidence level. For example, a 5% significance level is the complement of a 95% confidence level.

Illustration of a Confidence Interval

To illustrate the use of the *t* distribution for establishing a confidence interval suppose that the mean and standard deviation of a sample of 17 items from a large universe are 25 and 8, respectively. The estimated standard error of the mean is

$$\sigma_{\bar{x}} = \frac{\sigma_s}{\sqrt{N - 1}} = \frac{8}{\sqrt{17 - 1}} = \frac{8}{4} = 2$$

If we desire a 0.95 confidence interval for the universe mean we read in the 0.05 column of Table A-4 at 16 degrees of freedom (N-1) and find the ratio 2.12. Therefore the 0.95 confidence interval for the sample is

$$\overline{X}_s \pm 2.12\sigma_{\bar{x}} = 2.12(2) = 25 \pm 4.24 = 20.76 \text{ to } 29.24$$

Using the reading from the 0.01 column the 0.99 confidence interval is

$$\overline{X}_s \pm 2.92\sigma_{\bar{x}} = 25 \pm 2.92(2) = 25 \pm 5.84 = 19.16 \text{ to } 30.84$$

This *t* distribution, you will notice, gives readings for *two-tailed* significance levels.

Chart 8-7. 0.05 and 0.01 significance levels for the *t* distribution for 16 degrees of freedom.

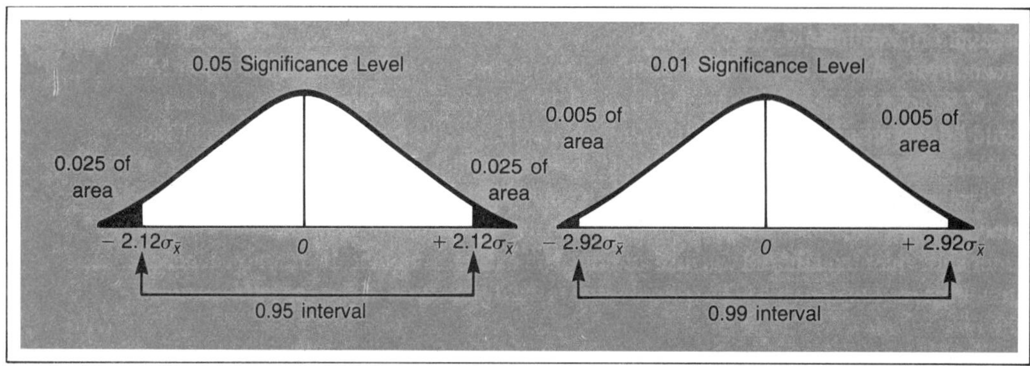

Chart 8-7 pictures the significance levels used to determine the 0.95 and 0.99 confidence intervals above.

The *t* table can be used to establish a one-sided confidence interval. If one wants a one-sided 0.99 interval he would get his reading from the 0.02 column, and, for a one-sided 0.95 confidence interval the reading would be made from the 0.10 column. For example, if $N = 17, \overline{X} = 25$ and $\sigma_{\bar{x}} = 2$ then

$$\overline{X}_s - 1.746\sigma_{\bar{x}} = 25 - 1.746(2) = 25\text{-}3.492 = 21.51$$

Therefore, we are 0.95 confident that the true mean is 21.51 or larger.

ANALYSIS OF SAMPLE PERCENTAGES

The Normal Curve of Sample Percentages

Not only do sample means and differences between sample means follow a normal curve when they derive from large samples of the same size from the same large population, but so do sample proportions or percentages.* If a large number of random samples of, say, 400 students each was selected from the university student population in the United States and the students were asked if they smoked, the percentages of students smoking computed from all the samples would be normally distributed around the true (universe) percentage.

If 55% of the university students smoke, then one half of the sample percentages would be less than 55% and one half would be more. Also, if the standard deviation of this normal distribution of sample percentages were added to and subtracted from the universe percentage the resulting interval would contain 68.26% of the sample percentages. Moreover, if we let p_u be the symbol for the universe percent and $\sigma_{\%}$ be the symbol for the standard deviation of the percentage distribution, we could set up the intervals $p_u \pm 1.96\sigma_{\%}$, $p_u \pm 2.58\,\sigma_{\%}$, and $p_u \pm 3\sigma_{\%}$, and these intervals would contain 95%, 99%, and 99.73%, respectively, of all the sample percentages (see Chart 8-8). Therefore, the basis for analysis of sample percentages is identical to that for an analysis of sample means.

The Standard Error of a Percentage

A standard deviation of a normal distribution of sample percentages, $\sigma_{\%}$, is usually called a *standard error of a percentage.* Since, in actual practice, we do not have a distribution of percentages, the standard error is computed with the formula

$$\sigma_{\%} = \sqrt{\frac{p_u q_u}{N}}$$

where p_u is the universe percentage, q_u is $100 - p_u$ and N is the sample size. In most situations, however, the universe percentage is not known, therefore the formula

$$\sigma_{\%} = \sqrt{\frac{p_s q_s}{N}}$$

is used as an estimate. In this formula p_s is the sample percentage and q_s is $100 - p_s$.

For the percentage distribution of smoking students from samples of 400, the calculation is

$$\sigma_{\%} = \sqrt{\frac{p_u q_u}{N}} = \sqrt{\frac{55 \times 45}{400}} = \sqrt{\frac{2475}{400}} = \sqrt{6.19} = 2.5$$

Therefore,

$$p_u \pm 3\sigma_{\%} = 55 \pm 3(2.5) = 55 \pm 7.5 = 47.5\% \text{ to } 62.5\%$$

This interval would contain 0.9973 of the sample percentages. Moreover, the probability is 0.9973 that the percentage of smokers from any random sample of 400 students would

*Percentages are analyzed in this chapter. However, the results and conclusion will be the same if sample proportions (decimal fractions) are used.

fall in the interval 47.5% to 62.5%. Also, the probability of a sample percentage falling in any specified interval could be determined from the table of areas of the normal curve. Suppose, for example, that we wanted to know the probability that 60% or more of the students in a sample will be smokers. First, we calculate

$$\frac{x}{\sigma} = \frac{p_s - q_u}{\sigma_{\%}} = \frac{60 - 55}{2.5} = \frac{5}{2.5} = 2$$

In this formula p_s is the hypothetical minimum limit of the sample percentage being tested. The result, 2, tells us that two or more standard errors separate the universe and hypothetical percentages, and Table A-3 in Appendix E reveals that a separation of two standard errors or less, in one direction, can be expected 47.72 times out of 100; therefore, a separation of two standard errors or more could be expected 2.28 times out of 100, so 0.0228 is the probability that a sample would include 60% or more smokers. Chart 8-9 pictures this analysis, with the shaded area showing the interval containing percentages of 60 and more

Chart 8-8. Normal curve of sample percentages around a universe percentage.

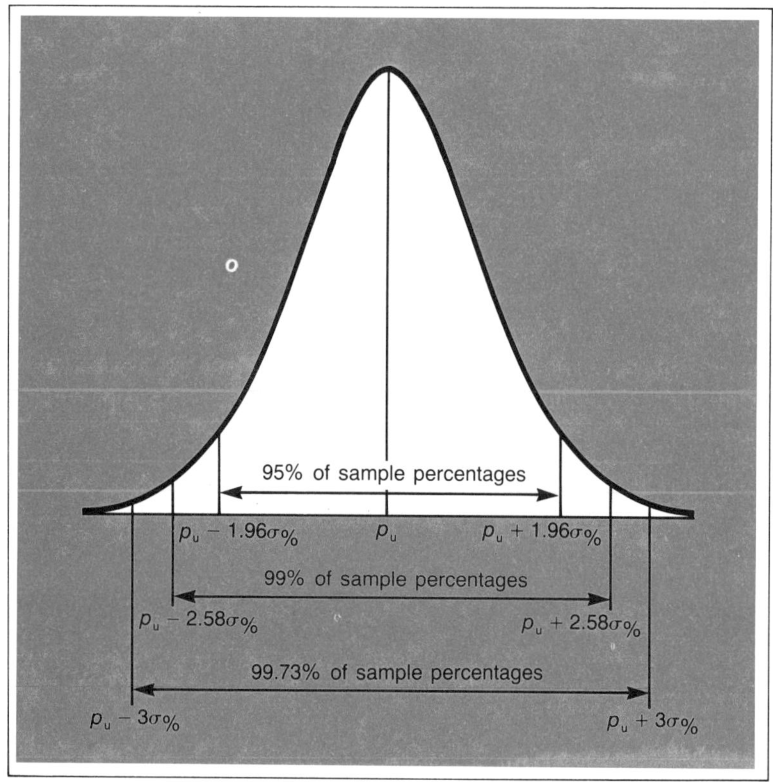

Chart 8-9. Normal curve of sample percentages around a universe percentage of 55.

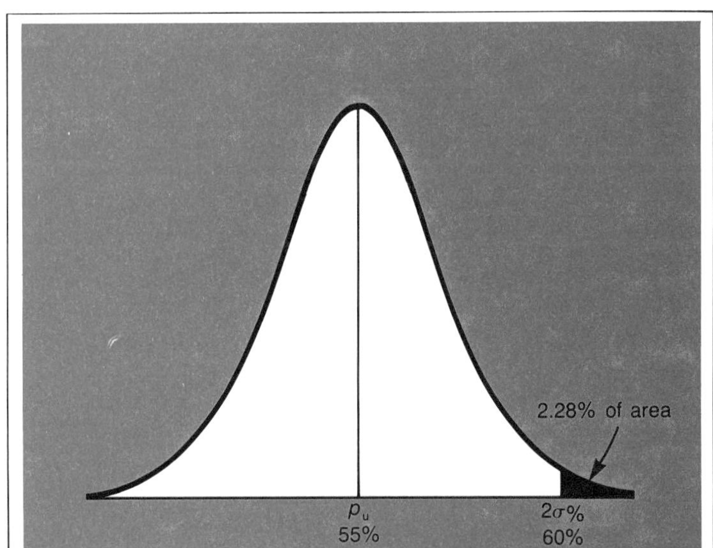

Confidence Intervals for Universe Percentages—Infinite Universe

In most practical sampling problems we do not know what the universe percentage is and will probably never know. In fact, a prime reason for sampling the universe is to learn the approximate value of the universe percent, and this can be done with confidence intervals. This methods of determining confidence intervals for universe percentages are similar to those for establishing confidence intervals for universe means. For example, we learned that $\overline{X}_s \pm 1.96\sigma_{\bar{x}}$ is the 0.95 confidence interval for the universe mean. Similarly, $p_s \pm 1.96\sigma_{\%}$ is the 0.95 confidence interval for the universe percentage. Two other common confidence intervals for a universe percentage are $p_s \pm 2.58\sigma_{\%}$ and p_s $3\sigma_{\%}$, which are respectively, the 0.99 and 0.9973 intervals.

An analysis of a random sample of 1000 women in the United States revealed that 480 of them drink beer. The estimate of the standard error of the percentage is

$$\sigma_{\%} = \sqrt{\frac{p_s q_s}{N}} = \sqrt{\frac{48 \times 52}{1000}} = \sqrt{\frac{2496}{1000}} = \sqrt{2.496} = 1.6$$

The interval $p_s \pm 1.96\sigma_{\%}$ is

$$48 \pm 1.96\ (1.6) = 48 \pm 3.2 = 44.8\% \text{ to } 51.2\%$$

therefore, we can be 95% confident that the true percentage of women beer drinkers lies between those two percentages. Moreover, we can be 2.5% confident that the true percentage is 44.8% or smaller and 2.5% confident that the true percentage of women beer drinkers is 51.2% or more.

If we want to know the degree of confidence that we can have that 50% or more of the women in the universe drink beer, we compute, using p_h to represent 50%,

$$\frac{x}{\sigma} = \frac{p_s - p_h}{\sigma_{\%}} = \frac{48 - 50}{1.6} = \frac{2}{1.6} = 1.25$$

According to Table A-3 (Appendix E), $x/\sigma = 1.25$ is 0.3944. Therefore, 0.5000 − 0.3944 = 0.1056 = 10.6 chances out of 100 that the true percentage of women beer drinkers is 50% or more.

Confidence Intervals for Universe Percentages—Finite Universe

If the random sample of 1,000 women in the previous example came from a city with only 5,000 women, then the computation of the standard error of the percentage would require the use of the finite correction factor previously discussed, because the sample comprises more than 1% of the universe. Under this situation,

$$\sigma_{\%} = \sqrt{\frac{p_s q_s}{N} \times \frac{M - N}{M - 1}} = \sqrt{\frac{48 \times 52}{1000} \times \frac{5000 - 1000}{4999}} = 1.4$$

and the interval $p_s \pm 1.96\sigma_{\%}$ is 48% ± 1.96(1.4%) = 48% ± 2.7% = 45.3% to 50.7%. Thus the 95% confidence interval for the true percentage of women beer drinkers is smaller than it was when the universe was large and the sample was relatively small.

Predetermining the Size of a Random Sample—Infinite Universe

The sample size needed to get a desired accuracy with a specified degree of confidence can be calculated with the formula

$$\sigma_{\%} = \sqrt{\frac{p_u q_u}{N}}$$

If, for example a research agency wanted to know within two percentage points, and with 95% confidence, what percentage of men in the United States use safety razors, the maximum size sample required would be calculated by substituting in the formula to get

$$\frac{2}{1.96} = \sqrt{\frac{50 \times 50}{N}}$$

In this formula, $\sigma_{\%} = 2/1.96$ because ±2% of the true percent equals $\pm 1.96\sigma_{\%}$, which is the 95% certainty interval. When the maximum percentage in the universe is not known, p_u is assumed to be 50%. A p_u of 50% will give the largest possible value of N. Solving for N gives

$$\frac{4}{3.8416} = \frac{2500}{N}$$

so

$$4N = 3.8416\,(2500) = 9604$$

and

$$n = 2401$$

Therefore, a random sample of 2401 men would give the desired precision. The general rule in a calculation of this kind is: Maximize p_u, that is make it as close to 50% as you would reasonably expect it to be.

Predetermining the Size of a Random Sample—Finite Universe

Suppose that the research agency wanted to know within two percentage points and with 95% confidence what percentage of the men in City *A* use safety razors if the city has only 2,000 men. One can see that the answer, 2401, calculated for the entire United States would be illogical because the sample size exceeds the size of the universe. The sample size for City *A* should be calculated with the standard error formula for a finite universe. The calculation is:

$$\sigma_{\%} = \sqrt{\frac{p_u q_u}{N} \times \frac{M - N}{M - 1}}$$

$$\frac{2}{1.96} = \sqrt{\frac{50 \times 50}{N} \times \frac{2000 - N}{1999}}$$

$$\frac{4}{3.8416} = \frac{2500}{N} \times \frac{2000 - N}{1999} = \frac{5{,}000{,}000 - 2500N}{1999N}$$

$$7996N = 19{,}208{,}000 - 9604N$$

$$17{,}600N = 19{,}208{,}000$$

$$N = 1091$$

Which means that a random sample of 1091 would be sufficient to achieve the required precision and confidence level.

STANDARD ERRORS AND SAMPLE SIZE

The larger a random sample, the closer the sample mean is to the universe mean. Therefore, as the sample size increases the standard error of the mean decreases. To illustrate, suppose that $\sigma_u = 10$ and $N = 100$. Then,

$$\sigma_{\bar{x}} = \frac{10}{\sqrt{100}} = 1$$

However, if $\sigma_u = 10$ and $N = 400$ then

$$\sigma_{\bar{x}} = \frac{10}{\sqrt{400}} = 0.5$$

This principle also applies to the standard error of a percentage. For example, if $p_u =$ 50% and $N = 100$, then

$$\sigma_{\%} = \sqrt{\frac{p_u q_u}{N}} = \sqrt{\frac{50 \times 50}{100}} = 5\%$$

But if $p_u = 50\%$ and $N = 400$ then

$$\sigma_{\%} = \sqrt{\frac{50 \times 50}{400}} = 2.5\%$$

These illustrations show that the error of a sample mean or sample percentage can be reduced by increasing the size of the sample. For example, assume that a random sample of 100 items that we have selected resulted in a standard deviation of \$150 and a standard error of the mean of \$15, and we desired to reduce the standard error of the mean to \$10. The sample size needed to achieve this reduction can be determined by the substitution of σ_u and the desired standard error into the formula $\sigma_{\bar{x}} = \sigma_u/\sqrt{N}$. Thus, $10 = 150/\sqrt{N}$. Solving, we find $N = 225$. Therefore, the sample must be increased by 125 items.

REVIEW QUESTIONS

1. What is a probability sample? What is a simple random sample?
2. Why are samples studied
3. Why might you use a cluster sample of households in an area rather than a simple random sample drawn from a directory giving addresses of households?
4. Which would be a better sample of a universe, a nonrandom sample of 50% of the universe or a random sample of 1% of the universe? Discuss and justify your answer.
5. Why is a table of random numbers useful in selecting probability samples?
6. What is a normal curve?

7. What types of data will be normally distributed?

8. Define standard error of the mean, standard error of a percentage, and standard error of a difference.

9. Discuss the role of the normal curve in analysis of sample data.

10. What is a confidence interval? What are the most commonly used confidence intervals?

11. What shape of curve will be formed by means of small samples when the samples are of the same size and are drawn from the same universe?

12. When would the Student's *t* distribution be used to analyze sample means?

PROBLEMS

1. A recent census of housing in an area with 50,000 units revealed that the mean monthly rent of the units is $287 and the standard deviation of the monthly rent is $50. What is the probability that a simple random sample of 100 of these units would reveal (1) a mean monthly rent of $275 or less, (2) a mean monthly rent between $272 and $302, (3) a mean monthly rent between $280 and $300?

2. A class studying wage and salary administration selected a sample of 100 secretaries in a large metropolitan area that has over 10,000 secretaries. The mean weekly earnings of the secretaries calculated from the sample was $152. If the mean weekly earnings (universe mean) and the standard deviation of the earnings of the universe were $150 and $25, respectively, could you believe that the sample of 100 was a simple random sample? Why?

3. A simple random sample of 625 camera batteries from a large production run shows that the mean life was 150 hours under normal use. If the sample standard deviation was 25 hours, what is the 0.95 confidence interval of the mean life of all batteries in the production run? Could the true mean be as high as 160 hours?

4. A simple random sample of students at a university with 40,000 students shows that the mean and standard deviation of the annual incomes of their families are $18,500 and $3,750, respectively. If 225 were in the sample, what is the 0.99 confidence interval for the mean of families of all the students in the university? What would the 0.99 interval be if the university had only 1,000 students?

5. A random sample of 500 of the 5,000 outstanding loans of a personal finance company reveals that the mean and the standard deviation of the amounts owed are $98 and $20, respectively. What are the chances that the true total amount owed on the 5,000 loans is $500,000 or more?

6. A large Wisconsin company looking for a new site wants to know the mean wage of typists in the Milwaukee metropolitan area within $4 of the true mean wage with 99% certainty. If it estimates the standard deviation of the typists' wages to be a maximum of $12, how many typists should the company include in a random sample to get the desired accuracy? If the company wanted the sample mean to be within $2 of the true mean, how large should the sample be?

7. A research agency needs to estimate the mean family income in area. It desired 95% certainty that the estimate will be within \$100 of the true mean family income. The agency feels that the standard deviation of the incomes could not exceed \$800. How many families are needed in a simple random sample to provide the desired precision if the population is infinite? If the population has only 1,000 families?

8. Devise a sampling plan and use it to calculate a 0.99 confidence interval for the total number of words in this text, from the first page of Chapter 1 to the last page of the last chapter.

9. A random sample of 17 auto damage claim records for the past year in a large insurance company shows the mean and standard deviation of the claims to be \$840 and \$200, respectively. Determine the 0.95 confidence interval for the mean of all of the company's damage claims for that year.

10. The number of customers served in one week in each of 10 restaurants in the Big Daddy chain is given below. If the 10 were randomly chosen what is the 98% confidence interval for the mean number served in all of the Big Daddy restaurants?

NUMBER OF CUSTOMERS	
800	600
700	1,000
1,100	1,200
900	500
1,200	1,300

11. A random sample of 26 transister radio batteries lasted an average of 112 hours under identical constant use. The standard deviation of the sample was 18 hours. Construct a 0.99 confidence interval for the true mean life of batteries in the inventory from which the sample was drawn. Also determine the minimum mean life that could be expected with 95% certainty.

12. According to the Municipal Gas Company in city X, 68% of the city's households heat with gas. The percent of a sample of 1,000 households in the City that heat with gas is 70%. Assuming the gas company figure is right, could this sample be a simple random sample? Why? What is the probability that a simple random sample of 1,000 households would show that 70% or more heat with gas?

13. If 50% of the one million auto drivers in a state have gasoline credit cards, what is the probability that a random sample of 1,000 drivers would yield a percentage of 52 or more?

14. A simple random sample of automobile owners in a state reveals that 60% use snow tires. If 225 were in the sample, what is the 0.95 confidence interval for the universe percent?

15. A simple random sample of 8,000 households in a metropolitan area of 400,000 showed that 55% own power lawn mowers. How likely is it that 56% or more in the universe own power mowers? Compute the 0.99 confidence interval for the universe percent.

16. What would the 0.99 confidence interval be in Problem 15 if the area had only 40,000 households?

17. A chamber of commerce will support a certain legislative bill if it can be 99% certain that 50% or more of its members favor the bill. In a simple random sample of 200 of its 1,000 members 55% say they favor the bill. Will the chamber give its support? Why?

18. A factory-locating company wants to know within five percentage points and with 99% certainty the percentage of the one million women in a labor market area that would work in a factory for $3.00 per hour. How large should a simple random sample of the women be to get the desired precision?

19. If the universe in Problem 18 consisted of only 800 women, how large a sample would be needed?

20. By what percentage must a simple random sample be increased to reduce the standard error of the percent by 10%? (Hint: set up your own problem.)

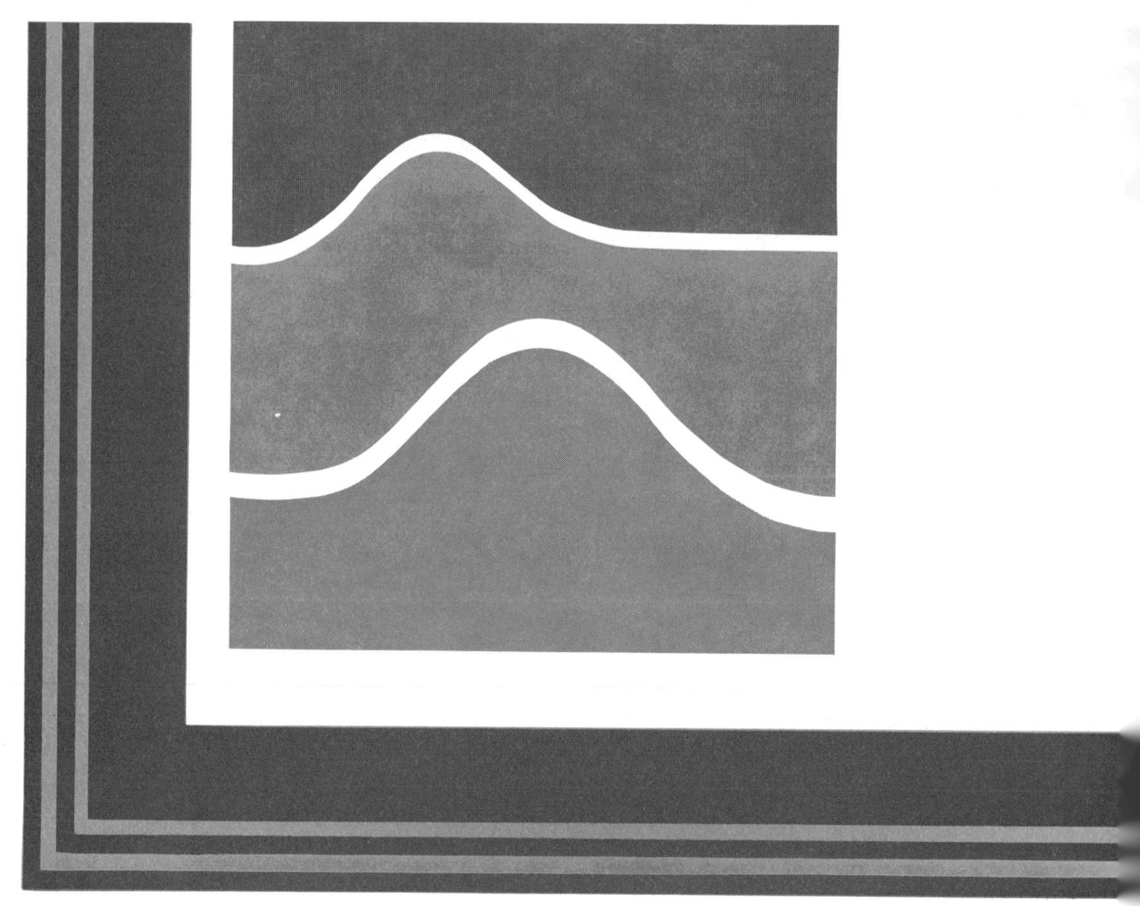

9

Hypothesis Testing

Chapter 8 discussed sampling, sampling, error and how the standard error of the mean and standard error of a percent are used for establishing confidence intervals which are useful for making decisions. In this chapter you can build on your understanding from Chapter 8 and learn more ways that the normal and *t* distributions are used in making decisions.

Decisions of business executives and professional people are often based on assumptions or statements they accept as true even though they cannot prove them to be true or do not wish to spend the time and money in a complete census study which would be required to prove or disprove the truth of the statements. Such statements are called *hypotheses*.

Hypothesis Testing with Samples

If a hypothesis concerns the value of the mean of a universe, a universe percentage or some other measure, it can often be "tested" for its validity with the use of a simple random sample of the universe. However, "Hypothesis" can never be *proved* nor *disproved* with sample data.

Both the normal distribution and the Student's *t* distribution are used to test hypotheses. When one or the other is to be used the normal distribution should be used when a large random sample is selected. The *t* distribution may or may not be used when a small sample is selected. The availability of information on the universe and the particular hypothesis will also be factors that will help determine which distribution should be used in a test.

TEST OF A HYPOTHESIS WHEN $\overline{X}_u$ AND σ_u ARE KNOWN

In Chapter 8 one of the problems stated that a census study six months ago showed that the mean of the weekly earnings of stenographers in a large city ($\overline{X}_u$) was $150 and the standard deviation of their earnings (σ_u) was $25. Assume that it has been suggested that the mean weekly earnings of the stenographers today is not the same as that of six months ago but we feel it is still the same and plan to test the *null hypothesis* that it is. We will do this, but first we will discuss the null hypothesis.

Null Hypothesis

A *null hypothesis* is a hypothesis of *no difference* between two means. A null hypothesis is never proved nor disproved when sample data are used in the test but a certain degree of doubt about its credibility can be established. If its credibility is highly doubted then it must be rejected and declared false. For every null hypothesis there is an alternative hypothesis that *there is a difference* and when the null hypothesis is rejected the alternative hypothesis is accepted. A null hypothesis is tested by computing the number of standard errors that separate two values, and then determining whether the difference between the two is significant. A significant difference is one that is too large to attribute to random errors of sampling. Therefore, to make the test we must decide what a significant difference will be. This should ordinarily be done, *before* we compute the sample mean, by choosing the probability level to be used for rejection of the null hypothesis. The probability level chosen depends on the risk we are willing to take in rejecting a true hypothesis. The choice will depend on the nature of the problem, but the most commonly used probability levels are 0.05 and 0.01. When an analyst uses a 0.05 level, he is willing to take 5 chances out of 100 that he will reject a *true hypothesis*.

Type I and Type II Errors

Rejecting a true hpothesis is called a *Type I error*. Accepting a false hypothesis is a *Type II error*. The smaller the chance of making a Type I error, the greater the chance of making a Type II error.

Both of these errors will be more fully explained after we discuss the two-tailed and one-tailed tests.

The Two-Tailed Test

In the problem above, assume that we select a sample of 625 stenographers to test our null hypothesis that their mean earnings are still \$150, and we find their mean weekly earnings to be \$155. This null hypothesis, H_o, and the alternative hypothesis, H_a, may be stated symbolically as:

$$H_o\colon \overline{X}_u = \$150 \quad \text{(There has been no change)}$$

$$H_a\colon \overline{X}_u \neq 150 \quad \text{(There has been a change)}$$

The 0.05 level for both tails of the normal curve will be used to make the test, which is a test of the difference between the universe mean of \$150 and the sample mean of \$155 to determine if it is significant. This will be a *two-tailed test* because we are not concerned whether the difference of $5 between the two means is negative or positive. To make this test the significance ratio, z, is computed, and if it is found to be less than 1.96, the hypothesis is accepted. If it is larger than 1.96, the hypothesis is rejected because a difference of 1.96 standard errors or more in either direction could occur only 5 times out of 100 because of sampling errors. The areas of the normal curve in which such differences could fall are shaded in Chart 9-1.

Calculations for our problem are

$$\sigma_{\bar{x}} = \frac{\sigma_u}{\sqrt{N}} = \frac{25}{\sqrt{625}} = 1$$

and

$$z = \frac{\bar{X}_s - \bar{X}_u}{\sigma_{\bar{x}}} = \frac{155 - 150}{1} = \frac{5}{1} = 5$$

The null hypothesis is rejected and the alternative hypothesis is accepted. This difference of 5 standard errors is significant because it is too large to attribute to random errors of sampling. In fact, the probability of getting a difference of 5 standard errors or more, in either direction, is so small that it is not included in Table A-3, Appendix E. Since the

Chart 9-1. Two-tailed test (0.05 level).

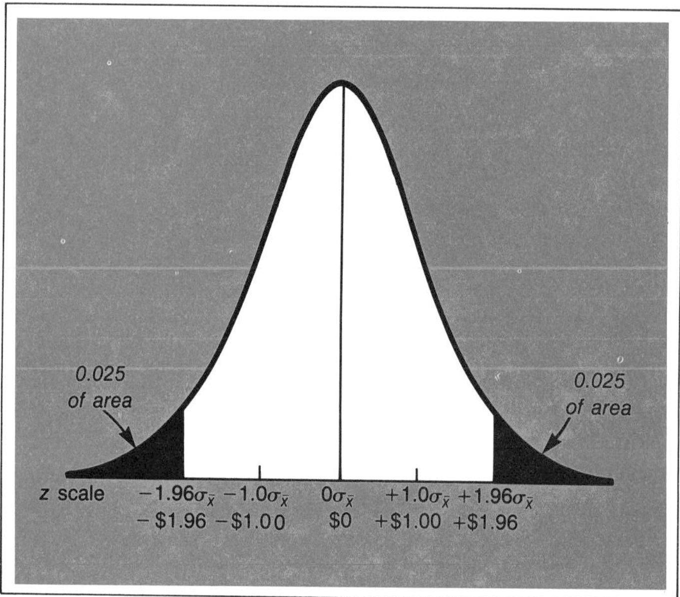

Standard error differences between $\bar{X}_u$ and $\bar{X}_s$ and differences between $\bar{X}_u$ and $\bar{X}_s$ in dollars

hypothesis has been rejected, we would conclude that the mean earnings of all stenographers in the city had *changed* since the census was taken.

The One-Tailed Test

The alternative hypothesis for the two-tailed test we just made was that the earnings had *changed*. If our alternative hypothesis had been that their earnings had *increased* then we would have made a one-tailed test of the null hypothesis. In a one-tailed test we always hypothesize that a change will be in one direction only.

Chart 9-2 shows the area of rejection for this test at the 0.05 level to be that beyond 1.645 standard errors in the right-hand tail of the curve. Therefore, if the significance ratio, z, were found to be 1.645 or more, the null hypothesis would be rejected. Since the ratio in our test is 5, the hypothesis is rejected and we would conclude that the sample is from a population with a mean greater than $150. However, this rejection could result in one of two types of errors.

Chart 9-2. One-tailed test, right side (0.05 level).

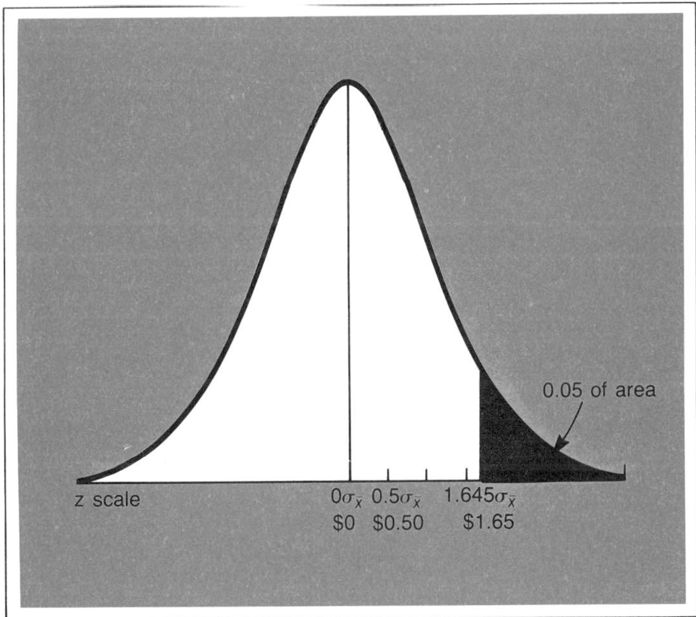

Standard error differences between $\bar{X}_u$ and $\bar{X}_s$ and differences between $\bar{X}_u$ and $\bar{X}_s$ in dollars

Type I and Type II Errors

Type I Error

If a null hypothesis is true but is declared to be false, then a Type I error has been made. The probability of making a Type I error is the significance level which is used to test the null hypothesis.

Since the analyst chooses the significance level for a test, he therefore chooses the probability of making a Type I error. For example, if he chooses a 0.05 significance level, then the probability that he will make a Type I error is 0.05. If he selects the 0.01 level, then the probability that he will make a Type I error is 0.01. If the probability of making a Type I error were 0.05 then the probability of making a Type II error would be less than it would be if the probability of making a Type I error were 0.01. However, the probability of making a Type II error is usually unknown.

Type II error. In both the two-tailed test and the one-tailed test of our previous examples, the probability of making a Type I error was 0.05, but the probability of making a Type II error was not known.

Type II Error

Since a Type II error is made by accepting a hypothesis as true when it is false, the exact probability of making a Type II error cannot be determined because we do not know how false the hypothetical value is—if it is false.

However, we can determine what the probability of making a Type II error would be given the true universe value. For example, if the true mean earnings of stenographers in the universe, $\overline{X}_u$, were \$151 rather than $\overline{X}_h$, the hypothesized mean of \$150, then we could calculate the probability of having made a Type II error, which is the probability that the hypothesized mean will fall in the acceptance area when the hypothesis is not true. Chart 9-3 pictures the acceptance area (unshaded) if the true mean were \$151. Using figures from the chart, calculations of the probability are as follows

$$z = \frac{151 - 148.04}{1} = +2.96$$ (which incorporates 0.4985 of the area under the curve)

$$z = \frac{151 - 151.96}{1} = -0.96$$ (which incorporates 0.3315 of the area under the curve)

Therefore, 0.4985 + 0.3315 = 0.8300, which is the probability of making a Type II error under the conditions stated.

It may not be necessary to calculate a Type II error. Given the value of the true mean the probability of making a Type II error can be read from an *operating characteristic curve*. A curve for reading the probability of making a Type II error at the 0.05 level in a two-tailed test is shown in Chart 9-4. The probability is read from the vertical scale and an example of how to get a reading when $\overline{X}_u - \overline{X}_h = 1\,\sigma_{\bar{x}}$ is shown. A further examination of Type II errors is beyond the scope of this text, but it should be mentioned that in a particular analysis one sometimes must compare the consequences of making a Type I and a Type II error before deciding on the significance level to use in the test of the hypothesis. Remember that in a real problem you will never know the probability of making a Type II error but you should remember that the smaller the probability of making a Type I error, the greater the probability of making a Type II error.

Chart 9-3. Probability of making a type II error in a two-tailed test at the 0.05 level when $\overline{X}_u$ = 151, $\overline{X}_h$ = 150 and $\sigma_{\bar{x}}$ = 1.

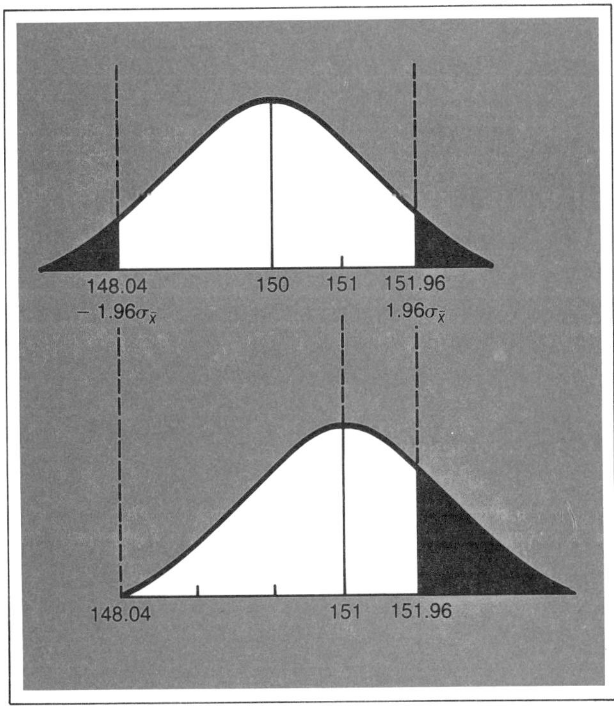

A Realistic Situation for Considering Type I and Type II Errors

A production process has been set up to produce thousands of steel balls with a mean diameter of 0.600 of an inch, which are to be used in the manufacture of roller bearings. Some small variation in diameter of the balls is expected due to a number of causes; nevertheless, the mean diameter should remain 0.600. Assume that production has been underway for some time and the production manager wishes to know if the process is still turning out balls with a mean of 0.600. To make this determination it would be possible to actually measure the diameter of all of the balls turned out by the process but this would be time-consuming and expensive. The alternative would be to make a judgement based on a sample selected from the universe which would consist of all the balls coming from the established production process.

To judge whether the universe mean diameter is still 0.600 of an inch, the manager hypothesizes that the universe mean is 0.600, selects the sample and tests the hypothesis.

If the hypothesis is true and is accepted, no error has been made and no readjustment of the production process is necessary. If the hypothesis is false and is rejected, no error has been made but a readjustment is needed. If the hypothesis is true and is declared to be false, then a Type I error has been made. If the hypothesis is false but has been accepted as true, a Type II error has been made.

If a Type I error has been made, the production process will be readjusted even though a readjustment is not needed. This could be expensive because production would cease during the readjustment period. If a Type II error has been made the process needs readjustment but will not be readjusted, which will result in the production of balls that are either too small or too large. Thus, the result will be faulty roller bearings which will mean sales returns and possible loss of customers. Therefore, the consequences and costs of making a Type I and Type II error should be considered and compared in order to establish the level of significance for testing the hypothesis.

TEST OF A HYPOTHESIS WHEN $\overline{X}_u$ AND σ_u ARE NOT KNOWN

In most sampling problems we do not know the universe mean, the standard deviation, or the value of any other parameter (universe value), so we make use of the sample information to test hypotheses. For example, when testing a hypothesis about a universe mean we use an estimate of standard error of the mean. The formula for a large sample from an infinite universe, which was explained in Chapter 8, is

$$\sigma_{\bar{x}} = \frac{\sigma_s}{\sqrt{N - 1}}$$

the following problem will exemplify the testing of hypotheses when $\overline{X}_u$ and σ_u are unknown.

Chart 9-4. Operating characteristic curve for a 0.05 significance test.

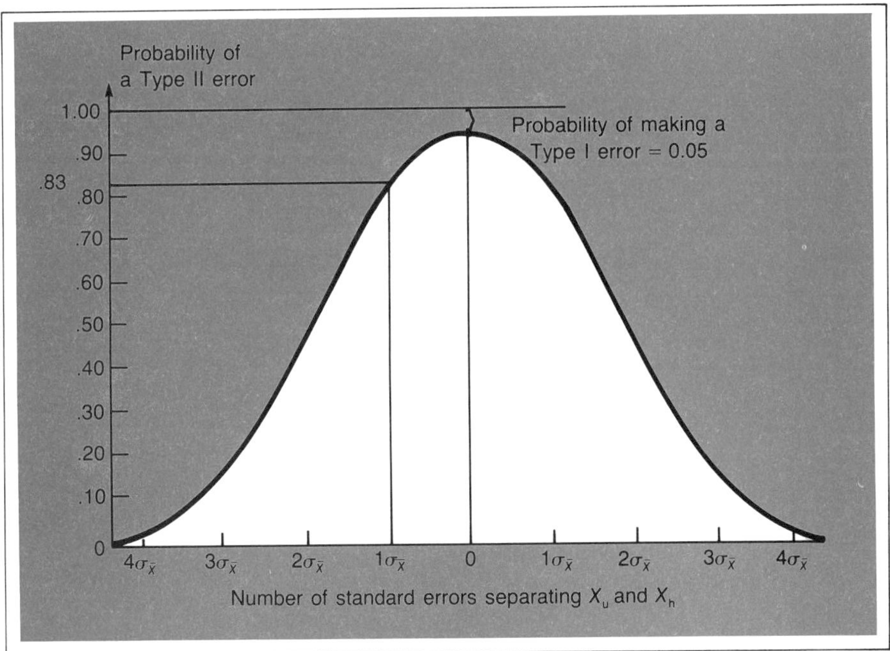

A home construction company has been told that the mean value of single family dwelling units in a large community is \$40,000. It decides to select a simple random sample of 226 of the homes to test at the 0.01 significance level the hypothesis that the mean is \$40,000. The 226 homes are found to have a mean value of \$39,000 and a standard deviation of \$9,000, therefore,

$$\sigma_{\bar{x}} = \frac{\sigma_s}{\sqrt{N-1}} = \frac{\$9{,}000}{225} = \frac{\$9{,}000}{15} = \$600$$

and if we let $\overline{X}_h$ be the hypothetical mean of \$40,000, then

$$z = \frac{\overline{X}_S - \overline{X}_h}{\sigma_{\bar{x}}} = \frac{39{,}000 - 40{,}000}{600} = \frac{-1{,}000}{600} = -1.67$$

which is larger than -2.58, the significance ratio for this two-tailed test at the 0.01 level. Therefore, the hypothesis is accepted.

A two-tailed test was made because the construction company did not know in advance whether the observed difference between $\overline{X}_S$ and $\overline{X}_h$ would be positive or negative. Thus, in a two-tailed test we consider the fact that the sample mean could be either larger or smaller than the universe mean. If the construction company had tested the multivalued Null hypothesis that the mean value of homes in the community was

$40,000 or more, then a one-tailed significance test would have been appropriate because the difference to be considered would be in one direction only. Here the significance ratio at the 0.01 level for the one-tailed test is −2.33 (see Table A3). So the null hypothesis that the mean is $40,000 or more would be accepted because the computed ratio, −1.67, is larger. If the sample mean had been larger than $40,000 no significance test would have been required in order to accept the null hypothesis.

Symbolic statements of the null hypothesis and the alternative hypothesis involved in this one-tailed test are as follows.

$$H_o : \overline{X}_h = \overline{X}_u \geqslant \$40{,}000$$

$$H_a : \overline{X}_h = \overline{X}_u < \$40{,}000$$

The hypothesis that the hypothetical mean equals the true mean which is equal to or larger than $40,000 is the null hypothesis because it is the one we attempt to validate or reject. The shaded area in the left tail of Chart 9-5 is the area of rejection of the null hypothesis. If the difference between $\overline{X}_S$ and $\overline{X}_h$ had been more than $1,398 (2.33 × $600), then $\overline{X}_o$ would have been rejected because such a difference would be too large to attribute to random errors of sampling.

Chart 9-5. One-tailed test, left side, 0.01 level.

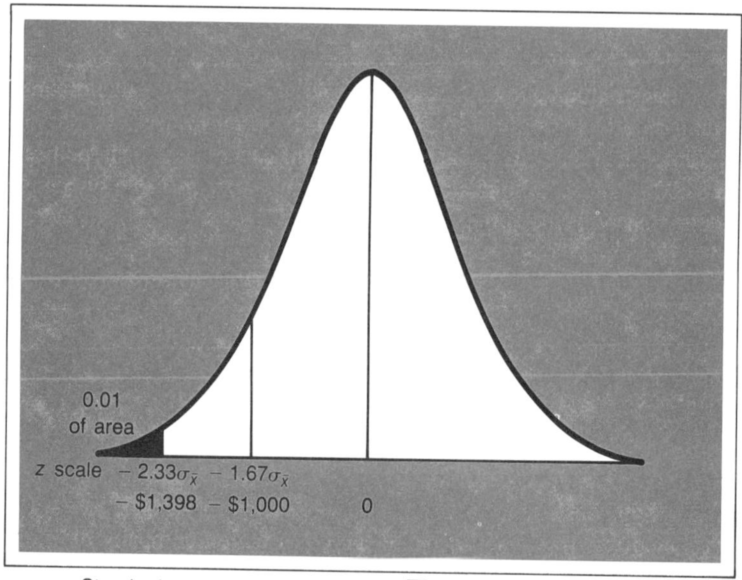

Standard error differences between $\overline{X}_s$ and $\overline{X}_h$ and differences between $\overline{X}_s$ and $\overline{X}_h$ in dollars.

Keep in mind that all significance tests such as we have made we are testing a *null hypothesis* by seeing whether the difference between a sample mean and a hypothetical universe mean is or is not significant. Whether the test should be a two-tailed or a one-tailed test depends upon the wording of our hypothesis.

Analysis of Differences Between Sample Means

Occasionally, an analysis of two sample means is made to determine if the two samples represent the same universe.* This type of analysis is made in relation to a normal distribution of differences between paired means computed from a large number of independently drawn random samples from the same universe. The standard deviation of this distribution of differences is called the *the standard error of a difference between means,* and when the samples are reasonably large and independent, it may be calculated with the formula

$$\sigma_{D_{\bar{x}}} = \sqrt{\sigma^2_{\bar{x}_1} + \sigma^2_{\bar{x}_2}}$$

where $\sigma_{D_{\bar{x}}}$ is the symbol for the standard error of the difference, $\sigma_{\bar{x}_1}$ is the square of the standard error of the mean computed for the first sample, and $\sigma_{\bar{x}_2}$ is the square of the standard error of the mean computed for the second sample. In an analysis of this sort, a test is made to determine if there is a significant difference between the two sample means. Suppose, for example, that a labor union claims that a random sample of 145 employees in manufacturing industries in a city revealed a mean hourly earning of $5.50 and a standard deviation of $0.60. Suppose also that an employer's association claimed that its own sample of 150 employees shows that they earn $5.20 per hour with a standard deviation of $0.66. Which is right? Based on the information given, we cannot know, but we can determine the likelihood that both the labor union and the employer's association sampled the same universe of manufacturing workers. Here the null hypothesis is that the difference between the two sample means is not significant.

If we let X_{u_2} represent the mean of the universe for the labor union sample and $\overline{X}_{u_2}$ represent the mean of the universe of the employers association then an equivalent statement of the null hypothesis would be $\overline{X}_{u_1} = \overline{X}_{u_2}$, and $\overline{X}_{u_1} \neq \overline{X}_{u_2}$ would be the alternative hypothesis. The standard error of the difference formula

$$\sigma_{D_{\bar{x}}} = \sqrt{\sigma^2_{\bar{x}_1} + \sigma^2_{\bar{x}_2}}$$

may be written

$$\sigma_{D_{\bar{x}}} = \sqrt{\frac{{\sigma_1}^2}{N_1} + \frac{{\sigma_2}^2}{N_2}}$$

*Also, an analysis can be made to determine if two populations have the same mean. When this is done it is assumed that the variances, σ^2, of the two populations are equal.

so that

$$\sigma_{D_{\bar{x}}} = \sqrt{\frac{(0.60)^2}{145} + \frac{(0.66)^2}{150}}$$

$$= \sqrt{\frac{0.3600}{145} + \frac{0.4356}{150}} = \sqrt{0.0054} = \$0.07$$

Now the hypothesis is tested by determining how many $\sigma_{D_{\bar{x}}}$ values separate the two means by computing

$$z = \frac{\overline{X}_{S_1} - \overline{X}_{S_2}}{\sigma_{D_{\bar{x}}}}$$

where $\overline{X}_{S_1}$ is the mean of the first sample and $\overline{X}_{S_2}$ is the mean of the second sample. The analyst must decide on the probability level for accepting or rejecting the hypothesis. Remember that the level chosen depends upon the chances the analyst is willing to take that he will err in his acceptance or rejection of the hypothesis. If the hypothesis is tested at the 1% level, the z ratio must be less than 2.58 to be accepted. In this illustration

$$z = \frac{5.50 - 5.20}{0.07} = \frac{0.30}{0.07} = 4.3$$

Therefore, at the 1% significant level, the null hypothesis is rejected; the difference between the two means is real and not due to random errors of sampling because 4.3 is greater than 2.58.

We cannot conclude from this analysis that the labor union's sample is better than the employer association's, or vice versa. All we can say is that the two samples represent different universes of manufacturing workers, that is, $\overline{X}_{u_1} \neq \overline{X}_{u_2}$

HYPOTHESIS TESTS—SMALL SAMPLES

Chapter 8 discussed the Student's t distribution and the general conditions under which it—rather than the normal distribution—would be used to analyze sample data. One condition was that when the standard error of the mean is estimated with the use of the sample standard deviation and another was that when the sample contained fewer than 30 items. The use of 30 as the dividing point between small samples and large samples is somewhat traditional with analysts and is based on the fact that the t distribution for samples of 30 items or more closely approximates the normal distribution. We will follow that tradition in the following tests of hypothesis using means of small samples.

Testing a Hypothesis About a Universe Mean

A large manufacturing firm needs an estimate of the mean number of times its employees have been late in the past year. The personnel director of the firm hypothesizes that the mean is 12. To test this hypothesis a random sample of the attendance records of 26 employees is selected. The mean and standard deviation of the tardinesses of these 26 employees in the past year are 10 and 4 respectively. Should the personnel director's hypothesis be accepted if the 0.05 level is used in a two-tailed test? To answer this question the following calculations are necessary.

$$\sigma_{\bar{x}} = \frac{\sigma_S}{\sqrt{N-1}} = \frac{4}{\sqrt{25}} = 0.8$$

and

$$t = \frac{\overline{X_S} - \overline{X_h}}{\sigma_{\bar{x}}} = \frac{10-12}{0.8} = \frac{-2}{0.8} = -2.5$$

The significance ratio for a two-tailed test at the 0.05 level from the t distribution table (Appendix E) for 25 degrees of freedom is 2.060. Therefore, the hypothesis is not accepted because the difference between the sample mean and the hypothetical universe mean is too large to attribute to random errors of sampling.

If the hypothesis in this problem had been that the mean was 12 or more than a one-tailed test would have been appropriate and the table reading for t at the 0.05 level would have been made from the 0.10 column, which is 1.708. Of course, the hypothesis would still be rejected and in fact be less tenable than it was for the two-tailed test.

Testing Differences Between Means of Small Samples

The procedure for testing differences between means of small samples is the same as that for large samples except the t distribution table for small samples is used. The following problem will exemplify such a test for small samples from large universes.

Random samples of file clerks from two cities were selected to test the null hypothesis that there is no difference in the mean earnings of the clerks in the two cities. In City A the mean and standard deviation of the weekly earnings of a sample of 17 clerks were found to be \$120 and \$20 respectively. In City B a sample of 10 clerks revealed a mean and standard deviation of their weekly earnings of \$128 and \$24, respectively. To test the null hypothesis we must determine if the difference between the two means could have resulted from chance (random errors of sampling). This requires the computation of the standard error of difference between paired means and the t ratio. The following procedure may be used. First, calculate

$$\sigma_{P_o} = \sqrt{\frac{N_1\,\sigma_{S_1}{}^2 + N_2\,\sigma_{S_2}{}^2}{N_1 + N_2 - 2}} = \sqrt{\frac{17(20)^2 + 10(24)^2}{17 + 10 - 2}}$$

$$= \sqrt{\frac{6800 + 5760}{25}} = 22.4143$$

which is a pooled estimate of the standard deviation of the two universes from which the samples were selected. Then calculate

$$\sigma_{\bar{x}_1} = \frac{\sigma_{p_o}}{\sqrt{N_1}} = \frac{22.4143}{\sqrt{17}} = 5.4363$$

and

$$\sigma_{\bar{x}_2} = \frac{\sigma_{p_o}}{\sqrt{N_2}} = \frac{22.4143}{\sqrt{10}} = 7.0880$$

Substituting these standard errors in the formula for the standard error of the difference between paired means we have

$$\sigma_{D_{\bar{x}}} = \sqrt{\sigma^2_{\bar{x}_1} + \sigma^2_{\bar{x}_2}}$$

$$= \sqrt{(5.4363)^2 + (7.0880)^2} = \sqrt{79.793} = 8.93$$

and

$$t = \frac{\overline{X}_{S1} - \overline{X}_{S2}}{\sigma_{\bar{x}}} = \frac{120 - 128}{8.93} = \frac{-8}{8.93} = -0.90$$

To determine if this difference of 0.90 standard errors is significant at the 0.05 level we read from the t table in the 0.05 column at 25 degrees of freedom. There are 25 degrees of freedom because two degrees of freedom were lost from the 27 sample items used in the calculation of the pooled estimate of the standard deviation of the two universes. The table reading is 2.060, therefore, the hypothesis is accepted. It would have been rejected if the two sample means had been separated by more than 2.060 standard errors.

Degrees of freedom. When analyzing the difference between the means of two small samples the degrees of freedom are always equal to the sum of the items in the two samples minus two. This is true because the two samples are combined to get the pooled estimate of the population standard deviation and two degrees of freedom are lost in its calculation. Also, tests of differences between sample means are usually two-tailed tests because we are not often concerned with whether the difference is positive or negative. In fact, since the choice of which sample is to be numbered 1 and which is to be numbered 2 is usually arbitrary, the sign (+ or −) of the difference between the two means is arbitrarily determined.

Shortcut Formula

Calculation of the standard error of the difference between paired means *may* be made quicker with the formula,

$$\sigma_{D_{\bar{x}}} = \sqrt{\left(\frac{N_1\,\sigma_{S1}{}^2 + N_2\,\sigma_{S2}{}^2}{N_1 + N_2 - 2}\right)\left(\frac{N_1 + N_2}{N_1N_2}\right)}$$

For the two samples in the preceding illustration the substitutions and calculations are

$$\sigma_{D_{\bar{x}}} = \sqrt{\left(\frac{17(20)^2 + 10(24)^2}{17 + 10 - 2}\right)\left(\frac{17 + 10}{17 \times 10}\right)}$$

$$= \sqrt{\frac{6800 + 5760}{25} \times \frac{27}{170}} = \sqrt{\frac{339120}{4250}} = 8.93$$

which is exactly the same answer previously calculated.

TESTS OF A HYPOTHESIS ABOUT A UNIVERSE PERCENTAGE

Two-Tailed Test

A hypothesis about a universe percentage can be tested in a manner similar to that used for means. For example, assume that we will test the null hypothesis at the 0.01 level that 60% of all production employees in a large city are unionized. To make the test, a random sample of 400 employees is selected and 55% are found to be unionized. Should we accept the hypothesis? To decide, we use the standard error formula for a sample percentage given in Chapter 8. We can use P_h, the hypothetical percentage, in the formula because, in essence, we want to know if a sample percentage of 55 could be one of all possible sample percentages from samples of 400 that would be distributed normally around a universe percent of 60. Thus,

$$\sigma_{\%} = \sqrt{\frac{P_h q_h}{N}} = \sqrt{\frac{60 \times 40}{400}} = \sqrt{6} = 2.4$$

and

$$z = \frac{x}{\sigma} = \frac{P_s - P_h}{\sigma_{\%}} = \frac{55 - 60}{2.4} = \frac{-5}{2.4} = -2.1$$

The significance ratio in this two-tailed test at the 0.01 level is −2.58, therefore, the hypothesis is accepted.

One-tailed test. Suppose that a manufacturer claims that *at least* 40% of all autos in a city uses its Brand X antifreeze and that we wish to test this claim at the 0.05 level and state:

$$H_o : p_h = p_u \geqslant 40\%$$

$$H_a : p_h = p_u < 40\%$$

Suppose further that we select a simple random sample of 600 auto owners to make the test. If the sample percent is 40% or more then the claim will be accepted. However, if it is less than 40% then a significance test must be made. To illustrate, assume that the sample shows that 38% use Brand X. In this case we wish to determine if the difference between the hypothetical percentage and the sample percent is significant. Since the difference is in one direction only, then the test is one-tailed. To make the test we can use the hypothetical percentage, P_h, to compute the standard error of a percent because in essence we want to know if a sample percentage of 38% could be one of all possible sample percentages from samples of 600 that would be distributed normally around a universe percent of 40%. Therefore,

$$\sigma_{\%} = \sqrt{\frac{P_h q_h}{N}} = \sqrt{\frac{40 \times 60}{600}} = 2$$

and

$$\frac{x}{\sigma} = \frac{P_S - P_h}{\sigma_{\%}} = \frac{38 - 40}{2} = \frac{-2}{2} = -1$$

In this one-tailed test -1.645 is our significance ratio. Since the two percentages are separated by less than 1.645 standard errors, we accept the claim that at least 40% or more use Brand X antifreeze.

Analyzing the Difference Between Two Sample Percentages

Earlier in this chapter, we learned that all possible differences between paired means of large samples from the same universe are normally distributed. So are differences between paired percentages, and because they are, we can determine the probability that two sample percentages have been drawn from the same or identical universes by determining how many standard errors separate the two sample percentages. The formula for the standard error of a difference between sample percentages, when the samples are large and independent, is

$$\sigma_{D\%} = \sqrt{\frac{\bar{p}\bar{q}}{N_{S_1}} + \frac{\bar{p}\bar{q}}{N_{S_2}}}$$

where $\bar{p}$ is the weighted average of the percentages for the two samples, and N_{S_1} and N_{S_2} are the sizes of the first and second samples.

To illustrate, suppose that in city X a random sample of 100 households showed that 36 heat with oil and that in city Y a random sample of 150 households revealed that 60 heat with oil. A logical question is, "Do a greater percentage of homes in city Y use oil heat than in city X?" To answer this question, we test the null hypothesis (whether formally stated or not) that there is no real difference between the true percentages in city X and city Y that heat with oil.

$$\bar{p} = \frac{36 + 60}{100 + 150} = \frac{96}{150} = 38.4\%$$

$$\sigma_{D\%} = \sqrt{\frac{38.4 \times 61.6}{100} + \frac{38.4 \times 61.6}{150}} = \sqrt{39.4239} = 6.3$$

Letting p_{s_1} and p_{s_2} represent the first and second sample percentages

$$z = \frac{x}{\sigma} = \frac{p_{S1} - p_{S2}}{\sigma_{D\%}} = \frac{36 - 40}{6.3} = \frac{4}{6.3} = 0.63$$

Thus, only 0.63 standard errors separate the two sample percentages. If this test were made at either the 0.01 or 0.05 significant levels, we would conclude that there is no significant difference between the two percentages—that is, the difference could easily be due to chance. Therefore, we would accept the hypothesis that the true percentages of homes heating with oil in city X and city Y are the same.

REVIEW QUESTIONS

1. What is a hypothesis? What is a null hypothesis?
2. At what point in the research procedure should a hypothesis be stated?
3. What is a significance level?
4. How does an analyst know which significance level to use in a test?
5. Are hypotheses ever proved? Why?
6. How does an analyst know whether to make a one-tailed test or a two-tailed test of a hypothesis.
7. Define Type I and Type II errors.
8. Can the probability of making a Type II error be determined in a real-life sampling problem?
9. Under what condition should the Student's *t* distribution be used for testing a hypothesis?
10. Under what condition should a hypothesis be accepted?

PROBLEMS

1. The office of vital statistics in a large city claims that the mean age of the citizens who died in the past year was 62 years. A random sample of 170 of the death records for that year showed that the mean and standard deviation of the ages at death to be 65 and 13, respectively. Use the 0.05 significance level and test the hypothesis that the claim is correct.
2. The graduate school of a university advertises that last year's mean starting salary for those receiving M.B.A. degrees was $14,000 per year. However, according to a random sample of 36 of the 360 that received the degrees the mean starting salary was $13,400 and the standard deviation was $3000. Can you believe the university's ad is truthful? Choose your own significance level to make the decision.
3. Calculations from random samples of employees in Company *X* and Company *Y* resulted in the following:

	COMPANY X	*COMPANY Y*
Sample size	145	170
Mean age of employees	37	33
Standard deviation of the ages of the employees	12	13

Use the 0.01 level and test the hypothesis that the mean age of all employees in Company *X* is 35 or less. Also test the hypothesis that the means of the ages of employees in the two companies is the same.

4. Assume that the means and standard deviations in Problem 3 are the same as given but that the sample sizes for Company *X* and Company *Y* are 10 and 17, respectively. Test the hypothesis that the means of the ages of the employees in the two companies are the same.
5. A labor union claims that the mean and standard deviation of the hourly earnings of maintenance carpenters in the United States are $6.00 and $1.50, respectively. A construction contractor's association claims that the mean and standard deviation of their hourly earnings is $7.00 and $2.00. Assuming that the claims of both the union and the contractor's association were based on their own simple random samples of 1000 maintenance carpenters, determine, using the 0.05 level, whether there is any real difference in their claims.
6. Seventeen slide-projector lamps were randomly selected from an inventory of 100,000 and placed in normal use until they burned out. The mean length of life was found to be 24 hours. The standard deviation of their lives was 3 hours. Using a 0.05 significance level, test the hypothesis that the true mean life of the bulbs is at least 25 hours.
7. The amounts of 10 meal checks from each of two cafeterias is presented in Exercise Table 9-1. Test at the 0.05 level the hypothesis that the mean amount of the meal checks in Cafeteria *X* was $2.25. Also, determine if the difference between the means of the two samples could be due to chance. Use the 0.05 level.

EXERCISE TABLE 9-1. Meal Checks from Two Cafeterias for the First Week in January (sample of 10 from each cafeteria).

CAFETERIA X (SAMPLE 1)	*CAFETERIA Y (SAMPLE 2)*
$1.55	$1.73
2.05	2.40
1.20	2.72
2.55	1.95
2.65	2.10
1.90	1.95
2.15	2.00
2.10	2.35
2.00	2.45
1.85	1.85

8. An electric utility claims that 45% of the households in a large metropolitan area have electric ranges. However, only 41% of a simple random sample of 400 households in the area have electric ranges. Using the 0.0l level, test the hypothesis that the utility's claim is correct.

9. A random sample of 225 of the 1200 faculty members at a state university shows that 65% have tenure. Test the hypothesis that 60% or fewer have tenure. Use the 0.05 level.

10. An advertising agency believes that men earning less than $10,000 per year are more apt to be beer drinkers than men earning $10,000 or more. To test whether that belief is plausible it selects samples of both groups of men in the United States and finds that 60% of the sample of 600 men earning less than $10,000 drink beer. It also finds that 50% of the sample of 400 men earning $10,000 or more are beer drinkers. Do these sample data validate the company's belief? Why?

11. In 1975 a simple random sample of 5,000 households in a large city revealed that 40% used Brand *X* fertilizer on their lawns. In 1976, a sample of the same size revealed that 43% used Brand *X* fertilizer. Use the 0.05 level and test the hypothesis that the real difference between the two sample percentages is zero. What conclusion can be drawn if the hypothesis is not accepted?

12. A random sample of 4000 of a state's motor vehicle records showed that 45% of the autos registered are more than 5 years old. A sample survey of 5000 auto owners in the state showed that 50% owned cars over 5 years old. Use the 0.05 significance level and determine whether the two percentages differ significantly.

13. Select a simple random sample of 50 numbers in Exercise Table 9-2 with the use of the table of random numbers in Appendix E. Construct a frequency distribution of your sample numbers and calculate the arithmetic mean, standard deviation, and standard error of the mean and use the 0.05 level to test the hypothesis that the mean of the universe is 40 or more.

EXERCISE TABLE 9-2. Sampling Numbers—Universe of 200

11	40	33	44	33	45	54	10
43	41	43	40	49	30	33	54
43	51	29	40	39	12	42	24
53	36	23	13	36	38	30	42
54	14	21	43	46	35	23	30
44	27	24	24	21	46	38	15
35	26	22	29	23	53	45	36
45	17	13	11	13	22	24	22
58	16	32	45	48	46	47	23
55	14	44	33	43	33	34	34
28	48	1	31	32	28	44	25
32	49	26	22	12	44	35	34
23	37	35	34	56	35	27	38
25	27	36	23	57	22	45	45
45	12	33	32	15	43	25	55
35	32	34	34	33	24	55	32
39	25	14	31	32	25	15	31
34	34	47	25	44	3	34	42
46	16	20	37	34	42	24	21
36	47	56	30	18	19	9	53
37	31	37	33	63	52	56	35
59	20	22	34	6	5	34	66
39	30	2	61	35	64	67	69
8	60	50	7	62	65	68	4
51	35	52	41	21	41	35	26

14. Use the sample data selected for Problem 13 and test the hypothesis that 50% of the numbers in the universe are below 30.

15. Select a simple random sample of 10 of the numbers in Exercise Table 9-2 and test the hypothesis that the universe mean is 35. Use the 0.01 level to make the test.

10

The F Distribution and Analysis of Variance

In Chapter 9 the z and t tests were used to test for the significance of difference between two sample means. Sometimes however, one desires to test for the significance of the differences between *three or more* means. The F distribution will allow us to do this.

The F Distribution

The F distribution is a probability distribution of ratios of sample variances.* It is used to determine if two sample variances represent the variance of the same population.

If variances are computed for two random samples from the same population they should be similar but we would expect them to differ because of random errors of sampling; therefore, the ratio of the two variances would be close to one. Moreover, if a large number of random samples were drawn from the same universe and ratios of all possible pairs of sample variances were computed these ratios would all differ but their mean would be one. This mean of one is the theoretical F ratio that would be expected for two sample variances if random errors of sampling did not occur. However, we know they will occur and that the ratio of any two sample variances is likely to be either less or more than one, depending upon which sample variance is placed in the numerator. For example, suppose that two random samples are selected and their variances are 15 and 20, respectively, and we wish to determine whether the difference between these two variances is too large to attribute to chance. To do this, two F ratios could be computed:

$$F = \frac{15}{20} = 0.75 \qquad \text{and} \qquad F = \frac{20}{15} = 1.33.$$

The interpretation of these ratios would be exactly the same because they have the same probability of occurrence. Because they would have the same meaning, however, the distribution for F ratios of larger than one is all that is needed to test a null hypothesis about the difference between two sample variances. Chart 10-1 depicts the general shape of the F distribution and table showing F ratios larger than one for the degrees of freedom for samples of various sizes is in Appendix E. The ratios are given for the 0.05 and 0.01 levels of significance only. This is done for practical reasons since a table for samples of various sizes and all significance levels would fill hundreds of pages.

Use of the F Table

Suppose that two random samples of 17 and 15 items have been selected and a test at the 0.05 level is to be made to determine if the difference between their variances is due to chance. The sample with the larger variance will be called sample one. The sample sizes

*The variance, σ^2, is the square of the standard deviation.

and their variances are: $N_1 = 17$ and $\sigma_{S_1}{}^2 = 12$, $N_1 = 15$ and $\sigma_{S_2}{}^2 = 10$, and F, the variance ratio, is

$$F = \frac{\text{Variance of Sample 1}}{\text{Variance of Sample 2}} = \frac{\sigma_{S_1}{}^2}{\sigma_{S_2}{}^2} = \frac{12}{10} = 1.2$$

To determine if a ratio of 1.2 could occur by chance we read the ratio in the F table, Table A-10, Appendix E for the degrees of freedom for the two sample variances. Since a degree of freedom was lost in the calculation of each sample variance the degrees of freedom for the two samples are $N_1 - 1 = 16, N_2 - 1 = 14$. Because the variance of the first sample was the numerator for computing the ratio we read the ratio in the table from the column under 16 degrees of freedom and from the row for 14 degrees of freedom. The ratio at the 0.05 level (light face type) is 2.44. A ratio of variances of this magnitude or larger could occur by chance only 5 times out of 100 due to the effects of random errors of sampling. Our computed ratio, 1.2, is less than this table value, therefore, we conclude that the difference in the two sample variances was due to chance and that the two samples are from the same population or from two populations with equal variances.

TESTING DIFFERENCES BETWEEN MEANS

If we had three or more random samples we might wish to know if they were drawn from the same universe or identical universes. This determination can be made by testing for

Chart 10-1. The *F* distribution and the 0.05 level of significance.

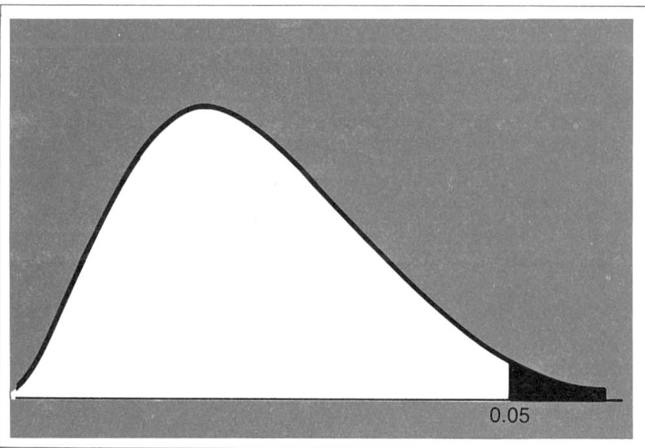

TABLE 10-1. Years of Life of Three Brands of Hot Water Tanks: Sample of Five of Each Brand.

	BRAND A COL. 1 X_{c1}	BRAND B COL. 2 X_{c2}	BRAND C COL. 3 X_{c3}
	10	10	14
	8	6	10
	7	9	13
	5	8	11
	10	7	12
Total	50	40	60
Mean	10	8	12

$$\overline{X}_{c_1} = \frac{\Sigma X_{c_1}}{N_{c_1}} = \frac{50}{5} = 10 \qquad \overline{\overline{X}}_c = \frac{10+8+12}{3} = 10$$

Also,

$$\overline{X}_{c_2} = \frac{\Sigma X_{c_2}}{N_{c_2}} = \frac{40}{5} = 8 \qquad \overline{\overline{X}}_c = \frac{\Sigma X_{c_1} + \Sigma X_{c_2} + \Sigma X_{c_3}}{N} = \frac{50+40+60}{15}$$

$$\overline{X}_{c_3} = \frac{\Sigma X_{c_3}}{N_{c_3}} = \frac{60}{5} = 12 \qquad = \frac{150}{15} = 10$$

the significance of differences *between* the several means.* To illustrate this type of analysis, which is called *analysis of variance,* we will use the data in Table 10-1, which shows the length of the lives of three brands of hot water tanks based on random samples of five of each brand. These samples were drawn to determine if the length of lives of the three brands differ significantly. If they do not, it would make no difference which brand was purchased if durability were the only consideration.

In making the significance test we assume that the variations of the data within each column (brand) are chance variations (because random samples were used) and then we determine if the variation between the column means (brands) *could be* due to random errors of sampling. To make this determination we test the null hypothesis that there is no significant difference between column means. This hypothesis is tested by computing the F ratio which is the ratio of the variance between column means to the variance within columns. If this ratio exceeds the significance ratio at a predetermined significance level for testing the null hypothesis, then the null hypothesis is rejected. The 0.05 level will be used for testing our hypothesis.

*Although the grammatically correct wording is "*among* the several means," it is customary to use the word *between*.

Analysis-method one. The first step in the analysis of the data in Table 10-1 is the computation of the mean life of each brand of hot water tank. These are 10, 8, and 12, respectively, and are shown below the table columns. Data for brands *A, B,* and *C* are listed in columns 1, 2, and 3; therefore X_{c_1}, X_{c_2}, and X_{c_3} represent the values of those respective columns and N_{c_1}, N_{c_2}, and N_{c_3} represent the number of values in each of the three columns. (The numbers of items in the columns do not need to be equal.) N is the total number of items in all three columns $\overline{X}_{c_1}$, $\overline{X}_{c_2}$, and $\overline{X}_{c_3}$ are the means of their respective columns. Next, the mean of the column means, $\overline{\overline{X}}_c$, has been computed. This is equal to the mean of all of the 15 values in the table,

$$\frac{\Sigma X}{N}$$

and is called the *grand* mean. The next step is to compute the *variation within columns,* which may be written as

$$\sum_{1}^{K_c}\left[\sum_{1}^{N_c}(X_c - \overline{X}_c)^2\right]$$

Here

$$\sum_{1}^{K_c}$$

indicates the sum for all of the columns and

$$\sum_{1}^{N_c}$$

represents the sum of all the values in a column. To use this formula thc differences between the mean of each column, $\overline{X}_c$, *and the values in the column,* X_c, are computed, squared, and summed, and these sums are added. These calculations which are below Table 10-2 show the *variation within columns* to be 58. The variation *between column means* can now be computed with the formula

$$\sum_{1}^{K_c}\left[N_c(\overline{X}_c - \overline{\overline{X}}_c)^2\right]$$

Here the difference between the mean of each colmun, $\overline{X}_c$ and the grand mean, $\overline{\overline{X}}_c$ is computed, squared, and multiplied by the number of values in the column, N_c, and these weighted square differences are summed. These computations are shown below Table 10-2 and the variation *between column means* (brands) is found to be 40. You will notice that the total variation is the sum of the variation within columns and the variation between columns, which is equal to 98. The total variation is also the sum of the squares of the differences between the mean of all the values (the *grand* mean) and each of the values. The formula is $\Sigma(X - \overline{X})^2$, where X represents a value without regard to any particular column, and $\overline{X}$ is the mean of all the values.

TABLE 10-2. Computation Needed for an Analysis of Variance of Years of Life of Three Brands of Hot Water Tanks: Sample of Five of Each Brand.

	BRAND A (COL. 1)			BRAND B (COL. 2)			BRAND C (COL. 3)		
	X_{C1}	$(X_{C1}-\overline{X}_{C1})$	$(X_{C1}-\overline{X}_{C1})^2$	X_{C2}	$(X_{C2}-\overline{X}_{C2})$	$(X_{C2}-\overline{X}_{C2})^2$	X_{C3}	$(X_{C3}-\overline{X}_{C3})$	$(X_{C3}-\overline{X}_{C3})^2$
	10	0	0	10	2	4	14	2	4
	8	2	4	6	2	4	10	2	4
	7	3	9	9	1	1	13	1	1
	15	5	25	8	0	0	11	1	1
	10	0	0	7	1	1	12	0	0
Total	50	—	38	40	—	10	60	—	10
Mean	10			8			12		

$$\overline{\overline{X}}_c = \frac{10+8+12}{3} = \frac{30}{3} = 10$$

Method One:

Variation within columns (within brands)

$$= \sum_{1}^{K_c}\left[\sum_{1}^{N_c}(X_c-\overline{X}_c)^2\right] = \Sigma(X_{c_1}-\overline{X}_{c_1})^2 + \Sigma(X_{c_2}-\overline{X}_{c_2})^2 + \Sigma(X_{c_3}-\overline{X}_{c_3})^2 = 38+10+10 = 58$$

Variation between column means (between brands)

$$= \sum_{1}^{K_c}[N_c(\overline{X}_c-\overline{\overline{X}}_c)^2] = N_{c_1}(\overline{X}_{c_1}-\overline{\overline{X}}_c)^2 + N_{c_2}(\overline{X}_{c_2}-\overline{\overline{X}}_c)^2 + N_{c_3}(\overline{X}_{c_3}-\overline{\overline{X}}_c)^2$$

$$= 5(10-10)^2 + 5(8-10)^2 + 5(12-10)^2 = 5(0)^2 + 5(2)^2 + 5(2)^2 = 0+20+20 = 40$$

Total Variation $= 58 + 40 = 98$ *Since* $\overline{\overline{X}}_c = \overline{X}$, then

Total Variation $= \Sigma(X-\overline{X})^2 = (10-10)^2 + (8-10)^2 + (7-10)^2 + (15-10)^2 + (10-10)^2 + (10-10)^2 + (6-10)^2$

$+ (9-10)^2 + (8-10)^2 + (7-10)^2 + (14-10)^2 + (10-10)^2 + (13-10)^2 + (11-10)^2 + (12-10)^2$

$= 98$

TABLE 10-3. Analysis of Variance of Years of Life of Three Brands of Hot Water Tanks.

SOURCE OF VARIATION	*AMOUNT OF VARIATION*	*DEGREES OF FREEDOM*	*VARIANCE*
Between column means (between brands)	40	2	20
Within columns (within brands)	58	12	4.83
Total	98	14	

$$F_{(2,12)} = \frac{20}{4.83} = 4.14$$

To complete the analysis of variance the measures of variation within columns and between column means have been placed in Table 10-3 and the variances have been computed by dividing each variation by the correct number of degrees of freedom. The variation between columns 40, is divided by two degrees of freedom, which results in a variance of 20. The variation within columns, 58, is divided by twelve degrees of freedom and is found to be 4.83. (For the computation of the variance between columns two degrees of freedom were used because there were three column means and any two of these were free to vary. The value of one mean was set by the value of the grand mean. Twelve degrees of freedom were used to calculate the variance within columns because there were three columns and one degree of freedom was lost in the computation of the variation for each column. For each column, four values were free to vary but one value was set by the value of the mean of the column.) To complete the analysis of variance, the *F* ratio is computed by dividing the variance between column means by the variance within columns and was found to be 4.14. This computed *F* ratio is compared to the *F* ratio at the 0.05 level in Table A-10, Appendix E for two and twelve degrees of freedom because there are two for the numerator and twelve for the denominator of the *F* fraction. The table reading is 3.88. A ratio this large or larger could occur by chance only 5 times out of 100. Since the computed ratio for our problem is larger, the null hypothesis must be rejected and we conclude that the difference in the length of life of the three brands is significant. (If we had tested the null hypothesis at the 0.01 level we would have accepted it because the significance ratio in the Table at this level is 6.93.)

Analysis—method two. A second and perhaps more expedient way of computing the total variation and the variation between column means and within columns is shown below Table 10-4. The variation between column means may be computed with the formula,

$$\sum_{1}^{K_c} \left[\frac{\left(\sum_{1}^{N_c} X_c \right)^2}{N_c} \right] - \frac{(\Sigma X)^2}{N}$$

TABLE 10-4. Computations Needed for an Analysis of Variance of Years of Life of Three Brands of Hot Water Tanks: Sample of Five of Each Brand.

	BRAND A (COL. 1)		*BRAND B (COL. 2)*		*BRAND C (COL. 3)*	
	X_{C_1}	$X^2_{C_1}$	X_{C_2}	$X^3_{C_2}$	X_{C_3}	$X^2_{C_3}$
	10	100	10	100	14	196
	8	64	6	36	10	100
	7	49	9	81	13	169
	15	225	8	64	11	121
	10	100	7	49	12	144
Column totals	50	538	40	330	60	730

$$\Sigma X = \Sigma X_{C_1} + \Sigma X_{C_2} + \Sigma X_{C_3} = 50 + 40 + 60 = 150 \quad (\Sigma X)^2 = (150)^2 = 22500 \quad \frac{(\Sigma X)^2}{N} = \frac{22500}{15} = 1{,}500$$

$$\Sigma X^2 = \Sigma X_{C_1}{}^2 + \Sigma X_{C_2}{}^2 + \Sigma x_{C_3}{}^2 = 538 + 330 + 730 = 1598$$

Variation within Columns

$$= \Sigma X^2 - \sum_{1}^{K_C}\left[\frac{\left(\sum_{1}^{N_C} X_C\right)^2}{N_C}\right] = \Sigma X^2 - \left(\frac{(\Sigma X_{C_1})^2}{N_{C_1}} + \frac{(\Sigma X_{C_2})^2}{N_{C_2}} + \frac{(\Sigma X_{C_3})^2}{N_{C_3}}\right) = 1598 - \left(\frac{(50)^2}{5} + \frac{(40)^2}{5} + \frac{(60)^2}{5}\right)$$

$$= 1598 - (500 + 320 + 720) = 1598 - 1540 = 58$$

Variation between Columns

$$= \sum_{1}^{K_C}\left[\frac{\left(\sum_{1}^{N_C} X_C\right)^2}{N_C}\right] - \frac{(\Sigma X)^2}{N} = \frac{(\Sigma X_{C_1})^2}{N_{C_1}} + \frac{(\Sigma X_{C_2})^2}{N_{C_2}} + \frac{(\Sigma X_{C_3})^2}{N_{C_3}} - \frac{(\Sigma X)^2}{N} = \left(\frac{(50)^2}{5} + \frac{(40)^2}{5} + \frac{(60)^2}{5}\right) = \frac{(150)^2}{15}$$

$$= 1{,}540 - 1{,}500 = 40$$

Total Variation

$$= \Sigma X^2 - \frac{(\Sigma X)^2}{N} = 1{,}598 - 1{,}500 = 98$$

Also, Total Variation

$$= 58 + 40 = 98$$

and the formula for the variation within columns is:

$$\Sigma X^2 - \sum_{1}^{K_c} \left[\frac{\left(\sum_{1}^{N_C} X_c \right)^2}{N_c} \right]$$

These computations do not require the calculation of differences between values and their means. The formulas result from derivations of the formulas used in the first method. For example, for the total variation,

$$\Sigma X^2 - \frac{(\Sigma X)^2}{N}$$

has been derived from $\Sigma(X - \overline{X})^2$. The subscript letters for these formulas have the same meaning as those used in the formulas for method one. You will notice that the answers obtained by the two methods are exactly the same.

TWO-WAY ANALYSIS OF VARIANCE

The analysis of variance of the data in Table 10-1 concerned only one criterion of classification—brand of hot water tank. However, an analysis of variance can be made when there are two classifications of the data. To illustrate how this is done we will use the same data on the years of life of the hot water tanks but will assume that the five rows represent five different sizes of tanks. In other words, we have a random sample of one of each size and brand of tank.*

Sources of Variation

There are three possible sources of variation: (1) chance variations, (2) variations due to differences in brands, and (3) variation due to differences in sizes.†

*A variance analysis could be made for more than one sample of each size and brand but this type of analysis is beyond the scope of this book.

†A two way analysis of variance may involve a source of variation called *interaction* which results from an interaction between the two factors. In such cases the analysis requires more than one observation for each factor combination and more complex calculations and is beyond the purpose of this book. For a brief discussion of interaction see Spurr, William A. and Bonini, Charles P. *Statistical Analysis for Business Decisions* (rev. ed.) Homewood, Ill., 1973, pp 315–318.

The two hypotheses to be tested are: (1) there is no difference in the years of life of the three brands, and (2) there is no difference in the years of life of the five sizes. To test these hypotheses we must determine whether the variation between the column means could be due to chance and whether the variation between row means could be due to chance. To do this we must compare each of the variations to the residual variation that is due to chance only. The residual variation is the total variation less the sum of the variation between column means and variation between row means.

Measuring Variation

Method one. The variation between *column* means (brands) was computed by *method one* below Table 10-2 was found to be 40.

TABLE 10-5. Computation of Variation of Years of Life between Five Sizes of Hot Water Tanks.

SIZE		*BRAND A*	*BRAND B*	*BRAND C*	*TOTAL*	*MEAN*
I	X_{r_1}	10	10	14	34	11.3
II	X_{r_2}	8	6	10	24	8.00
III	X_{r_3}	7	9	13	29	9.67
IV	X_{r_4}	15	8	11	34	11.33
V	X_{r_5}	10	7	12	29	9.67
	Total	50	40	60	150	10.00

Variation between row means $= \sum_{1}^{K_r} \left[N_r(\overline{X}_r - \overline{\overline{X}}_r)^2\right] = N_{r_1}(\overline{X}_{r_1} - \overline{\overline{X}}_r)^2 + N_{r_2}(\overline{X}_{r_2} - \overline{\overline{X}}_r)^2 + N_{r_3}(\overline{X}_{r_3} - \overline{\overline{X}}_r)^2 +$

$N_{r_4}(\overline{X}_{r_4} - \overline{\overline{X}}_r)^2 + N_{r_5}(\overline{X}_{r_5} - \overline{\overline{X}}_r)^2 = 3(11.33 - 10)^2 + 3(8.00 - 10)^2 + 3(9.67 - 10)^2 + 3(11.33 - 10)^2 +$

$3(9.67 - 10)^2 = 23.3$

Also, variation between row means $= \sum_{1}^{K_r} \left[\frac{\left(\sum_{1}^{N} X_r\right)^2}{N_r}\right] - \frac{(\Sigma X)^2}{N} =$

$$\frac{(\Sigma X_{r_1})^2}{N_{r_1}} + \frac{(\Sigma X_{r_2})^2}{N_{r_2}} + \frac{(\Sigma X_{r_3})^2}{N_{r_3}} + \frac{(\Sigma X_{r_4})^2}{N_{r_4}} + \frac{(\Sigma X_{r_5})^2}{N_{r_5}} - \frac{(\Sigma X)^2}{N}$$

$$\frac{(34)^2}{3} + \frac{(24)^2}{3} + \frac{(29)^2}{3} + \frac{(34)^2}{3} + \frac{(29)^2}{3} - \frac{(150)^2}{15} = 23.3$$

Residual variation $= 98 - (40 + 23.3) = 98 - 63.3 = 34.7$

The computation of the variation between row means (sizes) may be computed the same way. The symbolic expression would be

$$\sum_{1}^{K_r} \left[N_r(\overline{X}_r - \overline{\overline{X}}_r)^2\right]$$

where the r subscripts indicate that rows are being analyzed. Table 10-5 gives the means of the five rows. The number of a subscript r indentifies a particular row (r_1 refers to row one) and $\overline{\overline{X}}_r$ is the mean of the row means, which is 10. Since the calculation between row means is 23.3, then we make use of the total variation, 98, and find that the residual variation = 98 − (40 × 23.3) = 34.7.

Method two. The total variation, 98, and the variation between column means (brands), 40, were calculated below Table 10-2. Table 10-5 shows the calculations of the variation between row means by Method Two. The variation between row means (sizes) may be found in the same manner as that used for column means. The formula is,

$$\sum_{1}^{K_r} \left[\frac{\left(\sum_{1}^{N_r} X_r\right)^2}{N_r}\right] - \frac{(\Sigma X)^2}{N}$$

The calculations are shown below Table 10-5. The subscripts $r_1, r_2, \ldots, r_5$ identify the data in the five rows. For example

$$(\Sigma X_{r_1})^2$$

is the square of the sum of the values in the first row. The calculations show that the

TABLE 10-6. Analysis of Variance of Years of Life of Five Sizes and Three Brands of Hot Water Tanks.

SOURCE OF VARIATION	*AMOUNT OF VARIATION*	*DEGREES OF FREEDOM*	*VARIANCE*
Between column means (between brands)	40	2	20
Between row means (between sizes)	23.3	4	5.825
Residual	34.7	8	4.337
Total	98.0	14	

$$F_{(2,8)} = \frac{20}{4.337} = 4.611$$

$$F_{(4,8)} = \frac{5.825}{4.337} = 1.34$$

variation between row means is 23.3. Therefore, the residual variation = total variation − (variation between columns + variation between rows) = 98 − (40 + 23.3) = 98 − 63.3 = 34.7

The three types of variation have been placed in Table 10-6 and their respective variances have been computed. The degrees of freedom for computing the variances are: Two for the variance between column means, four for the variance between row means and eight for the residual variance. In fact, in any two-way analysis of variance the degrees of freedom for computing the residual variance is equal to the degrees of freedom for the total variance less the sum of the degrees of freedom for the variance between column means and the variance between row means. For our example, 14 − (2 + 4) = 8.

To calculate each of the F values the residual variance is the divisor since it is the variance that is due to chance only. To make the significance test for the column means

$$F_{(2,8)} = \frac{20}{4.337} = 4.61$$

and to make the test for the row means

$$F_{(4,8)} = \frac{4.825}{4.337} = 1.11$$

The value in the F Table for two and eight degrees of freedom at the 0.05 level is 4.46; therefore, the hypothesis that there is no difference in the years of life of the three brands of tanks is rejected. The table reading for F for four and eight degrees of freedom at the 0.05 level is 3.84; therefore, the hypothesis that there is no difference in the years of life of the five sizes of tanks is accepted.

REVIEW QUESTIONS

1. What is the F distribution? For what is it used?
2. What is meant by the term, "analysis of variance"?
3. What are the sources of variation in a one-way analysis of variance?
4. What are the sources of variation in a two-way analysis of variance?
5. How are the degrees of freedom determined in a two-way analysis of variance?

PROBLEMS

1. In an investigation of the truth or falsity of certain advertisements a government agency employs a testing service to determine if there is any difference in the gasoline mileage of three competing subcompact automobiles. The testing service collected the sample data in Exercise Table 10-1. Use these data and test the hypothesis that the gasoline mileage of the three cars is the same. Make the F test at the 0.01 level.

EXERCISE TABLE 10-1. Gasoline Mileage of Three Subcompacts for First 1000 Miles Driven (Sample of 10 of Each Make).

	MILES PER GALLON	
JETFIRE	*ZIPPER*	*SPRINTER*
20	25	33
18	27	34
21	26	30
17	24	28
22	29	33
23	22	32
22	24	29
19	23	26
18	24	28
20	26	27

2. A company has placed a new chain saw on the market in four sales areas. The saw is available in three different colors. Exercise Table 10-2 shows the number sold in the first week. Test the hypothesis that: (1) there is no difference between sales in the four areas, and (2) there is no difference between the sales of the three colors. Use the F test at the 0.05 level.

EXERCISE TABLE 10-2. Number of Brand X Chain Saws Sold, by Color and Sales Area.

	SALES BY COLOR		
SALES AREA	*RED*	*WHITE*	*BLUE*
1	16	6	12
2	17	8	14
3	19	6	11
4	20	3	19

3. Four newly employed typists for a large insurance company have typed many copies of a particular standard letter. The office manager claims that the typists make an equal number of errors. The assistant office manager feels his boss is wrong and presents the sample data in Exercise Table 10-3 to prove his boss is wrong. Is the manager's claim acceptable? Make the F test to make the determination. Use the 0.05 level.

EXERCISE TABLE 10-3. Number of Typing Errors on a Standard Form Typed by Four Beginning Typists (Sample of Six Letters for Each Typist).

TYPIST A	*TYPIST B*	*TYPIST C*	*TYPIST D*
3	3	5	2
2	4	2	4
4	4	2	1
3	4	4	2
2	3	6	2
4	3	5	4
18	21	24	15

4. In order to get income data for promotional purposes a marketing research agency needs to know the mean family income in each of three geographical areas. A marketing research agency hypothesizes that the mean income is the same in the three areas. To test this null hypothesis it selects a random sample of eight families in each area, and records the sample income data shown in Exercise Table 10-4. Should the company accept the null hypothesis? Make your own test to find out. Use the 0.05 significance level.

EXERCISE TABLE 10-4. 1978 Income of Samples of Families in Three Geographical Areas.

(INCOME ($000))		
AREA 1 (N = 8)	*AREA 2 (N = 10)*	*AREA 3 (N = 7)*
13	9	12
9	17	9
20	21	13
25	14	15
14	12	14
10	14	12
17	20	16
12	21	
	14	
	18	

5. A random sample of five homes from each of three suburban areas has been selected to test the hypothesis that the mean value of the homes in the three areas is the same. Exercise Table 10-5 shows the sample data. Test the hypothesis at the 0.05 level.

EXERCISE TABLE 10-5. Value of Five Homes in Three Different Suburban Areas, *a, b,* and *c*.

VALUE ($000)		
A	*B*	*C*
50	48	55
75	74	78
43	38	40
37	40	45
65	60	67

6. Three different brands of milk were priced in four different supermarkets. The results are shown in Exercise Table 10-6. Using the 0.05 level test if: (1) the prices vary significantly between supermarkets, and (2) if the prices vary significantly between brands. State your null hypothesis for each test.

EXERCISE TABLE 10-6. Price per Gallon of Three Brands of Milk in Four Different Supermarkets.

	PRICE PER GALLON		
SUPERMARKET	BRAND *A*	BRAND *B*	BRAND *C*
A	$1.39	$1.09	$1.29
B	1.28	1.29	1.39
C	1.45	1.49	1.45
D	1.40	1.19	1.39

11

Hypothesis Testing: Chi-square and Nonparametric Methods

The hypothesis tests made in Chapter 9 and 10 concerning means, percentages, differences between means and differences between percentages, used what might be called "parametric methods" because certain assumptions were made about the parameters of the populations which the samples represent. For example, when the z-test was used to test a hypothesis about a population mean it was assumed that the sample came from a normally distributed population with a mean of a specified value. Tests which do *not* require knowledge or asumptions about the shape of the universe or its population parameters are called *nonparametric tests.* Some of these tests will be illustrated in this chapter.

NOMINAL AND ORDINAL DATA

Most nonparametric tests require only nominal or ordinal data.

Nominal Data

Nominal data are observations that are classified into mutually exclusive groups which can be identified by numbers.

Examples are:

1) Answers classified as yes, no, and don't know that might be given the numbers 1, 2, and 3,
2) Classification by ages "under 40" and "40 and over" that might be numbered 1 and 2 respectively
3) The numbers in this book is an example of a nominal system of classification of objects.

Ordinal Data

Ordinal data are observations that have been placed in ranks from highest to lowest and identified by numbers.

For example, a dean may rank his best ten students, giving the best student the number 1 rank, the second, number 2, etc. Also, the 50 states could be ranked by population size with numbers 1 through 50, giving the largest state the Number 1 ranking. When data are ranked by numbers one cannot tell from the numbers how much Number 1 is better or larger than Number 2, or by how much the quality or quantity of the rankings differ between successive ranks.

We will first discuss the chi-square distribution and its use in testing hypotheses. Some chi-square tests involve the use of nominal data.

THE CHI-SQUARE DISTRIBUTION

The chi-square distribution is another probability distribution used to test for significant differences between two samples percentages; it results in the same conclusions as those drawn when significance tests are made with the normal distribution. Such tests usually involve construction of so-called contingency tables.

The chi-square distribution is also used to determine the goodness of fit of observed frequencies in a sample to the expected or theoretical frequencies. The term ''goodness of fit'' refers to how closely the curve of sample data conforms to some theoretical curve or expected curve. The expected frequencies may be the actual frequencies in a universe that has been sampled; therefore, we can determine whether to accept or reject the hypothesis that a particular sample is a random sample from a specified universe.

The Shape of the Chi-Square Distribution

The Chi-Square Distribution

A chi-square distribution is a skewed curve in which the degree of skewness decreases as the number of degrees of freedom increases. The shapes of chi-square distributions vary according to the degrees of freedom in the data being analyzed. Chart 11-1 exemplifies these shapes.

Chart 11-1. Chi-square distribution for two, five, and ten degrees of freedom.

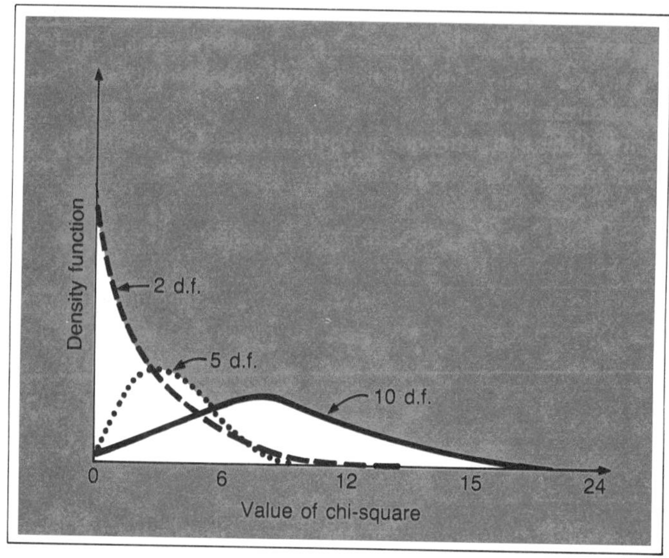

The basic formula for the value of chi-square is:

$$\chi^2 = \Sigma \frac{(f_o - f_c)^2}{f_c}$$

where χ^2 is the chi-square symbol, f_o is an observed frequency, and f_c is an expected, or theoretical, frequency. Table A-5 in Appendix E gives values for χ^2 at selected significance levels for several degrees of freedom. To test hypothesis with χ^2, we must choose the significance level for the test and determine the number of degrees of freedom in the observed frequencies. As we will see, when two distributions are compared in a chi-square test, the number of degrees of freedom is equal to the number of classes of the observed (sample) frequencies minus the number of restrictions imposed on the computed (expected or theoretical) frequencies to make them agree with the observed.

TABLE 11-1 Education Attained by Household Heads in a City: Percent Distribution of All Household Heads and Distribution of a Sample of 1000 Household Heads.

EDUCATION ATTAINED	PERCENT OF ALL HOUSEHOLDS	NUMBER IN SAMPLE OF 1000
Grade school or less	19	200
1–3 years high school	20	180
High school graduates	33	340
1–3 years college	15	172
College graduates	13	108
Total	100	1000

Chi-Square Tests

Chi-square tests fall into two categories. One is called *test of goodness of fit*, the other *test of independence of principles of classification*.

Testing for goodness of fit. Suppose an analyst finds from a sample of 1000 households in a city that the number of heads of households attaining different levels of education are as given in Table 11-1. Assume also that he knows the actual percentage distribution of households in the educational attainment groups, also listed in Table 11-1. With this information, he can test the hypothesis that he has a random sample of household heads in the city. He will accept this hypothesis if he can determine to his satisfaction that the difference between his observed (sample) frequencies and the expected (actual) frequencies could be due to random errors of sampling. First he computes the expected frequency from a random sample of 1000 by multiplying the percentages in the universe in each group by 1000, the size of the sample. These are shown in the f_c column in Table 11-2 next to the sample observations in the f_o column. Then the differences between the f_o and f_c values are calculated, squared, and expressed as ratios of the f_c values. The sum of these ratios, 9.779, is the chi-square value. If the hypothesis that there is no significant difference between the expected and observed frequencies is to be tested at the 0.02 level, then the χ^2 reading in the 0.02 column (see Appendix E, Table A-5) is taken at $N - 1 = 4$, the number of degrees of freedom. One degree of freedom was lost from the five classifications because the total of the expected frequencies was made to equal the total of the sample. The χ^2 value from the table is 11.668, which means that the hypothesis will be accepted. Had χ^2 been less than 9.779, the hypothesis would have been rejected. Had the computed χ^2 value been larger than 11.668, the hypothesis also would have been rejected because a value of 11.668 or larger could have occurred due to chance only two times out of 100.

TABLE 11-2. Computation of Chi Square for Educational Attainment Distribution of Household Heads in a City Obtained From a Sample of 1000 Compared to Expected Distribution.

EDUCATIONAL ATTAINMENT	*OBSERVED FREQUENCY* (f_o)	*EXPECTED FREQUENCY* (f_c)	$f_o - f_c$	$(f_o - f_c)^2$	$\frac{(f_o - f_c)^2}{f_c}$
Grade school or less	200	190	+10	100	0.526
1–3 years high school	180	200	−20	400	2.000
High school graduate	340	330	+10	100	0.303
1–3 years college	172	150	+22	484	3.227
College graduate	108	130	−22	484	3.723
					9.779

$$\chi^2 = \Sigma \frac{(f_o - f_c)^2}{f_c} = 9.779$$

Test of the independence of principles of classification. This test, which requires a *R*-by-*C* contingency table, also compares observed frequencies to expected frequencies.* Therefore, it is just a special case of a test for goodness of fit. This test is made in relation to the pre-stated hypothesis that the principles of classification are independent.

Suppose that a random sample of 200 men in an area showed that 110 smoke filter cigarettes and that a random sample of 200 women in the same area revealed that 104 smoke filter cigarettes. With these findings and a table of areas of the normal curve, we could make a test to determine if there is a significant difference in the percentage of men and the percentage of women who smoke filter cigarettes. With the chi-square test, however, we can draw the same conclusion much more easily.

The chi-square test is made with data expressed in original units rather than in percentages or ratios, and the data are set up in a 2-by-2 table showing the principles of classification. For our problem, the principles of classification are sex and use or nonuse of filter cigarettes. The sample frequencies in these classifications are shown in Table 11-3. From these data, the expected number of smokers of filter cigarettes is computed under the hypothesis that difference in sex has no effect on the number smoking them, that is, that the *principles of classification are independent*. The computations for the expected number of smokers and nonsmokers for both men and women are

$$\frac{214}{400} \times 200 = 107 \text{ smokers} \qquad \frac{186}{400} \times 200 = 93 \text{ nonsmokers}$$

These results are shown in Table 11-4. The expected frequencies and the observed frequencies (sample data) have been combined in Table 11-5 for computation of the chi-square, which is found to be 0.362. For the 0.05 level of significance for the test, we read the value of chi square for one degree of freedom in the 0.05 column of the chi-square table, which is 3.84. Therefore, we accept the hypothesis that the principles of classification are independent and conclude that sex has no effect on the smoking of filter cigarettes.

TABLE 11-3. Number of Men and Women Who Smoke and Do Not Smoke Filter Cigarettes, as Determined From Random Samples.

	SMOKERS	NONSMOKERS	TOTAL
Men	110	90	200
Women	104	96	200
Total	214	186	400

**R* is the number of rows and *C* is the number of columns in the table. A 2-by-2 table is one that has two rows and two columns that classify the data. A 3-by-4 table has three rows and four columns.

TABLE 11-4 Theoretical Number of Men and Women Who Smoke and Do Not Smoke Filter Cigarettes.

	SMOKERS	NONSMOKERS	TOTAL
Men	107	93	200
Women	107	93	200
Total	214	186	400

TABLE 11-5 Computation of Chi Square for Effect of Sex On Number of Smokers of Filter Cigarettes.

	OBSERVED FREQUENCY (f_O)	EXPECTED FREQUENCY (f_C)	$f_O - f_C$	$(f_O - f_C)^2$	$\frac{(f_O - f_C)^2}{f_C}$
Men smokers	110	107	3	9	0.084
Women smokers	104	107	3	9	0.084
Men nonsmokers	90	93	3	9	0.097
Women nonsmokers	96	93	3	9	0.097
					0.362

$$\chi^2 = \Sigma \frac{(f_O - f_C)^2}{f_C} = 0.362$$

For this analysis, we use one degree of freedom because there were three restrictions on the computations of the expected frequencies: the total, the number of men, and the number of smokers.

Notice that in Table 11-4 there are 4 cells. When a figure for one of the cells has been placed, the figures in the other three cells must be such that the totals 214, 186, 200, 200, and 400 are obtained. Therefore, only the first figure placed is free to vary. In fact, any 2-by-2 table has only one degree of freedom.

Another Chi-square Formula

If the cells in a 2-by-2 contingency table are lettered as in the following diagram

a	b	$a+b$
c	d	$c+d$
$a+c$	$b+d$	N

then the formula

$$\chi^2 = \frac{(ad - bc)^2 N}{(a+b)(c+d)(a+c)(b+d)}$$

may be used to compute the chi-square value. Substitutions from Table 11-3 and the calculations are

$$\chi^2 = \frac{(110 \times 96 - 90 \times 104)^2\ 400}{(200)(200)(214)(186)}$$

$$= \frac{(1200 \times 1200) \times 400}{(200)(200)(214)(186)}$$

$$= 0.362$$

This is the same answer obtained from the previously used formula. Theoretically, the calculated chi-square values should be exactly the same by the two methods of calculation, but sometimes a discrepancy will occur due to rounding of numbers.

Larger Contingency Tables

Contingency tables with any number of rows and columns may be analyzed to determine if the principles of classification are independent. This will be illustrated with the following problem.

In the spring semester a random sample of 200 freshmen, sophomores, and juniors at a large university was selected to ascertain whether they intended to attend summer school. Their answers, by class standing, are given in Table 11-6, which is a 3-by-3 table.

TABLE 11-6. Actual Distribution of Students by Attendance Plans for Summer School, as Determined by Random Samples.

	CLASS STANDING			
PLAN	*FRESHMEN*	*SOPHOMORE*	*JUNIORS*	*TOTAL*
Attend	5	8	7	20
Not attend	67	49	24	140
Undecided	8	13	19	40
Total	80	70	50	200

The hypothesis to be tested is if summer school attendance plans are independent of the class standing of the students. The formula

$$\chi^2 = \Sigma \frac{(f_o - f_c)^2}{f_c}$$

has been used to calculate the chi-square. The expected frequencies and the calculations are shown in Tables 11-7 and 11-8. However, the following derivation produces a formula that may expedite the computation of the chi-square value.

TABLE 11-7. Theoretical Distribution of Students by Attendance Plans for Summer School.

	CLASS STANDING			
PLAN	*FRESHMEN*	*SOPHOMORE*	*JUNIORS*	*TOTAL*
Attend	8	7	5	20
Not attend	56	49	35	140
Undecided	16	14	10	40
Total	80	70	50	200

TABLE 11-8. Computation of Chi-Square for Effect of Class Standing on Summer School Attendance Plans.

PLAN	*fo*	*fc*	*fo−fc*	$(fo-fc)^2$	$\frac{(fo-fc)^2}{fc}$
Attend	5	8	3	9	1.125
	8	7	1	1	0.143
	7	5	2	4	0.800
Not attend	67	56	11	121	2.161
	49	49	0	0	0.000
	24	35	11	121	3.457
Undecided	8	16	8	64	4.000
	13	14	1	1	0.071
	19	10	9	81	8.100
					19.857

$$\chi^2 = \Sigma \frac{(fo-fc)^2}{fc} = 19.857$$

$$\chi^2 = \Sigma \frac{(f_o - f_c)^2}{f_c} = \Sigma \frac{f_o^2 - 2f_of_c + f_c^2}{f_c}$$

$$= \Sigma \frac{f_o^2}{f_c} - 2\Sigma \frac{f_of_c}{f_c} - \Sigma \frac{f_c^2}{f_c}$$

$$= \Sigma \frac{f_o^2}{f_c} - 2\Sigma f_o - \Sigma f_c$$

but

$$\Sigma f_o = \Sigma f_c = N$$

therefore

$$\chi^2 = \Sigma \frac{f_o^2}{f_c} - \Sigma f_o = \Sigma \frac{f_o^2}{f_c} - N$$

Substitutions in this formula are made from Tables 11-6 and 11-7 which show the actual and theoretical distributions of the sample of 200 students. The theoretical distribution is what one would expect to get if class standing had no effect on attendance plans. The calculations are

$$\begin{aligned}
\chi^2 &= \Sigma \frac{f_o^2}{f_c} - N \\
&= \frac{(5)^2}{8} + \frac{(67)^2}{56} + \frac{(8)^2}{16} + \frac{(8)^2}{7} + \frac{(49)^2}{49} + \frac{(13)^2}{14} \\
&\quad + \frac{(7)^2}{5} + \frac{(24)^2}{35} + \frac{(19)^2}{10} - 200 \\
&= (3.125 + 80.161 + 4.000 + 9.143 + 49.000 \\
&\quad + 12.071 + 9.800 + 16.457 + 36.100) - 200 \\
&= 219.857 - 200 \\
&= 19.857.
\end{aligned}$$

The degrees of freedom are $(R - 1) \times (C - 1) = (3 - 1) \times (3 - 1) = 2 \times 2 = 4$.

The chi-square value read from Table A-5 Appendix E at 4 degrees of freedom for the 0.05 significance level is 9.488. Therefore, the hypothesis being tested is rejected because the differences between the observed and theoretical sample values are too large to attribute to chance. We conclude that class standing does affect summer-school attendance plans.

A Caution in Chi-Square Analysis

Since the Chi-square distribution is continuous and the number of possible combination of cell frequencies is finite, errors in a chi-square analysis may occur when the number of values in the cells are too small. A general rule used by many analysts is that the expected value in each cell be five or more. A table with fewer than five observations in a cell may be reconstructed by combining cells in two adjacent rows or an adjustment can be made by the use of *Yate's correction for continuity*.

The basic chi-square formula modified by Yate's correction factor reads

$$\chi^2 = \Sigma \frac{[(|f_o - f_c|) - \frac{1}{2}]^2}{f_c}$$

where $|f_o - f_c|$ is an absolute difference between an observed and expected cell frequency and $-\frac{1}{2}$ is the correction factor. This correction factor, $-\frac{1}{2}$, will usually have a minimal effect on the calculated chi-square value when the expected cell frequencies are large. It may be helpful when the expected cell frequencies are small but since there is some danger of over correction all analysts do not recommend its use.*

THE KRUSKAL-WALLIS *H* TEST

This test, commonly called the *H test*, is made on a ranked data and enables us to test, with ordinal data, the hypothesis that the several samples come from populations with the same means. It requires no assumptions about the distributions of the populations from which the samples were drawn except that the population data are continuous.

To make this test the data for all samples must be pooled and ranked in order of magnitude and then the H statistic is computed and examined to determine if it is significantly large.† The formula for H is

$$H = \frac{12}{N(N+1)} \Sigma \frac{R_k^2}{N_k} - 3(N+1)$$

where

N_k = the number of sample items in the kth column.
N = The total number of sample items in all columns.
R_k = total of the ranks of the sample items in the kth column.

The sample data in Table 11-9 will be used to exemplify the H test. The table shows random samples of the noon meal checks from each of three cafeterias for a particular day. The hypothesis to be tested is that the average noon meal checks in the three cafeterias were identical. If six or more observations are in each sample, H is distributed as chi-square, therefore the chi-square distribution will be used for the test. Since there are three columns of data the degrees of freedom are $C - 1 = 2$, for which the value of chi-square at the 0.05 level should be obtained for comparison with 11.377, the H value computed below the table. The chi-square value from Table A-5, Appendix E is 5.991. Therefore, the hypothesis is rejected, and the conclusion is that the populations from which the samples are drawn are not the same and the average noon meal checks differ among the cafeterias.

*For a more detailed discussion of Yate's correction see the references in the bibliography.

†The data may be ranked from lowest to highest or highest to lowest. The results of the test will be the same for both methods of ranking.

TABLE 11-9. Random Samples of Noon Meal Checks from Three Cafeterias, Ranked from Highest to Lowest—No Ties in Ranks.

CAFETERIA X		*CAFETERIA Y*		*CAFETERIA Z*	
AMOUNT	*RANK*	*AMOUNT*	*RANK*	*AMOUNT*	*RANK*
$2.55	3	$1.70	19	$2.05	11
3.21	1	1.63	20	1.85	16
1.99	12	1.80	17	2.25	7
2.40	5	1.75	18	2.10	10
2.75	2	2.15	9	1.90	15
1.95	13	1.50	21	2.30	6
2.50	4	1.93	14	2.20	8
Total	40		118		73

$$\frac{R_1^2}{N_1} = \frac{(40)^2}{7} = 228.6 \qquad \frac{R_2^2}{N_2} = \frac{(118)^2}{7} = 1989.1 \qquad \frac{R_3^2}{N_3} = \frac{(73)^2}{7} = 761.3$$

$$\Sigma \frac{Rk^2}{Nk} = 228.6 + 1989.1 + 761.3 = 2979.0$$

Substitution in the formula

$$H = \frac{12}{21(21+1)} \quad 2979.0 - 3(21+1)$$

$$= \frac{35{,}748}{462} - 66 = 77.4 - 66 = 11.377$$

The foregoing analysis was for ranked observations with no ties. If two or more observations are equal they are given the mean of the ranks. For example, if three observations tie for ranks 9, 10, and 11, each of three is assigned the rank of 10. When ties for ranks occur the H value is corrected by dividing it with the value computed from the formula

$$1 - \frac{\Sigma(t^3 - t)}{N^3 - N}$$

where t is the number of tied observations in one group of observations. To illustrate its use we will assume the mean meal check and ranks for the samples from Cafeterias X, Y, and Z are as shown in Table 11-10

There are two groups of ties. Two observations tied for 12th and 13th and were given the rank of 12.5. Three were tied for the ranks of 6, 7, and 8 were given the rank of 7. These are circled in the tables. Since the sum of the ranks in the three columns in Table 11-10 are the same as in Table 11-9 the unadjusted H value is still the same as that computed from Table 11-9. Substitutions in the adjustment formula are:

$$1 - \frac{(2^3 - 2) + (3^3 - 3)}{(21)^3 - 21} = 1 - \frac{6 + 24}{9{,}240} = 0.99675$$

TABLE 11-10. Random Samples of Noon Meal Checks from Three Cafeteria (Ranked from Highest to lowest with Ties in Some Ranks).

CAFETERIA X		*CAFETERIA Y*		*CAFETERIA Z*	
AMOUNT	*RANK*	*AMOUNT*	*RANK*	*AMOUNT*	*RANK*
$2.55	3	$1.70	19	$2.05	11
3.21	1	1.63	20	1.85	16
1.99	(12.5)	1.80	17	2.30	(7)
2.40	5	1.75	18	2.10	10
2.75	2	2.15	9	1.90	15
1.99	(12.5)	1.50	21	2.30	(7)
2.50	4	1.93	14	2.30	(7)
Total	40		118		73

Therefore, for the data in the table

$$H = \frac{11.377}{0.99675} = 11.414$$

This corrected value is not appreciably larger than the uncorrected H. This will be the case when few observations are tied and when N is large.

THE MANN-WHITNEY-TEST

The z-test and t-test are useful for testing whether two samples have been drawn from universes that are assumed to be normally distributed and which have equal means and variances. However, the *Mann-Whitney U-test* enables us to make a significance test without these assumptions, although the data for the Mann-Whitney test are assumed to be continuous. Since the ranks of the observations for the two samples are used in the test it is often called the *rank sum test*.

The sample data in Table 11-11 will be used to illustrate the test. The data show the SAT scores of random samples of engineering and business students attending a large university. The hypothesis to be tested is that the two samples represent the same universe of student scores (or scores drawn from identical universes). The test is always a two-tailed test and the normal distribution table may be used when both samples are larger than 10. Our test will be made at the 0.05 level.

TABLE 11-11. S.A.T. Scores in Mathematics Made by Freshmen in Engineering and Business Administration in a Large University (Sample of 12 from Each School).

ENGINEERING FRESHMEN	*BUSINESS FRESHMEN*
601	480
589	556
647	513
620	614
597	520
553	507
605	626
650	475
712	540
580	511
566	545
617	622

The first step in the analysis is to pool the two samples and rank their values in order of magnitude as shown in Table 11-12. Next the statistics U is calculated. The formula is

$$U = N_1N_2 + \frac{N_1(N_2 + 1)}{2} - R_1$$

where

N_1 = the size of the first sample
N_2 = the size of the second sample
R_1 = the total of the ranks of the values in the first sample

Which of the two samples is designated as sample No. 1 is an arbitrary choice. If we let the sample of engineering students be the first sample, then $N_1 = 12, N_2 = 12$, and $R_1 = 196$. Substitutions in the formula show,

$$U = 12(12) + \frac{12(12 + 1)}{2} - 196 = 26$$

This U must be compared to $\overline{X}_u$, the mean of the sampling distribution of U. The formula and calculations for the value is

$$\overline{X}_u = \frac{N_1 N_2}{2} = \frac{(12)(12)}{2} = 72$$

TABLE 11-12. S.A.T. Scores by Rank for Engineering and Business Administration Freshmen in a Large University.

SCORE	*RANK (LOWEST TO HIGHEST)*	*SCHOOL (B = BUSINESS) (E = ENGINEERING)*
480	1	B
475	2	B
507	3	B
511	4	B
513	5	B
520	6	B
540	7	B
545	8	B
553	9	E
556	10	B
566	11	E
580	12	E
589	13	E
597	14	E
601	15	E
605	16	E
614	17	B
617	18	E
620	19	E
622	20	B
626	21	B
647	22	E
650	23	E
712	24	E
Total of E Ranks	196	

The comparison of U and $\overline{X}_u$ is made with the use of the standard deviation of U, which is

$$\sigma_u = \sqrt{\frac{N_1N_2\,(N_1+N_2+1)}{12}} = \sqrt{\frac{(12)\,(12)\,(12\,+\,12\,+\,1)}{12}} = 17.3$$

To make the comparison (the test) we compute z to determine how many standard deviations separate U and $\overline{X}_u$. Thus

$$z = \frac{U - \overline{X}_u}{\sigma_u} = \frac{26 - 72}{17.3} = -2.66.$$

Since -2.66 shows a greater separation than -1.96, the significance ratio at the 0.05 level in a two-tailed test, the hypothesis is rejected.

THE SIGN TEST

When a z- or t-test is made for two sample means or two sample percentages it is assumed that the populations from which the two samples were drawn are normally distributed and have equal variances. However, the sign test enables us to test for significance of difference between paired observations without making any assumptions about the population which the samples represent. The following problem will illustrate the use of the sign test.

The sales manager of a large company, the *D* Corp. wishes to test a new sales presentation to potential customers that is supposed to enable salesmen to make more sales calls. To make the test he selects a random sample of twenty of his salesmen, who will try the new sales presentation. The null hypothesis to be tested is that the presentation will make no significant difference in the number of calls the salesmen can make. The twenty salesmen used the presentation for one month. The number of calls they made are recorded in Table 11-13 along with the calls they made the previous month.

An increase in the number of sales calls is indicated by a plus sign and a decrease in the number of calls is indicated by a negative sign. If the null hypothesis is true we would expect the number of plus signs in the universe to equal the number of minus signs in the universe. Thus the percentage in the universe, p_u, would be 0.5 and, q_u would be 0.5. Therefore,

$$\sigma = \sqrt{Np_uq_u} = \sqrt{20 \times 0.5 \times 0.5} = \sqrt{5} = 2.24$$

and since p_u is 0.5 and N is more than 10 the normal distribution can be used to approximate the binomial distribution. For making the test we compute

$$z = \frac{X - 0.5 - Np_u}{\sigma}$$

where X is the number of signs the most frequently occuring sign, 0.5 is a continuity correction factor, N is the number of paired observations, and p_u is the percentage expected in the universe.

Substitutions for our problem are

$$z = \frac{12 - 0.5 - 20(.5)}{2.24} = \frac{11.5 - 10}{2.24} = \frac{1.5}{2.24} = +0.67$$

Since +0.67 is less than 1.64 the hypothesis is accepted at the 0.05 level, and it can be concluded that the new sales presentation did not enable the salesmen to make more sales calls.

TABLE 11-13. Number of Sales Calls Made in Two Months by Twenty Salesmen of the D Corp. in the Month Before and the Month After the Institution of the New Presentation.

SALESMEN	*MONTH BEFORE*	*MONTH AFTER*	*SIGN OF DIFFERENCE*
1	50	52	+
2	41	39	−
3	73	75	+
4	60	63	+
5	57	55	−
6	26	28	+
7	35	32	−
8	41	44	+
9	65	70	+
10	38	34	−
11	40	43	+
12	55	57	+
13	48	40	−
14	42	38	−
15	35	40	+
16	29	33	+
17	62	55	−
18	33	35	+
19	30	40	+
20	45	39	−
12 increases	8 decreases		

Handling of Ties

When ties occur in paired observations these are deleted from the analysis. For example if 60 paired observations showed 30 pluses, 20 minuses, and 10 ties, the analysis would be made with the 30 pluses and 20 minuses only; therefore, N would be 50 rather than 60.

ONE-SAMPLE RUNS TEST

In the real research world the techniques described in Chapter 8 that assure randomness in sampling cannot always be used. However, a sample may be random concerning some attribute even though a random design was not preplanned.

One-Sample Runs Test

A test for testing for randomness is called the *runs test*. This test is based on the number of runs observed in the sample statistic concerning some attribute. A run is a series of like observations preceded and followed by a series of different like observations.

These runs are tested to determine if they are significantly different in number than would result if a random method had been used to select the sample. The subsequent problem illustrates an appropriate and effective use of the runs test.

A research organization desires to learn, among other things, what percentage of the adults attending a summer fair in a large city on a particular day are residents of that city. Fifty adults at the fair are interviewed on a "random" basis and were asked if they were residents. Letting Y = yes and N = no the order of the replies were

$\underline{YYYYY}\ \underline{NNN}\ \underline{Y}\ \underline{NN}\ \underline{YY}\ \underline{NNN}\ \underline{YY}\ \underline{N}\ \underline{YY}\ \underline{NNN}\ \underline{YYY}\ \underline{N}\ \underline{Y}\ \underline{NN}\ \underline{YYY}\ \underline{NN}\ \underline{YY}\ \underline{NNN}\ \underline{YY}\ \underline{NN}$
$\underline{YYYY}$

The 21 runs in the replies are underlined. In order to use the sample information the organization must show that the sample is random. Therefore it will test the null hypothesis that the order of the yes and no answers is random. This test, which is two-tailed, will be made at the 0.05 level. The formulas needed for making the test are,

$$E_R = \frac{2N_1N_2}{N_1 + N_2} + 1$$

$$\sigma_R = \sqrt{\frac{2N_1N_2(2N_1N_2 - N_1 - N_2)}{(N_1 + N_2)^2\,(N_1 + N_2 - 1)}}$$

$$z = \frac{R - E_R}{\sigma_R}$$

where

R = the number of runs
E_R = the expected number of runs
σ_R = the standard deviation of the number of runs
N_1 = number of yes answers
N_2 = number of no answers

These formulas make use of normal distribution to test for a difference between the actual number of runs and the expected number of runs. This may be done when the sample is large and, preferable when both N_1 and N_2 are larger than 20, but is often used if either N_1 or N_2 is larger than 20. Substitutions in the formulas,

$$E_R = \frac{2(28)\,(22)}{28 + 22} + 1 = \frac{1.232}{50} + 1 = 25.64$$

$$\sigma_R = \sqrt{\frac{2(28)\,(22)\,[2(28)\,(22) - 28 - 22]}{(28+22)^2\,(28+22-1)}}$$

$$= \sqrt{\frac{1232(1232 - 50)}{(50)^2\,(49)}} = \sqrt{\frac{1,456,224}{122,500}} = 3.45$$

$$z = \frac{21 - 25.64}{3.45} = -1.34$$

For this test -1.96 is the significance ratio; therefore the hypothesis is accepted and it is assumed that the sample of 50 is random. Thus the research organization will use the sample information with confidence.

Runs Above and Below the Median

The preceding illustration of the runs test used attribute data (residents or nonresidents) but the test is not limited to such data. It can be applied to runs above and below the median of a series of values. To illustrate this type of test we will assume that a Chamber of Commerce keeps a weekly record of the number of out-of-town visitors to its offices for one year. The recordings were as follows: 12,10,30,10; 17,41,18,19; 18,21,24,20; 28,27,26,32; 36,22,34,29; 40,47,39,43; 16,35,41,29; 14,29,36,22; 24,20,17,16; 27,26,19,24; 41,24,16,14; 12,10,32,15; 9,8,10,12. The chamber wishes to know if the numbers of weekly visits are random or if there is some rhythmic pattern or trend. Using the 0.05 significance level we will test the hypothesis that they are random. The median of the number is 23. Letting *A* and *B* represent the values above and below the median, respectively, the following run arrangement resulted:

BB A BB A BBBB A B AAAAA B AAAAAA B AAA B AA B A BBB AA B AAA BBBB A BBBBB

Counting, we find $N_1 = 26$, $N_2 = 26$, and $R = 23$, where N_1 = the number of *A*'s and N_2 = the number of *B*'s, and *R* is the number of runs. The computations are

$$E_R = \frac{2(26)\,(26)}{26 + 26} + 1 = 27$$

$$\sigma_R = \sqrt{\frac{2(26)\,(26)\,[2(26)\,(26) - 26 - 26]}{(26 + 26)^2\,(26 + 26 - 1)}} = 12.7$$

$$z = \frac{23 - 27}{12.7} = \frac{4}{12.7} = -.31$$

Since the significance ratio for this test is -1.96, the hypothesis is accepted.

In an analysis of time data of this sort we might reject the hypothesis of randomness and also find mostly A's occurred first, then mostly B's, indicating a downward trend or mostly B's at first, followed by mostly A's, suggesting an upward trend. Moreover, there could be a systematic alternation of A's and B's, with too many runs, suggesting a cyclical pattern of some sort.

REVIEW QUESTIONS

1. What are the two basic chi-square tests?
2. Describe the chi-square distribution.
3. What is meant by degrees of freedom? How are degrees of freedom calculated for a chi-square analysis?
4. What are the expected frequencies in a chi-square analysis?
5. What is the purpose of Yate's correction for continuity?
6. What is a nonparametric test?
7. What is the purpose of The Kruskal-Wallis H test. What types of data are used for this test?
8. What can be determined with the Mann-Whitney U test? What kind of data are used for this test?
9. What kind of observations are used for the sign test?
10. What conclusion can be made with the runs test?

PROBLEMS

1. Use the chi-square test to solve Problem 11 at the end of Chapter 9.
2. Use the chi-square test to work Problem 12 at the end of Chapter 9.
3. A typewriter distributor divided his sales territory into five smaller territories, A, B, C, D, and E, which he expects to have equal sales potentials. If he is correct, each territory, in the long run, should account for 20% of the typewriters sold. At the end of one month the number of typewriters sold in the territories were: A, 30; B, 25; C, 31; D, 36; and E, 28. By means of a chi-square test, determine whether this actual sales distribution differs significantly from the expected sales distribution. Use the 0.02 level to make the test. What conclusions might be drawn about the sales potentials of the five territories from the results of the significance tests?

4. A cigarette manufacturing company claims that smoker preference for plain and menthol cigarettes is independent of the sex of the smoker. A random sample of 1,000 men smokers and 800 women smokers produced the data in Exercise Table 11-1. Does a chi-square test of these data at the 0.05 level validate the claim of the company? To check the accuracy of your chi-square calculation use two different formulas.

EXERCISE TABLE 11-1. Percent of Men and Women Preferring Plain and Menthol Cigarettes (Random Sample of 1,000 Men and 800 Women).

	PERCENT PREFERRING	
TYPE OF CIGARETTE	*MEN*	*WOMEN*
Plain	66	59
Menthol	34	41
Total	100	100

5. A random sample of 600 registered voters in a community was selected to measure their attitudes concerning a certain legislative bill that would increase taxes. The sample data were classified by ages of the respondents because it was hypothesized that the attitudes of the voters in the community was independent of their age. The answers received are shown in Exercise Table 11-2. Use the chi-square test at the 0.01 level and determine if the hypothesis should be accepted.

EXERCISE TABLE 11-2. Attitude of 600 Voters in a Community Concerning a Legislative Bill.

	NUMBER OF VOTERS BY AGE			
ATTITUDE	*UNDER 25*	*25–49*	50 AND OVER	
Favorable	100	170	60	330
Unfavorable	20	75	85	180
Neutral	60	15	15	90
Total	180	260	160	600

6. A company desires to determine if the quality of the output of five employees operating identical machines is the same. To make this determination it examines a random sample of the pieces produced by each worker during the past year. The sample information is recorded in Exercise Table 11-3A. Make a chi-square analysis using the 0.05 level and test the hypothesis that there is no difference in the quality of the output of these five employees. Exercise Table 11-3B presents the theoretical (expected) frequencies to facilitate your analysis.

EXERCISE TABLE 11-3A. Actual Number of Pieces Produced by Five Workers Classified by Quality of Pieces (Random Samples of Annual Production of Each Worker).

QUALITY	*JOE*	*JOHN*	*JACK*	*BILL*	*DAN*	*TOTAL*
Above standard	610	629	626	619	479	2,963
Standard	614	598	641	619	595	3,067
Below standard	348	314	319	328	209	1,618
Total	1,572	1,541	1,586	1,566	1,383	7,648

EXERCISE TABLE 11-3B. Theoretical Number of Pieces Produced by Five Workers Classified by Quality of Pieces (Based on Samples of Annual Production of Each Worker).

	PIECES BY WORKER					
QUALITY	*JOE*	*JOHN*	*JACK*	*BILL*	*DAN*	*TOTAL*
Above standard	609	597	614	607	536	2,963
Standard	630	618	636	628	554	3,067*
Below standard	333	326	336	331	293	1,618*
Total	1,572	1,541	1,586	1,566	1,383	7,648

*Components do not add to these totals due to rounding.

7. Truck drivers for a large transport company have been using three different routes between two cities. Samples of ten of the speed averages on many trips on each route are shown in Exercise Table 11-4. Make the H test at the 0.05 level and test the hypothesis that the travel time between the two points is the same for the three different routes.

EXERCISE TABLE 11-4. Miles per Hours Experienced on Ten Trips in Three Different Truck Routes.

ROUTE 1	*ROUTE 2*	*ROUTE 3*
43.2	48.0	55.3
47.1	49.4	52.9
40.6	41.6	55.4
39.4	49.9	57.6
41.7	51.2	54.4
42.3	48.5	55.0
48.1	50.6	56.0
42.6	53.7	54.9
47.4	52.5	54.3
44.5	54.0	56.2

8. The following are the lifetimes (in hours) of samples of three brands of batteries. Make the Krushal-Wallis H test at the 0.05 level to test the null hypothesis that the mean lifetimes of the three brands of batteries is the same.

Brand A 80,87,69,74,83,76,84,76
Brand B 68,75,72,79,78,71,70,67
Brand C 88,91,86,88,85,94,93,89

9. An insurance company executive contends that women have scored as high as men on a particular insurance selling aptitude test that he has given to candidates for sales jobs. To examine this contention he selects a random sample of the files of both men and women who have taken the test in the past three years. The test scores from the samples are shown below. Use the Mann-Whitney test and the 0.05 level and determine if the executive's contention is acceptable.

Scores Made on Aptitude Test by 12 Men and 12 Women.

WOMEN	*MEN*
89, 87, 63, 77	96, 90, 65, 74
84, 69, 71, 85	83, 70, 80, 92
95, 72, 78, 81	68, 88, 73, 75

10. An oil company advertises that, on the average, a car can get more miles per gallon on its Brand X gasoline than on another company's Brand Y gasoline. To test the truth of this advertisement a consumer testing service selected a random sample of fifteen cars of various makes and models and each car was driven the same distance over the same road at the same speed using both brands. The miles per gallon for each car and each brand are shown below. Use the sign test at the 0.05 level and test the hypothesis that there is no difference in the gasoline mileage obtained with the two brands.

CAR	*MILES PER GALLON WITH BRAND X*	*MILES PER GALLON WITH BRAND Y*
1	18.6	18.9
2	17.6	17.2
3	16.8	16.4
4	20.2	20.5
5	13.4	13.7
6	8.9	8.5
7	14.0	13.8
8	15.1	15.6
9	15.9	15.3
10	30.4	31.7
11	16.2	16.0
12	25.4	25.7
13	19.7	20.0
14	22.6	22.9
15	11.5	10.9

11. A large manufacturing firm wishes to experiment with a four-day work week to determine if it will result in higher productivity than its current five-day work week. To make this experiment it selects a random sample of 30 employees, places them on a four-day work week, and keeps a record of their output for twelve weeks. This record is compared to their output for the previous twelve-week period. The comparison showed that 18 had higher production and 12 had lower production under the four-day work week basis. Make the sign test and determine if there was a significant change in production after the switch to the four-day week.

12. A gasoline service station which offers both full-service and self-service gasoline pumps is opened in a new location. Management desires to determine if the demand for the two types of service is random. The first day, 60 cars stopped for gasoline. Letting *F* represent full-service and *S* represent self-service the order of the demand for the two types of service was as follows:

$\underline{FF}\ \underline{SSSS}\ \underline{F}\ \underline{SS}\ \underline{FFF}\ \underline{SSS}\ \underline{FF}\ \underline{SSSS}\ \underline{F}\ \underline{SS}\ \underline{FFFF}\ \underline{SSSSSSS}$

$\underline{FFF}\ \underline{SS}\ \underline{FFFF}\ \underline{SS}\ \underline{FF}\ \underline{SSS}\ \underline{FF}\ \underline{SS}\ \underline{FFF}\ \underline{SS}$

Use this information and make the runs test of the hypothesis that the order of demand for the two types of service was random. Use the 0.05 level for the test.

13. A researcher interviewed 100 students at various locations on a university campus to gather information on cigarette smoking. He asked each student whether he or she smoke. Forty said yes and 60 said no. There were 27 reply runs. Determine at the 0.05 level if the difference between the actual number of runs and the expected number of runs is significant. What conclusion can you draw from your analysis?

12

Two-variable Regression and Correlation Analysis

Relationships among factors that can be measured quantitatively often serve as bases for estimating and forecasting. For example, the agriculturist can make reasonably accurate forecasts of crop yields based on such factors as weather conditions, type of soil, and amount of fertilizer applied to the soil. The businessman can make a sales forecast based on such factors as population and consumer income in his sales territory.

Variable Regression and Analysis

A factor that shows changes or differences in magnitude is a *variable*. An analysis of the nature and closeness of the movements of two variables is called a *simple* regression and correlation analysis

Analysis of more than two variables is called *multiple* regression and correlation analysis. Here, however, we are concerned only with simple regression and correlation analysis.

A simple regression analysis deals with the methods of deriving an estimating or regression equation that describes the functional relationship between the dependent variable and the independent variable. The equation then can be used to estimate values of the dependent variable with given values of the independent variable. A regression analysis can be made without any concern for the closeness of the relationship.

A simple correlation analysis refers to the methodology of measuring the closeness of the relationship between two variables, which is described by the regression equation. Moreover, the closeness of the relationship can be measured without computing the regression equation upon which the measurement is based. Usually, however, both a regression analysis and a correlation analysis of two variables are made. In fact, regression and correlation analysis combined is often called *correlation analysis* or just *correlation*.

A basic purpose of a regression analysis of two variables is to estimate or forecast the values of one variable from known values of the other and to measure the accuracy of the estimates and forecasts made. The estimated variable is called the *dependent variable*. The other is the *independent variable*. Two variables can be changing in the same direction (positive correlation) or in opposite directions (negative correlation), and the relationship of their movements can be linear or curved. Moreover, their movements may be closely synchronized or related. Such relationships of two variables can be due to one of the following reasons found in the list on the next page. It is important to be aware of the fact that close correlation of two variables does not *prove* the existence of a cause and effect relationship. In fact, one of the dangers of using correlation analysis as a tool for business decisions is making this assumption when it is not warranted. All correlation analysis does is to measure and describe the mathematical relationship; other studies are required to establish the existence of causality.

Relationships Between Two Variables

1) Changes in one variable can cause changes in the other variable. For example, variations in temperature cause variations in fuel consumed for the heating of homes

2) Changes in two variables may be affected in a similar manner by the same set of conditions or circumstances. Changes in retail sales and income are a good example. In general, the higher the sales in an economic area, the higher the income and vice versa. Changes in either of these series do not cause, entirely, the changes in the other, but changes in incomes do contribute to changes in sales and vice versa. The basic reason for close movements in income and sales is that the same economic forces affect both in a similar manner.

3) Changes in two variables may be closely associated by accident or chance. A teacher, for example, might find that in a given class there is a positive correlation between the heights of the students and their grades in the course. It would be difficult, however, to explain a reason for this condition.

TYPES OF DATA THAT CAN BE CORRELATED

Two variables that relate to the same unit identities for unchanging periods of time may be correlated. An example of such paired variables is income tax returns and retail sales, by county, for 1977. In this case, a unit identity is a county.

Two time series also may be correlated. For example, the number of income tax returns and the dollar volume of disposable income in the United States, by year, for the past 10 years could be paired and analyzed. Although a regression and correlation analysis of a time series will be illustrated in this chapter, the analysis of data not ordered by time will be given prime emphasis.

STEPS IN ANALYSIS OF TWO VARIABLES

A logical procedure should be followed in a complete regression and correlation analysis of two variables. The procedure presented below is both logical and expedient in relation to the formulas chosen for an analysis.

Analyzing Two Variables

1. *Construct a scatter diagram*. This is a chart that indicates: (a) whether the relationship is close enough to continue with the analysis; (b) whether the relationship is negative or positive; and (c) whether the relationship is basically linear or curved. This last determination is necessary in order to choose the proper equations for the analysis.

2. *Compute the estimating equation*, sometimes called the *regression equation*. This equation describes the general relationship between the two variables and enables us to construct a *regression line* on the scatter diagram. It is used also to estimate or predict values of the dependent variable from given values of the independent variable. In a regression analysis of sample data, the dependent variable is assumed to be random while the independent variable is fixed.

3. *Compute the standard error of estimate*. This computation gives a measure of the deviations of the actual values of the dependent variable from values computed with the estimating equation. With this measure we can determine intervals in which the actual values can be expected to fail with specified degrees of confidence. In fact, its use is similar to the use of the standard deviation discussed in Chapter 5.

4. *Compute the coefficient of correlation*. This is a "pure" number that measures the degree of the closeness of the movements of two variables. (A pure number is one that is not measured in units.) The maximum magnitude of the coefficient of correlation is 1. A coefficient of +1 means a perfect positive correlation of the two series. A coefficient of −1 means perfect negative correlation. A coefficient of 0 means no correlation. The sign of the coefficient is determined by the slope of the regression line. The coefficient of correlation can be defined also as the square root of the *coefficient of determination*, which measures the relative amount of variation in the dependent variable that has been explained by variations in the independent variable. In the computation of the coefficient of correlation of sample data, both variables are assumed to be random and the value of the coefficient is the same when either variable is designated as the dependent one.

The Scatter Diagram

On a scatter diagram, the scale for the independent variable is placed on the horizontal (X) axis and the scale for the dependent variable is placed on the vertical (Y) axis. One pair of an independent and dependent variable determines a point, which is plotted on the diagram.

The dependent Y variable is the one affected by movements of the causal or independent variable. If a cause-and-effect relationship does not exist, the dependent variable is defined as the one to be estimated or predicted. Examples of different scatter patterns are shown in Chart 12-1. When the plotted points fall on a straight line, as pictured in parts (a) and (b), perfect linear correlation exists. When the dots tend to cluster about an imaginary straight line, as in parts (c) and (d), there is a linear relationship; the closer they cluster about this imaginary straight line the closer the

Chart 12-1. Types of relationships between independent and dependent variables.

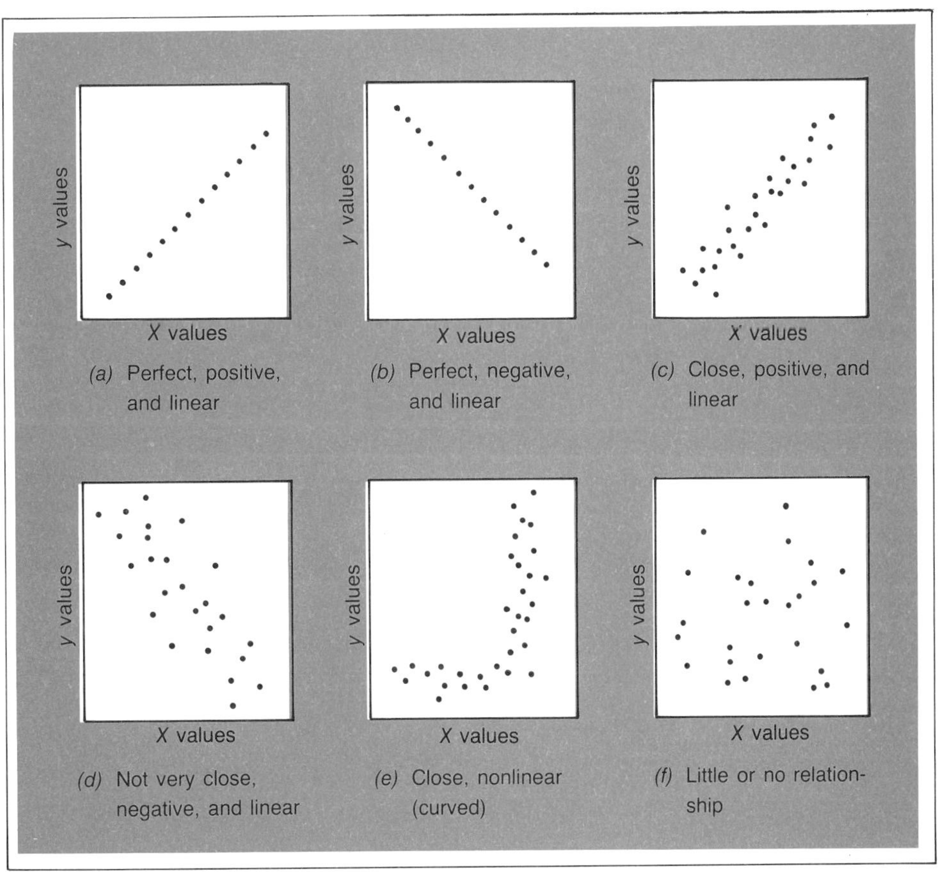

correlation. If the dots form a curved pattern as exemplified in part (e), there is a nonlinear or curved relationship; the closer the dots cluster about an imaginary curved line the closer the relationship. If the dots form no distinct pattern, straight or curved, as in part (f), then there is little or no relationship between the movements of the two variables.

The Estimating Equation

If a scatter diagram reveals a linear relationship, then the "average" or general relationship can be described by a straight line. This line, which is called a *regression line*, is usually constructed by plotting values estimated with the *least squares* estimating equation

$$Y_c = a + bX$$

If a and b are computed properly, this equation is such that the sum of the squares of the deviations of the actual Y values from the computed Y values (Y_c) is less than the sum of the squared deviations of the actual Y values from estimated Y values computed for any other straight line. In this equation the letters have the following meanings:

- Y_c Computed or estimated Y value. This is an estimate of the dependent variable.
- a Estimated value of the dependent variable (Y) when the value of the independent variable is 0.
- b Typical change in the dependent variable (Y) for every unit change in the independent variable (X).

To calculate a and b, the following equations must must be solved.*

$$\Sigma Y = Na + b\Sigma X$$

$$\Sigma XY = a\Sigma X + b\Sigma X^2$$

In these equations, Y represents the dependent variable, X represents the independent variable, and N is the number of paired observations.

When a scatter diagram shows a curved relationship, the equation for a parabola, $Y_c = a + bX + cX^2$, or some other curve might be used to describe it. The use of a parabola will be explained later in this chapter.

*These normal equations are derived from the general equation for the straight line, $Y = a + bX$, in the following manner.

To get the first equation, multiply the general equation by the coefficient of a and the sum. Since the coefficient of a is 1, the multiplication is

$$\Sigma(Y = a + bX)$$

The Standard Error of Estimate

The formula for the standard error of estimate

$$\sigma_{Y_u} = \sqrt{\frac{\Sigma(Y - Y_c)^2}{N}}$$

is not a practical one in most circumstances, but it is a good definitional formula, as we will see later in this chapter. In this formula, it is clear that the standard error of estimate is the square root of the squared deviations of the computed Y values (Y_c) from the actual Y values.

A convenient formula for computing the standard error of estimate after having calculated a and b in the equation $Y_c = a + bX$ is

$$\sigma_{Y_u} = \sqrt{\frac{\Sigma Y^2 - (a\Sigma Y - b\Sigma XY)}{N}}$$

The use of both of these formulas will be demonstrated. Also, $\sigma^2_{Y_u}$, which is a measure called *unexplained variance* will be used to calculate other correlation measures.

The Coefficient of Correlation

The coefficient of correlation is usually computed by extracting the square root of the *coefficient of determination*. The coefficient of determination measures the proportion of the total variance of the dependent values (Y) that have been explained by variations in the independent values (X). A formula for total variance is

$$\sigma_Y{}^2 = \frac{\Sigma(Y - \bar{Y})^2}{N}$$

---

which results in

$$\Sigma Y = Na + b\Sigma X$$

To get the second equation, multiply the general equation by the coefficient of b, which is X, and the sum. Multiplication by X yields

$$XY = aX + bX^2$$

and summation gives

$$\Sigma(XY = aX + bX^2)$$

or

$$\Sigma XY = a\Sigma X + b\Sigma X^2$$

where $\bar{Y}$ is the arithmetic mean of the Y values. A formula for *explained variance* is

$$\sigma^2_{Y_e} = \frac{\Sigma(Y_c - \bar{Y})^2}{N}$$

Therefore, the coefficient of determination, r^2, may be calculated as follows.

$$r^2 = \frac{\sigma^2_{Y_e}}{\sigma_Y{}^2} = \frac{\dfrac{\Sigma(Y_c - \bar{Y})^2}{N}}{\dfrac{\Sigma(Y - \bar{Y})^2}{N}} = \frac{\Sigma(Y_c - \bar{Y})^2}{\Sigma(Y - \bar{Y})^2}$$

Then

$$r = \sqrt{r^2}$$

Also, the coefficient of determination can be computed by subtracting the *coefficient of nondetermination*, $\sigma^2_{Y_u}/\sigma_{Y^2}$, from 1, because the coefficient of nondetermination is the proportion of the total variance that has *not* been explained by variations in the independent variable. The formula may be written.

$$r^2 = 1 - \frac{\sigma^2_{Y_u}}{\sigma_Y{}^2}$$

(The subscripts Y_u and Y_e identify measures of unexplained variation and explained variation, respectively, of the Y values.) Again, the coefficient of correlation is $r = \sqrt{r^2}$.

If a and b in the least squares straight line equation have been computed, a convenient formula for the coefficient of correlation is

$$r = \sqrt{\frac{(a\Sigma Y + b\ \Sigma\ XY) - \bar{Y}\ \Sigma\ Y}{\Sigma Y^2 - \bar{Y}\Sigma Y}}$$

All these formulas will be used in the examples that follow.

A TYPICAL PROBLEM

Table 12-1 shows the mean monthly rent and median family income in 15 sales areas of the Knick Company. If there is a close relationship between the movements of these two variables, then mean monthly rent in an area could be used to estimate median family income in the area, or vice versa. The purpose of the analysis in this illustration is to make estimates of family income from given values of mean monthly rent. Therefore, the mean monthly rent is the independent variable, X, and the median family income is the dependent variable, Y.

TABLE 12-1. Computation of Values Needed for Correlation Analysis of Mean Monthly Rent and Median Income in 15 Sales Areas of the Knick Company, 1976.

MEAN MONTHLY RENT (DOLLARS) X	MEDIAN FAMILY INCOME ($000) Y	X^2	XY	Y^2	Y_c
160	9.0	25,600	1440.000	81.00	11.5
146	10.0	21,316	1460.00	100.00	10.0
184	10.8	33,856	1987.20	116.64	14.1
162	14.2	26,244	2300.40	201.64	11.7
198	12.4	39,204	2455.20	153.76	15.6
220	21.8	48,400	4796.00	475.24	18.0
180	16.6	32,400	2988.00	275.56	13.6
284	24.0	80,656	6816.00	576.00	24.9
204	17.4	41,616	3549.60	302.76	16.2
250	17.0	62,500	4250.00	289.00	21.2
260	17.8	67,600	4628.00	316.84	22.3
180	15.0	32,400	2700.00	225.00	13.6
286	28.0	81,796	8008.00	784.00	25.1
220	16.0	48,400	3520.00	256.00	18.0
256	26.6	65,536	6809.60	707.56	21.8
3190	256.6	707,524	57,708.00	4861.00	257.6[1]

(1) $\Sigma Y = Na + b\Sigma X$

(2) $\Sigma XY = a\Sigma X + b\Sigma X^2$

Solving for b:

(1) $256.6 = 15a + 3190b$

(2) $57{,}708.0 = 3190a + 707{,}524\,b$

$\left[(1) \times \frac{3190}{15}\right]$ $54{,}570.3 = 3190a + 678{,}406.7b$

$3137.7 = 29{,}117.3b$

$$b = \frac{3{,}137.7}{29{,}117.3} = 0.1077606$$

$Y_c = -5.81 + 0.108X$

if $X = 160, Y_c = -5.81 + 0.108(160) = 11.5$

if $X = 220, Y_c = -5.81 + 0.108(220) = 17.9$

if $X = 286, Y_c = -5.81 + 0.108(286) = 25.1$

Solving for a:

(1) $256.6 = 15a + 3190\,(0.1077606)$

$256.6 = 15a + 343.8$

$15a = -87.2$

$a = -5.813333$

[1] $\Sigma Y_c = \Sigma Y$ (the difference in this case is due to rounding.)

The Scatter Diagram

To determine whether a complete analysis of the relationship might be worth while, a scatter diagram has been constructed in Chart 12-2. This chart shows a reasonably close relationship that is positive and linear because the dots are scattered upward and fairly close about an imaginary straight line. With this chart an experienced analyst could estimate quite accurately the value of the coefficient of correlation that measures the closeness of the relationship. He would probably compute the coefficient of correlation, however, to get the precise measure.

Chart 12-2. Mean monthly rent of dwelling units and median family income in 15 sales areas of the Knick Company, 1976.

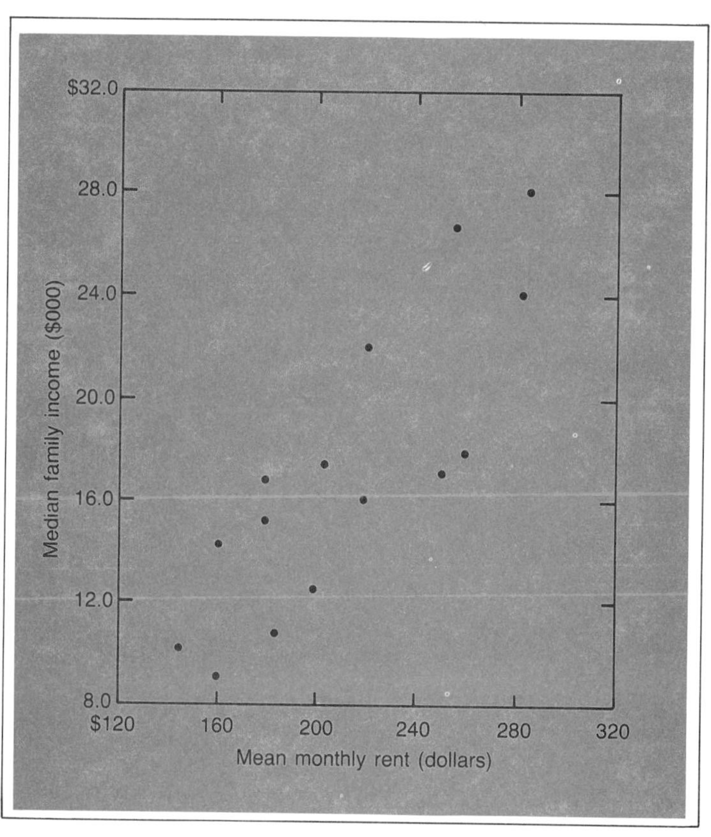

The Estimating Equation

The values needed to compute the least squares estimating equation are presented in Table 12-1 and the calculations are shown below the table. The sums of the products of X^2 and XY are substituted in the two equations, and then the equations are solved for the value of b. The coefficient of a in equation (1), which is 15, is divided into 3,190, the coefficient of a in equation (2) and each member of equation (1) is multiplied by the result. The products are placed below equation (2) and are subtracted, thus eliminating the constant a. The solution shows that the value of b is +0.1077606. This value is then substituted into equation (1) to calculate a, which is found to be −5.8133. The estimating equation then is $Y_c = -5.81 + 0.108X$. The values of b and a have been carried to six and four decimal places, respectively, in the original calculation because this accuracy will be needed in the subsequent calculation of the standard error of estimate. However, for making estimates with the estimating equation, the values of b and a carried to three and two decimal places, respectively, are sufficient because the Y_c values are to be rounded to one decimal place, the same degree of accuracy as the original Y values.*

Using the estimating equation. In order to make estimates of the dependent variable, Y, with given values of the independent variable, X, we need only to substitute the value of the independent variable for X in the equation. Three examples of the substitutions and

*The purpose of this text is not to show numerous derivations of formulas, but to illustrate their use. Two formulas, however, are convenient to use for computing b and a in the estimating equation for the lest squares straight line:

$$b = \frac{\Sigma XY - N\overline{X}\overline{Y}}{\Sigma X^2 - N\overline{X}^2}$$

$$a = Y - bX$$

where $\overline{Y}$ and $\overline{X}$ are the respective arithmetic means of the dependent and independent variables. Substituting values from Table 12-1, we have

$$\overline{Y} = \frac{\Sigma Y}{N} = \frac{256.6}{15} \quad \text{and} \quad \overline{X} = \frac{\Sigma X}{N} = \frac{3,190}{15}$$

and

$$b = \frac{57,708.0 - 15\left(\frac{3,190}{15} \times \frac{256.6}{15}\right)}{707,524 - 15\left(\frac{3,190}{15}\right)^2} = \frac{3,137.7}{29,117.3} = 0.1077606$$

$$a = \frac{256.6}{15} - 0.1077606\left(\frac{3,190}{15}\right) = 17.107 - 22.917 = -5.810$$

These are the same values obtained by substituting in the two normal equations and solving. Discrepancies in the answers are due to rounding.

the resulting values are shown below Table 12-1. These examples show that with mean monthly rents of \$160, \$220, and \$286, the estimated median family incomes in the areas would be \$11,500, \$17,900, and \$25,100, respectively.

The Y_c column in the table shows an estimate of median family income made for each value of mean monthly rent in the X column. These plotted values all fall on the straight line shown in Chart 12-3. To draw the line, however, only two values need be plotted if they are accurate. As a check on the accuracy of the calculations, the plotting of at least three Y_c values is preferable. These three should be a low value, a median value, and a high value of X so that they are spread on the diagram. When a ruler is placed along the three points, they should all fall on the edge of the ruler. If they do not, then there is an error in the calculations or in the plotting.

The solid line on Chart 12-3, which is called a *regression line,* describes the typical relationship between the dependent and independent variables. In fact, it may be thought of as a line of average relationship.

Chart 12-3.-Mean monthly rent of dwelling units and median family income in 15 sales areas of the Knick Company, 1976.

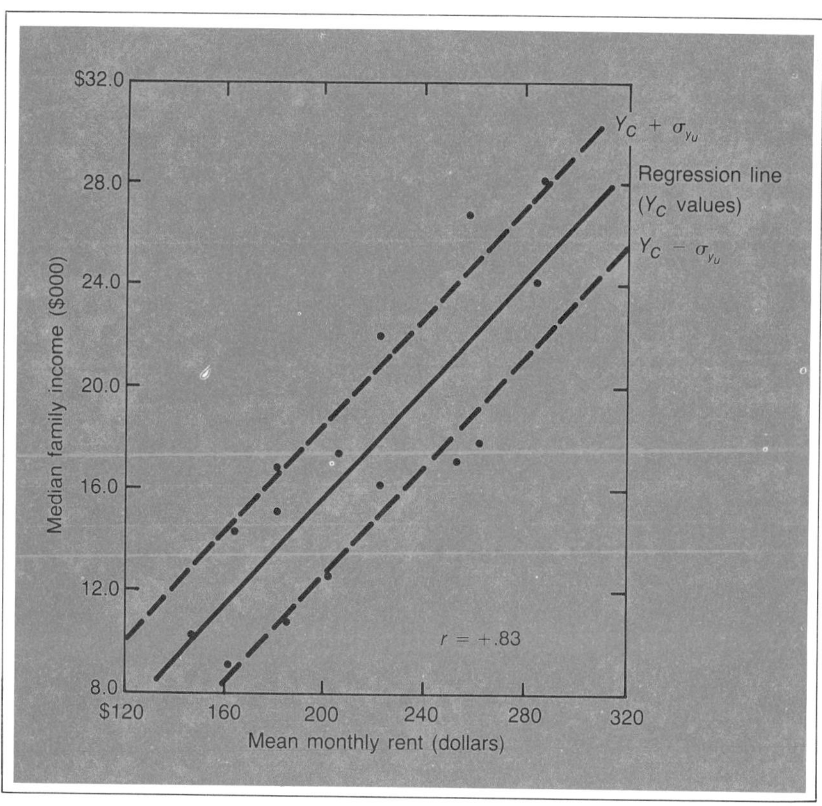

Caution in estimating. When making estimates of the dependent variable, the value of the independent variable should be within the range of the values of the independent variable. In Table 12-1, the smallest and largest X values are 160 and 286, respectively. Therefore, any X values used in estimating Y should not be smaller than 160 nor more than 286. The use of any values outside of this range would have to be under an assumption that the correlation between the observed independent and dependent variables exists for those unobserved values, which of course, may not be true.

The Standard Error of Estimate

After a brief study of Table 12-1 and Chart 12-3, we can see that the estimated median family income figures, Y_c, differ somewhat from the actual median family incomes. A summary measure of these differences is called the *standard error of estimate*. It is analogous to the standard deviation, except the standard deviation measures the deviations around an arithmetic mean whereas the standard error of estimate measures deviations around the Y_c values (or, graphically, the scatter of the dots about the regression line).

Since a and b are known, a practical formula for computing the standard error of estimate is the one previously stated,

$$\sigma_{Y_u} = \sqrt{\frac{\Sigma Y^2 - (a\Sigma Y + b\Sigma XY)}{N}}$$

Substituting values in this formula from Table 12-1 we have

$$\begin{aligned}
\sigma_{Y_u} &= \sqrt{\frac{\Sigma Y^2 - (a\Sigma Y + b\Sigma XY)}{N}} \\
&= \sqrt{\frac{4861.00 - [(-5.81333)(256.6) + (0.1077606)(57{,}708.00)]}{15}} \\
&= \sqrt{\frac{4861.00 - (-1491.70 + 6218.65)}{15}} = \sqrt{\frac{4{,}861.00 - 4{,}726.95}{15}} \\
&= \sqrt{\frac{134.05}{15}} = \sqrt{8.9366} = 2.99 = 3.0
\end{aligned}$$

If these data were a large and representative sample from a large universe we could say that the chances are about ⅔ that the actual family income, Y, would be within \$3,000 of the estimated income, Y_c, and it is almost certain that the actual income would be within three standard errors, \$9,000.

Other calculations of values of Y_c, in thousands of dollars, for X values of 160, 220, and 286 are shown below Table 12-1. Using these calculated values it can be said that

$$\text{If } X = 160,\ Y_c \pm \sigma_{Y_u} = 11.5 \pm 3.0 = 8.5 \text{ to } 14.5$$

$$\text{If } X = 160,\ Y_c \pm 3\sigma_{Y_u} = 11.5 \pm 9.0 = 2.5 \text{ to } 20.5$$

$$\text{If } X = 220,\ Y_c \pm \sigma_{Y_u} = 17.9 \pm 3.0 = 14.9 \text{ to } 20.9$$

$$\text{If } X = 220,\ Y_c \pm 3\sigma_{Y_u} = 17.9 \pm 9.0 = 8.9 \text{ to } 26.9$$

$$\text{If } X = 286,\ Y_c \pm \sigma_{Y_u} = 25.1 \pm 3.0 = 22.1 \text{ to } 28.1$$

$$\text{If } X = 286,\ Y_c \pm 3\sigma_{Y_u} = 25.1 \pm 9.0 = 16.1 \text{ to } 34.1$$

Using the last two as an example, what these calculations mean is this: If a sales area has a mean monthly rent of \$286, then the chances are about two out of three that the median family income in the area is between \$22,100 and \$28,100, and it is nearly certain that the median family income is between \$16,100 and \$34,100. These would be approximate prediction intervals for an actual Y value if a large sample had been used*. A more precise measure of a prediction interval which should be used for small samples will be presented later in this chapter.

Chart 12-4. Graphic illustration of the concept of the standard error of estimate.

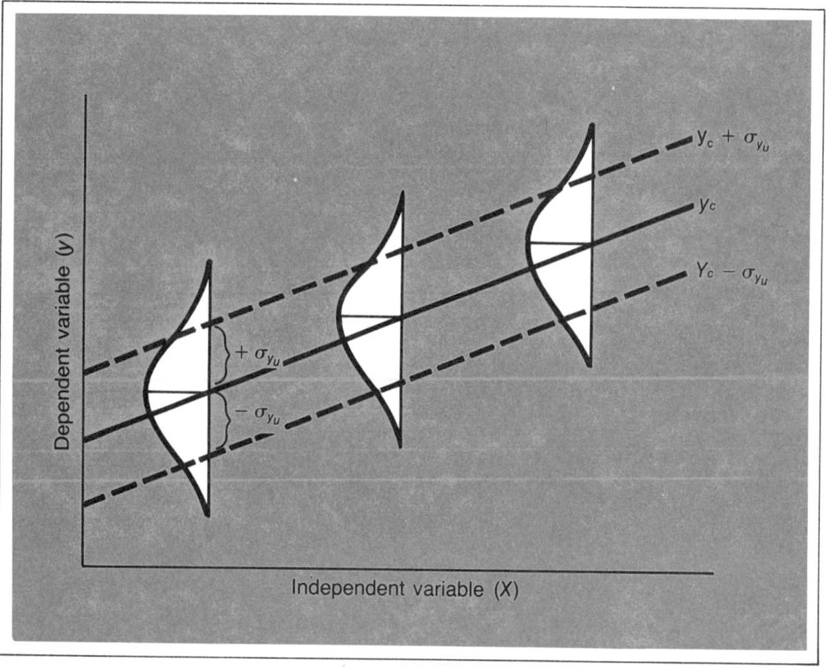

*Prediction intervals are analogous to confidence intervals discussed in Chapter 8. In fact some authers call them confidence intervals.

A graphic presentation of the standard error intervals for all Y values can be seen in Chart 12-3 (dashed lines). The standard error band includes 68.26 percent of the dots if the distribution around the regression line is normal.

The concept is graphically depicted in Chart 12-4. It is assumed that for any X value the Y values are distributed normally about their corresponding Y_c values and that the standard deviation of the distribution is equal to the standard error of estimate. The standard error of estimate, therefore, measures the error expected in the estimates made by the estimating equation. This measure of error is important if decisions are to be based on the estimates.

The Coefficient of Correlation

Earlier in this chapter, the coefficient of correlation was defined as the square root of the coefficient of determination. The coefficient of determination, as stated, measures the relative amount of variance in the dependent variable that has been explained by variations in the independent variable. A formula for computing the coefficient of determination using values already calculated for the standard error of estimate is

$$r^2 = \frac{(a\Sigma Y + b\Sigma XY) - \bar{Y}\Sigma Y}{\Sigma Y^2 - \bar{Y}\Sigma Y}$$

To substitute in this formula, the only new value that must be computed is $\bar{Y}$, which is the arithmetic mean of the dependent variable:

$$\bar{Y} = \frac{\Sigma Y}{N} = \frac{256.6}{15} = 17.1067$$

The value of $(a\ \Sigma Y + b\ \Sigma XY)$ has already been determined and the other sums are from Table 12-1. Substitution in the formula shows that

$$r^2 = \frac{4726.95 - (17.1067)\,(256.6)}{4861.00 - (17.1067)\,(256.6)} = \frac{337.37}{471.42} = 0.7156$$

This ratio indicates that 71.56% of the variations in median family income can be explained by variation in mean monthly rents. If a true cause and effect relationship existed between the two variables, it could be said that 71.56% of the variations in median family income were caused by variations in mean monthly rent. However, changes in mean monthly rent do not cause changes in median family incomes. Therefore, the explained variation is only a mathematical explanation.

The calculation of the coefficient of correlation is

$$r = \sqrt{0.7156} = +0.85$$

The coefficient computed with this formula is always positive, except that if the sign of b in the estimating equation is negative, a negative sign is given to the coefficient. In this case, however, the sign is positive because b is positive.

Whether or not +0.85 indicates a high degree of correlation is a matter for judgment. A coefficient of 0 means no correlation and a coefficient of 1 means perfect correlation. It is left to each analyst to interpret the meaning of the coefficient he obtains, but he should remember that, for the same two sets of data, the higher the coefficient of correlation the smaller the standard error of estimate and, therefore, the more accurate the estimates of the dependent variable made with the estimating equation.

Another formula for *r*. Sometimes an analyst desires to compute only the coefficient of correlation. When this is the case, the formula just discussed is impractical because it first requires the computation of a and b in the estimating equation. A more practical formula is:

$$r = \frac{N\Sigma XY - (\Sigma X)(\Sigma Y)}{\sqrt{[N\Sigma X^2 - (\Sigma X)^2][N\Sigma Y^2 - (\Sigma Y)^2]}}$$

All of the sums needed for this formula are found in Table 12-1. Substitution shows that

$$r = \frac{15(57{,}708.00) - (3{,}190)(256.6)}{\sqrt{[15(707{,}524) - (3{,}190)^2][15(4{,}861.00 - (256.6)^2]}}$$

$$= \frac{47{,}066.0}{\sqrt{(436{,}760)(7{,}071.44)}} = \frac{47{,}066.0}{55{,}574.5} + 0.85$$

As it should be, this is the same result as obtained previously. In this formula, the sign of the coefficient is derived directly by the calculation.

The Coefficient of Determination Explained

To clarify the meaning of the coefficient of determination, it will be computed another way.

Table 12-2 presents the calculations of the deviations of the Y values from the mean of the Y values $(Y - \bar{Y})$ in the correlation problem concerning mean monthly rent and median family income. It shows also the deviations of the $\bar{Y}$ values from the Y_c values, $(Y_c - \bar{Y})$, and the deviations of the Y_c values from the Y values, $(Y - Y_c)$. Each set of deviations is squared, and the sums of the squared deviations are used to compute measures of the total variation, explained variation, and unexplained variation of the dependent variable. The formulas for these three measures, called *variances*, are:

Total variance: $\sigma_Y{}^2 = \dfrac{\Sigma(Y - \bar{Y})^2}{N}$

Explained variance: $\sigma^2_{Y_e} = \dfrac{\Sigma(Y_c - \bar{Y})^2}{N}$

Unexplained variance: $\sigma^2_{Y_u} = \dfrac{\Sigma(Y - Y_c)^2}{N}$

TABLE 12-2. Computation of Values Needed to Measure Total, Explained and Unexplained Variance of Median Family Income in 15 Sales Areas of the Knick Company, 1976.

Y	Y_c	$Y-\bar{Y}$	$(Y-\bar{Y})^2$	$Y_c-\bar{Y}$	$(Y_c-\bar{Y})^2$	$Y-Y_c$	$(Y-Y_c)^2$
9.0	11.5	−8.1	65.61	−5.6	31.36	−2.5	6.25
10.0	10.0	−7.1	50.41	−7.1	50.41	0.0	0.00
10.8	14.1	−6.3	39.69	−3.0	9.00	−3.3	10.89
14.2	11.7	−2.9	8.41	−5.4	29.16	2.5	6.25
12.4	15.6	−4.7	22.09	−1.5	2.25	−3.2	10.24
21.8	18.0	4.7	22.09	0.9	0.81	3.8	14.44
16.6	13.6	−0.5	0.25	−3.5	12.25	3.0	9.00
24.0	24.9	6.9	47.61	7.8	60.84	−0.9	0.81
17.4	16.2	0.3	0.09	−0.9	0.81	1.2	1.44
17.0	21.2	−0.1	0.01	4.1	16.81	−4.2	17.64
17.8	22.3	0.7	0.49	5.2	27.04	−4.5	20.25
15.0	13.6	−2.1	4.41	−3.5	12.25	1.4	1.96
28.0	25.1	10.9	118.81	8.0	64.00	2.9	8.41
16.0	18.0	−1.1	1.21	0.9	0.81	−2.0	4.00
26.6	21.8	9.5	90.25	4.7	22.09	4.8	23.04
Total			471.43		339.89		134.62*

$$\sigma_Y^2 = \frac{\Sigma(Y-\bar{Y})^2}{N} = \frac{471.43}{15} = 31.43 \qquad \sigma_Y{}^2 = \sigma_{Y_e}^2 + \sigma_{Y_u}^2 = 22.66 + 8.97 = 31.63$$

$$\sigma_{Y_e}^2 = \frac{\Sigma(Y_c-\bar{Y})^2}{N} = \frac{339.89}{15} = 22.66 \qquad r^2 = \frac{\sigma_{Y_e}^2}{\sigma_Y^2} = \frac{22.66}{31.63} = 0.7164$$

$$\sigma_{Y_u}^2 = \frac{\Sigma(Y-Y_c)^2}{N} = \frac{134.62}{15} = 8.97 \qquad r = \sqrt{0.7164} = +0.85$$

$$\sigma_{Y_u} = \sqrt{8.97} = 3.0$$

* This sum is less than what would be obtained by taking the deviations around any other straight line.

The total variance, which is the square of the standard deviation of the Y values, is a summary measure of the deviations of the Y values from their mean. The explained variance measures the amount the Y_c values deviate from the mean of the Y values, and the unexplained variance measures the amount the computed Y values differ from the actual Y values. A graphic explanation of all three types of variations is presented in Chart 12-5.

Calculations of the three measures of variance, the standard error of estimate, and the coefficient of correlation are shown below Table 12-2. It can be seen that $\sigma_Y^2 = 31.43$ $\sigma_{Y_e}^2 = 22.66$ and $\sigma_{Y_u}^2 = 8.97$. Moreover, the total variance is a sum of these last two variances, or $\sigma_Y{}^2 = \sigma_{Y_e}^2 + \sigma_{Y_u}^2 = 22.66 + 8.97 = 31.63$. (The discrepancy between this sum and the answer, 31.43, obtained before is due to rounding of decimals when calculating the individual deviations.) Now that these measures have been calculated and

Chart 12-5. Total, explained, and unexplained variation: mean monthly rent and median family income.

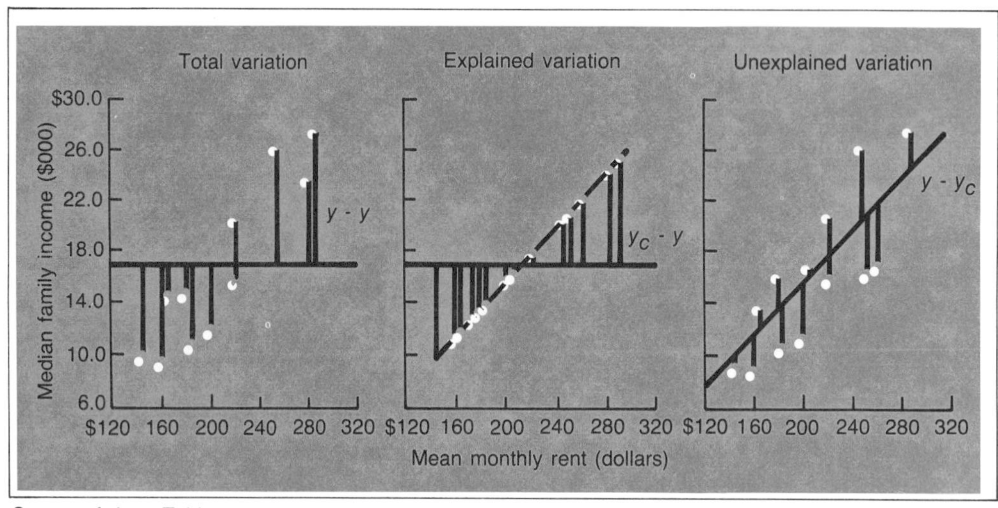

Source of data: Table 12-2.

their relationships explained, it should be clear that the coefficient of determination can be calculated as follows.

$$r^2 = \frac{\text{explained variance}}{\text{total variance}} = \frac{\sigma^2_{Y_e}}{\sigma_Y{}^2} = \frac{22.66}{31.63} = 0.7164$$

or the calculation could be

$$r^2 = 1 - \frac{\text{unexplained variance}}{\text{total variance}} = 1 - \frac{\sigma^2_{Y_u}}{\sigma_Y{}^2} = 1 - \frac{8.97}{31.63}$$

$$= 1 - 0.2836 = 0.7164$$

The coefficient of correlation, of course, is the square root of this value, +0.85, and the standard error of estimate is the square root of the unexplained variance, $\sigma^2_{Y_e}$, or 3.0. The slight discrepancy between this coefficient and the one obtained with the other formulas is due to rounding of deviations in Table 12-2.

ANALYZING SAMPLE DATA

Formulas for Sample Data

The formulas used in the preceding illustrations apply to sample data. When analyzing sample data, however, certain adjustments are made in the formulas if estimated values for the population are desired. These necessitate using the number of degrees of freedom as the denominator rather than the number of observations in the sample. For example, when calculating $\sigma_Y{}^2$, $N - 1$ rather than N should be used because a degree of freedom is lost by taking the deviations of the Y values from the arithmetic mean of the Y values. Moreover, when $\sigma^2_{Y_u}$ is computed, $N - 2$ rather than N should be used in the formulas because two degrees of freedom are lost by taking deviations of the actual Y values around the values computed with the estimating equation. The two degrees are lost by computing and using a and b in the equation.*

If the standard error of estimate, σ_{Y_e}, has already been computed from sample data with N instead of $N - 2$ then it can be adjusted by multiplying it by

$$\sqrt{\frac{N}{N - 2}}$$

The coefficient of correlation r, if already computed, can be adjusted by calculating

$$\sqrt{1 - (1 - r^2)\,\frac{N - 1}{N - 2}}$$

If, for example, the 15 sales areas of the Knick Co. are only a sample of a large number of sales areas, the adjustment of σ_{Y_u} (previously computed as 1.5) is

$$3.0\sqrt{\frac{N}{N - 2}} = 3.0\sqrt{\frac{15}{13}} = 3.2$$

and the calculation and estimate of r for the population is

$$\sqrt{1 - \left[1 - (0.85)^2\right]\,\frac{14}{13}} = \sqrt{0.7012} = +0.84$$

Theoretically, the adjustments just described should be made when any sample data are correlated. However, if the samples are large (over 30 items), then the adjustments are not worthwhile because they hardly change the results.

Significance of a Regression Coefficient

The coefficient b, in the regression equation $Y_c = a + bX$ measures the typical change in Y, the dependent variable, for every unit change in X, the independent variable. However, when sample data are used it is possible that the true regression coefficient is zero—that b results from chance alone.

*However, the formulas for computing a and b are not affected by the use of sample data because no degrees of freedom are lost in their computations. For an explanation of the meaning of *degrees of freedom*, refer back to the discussion on the calculation of standard error of the mean, analysis of variance and chi square in Chapters 8, 10, and 11.

It is possible to compute the standard error of the regression coefficient and that will determine if b, based on the sample, is significantly different from zero. This can be done for small samples by computing

$$t = \frac{b - 0}{\sigma_b}$$

where σ_b is the standard error of the regression coefficient. The formula is,

$$\sigma_b = \frac{\sigma_{Y_u}}{\sqrt{\Sigma(X - \overline{X})^2}}$$

Here, σ_{Y_u} is the sample standard error of estimate and $\Sigma(X - \overline{X})^2$ measures variation of the X values around their mean. We have found the sample σ_{Y_u} to be 3.2 and $\Sigma(X - \overline{X})^2$ computed from the X values in Table 12-1 is 29,117.33. Therefore,

$$\sigma_b = \frac{3.2}{29{,}117.33} = 0.019$$

Since b in the estimating equation (shown below Table 12-1) is 0.108, then

$$t = \frac{b - 0}{\sigma_b} = \frac{0.108 - 0}{0.019} = 5.68$$

Thus, b is 5.68 standard errors from 0. For a sample of 15 observations, as in Table 12-2, there are $N - 2$ degrees of freedom in the computation of σ_{Y_u}. The value of t for one tail at the 0.01 level from Table A-4 in Appendix E is 2.6. Therefore, 5.68 is significant at the 0.01 level and we can conclude that b is real and that there is a functional relationship between the two variables. If the difference had not been significant then we could have had no confidence in the estimates made with the regression equation.

Prediction Intervals for Small Samples

When establishing prediction intervals for small samples, consideration should be given to sampling error in the regression line as well as sampling error around the regression line. If several small samples were selected from the same universe their a coefficients would differ and their b coefficients would differ due to sampling error, making their regression lines differ. Therefore, the standard error for use in a prediction interval should make allowances for the presence of both types of errors. This can be done by adjusting the estimated standard error of estimate for the universe by the expression.

$$\sqrt{1 + \frac{1}{N} + \frac{(X - \overline{X})^2}{\Sigma X^2 - \frac{(\Sigma X)^2}{N}}}$$

Application for an X value of 160 from Table 12-1 and our standard error of 3.2 previously calculated for the 15 areas of the Knick Company results in

$$3.2\sqrt{1 + \frac{1}{15} + \frac{(160 - 212.67)^2}{707{,}524 - \frac{(3190)^2}{15}}} = 3.2\sqrt{1.169} = 3.5$$

Since 15 items constitute a small sample the establishment of a 0.95 prediction interval for an actual Y value when X is 160 and $Y_c = 11.5$ requires the use of the Student's t distribution. (Appendix Table A-4). The table reading for 13 degrees of freedom ($N - 2$) in the 0.05 column is 2.160. Therefore,

$$Y_c \pm t(3.5) = 11.5 \pm 2.160(3.5) = 3.9 \text{ to } 19.1$$

The closer the X value is to the mean the smaller the adjusted standard error. For example if X is 220 then,

$$3.2\sqrt{1 + \frac{1}{15} + \frac{(220 - 212.67)^2}{707{,}524 - \frac{(3190)^2}{15}}} = 3.2\sqrt{1.0687} = 3.3$$

The 0.95 prediction interval for Y when X is 220 and Y_c is 17.9 is:

$$Y \pm t(3.3) = 17.9 \pm 2.160(3.3) = 10.8 \text{ to } 25.0$$

Confidence Intervals for Coefficients of Correlation

If data from a random sample are used in a correlation analysis, then r is affected by random errors of sampling just as any other sample measure. Moreover, the distribution of sample r's follows the normal curve if r for the population is reasonably low and the samples are very large. When this is the case, confidence intervals can be established for r in the population in the same manner that confidence intervals are established for population means and percentages. The standard error of the coefficient is computed with the formula

$$\sigma_r = \frac{1 - r^2}{\sqrt{N - 1}}$$

where N is the size of the sample and r is the coefficient of correlation for the universe if it is known (this is seldom the case). When the universe coefficient of correlation is not known, the sample coefficient of correlation may be used with little sacrifice of accuracy if the sample is very large. This formula should not be applied to the problems in this chapter because none of the N values are large. However, if a coefficient of correlation of two variables was +0.62 and $N = 400$, then

$$\sigma_r = \frac{1 - (0.62)^2}{\sqrt{400}} = \frac{1 - 0.3844}{20} = \frac{0.6156}{20} = 0.03$$

and the 0.95 confidence interval for the universe r would be between

$$r \text{ (sample)} \pm 1.96\, \sigma_r = 0.62 \pm (1.96)\, 0.03$$
$$= 0.56 \text{ to } 0.68$$

Therefore, if we state that the universe r falls between these two values we have 95 chances out of 100 of being right.

Testing the Significance of a Coefficient of Correlation

When coefficients of correlation are based on small samples, the formula for estimating the standard error is

$$\sigma_r = \frac{\sqrt{1 - r^2}}{\sqrt{N - 2}}$$

This measure may be used in the formula

$$t = \frac{r - 0}{\sigma_r}$$

to determine whether r differs significantly from zero. Such a test is valuable because it is possible, due to random errors of sampling, to get a positive or negative coefficient of correlation when the coefficient for the universe is zero. If a test shows that the r based on a sample is significantly different from zero, then we can conclude that the universe r is not zero.

We will illustrate this test at the 0.05 level with r computed for the data from the sales areas of the Knick Co. (see Table 12-1). Assuming that these data come from a random sample of sales areas

$$\sigma_r = \frac{\sqrt{1 - 0.84^2}}{\sqrt{15 - 2}} = \frac{\sqrt{1 - 0.7056}}{\sqrt{13}} = \frac{.54}{3.605} = 0.15$$

and

$$t = \frac{0.84 - 0}{0.15} = \frac{0.84}{0.15} = 5.6$$

For 13 degrees of freedom ($n = N - 2 = 13$) at the 0.05 significance level, t, according to Table A-4, is 2.160. Therefore, it can be concluded that the difference is significant, that r is not zero, and that there is a true relation between the mean monthly rent and median family income in the sales areas of the Knick Co.

CORRELATION ANALYSIS OF GROUPED DATA

If a computer is not available and the number of paired observations to be correlated is large, time can be saved by grouping the data before performing the calculations.* The calculations will yield *estimates* of the values obtainable by correlating ungrouped observations.

Correlation of grouped data will be illustrated with the use of paired variables for 115 of the 157 U. S. metropolitan areas with 200,000 or more people. The variables are mean weekly earnings of production workers in manufacturing industries and per capita personal income. In this illustration, per capita personal income will be the dependent variable.

Tallying the Data

The first step in the procedure is to set up a two-way classification form as shown in Table 12-3. This table shows frequency classes on the horizontal axis for weekly earnings and on the vertical asix for per capita income. The cells that are formed by the crossed classifications are used to tally the number of paired observations that fall within the cells. Note that this table resembles a scatter diagram with the tally marks indicating the general direction of movement and giving a rough picture of the closeness of the relationship.

Tallying the paired observations is similar to plotting points on a scatter diagram. For example, in one metropolitan area—Akron, Ohio—mean weekly earning and per capita personal income were $166 and $5,220, respectively; therefore, a tally mark was placed in the cell formed by the X class of 150–175 and the Y class of 5000–5500.

Calculating the Sums Needed

After the data have been tallied, the marks are counted and the numbers, which are frequencies, are placed on another cross classified table for calculating values needed for the correlation analysis. The counted tally marks and the calculations needed for the formulas to be used are shown in Table 12-4. All but one of the calculations should look familiar because they are the ones used in Chapter 5 to compute the mean and standard deviation of a frequency distribution. The subscripts on the symbols identify the variables for which the calculations were made.

*In some cases the analysis may be made faster by grouping the data and making the calculation with a hand calculator than by gathering the ungrouped data and using a computer for the analysis.

TABLE 12-3. Cross-Classification Table for Tallying Mean Weekly Earnings of Production Workers and Per Capita Personal Income in 115 Metropolitan Areas with 200,000 or more People.

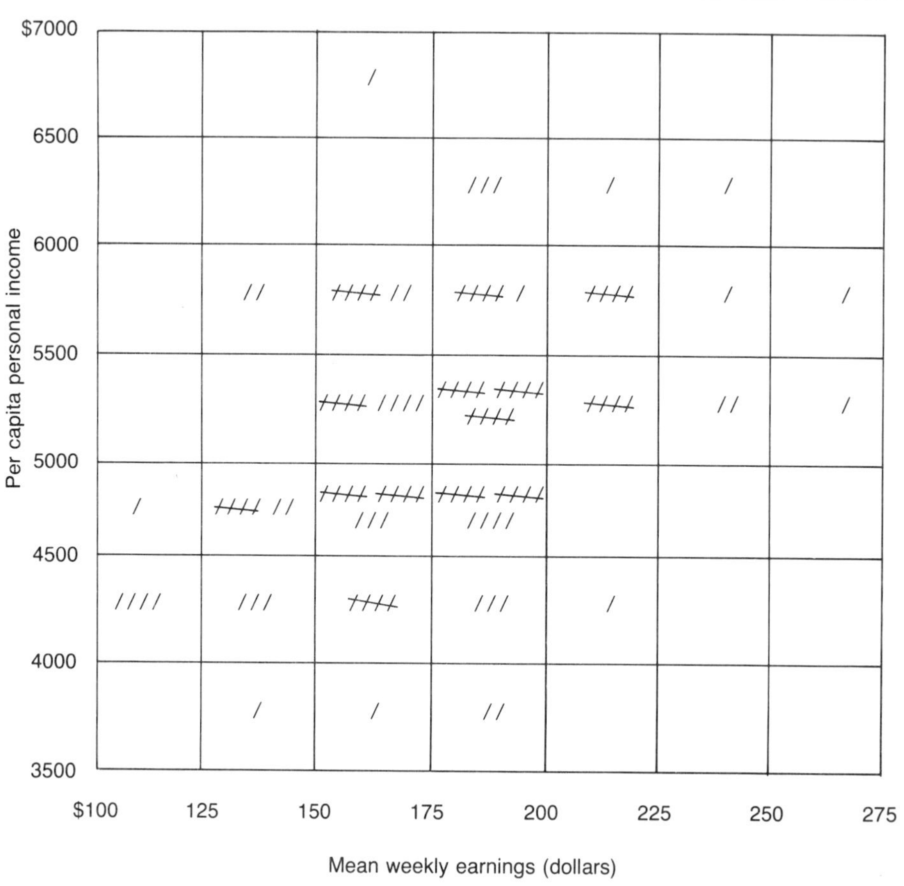

Source of data: *Statistical Abstract of the United States,* 1975, pages 892, 910, and 1928.

The number in the center of each cell in Table 12-4 is the sum of the tally marks in the corresponding cell in Table 12-3. The f_y values, the frequencies for the Y classes, were obtained by adding the center numbers horizontally. The f_x values, the frequencies for the X classes, were obtained by adding the center numbers vertically. The resulting figures are frequency distribution for the dependent and independent variables. The common total of each distribution, 115, is shown in the table. The other three rows and columns and their sums are self-explanatory calculations with which you should be familiar. However, the computation for $\Sigma f d'_X d'_Y$, shown in the lower right corner of the table, needs to be explained. The symbol f represents the frequency common to both the X and Y variables. This is the center value in the cell. The product $d'_X d'_Y$ are the left values in the cells. For example, the 4 in the upper right-hand cell is the product of the d'_Y and d'_X values for that cell, or 2×2. The right number in the same cell, 4, is the product $f d'_X d'_Y$, or 1×4. After similar calculations were made for each cell, the products were added and their sum is 85. This sum and other sums shown are used to compute the coefficient of correlation, the estimating equation, and the standard error of estimate. For grouped data, it is expedient to compute these measures in that order.

TABLE 12-4. Calculation of Values Needed for Correlating Mean Weekly Earnings of Production Workers and Per Capita Personal Income Placed in Frequency Classes.

PER CAPITA INCOME \ MEAN WEEKLY EARNINGS	$100–125	125–150	150–175	175–200	200–225	225–250	250–275	f_Y	d'_Y	$f_Y d'_Y$	$f_Y(d'_Y)^2$
$6500–$7000			−3×1= −3					1	3	3	9
6000–6500				0×3=0	2×1=2	4×1=4		5	2	10	20
5500–6000		−2×2= −4	−1×7= −7	0×6=0	1×5=5	2×1=2	3×1=3	22	1	22	22
5000–5500			0×9=0	0×15= 0	0×5=0	0×2=0	0×1=0	32	0	0	0
4500–5000	3×1=3	2×7= 14	1×13= 13	0×14= 0				35	−1	−35	35
4000–4500	6×4= 24	4×3= 12	2×5= 10	0×3=0	−2×1= −2			16	−2	−32	64
3500–4000		6×1=6	3×1=3	0×2=0				4	−3	−12	36
f_X	5	13	36	43	12	4	2	115	–	−44	186
d'_X	−3	−2	−1	0	1	2	3	–			
$f_X d'_X$	−15	−26	−36	0	12	8	6	−51	$\Sigma f d'_X d'_Y = 85$		
$f_X(d'_X)^2$	45	52	36	0	12	16	18	179			

Calculating the Coefficient of Correlation

The most convenient formula for computing the coefficient of correlation for grouped data is

$$r = \frac{N\Sigma fd'_X d'_Y - (\Sigma f_X d'_X)(\Sigma f_Y d'_Y)}{\sqrt{\left[N\Sigma f_X(d'_X)^2 - (\Sigma f_X d'_X)^2\right]\left[N\Sigma f_Y(d'_Y)^2 - (\Sigma f_Y d'_Y)^2\right]}}$$

Substitutions in this formula give

$$r = \frac{115(85) - (-51)(-44)}{\sqrt{\left[115(179) - (-51)^2\right]\left[115(186) - (-44)^2\right]}}$$

$$= \frac{9775 - 2{,}244}{\sqrt{(17{,}984)(19{,}454)}} = \frac{7511}{18{,}705} = +0.40$$

Calculating the Estimating Equation

The formula to use for the estimating equation makes use of r:

$$Y_c = \overline{Y} + \frac{r\sigma_Y}{\sigma_X}(X - \overline{X})$$

In this formula the means and standard deviations of the X and Y values are needed.*

$$\overline{X} = \overline{X}_a \times \frac{\Sigma f_X d'_X}{N} i_X = 187.50 \times \frac{-51}{115} 25 = 187.50 - 11.09 = 176.41$$

$$\overline{Y} = \overline{Y}_a + \frac{\Sigma f_Y d'_Y}{N} i_Y = 5250 + \frac{-44}{115} 500 = 5250 - 191.30 = 5058.70$$

$$\sigma_X = i_X \sqrt{\frac{\Sigma f_X (d'_X)^2}{N} - \left(\frac{\Sigma f_X d'_X}{N}\right)^2} = 25\sqrt{\frac{179}{115} - \left(\frac{-51}{115}\right)^2} = 29.15$$

$$\sigma_Y = i_Y \sqrt{\frac{\Sigma f_Y (d'_Y)^2}{N} - \left(\frac{\Sigma f_X d'_X}{N}\right)^2} = 500\sqrt{\frac{186}{115} - \left(\frac{-44}{115}\right)^2} = 606.42$$

Substituting these values and the value of r in the estimating equation, we have

$$Y_c = 5058.70 + 0.40\left(\frac{606.42}{29.15}\right)(X - 176.41)$$

$$Y_c = 5058.70 + 8.32(X - 176.41) = 5058.70 + 8.37X - 1467.73$$

$$Y_c = 3590.91 + 8.32X$$

*These formulas were discussed in Chapter 5.

Therefore, $a = 3590.91$ and $b = 8.32$. These should be close to the a and b that would result from an analysis of the ungrouped observations.

Calculating the Standard Error of Estimate

An expeditious computation of the standard error of estimate can be made with the formula

$$\sigma_{Y_u} = \sigma_Y \sqrt{1 - r^2}$$

which gives

$$\sigma_{Y_u} = 606.42 \sqrt{1 - (0.40)^2} = 555.79$$

This formula is easy to understand if you recall that r^2 is the proportion of the total variance of Y that has been explained by variations in X, and therefore, $1 - r^2$ is the proportion of the total variance that has not been explained. This being the case.

$$\sigma^2_{Y_u} = \sigma^2_Y (1 - r^2)$$

or, in other words, the unexplained variance equals the total variance times the proportion of the total variance that has not been explained.

CORRELATING DATA THAT ARE RANKED

Sometimes exact magnitudes for paired observations cannot be determined but ranks of magnitudes can be assigned. (That is, if there are N observations, each observation is given a number from 1 to N in the order of its magnitude; this number is its *rank* in N observations.) When such is the case, the coefficient of correlation previously explained should not be computed. However, to get a measure of the closeness of the association of the two ranked series *Spearman's rank correlation coefficient* can be used. The formula is

$$r_{\text{rank}} = 1 - \frac{6\Sigma D^2}{N(N^2 - 1)}$$

with D representing the differences in the paired rankings of the two series.

Table 12-5 has been set up to illustrate the use of Spearman's coefficient.

TABLE 12-5. Calculation of Values Needed for Correlation of Rankings of Ten Sales Areas of the Kaye Company by Sales Potentials and Actual Sales, 1976.

SALES AREA	*POTENTIAL RANKING*	*ACTUAL SALES RANKING*	*DIFFERENCE (D)*	D^2
A	1	1	0	0
B	2	3	−1	1
C	3	2	+1	1
D	4	7	−3	9
F	5	5	0	0
G	6	4	+2	4
H	7	6	+1	1
I	8	8	0	0
J	9	10	−1	1
K	10	9	+1	1
Total				18

Substituting in the formula we have

$$r_{\text{rank}} = 1 - \frac{6(18)}{10(100-1)} = 1 - \frac{102}{990} = +0.9$$

which is quite high.

If the potential and actual rankings had been identical, ΣD^2 would have been 0 and the rank correlation coefficient would have been +1. If the rankings had been inverse, the coefficient would have been negative. This formula gives the correct sign, which is positive in this case. If there is a tie in rank, the average (mean) of the ranks is given to the positions. Thus, if actual sales of areas B and C had been equal, they would have tied for a second place and the rank values for both would have been 2.5.

We might ask why rankings of sales and sales potential are correlated, rather than actual sales and sales potentials. A good reason is that precise measurements, and frequently even close measurements, of sales potentials are difficult; therefore, correlating the estimated potentials and actual sales would produce spurious accuracies that, in turn, could lead to wrong decisions. When data pertaining to one or both series to be correlated provide only rough estimates of actual magnitudes, the computation of r_{rank} is justified.

Furthermore, some rankings of individuals or other entities can be based on qualitative characteristics not subject to exact measurement. For example, a dean might rank the top ten students in a graduating class using criteria such as grade point average and extracurricular activities as guides in making his judgments. Rankings of this nature are suitable for the rank correlation technique described.

SIMPLE LINEAR CORRELATION OF TIME SERIES

Time series data are often correlated to determine whether a value of one series can be used to estimate or predict the value of the other. To illustrate, we will make a complete regression and correlation analysis of the U.S. Consumer Price Index and mean weekly earnings of production workers in the United States from 1966 to 1975 presented in Table 12-6. If there is a close correlation in the movements of the two series, we might feel comfortable in predicting either series from the other. We will assume, however, that the purpose of the analysis is to predict the value of the price index from a given value for average weekly earnings. Chart 12-6 shows that the relationship of the movements of the two series is positive, linear, and close.

Table 12-6 shows the necessary calculations for substitution in the formulas for the linear regression equation, standard error of estimate, and coefficient of correlation.

Chart 12-6. Mean weekly earnings of production workers in manufacturing industries and the consumer price index, United States, 1966–1975.

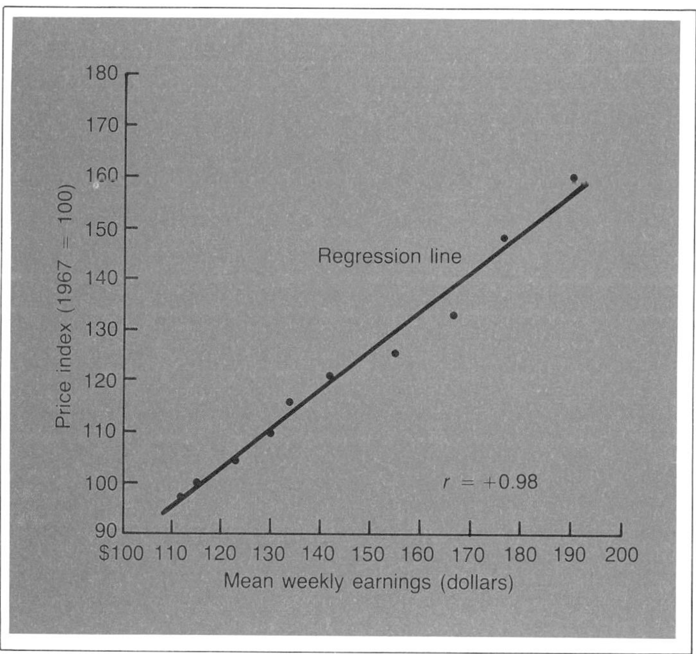

TABLE 12-6. Computation of Values Needed for Correlation Analysis of Production Worker Earnings in Manufacturing Industries and the Consumer Price Index, United States, 1966—1975.

YEAR	MEAN WEEKLY EARNINGS (DOLLARS)	CONSUMER PRICE INDEX 1967+100			
	X	Y	X^2	XY	Y^2
1966	112	97	12,544	10,864	9,409
1967	115	100	13,225	11,500	10,000
1968	123	104	15,129	12,792	10,816
1969	130	110	16,900	14,300	12,100
1970	134	116	17'956	15,544	13,456
1971	142	121	20,164	17,182	14,641
1972	155	125	24,025	19,375	15,625
1973	166	133	27,556	22,078	17,689
1974	176	148	30,976	26,048	21,904
1975	190	161	36,100	30,590	25,921
	1443	1,215	214,575	180,273	151,561

(1) $\Sigma Y = Na + b\Sigma X$

(2) $\Sigma XY = a\Sigma X + b\Sigma X^2$

Solving for b:

(1) $1215 = 10a + 1443b$

(2) $180{,}273 = 1443a + 214{,}575b$

$[(1) \times 144.3]$ $175{,}324 = 1443a + 208{,}225b$

$4{,}949 = 6350b$

$b = 0.77937$

Solving for a:

(1) $1215 = 10a + 1443(0.77937)$

$1215 = 10a + 1125$

$10a = 90$

$a = 9.0$

$Y_C = 9.0 + 0.78X$

The Estimating Equation

The solution of the two equations to obtain a and b for use in the equation $Y_c = a - bX$ are shown below the table. The equations are first solved for b by subtracting equation (1) from (2). Subtraction eliminates a, and b is found to be +0.77937.

This figure is then substituted in equation (1) in Table 12-6, and a is found to be 9.0. The estimating equation, therefore, is $Y_c = 9.0 + 0.78X$. To establish the regression line on Chart 12-6, the following calculations were made for weekly earnings of \$130, \$155, and \$190.

$$Y_c = 9.0 + 0.78(130) = 110.4$$

$$Y_c = 9.0 + 0.78(155) = 129.9$$

$$Y_c = 9.0 + 0.78(190) = 157.2$$

When these values were plotted on the scatter diagram, a straight line was drawn through them.

The Standard Error of Estimate

The standard error of estimate computed with the equation that makes use of the values of a and b is

$$\sigma_{Y_u} = \sqrt{\frac{\Sigma Y^2 - (a\Sigma Y + b\Sigma XY)}{N}}$$

$$= \sqrt{\frac{151{,}561 - \left[(9.0)\,(1215)\right] + (0.77937)\,(180{,}273)}{10}}$$

$$= \sqrt{\frac{151{,}561 - (10{,}935 + 140{,}499.4)}{10}}$$

$$= \sqrt{\frac{151{,}561 - 151{,}434.4}{10}} = \sqrt{\frac{126.6}{10}} = \sqrt{12.66} = 3.6$$

The standard error of estimate for correlated time series data can be used in the same way as for data not ordered by time if we assume the observations are scattered normally about the regression line. Such an assumption is usually practical, but the exact precision of the probabilities of the normal curve should not be applied. For example, when mean weekly earnings are \$190, Y_c is calculated to be 157.2. Therefore,

$$Y_c \pm \sigma_{Y_u} = 157.2 \pm 3.6 = 153.6 \text{ to } 160.8$$

which is the interval in which the likelihood is *about* two thirds that the Consumer Price Index would fall. Moreover, the chances are *about* 95 to 100 that $Y_c \pm 1.96\sigma_{Y_u}$ will contain the actual Y value.

The Coefficient of Correlation

The coefficient of correlation computation for the price and earnings data is

$$r = \sqrt{\frac{(a\Sigma Y + b\Sigma XY) - \bar{Y}\Sigma Y}{\Sigma Y^2 - \bar{Y}\Sigma Y}}$$

$$= \sqrt{\frac{151{,}434.4 - (121.5)\,(1215)}{515{,}561 - (121.5)\,(1215)}} = \sqrt{\frac{151{,}434.4 - 147{,}622.5}{151{,}561 - 147{,}622.5}}$$

$$= \sqrt{\frac{3811.9}{3938.5}} = \sqrt{0.9679} = +0.98$$

This coefficient, which seems to be reasonably high, indicates that predictions or estimates of the price index based on given values of mean weekly earnings should be quite accurate as long as the weekly earnings figures are within the range of the earnings figures correlated. Thus we could feel fairly safe using the calculated estimating equation for making estimates of the price index from given values of the average weekly earnings.

Caution in Estimating

Although we should not use X to estimate Y if it is outside the range of the X values used in the analysis, most analyst might venture outside that range by a small amount to make predictions. To illustrate, suppose that a reliable source has predicted that weekly earnings of production workers will rise to $200 in 1976. Using this figure, which is higher than any of the actual figures, we might calculate $Y_c = 9.0 + 0.78\ (200) = 165$, which would be a 1976 prediction for the price index. Going further, we might say that chances are about two out of three that the price index will be between 165 ± 3.6, or between 161.4 and 168.6.

Not only would it be dangerous to take too much liberty in using values beyond the observed values, but we should not predict too far into the future because the relationships that exist at a given time are not likely to continue indefinitely.

Caution in Correlating Time Series

An analyst may make a correlation analysis of time series and use the results in decision making. However, the interpretation of the meaning of the correlation measures is somewhat subjective because the values of a time series are not random and independent of each other. Before time series are correlated certain components may need to be removed from each variable. Time series components are discussed in Chapters 15–18 and Chapter 18 illustrates the correlation of two time series after the removal of trend.

NONLINEAR REGRESSION AND CORRELATION ANALYSIS

Occasionally, a scatter diagram reveals a curved pattern of dots, indicating that the relationship between the independent and dependent variables should be described by a curve. When this is the case, one of several equations can be used to describe that relationship. Sometimes the choice is difficult and requires calculation of two or more different equations and drawing several regression lines to determine which is the best. A discussion of the various nonlinear estimating equations is beyond the scope of this book.

However, to exemplify the nonlinear concept, a parabolic estimating equation will be illustrated, and the standard error of estimate and coefficient of correlation based on that equation will be calculated. The data on total expenditures and expenditures for food for ten families presented in Table 12-7 will be used for this purpose. In this illustration, we will make food expenditures the dependent variable. A scatter diagram of these ten paired values is shown with a curved regression line in Chart 12-7. The information gained from the scatter diagram is that as total spending increases so does spending for food, but at a slower rate. This relationship is to be expected. The human capacity for food consumption is limited, but higher-income people, with larger spending potential, are likely to buy more expensive food and eat out more often than poorer people with lower spending potential.

The Second Degree Estimating Equation

The regression line on Chart 12-7 was constructed with values calculated with the second degree equation

$$Y_c = a + bX + cX^2$$

Chart 12-7. Total expenditures and expenditures for food of ten childless families.

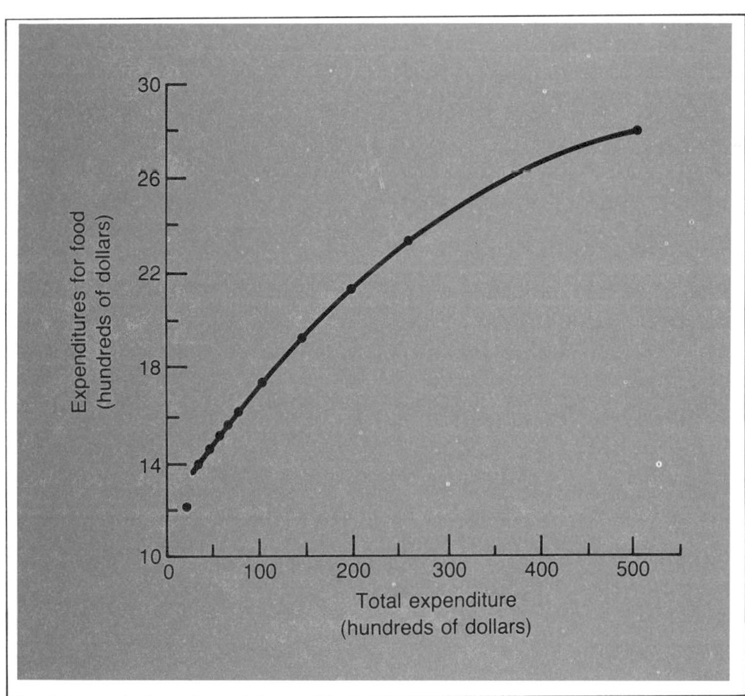

TABLE 12-7. Correlation of Annual Total Expenditures and Food Expenditures of Ten Childless Families.

TOTAL EXPEND-ITURES ($00) X	FOOD EXPEND-ITURES ($00) Y	X^2	Y^2	XY	X^2Y	X^3	X^4	Yc
34	12	1156	144	408	13,872	39,304	1,336,336	13.6
45	14	2025	196	630	28,350	91,125	4,100,625	14.2
50	15	2500	225	750	37,500	125,000	6,250,000	14.5
62	16	3844	256	992	61,504	238,328	14,776,336	15.2
75	17	5625	289	1275	95,625	421,875	31,640,625	16.0
100	18	10,000	324	1800	180,000	1,000,000	100,000,000	17.1
150	19	22,500	361	2850	427,500	3,375,000	506,250,000	19.7
200	21	40,000	441	4200	840,000	8,000,000	1,600,000,000	21.8
250	24	62,500	576	6000	1,500,000	15,625,000	3,906,250,000	23.6
500	28	250,000	784	14,000	7,000,000	125,000,000	62,500,000,000	28.0
1,466	184	400,150	3,596	32,905	10,184,351	153,915,632	68,670,603,922	

This equation will produce a curve with one bend. The shape of the curve depends on the values of the constants a, b, and c. The b value gives the general direction of the slope of the line and c produces a change in that slope.

To calculate these constants the following equations can be used:

$$
\begin{aligned}
&(1) \quad \Sigma Y = Na + b\Sigma X + c\Sigma X^2 \\
&(2) \quad \Sigma XY = a\Sigma X + b\Sigma X^2 + c\Sigma X^3 \\
&(3) \quad \Sigma X^2Y = a\Sigma X^2 + b\Sigma X^3 + c\Sigma X^4
\end{aligned}
$$

The values to be substituted into these two equations are given in Table 12-7.

Substituting,

$$
\begin{aligned}
&(1) \quad 184 = 10a + 1{,}466b + 400{,}150c \\
&(2) \quad 32{,}905 = 1{,}466a + 400{,}150b + 153{,}915{,}632c \\
&(3) \quad 10{,}184{,}351 = 400{,}150a + 153{,}915{,}632b + 68{,}670{,}603{,}922c
\end{aligned}
$$

The first step in the solution is to derive two new equations, (4) and (5), with only two constants each. This can be done by eliminating the constant a. We first multiply each term of equation (1) by 1466/10 or 146.6 and subtract the resulting equation from equation (2) to get equation (4). Thus,

$$
\begin{array}{lrcrcrcr}
(2) & 32{,}905 & = & 1466a & + & 400{,}150b & + & 153{,}915{,}632c \\
 & 26{,}974 & = & 1466a & + & 214{,}916b & + & 58{,}661{,}990c \\
\hline
(4) & 5{,}931 & = & 0 & + & 185{,}234b & + & 95{,}253{,}642c
\end{array}
$$

Secondly, we multiply each term in equation (2) by 400,150/1466 or 272.9536 and substract the resulting equation from equation (3) to get equation (5). The calculations are:

$$
\begin{array}{lrcrcrcr}
(3) & 10{,}184{,}351 & = & 400{,}150a & + & 153{,}915{,}632b & + & 68{,}670{,}603{,}922c \\
 & 8{,}981{,}539 & = & 400{,}150a & + & 109{,}222{,}389b & + & 42{,}011{,}828{,}202c \\
\hline
(5) & 1{,}202{,}812 & = & 0 & + & 44{,}693{,}243b & + & 26{,}658{,}775{,}720c
\end{array}
$$

Now equations (4) and (5) can be solved for either of the constants, b or c. We will solve for c. To do this, each term in equation (4) is multiplied by 44,693,243/185,234 or 241.279911 and the new equation is subtracted from equation (5)

$$
\begin{array}{lrcrcr}
(5) & 1{,}202{,}812 & = & 44{,}693{,}243b & + & 26{,}658{,}775{,}720c \\
 & 1{,}431{,}031 & = & 44{,}693{,}243b & + & 22{,}982{,}790{,}247c \\
\hline
 & -228{,}219 & = & 0 & + & 3{,}675{,}985{,}473c
\end{array}
$$

so

$$c = -0.0000621$$

Substituting the value for c in equation (5) to get b, we have

$$
\begin{aligned}
1{,}202{,}812 &= 44{,}693{,}243b + 26{,}658{,}775{,}720\,(-0.0000621) \\
1{,}202{,}812 &= 44{,}693{,}243b - 710{,}188 \\
44{,}693{,}243b &= 2{,}858{,}322
\end{aligned}
$$

so

$$b = 0.0640$$

By substituting the values for b and c into equation (1) we can calculate a:

$$\begin{aligned}(1) \quad 184 &= 10a + 1466\,(0.0640) + 400{,}150\,(0.0000621)\\ 10a &= 115.02\end{aligned}$$

so

$$a = 11.502$$

The estimating equation, then, is

$$Y_c = 11.502 + 0.0640X - 0.0000621X^2.$$

All of the Y_c values computed with this equation, by substituting in the X and X^2 values for each of the ten observations, are shown in the right-handed column of Table 12-7.

The Standard Error of Estimate

The amount of error that can be expected in the Y_c values is measured by the standard error of estimate. The equation

$$\sigma_{Y_u} = \sqrt{\frac{\Sigma Y^2 - (a\Sigma Y + b\Sigma XY + c\Sigma X^2Y)}{N}}$$

is convenient because it makes use of the constants a, b, and c, which have already been computed. Substitutions in this formula after $a\Sigma Y$, $b\Sigma XY$, and $c\Sigma X^2Y$ have been determined give

$$\sigma_{Y_u} = \sqrt{\frac{3596.0 - (2{,}116.368 + 2{,}105.920 - 632.448)}{10}}$$

$$= \sqrt{\frac{6.16}{10}} = \sqrt{0.616} = 0.78$$

Just as in simple linear regression analysis, this standard error of estimate may be used with Y_c to set up intervals within which the actual Y values would be expected to fall with given degress of certainty. For example, the probability is about two thirds that any $Y_c \pm \sigma_{Y_u}$ will contain the actual Y value if a large sample is used.

The Coefficient of Correlation

It is expedient to compute the coefficient of correlation with a formula that makes use of the values already available from computation of the standard error of estimate. The formula is

$$\rho = \sqrt{\frac{(a\Sigma Y + b\Sigma XY + c\Sigma X^2 Y) - \bar{Y}\Sigma Y}{\Sigma Y^2 - \bar{Y}\Sigma Y}}$$

The Greek letter ρ (rho) is used as the symbol for the coefficient of nonlinear correlation to differentiate it from the symbol for the linear correlation coefficient, r. Substitution gives

$$\rho = \sqrt{\frac{(2{,}116.368 + 2{,}105.920 - 632.448) - (18.4)(184)}{3{,}596.0 - (18.4)(184)}}$$

$$= 0.9714 = 0.99$$

This coefficient is not given a sign because it is possible for the regression line to be positive in one part and negative in another.

Adjustment for Sample Data

The formulas in the foregoing calculations can be applied to any paired series. If the two series represent *sample* observations, then the standard error of estimate can be adjusted by multiplying it by

$$\sqrt{\frac{N-1}{N-3}}$$

This adjustment will result in an estimate of the standard error of estimate for the population from which the sample was drawn.

The coefficient of correlation for the population can be estimated by calculating

$$\sqrt{1 - (1 - \rho^2)\left(\frac{N-1}{N-3}\right)}$$

Both adjustments are for the degrees of freedom lost in calculating the measures from sample data. If the sample is very large, however, these adjustments would be so negligible as to be unnecessary.

REVIEW QUESTIONS

1. Define regression analysis and correlation analysis.
2. Why would you make a regression analysis of two variables?
3. Why would you make a correlation analysis of two variables?

4. If an analyst has computed the equation $Y_c = a + bX$ for two variables, has he made a correlation analysis or a regression analysis?

5. Is the computation of a coefficient of correlation part of a regression analysis?

6. Is a coefficient of correlation in any way related to a regression equation even though a regression equation has not been computed?

7. What is meant by the term *correlation?*

8. What is the purpose of correlation analysis?

9. Why are two variables sometimes closely correlated?

10. True or false: If two variables are closely correlated, then the movements in one variable cause the movements in another. Why?

11. Can a coefficient of correlation be computed without computing a regression equation?

12. Why is it important to construct a scatter diagram before computing a regression line or coefficient of correlation?

13. Define and give the uses of the following: estimating equation, regression line, standard error of estimate, coefficient of determination, coefficient of correlation.

14. Define: total variance, explained variance, unexplained variance.

15. Before correlating two series, how can you determine which will be the dependent variable?

16. Under what conditions can Spearman's rank correlation coefficient be used effectively?

17. Why would you group two variables before computing the various regression and correlation measures?

PROBLEMS

1. Construct a scatter diagram of the data in Exercise Table 12-1. Make the number of deaths the dependent variable. Carefully inspect the diagram and answer the following questions.
   (a) Is the relationship of the two variables close enough so that accurate estimates of deaths from motor vehicle accidents could be based on known auto registrations?
   (b) Is the relationship of the two variables positive or negative?
   (c) If you were to describe the functional relationship between the two variables with a regression line would it be linear or curved?

EXERCISE TABLE 12-1. Motor Vehicles Registered and Deaths from Motor Vehicle Accidents, by States, 1973.

STATE	VEHICLES REGISTERED (000)	NO. OF DEATHS	STATE	VEHICLES REGISTERED (000)	NO. OF DEATHS
Ala.	2,354	1,376	Mont.	567	334
Alaska	172	78	Nebr.	1,097	425
Ariz.	1,419	1,008	Nev.	437	292
Ark.	1,185	664	N. H.	462	145
Calif.	13,413	5,049	N. J.	4,074	1,341
Colo.	1,803	699	N. Mex.	726	645
Conn.	1,891	516	N. Y.	7,319	2,929
Del.	333	137	N. C.	3,445	1,942
Fla.	5,347	2,704	N. Dak.	489	230
Ga.	3,170	1,894	Ohio	6,679	2,237
Hawaii	478	146	Okla.	1,984	776
Idaho	590	342	Oreg.	1,606	658
Ill.	5,952	2,293	Pa.	6,675	2,424
Ind.	3,231	1,629	R. I.	563	141
Iowa	1,979	832	S. C.	1,601	995
Kans.	1,778	648	S. Dak.	486	299
Ky.	2,091	1,155	Tenn.	2,467	1,599
La.	2,057	1,176	Tex.	7,816	3,699
Me.	596	252	Utah	751	377
Md.	2,259	847	Vt.	275	137
Mass.	2,952	1,029	Va.	2,793	1,264
Mich.	5,240	2,186	Wash.	2,371	826
Minn.	2,453	1,045	W. Va.	911	498
Miss.	1,312	932	Wisc.	2,472	1,129
Mo.	2,745	1,487	Wyo.	294	200

Source: U. S. Bureau of the Census, *Statistical Abstract of the United States, 1975.*

2. Using the family budgets as the dependent variable, construct a scatter diagram of the data in Exercise Table 12-2 and visually determine if (a) there is a fairly close relationship (b) the relationship is linear or curved, and (c) the relationship is positive or negative. Calculate a and b for the equation $Y_c = a + bX$. Compute three Y_c values where X equals 163, 200, 220. Plot these values on the scatter diagram, and draw a regression line.

3. Using the a and b values calculated in Problem 2, compute the standard error of estimate and the coefficient of correlation by the following formulas:

$$\sigma_{Y_u} = \sqrt{\frac{\Sigma Y^2 - (a\Sigma Y + b\Sigma XY)}{N}}$$

$$r = \sqrt{\frac{(a\Sigma Y + b\Sigma XY) - \bar{Y}\Sigma Y}{\Sigma Y^2 - \bar{Y}\Sigma Y}}$$

EXERCISE TABLE 12-2. Annual Cost of Budgets for a Family of Four and Mean Weekly Earnings of Production Worders in Manufacturing Industries, Selected Metropolitan Areas, 1974.

METROPOLITAN AREA	COST OF BUGET ($000)	MEAN WEEKLY EARNINGS (DOLLARS)	METROPOLITAN AREA	COST OF BUDGET ($000)	MEAN WEEKLY EARNINGS (DOLLARS)
Atlanta	$13.1	$163	Indianapolis	$12.9	$205
Baltimore	14.4	191	Kansas City	13.9	193
Baton Rouge	12.9	228	Los Angeles	14.1	179
Buffalo	15.4	222	Milwaukee	15.0	216
Cincinnati	13.8	199	Philadelphia	14.8	184
Cleveland	14.6	220	Pittsburgh	13.9	222
Dayton	13.4	219	San Francisco	15.1	219
Detroit	14.4	252	Seattle	14.5	209
Honolulu	17.0	163	St. Louis	13.8	200
Houston	12.9	205	Washington D.C.	15.0	199

Source: *Statistical Abstract of the United States,* 1975, pp. 427, 892, 910, and 928.

Also, for each of the Y_c values computed in Problem 2 above calculate $Y_c \pm \sigma_{YU}$, plot these six values, and draw a standard error band. Do about two-thirds of the dots fall inside the band? Why or why not? Was the value of r as high as you expected it to be from observation of the scatter on the scatter diagram? Do you think fairly accurate estimates of family budgets could be made for a metropolitan area if the weekly earnings of production workers in the metropolitan area were known? Why?

4. Use the information in Exercise Table 12-3 to do the following
   (a) Construct a scatter diagram using gasoline sales as the dependent variable.
   (b) Estimate gasoline sales with the equation $Y_c = a + bX$ using motor vehicle registrations in counties 2, 10, and 6, and compare these estimated sales to actual sales in those counties. Plot the three Y_c values on the scatter diagram and draw a regression line.
   (c) Compute the coefficient of determination and explain what it means.
   (d) Calculate the coefficient of correlation. What sign did you give to the coefficient. Why? What does this coefficient indicate?

5. Use the formula

$$r = \frac{N\Sigma XY - (\Sigma X)(\Sigma Y)}{\sqrt{\left[N\Sigma X^2 - (\Sigma X)^2\right]\left[N\Sigma Y^2 - (\Sigma Y)^2\right]}}$$

to measure the degree of closeness of the movements of the two variables in Exercise Table 12-4. Make personal income the dependent variable. After you have computed r, adjust it with the formula

$$\sqrt{1 - (1 - r^2)\frac{N - 1}{N - 2}}$$

What is the purpose of this adjustment? Is the relationship of the two variables close enough to make you feel that personal income in a metropolitan area could be accurately estimated with the number of tax returns in the area? Why?

EXERCISE TABLE 12-3. Motor Vehicle Registrations on July 1, and Gallons of Gasoline Sold During the Entire Year by the Gasco Company in 12 Counties, 1976.

COUNTY	THOUSANDS OF MOTOR VEHICLE REGISTRATIONS ON JULY 1	MILLIONS OF GALLONS OF GASOLINE SOLD
1	118	16.3
2	90	12.2
3	121	16.9
4	107	13.4
5	85	11.6
6	150	21.4
7	95	11.5
8	125	17.4
9	128	18.7
10	110	15.1
11	123	16.6
12	98	13.7

Source: The Gasco Company.

EXERCISE TABLE 12-4. Personal Income and Retail Sales in Twelve U.S. Metropolitan Areas, 1972 (a random sample of metropolitan areas with 250,000 or more people).

AREA	PERSONAL INCOME (BILLIONS)	RETAIL SALES (BILLIONS)
Akron, Ohio	3.2	1.5
Bakersfield, Calif.	1.4	0.7
Buffalo, N.Y.	63	2.8
Dallas, Tex.	11.3	6.1
Greenville, S.C.	1.9	1.1
Knoxville, Tenn.	1.6	1.0
Louisville, Ky.	4.0	2.0
Newark, N.J.	11.4	4.6
Reading, Pa.	1.4	0.7
Seattle/Everett, Wash.	6.8	3.3
Tucson, Ariz.	1.6	1.0
Wichita, Kans.	1.7	0.9

Source: U.S. Dept. of Commerce, *Statistical Abstract of the United States*, 1975; and *Survey of Current Business*, (Local Area Personal Income), May, 1974.

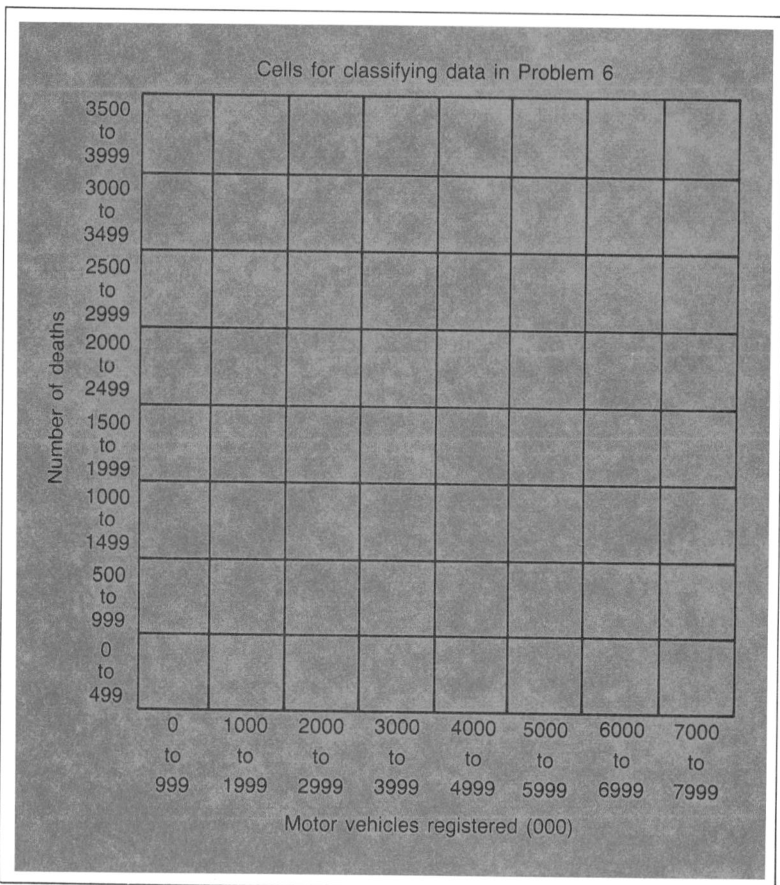

6. Eliminate California and classify the data in Exercise Table 12-1 in the cells above, set up a cross classification as illustrated in Table 12-4 and calculate the regression equation, the standard error of estimate, and the coefficient of correlation. The number of deaths is the dependent variable

7. Set up a two-way classification tally table and cross-classification table for grouping the data in Exercise Table 12-2. Compute the coefficient of correlation of these grouped data with the formula used for the illustration in the chapter. Does this coefficient have the same value as that computed from the ungrouped data in Problem 3? Why?

8. Seven applicants for a job with the Thielges Company were given a written aptitude test and each was interviewed. Based on the interviews, the applicants were ranked by the interviewer as to preference for job. The ranks are shown in Exercise Table 12-5, together with the ranks in scores made on the written aptitude tests. Compute Spearman's rank correlation coefficient and determine whether there is a close association between the ranked series. If there is, what does the analysis "prove" or indicate? Why?

EXERCISE TABLE 12-5. Seven Applicants for a Job in the Thielges Company Ranked According to Preference Based on Interviews and Scores on Written Aptitude Tests.

APPLICANT	*RANK BASED ON INTERVIEW*	*RANK BASED ON TEST SCORE*
A	1	4
B	2	3
C	3	1
U	4	7
E	5	6
F	6	5
G	7	2

Source: The Thielges Company.

9. Compute r_{rank} for the figures in Exercise Table 12-6. Explain the meaning of the result.

EXERCISE TABLE 12-6. 1976 Preseason Rankings of Ten Football Teams by the Associated Press and the United Press International.

	RANK GIVEN BY POLLS OF:	
	A.P. POLL (SPORTSWRITERS AND SPORTSCASTERS)	*U.P.I. POLL (COACHES)*
Nobraska	1	1
Michigan	2	2
Arizona State	3	7
Ohio State	4	3
Oklahoma	5	6
Alabama	6	4
Texas	7	5
Southern California	8	8
Pittsburgh	9	10
Penn State	10	9

Source: *The Milwaukee Journal*, August 28, 1976 and August 26, 1976.

10. Rank the two series from highest to lowest for the twelve countries in Exercise Table 12-3 and compute Spearman's rank correlation coefficient.

11. Construct a scatter diagram of the two time series shown in Exercise Table 12-7. Make the Index of Industrial Products the independent variable. Compute a and b for the equation $Y_c = a + bX$ and estimate the unemployment rate in 1976, based on the 1976 Industrial

Production Index of 125. Compute the coefficient of correlation and decide whether close estimates of the unemployment rate could be made for a year when the industrial production index is available. What general rule have you violated by using a value of the independent variable of 125 for estimating a value of the dependent variable? Do you think this rule should ever be violated? Why?

EXERCISE TABLE 12-7. Unemployment Rate and Index of Industrial Production, United States, 1968—1975.

YEAR	*UNEMPLOYMENT RATE*	*INDEX OF INDUSTRIAL PRODUCTION (1967=100)*
1968	3.6	106
1969	3.5	111
1970	4.9	107
1971	5.9	107
1972	5.6	115
1973	4.9	126
1974	5.6	125
1975	8.5	114

Source: *Federal Reserve Bulletin,* March, 1976 and April, 1974.

12. Construct a scatter diagram of the two time series in Exercise Table 12-8. Compute an estimating equation to describe the functional relationship between two variables. Make preferred stock yields the dependent variable. Obtain the yield for U.S. Bonds (long-term) for 1976 and use it to estimate the 1976 yield for preferred stock. Check on the accuracy of the estimate by getting the actual yield for 1976. Explain why your estimate was or was not reasonably accurate. Would the calculation of a standard error of estimate and coefficient of correlation be necessary for you to judge the accuracy of the estimate? Why?

EXERCISE TABLE 12-8. Yields of U.S. Government Bonds and Preferred Stocks, 1968—1975 (percent per annum).

YEAR	*U.S. BONDS (LONG-TERM)*	*PREFERRED STOCKS (DIVIDEND PRICE RATIO)*
1968	5.25	5.78
1969	6.10	6.41
1970	6.59	7.22
1971	5.74	6.75
1972	5.63	7.27
1973	6.30	7.23
1974	6.99	8.23
1975	6.98	8.38

Source: *The Federal Reserve Bulletin,* April 1970 and March 1976.

13. Math scores on the College Entrance Examination Board tests are supposed to be indicators of a student's ability in math. Exercise Table 12-9 shows CEEB scores and grades in a course in math made by 15 students. Assume that this is a simple random sample from 200 students and determine whether the CEEB math scores could be used to predict grades of other students who will take the math course. Carry your analysis only as far as is necessary for your to draw your conclusions. Qualify your answer in any way you think necessary.

EXERCISE TABLE 12-9. Math Scores on College Entrance Examination Boards and Grades in a Mathematics Course Earned by 15 Students.

CEEB MATH SCORES	*COURSE GRADE*
588	58
416	72
646	94
564	83
492	70
668	88
478	76
675	55
598	76
487	67
582	75
684	85
586	73
599	82
422	64

Source: A midwestern university.

14. Construct a scatter diagram of the ages and death rates in Exercise Table 12-10. Make death rates the dependent variable and use the methods and formulas demonstrated in this chapter, then fit a regression line to the dots on the diagram with Y_c values calculated with the equation:

$$Y_c = a + bX + cX^2$$

Compute the coefficient of correlation with the formula:

$$\rho = \sqrt{\frac{(a\Sigma X + b\Sigma XY + c\Sigma X^2Y) - \bar{Y}\Sigma Y}{\Sigma Y^2 - \bar{Y}\Sigma Y}}$$

EXERCISE TABLE 12-10. Death Rates per 1000 Persons, by Age, United States, 1960.

AGE	*RATE*
10	0.5
20	1.0
30	1.4
40	3.0
50	7.3
60	17.0
70	71.2
80	87.0

Source: U.S. Bureau of the Census.

15. Gather and analyze the necessary data and determine if reasonably accurate retail sales estimates for the 50 states could be made with known values of personal income for the states.

16. Select a simple random sample consisting of 20 of the counties in California. Gather data on median years of school completed and median family income for each of these 20 counties to see if there is a close relationship between the two variables. Do the findings support the adage that "education pays"?

17. With the calculations you made in Problems 2 and 3, compute the following for the data in Exercise Table 12-2.

$$\sigma_Y^2 = \frac{\Sigma(Y - \bar{Y})^2}{N}$$

$$\sigma_{Y_e}^2 = \frac{\Sigma(Y_c - \bar{Y})^2}{N}$$

$$\sigma_{Y_u}^2 = \frac{\Sigma(Y - Y_c)^2}{N}$$

$$r^2 = \frac{\sigma_{Y_e}^2}{\sigma_Y^2}$$

$$r^2 = 1 - \frac{\sigma_{Y_u}^2}{\sigma_Y^2}$$

Identify these measures.

18. Using the appropriate measures from Problem 17, compute the coefficient of correlation for the data in Exercise Table 12-2. Is it the same as that computed in Problem 2? Why?

19. Use the calculations you make in Problems 2 and 3 and compute 0.95 confidence intervals for X-values of 160, 190, and 220, and 250. How do these intervals differ? Why?

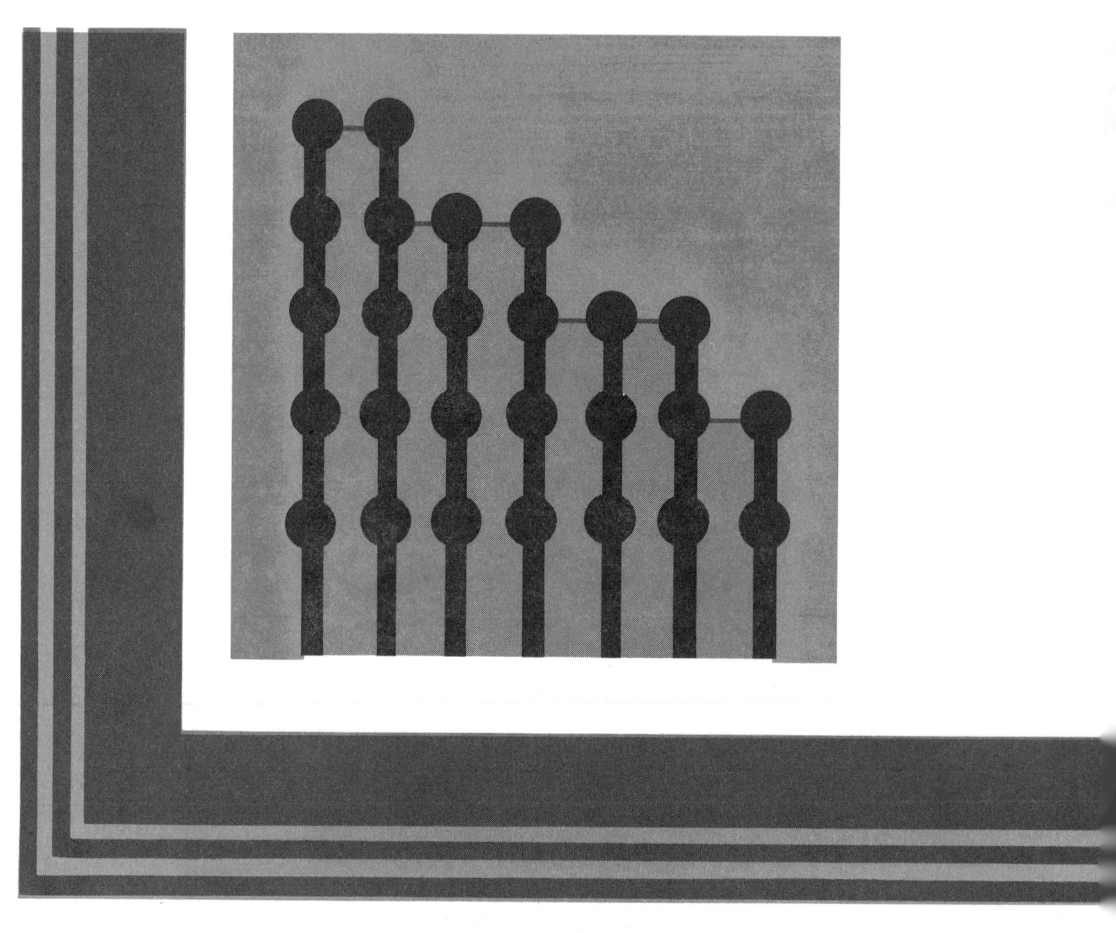

13

Multiple Regression and Correlation

MULTIPLE REGRESSION AND CORRELATION

An agricultural scientist may wish to examine the combined effects of varying amounts of water, fertilizer, and sunshine on the growth of a plant. A businessman may wish to determine what happens to sales of a product when he changes both the price and the advertising expenditures for the product. In both cases the desire would be to examine the combined effect of more than one independent variable on one dependent variable. For the agricultural scientist the growth of the plant is considered to depend upon the *combined* effects of water, soil fertility and sunshine. The businessman believes that changes in the price and advertising expenditures for the product will affect the amount of sales.

Regression Versus Correlation

When the combined effect of two or more independent variables on one dependent variable is measured, it is called *multiple regression analysis*. When the degree of the closeness of the combined movements of two or more independent variables and the dependent variable is measured it is called *multiple correlation analysis*.

However, the general term, *multiple correlation*, usually refers to an incorporation of both a multiple regression and multiple correlation analysis.

MULTIPLE REGRESSION

Net Regression Coefficients

Net Effects of Variables

The combined effects of several independent variables on a dependent variable is the sum of the net effects of each of the independent variables. The *net* effect of one independent variable is the effect it has on the dependent variable when the other independent variables are held constant.

For example, if the agricultural scientist holds the amount of water and the amount of fertilizer constant but allows the amount of sunshine to vary then he can measure the net effect of changes that sunshine has on plant growth. Moreover, if the businessman keeps the price of his product constant, he can measure the net effect of changes in advertising expenditures on sales. Also, if he changes his price and keeps advertising expenditures constant, he can measure the net effect of price change on his sales volume. A statistical measure which shows the typical net effect of an independent variable is called a *net regression coefficient*, which is a part of the multiple regression equation.

The Multiple Regression Equation

The number of terms in a multiple regression equation depends upon the number of independent variables to be used in the regression analysis. For example if we have only two independent variables, X_2 and X_3, we could write the multiple regression equation for estimating the dependent variable, X_1, as

$$X_{c1.23} = a_{1.23} + b_{12.3} X_2 + b_{13.2} X_3$$

where:

1) $X_{c1.23}$ is a computed (estimated) value of the dependent variable X_1 made with the independent variables X_2 and X_3.
2) $a_{1.23}$ is a constant in the equation in which X_1 is the dependent variable, and X_2 and X_3 are independent variables.
3) $b_{12.3}$ is the typical change in the dependent variable associated with a unit change in X_2 when the influence of X_3 is held constant.
4) $b_{13.2}$ is the typical change in the dependent variable associated with a unit change in X_3 when the influence of X_2 is held constant.

The terms $b_{12.3}$ and $b_{13.2}$ are *net regression coefficients* and the number behind the decimal point in a b subscript is the variable that is being held constant. The number to the left of the decimal point indicates the variables to which the net regression relates.

Equations for a larger number of independent variables would be written in a similar fashion. For example, the equation for three independent variables would be:

$$X_{c1.234} = a_{1.234} + b_{12.34} X_2 + b_{13.24} X_3 + b_{14.23} X_4$$

Here also, the b subscripts tell which variables are being related and which are held constant. Thus, $b_{12.34}$ measures the typical net effect of changes in X_2 on X_1 while variables X_3 and X_4 are not allowed to change. The student should be able to write an equation for a dependent and four independent variables.

Holding a variable constant

In certain scientific experiments each of the independent variables can be held constant. For example, the agricultural scientists can keep the amount of water constant when measuring the net effects of varying amounts of fertilizer and sunshine on the growth of a particular plant. However, in the fields of business, economics, and marketing this usually cannot be done. However, in a multiple regression analysis, a variable can be held constant mathematically. For example, if we desired to measure the effects of the number of auto registration and advertising expenditures in several cities on the sales of auto tires in those cities, we cannot experiment and literally hold auto registrations constant, because that would be beyond our control. Moreover, advertising expenditures could not be held constant if independent tire dealers make their own advertising decisions. However, in a subsequent example we shall learn that such variables are held constant in the mathematics of the regression analysis.

Multiple Regression Versus Simple Regression

In Chapter 12 we learned the meaning of simple regression and correlation. We used the simple regression equation, $Y_c = a + bX$, where Y_c was the computed (estimated) value of the dependent variable, and b was the regression coefficient that measured the typical change in Y for every unit change in X. However, the b value was in essence a gross regression coefficient because its computation did not take into consideration other variables that might affect Y, the dependent variable, nor did it involve the possible influence of other independent variables on the movements of the one independent variable being used. In fact, in a simple regression analysis the real effect or importance of the one independent variable is obscured for these reasons. Later in this chapter we will illustrate the difference between a simple regression coefficient and its corresponding net regression coefficient, and show how the net regression coefficient measures the "true" influence of an independent variable on the dependent variable.

MULTIPLE AND PARTIAL CORRELATION

Coefficients of Multiple Determination and Correlation

In a simple correlation of two variables, the coefficient of determination is the proportion of the total variation in the dependent variable that has been explained by variations in the independent variable.

The Coefficients Defined

However, in a multiple correlation the *coefficient of multiple determination* measures the proportion of the total variation in the dependent variable that has been explained by the combined movements of the several independent variable. The *coefficients of multiple correlation*, which is the square root of this coefficient, measures the degree to which the movements of the several independent variables are synchronized with the movements of the dependent variable.

The coefficient of correlation is a "pure" number between 0 and 1. No sign (+ or −) is affixed to the coefficient, since the association of the dependent variable may be positive with some independent variables but negative with others. A coefficient of one would result when all pertinent independent variables were included in a multiple correlation analysis. A coefficient of zero would result when none of the independent variables were pertinent. However, when actual data are used it is an extreme rarity for a coefficient of multiple correlation to be either 0 or 1.

Coefficients of Partial Determination and Correlation

Most computer programs for a complete multiple regression and correlation analysis include the computation of *coefficients of partial determination and correlation*.

Net Influence

These coefficients measure the degree of the *net* influence of the movements of each of the independent variables on the movements of the dependent variable.

The coefficient of partial determination for a particular variable reveals the proportion of the total variation in the dependent variable which is not explained by variation in other independent variables but is explained by that particular independent variable. The coefficient of partial correlation, which is the square root of the coefficint of partial determination, may be positive or negative. We will learn how the sign (+ or −) is determined.

MULTIPLE CORRELATION PROBLEM

Multiple correlation problems often involve observations from random samples. In the following problem the formulas applied will be those that would be applied to three sets of data from large samples from normally distributed universes, but to keep the analysis simple, only 19 observations will be used. Moreover, the illustrative problem will use hypothetical data (with a realistic tone) in order to bring out the meaning of the various regression and correlation measures. Later, a second illustration will exemplify the analysis of data of the type that is often found in the "real" world of business.

AN ANALYSIS OF THREE VARIABLES

Because of the tediousness and complexity of the computations required for a multiple regression and correlation analysis, to illustrate the computational procedure and the meaning of the various measures we will use only three variables. The three variables in Table 13-1 were designed so that the results would clearly reveal the purposes and uses of the regression and correlation coefficients to be examined.

The dependent variable—the one to be estimated or predicted—is the number of units produced with the use of 19 different combinations of machines and men. The number of machines and number of men, X_2 and X_3, are the independent variables. It is our desire to measure the relationship that these two variables have with the number of units produced, X_1.

The Analysis Procedure

A suggested procedure for making a complete multiple regression and correlation analysis is to first compute the multiple regression equation and then compute the standard error of estimate and, lastly, compute the coefficients of multiple determination and correlation. Also, it may be helpful to compute certain simple correlation measures for the dependent variable and each of the independent variables and for the different pairs of independent variables.

Scatter Diagrams

If only a few variables are involved, say three or four, scatter diagrams that show the simple relationships between paired variables may be helpful in the interpretation of the analysis. Scatter diagrams have been constructed from the data in Table 13-1 and they are shown in Chart 13-1. Diagram (*a*) shows the relationship between units produced and the number of machines. Diagram (*b*) shows the relationship between the units produced and the number of men. Diagram (*c*) shows the relationship between the two independent variables—number of men and number of machines. On each of the diagrams the simple coefficient of correlation between the two variables is given. The subscripts on the *r*'s indicate which variables are correlated. For example, r_{12} is the coefficient of correlation for variable X_1, the dependent variable, and X_2, one of the independent variables. Scatter diagrams of the independent variables, and computation of the simple coefficient of correlation for the two, as shown in diagram (*c*), may be helpful in interpreting the results of the multiple and partial correlation measures.

TABLE 13-1. Computation of Values Needed for Correlation Analysis of Production, Number of Machines and Number of Men.

	NO. OF UNITS PRODUCED X_1	NO. OF MACHINES X_2	NO. OF MEN X_3	X_1^2	X_1X_2	X_1X_3	X_2^2	X_2X_3	X_3^2
	4	1	2	16	4	8	1	2	4
	5	2	1	25	10	5	4	2	1
	5	1	3	25	5	15	1	3	9
	6	2	2	36	12	10	4	4	4
	6	1	4	36	6	24	1	4	16
	7	3	1	49	21	7	9	3	11
	7	2	3	49	14	21	4	6	9
	7	1	5	49	7	35	1	5	25
	8	3	2	64	24	16	9	6	4
	8	2	4	64	16	32	4	8	16
	8	1	6	64	8	48	1	6	36
	9	4	1	81	36	9	16	4	1
	9	3	3	81	27	27	9	9	9
	9	2	5	81	18	45	4	10	25
	9	1	7	81	9	63	1	7	49
	10	4	2	100	40	20	16	8	4
	10	3	4	100	30	40	9	12	16
	10	2	6	100	20	60	4	12	36
	10	1	8	100	10	80	1	8	64
Total	147	39	69	1,210	317	567	99	119	329

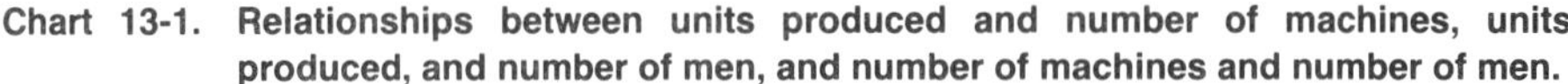

Chart 13-1. Relationships between units produced and number of machines, units produced, and number of men, and number of machines and number of men.

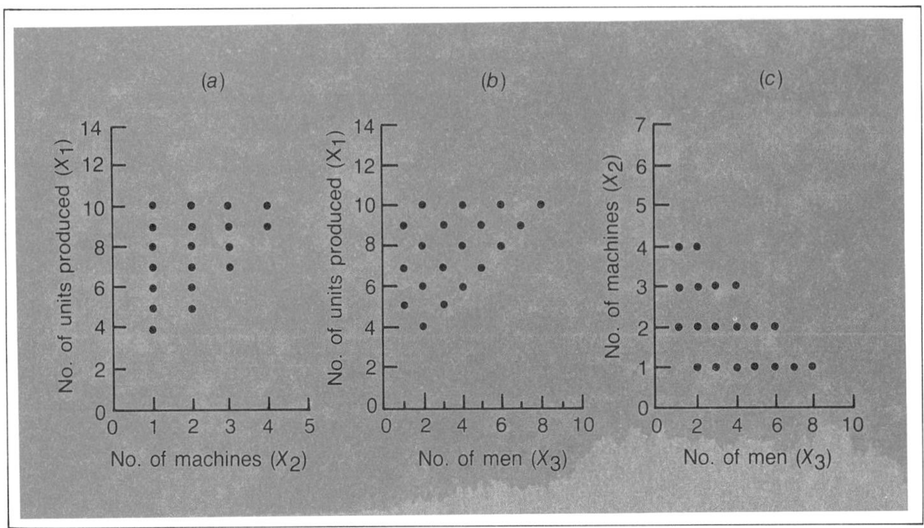

Revelations of the diagrams. From each of the scatter charts we can see the shape, direction, and to some extent, the closeness of the paired relationships. The shape of the relationships, linear or nonlinear, help the analyst decide which equations to use in the analysis. The scatter on the diagrams in Chart 13-1 seems to be linear so the analysis to follow will be for linear relationships. A curvilinear multiple regression and correlation analysis is beyond the scope of this book.

Scatter diagrams (*a*) and (*b*) in Chart 13-1 show low and positive correlations coefficients for the dependent variable and each of the independent variables. However, it would be incorrect to conclude that the number of machines or men used has little influence on the number of units produced. Simple relationships, such as depicted here, often obscure the real or *net* relationships between the dependent and an independent variable. Such relationships may be hidden by the relationships between independent variables. For example, an experienced analyst would surmise that the low simple correlation between X_1 and X_2 and X_1 and X_3, might have resulted from the negative relationship between X_2 and X_3, the two independent variables.

The Regression Equation

The obscurity of the relationship between the dependent variable and each of the independent variables can be eliminated by computing the multiple regression equation which shows the *net* regression coefficients for each of the independent variables. To compute the values for the regression equation for three variables, which is

$$X_{c1.23} = a_{1.23} + b_{12.3}X_2 + b_{13.2}X_3$$

the following three equations must be solved:

1) $\Sigma X_1 = Na_{1.23} + b_{12.3}\,\Sigma X_2 + b_{13.2}\,\Sigma X_3$

2) $\Sigma X_1 X_2 = a_{1.23}\,\Sigma X_2 + b_{12.3}\,\Sigma X_2^2 + b_{13.2}\,\Sigma X_2 X_3$

3) $\Sigma X_1 X_3 = a_{1.23}\,\Sigma X_3 + b_{12.3}\,\Sigma X_2 X_3 + b_{13.2}\,\Sigma X_3^2$

Table 13-1 shows the computations of the sums required for their solutions. Substitutions must be made in these equations and two new equations, A and B, must be computed. Equations A and B must be solved for $b_{13.2}$, which is then substituted in equation A to find $b_{12.3}$. Finally, $a_{1.23}$ is computed by substituting the values of $b_{12.3}$ and $b_{13.2}$ into equation (1) above. The substitutions and the computations are listed below. The addition (or subtraction) method, with which the student should be familiar, is used for solving the equations.

Substitutions needed to compute estimating equation are as follows.

1) $147 = 19a_{1.23} + 39b_{12.3} + 69b_{13.2}$

2) $317 = 39a_{1.23} + 99b_{12.3} + 119b_{13.2}$

3) $567 = 69a_{1.23} + 119b_{12.3} + 329b_{13.2}$

Solving for a new equation A:

1) $147 = 19a_{1.23} + 39b_{12.3} + 69b_{13.2}$

2) $317 = 39a_{1.23} + 99b_{12.3} + 119b_{13.2}$

1′) $\underline{301.7 = 39a_{1.23} + 80.1b_{12.3} + 141.6b_{13.2}}$ $\quad (1') = (1) \times \frac{39}{19}$

A $\quad 15.3 = 18.9b_{12.3} - 22.6b_{13.2}$

Solving for a new equation B:

2) $317 = 39a_{1.23} + 99b_{12.3} + 119b_{13.2}$

3) $567 = 69a_{1.23} + 119b_{12.3} + 329b_{13.2}$

2′) $\underline{560.8 = 69a_{1.23} + 175.2b_{12.3} + 210.5b_{13.2}}$ $\quad (2') = (2) \times \frac{69}{39}$

B $\quad 6.2 = -\ 56.2b_{12.3} + 118.5b_{13.2}$

Solving for $b_{13.2}$

A $\quad 15.3 = 18.9b_{12.3} - 22.6b_{13.2}$

B $\quad 6.2 = -56.2b_{12.3} + 118.5b_{13.2}$

A' $\quad \underline{-45.5 = -56.2b_{12.3} + 67.2b_{13.2}}$ $\quad A' = A \times \frac{-56.2}{18.9}$

$\quad 51.7 = 51.3b_{13.2}$

$$b_{13.2} = \frac{51.7}{51.3} = 1.008 = 1.0$$

Solving for $b_{12.3}$

$$A \qquad 15.3 = 18.9b_{12.3} - 22.6(1.0)$$

$$37.9 = 18.9b_{1.23}$$

$$b_{1.23} = \frac{37.9}{18.9} = 2.005 = 2.0$$

Solving for $a_{1.23}$

$$1) \qquad 147 = 19a_{1.23} = 39(2.0) + 69(1.0)$$

$$147 = 19a_{1.23} + 78 + 69$$

$$147 = 19a_{1.23} + 147$$

$$a_{1.23} = \frac{0}{19} = 0$$

Substituting in the multiple regression equation:

$$X_{c_{1.23}} = a_{1.23} + b_{12.3}X_2 + b_{13.2}X_3$$

$$X_{c_{1.23}} = 0 + 2X_2 + 1X_3$$

The 0 value for $a_{1.23}$ means that production would be zero if no machines and no men are used. The $b_{12.3}$ of (2) means that units of output increase by two for every increase in one machine and the $b_{13.2}$ of (1) means that the units produced increase by one for every additional man. The multiple regression equation may be used for estimating the number of units that would be produced given the number of machines and men to be used. For example, if three machines and two men are to be used then,

$$X_{c1.23} = 0 + 2(3) + 1(2) = 8$$

Therefore, the estimated production would be eight units.

The Standard Error of Estimate

Estimates made with the estimating (regression) equation are subject to sampling error when random samples of actual data are used.

Standard Error of Estimate

A standard measure of the sampling error is called the *standard error of estimate*. It indicates the reliability of the estimates made with the estimating equation. Its use is identical to that explained in Chapter 12 for a simple relationship between two variables, that is, it can be used to calculate prediction intervals for an actual value of the dependent variable.

Since the coefficients for the multiple regression equation have already been computed a formula for an expeditious computation of the standard error of estimate for three variables is

$$\sigma_{u_{1.23}} = \sqrt{\frac{\Sigma X_1^2 - a_{1.23}\,\Sigma X_1 - b_{12.3}\,\Sigma X_1X_2 - b_{13.2}\,\Sigma X_1X_3}{N}}$$

and substitutions for our problem are

$$= \sqrt{\frac{1{,}210 - 0(147) - 2.0(317) - 1.0(567)}{19}}$$

$$= \sqrt{\frac{1{,}210 - 634 - 567}{19}} = 0$$

This standard error of 0 reveals that there will be no error in the estimates of production made with the estimating equation and that *all* of the variation in production is explained by the combined variations in the number of machines and men. However, in a "real world" problem the standard error will not be 0 and two times out of three one would expect to find an actual X_1 value between $X_{c1.23} \pm \sigma_{u_{1.23}}$ when three variables from a large sample are being correlated.

The Coefficients of Multiple Determination and Correlation

The coefficient of multiple determination, $R^2_{1.23}$, will reveal the proportion of the total variation in the number of units produced that is associated with the variations in the number of machines and men, when considered together. The following formula is suggested because it makes use of values that were used in the computation of the standard error of estimate:

$$R^2_{1.23} = \frac{a_{1.23}\,\Sigma X_1 + b_{12.3}\Sigma X_1X_2 + b_{13.2}\,\Sigma X_1X_3 - N\overline{X}_1^2}{\Sigma X_1^2 - N\overline{X}_1^2}$$

The only new term in the formula is $\overline{X}_1$, the mean of the dependent variable, which equals

$$\frac{\Sigma X_1}{N} = \frac{147}{19}$$

Substitutions in the formula and the calculations are:

$$\frac{0(147) + 2.0(317) + 1.0(567) - 19\left(\frac{147}{19}\right)^2}{1201 - 19\left(\frac{147}{19}\right)^2} = \frac{63.7}{63.7} = 1$$

Since $R^2_{1.23} = 1$ then all of the variations in the units produced have been explained by the variations in the number of machines and the number of men. This result was expected because the standard error of estimate, which is a measure of the unexplained variation in the dependent variable was, 0. In fact, if a standard error of estimate in *any* analysis is 0, then the coefficient of multiple determination is 1. Moreover, in any multiple regression and correlation analysis the smaller the standard error of estimate the larger the coefficients of multiple determination and correlation. In this problem,

$$R_{1.23} = \sqrt{R^2_{1.23}} = \sqrt{1} = 1$$

which is perfect correlation.

Coefficients of Partial Determination

How did perfect correlation result when the simple correlation between X_1 and X_2 ($r_{12} = 0.44$) and between X_1 and X_3 ($r_{13} = 0.47$) were low, as depicted in Chart 13-1? The answer is that the effect of the variation in the number of machines was obscured by the variations in the number of men and the effect of the variation in the number of men was obscured by the variation in the number of machines. This was expected because of the negative simple correlation between X_2 and X_3 which is shown in scatter diagram (*c*). When this relationship is accounted for we can see the net influence of each variable, which has already been measured, in an *absolute* sense, by the net regression coefficients. However, one can measure the *relative* contribution of each of the several independent variables in explaining variations in the dependent variable not explained by the other variables. This can be done with partial (or net) coefficients of determination.

Coefficient of Partial Determination

A coefficient of partial determination is the net increase in the explained variation from the newly introduced independent variable, expressed as a proportion of the variation in the dependent variable which was not explained before the introduction of the new independent variable.

Computations using the variances.

Since the *variance* is a measure of variation, the following formulas may be used to compute the two coefficients of partial determination in an analysis involving one dependent and two independent variables:

$$r^2_{12.3} = 1 - \frac{\sigma^2_{u1.23}}{\sigma^2_{u1.3}} \qquad \text{and} \qquad r^2_{13.2} = 1 - \frac{\sigma^2_{u1.23}}{\sigma^2_{u1.2}}$$

In these formulas $r^2_{12.3}$ is the partial coefficient of determination resulting from the introduction of X_2 and $r^2_{13.2}$ is the partial coefficient of determination resulting from the introduction of X_3. The symbol $\sigma^2_{u1.23}$ is the unexplained variance for the multiple case, $\sigma^2_{u1.3}$ is the unexplained variance in the simple relationship between X_1 and X_3, and $\sigma^2_{u1.2}$ is the unexplained variance in the simple relationship between X_1 and X_2.

Computations using r and R. Using the procedure explained in Chapter 12 for computing the standard error of estimate in the sample case, $\sigma_{u_{1.2}}$ was found to be 1.6168. Since we previously found $\sigma_{u_{1.23}}$ to be 0, then

$$r^2_{12.3} = 1 - \frac{0}{(1.6168)^2} = 1 \qquad \text{and} \qquad r^2_{13.2} = 1 - \frac{0}{(1.6446)^2} = 1$$

The other formulas for $r^2_{12.3}$ and $r^2_{13.2}$ which are often expedient to use are:

$$r^2_{12.3} = \frac{R^2_{1.23} - r^2_{13}}{1 - r^2_{13}} \qquad \text{and} \qquad r^2_{13.2} = \frac{R^2_{1.23} - r^2_{12}}{1 - r^2_{12}}$$

In the formula for $r^2_{12.3}$ the numerator of the formula measures the net increase in the proportion of the variation in X_1 that can be attributed to the introduction of X_2 and the denominator measures the proportion of the variation in X_1 that was not explained by the exclusive use of X_3. An analogous wording would apply to the formula for $r^2_{13.2}$.

Substitution in these formulas are,

$$r^2_{12.3} = \frac{1 - (0.47)^2}{1 - (0.47)^2} = 1 \qquad \text{and} \qquad r^2_{13.2} = \frac{1 - (0.44)^2}{1 - (0.44)^2} = 1$$

Since $r^2_{12.3} = 1$, we know that all of the variation in X_1 that was not explained by the exclusive use of X_3 has been explained by variations in X_2 and since $r^2_{13.2} = 1$, then we know that all of the variation in X_1 that was not explained by the exclusive use of X_2 was explained by the variation in X_3.

This is clearly revealed in Table 13-2, which shows the removal of the influence of each of the independent variables on the number of units produced. Column (4) shows the contribution of machines to the number of units produced and Column (5) shows the number of units produced when this contribution is taken out. Notice that the values in Column (3) and Column (5) are identical, which means perfect correlation between the number of men and the remaining units produced. Column (6) shows the contribution of men to the number of units produced, and (7) shows this contribution removed. Note that the values in this column are exactly double their corresponding values in Column (2), which means perfect correlation between the number of machines and the remaining number of units produced.

TABLE 13-2. Removal of the Influence of Machines and Men on the Number of Units Produced.

(1) NO. OF UNITS PRODUCED X_1	(2) NO. OF MACHINES X_2	(3) NO. OF MEN X_3	(4) $b_{12.3}X_2$ $(2X_2)$	(5) COL. (1) − COL. (4) NO. OF UNITS WITH MACHINE INFLUENCE REMOVED	(6) $b_{13.2}X_3$ $(1X_3)$	(7) COL. (1) − COL. (6) NO. OF UNITS WITH INFLUENCE OF MEN REMOVED
4	1	2	2	2	2	2
5	2	1	4	1	1	4
5	1	3	2	3	3	2
6	2	2	4	2	2	4
6	1	4	2	4	4	2
7	3	1	6	1	1	6
7	2	3	4	3	3	4
7	1	5	2	5	5	2
8	3	2	6	2	2	6
8	2	4	4	4	4	4
8	1	6	2	6	6	2
9	4	1	8	1	1	8
9	3	3	6	3	3	6
9	2	5	4	5	5	4
9	1	7	2	7	7	2
10	4	2	8	2	2	8
10	3	4	6	4	4	6
10	2	6	4	6	6	4
10	1	8	2	8	8	2

Coefficients of Partial Correlation

Since the coefficient of partial correlation is the square root of the coefficient of partial determination then $r_{12.3} = +1$ and $r_{13.2} = +1$.

Signs of the Coefficients

The signs of coefficients of partial correlation are determined by their corresponding net regression coefficients. Therefore, $r_{12.3}$ receives the same sign as $b_{12.3}$, and $r_{13.2}$ receives the same sign as $b_{13.2}$.

Both of these coefficients show perfect partial correlation, because the variations in X_2 and X_3 explained all of the variation in X_1.

A TYPICAL PROBLEM

Let us investigate another correlation problem of the type that exemplifies realistic data, using computations from a computer program because such a program gives the same answers as the formulas used in the preceding discussion. This program is similar to other correlation programs in use.

The data to be analyzed are in Table 13-3. This is a random sample of only 20 of the thousands of sales areas of the Xero Company. However, let us first treat the data as if they were for a large sample, and then make adjustments necessary for small samples. A practical objective of the analysis would be to determine if reasonably accurate estimates of tire sales could be made for a sales area if the number of autos registered and the advertising expenditures for the sales area were known. However, the main objective here is to further explain the meaning of the regression and correlation measures.

TABLE 13-3. Xero Brand Tire Sales, Thousands of Autos Registers, and Tire Advertising Expenditures in 20 Sales Areas of the Xero Company.

XERO BRAND TIRE SALES ($000)	*THOUSANDS OF AUTOS REGISTERED*	*ADVERTISING EXPENDITURES FOR XERO BRAND TIRES ($000)*
50	77	1 1
580	670	13.5
960	915	17.4
182	210	3.2
210	293	4.0
325	308	5.5
310	348	5.5
600	712	10.0
300	296	4.6
720	667	11.4
190	212	3.0
255	282	4.8
385	405	5.9
305	266	6.0
800	953	14.2
315	376	4.9
275	284	5.2
400	422	7.1
104	138	2.2
480	579	8.4

Computer Program Computations

In this analysis the sales of Xero Brand tires is the dependent variable, X_1. Auto registrations, X_2, and advertising expenditures, X_3, are the independent variables.

TABLE 13-4. Computer Computation of Regression from Table 13-3.

INPUT DATA

50.0000	77.0000	1.1000
580.0000	670.0000	13.5000
960.0000	915.0000	17.4000
182.0000	210.0000	3.2000
210.0000	293.0000	4.0000
325.0000	308.0000	5.5000
310.0000	348.0000	5.5000
600.0000	712.0000	10.0000
300.0000	296.0000	4.6000
720.0000	667.0000	11.4000
190.0000	212.0000	3.0000
255.0000	282.0000	4.8000
385.0000	405.0000	5.9000
305.0000	266.0000	6.0000
800.0000	953.0000	14.2000
315.0000	376.0000	4.9000
275.0000	284.0000	5.2000
400.0000	422.0000	7.1000
104.0000	138.0000	2.2000
480.0000	579.0000	8.4000

SUMS OF PRODUCTS

4066290.000	4344077.000	72421.500
.000	4699279.000	77578.187
.000	.000	1305.428

SIMPLE CORRELATION

$X(1) = -0.62958736E$ 01 + 0.93568486E 00 * $X(2)$
STANDARD ERROR 50.1852
$RSQ = 0.95276$ $R = 0.97609$

$X(1) = 0.17615036E$ 02 + 0.53616547E 02 * $X(3)$
STANDARD ERROR 48.4014
$RSQ = 0.95606$ $R = 0.97778$

$X(2) = 0.40120544E$ 02 + 0.55189117E 02 * $X(3)$
STANDARD ERROR 63.3538
$RSQ = 0.93082$ $R = 0.96479$

Tables 13-4 and 13-5 resulted from the running of a computer program to analyze the variables. Table 13-4 shows the computer computation of simple regression and correlation measures and Table 13-5 shows the computer computation of the coefficients of partial determination and correlation, the net regression coefficients, and the coefficients of multiple determination and correlation.

Chart 13-2 pictures the simple relationship between each of the independent variables and the dependent variable and the relationship between the two independent variables. Close, linear, and positive relationships are revealed for each of the paired variables, indicating that numerical measurements of the relationships may provide an equation useful for estimating and forecasting tire sales.

TABLE 13-5. Computer Computation of Correlation from Table 13-3.

PARTIAL CORRELATION

	RSQ	*R*
R(13.2)	0.3976668	0.6306082
R(12.3)	0.3524559	0.5936799

MULTIPLE CORRELATION

X(1)=*A*(1) + *A*(2)**X*(2) + *A*(3)**X*(3) + . . . ETC

A(1) = −0.58861285*E* 00
A(2) = 0.45370048*E* 00
A(3) = 0.28577164*E* 02

STANDARD ERROR 38.9487

RSQ = 0.97155 *R* = 0.98567

ACTUAL	ESTIMATED	RESIDUAL	PCT. ERROR
50.00	65.78	−15.78	−31.56
580.00	689.18	−109.18	−18.82
960.00	911.79	48.21	5.02
182.00	186.14	−4.14	−2.27
210.00	246.65	−36.65	−17.45
325.00	296.33	28.67	8.82
310.00	314.47	−4.47	−1.44
600.00	608.22	−8.22	−1.37
300.00	265.16	34.84	11.61
720.00	627.81	92.19	12.80
190.00	181.33	8.67	4.56
255.00	264.53	−9.53	−3.74
385.00	351.77	33.23	8.63
305.00	291.56	13.44	4.41
800.00	837.58	−37.58	−4.70
315.00	310.03	4.97	1.58
275.00	276.86	−1.86	−0.68
400.00	393.77	6.23	1.56
104.00	124.89	−20.89	−20.09
480.00	502.15	−22.15	−4.61

Chart 13-2. **Relationships between Xero Brand tire sales and auto registrations, Xero Brand tire sales and advertising expenditures for Xero Brand tires, and thousands of auto registrations and advertising expenditures for Xero Brand tires: 20 sales areas of the Xero Company.**

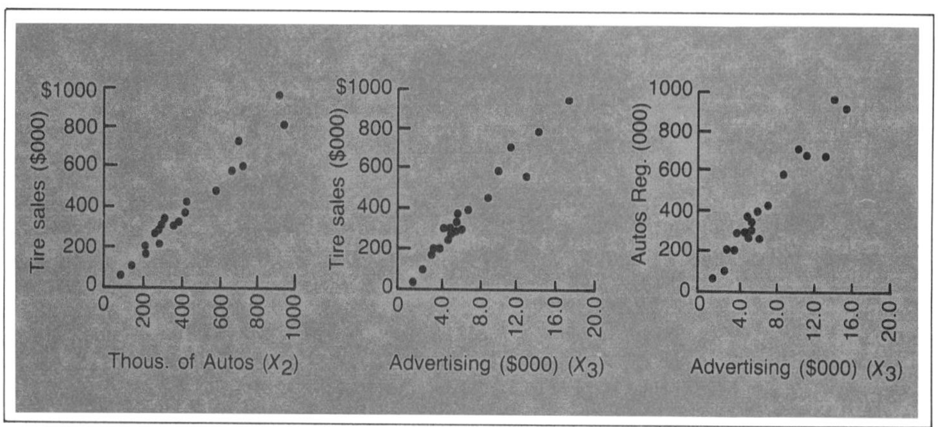

Simple Regression and Correlation Measures

The simple regression and correlation measures in Table 13-4 give for each pair of variables (a) the estimating equation, (b) the standard error of estimate, and (c) the coefficients of determination and correlation. For example, for the analysis of X_1 and X_2, the simple regression equation is $X_{c1.2} = a_{1.2} + b_{12}X_2 = -6.2959 + 0.9357X_2$. The standard error of estimate, $\sigma_{1.2}$, is 50.1852, the coefficient of determination ($RSQ = r^2_{12}$) is 0.95276, and the coefficient of correlation ($R = r_{12}$) is 0.97609. The subscripts of the symbols identify the two variables involved in the analysis.

The other simple correlation measures on the computer sheet are for variables X_1 and X_3 [identified as $X(1)$ and $X(3)$] and for variables X_2 and X_3. All of these measures of simple regression and correlation are helpful in understanding certain multiple regression and correlation measures and in determining the contributions of the independent variables in a multiple regression and correlation analysis.

Coefficients of Partial Determination and Correlation

The partial coefficients of determination and correlation in Table 13-5 ($r^2_{13.2}$, $r_{13.2}$, $r^2_{12.3}$, and $r_{12.3}$) are easily identified. *RSQ* and *R* are synonymous with r^2 and r, which have been used previously to symbolize those measures. For example, $r^2_{13.2} = 0.3976668$ and $r_{13.2} = 0.6306082$.

Multiple Regression and Correlation Measures

The multiple regression equation we have been using, $X_{c1.23} = a_{1.23} + b_{12.3}X_2 + b_{13.2}X_3$, is symbolized in the computer calculation as $X(1) = a(1) + A(2) \cdot X(2) + A(3) \cdot X(3)$. Therefore, the regression equation is:

$$X_{c1.23} = -0.58861285 + 0.45370048X_2 + 28.577164X_3$$

The standard error of estimate for the multiple case, $\sigma_{u1.23}$, is 38.9487 and $R^2_{1.23}$ and $R_{1.23}$, the coefficients of multiple determination and correlation are 0.97155 and 0.98567, respectively.

The regression coefficients. We will now interpret the meaning of the multiple correlation measures and see how they relate to the simple correlation measures.

In the multiple regression equation, $b_{12.3} = +0.4537$. This is the typical net change in sales per unit change in auto registration. In other words, when there is a change of 1000 in auto registrations, the net increase in sales is $0.4537 \times 1{,}000 =$ \$453.70. Since $b_{13.2} = 28.5772$, we know that the net increase in sales is \$28,577.20 for every \$1000 change in advertising expenditures. If there were an increase of 1000 in both $b_{12.3}$ and $b_{13.2}$ then tire sales would rise by \$29,030.90. (\$28,577.20 + \$453.70). To demonstrate this increase with the use of the multiple regression equation, we will assume that auto registration (in thousands) are 210 and advertising expenditures (in thousands of dollars) are \$3.2. Therefore, estimated tire sales are,

$$X_{c1.23} = -0.5886 + 0.4537(210) + 28.5772(3.2) = 186.13144$$

Now, if we let auto registrations be 211 thousand and advertising expenditures be \$4.2 thousand then,

$$X_{c1.23} = -0.5886 + 0.4537(211) + 28.5772(4.2) = 215.16634$$

and $215.16634 - 186.13544 = 29.0309$, which is a \$29,030.90 increase. In this multiple regression equation $a_{1.23} = -0.5886$, which is the expected sales of tires, in thousands of dollars, when no autos are registered and no advertising expenditures are made. Alone, this value is unrealistic because one would expect zero sales rather than an impossible negative sales when there were no autos and no advertising expenditures.

The standard error of estimate. An $X_{c1.23}$ value (estimated value) has been computed for each actual X_1 value. These, together with the differences between them, are given in the residual column of Table 13-5. These residual values are the unexplained deviations. If these deviations are squared, summed, and divided by 20 (the number of observations) the result will be the measure called *unexplained variance*, $\sigma^2_{u1.23}$. The square root of this measure, $\sigma_{u1.23}$, is the *standard error of estimate*. A formula for the standard error of estimate may be written.

$$\sigma_{u1.23} = \sqrt{\frac{(X_1 - X_{c1.23})^2}{N}}$$

This value, given in Table 11-5, is 38.9487, and its use is analogous to the use of the standard error of estimate in a simple regression and correlation analysis. Therefore $X_{c1.23} \pm \sigma_{u_{1.23}}$ is the interval in which we would expect as actual X_1 value to fall two times out of three when the variables are for a large sample.

Coefficients of multiple determination and correlation. The coefficient of multiple determination, $R^2_{1.23} = 0.97155$, indicates that nearly all (97.2%) of the variation in the dependent variable (tire sales) has been explained by variations in auto registrations and tire advertising expenditures. $R_{1.23}$ is very high (0.98567), which indicates that combined fluctuations of autos registered and tire advertising have much influence on the fluctuations in tire sales.

Coefficients of partial determination. Both of the coefficients of partial determination are greater than zero, therefore each independent variable, X_2, and X_3, explains part of the variation in X_1 that was not explained by the other independent variables. In our example, $r^2_{13.2} = 0.3977$, and $r^2_{12.3} = 0.3525$. This means that 39.77% of the variation in X_1 that was not explained by variation in X_2, has been explained by the variation in X_3, and that 35.25% of the variation in X_1 that was not explained by variation in X_3 has been explained by the variation in X_2.

You will recall that for a three-variable analysis, coefficients of partial determination can be computed with the formulas,

$$r^2_{12.3} = 1 - \frac{\sigma^2_{u_{1.23}}}{\sigma^2_{u_{1.3}}} \qquad r^2_{13.2} = 1 - \frac{\sigma^2_{u_{1.23}}}{\sigma^2_{u_{1.2}}}$$

$$r^2_{12.3} = \frac{R^2_{1.23} - r^2_{13}}{1 - r^2_{13}} \qquad r^2_{13.2} = \frac{R^2_{1.23} - r^2_{12}}{1 - r^2_{12}}$$

These computations, of course, will not be necessary if a computer program provides the measures. However, they should help one understand what partial coefficients measure. For example, if the ratio $\sigma^2_{u_{1.23}}/\sigma^2_{u_{1.3}}$ is less than one, the independent variable X_2 provides information about X_1 in addition to that provided by X_3, which results in a reduction of the unexplained variance of the dependent variable and an increase in the explained variations. Also, in words the expression

$$\frac{R^2_{1.23} - r^2_{13}}{1 - r^2_{13}} = \frac{\text{The net increase in the proportion of the total variation of the dependent variable, } X_1\text{, that resulted from the introduction of the independent variable } X_2.}{\text{The proportion of the total variation of the dependent variable not explained by the exclusive use of } X_3.}$$

Substitutions in these two formulas from Tables 13-4 and 13-5 and the calculations are:

$$r^2_{12.3} = 1 - \frac{\sigma^2_{u_{1.23}}}{\sigma^2_{u_{1.3}}} = 1 - \frac{(38.948)^2}{(48.4014)^2} = 1 - \frac{1{,}516.9467}{2{,}342.6955} = 0.3525$$

also

$$r^2_{12.3} = \frac{R_{1.23} - r^2_{13}}{1 - r^2_{13}} = \frac{0.97155 - 0.95606}{1 - 0.95606} = \frac{0.01549}{0.04394} = 0.3525$$

These are the same answers, accurate to four decimal places, as those provided by the computer program.

Comparison of the Simple and Multiple Measures

Regression coefficients. A study of Table 13-4 and 13-5 will reveal differences in the simple regression coefficients and their corresponding net regression coefficients. You will note that $b_{12} = +0.9357$ while $b_{12.3} = +0.4537$, and $b_{13} = +53.6165$ while $b_{13.2} = +28.5772$. Note that both of the net regression coefficients are smaller than their corresponding simple regression coefficients. This is a tendency in a three-variable multiple regression analysis when there is positive simple correlation between the two independent variables, which is revealed on the computer sheet by the b_{23} value of +55.1891. This positive relationship between X_2 and X_3 is also revealed in diagram (c) of Chart 13-2. If there were a negative relationship between X_2 and X_3 the expectation would have been $b_{12.3} > b_{12}$ and $b_{13.2} > b_{13}$. These relationships between the simple and net regression coefficients result from the fact that in the simple regression equation the single independent variable being used will reveal not only the relationship it has with the dependent variable but will also be mathematically credited for some of the influences of the other independent variable. Thus, in a regression analysis the simple relationship between X_2 and X_3 will hide the net relationships between X_1 and X_2 and between X_1 and X_3 in a three-variable correlation analysis.

Beta coefficients. How can one determine which of the independent variables in a multiple regression has the most influence on the dependent variable? If they are expressed in the same units and magnitudes (for example, dollars) this can be done by comparing the net regression coefficients. The variable with the largest coefficient is the most influential.

When the independent variables are expressed in different units the importance of the dependent variables can be compared with β (beta) coefficients which express the net regression coefficients in comparable units. The two beta coefficient formulas needed for our Xero Company problem are

$$\beta_1 = b_{12.3} \left(\frac{\sigma_{X_2}}{\sigma_{X_1}}\right)$$

$$\beta_2 = b_{13.2} \left(\frac{\sigma_{X_3}}{\sigma_{X_1}}\right)$$

where σ_{X_1}, σ_{X_2}, and σ_{X_3} are the respective standard deviations of X_1, X_2, and X_3*. These formulas adjust the net regression coefficients to standard deviation units. Substitutions in these formulas are

$$\beta_1 = 0.4537 \left(\frac{240.87}{230.90}\right) = 0.4733$$

$$\beta_2 = 28.5772 \left(\frac{4.21}{230.90}\right) = 0.5212$$

Therefore, for each standard deviation increase in auto registrations, tire sales increase by 0.4733 standard deviations, while tire sales increase by 0.5212 standard deviations for every standard deviation increase in tire advertising expenditures. Therefore, advertising expenditures for tires are relatively more important than auto registrations in explaining variation in tire sales.

Standard errors of estimate.

The Standard Error of Estimate

A major advantage of a multiple regression equation is that it will reduce the error in estimates made with it if each of the independent variables has some influence on the dependent variable. Whether this is true in a particular case can be determined by comparing the standard error for the multiple case to the standard errors for the simple cases.

In our problem concerning the tire sales of the Xero Company $\sigma_{u_{1.2}}$ and $\sigma_{u_{1.3}}$, the standard errors for the simple regression equations for X_1 and X_2, and X_1 and X_3, are 50.1852 and 48.4014, respectively. Since both of these are larger than $\sigma_{u_{1.23}}$, which is 38.9487, each of the independent variables has some influence on the movements of the dependent variable. If a standard error of estimate is not reduced by the introduction of a new independent variable then that independent variable contributes nothing.

Simple and multiple correlation coefficients. The simple correlation coefficients for X_1 and X_2, and X_1 and X_3 are +0.97609 and +0.97778 respectively. Since $R_{1.23}$, the correlation coefficient for the multiple case, is higher (0.98567), this is another indication that movements in each of the independent variables helps explain the movements in the dependent variable. There would be no point in introducing an independent variable in an analysis if its addition did not increase the multiple correlation coefficient.

*The calculations of these standard deviations are not shown. However, they were computed by methods shown in Chapter 5.

Understanding the Coefficient of Multiple Determination

The coefficient of multiple determination is the proportion of the total variation of the dependent variable that has been explained by variations in the several independent variables. Therefore, if we let $\sigma^2_{e1.23}$ and $\sigma^2_{1.23}$represent the explained variance and total variance, respectively, then

$$R^2_{1.23} = \frac{\sigma^2_{e1.23}}{\sigma^2_{1.23}}$$

and since the explained variance plus the unexplained variance equals the total variance we can write

$$\sigma^2_{1.23} = \sigma^2_{e1.23} + \sigma^2_{u1.23}$$

and

$$\sigma^2_{e1.23} = \sigma^2_{1.23} - \sigma^2_{u1.23}$$

Therefore,

$$R^2_{1.23} = \frac{\sigma^2{}_{1.23} - \sigma^2_{u1.23}}{\sigma^2_{1.23}}$$

and

$$R^2_{1.23} = 1 - \frac{\sigma^2_{u1.23}}{\sigma^2_{1.23}}$$

To illustrate this latter formula X_1 and $X_{c1.23}$ values were taken from Table 13-5, placed in 13-6 and the values necessary for calculations of $\sigma^2_{1.23}$ and $\sigma^2_{u1.23}$ were made. The calculations of the total and unexplained variances are shown below the table. Therefore,

$$R^2_{1.23} = 1 - \frac{\sigma^2_{u1.23}}{\sigma^2_{1.23}} = 1 - \frac{1{,}516.6638}{51{,}277.205} = 0.9704$$

and since $\sigma^2_{1.23} - \sigma^2_{u1.23} = 51{,}277.205 - 1{,}516.6682 = 49{,}760.537$ which is the explained variance, $\sigma^2_{e1.23}$, then

$$R^2_{1.23} = \frac{\sigma^2_{e1.23}}{\sigma^2_{1.23}} = \frac{49{,}760.537}{51{,}277.205} = +0.9704$$

and

$$R = \sqrt{0.9704} = 0.9851$$

Except for errors due to rounding this coefficient should be the same as that made by the computer as shown in Table 11-5.

TABLE 13-6. Values Needed to Calculate the Total Variance and Unemplained Variance of the Dependent Variable.

(1) $X_1 - \overline{X}_1$	(2) $(X_1 - \overline{X}_1)^2$	(3) $X_1 - X_{c_{1.23}}$	(4) $(X_1 - X_{c_{1.23}})^2$
−337.3	113,771.29	−15.78	249.0084
+192.7	37,133.29	−109.18	11,920.2720
+572.7	327,985.29	48.21	2,324.2041
−205.3	42,148.09	−4.14	17.1396
−177.3	31,435.29	−36.65	1,343.2225
−62.3	3,881.29	28.67	821.9689
−77.3	5,975.29	−4.47	19.9809
212.7	45,241.29	−8.22	67.5684
−87.3	7,621.29	34.84	1,213.8256
332.7	110,689.29	92.19	8,498.9961
−197.3	38,927.29	8.67	75.1689
−132.3	17,503.29	−9.53	90.8209
−2.3	5.29	33.23	1,104.2329
−82.3	6,773.29	13.44	180.6336
412.7	170,321.29	−37.58	1,412.2564
−72.3	5,227.29	4.97	24.7009
−112.3	12,611.29	−1.86	3.4596
12.7	161.29	6.23	38.8129
−283.3	80,258.89	−20.89	436.3921
92.7	8,593.29	−22.15	490.6225
Total	1,025,544.1		30,333.276

$$\overline{X}_1 = \frac{\Sigma X}{N} = \frac{7746}{20} = 387.3$$

$$\sigma^2_{1.23} = \frac{\Sigma(X_1 - \overline{X}_1)^2}{N} = \frac{1,025,544.1}{20} = 51,277.05$$

$$\sigma_{1.23} = \sqrt{51,277.205} = 226.4447$$

$$\sigma^2_{u_{1.23}} = \frac{30,333.276}{20} = 1,516.6638$$

$$\sigma_{u_{1.23}} = \sqrt{1516.6638} = 38.94$$

The Standard Error of Estimate

The computation of the standard error of estimate, $\sigma_{u_{1.23}}$, for the tire sales of the Xero Company, is shown below Table 13-6. This computation helps the student understand the meaning of the measure. It is merely an "average" of the squared differences between $X_1$and $X_{c_{1.23}}$ that are shown in Table 13-6. This "average" is obtained by squaring the deviations, summing them, dividing by N, and then taking the square root of the result.

ANALYZING SAMPLE DATA

Adjustments for Sample Data

If sample data are being used in a multiple regression and correlation analysis adjustments to certain formulas that have been used should be made if estimated values for the population are desired.

These adjustments may not be necessary for very large samples, particularly if only two or three independent variables are used, because the adjustments would result in insignificant changes. However, it is advisable to make them for small samples. For example, when calculating $\sigma_{u_{1.23}}$, $N-m$, where m is the number of constants in the multiple regression equation, should be used rather than N, because m degrees of freedom are lost by taking deviations of the actual X_1 values from the computed X_1 values.

For our sample data for the Xero Company,

$$\sigma_{u_{1.23}} = \sqrt{\frac{(X_1 - X_{c_{1.23}})^2}{N - m}} = \sqrt{\frac{30{,}333.276}{20 - 3}} = \sqrt{1{,}784.3104} = 42.24$$

If $\sigma_{u_{1.23}}$ has already been computed with N instead of $N-m$ then the adjustment can be made by multiplying it by

$$\sqrt{\frac{N}{N - m}}$$

For our data $\sigma_{u_{1.23}}$ was found to be 38.94 before any adjustment. Therefore,

$$38.94\sqrt{\frac{20}{20 - 3}} = 38.94\sqrt{\frac{20}{17}} = 42.24$$

The formula for $\sigma_{1.23}$ for sample data would be

$$\sqrt{\frac{\Sigma(X_1 - \overline{X}_1)^2}{N - 1}}$$

because one degree of freedom is lost by taking the deviation of the X_1 values from their mean. Using 20 sample observations for the Xero Company,

$$\sigma_{1.23} = \sqrt{\frac{1{,}025{,}544.1}{20 - 1}} = \sqrt{53{,}976.005} = 232.327$$

or our previously calculated $\sigma_{1.23}$ of 226.447 can be adjusted by multiplying it by

$$\sqrt{\frac{N}{N - 1}}$$

Thus

$$226.447\sqrt{\frac{20}{19}} = 232.327$$

Using the unexplained variance and total variance adjusted for the sample we can estimate the coefficients of multiple determination and correlation for the universe. The calculations are,

$$R^2_{1.23} = 1 - \frac{\sigma^2_{u1.23}}{\sigma^2_{1.23}} = 1 - \frac{(42.24)^2}{(232.327)^2} = 1 - \frac{1{,}784.218}{53{,}976.005} = 0.9669$$

and

$$R_{1.23} = \sqrt{0.9669} = 0.9833$$

If $R_{1.23}$ has already been computed without considering the degrees of freedom it can be adjusted for sample data with the formula

$$\sqrt{1 - (1 - R^2_{1.23})\left(\frac{N - 1}{N - m}\right)}$$

For our data the adjustment would be

$$\sqrt{1 - (1 - 0.9704)\left(\frac{19}{17}\right)} = \sqrt{1 - 0.0330823}$$

$$= \sqrt{0.9669} = 0.9833$$

Making Estimates from the Sample

We know that the coefficient of a multiple correlation, 0.9833, is high, but how accurate would estimates of Xero Company tire sales be for a particular sales area if we knew the number of autos registered and the tire advertising expenditures to be made? There is no way of knowing with certainty. However, we can know with various degrees of confidence how much error would be involved in the estimate.

Since $\sigma_{u_{1.23}}$ for the sample of 20 sales areas is 42.24 we can say that the chances are about two-thirds that tire sales would fall within \$42,240 of the value estimated with the regression equation. If we use the *t* distribution (Appendix A-4) for small samples (and ignore minor sampling error in the regression plane) we can be 95% confident that sales for a particular area would be within $X_{c_{1.23}} \pm t\sigma_{u_{1.23}}$. Since three degrees of freedom are lost in the computation of $\sigma_{u_{1.23}}$, because of the three constants in the regression equation, the *t* value would be read at 17 degrees of freedom in the 0.05 column. For example, if for a particular sales area $X_2 = 500$ and $X_3 = 8$, then

$$\begin{aligned} X_{c_{1.23}} &= a_{1.23} + b_{12.3} X_2 + b_{13.2} X_3 \\ &= -0.5886 + 0.4537(500) + 28.5772(8) = 454.88 \end{aligned}$$

and

$$\begin{aligned} X_{c_{1.23}} \pm t\sigma_{u_{1.23}} &= 454.88 \pm 2.110(42.24) = 365.8 \text{ to } 544.0 \\ &= \$365{,}800 \text{ to } \$544{,}000 \text{ in sales.} \end{aligned}$$

Whether this prediction is accurate enough to be useful would have to be decided by the one who would use it in the decision-making process.

Significance of the Net Regression Coefficient

Regression and Sampling Error

Like sample means and other measures the net regression coefficients are affected by sampling error. In fact, it is possible for sample data to show net regression when there is no net regression in the universe from which the sample was drawn.

If the net regression coefficients $b_{12.3}$ and $b_{13.2}$ are due to chance then they should not differ significantly from zero. The *t* test of significance can be made to determine whether the difference is significant. To make the test the standard error of each regression coefficient must be computed. The formulas are

$$\sigma_{b_{12.3}} = \frac{\sigma_{u_{1.23}}}{\sqrt{\Sigma(X_2 - \bar{X}_2)^2 (1 - r_{23}^2)}}$$

$$\sigma_{b_{13.2}} = \frac{\sigma_{u_{1.23}}}{\sqrt{\Sigma(X_3 - \bar{X}_3)^2 (1 - r_{23}^2)}}$$

where $\Sigma(X_2 - \overline{X}_2)^2$ and $\Sigma(X_3 - \overline{X}_3)^2$ are measures of variation of the values of the dependent variables from their means and r^2_{23} is the coefficient of determination for X_2 and X_3. This coefficient, in Table 13-4 (which ignores correction for sample) is 0.93082
Also, using the figures from Table 13-4, we find

$$\Sigma(X_2-\overline{X}_2)^2 = \Sigma X_2^2 - \frac{(\Sigma X_2)^2}{N} = 4{,}699{,}279 - \frac{(8413)^2}{20} = 1{,}160{,}351$$

and

$$\Sigma(X_3-\overline{X}_3)^2 = \Sigma X_3^2 - \frac{(\Sigma X_3)^2}{N} = 1305.428 - \frac{(137.9)^2}{20} = 354.06$$

Substituting in the two formulas we have

$$\sigma_{b12.3} = \frac{42.24}{\sqrt{1{,}160{,}351\ (1-0.93082)}} = \frac{42.24}{283.33} = 0.15$$

$$\sigma_{b13.2} = \frac{42.24}{\sqrt{354.6\ (1-0.93082)}} = \frac{42.24}{4.95} = 8.53$$

The t tests for $b_{12.3}$ and $b_{13.2}$ are

$$t = \frac{b_{12.3} - 0}{\sigma_{b_{12.3}}} = \frac{0.4537 - 0}{0.15} = 3.025$$

and

$$t = \frac{b_{13.2} - 0}{\sigma_{b_{13.2}}} = \frac{28.5772}{8.53} = 3.350$$

In Table 11-4, $N = 20$ and $m = 3$, so there are 17 degrees of freedom. The one-tailed t value at the 0.01 level for 17 degrees of freedom from Table A4, Appendix E is 2.567. Therefore, the computed t values show that the two net regression coefficients differ significantly from zero.

Significance of a Coefficient of Multiple Correlation

Chance Correlation

When sample data are used in a multiple correlation analysis, the resulting coefficient of determination may occur due to chance even though there may be no correlation between the dependent variable and independent variables in the universe.

A test to determine whether the multiple coefficient of determination is significant can be made by using the F distribution. For this analysis

$$F = \frac{(R^2_{1.234...m}) \div (m - 1)}{(1 - R^2_{1.234...m}) \div (N - m)}$$

where m is the number of constants in the multiple regression equation. In the sample of 20 observations for the Xero Company

$$F = \frac{0.9669 \div 2}{(1 - 0.9669) \div 17} = 248.3$$

The F ratio for 2 and 17 degrees of freedom in Table A10, Appendix E is only 6.11. Therefore, the computed F ratio is significant and $R^2_{1.23}$ is not zero.

CAUTIONS

Cautions in Estimating

An analyst may err seriously when estimating with the multiple regression equation if he uses values of the independent variables beyond the range of the data used in the regression analysis. He should use such values carefully and only under a reasonable assumption that the regression correlation measures would not have changed if the values had been used in the analysis.

Caution in Correlating Time Series

A multiple regression and correlation analysis of time series data can be made. However, special problems exist for correlation of time series. It is beyond the scope of this book to discuss in detail the interesting techniques available and the pitfalls to be avoided. However, the cautions mentioned in the previous chapter concerning simple correlation apply in general to multiple correlation of time series.*

*For a somewhat detailed discussion of the problems of correlating time series, see Spurr, W. A., and Bonini, C. P., *Statistical Analysis for Business Decisions*, Homewood, Illinois: Richard D. Irwin, Inc., pp. 477–483 and 518–519.

REVIEW QUESTIONS

1. Define multiple regression and multiple correlation.
2. What are net regression coefficients?
3. What does a coefficient of multiple determination measure? What does a coefficient of multiple correlation measure?
4. What does a coefficient of partial correlation measure?
5. Of what use is a standard error of estimate in a multiple regression analysis?
6. Under what conditions will the standard error of estimate for a multiple regression analysis be smaller than for simple regression when the same dependent variable is used?
7. Under what condition will the net regression coefficients be smaller than their corresponding simple regression coefficients?
8. How is the sign (+ or −) determined for a coefficient of partial correlation?
9. A sign should not be affixed to a coefficient of multiple correlation. Why?
10. What caution should an analyst take when estimating values of the dependent variable with the multiple regression equation?
11. When should adjustments for sample data be made for the coefficient of multiple correlation and the standard error of estimate?
12. What assumptions must be made when correlating time series data?

PROBLEMS

1. Make a complete multiple regression and correlation analysis of the data in Exercise Table 13-1, and interpret your findings. First, make scatter charts of the simple relationships between X_1 and X_2, X_1 and X_3, and X_2 and X_3. Second, use the sums of products shown below the table and the three equations given in the chapter and compute the values for the multiple regression equation $X_{c1.23} = a_{1.23} + b_{12.3}X_2 + b_{13.2}X_3$. Third, compute the standard error of estimate with the equation

$$\sigma_{u_{1.23}} = \sqrt{\frac{\Sigma X_1^2 - a_{1.23}\,\Sigma X_1 - b_{12.3}\Sigma X_1X_2 - b_{13.2}\,\Sigma X_1X_3}{N}}$$

Fourth, compute the coefficients of multiple determination and correlation with the formulas

$$R^2_{1.23} = \frac{a_{1.23}\,\Sigma X_1 + b_{12.3}\,\Sigma X_1X_2 + b_{13.2}\,\Sigma X_1X_3 - N\overline{X}_1^2}{\Sigma X_1^2 - N\overline{X}_1^{\,2}}$$

$$R_{1.23} = \sqrt{R^2_{1.23}}$$

EXERCISE TABLE 13-1. Median Family Income, Mean Monthly Rent, and Per-Family Sales Taxes in 15 Sales Areas of the Knick Company, 1976.

MEDIAN FAMILY INCOME ($000) X_1	*MEAN MONTHLY RENT (DOLLARS)* X_2	*PER-FAMILY SALES TAX (DOLLARS)* X_3
9.0	160	152
10.0	146	170
10.8	184	186
14.2	162	234
12.4	198	206
21.8	220	300
16.6	180	250
24.0	284	320
17.4	204	240
17.0	250	220
17.8	260	260
15.0	180	238
28.0	286	360
16.0	220	244
26.6	256	380

$\Sigma X_1{}^2 = 4{,}860.996$ $\Sigma X_1X_2 = 57{,}707.996$ $\Sigma X_1X_3 = 69{,}529.938$

$\Sigma X_1{}^2 = 707{,}524.000$ $\Sigma X_2X_3 = 832{,}260.000$ $\Sigma X_3^2 = 1{,}002{,}472.000$

2. Use the regression equation computed in Problem 1 and make an estimate of median family income for a sales area where the mean monthly rent is $200 and the per-family sales tax is $300. Do you feel that this estimate would be fairly reliable? Why?
3. Adjust the standard error of estimate computed in problem one by multiplying it by formula

$$\sqrt{\frac{N}{N - m}}$$

and adjust the coefficient of multiple determination computed in Problem 1 with the formula

$$\sqrt{1 - (1 - R^2_{1.23})\left(\frac{N - 1}{N - m}\right)}$$

Under what conditions would these adjustments be practical?

4. If you have access to a computer program for a complete multiple regression and correlation analysis, use it to analyze the data in Exercise Table 13-1. Compare the computer answers to those obtained in Problem 1 and Problem 3.

5. Use the data in Exercise Table 13-2 and make a multiple regression and correlation analysis on your school's computer or by using the formulas in the text. Interpret your findings.

EXERCISE TABLE 13-2. Data for Three Variables.

X_1	X_2	X_3
1	2	10
2	4	9
3	6	8
4	8	7
5	10	6
6	12	5
7	14	4
8	16	3
9	18	2
10	20	1

$\Sigma X_1^2 = 385$ $\quad \Sigma X_1X_2 = 770$ $\quad \Sigma X_1X_3 = 220$

$\Sigma X_2^2 = 1540$ $\quad \Sigma X_2X_3 = 440$ $\quad \Sigma X_3^2 = 385$

6. Using either a computer program or hand calculator, make a multiple regression and correlation analysis of X_1, X_2, and X_3 in Exercise Table 13-3. Interpret your findings. If your school has a multiple regression and correlation program, make an analysis of the four variables. Does X_4 contribute any influence on the number of batteries sold? Do you believe that the regression equation will give reasonably accurate estimates of battery sales for a particular sales area? Why?

7. Use your school's multiple regression and correlation program and analyze the data in Exercise Table 13-4. Do you think that manufacturing payrolls for 1976 could be closely estimated if the 1976 values of the independent variables are known? If so, get the 1976 values from the March issue of the *Federal Reserve Bulletin* to make the estimate and see how close the estimate is to the actual value.

EXERCISE TABLE 13-3. Automobile Bettery Sales, Motor Vehicle Registrations, Weekly Earnings of Factory Workers, and Battery Advertising Expenditures in 30 Sales Areas of the EBA Company, 1976.

SALES AREA	NO. OF BATTERIES SOLD X_1	MOTOR VEHICLE REGISTRATIONS X_2	WEEKLY MEAN EARNINGS FACTORY WORKERS X_3	BATTERY ADVERTISING EXPENDITURES X_4
1	135	111	$ 217	$ 850
2	122	112	193	700
3	137	112	220	880
4	131	113	206	730
5	116	114	186	600
6	163	114	254	1,050
7	122	115	195	550
8	142	109	225	880
9	140	115	226	750
10	128	112	211	690
11	139	116	223	760
12	125	116	197	610
13	130	116	204	710
14	136	117	209	790
15	121	107	202	720
16	124	108	206	750
17	149	118	230	900
18	130	118	223	1,330
19	164	109	247	950
20	144	110	234	920
21	139	120	213	770
22	128	120	204	600
23	144	121	216	1,040
24	112	121	217	1,330
25	129	148	184	510
26	132	133	200	540
27	114	142	216	1,480
28	116	131	215	1,480
29	131	122	222	780
30	145	135	220	620
Total	3,988	3,555	6,415	25,260

$\Sigma X_1^2 = 534{,}876$ $\quad \Sigma X_1 X_2 = 471{,}744$ $\quad \Sigma X_1 X_3 = 857{,}158$

$\Sigma X_2^2 = 424{,}153$ $\quad \Sigma X_2 X_3 = 759{,}055$ $\quad \Sigma X_3^2 = 1{,}379{,}153$

EXERCISE TABLE 13-4. Selected Business Indexes, U.S., 1960–1975 (1967 = 100).

YEAR	*MFG. PAYROLLS (PRODUCTION WORKERS)*	*INDUSTRIAL PRODUCTION*	*MFG. EMPLOYMENT (PRODUCTION WORKERS)*	*CONSUMER PRICES*
	X_1	X_2	X_3	X_4
1960	68.8	66.2	88.0	88.7
1961	68.0	66.7	84.5	89.6
1962	73.3	72.2	87.3	90.6
1963	76.0	76.5	87.8	91.7
1964	80.1	81.7	89.3	92.9
1965	88.1	89.2	93.9	94.5
1966	97.8	97.9	99.9	97.2
1967	100.0	100.0	100.0	100.0
1968	108.3	105.7	101.4	104.2
1969	116.6	110.7	103.2	109.8
1970	114.2	106.7	98.1	116.3
1971	116.3	106.8	93.9	121.2
1972	130.2	115.2	96.7	125.3
1973	146.9	125.6	101.9	133.1
1974	157.1	124.8	102.1	147.7
1975	151.0	113.8	91.4	161.2

Source: *Federal Reserve Bulletin,* March, 1976, Page A50.

8. If $R_{1.23} = 0.8976$ and $r_{12} = 0.6874$ what does $r^2_{13.2}$ equal?

9. If $\sigma_{u_{1.23}} = 25$ and $\sigma_{1.3} = 36$, what does $r^2_{12.3}$ equal?

10. If $r^2_{12.3} = 0.893$ and $r_{13} = 0.25$, what does $R^2_{1.23}$ equal?

14

Index Numbers for Business Measurements

Economic and business indexes are tools for measuring relationships among numerical data. Most indexes in use today record changes in economic and business data over a period of time and are useful for comparing changes in prices, production, income, sales and other economic indicators.

GENERAL TYPES OF INDEXES

The three main classifications of index numbers are price, physical volume, and dollar volume. Indexes can be simple or composite. A simple index, which is illustrated in Table 14-1, can be used to show changes in the price, quantity or dollar value of a single commodity. It can be used also to show changes in quantities expressed in the same units such as pounds or dollars.

Composite indexes are especially valuable because they enable one to measure changes in averages made up of quantities that are not expressed in the same units. Average prices cannot usually be found by totaling the prices of the products and dividing by the number of products because prices are often quoted in varied units, such as price per pound, price per bushel, and price per dozen. Also, because quantities of goods are expressed in different units, simple averages (arithmetic means) usually cannot be calculated or compared. However, changes in the average level of prices or quantities of a large number of goods can be measured by proper index number construction, which puts to use the concept of the weighted average discussed in Chapter 4.

Index numbers of dollar volumes, such as sales, are valuable because they express changes in magnitudes in a way that is easily interpreted and they facilitate comparisons of two or more series of data originally expressed in different magnitudes, such as thousands of dollars and billions of dollars.

Probably the most widely known and used composite price index is the Consumer Price Index published by the U.S. Bureau of Labor Statistics. The best known physical volume index is the Index of Industrial Production computed by the Board of Governors of the Federal Reserve System. A good example of a dollar volume index is the Index of Weekly Payrolls of Production Workers in Manufacturing Industries published by the U.S. Bureau of Labor Statistics. Several indexes such as these will be discussed in detail.

THE BASE PERIOD OF AN INDEX

Index numbers are usually expressed as percentages of some fixed base period. Table 14-1 shows annual steel production in the United States from 1970 to 1975 and an index of steel production using 1970 as the base. This is a simple physical volume index. To compute the index numbers, the 1970 value of 131.5 was divided into each value for each year and the resulting quotients were multiplied by 100. For this illustration, the base year, 1970, was arbitrarily chosen. In practice, however, several criteria should be considered in the selection of the base of an index.

Normal Period Criterion

Generally, a base period should represent a "normal" period; that is, a price index should have a base period when the prices of the commodities used in the index were "normal."

There is no absolute normal, only a relative normal. Therefore, "normal" should be taken to mean *not extreme*. For example, an index showing changes in the prices of citrus fruits over a period of time ordinarily should not have as the base period a year when late freezing weather destroyed crops, thus raising prices considerably. Moreover, an index showing changes in gross national product in the United States over the past five decades should not ordinarily have either the value for 1933 or 1977 as the base because both years show extreme values in relation to most other years.

One help in developing a statistically normal base value for an index is to use a mean of several years that represent different phases of the business cycle. The most widely used base period for economic indicators published by U.S. government agencies is 1967. During most of the 1960's the three-year average for 1957, 1958, and 1959 (usually written 1957-59 = 100) was the base. These three years give values for the boom year of 1957, the recession year of 1958, and the business recovery year of 1959. Other popular base periods used in the past to average out values for different phases of the business cycle were 1947, 1948, and 1949 (1947-49 = 100) and 1935, 1936, 1937, 1938, and 1939 (1935-39 = 100).

TABLE 14-1 Annual Steel Production in the United States, 1970–1975.

YEAR	*MILLIONS OF TONS*	*INDEX (1970 = 100)*
1970	131.5	100.0
1971	120.4	91.6
1972	133.2	101.3
1973	150.8	114.7
1974	145.7	110.8
1975	116.6	88.7

Source: U.S. Department of Commerce: *Business Statistics,* 1975 and *Survey of Current Business,* July 1976.

Time Criterion

A base period should be timely, In other words, a base period should be a fairly recent period.

Timeliness is important for several reasons. For one thing, it is difficult to find an aggregate of commodities that are common to base periods in the far past and in recent periods. For example, if the Consumer Price Index still used its old base, 1935-39 = 100, the price of commodities important to the consumer today, such as television sets and nylon hosiery, could not be included because these commodities did not exist in the 1930's.

Secondly, over a long period of time the qualities and styles of many products change so much that no comparison of prices today and in the far past would be meaningful. For example, we cannot effectively compare prices of automobiles today to prices of those made in the 1920's. Moreover, we cannot accurately compare the price of women's hose today, made of nylon, to their prices in the 1930's when they were made of silk. Theoretically, price indexes should be computed for commodities of constant qualities. In practice, this is impossible for many commodities, except in the short run.

Finally, base periods are more meaningful if they have been lived through by the user of the index. Many economists and business analysts using indexes based on the year 1967 experienced the economic conditions of that year as adults and, therefore, have a ''feeling'' for the base period. Few analysts living today, however, remember economic conditions during 1910-14, which is the base for an index of prices farmers receive for their products.

Comparison Criterion

Two or more indexes, if they are to be compared, must have the same base period.

If we wanted to compute an index of retail prices to compare to the U.S. Consumer Price Index (1967 = 100) we should use this same period as the base for our index of retail prices.

Moreover, if we desire to compare two indexes calculated on different bases, we must shift the base of one to that of the other. As an illustration, the Index of Annual Steel Production on the 1970 base that appears in Table 14-2 is also shown after shifting to the 1970 and the 1970-72 bases. To shift the base of an index we divide the index number for the new base period into the index number for each of the periods. In Table 14-2, the index on the 1975 base was obtained by dividing 88.7, the index number for 1975 on the 1970 base, into each index number calculated on the 1970 base. For example.

$$\frac{1970}{1975} = \frac{100.0}{88.7} = 1.127 = 112.7\%$$

which is the new index number for 1970 (where 1975 = 100) shown in Column (2). Similarly, to shift the 1970 base to the 1970-72 base, the mean of the index numbers for 1970, 1971, and 1972, that is

$$\frac{100 + 91.6 + 101.3}{3} = 97.6$$

is divided into each index number calculated on the 1970 base. To illustrate,

$$\frac{1975}{1970-72 \text{ mean}} - \frac{88.7}{97.6} - 9.09 - 90.9\%$$

which is the new index number for 1975 shown in Column (3).

TABLE 14-2. Shifting the Base of an Index (Index of annual steel production in the United States).

YEAR	*(1)* *INDEX (1970=100)*	*(2)* *INDEX BASE SHIFTED (1975=100)*	*(3)* *INDEX BASE SHIFTED (1970–72=100)*
1970	100.0	112.7	102.5
1971	91.6	103.3	93.9
1972	101.3	114.2	103.8
1973	114.7	129.3	117.5
1974	110.8	124.9	113.5
1975	88.7	100.0	90.9

Reliable Data Criterion

The base period should be a period for which accurate and reliable data are available.

For example, an index showing changes in value added by manufacture over several years might better use as a base value added by manufacture for a year when a census of manufactures was conducted than value for a year in which only sample data were gathered.

COMPOSITE PRICE INDEXES

A price index that measures the aggregate or "average" prices of several commodities and services is known as a *composite price index*. In such an index, the prices of several commodities and services are reduced to a single summary figure, either aggregate or average for each time period, and these summary figures are expressed as percentages of the base period value.

The Simple Aggregative Method

Under certain conditions, an acceptable composite price index of N items can be computed with the formula

$$I = \frac{\Sigma p_n/N}{\Sigma p_o/N}$$

which reduces to

$$I = \frac{\Sigma p_n}{\Sigma p_o}$$

where p_n and p_o are the respective prices of a commodity in a given period and in the base period. Two conditions are necessary before the simple aggregative method can be used:

1) Prices of all commodities used in the calculation must be expressed in the same unit.
2) The relative importance of the commodities must be equal and unchanging during the time period covered by the index.

TABLE 14-3. Calculation of a Simple Aggregative Price Index of Selected Business Supplies for 1977 (1975=100).

SUPPLIES	UNIT	PRICES PER UNIT 1975 (p_o)	1977 (p_n)
Pencils	Gross	$ 8.64	$11.52
Paper	Ream	1.40	1.60
Duplicating fluid	Gallon	1.60	1.90
Total		$11.64	$15.02

$$I_{1975} = \frac{\Sigma p_n}{\Sigma p_o} = \frac{15.02}{11.64} = 1.29 = 129\%$$

It is difficult, however, to find a group of commodities for which both of these conditions exist. An illustration will clarify this.

Suppose that a business organization needed to know the change between 1975 and 1977 in the average prices it paid for certain business supplies, say pencils, paper, and ink. To measure this change, it might be suggested that the method of simple aggregates be used. The resultant computations are shown in Table 14-3. The calculations show that $15.02 is the sum of the prices in the given period, 1975, and the $11.64 is the sum of the prices in the base period; therefore, the simple aggregative price index for 1977 is

$$\frac{\Sigma p_n}{\Sigma p_o} = \frac{15.02}{11.64} = 1.29 = 129\%$$

which shows an increase of 29%. However, this calculation is biased because the prices of the products are quoted in different units. For example, if prices per pencil of 6 cents in 1975 and 8 cents in 1977 were used instead of prices per gross the index calculation would be

$$\frac{\Sigma p_n}{\Sigma p_o} = \frac{0.08 + 1.60 + 1.90}{0.06 + 1.40 + 1.60} = \frac{3.58}{3.06} = 1.17 = 117\%$$

which is an entirely different answer.

We might suggest changing the prices of all commodities to the same unit to eliminate the bias that can result from aggregating prices expressed in different units. This would be highly impractical, however, even though, in theory, it is possible. Imagine having to convert the prices of hundreds of consumer goods such as shirts, beer, automobiles, cigarettes, and television sets to prices per pound. Moreover, even when prices are customarily quoted in the same unit, the method of simple aggregates would still produce a biased index in most cases because of the difference in the importance of the commodities being aggregated. To exemplify, suppose a chain of

TABLE 14-4. Calculation of a Simple Aggregative Price Index of Three Meat Products for 1976 (1971=100).

PRODUCT	PRICE PER POUND 1971 (p_o)	1976 (p_n)
Hamburger	\$0.80	\$1.00
Frankfurters	0.75	0.90
Minute Steak	1.25	2.00
Total	\$2.80	\$3.90

$$I_{1976} = \frac{\Sigma p_n}{\Sigma p_o} = \frac{3.90}{2.80} = 1.39 = 139\%$$

short-order restaurants computes by the simple aggregative method an index of the prices it paid for three meat products, as shown in Table 14-4. We can see that minute steak influences the price index more than hamburger or frankfurters because of its higher price and higher percentage change. Furthermore, if the restaurant chain serves ten times as many pounds of hamburger as minute steak and five times as many pounds of frankfurters as minute steak, we certainly would not accept the index of 139 as a useful measure of the average price change of these meat products between 1971 and 1976. To accurately measure this, the relative importance of these three products should be introduced in the computations.

The Weighted Aggregative Method

Importance of Products

The relative importance of products is introduced into the calculation of aggregative price indexes by weighting the prices with the quantities of the products.

For example, if in 1971 the restaurant chain used 100,000 pounds of hamburger, 50,000 pounds of frankfurters, and 10,000 pounds of minute steak, its price index could be computed by the formula for N items

$$I = \frac{\Sigma p_n q_o / N}{\Sigma p_o q_o / N}$$

which reduces to

$$I = \frac{\Sigma p_n q_o}{\Sigma p_o q_o}$$

where p_n and p_o are prices of product in a given year and the base year, respectively, and q_o is the quantity of a product in the base year.* Calculation of the weighted values and their sums in Table 14-5 and substitution in the formula reveal that

$$I = \frac{\$165{,}000}{\$130{,}000} = 1.27 = 127\%$$

TABLE 14-5. Calculation of a Weighted Aggregative Price Index of Three Meat Products for 1976 Using Base Year Quantities as Weights (1971 = 100).

PRODUCT	POUNDS BOUGHT 1971 (q_o)	PRICE PER POUND 1971 (p_o)	PRICE PER POUND 1976 (p_n)	VALUE IN 1971 ($p_o q_o$)	VALUE OF 1971 QUANTITIES AT 1976 PRICES ($p_n q_o$)
Hamburger	100,000	$0.80	$1.00	$ 80,000	$100,000
Frankfurters	50,000	0.75	0.90	37,500	45,000
Minute Steak	10,000	1.25	2.00	12,500	20,000
Total				$130,000	$165,000
Index				100	127

$$I_{1976} = \frac{\Sigma p_n q_o}{\Sigma p_o q_o} = \frac{165{,}000}{130{,}000} = 1.27 = 127\%$$

TABLE 14-6. Calculation of a Weighted Aggregative Price Index of Three Meat Products for 1976, Using 1976 Quantities as Weights. (1971 = 100).

	POUNDS BOUGHT 1976 (q_n)	PRICE PER POUND 1971 (p_o)	PRICE PER POUND 1976 (p_n)	VALUE OF 1976 QUANTITIES AT 1971 PRICES $p_o q_n$	VALUE IN 1976 $p_n q_n$
Hamburger	10,000	$0.80	$1.00	$ 8,000	$ 10,000
Frankfurters	50,000	0.75	0.90	37,500	45,000
Minute Steaks	100,000	1.25	2.00	125,000	200,000
Total				$170,500	$255,000
Index				100	150

$$I_{1976} = \frac{\Sigma p_n q_n}{\Sigma p_o q_n} = \frac{255{,}000}{170{,}500} = 1.50 = 150\%$$

*This weighted aggregative method, using base year quantities as weights, is known as the *Laspeyres' method*.

which is the 1976 index number. Therefore, the average prices of the three products rose only 27% between 1971 and 1976. This must be true because, the quantities being held constant, the only reason for the change in the sums from $130,000 to $165,000 was the changes in prices.

Constant Relative Importance

The weighted aggregative method is most effective when the relative importance of the commodities changes very little over a period of time.

In the foregoing illustration, for the price index to be an unbiased measure of price change, the relative amounts of the meat products should be the same in 1976 as in 1971. If the restaurant chain was using more pounds of minute steaks than hamburger by 1976, then the calculated change of 27% would be misleading.

Suppose quantities, q_n, for a given year are used as weights, as shown in Table 14-6.* In this table, the quantities of hamburger and minute steaks have been interchanged between 1971 and 1976 to illustrate the effect of changing weights. The weighted aggregate formula, using given-year weights, is

$$I = \frac{\Sigma p_n q_n}{\Sigma p_o q_n}$$

Substituting in this formula from Table 14-6, the 1971 index is

$$I_{1971} = \frac{255{,}000}{170{,}500} = 1.50 = 150\%$$

This index indicates that prices of the three meat products rose 50% between 1971 and 1976.

Now a valid question is: Did prices rise 27% or 50%? Either is correct if the result is qualified. Twenty-seven percent is correct if the same quantity of each of the products that was bought in 1971 was bought in 1976 at 1976 prices. Fifty percent is correct if the 1976 quantity of each product was bought in 1971 at 1971 prices. Therefore, the weighting system chosen depends upon what we want to measure, or in other words, what question we want to answer.

Choice of weights. The calculation of the weighted aggregative price index of the three meat products illustrated use of base year and given pounds as weights. It is not necessary to use either, however, and in fact, it is seldom done in actual practice.

*This weighted aggregative method, using given period quantities as weights, is known as *Paasche's method*.

Use "Normal" Weights

Quantities used as weights should ideally represent "normal" amounts of the commodities involved in the computation and, therefore, might be the average (mean) amounts for several time periods or for any given period.

We should choose weights carefully to assure their maximum representativeness. For example, the weights for a price index of agricultural grain products ordinarily should not be the amounts produced in a year when wheat production was drastically reduced by severe drought in wheat-growing states and corn production was exceptionally high due to favorable growing conditions in corn-producing states.

The Simple Average-of-Relatives Method

Price relatives of several commodities are sometimes combined in a composite price index. (A *price relative* is the ratio of present price to base-year price.) One way this can be done is by calculating a simple mean of price relatives, as in Table 14-7 for the three meat products used by the restaurant chain. The formula is

$$I = \frac{\sum \frac{p_n}{p_o}}{N}$$

TABLE 14-7. Calculation of a Simple Average of Relatives Price Index of Three Meat Products for 1976 (1971=100).

PRODUCT	PRICE PER POUND 1971 p_o	1976 p_n	PRICE RELATIVE $\frac{p_n}{p_o}$
Hamburger	$0.80	$1.00	1.25
Frankfurters	0.75	0.90	1.20
Minute steak	1.25	2.00	1.60
Total			4.05
Index	100	135	

$$I_{1976} = \frac{\sum \frac{p_n}{p_o}}{N} = \frac{4.05}{3} = 1.35 = 135\%$$

where N is the number of price relatives and

$$\frac{p_n}{p_o}$$

is a given period price relative for a product.

Substituting in the formula, we have

$$I_{1976} = \frac{4.05}{3} = 1.35 = 135\%$$

which means that the calculated average price increase was 35% between 1971 and 1976. However, a glance at the table shows that a price relative of 1.60 for minute steak influences the average more than the price relatives for hamburger and frankfurters, and yet, as was previously noted, minute steaks are relatively less important in usage than hamburger and frankfurters.

The Weighted Average-of-Relatives Method

To remove the upward bias caused by one or more high-priced items from the index, weights must be applied to the relatives. If available, the weights should be the dollar values of the products, because the money measurements of the prices were lost when the relatives were computed. When this is done, using base-year values, the resulting composite index is the same as would be obtained by the weighted aggregative method using base-year quantities. To show that this is so, we weight the price relatives with the dollar values of the three meat products in the base year 1971 (see Table 14-8). The formula for the weighted average of relatives index is

TABLE 14-8. Calculation of a Weighted Average of Relatives Price Index of Three Meat Products for 1976 (1971=100).

PRODUCT	PRICE RELATIVE $\frac{p_n}{p_o}$	BASE YEAR VALUE (V_o)	WEIGHTED RELATIVE $\frac{p_n}{p_o}V_o$
Hamburger	1.25	$ 80,000	$100,000
Frankfurters	1.20	37,500	45,000
Minute steak	1.60	12,500	20,000
		$130,000	$165,000

$$I_{1976} = \frac{\Sigma \frac{p_n}{p_o} V_o}{\Sigma V_o} = \frac{165{,}000}{130{,}000} = 1.27 = 127\%$$

$$I = \frac{\Sigma \frac{p_n}{p_o} V_o}{\Sigma V_o}$$

where V_o is the symbol for (dollar) values in the base period. The substitutions are

$$I_{1976} = \frac{165{,}000}{130{,}000} = 1.27 = 127\%$$

This is the same index number obtained with the weighted aggregate formula. We can see, working with symbols, that the formulas give identical results. Since value represents price times quantity,

$$V_o = p_o q_o$$

and

$$\frac{p_n}{p_o} V_o = \frac{p_n}{p_o} p_o q_o = p_n q_o$$

Therefore

$$\Sigma \frac{p_n}{p_o} V_o = \Sigma p_n q_o$$

and thus

$$\frac{\Sigma \frac{p_n}{p_o} V_o}{\Sigma V_o} = \frac{\Sigma p_n q_o}{\Sigma p_o q_o}$$

Advantages of the weighted average-of-relatives method. We might ask, ''If the weighted average-of-relatives method gives the same results as the weighted aggregative method why use it?'' There are three reasons. One is that only price relatives, not prices from which the relatives were computed, may be available, or the actual prices may be difficult to get. Another reason is that only dollar values of commodities may be available for weights. This would be the case if we were to use data from the census of manufactures to construct an index of manufacturers' prices because this census does not give quantities produced, only value added by manufacture. A third reason is that the weighted average-of-relatives method produces a price index for each commodity (the individual commodity price relatives) as well as the composite index. This enables the analyst to compare price changes among the individual commodities and changes in the composite. For example, by multiplying each price relative in Table 14-7 by 100, we have indexes for hamburger, frankfurters, and minute steak of 125, 120, and 160, respectively, to compare.

THE PHYSICAL-VOLUME COMPOSITE INDEX

The weighted aggregative and weighted average-of-relatives methods can be used to compute acceptable indexes of physical volume. For the weighted aggregative method, the quantities used in the computation are weighted with prices. The formula, using base-year prices as weights, is

$$I = \frac{\Sigma p_o q_n}{\Sigma p_o q_o}$$

TABLE 14-9. Calculation of a Weighted Aggregative Index of the Production of Three Farm Products for 1975, Using Base Year Prices as Weights (1970=100).

PRODUCT	*UNIT*	*PRICE PER UNIT 1970 (p_o)*	*QUANTITY (000,000) 1970 (q_o)*	*QUANTITY (000,000) 1975 (q_n)*	*VALUE IN 1970 p_oq_o*	*VALUE OF 1975 QUANTITIES AT 1970 PRICES p_oq_n*
Wheat	bu.	$ 1.33	1,352	2,134	$1,798.16	$2,838.22
Rice	cwt.	5.17	84	128	434.28	661.76
Sugar beets	short ton	14.82	26	29	385.32	429.78
Total					$2,617.76	$3,929.76
Index					100	150

When the weighted average price relatives is used, the quantity relatives are weighted with dollar values. The formula when base-year dollar values are the weights is

$$I = \frac{\Sigma \frac{q_n}{q_o} V_o}{\Sigma V_o}$$

All symbols in these two formulas have already been defined.

The Weighted Aggregative Method

Table 14-9 shows the computation of an index by the weighted aggregative method with base-year (1970) prices used as weights. The 1975 index is

$$\frac{\Sigma p_o q_n}{\Sigma p_o q_o} = \frac{\$3929.76}{\$2617.76} = 1.50 \text{ or } 150\%$$

This means that the physical quantities of the products increased by an average of 50% between 1970 and 1975 because the price weights remained constant.

The Weighted Average-of-Relatives Method

Quantity relatives can be combined into a single summary figure for computation of a composite physical-volume index by weighting them with dollar values. Table 14-10 shows how this is done with the three farm products when base-year values are the weights. In the table, the V_o column is multiplied by the

$$\frac{q_n}{q_o}$$

column, resulting in the

$$\frac{q_n}{q_o}V_o$$

column. The calculation of the composite index for 1975 is, therefore,

$$I_{1967} = \frac{\Sigma \frac{q_n}{q_o} V_o}{\Sigma V_o} = \frac{3928.97}{2617.76} = 1.50 = 150\%$$

Note that the substitutions in this formula are the same as those in the formula for weighted aggregates except for minor discrepancies, which are due to rounding of quantity relatives in Table 14-10.

TABLE 14-10. Calculation of a Weighted Average-of-Relatives Index of the Production of Three Farm Products for 1975, Using Base Year Values as Weights (1970=100).

PRODUCT	UNIT	QUANTITY (000,000) 1970 (q_o)	QUANTITY (000,000) 1975 (q_n)	1970 VALUE ($000,000) V_o	QUANTITY RELATIVES $\frac{q_n}{q_o}$	WEIGHTED RELATIVES $\frac{q_n}{q_o}V_o$
Wheat	bu.	1,352	2,134	$1,798.16	1.578	$2,837.50
Rice	cwt.	84	128	434.28	1.524	661.84
Sugar beets	short tons	26	29	385.32	1.115	429.63
Total				$2,617.76		$3,928.97*
Index				100		150

*This sum should equal $3,929.76 but does not because the quantity relatives were rounded to three decimals. The weighted relatives for the three commodities computed with unrounded relatives would be the same as the p_oq_n values in Table 14-9.

Weighted Relatives

This method of weighted relatives is used when only quantity relatives, rather than quantities, are available or when only dollar values of the products can be found for weights.

Moreover, this method produces quantity indexes for the individual commodities. These are 157.8 for wheat, 152.4 for rice and 111.5 for sugar beets, respectively, in this illustration.

THE CHAIN INDEX

Sometimes an index of a series is desired, but actual prices, quantities or dollar values are not available for calculating them. However, if percentage changes between each time period and each preceding time period are available, these percentages can be converted to ratios of change and mathematically linked together in what might be called a *chain index*. The year to year percentage changes in annual steel production in the United States shown in Column (1) of Table 14-11 will suffice to illustrate the procedure. The first step is to convert the percentage changes to the percentage relatives shown in Column (2). For example, the percentage decrease of 8.4% in steel production between 1970 and 1971 means that steel production in 1971 was 91.6% of steel production in 1970. Likewise, the 10.6% increase between 1971 and 1972 means that production of steel in 1972 was 110.6% of 1971 production. When all of the percentage relatives have been determined they are linked together to a 1970 base of 100, which was the base for the first relative of 91.6. The logic behind the linking process indicated by the arrows, multiplication signs, and equals signs in the table is simple: 91.6 is the index number for 1971 with 1970 as the base. The 110.6 for 1972 means that production in 1972 was 110.6% of production in 1971; therefore it was $1.106 \times 91.6 = 101.3\%$ of production in 1970. Similarly $1.132 \times 101.3 = 114.7$, the index for 1973 on a 1970 base. The other index numbers in Column (3) were calculated by continuing this procedure. This chain index results in the same index numbers that were obtained by working with the original production figures, as a look at Table 14-1 shows.

TABLE 14-11. Chaining Relatives of Annual Steel Production in the United States.

YEAR	STEEL PRODUCED (MILLIONS OF TONS)	(1) PERCENT CHANGE IN PRODUCTION FROM PREVIOUS YEAR	(2) PRODUCTION AS A PERCENT OF PREVIOUS YEAR (RELATIVES)	(3) INDEX (1970=100) CHAINED RELATIVES
1970	131.5	—	—	100.0
1971	120.4	−8.4	91.6	91.6
1972	133.2	+10.6	110.6	101.3
1973	150.8	+13.2	113.2	114.7
1974	145.7	−3.4	96.6	110.8
1975	116.6	−20.0	80.0	88.6

FISHER'S "IDEAL" INDEX NUMBER FORMULA

A well-known statistician, Irving Fisher, devised a formula for computing an "ideal" index, so-called because it meets two tests, the *factor reversal test* and the *time reversal test*.

The factor reversal test determines whether the product of a price index and its corresponding quantity index is equal to a value index for the same products. The test, made with the weighted aggregative formulas using base figures as weights, is

$$\frac{\Sigma p_n q_o}{\Sigma p_o q_o} \times \frac{\Sigma q_n p_o}{\Sigma q_o p_o}$$

but the product of these two indexes is not

$$\frac{\Sigma p_n q_n}{\Sigma p_o q_o}$$

which is the index formula for value.

The time reversal test determines whether an index works backward as well as forward. For example, if a price index for 1970 on the 1960 base is 200, the price index for 1960 on the 1970 base should be 50. If this were true, then the product of these two indexes would be $2.00 \times 0.5 = 1$. However, using the weighted aggregative price index formulas

$$\frac{\Sigma p_n q_o}{\Sigma p_o q_o} \times \frac{\Sigma p_o q_n}{\Sigma p_n q_n} \neq 1$$

Fisher's ideal index formula,

$$\sqrt{\frac{\Sigma p_n q_o}{\Sigma p_o q_o} \times \frac{\Sigma p_n q_n}{\Sigma p_o q_n}}$$

meets both the factor reversal and the time reversal tests. His index is impractical to use, however, because it requires both price and quantity values for each period covered in the index. These would be costly, if not impossible to get for many indexes computed today.

Demonstrations of the Tests

The following figures are used to demonstrate the factor reversal tests

	PRICE ($)		*QUANTITY*					
	1960	*1975*	*1960*	*1975*				
PRODUCT	p_o	p_n	q_o	q_n	$p_o q_o$	$p_n q_o$	$q_n p_o$	$p_n q_n$
A	1	2	5	10	5	10	10	20
B	2	3	10	15	20	30	30	45
C	3	4	15	20	45	60	60	80
Total					70	100	100	145

Substituting in the formulas for the factor reversal test,

$$\frac{100}{70} \times \frac{100}{70} = 204.1$$

but this product is not equal to

$$\frac{145}{70} = 207.1$$

the index of value.

Substituting in the formulas for the time reversal test,

$$\frac{100}{70} \times \frac{100}{145} = 0.985 \neq 1$$

Substituting in Fisher's ideal index formula,

$$\sqrt{\frac{100}{70} \times \frac{145}{100}} = \sqrt{\frac{145}{70}}$$

Fisher's formula with the factors reversed is

$$\sqrt{\frac{\Sigma q_n p_o}{\Sigma q_o p_o} \times \frac{\Sigma q_n p_n}{\Sigma q_o p_n}} = \sqrt{\frac{100}{70} \times \frac{145}{100}} = \sqrt{\frac{145}{70}}$$

and

$$\sqrt{\frac{145}{70}} \times \sqrt{\frac{145}{70}} = 207.1$$

which is the index value. Fisher's formula with the time reversed is

$$\sqrt{\frac{\Sigma p_o q_n}{\Sigma p_n q_n} \times \frac{\Sigma p_o q_o}{\Sigma p_n q_o}} = \sqrt{\frac{100}{145} \times \frac{70}{100}} = \sqrt{\frac{70}{145}}$$

and

$$\sqrt{\frac{145}{70}} \times \sqrt{\frac{70}{145}} = 1$$

SOME USEFUL CALCULATIONS

Measuring the Value of a Dollar

Price indexes are often used to measure the purchasing power of a dollar. The idea behind this is that, if prices rise, the value of the dollar falls, and vice versa. For example, if the prices of goods double, the value of the dollar used to buy those goods is halved.

To determine the value or purchasing power of a dollar, the reciprocal of the price index is calculated as in the following simple illustration:

YEAR	*PRICE INDEX (1970 = 100)*	*RECIPROCAL (VALUE OF DOLLAR)*
1970	100	$\frac{100}{100}$ = 100 cents
1976	125	$\frac{100}{125}$ = 80 cents

The price increase of 25% results in a 20-cent drop in the dollar's value; it is worth only 80 cents.

It is important to remember that the value of a dollar depends on what dollar we are trying to measure and the base period of the index used to make the calculations. Later in this chapter, we will see how much the U.S. consumer dollar is worth when measured with the U.S. Consumer Price Index.

Adjusting Dollar Volumes

When prices of goods change, the dollar volume of the sales of a constant quantity of those goods changes; therefore, if we have a time series of sales figures, we can adjust the figures for the effects of price changes by dividing the price index for goods sold into the dollar sales volumes as in the following illustration:

YEAR	SALES ($000)	PRICE INDEX (1960 = 100)	ADJUSTED SALES ($000)
1970	$50	100	$\frac{50}{1.00} = \$50$
1976	$80	125	$\frac{80}{1.25} = \$64$

Thus, 1976 sales would have amounted to only $64 thousand if prices had remained constant between 1970 and 1976. Calculations of this type are often called "deflating" because the original dollar volumes are reduced. If the price index were below 100, however, the sales figure would be increased or "inflated." In any case, the adjusted sales figures are referred to as "real" sales. Further on in this chapter, we will learn how to measure "real" earnings of workers by "deflating" with the Consumer Price Index.

Splicing Two Indexes

Sometimes the base of an index is changed to a more current period. If this has been done, the index on the new base can be "spliced" to the index on the old base, or vice versa, to get a continuous index on one base only. In the tabulation below, the index on the 1974 base has been spliced to the index on the 1971 base to produce the index in the right column.

YEAR	INDEX (1971 = 100)		INDEX (1974 = 100)		SPLICED INDEX (1971 = 100)
1971	100.0		—		100.0
1972	116.3		—		116.3
1973	120.3		—		120.3
1974	122.7		100.0		122.7
1975	—	×	94.9	=	116.4
1976	—	×	97.7	=	119.9

This was accomplished by multiplying the 1974 index number in the first column, expressed as a decimal, by the indexes for 1975 and 1976 in the second column as indicated by the arrows and multiplication signs.* This calculation is logical because the indexes on the 1974 base tell us that the 1975 value is 94.9% of the 1974 value and that the 1976 value is 97.7% of the 1974 value.

CALCULATION AND APPLICATIONS OF THREE POPULAR INDEXES

Earlier in this chapter, references were made to the Consumer Price Index, the Wholesale Price Index, and the Index of Industrial Production. These three indexes are probably used more often by more people than any of the other many indexes computed by government or private organizations. Because these three indexes are important tools for business and economic analysis their construction, characteristics, and applications will be discussed.

The Consumer Price Index

Consumer Price Index

The U.S. Bureau of Labor Statistics has computed the Consumer Price Index since 1919. It is currently being updated and revised and the new index will be introduced in 1977. A major result of the revision will be two indexes. One will be the present index for urban wage earners and clerical workers, and the other will be a new index for all urban households. The consumer price index has often been called a "cost of living" index. However, it measures only *changes* in prices or important consumer goods and services. It does not measure how much it costs to live. Since the indexes used in Tables 14-12, 14-13, and 14-14 make use of the unrevised consumer price index, our discussion will concern that index.*

*The algebraic equations for making these computations for 1975 and 1976 are

$$\frac{122.7}{100.0} = \frac{x}{94.9} \quad \text{and} \quad \frac{122.7}{100.0} = \frac{x}{97.7}$$

where x is the index for 1971 = 100.

*At this writing the revised index for the current period has just been released and complete details in the revision are not available. However, new weights will be used, prices will be collected from more establishments, and rent rates will be collected from more tenants. For more information see: U.S. Department of Labor, Bureau of Labor Statistics, *The Consumer Price Index:* How will the 1977 Revision Affect It? 1975 (Report 449)

About 400 goods and services are priced for the index. Examples are food, clothing, automobiles, houses, furniture, repair services, rent, bus fares, and medical care.

TABLE 14-12. Consumer Price Indexes, by Commodity Group, 1960, 1970, 1975 (1967=100).

COMMODITY GROUP	1960	1970	1975
All items	88.7	116.3	161.2
Food	88.0	114.7	175.4
Housing	90.2	118.9	166.8
Apparel and upkeep	89.6	116.1	142.3
Transportation	89.6	112.7	150.6
Health and recreation	85.1	116.2	153.5

Source: *Federal Reserve Bulletin,* April, 1976.

Table 14-12 gives the index for all items and five important commodity groups for three selected years. Until December 1963, the index applied to purchases by families of two or more. Since January 1964, the index coverage has included single workers living alone.

A monthly city average index represents all urban areas in the United States. This average was based on 34 cities prior to 1955, 46 cities from 1955 to 1964, 50 urban areas in 1965, and 56 areas since 1966. Separate indexes are computed for each of 25 metropolitan areas and can be used to compare changes in consumer prices among the areas. Most of these indexes are computed quarterly.

Base year and weights. The current base for the Consumer Price Index is 1967. The average of the three years 1957, 1958, and 1959 (written 1957–59 = 100) was used from 1962–1970. From 1952 to 1962, 1947, 1948, and 1949 (1947–49 = 100) served as the base' and prior to that' the average for 1935–39 was the base. The index for all items is still calculated on the 1957–59 base because some users desire it.

Like the base period, the weighting factors are updated from time to time. The weights for the index since 1964 were derived from a study of expenditures actually made by a carefully selected sample of wage earners and clerical workers and their families. From January 1953 to 1964, weights were based on 1950 expenditures. Changes in weights are needed from time to time because of changes in the relative importance of many consumer goods and services. For example, the weight for food declined significantly from the old index series to the new with accompanying increases in weights for housing, transportation, and health and recreation.

Collection of price data. The goods and services priced for the index calculations are called the "market basket." Price changes for these commodities are used to represent price changes for the thousands of goods and services bought by wage earners and clerical workers and their families. With each revision of the index, some items are dropped and others are added in order to maintain the best representation of all consumer items.

So that the index measures only changes in prices and is not affected by quality and quantity changes, detailed specifications describing each item are used to gather the data.

Prices were obtained from about 16,500 establishments and professional people from whom wage and clerical people make purchases. Rental rates are obtained from approximately 34,000 tenants. Some prices are gathered by mail questionnaire and some by personal visit.

Calculating the index. The basic method used to calculate the index is the weighted average of relatives with a chain computation procedure. The formula for computing a relative change from one month to another is

$$I = I_{i-1} \frac{(\Sigma q_a p_{i-1})\,(p_i/p_{i-1})}{\Sigma q_a p_{i-1}}$$

with q_a representing the average annual quantity of a commodity bought by the wage earners and clerical workers in 1960–61, p_i representing the average price of the commodity in the current period, and p_{i-1} the price in the period prior to the current one. The q_a values are not actually available but the $q_a p_{i-1}$ dollar values are; these are based on expenditure studies made during 1960–61.

Limitations of the index. The Consumer Price Index is not a precise measure of changes in consumer prices. It is subject to sampling errors resulting from the sample selection of wage earners and clerical workers and the "market basket" items. Some error may creep in due to human error in price reporting, but this is thought to be minimal. Moreover, despite efforts to keep constant the quality of all the goods priced, this impossible over the long run. Despite these limitations, however, the index is accurate enough for most purposes.

Consumer Price Index

The Consumer Price Index is used to measure inflationary trends in the national and local economies. It is a particularly valuable aid for understanding what is happening to family finances; therefore, the general public, as well as the economist, is interested in changes in the index.

The index is used also as a guide for adjusting wages. Some labor management contracts contain "escalator" clauses that provide for automatic adjustments in

TABLE 14-13. Measuring the Value of the U.S. Consumer Dollar, 1967—1975.

YEAR	(1) CONSUMER PRICE INDEX (1967=100)	(2) VALUE OF THE CONSUMER DOLLAR (1967 $=100¢)	(3) CONSUMER PRICE INDEX BASE SHIFTED (1970=100)	(4) VALUE OF THE CONSUMER DOLLAR (1970 $=100¢)
1967	100.0	100.0¢	86.0	115.3¢
1968	104.2	96.0	89.6	111.6
1969	109.8	91.1	94.4	105.9
1970	116.3	86.0	100.0	100.0
1971	121.3	82.4	104.3	95.8
1972	125.3	79.8	107.7	92.9
1973	133.1	75.1	114.4	87.4
1974	147.7	67.7	127.9	78.2
1975	161.2	62.0	138.6	72.2

wages, based on changes in the index. Because the reciprocal of the index measures the purchasing power of the dollar, it is used in adjusting royalties, pensions, welfare payments, and ocasionally, alimony payments. Column (1) of Table 14-13 shows the annual index on the 1967 base for 1967–75 period and Column (2) the value of the consumer dollar in each year compared to a dollar with an average value of 100 cents in the base period 1967. The value of the dollar for each year was obtained by dividing the index for each year into 100. For example, the 1975 index of 161.2 divided into 100 gives 62.0 cents, the value of the 1975 dollar compared to a 100-cent dollar in the 1967 base period.

To measure the value of the U.S. Consumer dollar in each year 1967–1975, compared to a dollar with 100 cents in some other period, the base of the index is shifted, and then each new index number is divided into 100. An illustration of this procedure is also presented in Table 14-13. In Column (3) the base of the index is 1970, having been shifted from 1967 based index shown in Column (1) by the procedure given on p. 367. After this was done the value of the dollar in each year compared to a 100-cent 1967 dollar was computed by dividing the indexes into 100. The resulting values are shown in Column (4) of Table 14-13. The measure of the dollar's value is not difficult to interpret when we realize that if prices double, the dollar will buy only one half as much. Explaining further, the 72.2-cent value of the dollar in 1975, shown in Column (4) of Table 14-13, means that by spending a dollar in 1975 we would have bought the same amount of goods and services we could have gotten for 72.2 cents in 1970.

When measuring the value of the dollar, we should identify the base for the measurement. The dollar today is worth any number of cents, depending upon the dollar to which it is compared. Compared to the present, a dollar is worth 100 cents, but its value generally declines the further back in time we go for the comparison.

Also, when discussing the value of the dollar, the kind of dollar should be identified. Compared to the same base, the consumer dollar may differ in value from the wholesale dollar. Moreover, the consumer food dollar may differ in value from the consumer housing dollar or clothing dollar. These differences result from differences in price increases for food, housing, clothing, etc.

The index is important also in removing the effect of price changes from dollar series. This operation is often called ''deflating'' because the magnitudes of rising dollar figures are reduced by the operation when the price indexes are above 100. Dollar figures are ''inflated'' when price indexes are below 100. When wage and sales figures are ''deflated'' the resulting values are often referred to as ''real'' wages and ''real'' sales. ''Real'' wages are a measure of the purchasing power of the wages. ''Real'' sales is a measure of what the sales volumes would have been at constant prices.

Table 14-14 illustrates the deflation of the mean weekly earnings of production workers in United States manufacturing industries, 1970–1975, with the use of the U.S. Consumer Price Index on the 1970 base. The first column gives the actual earnings, the common term for such figures being ''current'' dollars. The earnings figure for each year is divided by the consumer price index for that year to remove the effect of inflationary forces on the purchasing power of the earnings. For example, $190, the mean earnings for 1975, is divided by 1.386, the index for 1975 expressed as a decimal, and the resulting quotient is $137. This $137 measures the real purchasing power of the 1975 earnings compared to the $134 earned in 1970: Looking at it another way: Average weekly earnings increased by 41.8% between 1970 and 1975 (190/134 = 1.418), but because price rose by 38.6% during that time, the purchasing power of the earnings increased only 2.2% (137/134 = 1.022).

In the past three decades, price trends of most products have been upward. Therefore, for most dollar value series, upward movements are biased by price increases. In economic analyses of time series, the effects of price changes must be removed in order to see the effect of other economic forces on the series.

TABLE 14-14. Deflating with the Consumer Price Index (Measuring the Purchasing Power of U.S. Production Workers Mean Weekly Earnings in 1970 Dollars).

YEAR	(1) MEAN WEEKLY EARNINGS OF PRODUCTION WORKERS (CURRENT DOLLARS)	(2) U.S. CONSUMER PRICE INDEX (1970=100)	(3) MEAN WEEKLY EARNINGS OF PRODUCTION WORKERS (1970 DOLLARS)
1970	$134	100.0	$134
1971	142	104.3	136
1972	155	107.7	144
1973	166	114.4	145
1974	176	127.9	138
1975	190	138.6	137

The Wholesale Price Index

Wholesale Price Index

A Wholesale Price Index has been computed by the U.S. Bureau of Labor Statistics since 1880 to measure the changes in prices of goods sold in large quantities

The monthly index is now based on prices of about 2800 commodities.* In the 1947-60 period, about 1900 commodities were included and about 900 for the period prior to 1947. Prices used in the index are collected from primary market sources, such as manufacturer's agents and commodity exchanges. In addition to a composite index for all commodities, indexes for numerous commodity groups and subgroups are calculated. Table 14-15 presents indexes for selected years 1960–75 for the commodity groups and Table 14-16 shows, for example, subgroups in the machinery and equipment group.

No Wholesale Price Index is constructed for cities or metropolitan areas.

TABLE 14-15. Wholesale Price Indexes by Commodity Group, Selected Years, 1960—1975 (1967=100).

COMMODITY GROUP	1960	1970	1975
All commodities	96.6	110.4	174.9
Farm products and processed food and feeds	93.7	111.7	184.2
Farm Products	97.2	111.0	186.7
Processed foods and feeds	89.5	112.1	182.6
Industrial commodities	95.3	110.0	171.5
Textile products and apparel	99.5	107.1	137.9
Hides, skins, leather, and related products	90.8	110.3	148.5
Fuels, power, and related products	96.1	106.2	245.1
Chemical and allied products	101.8	102.2	181.3
Rubber and plastic products	103.1	108.3	150.2
Lumber and wood products	95.3	113.6	176.9
Pulp, paper, and allied products	98.1	108.2	170.4
Metal and metal products	92.4	116.6	185.6
Machinery and equipment	92.0	111.4	161.4
Furniture and household durables	99.0	107.5	139.7
Nonmetallic mineral products	97.2	112.9	174.0
Transportation equipment:			
Motor vehicles and equipment	98.8	108.7	144.6
Railroad equipment	N.A.*	115.1	201.2
Miscellaneous products	93.0	109.6	147.7

*Not available.

Source: U.S. Department of Commerce, Bureau of the Census, *Statistical Abstract of the United States*, 1976.

*A weekly index based on about 250 commodities is computed also.

Base year and weights. The Wholesale Price Index is computed on the 1967 base. Weights used in the index for the 1947–54 period were based mostly on the dollar value of transactions reported in the 1947 *Census of Manufactures*. Weights for 1955–57 were computed from primary market transactions in 1952 and 1953.

TABLE 14-16. Wholesale Price Indexes for Machinery and Equipment, Selected Years, 1960—1975 (1967=100).

COMMODITY GROUP	*1960*	*1970*	*1975*
Machinery and equipment	92.0	111.4	161.4
Agricultural	86.1	113.2	168.6
Construction	85.9	115.9	185.2
Metal working	85.1	114.1	171.6
General purpose	91.2	113.7	178.5
Special industry	N.A.*	115.7	175.0
Electrical	99.5	106.4	162.3

*Not available

Source: U.S. Department of Commerce, Bureau of the Census, *Statistical Abstract of the United States*, 1976.

Weights for other years have been revised from time to time and, effective January 1967, they represent values of net shipments of commodities in 1963.

Collection of price data. Over 10,000 price quotations on about 2300 commodities are used to construct the index. Most price quotations come from a representative group of manufacturers or producers, but some are obtained from organized exchanges or at central markets. Prices of imported commodities come from importers. Detailed specifications for the commodities priced assure the same quality of product so that only ''pure'' price changes are measured. Also, for the most part, actual transaction prices are used because the Bureau of Labor Statistics requests reports of prices less all discounts, allowances, rebates, and free offers. Price data are gathered by mail questionnaire.

Calculation of the index. The weighted average-of-relatives formula

$$I_i = \frac{\Sigma p_o q_a p_i / p_o}{\Sigma p_o q_a}$$

best describes the computational procedure. In this formula the $p_o q_a$ are the dollar-value weights and the p_i / p_o are the price relatives. New weights are introduced from time to time and the index with the new weights is linked to the index with the old weights.

Wholesale Price Index

The Wholesale Price Index is a reliable indicator of price trends in the economy and a tool for general economic analysis. Many organizations use it as a price adjustment factor in long-term contracts for the purchase of commodities.

The index may be changed to a measure of the purchasing power of the wholesale dollar by computing the reciprocals of the index numbers. Also, the index is a valuable tool for "deflating" dollar figures of certain economic data. Table 14-17 exemplifies this. In Column (1), the value of shipments of farm machinery and equipment by U.S. manufacturers since 1955 are tabulated. Since the increases in this series are due in part to rising prices, the effects of price changes must be removed if a measure of the "real" increase in shipments is desired. The most appropriate price index to use for this purpose is the Wholesale Price Index for Agricultural Machinery and Equipment, listed in Column (2). In this illustration a measure of the shipments in 1955 dollars is desired, therefore the base of the index must be shifted to 1955 before making the necessary calculation. The base 1967 is shifted to 1955 by dividing the 1955 index number, 72.6, into the index number for each year and multiplying by 100. This has been done and the index on the 1955 base is shown in Column (3). The new index numbers, expressed as decimals, were divided into the shipments in Column (1) to produce the deflated shipments in Column (4). These constant dollar values can be used to measure changes in the physical volume of shipments of farm machinery and equipment. For example, the physical volume of shipments in 1974 was 79.8% greater than in 1970, since, from Column (4),

$$\frac{1791}{996} = 1.798 = 179.8\%$$

TABLE 14-17. Deflating with the Wholesale Price Index (Measuring the "Real" Value of Shipments of U.S. Farm Machinery and Equipment, 1955—1974.)

YEAR	SHIPMENTS OF FARM MACHINERY AND EQUIPMENT IN CURRENT DOLLARS ($000,000)	WHOLESALE PRICE INDEX OF AGRICULTURAL MACHINERY AND EQUIPMENT		SHIPMENTS OF FARM MACHINERY AND EQUIPMENT IN 1955 DOLLARS ($000,000)
		(1967=100)	(1955=100)	
	(1)	(2)	(3)	(4)
1955	$ 912	72.6	100.0	$ 912
1960	1001	86.1	118.6	844
1965	1432	94.0	129.5	1106
1970	1553	113.2	155.9	996
1974	3548	143.8	198.1	1791

Source: U.S. Department of Commerce, *Statistical Abstract of the United States,* 1972 and 1976.

The Index of Industrial Production

Index of Industrial Production

The Board of Governors of the Federal Reserve System computes and publishes the Index of Industrial Production, which measures the changes in the physical volume or quantity of output of the manufacturing and mining industries and of electric and gas utilities. The agricultural, construction, transportation, trade, and service industries are not represented in the index.

First computed in the 1920's, this index has been revised several times to account for changes in the economy and to take into account more data and refinements in methods of analysis. The latest revision was in 1976.

Separate indexes are computed for a number of groups and subgroups, such as those illustrated in Table 14-18. The number of individual indexes in the groups and subgroups increased from 227 to 235 as a result of the 1976 revision. The 1976 revision added about 30 subgroups.

Base year and weights. The index is now on the popular 1967 base. In several years in the 1960's the 1957–59 average was the base. Prior to a 1962 revision, 1957 was the base and the base used in the early 1950's was the 1947–49 average.

Weights for the index are based on value added data from the Census of Manufactures and Census of Mineral Industries. Weights for utility data were derived from data supplied by the Federal Power Commission.

TABLE 14-18. Index of Industrial Production by Major Industry and Market Groups, Selected Year, 1960—1975 (1967=100).

MAJOR GROUP	*1960*	*1970*	*1975*
Total Index	66	107	114
Industry groups:			
Manufacturing, total	65	105	112
Durable manufactures	63	101	106
Nondurable manufactures	69	111	121
Mining	83	110	107
Utilities	62	128	154
Market groups:			
Final products, total	65	104	116
Consumer goods	71	110	124
Equipment	56	96	104
Materials	66	107	110

Source: U.S. Department of Commerce, Bureau of the Census, *Statistical Abstract of the United States,* 1976.

Collection of data Data for computing the index are received from manufacturers, mining companies, and utilities. The industries covered in the index are responsible for 35% of the total value of production in the United States.

Calculation of the index. The weighted average-of-relatives method is used to combine individual series into composite indexes. Dollar-value weights are used, but they are expressed as percentages of the total of the weights assigned to all the series.

The index is adjusted for differences in the number of working days from month to month and for seasonal variations. The working-day adjustment converts the measures to a daily average basis so that the index better reflects changes in the rate of production. The seasonal adjustment causes the index to reflect basic month-to-month changes that are not temporary due to seasonally heavy and low periods of activity.

Index of Industrial Production

The Index of Industrial Production serves mainly as a tool for general economic analysis.

The composite index is watched closely by economists because it is a good indicator of the level of general economic activity. Any significant downturn or upturn in output of the nation's factories, mines, and utilities signifies changes in employment, income, retail trade, and other economic segments.

The indexes for individual groups and subgroups help firms classified in those groups to measure their own performances and forecast their output. For example, a firm that manufactures machinery may compare changes in its output to changes in the industrial production index for the machinery group to see if it is keeping pace with its industry.

OTHER ECONOMIC INDEXES

Many indexes other than the three that have been described have important uses in specialized areas. Examples are: Help Wanted Advertising Index (1967 = 100), published by the National Industrial Conference Board; Index of Exports and Imports (1967 = 100), published by the Bureau of International Commerce, U.S. Department of Commerce; Construction Cost Index (1967 = 100), published by the American Appraisal Company; and Index of National Advertising Expenditures (1967 = 100), compiled by McCann-Erickson, Inc., for Decher Communications, New York. Any recent issue of the U.S. Department of Commerce's *Survey of Current Business* lists many other indexes used for economic and business analysis.

REVIEW QUESTIONS

1. What is an index?
2. For what are indexes used?
3. What are the three basic types of indexes?
4. What is the most widely used index base period?
5. Discuss the criteria for choosing the base of an index.
6. Discuss the considerations for choosing weights for composite indexes.
7. Under what conditions is the simple aggregative method satisfactory for construction of a composite price index?
8. Why might we use the weighted average-of-relatives method to compute an index rather than the weighted aggregative method?
9. Briefly describe the Consumer Price Index, the Wholesale Price Index, and the Index of Industrial Production.
10. Why might it be necessary to shift the base of an index?

PROBLEMS

1. Exercise Table 14-1 gives data on durable and nondurable goods sales of wholesale establishments. Compute an index for each series using the 1967 value as the base. Plot the two indexes on the same chart and briefly comment on the comparative growth of the two series.

EXERCISE TABLE 14-1. Sales of Durable and Nondurable Goods in Wholesale Establishments, United States 1965—1975.

YEAR	BILLIONS OF DOLLARS DURABLE GOODS	NONDURABLE GOODS
1965	$ 82.9	$104.5
1966	91.1	112.7
1967	90.6	114.7
1968	100.2	120.9
1969	109.7	127.3
1970	112.0	135.0
1971	122.4	145.2
1972	138.5	159.9
1973	168.1	196.7
1974	202.3	245.8
1975	185.9	253.1

2. Average weekly earnings of production workers in the United States rose from $176 in 1974 to $190 in 1975. During the same time, the nations's Consumer Price Index (1967 = 100) rose from 127.9 to 138.6. Calculate the percent change in ''real'' earnings of the production workers.

3. Shift the base of the price index for medical care shown in Exercise Table 14-2 to 1970 and then compute the value of the medical care dollar in each year compared to a 100-cent 1970 medical care dollar.

EXERCISE TABLE 14-2. Consumer Price Index for Medical Care, United States, 1970—1975 (1967=100).

YEAR	INDEX
1970	120.6
1971	128.4
1972	132.5
1973	137.7
1974	150.5
1975	168.6

Source: *Federal Reserve Bulletin,* April 1976.

4. Exercise Table 14-3 gives the U.S. Consumer Price Index on the 1970 base and sales of retail stores in the U.S. from 1970 to 1975. Deflate the sales figures so that they are expressed in 1970 dollars. Do you think the Consumer Price Index is a good deflater for retail sales? Why?

5. A company's exports rose as follows: Between 1971 and 1972, 14.3%; between 1972 and 1973, 3.6%; between 1973 and 1974, 10.8%; and between 1974 and 1975, 5.5%. Using this information, construct an index of exports with 1971 as the base.

EXERCISE TABLE 14-3. Consumer Price Index and Sales of Retail Stores, United States, 1970—1975.

YEAR	*CONSUMER PRICE INDEX (1970=100)*	*SALES OF RETAIL STORES (BILLIONS)*
1970	100.0	381
1971	104.3	410
1972	107.7	449
1973	114.4	505
1974	127.0	538
1975	138.6	585

Source: *Federal Reserve Bulletin,* April 1976, *Business Statistics* 1975, and *Survey of Current Business,* July, 1976.

6. Using the information in Exercise Table 14-4, construct a composite price index for the selected mineral products. Use the 1965 quantities as weights and make 1965 the base period.

EXERCISE TABLE 14-4. Prices of Selected Mineral Products in 1965, 1970, and 1974, with 1965 Quantities Produced in the United States.

PRODUCT	*UNIT*	*1965 QUANTITIES (000,000)*	*PRICE PER UNIT 1965*	*1970*	*1974*
Sulphur	Long ton	7	$25.50	$23.14	$29.50
Bituminous coal	Short ton	512	4.44	6.26	15.00
Crude petroleum	Barrel	2,848	2.86	3.18	6.85

Source: U.S. Department of Commerce, *Statistical Abstract of the United States,* 1975.

7. Exercise Table 14-5 gives the quantity and dollar value of United States exports of three kinds of fish in 1970 and 1974. Compute a composite physical-volume index of these products using the 1970 values as the weights and 1970 as the base. Also compute an index on the 1974 base, but use 1974 values as the weights. Explain the meaning of the two index numbers for 1974 derived by using the different weights.

(a) Could a satisfactory quantity index be computed from the data in Exercise Table 14-5 by dividing the sum of the 1974 quantities by the sum of the 1970 quantities? Why?

(b) If the information in Exercise Table 14-5 is all that is available on the three seafoods for those years, could the weighted aggregative method be used to compute a quantity index? Why?

(c) Could the mean value of each product for 1970 and 1974 be used as weights for computing an index of quantity from the data in Exercise Table 14-5?

EXERCISE TABLE 14-5. Quantity and Value of U.S. Catch of Three Selected Fish, 1970 and 1974.

FISH	1970 POUNDS CAUGHT (000,000)	1970 VALUE ($000,000)	1974 POUNDS CAUGHT (000,000)	1974 VALUE ($000,000)
Salmon	410	99	197	121
Mackerel	48	2	22	1
Tuna	393	75	386	118

Source: U.S. Department of Commerce, *Statistical Abstract of the United States,* 1975.

8. Use the information in Exercise Table 14-6 to compute a composite index of the physical volume of imports for 1965, 1970, and 1974. Make 1965 the base and use 1965 dollar values as the weights.

EXERCISE TABLE 14-6. Imports of Coffee, Tea, and Cocoa 1965, 1970, and 1974 (Quantities in millions of pounds and values in millions of dollars).

ITEM	1965 QUANTITY	1965 VALUE	1970 QUANTITY	1974 QUANTITY
Coffee	2,834	$1,069	2,690	2,545
Tea	130	57	137	178
Cocoa	934	146	847	728

Source: U.S. Department of Commerce, *Statistical Abstract of the United States,* 1975.

9. Use data from Exercise Table 14-7 to compute an index of price for the grain products for 1965, 1970, and 1974 by the weighted aggregative method. Use the production averages for 1961–65 as weights and make 1961–65 the base. Also, compute a price index for the same grain products for 1965, 1970, and 1974 by the weighted average-of-relatives method. Make 1961–65 average values the weights. Compare the index numbers computed by the two methods. Are they identical? If not, why? Should they be identical? Explain.

10. Compute an index that shows the average change in shipments of all structural clay products between 1965 and 1974. Use the 1965 values as weights. Data for these computations are presented in Exercise Table 14-8.

EXERCISE TABLE 14-7. Production and Value of Four Grain Products in the United States, Selected Years.

	MILLIONS OF BUSHES PROD.				*PRICE PER BUSHEL*			
CROP	*1961–65 AVERAGE*	*1965*	*1970*	*1974*	*1961–65 AVERAGE*	*1965*	*1970*	*1974*
Corn	3,758	4,084	4,152	4,651	$1.13	$1.16	$1.33	$3.51
Wheat	1,214	1,316	1,352	1,793	1.60	1.35	1.33	4.32
Oats	953	917	917	621	0.63	0.62	0.62	1.66
Rice	68	76	84	114	5.00	4.93	5.17	10.78

Source: U.S. Department of Commerce, *Statistical Abstract of the United States,* 1975, p.635.

EXERCISE TABLE 14-8. Quantity and Value of Structural Clay Products Shipped, United States, 1965, 1970, 1974.

PRODUCT	*1965*	*1970*	*1974*
Brick (building or common and face):			
Shipments (mil. of std. brick)	8,089	6,496	6,681
Value (millions of dollars)	301	288	380
Facing tiles (structural):			
Shipments (mil. of brick equiv.)	314	169	97
Value (millions of dollars)	26	16	13
Structural clay tile:			
Shipments (1,000 sh. tons)	313	181	100
Value (millions of dollars)	5	6	4
Vitrified clay sewer pipe and fittings:			
Shipments (1,000 sh. tons)	1,732	1,622	1,455
Value (millions of dollars)	103	119	134
Clay floor and wall tile and accessories:			
Shipments (millions of sq. ft.)	282	250	273
Value (millions of dollars)	142	126	168

Source: U.S. Department of Commerce: *Statistical Abstract of the United States,* 1975, p. 759.

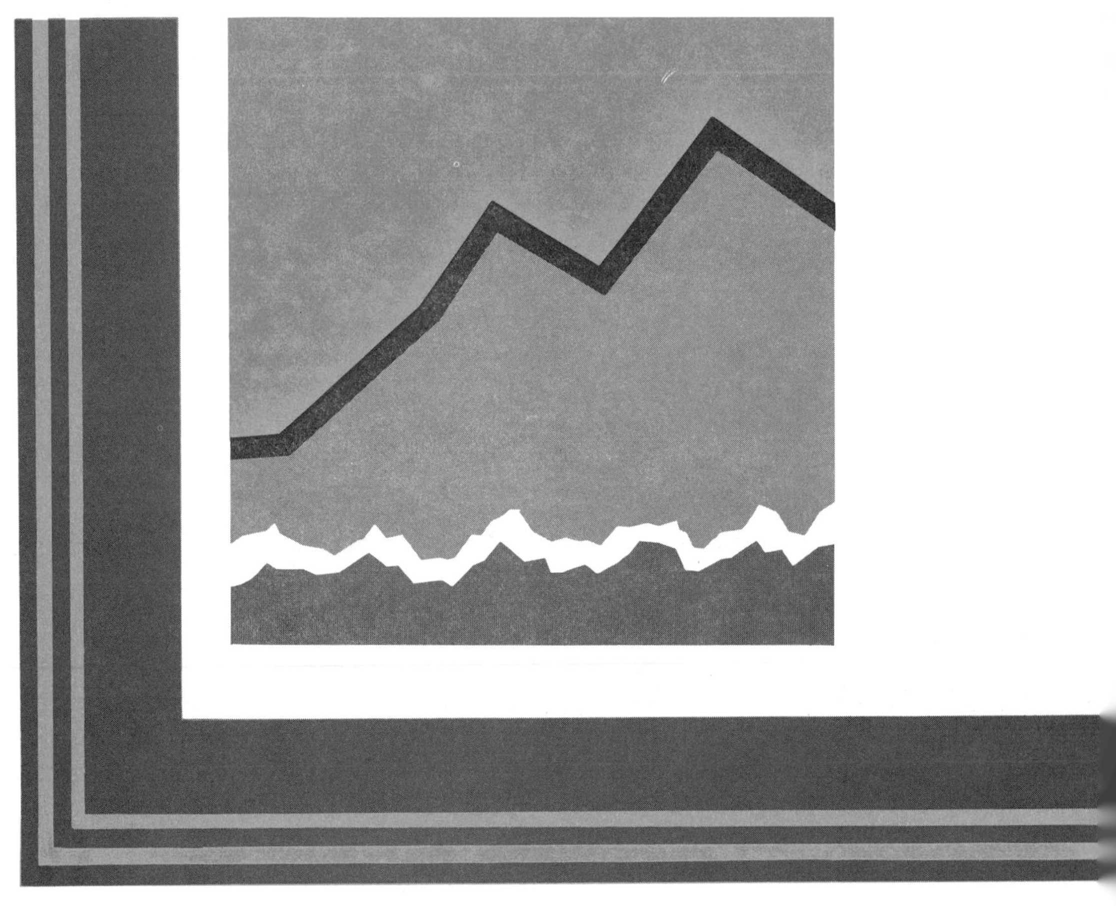

15

Time Series Analysis

Chapter 12, on regression and correlation analysis, was concerned with the functional relationship of two variables, one dependent and one independent, that related to thc same ordered units. In correlation analysis the dependent variable, Y, is a function of the independent variable, X, but the independent variable is not time, even when two time series are correlated.

Time Series Analysis

Analysis of a single variable classified by time in which the values of the variable are functions of the time periods is called time series analysis.

Any variable classified chronologically is a time series. The time periods may be years, quarters, months, weeks, and in some cases days or hours.

PURPOSE OF TIME SERIES ANALYSIS

Frequently, we may desire to analyze a time series to discover past patterns of growth and change that can be used to predict future patterns and needs for business operations and economic events. Such predictions are necessary for making business decisions. Time series analysis does not provide the answer to what the future holds, but it is valuable in the forecasting process—and helps to reduce errors in forecasts.

Every minute of the day someone is making decisions. Knowingly or unknowingly, consciously or unconsciously, these decisions are based on predictions. And these predictions are usually based on what has happend in the past. For example, when a student goes to class, he predicts, without thinking of it as such, that the instructor will be there. His prediction is based on the fact that the instructor has always, or usually, met his classes. A housewife goes to the porch to get the milk at 7:30 in the morning. She expects the milk to be there because the milkman has been punctual and periodic in his delivery of the milk. Her *action* results from a *decision* based on a *forecast*, which in turn was based on *past events*.

Analogously, a businessman with decisions to make relies on forecasts based in part on past patterns of change in business operations. If his sales have risen from November to December every year in the past ten years, he is likely to predict that this will happen next year, unless he knows of certain plans or economic events that are likely to disrupt the traditional sales pattern. Of course, it is important for the business forecaster to be aware of economic changes that could interfer with the traditional growth or periodicity of his business operations. He, therefore, should be a part of the management team so that he will be apprised of management plans. Moreover, he needs to know what is happening in the over-all economy and in the industry in which his firm operates. Most of all, the effective forecaster needs experience and good judgment, as well as sound knowledge of analytical tools. Analytical tools are as necessary to the forecaster as pliers, screwdrivers, and wrenches are necessary to the mechanic. Like the mechanic, the analyst must know his business well enough to choose the proper tool to solve the problem at hand.

COMPOSITION OF A TIME SERIES

Time series are composed of distinct movements that can be measured separately. Three movements are found in an annual time series. These are: *secular trends, cyclical movements,* and *irregular fluctuations*. An additional movement, called *seasonal*, is found in time series classified by quarters, months, and weeks.

Secular Trends

Secular trends are the basic long-term movements in a time series that can be described by a straight line or curve.

The trend may be upward or downward or in both directions. Chart 15-1 illustrates various shapes of secular trends.

The basic forces producing or affecting the trends of a series are: population change, price change, technological change, and productivity increases.

The total retail sales of a community may have risen each year for several years because its population continued to grow. Moreover, the sales in current dollars may have been pushed upward because of general increases in prices of retail goods—even if the physical volume of goods sold did not change.

Technological change may cause a time series to move generally upward or downward. The development and improvement of the automobile, accompanied by improvements in roads, permitting winter driving, has increased gasoline sales. The same automobile, however, produced in increasing volumes, caused a downward trend in the production of horse-drawn wagons and buggies.

Chart 15-1. Illustration of types of secular trends.

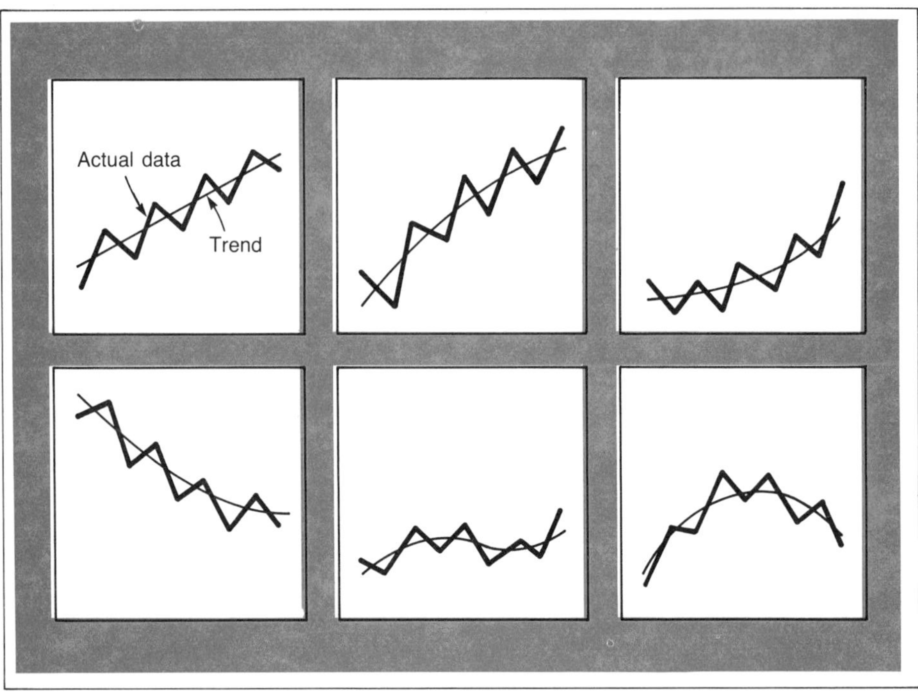

Productivity increases, which, in turn, may be due to technological change, give an upward slope to many time series. Any measure of total output, such as manufacturers' sales, are affected by changes in productivity.

Cyclical Fluctuations

A movement is cyclical only in the sense that it has been historically recurrent. The durations of cyclical fluctuations are longer than a year and cycles are usually irregular in timing and amplitude.

Cyclical fluctuations occur in most quarterly, monthly, and weekly time series, as well as in annual series. Almost everyone has heard of and felt the effects of the general business cycle in the nations's economic activity. Because of the absence of a regular periodic pattern, however, the forecasting of the turning points and magnitudes of such

Chart 15-2. Number of dwelling unit construction permits in the Milwaukee Metropolitan Area, 1957—1975.

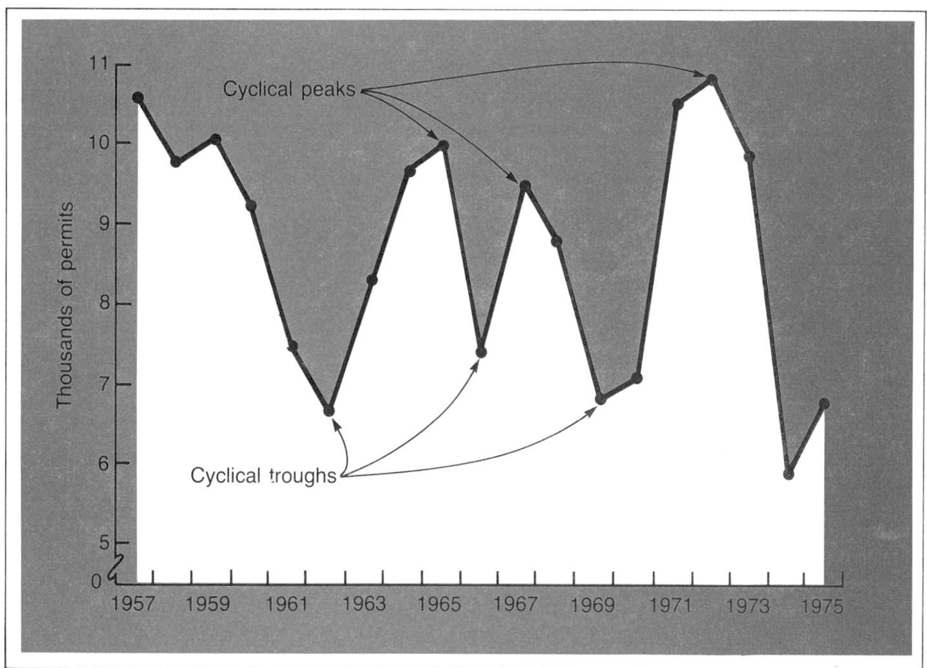

cycles is extremely difficult. Chart 15-2 illustrates the cyclical swings in a time series. In Chapter 18 we shall learn how cyclical fluctuations can be isolated from a time series.

An economic cycle may be thought of as having four phases: recovery, boom, recession, and depression. However, the layman usually hears only the terms prosperity and recession. Recession usually means mild depression, or simply that business is down from a higher level.

Many books have been written about the economic forces that produce the business cycle, and much controversy still exists concerning the importance and the effects of each of these forces. Although a discussion of business cycle theory is out of place in this textbook, it should be pointed out that some of the key factors affecting cyclical economic activity in the nation are government spending, investment in new plant and equipment, consumer purchases, price changes and interest rates. Also, there may be unusual factors producing cyclical swings in a particular industry.

Irregular Fluctuations

Irregular or random fluctuations, a third component of annual, quarterly, monthly, and weekly time series are, as the name implies, nonperiodic. They cannot be predicted because, for the most part, they are caused by unpredictable or nonperiodic events such as weather changes, strikes, wars, rumors of wars, elections and the passage of legislative bills.

For example, a snow storm will cause a drop in retail sales because shoppers cannot get to the stores; a strike will produce a drop in production; and a war rumor may cause stock prices to fall and sales of certain consumer items to rise. In monthly time series, we find numerous irregular fluctuations. One of an unusually high or low magnitude can often be identified with some particular event. Most random fluctuations, however, remain unexplained.

Seasonal Fluctuations

Seasonal fluctuations, a fourth component of time series, are usually found in data classified quarterly, weekly, and monthly. These fluctuations are quite regular in timing and magnitude and, therefore, are easier to predict than cyclical fluctuations. Because of their regular perodic pattern, the average or typical pattern can be measured and used to forecast future seasonal increases and decreases.

For example, a large department store should, based on its past monthly sales patterns for several years, be able to predict quite accurately an increase in sales from November to December and a decline in sales for the following January. Only unusual weather or other unforeseen events could cause such a forecast to be far wrong. Chart 15-3 reveals the pattern of the monthly sales volumes of department stores in the United States each year for a five-year period. The pattern of fluctuation for each year is essentially the same.

Seasonal movements show regularity in timing and amplitude because they are caused by changes in seasonal weather conditions and people's habits. For example, weather causes sales of ice to be higher in summer than in winter and consumer fuel bills to be higher in winter than in summer. Frozen fruit stocks are heavier in October, right

Chart 15-3. Department store sales in the United States, by months, 1971—1975 (Billions of dollars).

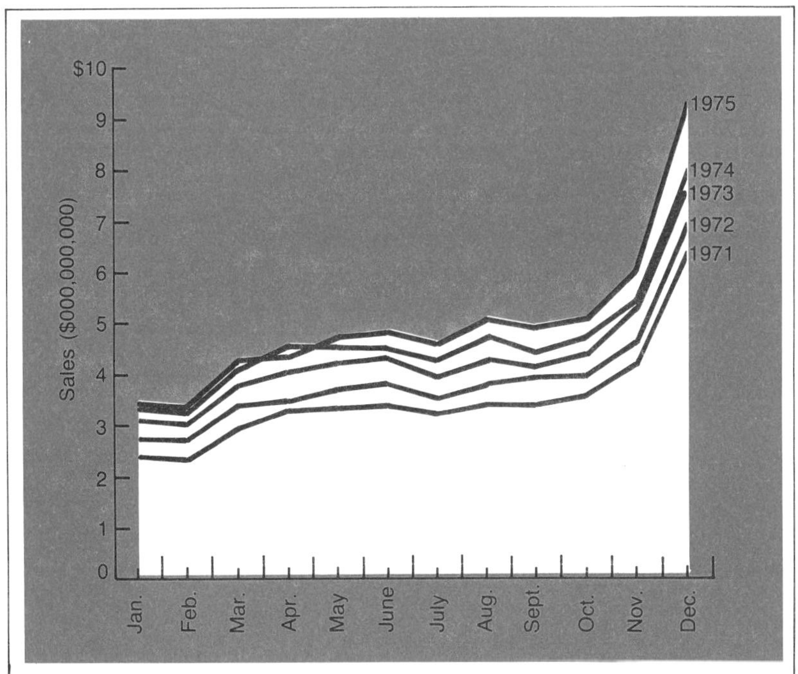

after the fruit harvest, than in April when much of stock has been consumed. People's custom of observing Christmas by exchanging gifts results in significant increases in the total retail sales of the nation each December. Sales of children's clothing and school supplies rise from August to September because September is the traditional period for school to begin in the United States.

If events that cause seasonal fluctuations are naturally or traditionally regular in occurrence, a forecaster can rely upon future regularity in the seasonal fluctuations of the economic data affected. If the timing of a customary practice is changed, then the seasonal pattern of business data affected by the practice will be changed. For example, if a community decided to open its school in August, instead of September, the peak of sales of school supplies in that community would change from September to August, and errors in forecasts based on the traditional custom would be large.

In Chapter 17 we shall learn how to compute seasonal indexes, which measure the average or typical seasonal fluctuations in a time series. We shall also learn how to use such indexes in deseasonalizing data and in short range forecasting and decision-making.

MATHEMATICAL RELATIONSHIPS OF TIME SERIES COMPONENTS

In order to study the seasonal and other components of a time series, a consideration of the mathematical relationships of the components is necessary. Analysts almost universally agree that the original data of a time series are a product of the components; that is, an annual series is a product of trend, cycle, and irregular fluctuations, expressed symbolically as $T \times C \times I$. In data where seasonal variations are present, the composition is $T \times C \times S \times I$. In this multiplicative composition, T is measured in the units of the actual data and the other components, C, S, and I are index values. In certain time series, it might be agreed that the original data are best represented as a sum of the components, $T + C + S + I$, each of which is expressed in units of the actual values. However, we shall make use of the product concept in this text.

The next two chapters will show how T, the trend, and S, the seasonal variation, can be measured directly, and how C, the cyclical, and I, the irregular, movements can be isolated by removing T and S. The following symbolically illustrates the main types of analysis that will be made. Trend will be measured directly from annual data and then removed from the original data by division; that is,

$$\frac{T \times C \times I}{T} = C \times I$$

Trend and seasonal variations will be measured for monthly data and removed from original data as follows:

$$\frac{T \times C \times S \times I}{T \times S} = C \times I$$

The irregular component, I, can be removed by a moving average, resulting in a measure of C. Theoretically, any of the components of a time series can be removed by division, but in actual practice, C and I are seldom, if ever, so removed because of the difficulty or impossibility of directly measuring them. However, a good direct measure of trend and cycle, $T \times C$, combined can be made with a moving average (illustrated in Chapter 17) and then removed by division as a step in the calculation of seasonal indexes. The formula for this is

$$\frac{T \times C \times S \times I}{T \times C} = S \times I$$

Moving averages will be discussed in Chapter 17.

CHARTING TIME SERIES

As we can see from Charts 15-2 and 15-3, line charts are useful for depicting fluctuations in data covering several time periods. It is usually necessary for an analyst to chart his data on both arithmetic and logarithmic scales before choosing methods of analysis. By doing this he gets an additional guide for selecting equations and other methods for measuring and describing the fluctuations revealed on the chart.

Time series line charts, like bar charts, are constructed in reference to two intersecting lines called axis, which divide a plane into four parts called quadrants (see rules for bar charts, Chapter 3). Plotting is usually in the first quadrant.

Time series line charts are traditionally constructed with the time periods (years, months, etc.) placed on the horizontal axis and the scale for the data placed on the vertical axis. Any other arrangement of the time and data intervals would produce an awkward chart that would be difficult to read.

Time Series Rules

1) Place time on the horizontal axis and the scale for the values to be plotted on the vertical axis.
2) Make the chart slightly wider than high. Use of this rule helps avoid distortion of facts.
3) Place a few scale values at guide lines on the chart. This facilitates reading the chart.
4) Set the scale values on the vertical axis so that the line depicting movements of the data will be approximately in the center of the chart, giving the chart a balanced appearance.
5) Start the scale numbering with zero unless index numbers are being charted or a logarithmic scale is being used. This must be done to avoid distortion. The reference base is zero, therefore it must be shown. (Charting of index numbers and the logarithmic scale are explained later.)
6) Make equal distances on the vertical scale represent equal, absolute amounts so that the chart can be read accurately.
7) Plot points to the middle of the time periods when comulative data (period data) are being charted, but plot noncumulative data (point data) to the point in time to which the data refer.
8) Connect plotted points on the chart with straight lines. Do not use curved lines because you do not know what kind of curve to make.

In the observance of rule 7, either spaces of lines may be used to represent time periods. To illustrate, a chart of the same *cumulative* figures for four years could appear in either of two ways:

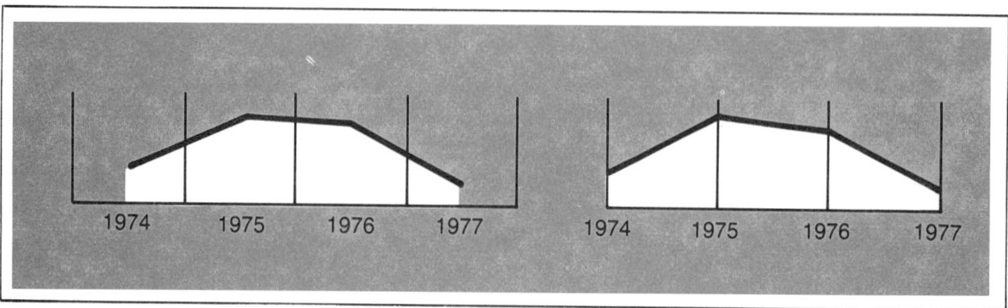

Charts 15-4*a* through 15-4*b* have spaces representing years. The points are plotted to the middle of the spaces because the data are *cumulative*. Cumulative data, or period data, are those that result from a cumulation from the beginning of a time period, such as a year, to the end of the time period. Examples are total annual sales and total annual production. *Noncumulative* data, or point data, measure magnitudes at particular points of time, for example, population on April 1 or inventories on December 31, for several years. If spaces are used for plotting noncumulative data, the plotted points should be placed in the space where the point of time would fall. For example, potato prices on September 30 would be plotted three fourths of the way over from the beginning of the space. When plotting noncumulative data, however, it may be less confusing to use lines rather than spaces to represent time periods.

These eight rules apply to any time series line chart. There are other rules for particular types of time series charts, some of which will be discussed later.

TABLE 15-1 Sales of the CBA Co., 1970–1976.

YEAR	*SALES ($000,000)*
1970	$15
1971	20
1972	27
1973	23
1974	29
1975	35
1976	32

Source: The CBA Company.

Charts 15-4*a*, 15-4*b*, 15-4*c*, 15-4*d*, and 15-4*e* have all been constructed from the data in Table 15-1. Some of the rules have been ignored or violated in all except Charts 15-4*a* and 15-4*e*, which are labeled "right" and "acceptable," respectively. Chart 15-4*b* is "wrong" because it is too flat and thus under-emphasizes the growth in the sales of the CBA Co. Chart 15-4*c* distorts the growth trend in the other direction by its tall narrow dimensions and Chart 15-4*d* gives an impression of extremely rapid growth because of the tall narrow grid and because the scale beginning is not zero. Chart 15-4*a* does not seem to distort the growth of the sales of the CBA Co. in any way with its

Chart 15-4. Sales of the CBA Co., 1970–1976 (millions of dollars).

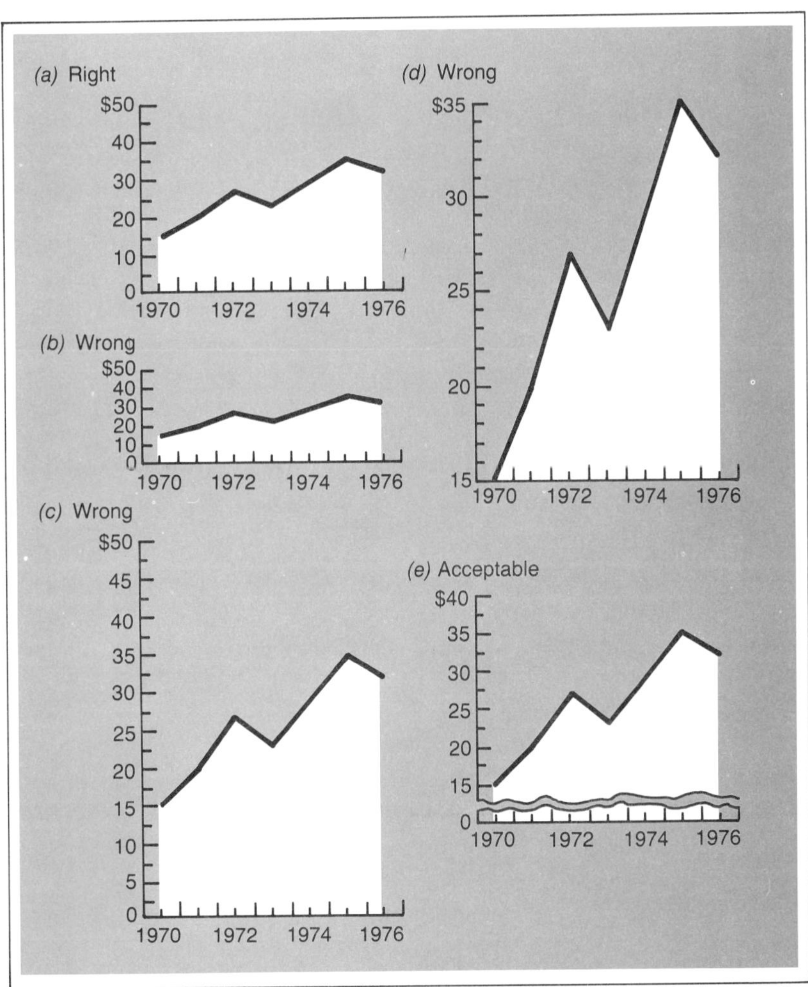

Source of data: Table 15-1

moderate slope. Just how much slope a time series line should show is a judgment for the analyst to make. His purpose should be to present the facts as they are, not as he wishes the reader to see them.

Occasionally, an analyst needs to chart a time series where the magnitudes of change between consecutive time periods are small in relation to the general magnitude of the data. If he considers the changes highly important, he can bring out this importance ethically by using a broken scale, which indicates that a large area of the chart is not used. Another glance at Chart 15-4*c* will reveal that much of the space, between 0 and 15 and 40 and 50, is not used. An untrained chart maker would probably start the bottom line at 15, as in Chart 15-4*d*, to picture the same growth, rather than start with zero and use the broken scale. His reader, though, might not notice that the scale starts with 15 and, consequently, might misinterpret the sales growth. If the chart marker, however, believes that the growth picture in Chart 15-4*c* is the correct one, he can present it as in Chart 15-4*e*, where the break between 0 and 15 shows the reader that the chart maker purposely magnified the fluctuations without intending to trick the reader.

Using two scales. It is usually unwise to compare two time series that are expressed in different units or widely different magnitudes in the same arithmetic chart. To do this would require two different scales, and thus would enable the chart maker to present almost any picture he desired. To illustrate this fact, the data in Table 15-2 are presented in Charts 15-5*a* and 15-5*b*. We can readily see that the two charts give different impressions even though the rules for chart construction have been observed—except, of course, that two different scales on the arithmetic grid have been used. If we desire to compare the two series in Table 15-2 we can do it effectively by converting each series to an index, using the same base for both, or we can plot the two series on a logarithmic scale; both methods enable us to compare rates of change.

TABLE 15-2 Gross National Product and Passenger Cars Registered, United States, 1950–1975.

YEAR	*GROSS NATIONAL PRODUCT (BILLIONS OF DOLLARS)*	*CARS REGISTERED DEC. 31 (MILLIONS)*
1950	$ 286	40
1955	399	52
1960	506	61
1965	688	75
1970	982	89
1975	1499	109 (est.)

Source: U.S. Department of Commerce, *Statistical Abstract of the United States*, 1975; and Automobile Manufactures Association, *Automobile Facts and Figures*, 1967

Index

An index is a device for measuring relationships among values. To construct an index of a time series, a base figure must be chosen, then divided into the figure for each time period.

Table 15-3 shows indexes constructed from Table 15-5 with the figure for 1950 as the base. The Gross National Product for 1950, 286, was divided into the Gross National Product for each of the other years, and the quotients were multiplied by 100. Also, the passenger car registration figure for each year was expressed as a percentage of the 1950 figure, 40. These two indexes are plotted in Chart 15-6, making it possible to make a proper and meaningful analysis and interpretation of the growth of the two series.

For this illustration, the choice of 1950 as the base for the two indexes was arbitrary. Any other year, or an average of two or more years, could have been chosen. Choice of a base period for an index depends partly upon the reason for its calculation. Criteria for choosing bases of indexes are thoroughly discussed in Chapter 14. It should be exphasized here, however, that indexes must have the same base periods in order to be compared.

Note that in Charts 15-5*a*, 15-5*b*, and 15-6 the years are designated by lines, rather than spaces, as in Charts 15-4*a* through 15-4*e*. The line represents the entire year for Gross National Product, but December 31 of the year for passenger cars registered.

Chart 15-5. Gross National Product and passenger cars registered, United States, 1950—1975.

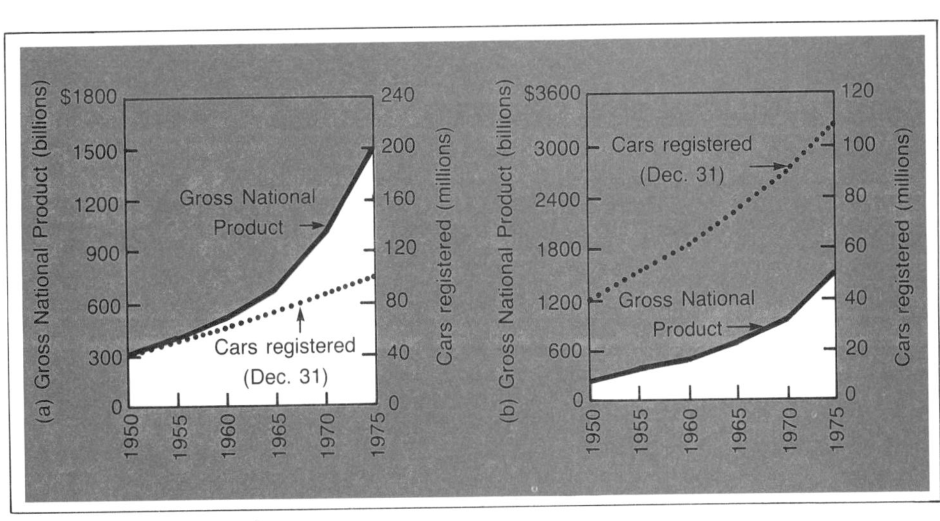

Source of data: Table 15-2

TABLE 15-3 Indexes of Gross National Product and Passenger Cars Registered, United States, 1950–1975 (1950 = 100).

YEAR	*INDEX OF GROSS NATIONAL PRODUCT*	*INDEX OF CARS REGISTERED*
1950	100	100
1955	140	130
1960	177	152
1965	241	188
1970	343	222
1975	524	272

Source: Computed from data in Table 15-2.

Semi-Logarithmic Chart

In a semi-log chart the vertical scale is ruled logarithmically and the horizontal scale is ruled arithmetically. The vertical scale shows graphically the rates of change in the time series plotted while the horizontal scale shows the time period.

Since the vertical scale of a semi-log chart shows rates of change, it can be used to compare the rates of change in two or more series on the same graph. Also, two different vertical scales may be used. Two rules for placing vertical scale values make it impossible to distort comparative growth trends in the semi-log chart by changing scale values when using two different scales: The starting vertical scale value must be larger than zero; and the number at the top of a cycle must be 10 times the number at the bottom of the same cycle. The first rule is logical since the vertical scale reveals rates of change and a rate cannot be computed with zero. The second rule must be observed because the scale for a cycle is ruled according to the logarithms of the numbers 1 through 10.* To follow this rule, the values on the 10 major grid lines of the scale must be an arithmetic progression of values from the starting value; an increment must equal the starting value. Three examples of numbering a scale on two-cycle semi-log paper are shown on the opposite page, where the starting point is 10, the arithmetic progression is 10, 20, 30, etc., until the second cycle is reached and then the arithmetic progression is 100, 200, 300, etc. Notice that the distance between 10 and 20 on the vertical scale is the same as the distance from 20 to 40 and 40 to 80. Equal distances on the logarithmic scale represent equal *percent changes*. (Equal distances on an arithmetic scale represent equal *absolute amounts*.)

*For a review of logarithms, see Appendix.

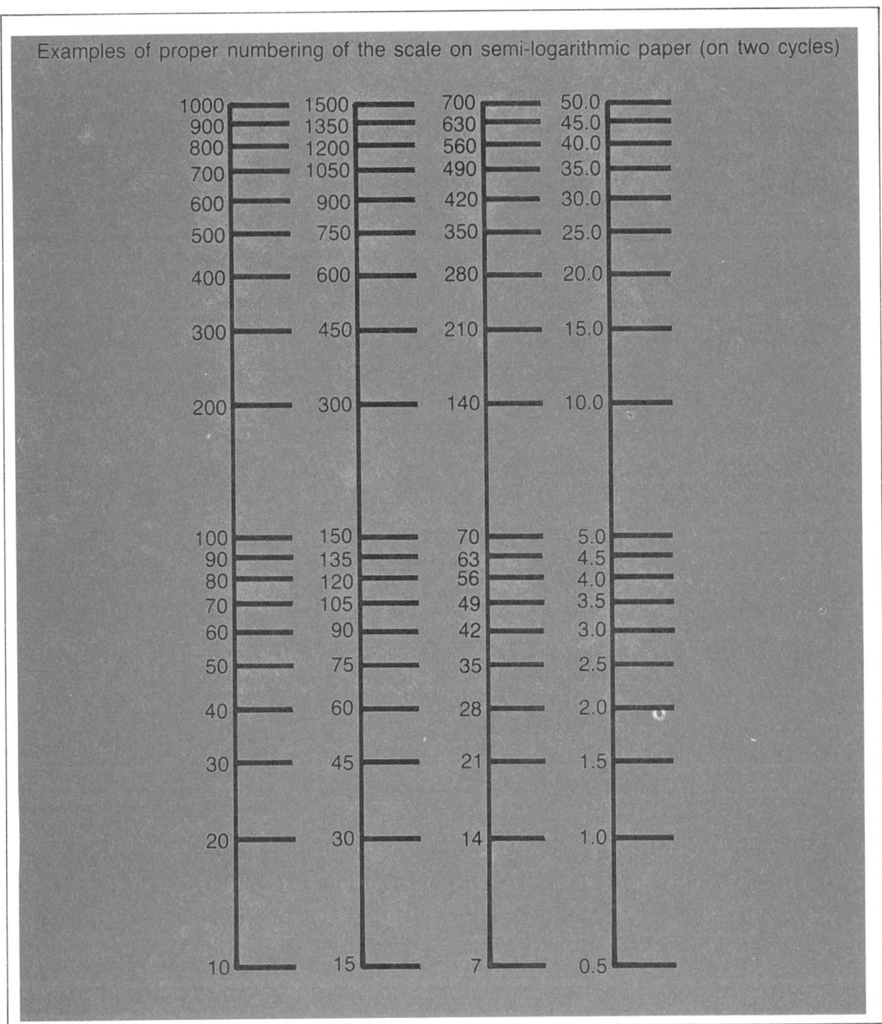

No instruction will be given on the actual construction of semi-log paper because its construction is required very rarely. Most stores selling business supplied carry semi-log paper with one or more cycles. Since one cycle represents an increase of 900%, it would be an unusual chart that would require semi-log paper with more than three cycles.

Because the logarithmic scale shows rates of change in time series, it can be used very effectively to compare the rates of change in two series that are: expressed in the same units, but different magnitudes; or expressed in different units. Chart 15-7 shows a semi-log chart of the data plotted arithmetically in Chart 15-6. The scale numbers in Chart 15-7 were set up so that the two lines would fall close together near the middle of the paper. Changing the scale values does not change the magnitudes of the fluctuations

Chart 15-6. Indexes of Gross National Product and passenger cars registered. United States, 1950–1975.

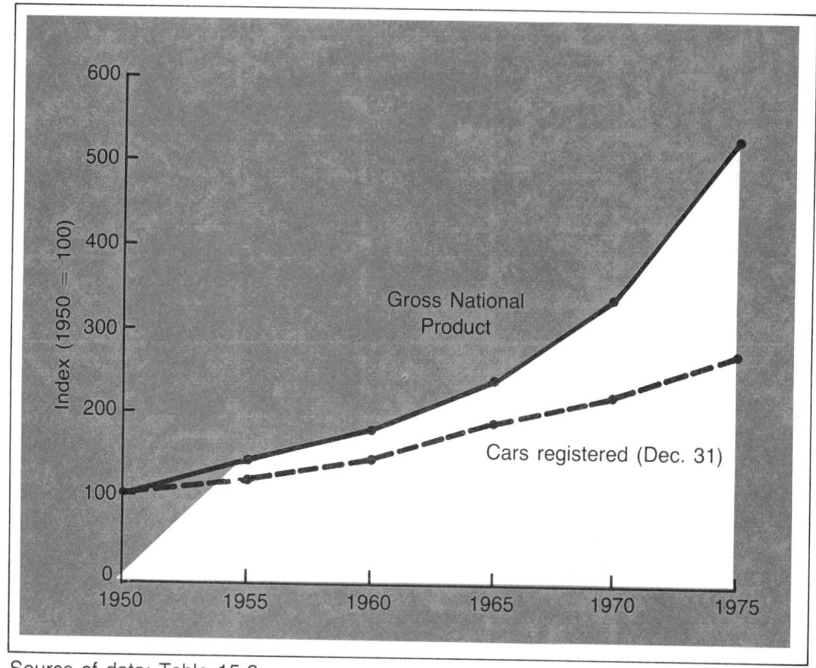

Source of data: Table 15-3.

revealed by the lines, but merely changes the positions of the lines on the chart. For example, had the scale numbers for "passenger cars registered" started with 15, its line would have been parallel to that shown, but it would have been higher on the chart.

Chart 15-8 shows a comparison of the growth in average weekly earnings of production workers, in dollars, and value added by manufacture, in millions of dollars, in the Milwaukee metropolitan area. It makes no difference which line is above the other or on which side the scale numbers are placed. The goal is to get the two lines close together to compare their slopes: the steeper the slope, the greater the rate of change.

In Chart 15-7 the slope of the "Gross National Product" line is generally steeper than that of "passenger cars registered"; therefore, during the 25-year period 1950–1975, Gross National Product increased at a faster rate than did passenger car registrations. Also, in Chart 15-8, the general slope of the line "value added by manufacture" from 1971 to 1974 is slightly steeper than the slope of "average weekly earnings," meaning that value added by manufacture rose at a faster rate during that period.

Comparing increases between consecutive years shows that between 1973 and 1974 values added by manufacture increased by a smaller percentage than did average weekly earnings. Moreover, between 1974 and 1975 there was no percentage change in value added by manufacture, but a percentage rise in average weekly earnings.

Chart 15-7. Gross National Product and passenger cars registered, United States, 1950–1975 (ratio scale).

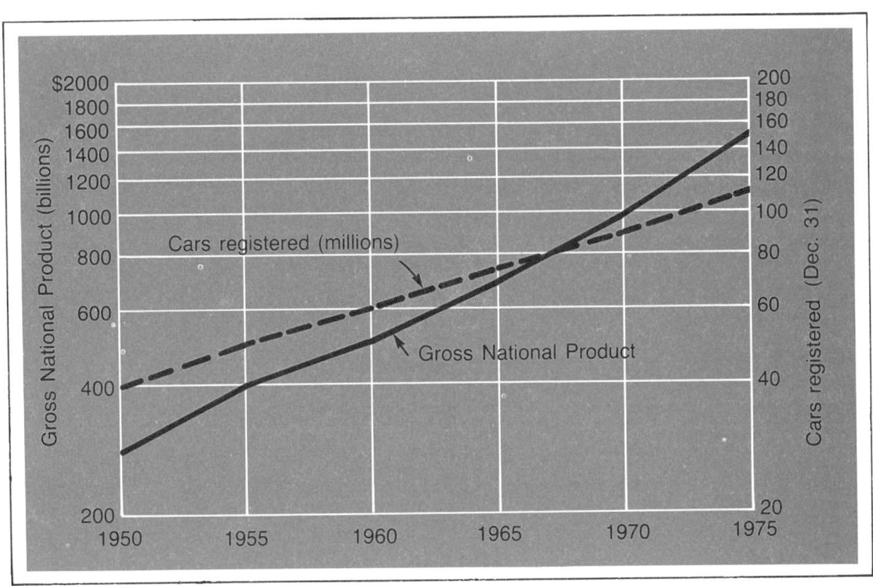

Source of data: Table 15-2.

Chart 15-8. Value added by manufacture and average weekly earnings of production workers in manufacturing industries, Milwaukee metropolitan area, 1966—1975 (ratio scale).

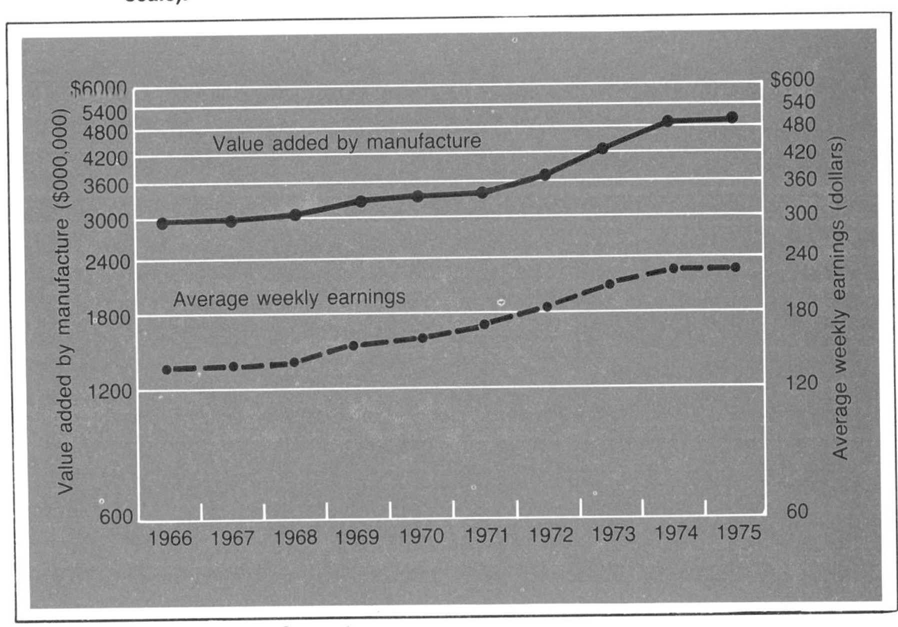

Source of data: Table 14 in Chap. 3.

The semi-log chart should not be used indiscriminately. We should be reasonably sure that most readers will understand the chart before presenting it to them. Moreover, it is wise to alert the reader to the fact that the vertical scale reveals ratios of change, not arithmetic changes. This is done on Charts 15-7 and 15-8 by writing (ratio scale) after the title.

Component-Parts Line Chart

The component-parts line chart shows the changes in the components that make up a time series, along with the changes in the totals of the components. It is used mainly for subjective analysis and comparisons of components.

Chart 15-9, which was constructed from the data in Table 14 of chapter 3 is a component-parts line chart. In constructing this chart, the manufacturing figures were plotted first. To get the ''wholesale and retail trade'' segment, the figures for manufacturing and wholesale and retail trade were added together and these totals were plotted. The line at the top of the ''government'' segment represents the total number of employees in manufacturing, wholesale and retail trade, and government.

Chart 15-9. Employees in nonagricultural establishments, by industry, United States, 1950—1975.

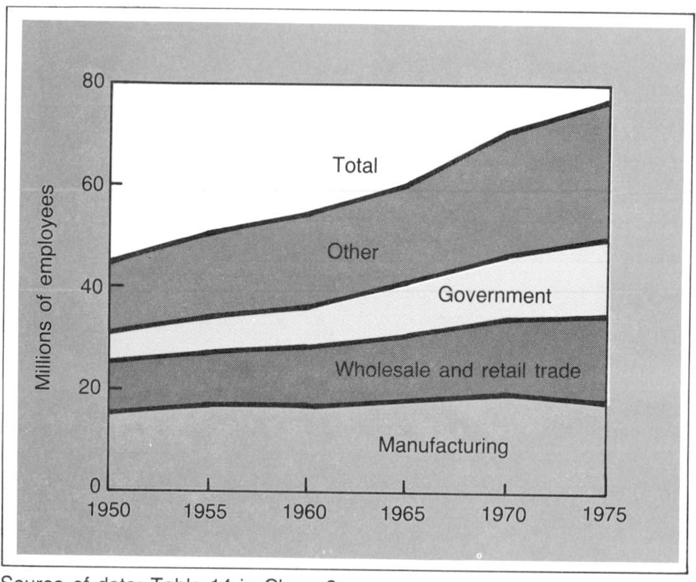

Source of data: Table 14 in Chap. 3.

Chart 15-10. Percentage distribution of employees in nonagricultural establishments, by industry, United States, 1940—1965.

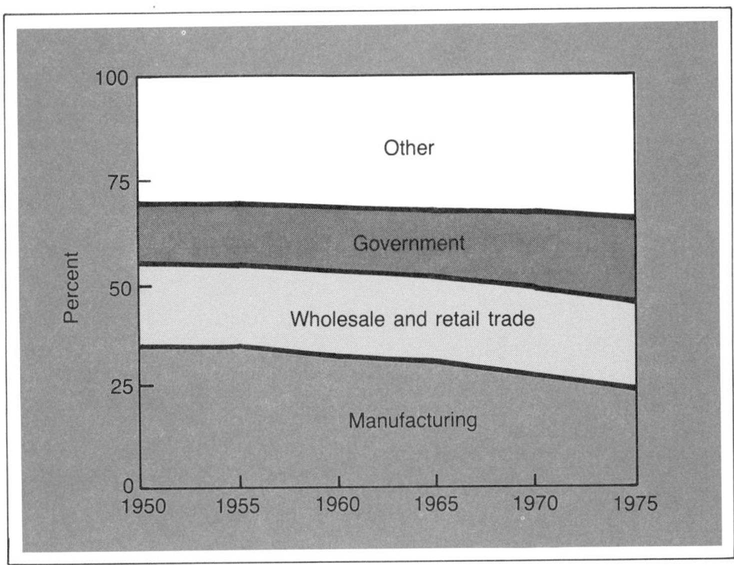

Source of data: Table 14 in Chap. 3.

These component parts expressed as a percent of total can be charted too. This has been done in Chart 15-10 with the percentages having been taken from Table 14 in Chap. 3. Now the vertical scale must run from 0 to 100 percent, covering the entire grid with charted data.

REVIEW QUESTIONS

1. What is the purpose of time series analysis?
2. On what do we frequently base our predictions and decisions?
3. Define the four basic movements in a monthly time series and briefly give the causes for each movement.
4. In what directions do secular trends move?
5. What is the mathematical composition of time series?
6. What does a seasonal index measure?

7. How can technological change affect the trend of a time series?

8. If a snow storm prevents people from shopping for two days, what type of fluctuation in sales would this cause: trend, seasonal, cyclical, irregular? Why?

9. What are the four phases of a business cycle?

10. Give an example of a business that experiences large seasonal changes in sales or production. Tell why the seasonal changes occur.

11. Give an example of an industry that experiences large irregular fluctuations in activity. Tell why these fluctuations occur.

12. Look at Chart 17-5 and determine the months for which department store sales in the United States typically reach seasonal highs and lows.

13. The data of Chart 16-1 shows an upward trend in sales between 1968 and 1976. What economic changes helped produce the upward direction of the trend?

14. Can you recognize any cyclical fluctuations in Chart 16-2. If so, identify, if possible, the months when cyclical troughs and peaks were reached.

15. Why would it be difficult to predict the point in time when a business cycle will reach a peak or a trough?

16. Why are irregular fluctuations in a business activity impossible to forecast?

17. What types of time series have the composition $T \times C \times S \times I$.

18. Show symbolically how the influence of seasonal variations may be removed from a monthly time series.

19. If direct measures of the cyclical and irregular movements of a time series could be calculated, state symbolically how their combined influence could be removed from (1) an annual time series, (2) a monthly time series, (3) a quarterly time series.

20. Give five rules for constructing time series line charts.

21. Why should the numerical scale of a time series line chart begin with 0? Are there any exceptions?

22. What does a semi-logarithmic scale show? What types of data are better compared on a semi-logarthmic scale than on an arithmetic scale?

23. Define cumulative and noncumulative data.

24. What does a component-parts line chart show?

CHART CONSTRUCTION

1. Construct a simple line chart of electric power sales figures in Exercise Table 15-1.

EXERCISE TABLE 15-1 Electric Power and Gas Sales to Residential Consumers in the United States, 1965–1975.

YEAR	*ELECTRIC POWER SALES (BILLIONS OF KWH)*	*GAS SALES (TRILLIONS OF BTU'S)*
1965	281	3,999
1966	307	4,175
1967	332	4,365
1968	368	4,553
1969	408	4,820
1970	448	4,924
1971	479	5,040
1972	511	5,144
1973	554	4,994
1974	555	4,865
1975	586	4,977

Source: U.S. Department of Commerce, Bureau of Economic Analysis, *Business Statistics*, 1975; and *Survey of Current Business*, November, 1976.

2. Construct a simple line chart of newspaper advertising expenditures in the United States shown in Exercise Table 15-2.

EXERCISE TABLE 15-2 Expenditures for Newspaper and Magazine Advertising in the United States, 1970–1975 (Millions of Dollars).

YEAR	*NEWSPAPER*	*MAGAZINE*
1970	$3,120	$1,186
1971	3,208	1,191
1972	3,496	1,211
1973	3,668	1,316
1974	3,845	1,372
1975	4,100	1,336

Source: U.S. Department of Commerce, Bureau of Economic Analysis, *Business Statistics*, 1975; *Survey of Current Business*, Nov., 1976.

3. Compare the data in Exercise Table 15-1 on a semi-logarithmic chart. Use two different scales.
4. Compare the figures in Exercise Table 15-2 on a semi-logarithmic chart. Use only one scale.
5. Depict all of the information in Exercise Table 4 of Chapter 3 as a component-parts line chart.

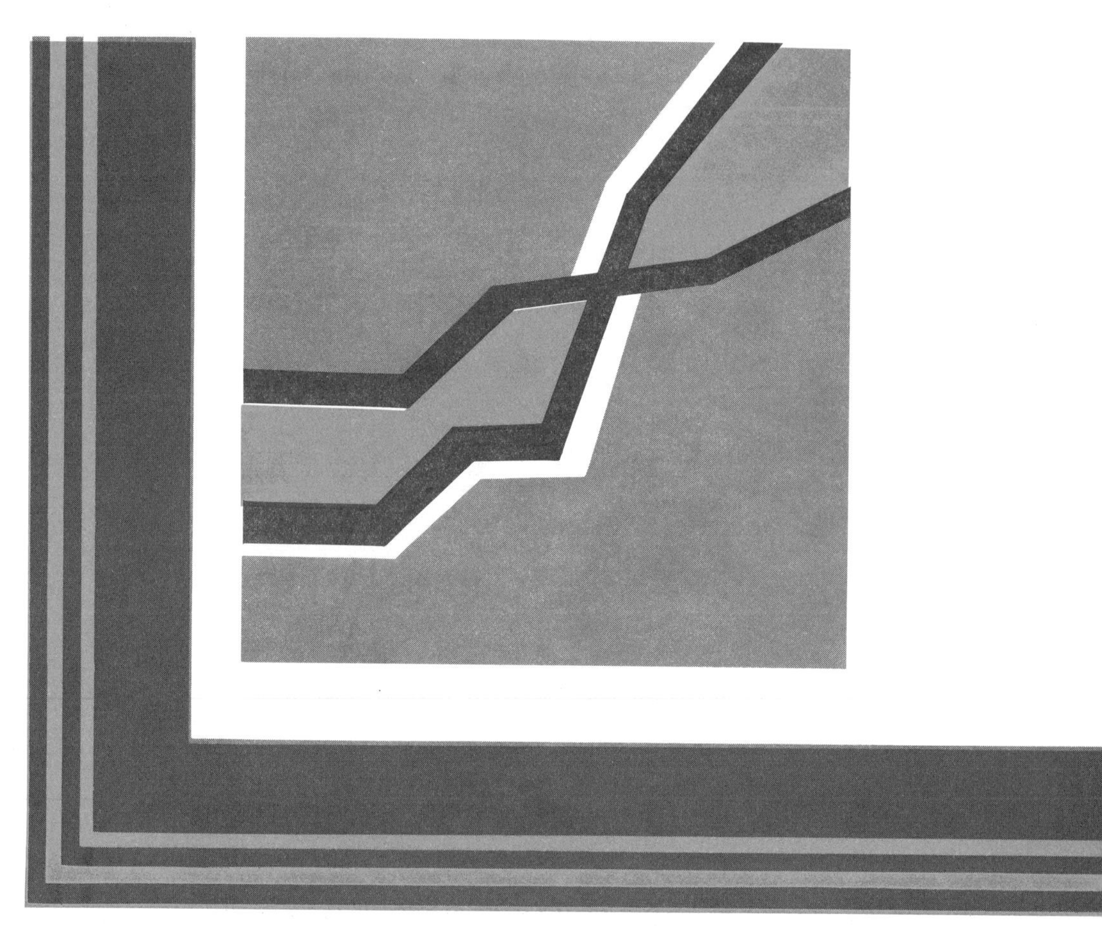

16

Secular Trend Analysis

In Chapter 15, the secular trend was defined as the long term movement in a time series. Now we shall illustrate the widely used methods of measuring trends.

PROCEDURE FOR TREND MEASUREMENT

State the Purpose

Purpose of Trend

Before measuring the trend of a time series it is important to know the purpose for measuring it. Two basic purposes are to project it and to eliminate it from the original data.

Knowledge of the purpose guides the analyst in his choice of method and in the length of the time series to be used for the measurement. If projection is the purpose for measurement, it is important to know the projection date. A trend projection for five years may require the use of a time series of shorter length than a projection for 20 years.

Chart the Data

The analyst should chart his data on both arithmetic and semi-log scales before choosing the method of measurement. By doing this, he gets an additional guide for choosing the trend equation because he can see the general shape of the trend.

Choose the Trend Equation

If the series shows basically a straight line movement on the arithmetic scale, the analyst will probably fit a straight trend line to the data. If a curved trend is revealed, he can determine which of several trend formulas that give curves might be the most appropriate. If the data plotted on semi-logarithmic paper indicate a basic constant rate of growth, he may compute a straight trend line for the logarithms of the original data.

A chart of the data and a statement of purpose for measuring the trend do not always enable the analyst to make a final choice of trend formula. Sometimes two or more trends must be computed and plotted with the original data to see which fits the time series best.

What constitutes a "best" fit is a matter of judgment. The trend that fits best is the one that best does the job the analyst has to do. There are no superior methods for measuring trends. Sometimes a trend drawn freehand through a time series is sufficient to reveal a picture of the general shape and direction. To draw a freehand trend properly, however, the analyst must be able to recognize the major cycles and seasonal fluctuations through which the trend must pass. Sometimes this is hard to do unless he is very familiar with the particular series being analyzed. Most analysts, therefore, choose an objective method that can be stated as an equation, in order to avoid the subjective decisions required for the freehand method.

THE LEAST SQUARES STRAIGHT LINE TREND

The method most widely used to describe straight line trends is called the "least squares" method. This trend equation is

$$Y_c = a + bX$$

where: *

- Y_c is a computed trend value for a given time period.
- a is the value of the trend at its mathematical origin.
- b is the typical change in the data per time period. (It gives the "average" amount of change per period and measures the slope of the line.)
- X is the number of time units from the trend's origin. The selection of the origin is arbitrary.

The values for a and b in this straight line equation are obtained by solving the following simultaneous linear equations, which were derived in Chapter 10.

$$(1)\ \Sigma Y = Na + b\Sigma X$$

$$(2)\ \Sigma XY = a\Sigma X + b\Sigma X^2$$

where Y is the symbol for the original data and N is the number of time periods to be analyzed.

It will be recalled from Chapter 12 that the term "least squares" comes from the fact that the sum of the squares of the deviations of the original values, Y, from the computed trend values, Y_c, is less than the sum of the squares of the deviations of the original values from any other straight line that might be used to measure the trend. Because of this characteristic, the least squares trend has been called the "line of best fit."

*This is the same equation used in Chapter 12 for computing a least squares regression line.

Straight Line Trend Calculation—Long Method

Table 16-1 gives the annual sales of the Metro Company from 1968 to 1976, and shows the computations necessary to solve the two equations to obtain a and b in the straight line equation. Chart 16-1 shows the plotted sales data and the resulting trend line with a projection to 1980.

Step 1 in the analysis is to state the equations to be used, set up the work table, and make calculations to obtain the values in the equations. In the work table, (Table 16-1) the original data are designated as Y and the X values are the number of years from the trend's origin, which was chosen to be 1968. Step 2 requires substituting into the

TABLE 16-1. Computation of a Least Squares Straight Line Trend to Sales of the Metro Company, 1968—1976 (Long Method).

YEAR	SALES (MILLIONS OF DOLLARS Y	X	X^2	XY	TREND Y_c
1968	358.4	0	0	0	393.0
1969	453.4	1	1	453.4	420.2
1970	474.3	2	4	948.6	447.4
1971	451.6	3	9	1,354.8	474.6
1972	530.6	4	16	2,122.4	501.8
1973	503.0	5	25	2,515.0	529.0
1974	531.5	6	36	3,189.0	556.2
1975	592.2	7	49	4,145.4	583.4
1976	621.5	8	64	4,972.0	610.6
Total	4,516.5	36	204	19,700.6	

Step 1: (1) $\Sigma Y = Na + b\,\Sigma X$

(2) $\Sigma XY = a\Sigma X + b\Sigma X^2$

Step 2: (1) $4{,}516.5 = 9a + 36b$

(2) $19{,}704.1 = 36a + 204b$

Step 3: (2) $19{,}700.6 = 36a + 204b$

(1) × 4 $18{,}066.0 = 36a + 144b$

$16{,}346 = 60b$

Step 4: $b = \dfrac{1{,}634.6}{60} = 27.2$

Step 5: (1) $4{,}516.5 = 9a + 36(27.2)$

$9a = 3537.3$

$a = 393.0$

Step 6: $Y_C = a + bX$ or $Y_C = 393.0 + 27.2X$

Step 7: $Y_C(1980) = 393.0 + 27.2(12) = 719.4$

Chart 16-1. Sales of the Metro Company, 1968—1976, with least squares straight line trend and projection to 1980.

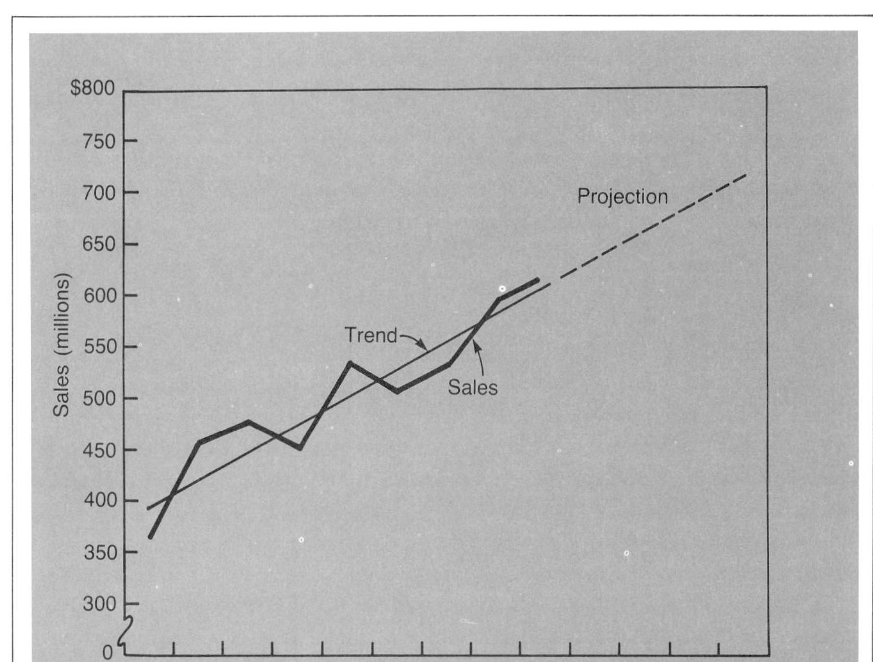

equations the figures calculated in the work table. Step 3 shows the elimination of the unknown, a, from the equations in order to solve for b. This is done by multiplying each member of equation (1) by 4 and subtracting the resulting equation from equation (2). The multiplication factor, 4, was obtained by dividing the numerical coefficient of a in equation (1) into the numerical coefficient of a in equation (2), which is $36 \div 9 = 4$. Step 4 shows the calculation of b from the data obtained in step 3. The value of the coefficient a is then found in step 5 by substituting the value of b into the original equation (1) and solving it algebraically.

Step 6 is a statement of the equation for the least squares straight line trend. The Y_c value (trend value) for any year can be calculated with this equation by substituting in the proper value of X. For example, if we wanted to compute the trend value for 1974, the equation would read $Y_c = 393.0 + 27.2(6)$, because 1974 is six years after the trend origin of 1968.

A practical way to calculate trend values for all of the years 1968 through 1976 requires, first, establishment of the trend value for 1968. This is the value of a, or 393.0.

Since b, or 27.2, is the "typical" or "average" growth per year, all we must do is add 27.2 to the 1968 trend value to get 420.2, the value for 1969. The 1970 trend value is then obtained by adding the value of b, or 27.2, to 420.2 to get 447.4. The trend values for other years are obtained in the same manner, that is, by cumulating with the value of b. This cumulation process is easily done on a desk calculator.

Step 7 shows a projection to 1980 with the straight line equation. The value of X is 12 because 1980 is 12 years after the 1968 trend origin. This same 1980 trend projection, 719.4, could be obtained by extending the trend line on Chart 16-1 to 1980 and reading the value from the chart. However, we might not be able to read a chart scale value as accurately as we could calculate the trend with the equation.

Straight Line Trend—Short Method

The "long method" just explained is not ordinarily used to calculate trend values, because the same results can be obtained by the "short method." One case, however, in which the long method is used is to revise the trend calculation from the same origin in succeeding years. For example, when 1977 sales are known for the Metro Company, it would be simple to add the 1977 value to the totals shown in Table 16-1 to get the totals for the years 1968 through 1977. The short method does not lend itself to continuous revision with the same ease.

In the short method, the calculations are easier because the need for simultaneous solution of the two equations is eliminated by placing the origin of the trend at the exact middle of the time period being used to calculate the trend. When this is done the sum of the X values in the work table is zero, as illustrated in Table 16-2. (The negative X values represent the numbers of years before the trend origin, which is July 1, 1972, and the positive X values represent the numbers of years after the trend origin.) When the sum of X (ΣX) is zero, $b\Sigma X = 0$ and $a\Sigma X = 0$ and, therefore, the two equations

$$(1) \quad \Sigma Y = Na + b\Sigma X$$

$$(2) \quad \Sigma XY = a\Sigma X + b\Sigma X^1$$

become

$$(1) \quad \Sigma Y = Na \quad \text{or } a = \frac{\Sigma Y}{N}$$

and

$$(2) \quad \Sigma XY = b\Sigma X^2 \text{ or } b = \frac{\Sigma XY}{\Sigma X^2}$$

With the equations in this form, a and b can be obtained independently.

Table 16-2 shows the step-by-step calculations of the trend values for the sales of the Metro Company for each year 1968 through 1976 and a projection to 1980, using the short method. Note that the value of b, 27.2, is the same for the short and long methods. However, the values of a differ—501.8 by the short method and 393.0 by the long method—because the trend origins are different. This does not affect the trend equation.

TABLE 16-2. Computation of a Least Squares Straight Line Trend to Sales of the Metro Company, 1968—1976 (Short Method-Odd Number of Years).

YEAR	SALES (MILLIONS OF DOLLARS) Y	X	X^2	XY	TREND Y_C
1968	358.4	−4	16	−1,433.6	393.0
1969	453.4	−3	9	−1,360.2	420.2
1970	474.3	−2	4	−948.6	447.4
1971	451.6	−1	1	−451.6	474.6
1972	530.6	0	0	0	501.8
1973	503.0	1	1	503.0	529.0
1974	531.5	2	4	1,063.0	556.2
1975	592.2	3	9	1,776.6	583.4
1976	621.5	4	16	2,486.0	610.6
	4,516.5	0	60	1,634.6	

Step 1: $a = \frac{\Sigma Y}{N}$

$b = \frac{\Sigma XY}{\Sigma X^2}$

Step 2: $a = \frac{4{,}516.5}{9} = 501.8$

$b = \frac{1{,}634.6}{60} = 27.2$

Step 3: $Y_C = a + bX$

Step 4: $Y_C(1968) = 501.8 + 27.2(-4) = 393.0$

Step 5: $Y_C(1980) = 501.8 + 272.(8) = 719.4$

Step 4 in Table 16-2 shows the calculation of the trend value for 1968, which is obtained by substituting −4, the X value for 1968, in the trend equation. This 1968 trend value is 393.0, the same as the value calculated by the long method.

Step 6 shows that the direct calculation of the trend for 1980, using the equation calculated by the short method, requires an X value of 8 because 1980 is eight years from the trend origin of 1972.

Short Method—Even Number of Years

Table 16-3 illustrates a generally preferred way to calculate trend values by the short method when an even number of years is being analyzed. The procedure is exactly the same as that for an odd number of years except that X in the equation $Y_c = a + bX$ is defined as the number of half-year periods from the trend origin. In Table 16-3, the trend origin is January 1, 1973. The −1 value for 1972 represents the six months period before the origin, that is, from January 1, 1973, back to July 1, 1972. The −3 for 1971 is the eighteen months (3 half-year periods) before the trend origin, from January 1, 1973, to July 1, 1971. The positive X values represent the number of half-year periods from the trend origin to the middles of the years after the trend origin.

TABLE 16-3. Computation of a Least Squares Straight Line Trend to Expenditures for New Plant and Equipment, United States, 1970—1975 (Short Method—Even Number of Years).

YEAR	EXPENDITURES (BILLIONS OF DOLLARS Y	X	X^2	XY	TREND Y_C
1970	80	−5	25	−400	76.4
1971	81	−3	9	−243	84.1
1972	88	−1	1	−88	91.8
1973	100	1	1	100	99.6
1974	112	3	9	336	107.3
1975	113	5	25	565	115.0
	574		70	270	

Step 1: $a = \frac{\Sigma Y}{N}$

$b = \frac{\Sigma XY}{\Sigma X^2}$

Step 2: $a = \frac{574}{6} = 95.7$

$b = \frac{270}{70} = 3.86$

Step 3: $Y_C = a + bX$

Step 4: $Y_C(1970) = 95.7 + 3.86(-5) = 76.4$

Step 5: $3.86 \times 2 = 7.72$ = increase per year

Step 6: $Y_C(1978) = 95.7 + 3.86(11) = 138.2$

We could let X represent the number of years, but then the X values would read −2.5, −1.5, −0.5, 0.5, 1.5, 2.5, etc. This would necessitate the use of two-digit figures and decimals, which would be an inconvenience in making the calculations.

Also, we may ask why the X values are measured to the middle of each year. This is done because a trend value is an "average" value that represents the entire year and the middle of a year represents the entire year better than any other time period.

The value of b calculated from Table 16-3 is 3.86. This means that the typical increase in the expenditures for new plant and equipment during each six-months period of the years 1970–1975 was \$3.86 million. The typical increase per year, of course, was \$7.72 million. To use the equation $Y_c = 95.7 \times 3.86X$ to make estimates and projections, we must substitute for X the number of half-year periods from the trend origin, January 1, 1973, to the middle of the year for which we want to find a trend value. Step 6, for example, shows the calculation for 1978. In this calculation, the middle of 1978 is 11 half-year periods from the trend origin.

Computation of Monthly Trend Values

To compute trend values for monthly data with the equation $Y_c = a + bX$, we can compute the values of a and b with the monthly data by the procedure just outlined for annual data. The job is tedious and time consuming, however, unless a computer is used. Fortunately, least squares straight line trend values for monthly data can be obtained quite easily by computing the values of a and b in annual terms and then converting these to monthly terms. There are four conversion methods. The choice depends upon the nature of the data. The four methods are:

1) Divide a by 12 and divide b by 144 when the annual data are cumulative (the sum of 12 monthly values), an odd number of years is being analyzed, and X represents the number of years from the trend origin.
2) Divide a by 12 and divide b by 72 when the data are cumulative, an even number of years is being analyzed, and X represents the number of half-year periods from the trend origin.
3) a remains the same and b is divided by 12 when the data are index numbers, noncumulative (point data) or the annual figures are monthly averages, when an odd number of years is being analyzed, and when X represents the number of years from the trend origin.
4) a remains the same and b is divided by 6 when the data are index numbers, noncumulative or the annual figures are monthly averages, when an even number of years is being analyzed, and when X represents the number of half-year periods from the trend origin.

In method 1, it is fairly obvious why a is divided by 12, but the reason for dividing b by 144 is not obvious. If b is divided by 12 the resulting figure gives the monthly change in annual magnitudes; therefore, to reduce this figure to the monthly change in monthly magnitudes it must be divided by 12 again. These two divisions are equivalent to a single division by 144.

In method 2, b is divided by 72, which is equivalent to a division by 12 to get the half-year change in monthly magnitudes and another division by 6 to get the monthly change in monthly magnitudes.

In methods 3 and 4, a remains the same because the annual data are not sums of 12 monthly figures, but b is divided by 12 in method 3, and 6 in method 4, to convert increments in the annual and six-months (half-year) terms to monthly terms.

After a and b have been converted to monthly terms, the monthly equation $Y_c = a + bX$ can be used to make an estimate or projection by substituting for X the number of months between the trend origin and the month for which the calculation is being made.

We shall illustrate monthly trend calculation for the data in Table 16-2 where the data are cumulative and there is an odd number of years. The annual equation computed from the table is $Y_c = 501.8 + 27.2X$. The monthly equation, therefore, is

$$Y_c = \frac{501.8}{12} + \frac{27.2}{144}X \text{ or } Y_c = 41.8 + 0.19X$$

To compute a trend value for any month, we substitute for X the number of months from July 1, 1972, the trend origin, to the middle of the month for which the trend value is desired. For example, the calculations for January 1968, July 1972, and December 1976 are

$$Y_c \text{ (Jan. 1968)} = 41.8 + 0.19\,(-53.5) = 31.6$$
$$Y_c \text{ (July 1972)} = 41.8 + 0.19\,(0.5) = 41.9$$
$$Y_c \text{ (Dec. 1976)} = 41.8 + 0.19\,(53.5) = 52.0$$

These three trend values have been plotted on Chart 16-2 and a straight line has been drawn through them. These plotted points are enough to chart the trend. If we desired to eliminate the trend of the monthly data, however, we would have to compute a trend value for each month.

Computation of Quarterly Trend Values

The least squares straight line trend equation in annual terms can be converted to quarterly terms by using the same basic concepts outlined for conversion to monthly terms. The procedure is:

1) Divide a by 4 and divide b by 16 when the annual data are cumulative, an odd number of years is being analyzed, and X represents the number of years from the trend origin.
2) Divide a by 4 and divide b by 8 when the data are cumulative, an even number of years is being analyzed, and X represents the number of half-years from the trend origin.
3) a remains the same and b is divided by 4 when the annual data are index numbers, noncumulative, or quarterly averages are being analyzed, with X representing the number of years from the trend origin.
4) a remains the same and b is divided by 2 when the annual data are index numbers, noncumulative or quarterly averages and an even number of years is being analyzed, with X representing the number of half-years from the trend origin.

Chart 16-2. Sales of the Metro Company, by months, 1968—1976, with least squares trend.

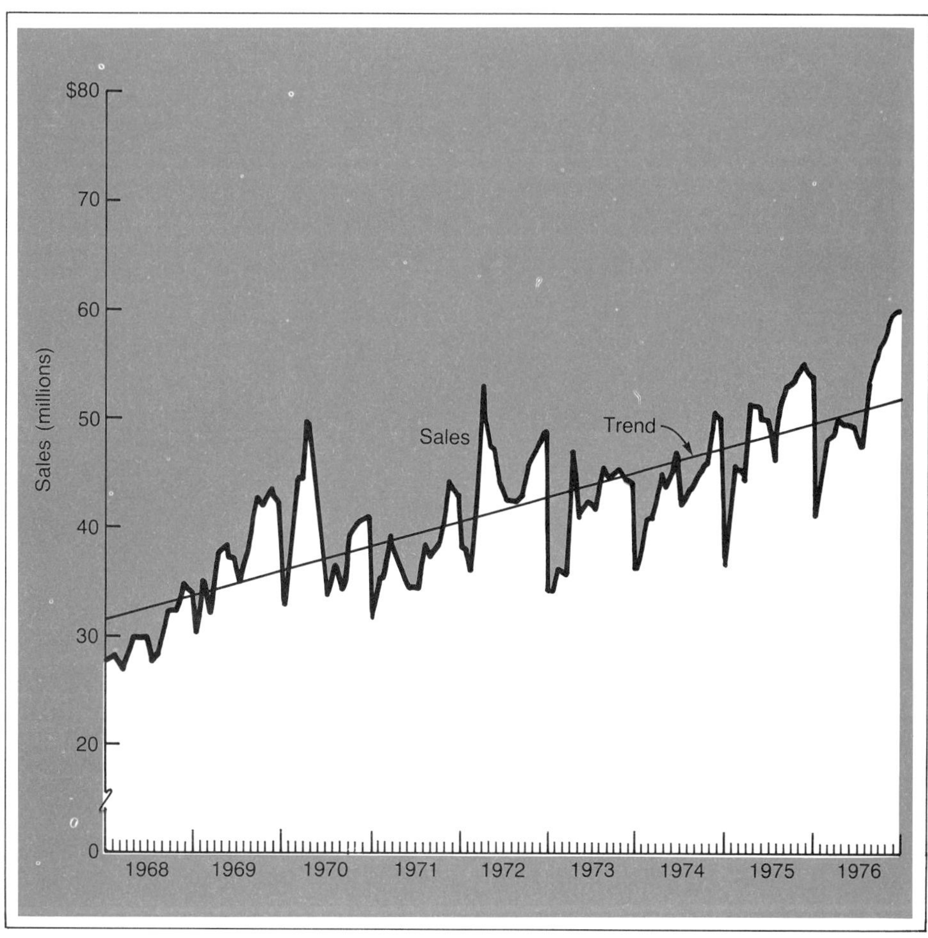

For the sales of the Metro Company the quarterly equation would be

$$Y_c = \frac{501.8}{4} + \frac{27.2}{16} = 125.4 + 1.70X$$

To compute a quarterly trend value the number of quarters from the trend origin to the middle of the quarter is substituted for X. For example, there are 14.5 quarters from the trend origin, July 1, 1972, to the middle of the first quarter of 1976. Therefore the calculation of the trend for that quarter is

$$Y_c = 125.4 + 1.70\,(14.5) = 150.0$$

This quarterly trend equation will be used again in Chapter 17 in a forecasting technique.

A Caution about the Least Squares Straight Line

It may not be advisable to use a least squares trend line for time series with a few extremely large fluctuations, because the least squares method gives so much weight to them that the resulting trend does not follow the general pattern of most of the fluctuations. Also, as a rule trends of monthly data, as illustrated in Chart 16-2, are not good forecasting tools when used alone. However, when monthly trends are used in conjunction with measurements of seasonal variation, they may be valuable. Should this trend be used for these data? There is no unqualified yes or no answer to this question. The analyst's judgment of how well the trend line fits and his purpose in making the trend measurement would be his criteria for choosing to use or not use it.

NONLINEAR TRENDS

Although the least squares trend line is probably used more often than any other to describe the long-term growth of a time series, the use of curved trends is sometimes necessary for a logical description of change. A large variety of equations are available to compute trends with one or more curves, but a second degree equation—the equation for a parabola—is the most common one. The equation is

$$Y_c = a + bX + cX^2$$

where Y_c is a computed trend value, a is the value of the trend at its origin, b is the slope of the line, c is the change in the slope per time period, and X is the number of time periods from the trend's origin.

Another frequently used equation that produces a trend with one bend is the exponential equation

$$Y_c = ab^X$$

This equation is useful when the long run growth or decline in a time series is at a constant rate. In this equation, Y_c is a trend value, a is the value of the trend at its origin, and b is the typical ratio of the value in one year to the value in the preceding year.

Other equations for curved trends are: $Y_c = a + bX + cX^2 + dX^3$, which gives a trend with two bends; $Y_c = ab^Xc^{X^2}$, which gives a trend that increases or decreases at an increasing rate; $Y_c = Ka^{b^X}$, named the Gompertz curve, which produces trends asymptotic to upper and/or lower values. The use of these trends will not be demonstrated in this text.

Calculation of a Second Degree Curve

Chart 16-3 shows exports of merchandise from the United States from 1967 to 1975 with a trend fitted and projected to 1976. This trend, which fits the data nicely, was computed with the second degree equation $Y_c = a + bX + cX^2$. The calculations of the sums needed to compute the values for a, b, and c are shown in Table 16-4.
The formulas for computing a, b, and c when the trend origin is started at the middle of the time period are:

$$(1) \qquad \Sigma Y = Na + c\Sigma X^2$$

$$(2) \qquad b = \frac{\Sigma XY}{\Sigma X^2}$$

$$(3) \qquad \Sigma X^2Y = a\Sigma X^2 + c\Sigma X^4$$

Equation (2) for calculating b is the same as that for computing b for the straight line trend. Equations (1) and (3) must be solved simultaneously for the value of a or c. When a or c is thus obtained, it may be substituted into either equation (1) or (3) to get the remaining constant.

Chart 16-3. Exports of Merchandise, United States, 1967—1975, with second degree trend and projection to 1976.

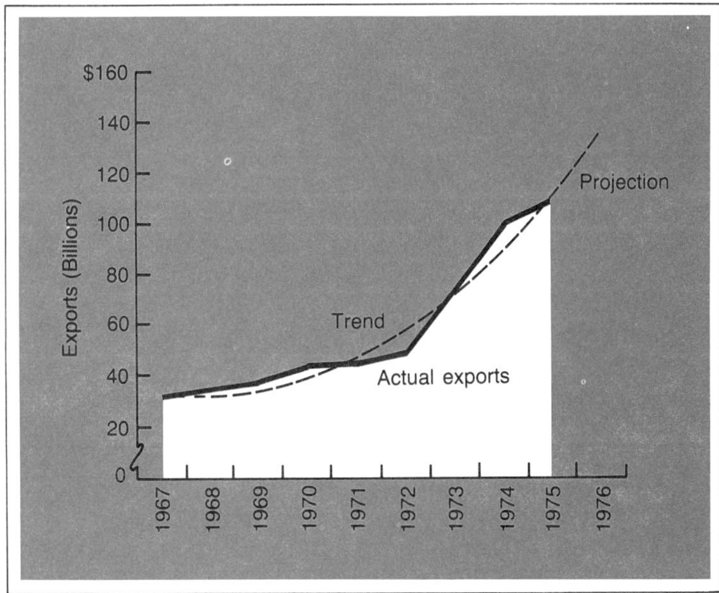

TABLE 16-4. Computation of a Second Degree Curve to Exports of Merchandise, United States, 1967—1975.

YEAR	EXPORTS (BILLIONS OF DOLLARS) Y	X	X^2	X^4	XY	X^2Y	TREND Y_c
1967	31	−4	16	256	−124	496	34
1968	34	−3	9	81	−102	306	32
1969	37	−2	4	16	−74	148	34
1970	43	−1	1	1	−43	43	38
1971	44	0	0	0	0	0	46
1972	49	1	1	1	49	49	58
1973	71	2	4	16	142	284	72
1974	98	3	9	81	294	882	89
1975	107	4	16	256	428	1712	110
	514	0	60	708	570	3920	

Step 1:
(1) $\Sigma Y = Na + c\Sigma X^2$
(2) $b = \dfrac{\Sigma XY}{\Sigma X^2}$
(3) $\Sigma X^2Y = a\Sigma X^2 + c\Sigma X4$

Step 2:
(1) $514 = 9a + 60c$
(3) $3920 = 60a + 708c$
(1) × 11.8 $6065.2 = 106.2a + 708c$

Step 3: $-2145.2 = -46.2a$
$a = 46.4$

Step 4: (2) $b = \dfrac{570}{60} = 9.50$

Step 5: (1) $514 = 9(46.6) + 60c$
$514 = 417.6 + 60c$
$96.4 = 60c$
$c = 1.607$

Step 6: $Y_c = 46.4 + 9.50X + 1.607X^2$
$Y_C(1967) = 46.4 + 9.50(-4) + 1.607(16)$
$Y_C(1967) = 46.4 - 38.0 + 25.7 = 34.1$

Step 7: $Y_C(1976) = 46.4 + 9.50(5) + 1.607(25)$
$Y_C(1976) = 46.4 + 47.5 + 40.2 = 134.1$

The solutions of the equations for *a, b,* and *c* and illustrations of the calculation of trend values, Y_c, are shown below Table 16-4.

The first step is to state the equations for computing *a, b,* and *c* and set up the work table for calculating the needed sums. The second step is to substitute in equations (1) and (3) for the simultaneous solution of *a* or *c*. In the illustration, the value of *a* has been obtained first by multiplying each term in equation (1) by 11.8, which is 708/60. The resulting equation is subtracted from equation (3) to eliminate *c*. Step 3 is to solve for *a* by using the results of this subtraction. The fourth step is the calculation of *b* with equation (2), and step 5 is the computation of *c* by substituting the value of *a* in equation

(1). Now that the values in the equation $Y_c = a + bX + cX^2$ are known, step 6 is the calculation of trend values (Y_c) for each year. The calculation for 1967 is demonstrated.

All we need to do to make a trend calculation for any year is to substitute the value of X for that year in the equation $Y_c = 46.4 + 9.50X + 1.607X^2$. The value of X is determined by counting the number of years from the trend origin, July 1, 1971, to the middle of the year for which the trend is desired. Since 1967 is four years before the 1971 trend origin, the value of X for 1967 is -4 and X^2 is 16.

Step 7 shows the calculation of a projection to 1976. Here X is 5 and X^2 is 25, because 1976 is five years after the trend origin. A projection to 1979 would require an X of 8.

In this particular illustration, the trend is concave. However, if the value of b is positive and c is negative, the second degree equation will produce a convex curve. One of the assignments at the end of this chapter requires you to compute such a curve.

The Logarithmic Straight Line Trend

The equation $Y_c = ab^X$ produces trend values that plot as a curve on arithmetic paper and as a straight line on semi-log paper. A straight line results because the equation produces a trend that increases by a constant rate. In logarithm form, the equation is

$$\log Y_c = \log a + X \log b$$

where the $\log Y_c$ values are calculated first and from these the Y_c values are determined. Since this equation is a straight line for logarithms the following equations are used to find $\log a$ and $\log b$.

1) $\Sigma \log Y = N \log a + \log b \; \Sigma X$
2) $\Sigma X \log Y = \log a \; \Sigma X + \log b \; \Sigma X^2$

The equations in the short form, which may be used when the trend origin is taken as the middle of the time period, are

$$(1)\ \log a = \frac{\Sigma \log Y}{N}$$

$$(2)\ \log b = \frac{\Sigma X \log Y}{\Sigma X^2}$$

The use of these two equations is demonstrated in Table 16-5; Chart 16-4 shows the trend resulting from the calculations. The equations are stated first. Then the logarithms of the Y values are determined, the table is set up and the necessary calculations are made. Substitutions, as shown in step 1, result in calculation of $\log a = 1.7145$ and $\log b$

TABLE 16-5. Computation of a Least Squares Straight Line Trend to the Logarithms of Exports of Merchandise, United States, 1967—1975.

YEAR	EXPORTS (BILLIONS OF DOLLARS) Y	$\log Y$	X	X^2	$X \log Y$	$\log Y_c$	TREND Y_c
1967	31	1.4914	−4	16	−5.9656	1.4377	27.4
1968	34	1.5315	−3	9	−4.5945	1.5069	32.1
1969	37	1.5682	−2	4	−3.1364	1.5761	37.7
1970	43	1.6336	−1	1	−1.6336	1.6453	44.2
1971	44	1.6435	0	0	0	1.7145	51.8
1972	49	1.6902	1	1	1.6902	1.7837	60.8
1973	71	1.8513	2	4	3.7026	1.8529	71.3
1974	98	1.9912	3	9	5.9736	1.9221	83.6
1975	107	2.0294	4	16	8.1176	1.9913	98.0
Total		15.4303		60	4.1539		

Step 1: (1) $\log a = \frac{\Sigma \log Y}{N} = \frac{15.4303}{9} = 1.7145$

(2) $\log b = \frac{\Sigma X \log Y}{\Sigma X^2} = \frac{4.1539}{60} = 0.0692$

Step 2: $\log Y_C = \log a + X \log b$

Step 3: $\log Y_{C(1967)} = 1.7145 + -4(0.0692) = 1.4377$
$Y_{(1967)} = 27.4$

Step 4: $\log Y_{C(1976)} = 1.7145 + 5(0.0692) = 2.0605$
$Y_{C(1976)} = 115.0$

$= 0.0692$. Therefore, the trend equation for exports from the United States for the period 1967–1975 is $\log Y_c = 1.7145 + 0.0692X$. Calculations are made by substituting the proper values of X. Step 3 shows a calculation for 1967 resulting in $\log Y_c = 1.4377$. Y_c is the anti-log of 1.4377 or 27.4. The fourth step shows the computation of a 1976 projected trend value.

The Y_c values in Table 16-5 can be obtained also by using the equation $Y_c = ab^X$. The anti-log of $\log a$ (1.7145) is 51.8. The anti-log of $\log b$ (0.0692) is 1.17. Therefore, the equation $Y_c = 51.8\,(1.17)^X$ should give the same value as the equation in logarithmic form, except for discrepancies due to rounding. For example, the Y_c value for 1972, where $X = 1$, is $Y_c = 51.8\,(1.17) = 60.6$. The Y_c value for 1973 is $51.8\,(1.17)^2$ or 70.9. The calculation for 1973 with logs resulted in a Y_c of 71.3. You should have observed that the 1.17 value for b means that, on the average, business expenditures for new plants and equipment in any one year were 117% of the expenditures in the previous year, or

Chart 16-4. Exports of merchandise, United States, 1967—1975, with logarithmic straight line trend and projection to 1976.

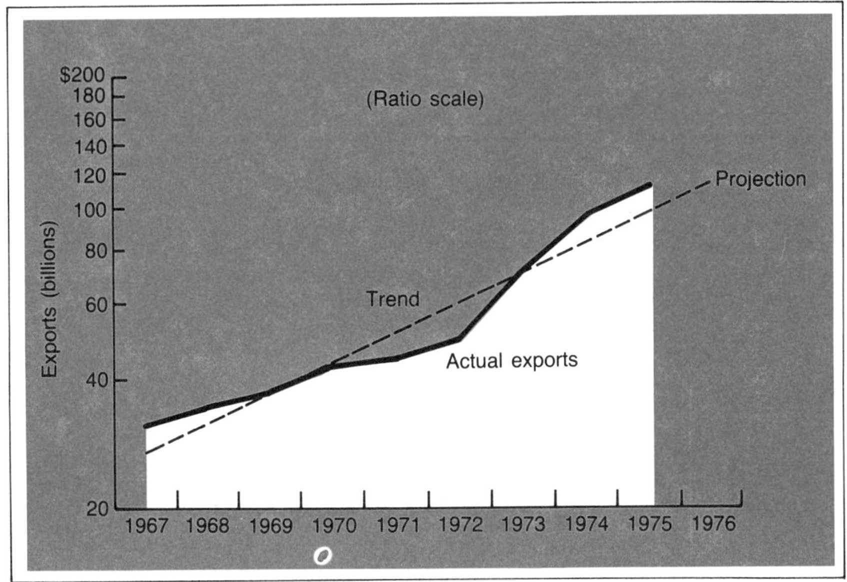

Source of data: Table 16-5.

stated another way, the average rate of increase per year during the nine-year period was 17%.

Chart 16-5 shows the original and trend values in Table 16 5 charted on an arithmetic scale. Note that the trend curves upward.

Choosing the Trend

Which trend equation, $Y_c = a + bX + cX^2$ or $Y_c = ab^X$, is the best one for measuring the trend of exports from 1967 to 1975? There is no accurate, unqualified answer, although the second degree equation seems to give a trend that follows the original data more closely than the exponential trend. In deciding which trend to use, we must know why we are computing the trend. For example, if the purpose is to project and get an estimate of expenditures for a future year, we need a knowledge of the many economic relationships and conditions currently prevailing and to have some subjective idea what general economic conditions might be in the projected year. In other words, the right choice of trend is a matter of judgment and, therefore, usually requires experience on the part of the analyst.

Chart 16-5. Exports of Merchandise, United States, 1967—1975, with logarithmic trend and projection to 1976 on an arithmetic scale.

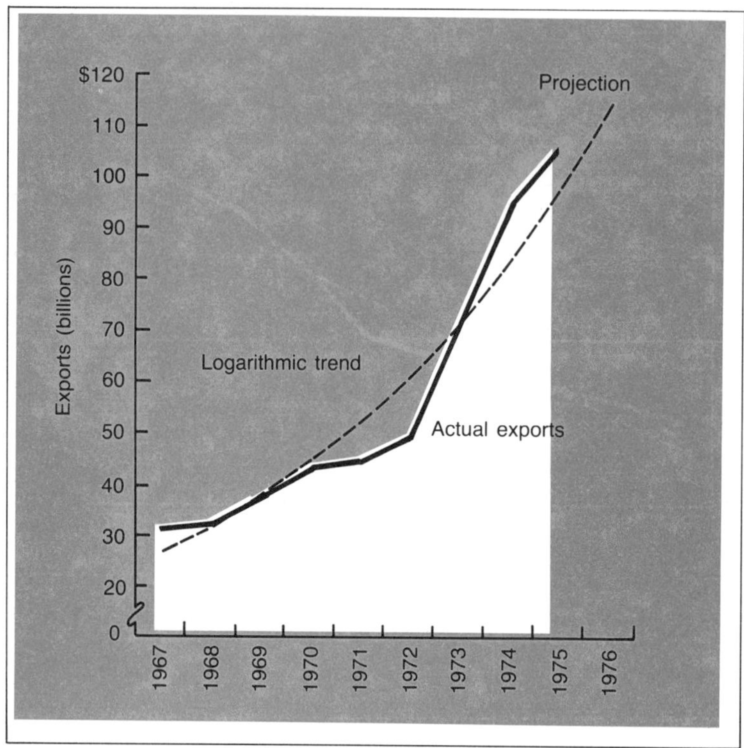

Source of data: Table 16-5.

REVIEW QUESTIONS

1. What are the two basic reasons for measuring the trend of a time series? Why is it important to know the reason?

2. Why is it important to chart a time series before choosing the type of trend to fit to the series?

3. What type of trend is the best one to use?

4. What is the most widely used trend line? What equation is generally used to describe a trend with one bend?

5. Explain the meaning of the coefficient of the equation $Y_c = a + bX$.

6. What does b show in the equation $Y_c = ab^X$?

7. Explain the meaning of the coefficients in the equation $Y_c = a + bX + cX^2$.

PROBLEMS

1. Chart the annual totals of the retail sales figures in Exercise Table 16-1. Compute a least squares straight line trend from the data and show the trend on the chart. Project the trend to 1978 and show the projection on the chart.

EXERCISE TABLE 16-1. Retail Sales in the United States, by Month, 1969—1975 (Billions of Dollars).

YEAR	J	F	M	A	M	J	J	A	S	O	N	D	TOTAL
1969	27	25	28	29	31	30	30	30	29	31	30	37	357
1970	28	26	30	31	32	32	32	31	31	33	36	39	381
1971	29	28	32	34	34	35	35	34	34	36	36	43	410
1972	31	31	36	35	38	39	37	38	38	39	40	47	449
1973	36	35	41	41	43	44	42	43	41	44	45	50	505
1974	38	37	43	44	47	46	46	48	44	47	46	52	538
1975	41	40	45	46	51	49	50	51	48	52	51	61	585

Source: U.S. Department of Commerce, *Business Statistics*, 1973 and 1975; and *Survey of Current Business*, Feb. 1976.

2. Chart the data in Exercise Table 16-2 on both arithmetic and semi-log paper. Compute a second degree trend for the data and a straight line trend for the logarithms of the data. Show these respective trends on the charts. Which trend do you think fits the data best? Which trend do you think would give the best forecast for 1976? Why?

EXERCISE TABLE 16-2 Corporate Profits Before Taxes, 1968—1974.

YEAR	PROFITS (BILLIONS OF DOLLARS)
1968	$ 86
1969	84
1970	72
1971	82
1972	96
1973	117
1974	132

Source: *Federal Reserve Bulletin*, April 1976, p. A41.

3. Gather population data on the U.S., by decade, for 1900 to 1970. Using these data, project the population of the U.S. to 1980. (Find your own source for these data and decide what type of trend to use to make the projection.) After you have made your projection, criticize it—both constructively and destructively.

4. Using the data in Exercise Table 16-3, project the population of Kenosha County, Wisconsin, to 1980. Choose your own method for projecting and defend it. Show the original data, your computed trend, and projection on the same chart.

EXERCISE TABLE 16-3 Population of Kenosha County, Wisconsin, by decade, 1890 to 1970.

YEAR	*THOUSANDS OF PEOPLE*
1890	15.6
1900	21.7
1910	32.9
1920	51.6
1930	63.3
1940	63.5
1950	75.2
1960	100.6
1970	117.9

Source: U.S. Bureau of the Census.

5. Fit a trend to the data in Exercise Table 16-4, using the equation $Y_c = a + bX + cX^2$, and project it to 1980. Consult the United States Brewers Association or the source given at the bottom of the table and check the accuracy of the projections for 1975, 1976, and 1977 if the data are available.

EXERCISE TABLE 16-4. Per Capita Consumption of Malt Beverages in the United States, 1952—1974.

YEAR	*GALLONS*	*YEAR*	*GALLONS*	*YEAR*	*GALLONS*
1952	16.8	1960	15.1	1969	17.8
1953	16.7	1961	15.0	1970	18.6
1954	15.9	1962	15.1	1971	19.0
1955	15.9	1963	15.3	1972	19.4
1956	15.7	1964	15.9	1973	20.2
1957	15.1	1965	15.9	1974	21.1
1958	15.0	1966	16.4		
1959	15.3	1967	16.7		
		1968	17.2		

$\Sigma Y = 385.1$ $\Sigma XY = 198.2$ $\Sigma X^2Y = 17{,}957.2$

$\Sigma X = 0$ $\Sigma X^2 = 1012$ $\Sigma X^4 = 79{,}948$

Source:-United States Brewers Association, Inc., Brewers Almanac, 1975.

6. Compute a and b in the least squares trend equation for the annual totals in Exercise Table 16-5. Convert a and b to monthly terms. Chart the monthly figures, and show on the same chart a trend for the monthly data that result from use of the converted a and b values.

EXERCISE TABLE 16-5. Manufacturers' Shipments of Mobile Homes, by Months, 1968—1974 (Thousands).

	1968	*1969*	*1970*	*1971*	*1972*	*1973*	*1974*
January	19	27	24	25	34	40	26
February	21	29	24	29	40	42	27
March	24	32	30	36	49	56	33
April	27	36	40	43	54	60	38
May	28	35	33	41	52	56	37
June	27	36	36	48	55	56	36
July	27	35	37	46	48	49	31
August	30	38	38	50	52	53	29
September	30	40	41	54	49	44	24
October	34	43	41	51	54	45	21
November	28	33	30	40	51	39	15
December	24	27	27	34	38	28	12
Total	319	411	401	497	576	568	329

Source: U.S. Department of Commerce, *Business Statistics*, 1975.

7. Gather annual figures on Gross National Product for the years 1960 to 1974 from a reliable source. Calculate a least squares straight line trend for these figures and project the trend to 1976. Compare your projection with the 1976 figure published by the U.S. Department of Commerce. Was your projection reasonably accurate? Do you think a curved trend would have been better for projecting the GNP?

8. Exercise Table 16-6 shows annual farm population in the United States from 1964 to 1974. Compute a least squares straight line trend and a second-degree trend for these figures and make projections for 1976. Do you believe either projection is reasonably accurate? Why?

EXERCISE TABLE 16-6. Farm Population in the United States, 1964—1974.

YEAR	*POPULATION ON APRIL 1 (MILLIONS)*
1964	12.9
1965	12.4
1966	11.6
1967	10.9
1968	10.5
1969	10.3
1970	9.7
1971	9.4
1972	9.6
1973	9.5
1974	9.3

Source: *Statistical Abstract of the United States*, 1975

EXERCISE TABLE 16-7. Birth Rates in the United States, 1935—1975 (rate per 1000 population).

YEAR	*RATE*
1935	18.7
1940	19.4
1945	20.4
1950	24.1
1955	25.0
1960	23.7
1965	19.3
1970	18.4
1975	14.5

Source: U.S. Department of Commerce, *Statistical Abstract of the United States,* 1975, p. 51.

9. Compute a second degree trend for the birth rates shown in Exercise Table 16-7, and project the birth rate to 1980. Make a line chart which shows the actual data and the trend with the 1980 projection. Is the trend a good fit? Do you think the projection will be reasonably accurate? Why?

10. Exercise Table 2 of Chapter 17 gives the value of expenditures for new plants and equipment in the United States, by quarter, 1968–1975. Compute a least squares straight line trend for the annual totals and project the trend to 1977. Make a line chart which shows the actual annual expenditures and the trend with the 1977 projection.

11. Draw a line chart of the quarterly figures in Exercise Table 17-2. Convert the annual trend equation computed for problem 10 to quarterly terms and calculate the trend values for the first quarters to 1969, 1972, and 1975 and for each quarter of 1976. Plot these trend values on your chart and draw a line through them.

17

Seasonal Variation

In Chapter 15, we learned that seasonal variations are usually found in monthly, quarterly, and weekly time series. These variations are periodic enough so that their averages can be used to predict future seasonal business patterns.

Seasonal fluctuations show a high degree of regularity, in both timing and amplitude. For example, a typical department store's sales drop from December to January every year and the percentage decline is about the same from year to year. Because of this, the percentage seasonal decline for the forthcoming December-January period can be quite accurately predicted.

Over a long period of time seasonal patterns may change as a result of technological innovations or gradual changes in people's customs and habits. When this happens, we must measure that gradual changing seasonal pattern to establish an estimating model for future seasonal fluctuations. Measurements of both stable and moving seasonal patterns are called *seasonal indexes*.

DATA ADJUSTMENTS

Adjustments for Days in a Month

Time series data may need to be adjusted before a seasonal index is computed. Sometimes it is necessary to make adjustments for the difference in the numbers of days in some months.* If a business operates every day, then months with 31 days, all other things held constant, should show larger figures than months with fewer days, revealing a certain monthly periodicity of total activity.

To adjust for these differences, a factor is computed for each month and multiplied times the data for that month. The factor is computed by dividing the average number of days in a month, 30.4167, by the actual number of days in the month. For example, the adjustment factor for the 31-day months is

$$\frac{30.4167}{31} = 0.98118$$

Since this factor is less than 1, the data for each of the 31-day months will be lowered. Moreover, data for February and the 30-day months will be raised.

*Point data do not require this adjustment. Period data and point data were defined in Chapter 15.

Adjustments for Working Days

We might find it necessary to make a second adjustment for the number of working days in a month.* For a business that does not operate every day, there are more working days in some months than in others because of weekends, holidays, and closings due to strikes, bad weather, etc. The adjustment factors for the monthly data for a particular year can be calculated by dividing the average number of working days per month for the year by the actual number of working days in each month.

Whether or not such adjustments need to be made before computing a seasonal index depends on the *purpose* for computing the index. If we are interested in measuring the *rate* of seasonal activity, adjustments must be made. If our intent is to measure *total* seasonal activity the adjustments are unnecessary.

The data in this chapter have not been adjusted because the purpose here is to show the computation of seasonal indexes and illustrate their general use.

METHODS OF COMPUTATION

A large variety of seasonal indexes have been developed, but our discussion will be limited to two computational methods. The first is the "percent-of-monthly-averages method" and the second the "percent-of-12-month-moving-averages method." The percent-of-monthly-averages method will be explained first so that you can grasp the basic idea of what a seasonal index measures. The percent-of-12-month-moving-averages method provides one of the better measures of the typical seasonal pattern of a series and is, as a result, used more often than any other method.

The Percent-of-Monthly-Averages Method

Table 17-1 gives the monthly sales of the Metro Company for 1968 through 1976. A close examination of the figures shows that, except for 1969, sales in the autumn were generally higher than in the spring. However, it is difficult to determine by looking at all of the figures which month was typically the best one, which was the worst one, and how the other months ranked in sales volumes for the entire nine-year period. This difficulty is handled by averaging the figures for each month. The mean row $(\overline{X})$ at the bottom of

*Point data do not require working day adjustments.

TABLE 17-1. Sales of the Metro Company, by Months, 1968—1976 (millions of dollars).

YEAR	JAN.	FEB.	MAR.	APR.	MAY	JUNE	JULY	AUG.	SEPT.	OCT.	NOV.	DEC.	TOTAL
1968	26.7	27.3	26.3	29.8	29.8	29.9	27.3	28.1	32.3	32.1	34.8	34.0	358.4
1969	30.1	35.1	32.3	37.8	38.4	37.1	35.1	37.5	42.9	41.8	43.3	42.0	453.4
1970	32.9	37.5	44.7	49.5	45.5	39.5	33.5	36.5	34.4	39.1	40.3	40.9	474.3
1971	31.5	36.4	39.5	37.4	35.9	34.3	34.3	38.5	37.1	39.3	44.4	43.0	451.6
1972	37.8	35.9	41.8	53.0	47.8	44.0	42.5	42.3	42.9	45.9	47.8	48.9	530.6
1973	34.2	36.4	35.7	47.4	41.2	42.6	41.5	45.4	44.4	45.4	44.7	44.1	503.0
1974	36.1	40.7	40.9	45.0	43.5	47.2	42.1	43.8	44.7	46.3	50.9	50.3	531.5
1975	36.5	45.7	44.5	51.4	51.0	49.9	45.9	51.5	53.1	53.7	55.1	53.9	592.2
1976	41.8	47.8	48.8	50.1	49.7	49.2	47.6	53.4	55.9	57.5	59.6	60.1	621.5
Total	307.6	342.8	354.5	401.4	382.8	373.7	349.8	377.0	387.7	401.1	420.9	417.2	4516.5
$\overline{X}$	34.2	38.1	39.4	44.6	42.5	41.5	38.9	41.9	43.1	44.6	46.8	46.4	41.8
S. Index	81.8	91.1	94.3	106.7	101.7	99.3	93.1	100.2	103.1	106.7	112.0	111.0	1201.0[1]
S. Index (Adj.)	81.7	91.0	94.2	106.6	101.6	99.2	93.0	100.1	103.0	106.6	111.9	110.9	1199.8

[1] $\frac{1201}{1200} = 1.00083333$ (adjustment factor).

the table gives the averages used. The means themselves are a kind of index that enable us to see, on the average, how the monthly sales volumes compare. Comparison of the monthly performances can be improved, however, if the means for the months are expressed as percentages of some norm, in this case, the *grand mean*. The grand mean is the mean of all the months or the mean of the 12 monthly means, which is 41.8. To compute the final index we divide this mean into each of the 12 monthly means and multiply the quotients by 100. For example, the seasonal index number for January is

$$\frac{34.2}{41.8}(100) = 81.8$$

To check the accuracy of the calculations, the 12 index numbers computed this way should be totaled; the total should equal 1200%. In this illustration, there is a discrepancy of 1.0% due to rounding. The last row in the table shows the seasonal index which was adjusted for this discrepancy by multiplying each of the twelve index numbers by 1.0008333, which is 1201 ÷ 1200. The adjusted index total is as close to 1200 as possible unless the numbers are carried to more decimal places. If the total of the 12 indexes is off by more than 1.2%, the error most probably is due to something other than rounding.

The seasonal index is shown on Chart 17-1. It is the heavy solid line labeled A. The other lines on the chart show seasonal indexes computed by methods to be explained subsequently.

Chart 17-1. Seasonal indexes of sales of the Metro Company, computed by different methods.

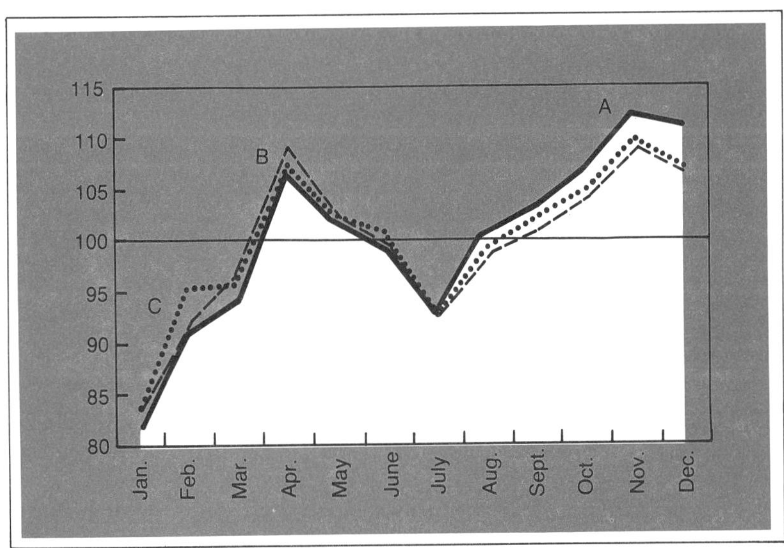

Index Bias

The percent-of-monthly-averages method may be sufficiently accurate for calculating seasonal indexes for some data. However, this method results in biases due to the influence of trend and cyclical fluctuations found in the data.

Trends usually go in one direction; therefore, it is impossible to average them out. Also, a given set of data might have more upward phases of cyclical fluctuations than receding phases, or vice versa, so that an average of such data produces an upward or downward bias in the seasonal index numbers for certain months. Movements in data can be averaged out only when they are about equally divided as to number and magnitude of ups and downs.

Percent-of-12-Month-Moving-Averages Method

Most of the biases due to trend and cyclical fluctuations can be removed from a seasonal index by means of the "percent-of-12-month-moving-averages method." This method gives mathematical measures of the trend and cyclical fluctuations (see Chart 17-2) and then removes them mathematically before averaging the data for each of the months. Symbolically, $T \times C$ is computed and then

$$\frac{T \times C \times S \times I}{T \times C} = S \times I$$

where T is the trend, S the seasonal variation, and C and I the cyclical and irregular movements, respectively. The I's, are averaged out, leaving S, the seasonal index.

Steps in the calculations. Table 17-2 shows the steps in the calculation of the percentages of 12-month moving averages ($S \times I$) of the monthly sales of the Metro Company. Column (1) shows the original sales figures in chronological order. Column (2) gives 12-month *moving* totals of the figures in Column (1). These moving totals can be computed by the following procedure. First, compute the total for 1968, which is 358.4, as shown in Column (2); next, move down one month and compute the total for the 12-month period February 1968 through January 1969, which is 361.8; next, move down one month and compute the total for the 12 month period March 1968 through February 1969; continue this process until all the moving totals have been computed. This method is laborious and not necessary. The practical way to compute the moving totals is: First, compute the total for 1968, 358.4. Secondly, subtract the figure for January 1968, 26.7, from 358.4 and add the figure for January 1969, 30.1, to the result. This gives the total 361.8, the second figure in Column (2). From this the total sales in February 1968, 27.3, is subtracted and sales in February 1969, 35.1, is added, to give 369.6, the third total in Column (2). This subtraction and addition process is easily

Chart 17-2. Sales of the Metro Company, by months, with 12-month moving average.

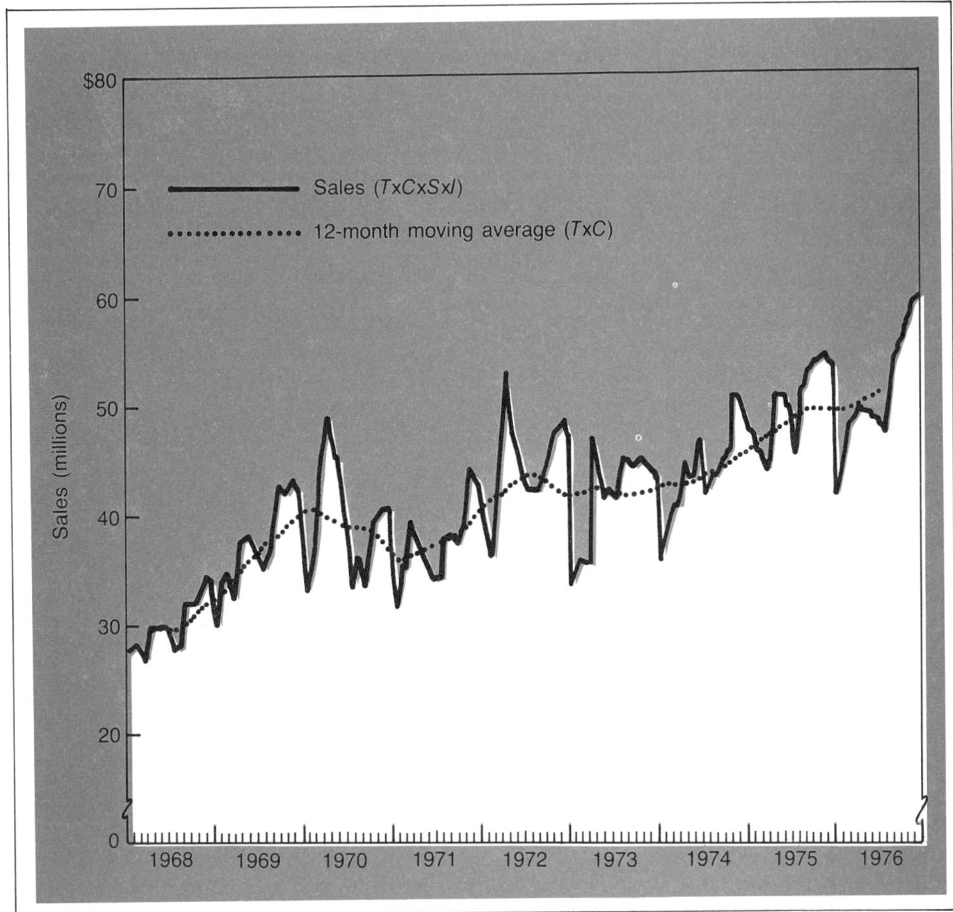

accomplished by placing a small slip of paper over the figures in Column (1) so that the figure to be subtracted is just above the top end and the figure to be added is just below the bottom end.

Before calculating the moving totals, the analyst should compute the total for each year and place it at the center of the year (between June and July). These totals are the ones which are footnoted. They are used to check the accuracy of the moving total calculations. As we move down to these points with the addition-subtraction process, we should get the total shown. If not, the error can be found by recalculating, at the most, the moving total for the previous 12 months. These check points are very important because without them, if we discovered an error in the figures toward the end, we would have to recalculate all of the moving totals to find it.

TABLE 17-2. Computations of Percentages of 12-Month Moving Averages for Sales of the Metro Company, 1968—1976.

YEAR AND MONTH	(1) SALES (MILLIONS)	(2) 12-MONTH MOVING TOTAL OF COL. (1)	(3) 2-MONTH MOVING TOTAL OF COL. (2)	(4) COL. (3) ÷ 24 (12-MONTH MOVING AVERAGE)	(5) (COL. (1) ÷ COL. (4)) × 100 (PERCENT 12-MONTH MOVING AVERAGE)
Jan. 1968	26.7				
Feb.	27.3				
Mar.	26.3				
Apr.	29.8				
May	29.8				
June	29.9				
		358.4*			
July	27.3		720.2	30.01	91.0
		361.8			
Aug.	28.1		731.4	30.48	92.2
		369.6			
Sept.	32.3		745.2	31.05	104.0
		375.6			
Oct.	32.1		759.2	31.63	101.5
		383.6			
Nov.	34.8		775.8	32.32	107.7
		392.2			
Dec.	34.0		791.6	32.98	103.1
		399.4			
Jan. 1969	30.1		806.6	33.61	89.6
		407.2			
Feb.	35.1		823.8	34.32	102.3
		416.6			
Mar.	32.3		843.8	35.16	91.9
		427.2			
Apr.	37.8		864.1	36.00	105.0
		436.9			
May	38.4		882.3	36.76	104.5
		445.4			
June	37.1		898.8	37.45	99.1
		453.4*			
July	35.1		909.6	37.90	92.6
		456.2			
Aug.	37.5		914.8	38.12	98.4
		458.6			
Sept.	42.9		929.6	38.73	110.8
		471.0			
Oct.	41.8		953.7	39.74	105.2
		482.7			
Nov.	43.3		972.5	40.52	106.9
		489.8			
Dec.	42.0		982.0	40.92	102.6
		492.2			

TABLE 17-2. Computations of Percentages of 12-Month Moving Averages for Sales of the Metro Company, 1968—1976.

YEAR AND MONTH	(1) SALES (MILLIONS)	(2) 12-MONTH MOVING TOTAL OF COL. (1)	(3) 2-MONTH MOVING TOTAL OF COL. (2)	(4) COL. (3) ÷ 24 (12-MONTH MOVING AVERAGE)	(5) (COL. (1) ÷ COL. (4)) × 100 (PERCENT 12-MONTH MOVING AVERAGE)
		557.1			
Jan. 1975	36.5		1118.0	46.58	78.4
		560.9			
Feb.	45.7		1129.5	47.06	97.1
		568.6			
Mar.	44.5		1145.6	47.73	93.2
		577.0			
Apr.	51.4		1161.4	48.39	106.2
		584.4			
May	51.0		1173.0	48.87	104.4
		588.6			
June	49.9		1180.8	49.20	101.4
		592.2			
July	45.9		1189.7	49.57	92.6
		597.5*			
Aug.	51.5		1197.1	49.88	103.3
		599.6			
Sept.	53.1		1203.5	50.15	105.9
		603.9			
Oct.	53.7		1206.5	50.27	106.8
		602.6			
Nov.	55.1		1203.9	50.16	109.8
		601.3			
Dec.	53.9		1201.9	50.08	107.6
		600.6			
Jan. 1976	41.8		1202.9	50.12	83.4
		602.3			
Feb.	47.8		1206.5	50.27	95.1
		604.2			
Mar.	48.8		1211.2	50.47	96.7
		607.0			
Apr.	50.1		1217.8	50.74	98.7
		610.8			
May	49.7		1226.1	51.08	97.3
		615.3			
June	49.2		1236.8	51.53	95.5
		621.5			
July	47.6				
Aug.	53.4				
Sept.	55.9				
Oct.	57.5				
Nov.	59.6				
Dec.	60.1				

*Checkpoints for accuracy of moving totals.

The third step in calculating a seasonal index using percentages of 12-month moving averages is to compute a two-month total of the 12-month totals as shown in Column (3) of Table 17-2. This step enables the analyst to center the moving averages on the months, rather than have them between months, as would be the case if each figure in Column (2) were divided by 12. The figure 720.2 in Column (3) is the total of 358.4 and 361.8. The next figure, 731.4, is the total of 361.8 and 369.6. All the other figures were obtained by this moving-down-and-totaling process. Each figure in Column (3) is a 24-month total—11 months included twice and two months included once. For example, 720.2, the first figure in Column (3), is the figure for January 1968 given a weight of one, plus the figures for February through December, 1968, given weights of 2, plus the figure for January 1969 given a weight of one. To get the averages in Column (4), each total in Column (3) is divided by 24. These calculations result in each of these averages being centered on a specific month.

You may wonder why these averages are not called 24-month moving averages since we divide by 24. Actually, 12 months, *by name*, are involved and 13 different figures are used to calculate each average in Column (4). If you want to pursue this question further, you might consult a source that illustrates the "long" method of computing the 12-month moving averages.*

Column (5) of Table 17-2 shows the data in Column (1) expressed as percentages of the moving averages in Column (4). The sales data in Column (1) are, symbolically $T \times C \times S \times I$. The averages in Column (4) are a measure of $T \times C$. Column (5) then is

$$\frac{\text{Column (1)}}{\text{Column (4)}} = \frac{T \times C \times S \times I}{T \times C} = S \times I$$

These $S \times I$ values in Column (5) have been placed in Table 17-3 in order to compute a mean for each month to eliminate some of the I components. The arithmetic means for the 12 months are shown at the bottoms of the columns. These are our preliminary seasonal index numbers. Due to the centering process and rounding of numbers, however, they must be adjusted so that they total 1200%. The total of the means is 1198.1. The adjustment factor is computed by dividing this into 1200. The resulting factor, 1.0015858, is multiplied by each mean to get the adjusted means, shown in the last row of Table 17-3, that comprise the seasonal index.

Other methods of averaging. This seasonal index, using arithmetic means of all the percentages for each month, probably is not as accurate a measure of the typical seasonal variation of the sales of the Metro Company as could be obtained with a modified mean or median, which would eliminate the extreme figures that bias arithmetic means. The percentages of 12-month moving averages, you will remember, are composed of seasonal and irregular fluctuations. The purpose of the averaging of the percentages is to eliminate the irregular fluctuations. If the irregular fluctuations are not extreme in amplitude and are balanced between upward and downward movements, then they can be "averaged" out with unmodified means. However, extreme irregular fluctuations

*See Croxton, Cowden, and Klein, *Applied General Statistics*, Third Edition (Englewood Cliffs, N.J.: Prentice-Hall, Inc.), p. 293.

TABLE 17-3. Percentages of 12-Month Moving Averages of Sales of the Metro Company, 1968—1976.

YEAR	*JAN.*	*FEB.*	*MAR.*	*APR.*	*MAY*	*JUNE*	*JULY*	*AUG.*	*SEPT.*	*OCT.*	*NOV.*	*DEC.*
1968	—	—	—	—	—	—	91.0	92.2	104.0	101.5	107.7	103.1
1969	89.6	102.3	91.9	105.0	104.2	99.1	92.6	98.4	110.8	105.2	106.9	102.6
1970	80.3	91.8	110.5	123.8	114.5	99.8	84.9	92.7	88.0	101.9	107.5	111.0
1971	85.9	98.9	106.8	100.8	96.3	91.4	90.5	101.0	97.1	100.9	110.7	104.9
1972	90.5	85.0	98.0	122.8	109.7	100.1	96.4	96.3	98.2	106.2	111.9	115.4
1973	80.9	85.9	83.9	111.3	97.1	101.1	98.8	107.4	104.1	106.2	104.5	102.4
1974	83.4	94.2	94.7	104.2	100.0	107.2	95.0	98.4	99.6	102.2	110.9	108.6
1975	78.4	97.1	93.2	106.2	104.3	101.4	92.6	103.2	105.9	106.8	109.8	107.6
1976	83.4	95.1	96.7	98.7	97.3	95.5	—	—	—	—	—	—
$\overline{X}$	84.1	93.8	97.0	109.1	102.9	99.4	92.7	98.7	100.9	103.8	108.7	107.0
Seasonal index	84.2	93.9	97.2	109.3	103.1	99.6	92.8	98.9	101.1	104.0	108.9	107.2

$\frac{1200}{1198.1} = 1.0015858$ (adjustment factor).

should be removed by some other averaging process. To discover the extent of extreme figures in the percentages of 12-month moving averages, the percentages should be arrayed by months, as shown for the Metro Company in Table 17-4, where some of the most extreme figures are circled. Using modified means or medians as the averages for the monthly columns minimizes the effect of extremes on the seasonal measurement.

Modified Mean

Remember from Chapter 4 that the mean is most appropriate for data that are quite homogeneous. Extreme figures, not typical of the group, should be eliminated before means are computed. This is called "modifying." Just how to modify is a matter of judgment on the part of the analyst.

Usually, in computing a seasonal index, a few of the central percentages from each of the arrayed columns are averaged. The analyst might take, for example, two from one, three from another, etc. Usually, however, he decides to take the same number from each monthly column to eliminate judgment decisions as to what are extreme figures in each column. For example, a study of the arrayed percentages in Table 17-4 shows that the four central percentages for most of the 12 columns make up quite homogeneous groups.

TABLE 17-4. Arrayed Percentages of 12-Month Moving Averages of Sales of the Metro Company, 1968—1976.

	JAN.	*FEB.*	*MAR.*	*APR.*	*MAY*	*JUNE*	*JULY*	*AUG.*	*SEPT.*	*OCT.*	*NOV.*	*DEC.*
	78.4	85.0	83.9	98.7	96.3	91.4	84.9	92.2	88.0	100.9	104.5	102.4
	80.3	85.9	91.9	100.8	97.1	95.5	90.5	92.7	97.1	101.5	106.9	102.6
	80.9	91.8	93.2	104.2	97.3	99.1	91.0	96.3	98.2	101.9	107.5	103.1
	83.4	94.2	94.7	105.0	100.0	99.8	92.6	98.4	99.6	102.2	107.7	104.9
	83.4	95.1	96.7	106.2	104.2	100.1	92.6	98.4	104.0	105.2	109.8	107.6
	85.9	97.1	98.0	111.3	104.3	101.1	95.0	101.0	104.1	106.2	110.7	108.6
	89.6	98.9	106.8	122.8	109.7	101.4	96.4	103.2	105.9	106.2	110.9	111.0
	90.5	102.3	110.5	123.8	114.5	107.2	98.8	107.4	110.8	106.8	111.9	115.4
Modified mean*	83.4	94.6	95.6	106.7	101.4	100.0	92.8	98.5	101.5	103.9	108.9	106.1
Seasonal index	83.9	95.1	96.1	107.3	102.0	100.6	93.3	99.0	102.1	104.5	109.5	106.7
Median	83.4	94.6	95.7	105.6	102.1	100.0	92.6	98.4	101.8	103.7	108.8	106.2
Seasonal index	83.9	95.2	96.3	106.2	102.7	100.6	93.2	99.0	102.4	104.3	109.4	106.8

*Four central percentages

$\frac{1200}{1193.4}$ = 1.0055304 (adjustment factor for modified means).

$\frac{1200}{1192.9}$ = 1.0059518 (adjustment factor for medians).

Means of these four central figures have been computed for each month and are shown at the bottom of the table. The median, which is, in this case, the mean of the two central percentages, is also shown. This median also eliminates the effect of the extreme percentages.

Errors due to the nature of the moving average, rounding of numbers, and modifying the means prevent the modified means (and medians) from totaling 1200%.

The modified means total 1193.4 and the medians total 1192.9. Therefore, the row of 12 means and the row of 12 medians both have been adjusted to total 1200. The adjustments, shown below the table, are made by multiplying the modified means and median by the adjustment factors. The adjusted data constitutes the final seasonal index.

Comparison of Results of Methods Used

With Table 17-5 we can compare the seasonal indexes of the sales of the Metro Company computed by the four methods just illustrated. Column A shows the indexes computed by the percent-of-monthly-averages method in Table 17-1. Columns B, C, and D show the three seasonal indexes computed by the percent-of-12-month-moving-averages method using means (Column B), modified means (Column C), and medians (Column D) as the averages of the percentages. Columns C and D differ only slightly, but Column B shows greater variation from both C and D than the variation between C and D. This is caused by the extreme, irregular variations that were not averaged out when the B Column was computed. The student should compare the April seasonal index number in Column B with the April seasonal numbers in Columns C and D. The number in Column B is somewhat larger because of the extreme ratios that were included in that average. (These are the extremes circled in Table 17-4.)

TABLE 17-5. Seasonal Index of Sales of the Metro Company, Computed by Four Methods.

MONTH	*A*[a]	*B*[b]	*C*[c]	*D*[d]
Jan.	81.7	84.2	83.9	83.9
Feb.	91.0	93.9	95.1	95.2
Mar.	94.2	97.2	96.1	96.3
Apr.	106.6	109.3	107.3	106.2
May	101.6	103.1	102.0	102.7
June	99.2	99.6	100.6	100.6
July	93.0	92.8	93.3	93.2
Aug.	100.1	98.9	99.0	99.0
Sept.	103.0	101.1	102.1	102.4
Oct.	106.6	104.0	104.5	104.3
Nov.	111.9	108.9	109.5	109.4
Dec.	110.9	107.2	106.7	106.8

[a] Computed by the monthly averages method.
[b] Computed by the percent of 12-month moving averages method, using means as the averages of the percentages.
[c] Computed by the percent of 12-month moving averages method, using modified means as the averages of the percentages.
[d] Computed by the percent of 12-month moving averages method, using medians as the averages of the percentage.

Column A differs considerably from the other columns. The seasonal index numbers in this column are biased due to cyclical and trend components that were not removed. The influence of the upward trend in the sales of the Metro Company can be seen in Column A: The percentages in the first half of the year are smaller and in the last half are larger than those shown in the other columns. This upward bias due to the unremoved trend is evident in Chart 17-1, which compares three of the four seasonal indexes.

THE STABLE SEASONAL INDEX

A seasonal index computed by one of the methods illustrated is sometimes called a "stable" seasonal index. A stable seasonal index is one in which there is only one index number for each month. As a rule, we use a short time period, perhaps 5 to 10 years, for computing stable indexes, because (1) the seasonal pattern in the near future is likely to be similar to the seasonal pattern of the recent past and (2) over a long period of time there may have been a gradual change in the seasonal pattern that would first appear in the magnitudes of the seasonal fluctuations and eventually in their timing.

THE MOVING SEASONAL INDEX

To measure changes in seasonal patterns we can compute a "moving" seasonal index. For the sales of the Metro Company, we might compute the percentages of 12-month moving averages as shown in Table 17-2 and then proceed with the following steps:

1) Chart the percentages of 12-month moving averages by months (shown on Chart 17-3).
2) Describe the trend of the percentages for each month, using a trend equation or a freehand description. Some of the trends may be straight lines and some may be curved. All of those shown on Chart 17-3 are computed least squares straight line trends.
3) Read the monthly trend values from the charts for each year if freehand trends are used. If they are computed, use the computed values (see Table 17-6).
4) Adjust the 12-monthly percentages for each year so that the total will be 1200%. The adjustment is made in a manner similar to that described for stable seasonal indexes. The adjusted values are shown in Table 17-7.

To forecast the seasonal index, we can extend the trend lines on the charts and read and adjust the ratios to total 1200%. This has been done for 1977.

Chart 17-3. Percentages of 12 month moving averages of sales of the Metro Co., with least squares straight line trends.

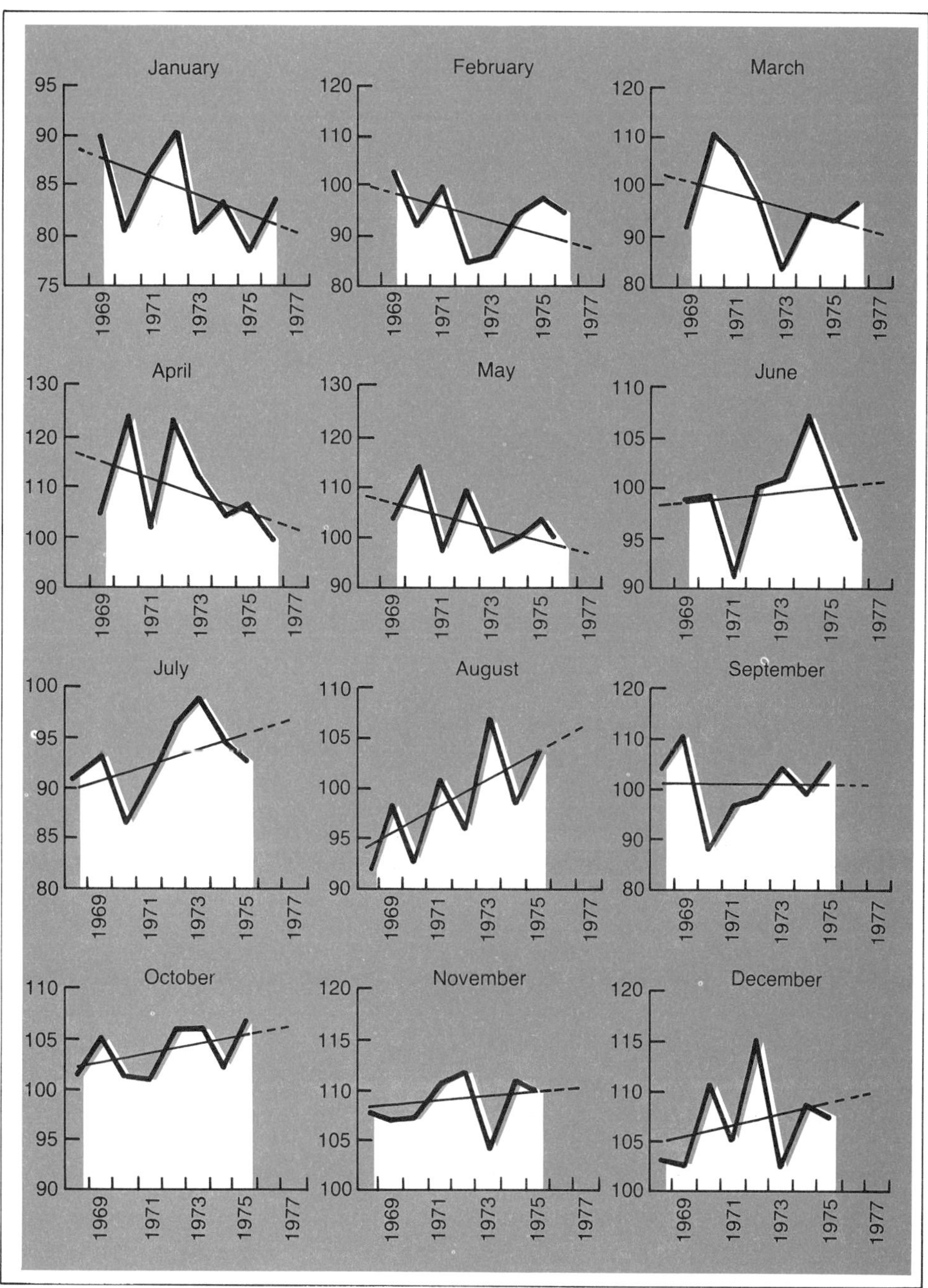

TABLE 17-6. Least Squares Straight Line Trend Values for the Percentages of 12-Month Moving Averages of the Sales of the Metro Company.

MONTH	*1968*	*1969*	*1970*	*1971*	*1972*	*1973*	*1974*	*1975*	*1976*	*PROJECTED 1977*
Jan.	87.9*	87.0	86.2	85.4	84.5	83.7	82.8	82.0	81.2	80.3
Feb.	99.9*	98.6*	97.2	95.8	94.5	93.1	91.8	90.4	89.0	87.7
Mar.	102.6*	101.3	100.1	98.8	97.6	96.3	95.1	93.9	92.7	91.4
Apr.	116.2*	114.6	113.0	111.5	109.9	108.3	106.7	105.2	103.4	102.0
May	108.3*	107.1	105.9	104.7	103.5	102.3	101.1	99.9	98.7	97.5
June	97.7*	98.1	98.4	98.8	99.2	99.6	100.0	100.4	100.7	101.1
July	89.8	90.6	91.4	92.3	93.1	94.0	94.8	95.6	96.4*	97.2
Aug.	93.9	95.2	96.6	98.0	99.4	100.8	102.2	103.5	104.9*	106.3
Sept.	100.6	100.7	100.8	100.9	100.9	101.0	101.1	101.2	101.3*	101.3
Oct.	102.1	102.6	103.1	103.6	104.0	104.5	105.0	105.5	106.0*	106.4
Nov.	107.6	107.9	108.2	108.5	108.9	109.2	109.5	109.8	110.1*	110.5
Dec.	105.1	105.6	106.2	106.7	107.3	107.8	108.4	108.9	109.4*	110.0
Total	1211.7	1209.3	1207.1	1205.0	1202.8	1200.6	1198.5	1196.3	1193.8	1191.7

*Extrapolated

TABLE 17-7. Moving Seasonal Index of Sales of the Metro Company, with Projection to 1977[a].

MONTH	1968	1969	1970	1971	1972	1973	1974	1975	1976	PROJECTED 1977
Jan.	87.0[b]	86.3	85.7	85.0	84.3	83.7	82.9	82.3	81.6	80.9
Feb.	98.9[b]	97.8	96.6	95.4	94.3	93.1	91.9	90.7	89.4	88.3
Mar.	101.6[b]	100.5	99.4	98.6	97.4	96.3	95.2	94.2	93.1	92.0
Apr.	115.1[b]	113.7	112.3	111.0	109.6	108.2	106.8	105.5	103.9	102.7
May	107.3[b]	106.3	105.3	104.2	103.2	102.1	101.2	100.2	99.2	98.2
June	96.7[b]	97.3	97.8	98.4	99.0	99.6	100.1	100.7	101.2	101.8
July	88.9	89.9	90.9	91.9	92.9	94.0	94.9	95.9	96.9[b]	97.9
Aug.	93.0	94.5	96.0	97.6	99.2	100.8	102.3	103.8	105.4[b]	107.0
Sept.	99.6	99.9	100.2	100.5	100.7	100.9	101.2	101.5	101.8[b]	102.0
Oct.	101.1	101.8	102.5	103.2	103.8	104.4	105.1	105.8	106.5[b]	107.1
Nov.	106.6	106.3	107.6	108.0	108.6	109.1	109.6	110.1	110.7[b]	111.3
Dec.	104.1	104.8	105.6	106.3	107.1	107.7	108.5	109.2	110.0[b]	110.8
Total[c]	1200.0	1200.0	1200.0	1200.0	1200.0	1200.0	1200.0	1200.0	1200.0	1200.0

[a] These are the least squares straight line trend values for the percentages of 12-month moving averages. The percentages for each year have been adjusted to total 1200%.
[b] Extrapolated.
[c] Components may not add to totals due to rounding.

USES OF SEASONAL INDEXES

Purpose of Seasonal Indexes

There are two basic purposes for computing seasonal indexes. One is for use as a forecasting tool. The other is to eliminate the seasonal variation from original data so that the other movements can be observed.

Forecasting with a Seasonal Index

Certain mathematical forecasts that can be made with a seasonal index help the businessman in short-range planning. You will recall that a seasonal index measures the typical periodic pattern of activity within a year's time. If a seasonal index is computed from monthly data, it measures the typical monthly seasonal fluctuations of the data. Therefore, the monthly index values can be used to forecast monthly values.

A monthly forecast based on annual average forecast. Below is the seasonal index of the sales of the Metro Company from Column B of Table 17-5:

MONTH	*SEASONAL INDEX*
Jan.	84.2
Feb.	93.9
Mar.	97.2
Apr.	109.3
May	103.1
June	99.6
July	92.8
Aug.	98.9
Sept.	101.1
Oct.	104.0
Nov.	108.9
Dec.	107.2

This index shows, for example, that January sales of the Metro Company are typically 84.2% of the normal monthly volume. Therefore, if we knew the normal monthly volume for a year, we could calculate the expected January sales by taking 84.2% of it. To illustrate forecasting procedure, assume that a researcher in the Metro Company has predicted that the company's annual sales in 1977 would amount to $720 million, for a mean monthly volume of $60 million. Multiplying this $60 by each of the seasonal index numbers (each expressed as a decimal) gives the monthly forecasts for 1977. The calculations are given in Table 17-8.

TABLE 17-8. Calculating Monthly Forecasts with a Seasonal Index and Monthly Average.

MONTH	*SEASONAL INDEX EXPRESSED AS A DECIMAL*	*1977 FORECAST: SEASONAL INDEX × $60 (MILLIONS OF DOLLARS)*
Jan.	0.842	50.5
Feb.	0.939	56.3
Mar.	0.972	58.3
Apr.	1.093	65.6
May	1.031	61.9
June	0.996	59.8
July	0.928	55.7
Aug.	0.989	59.3
Sept.	1.011	60.7
Oct.	1.040	62.4
Nov.	1.089	65.3
Dec.	1.072	64.3
Total		720.0

The total, $720, is the annual sales for the year. The accuracy of this method depends on the accuracy of the annual total and on the size of the cyclical and irregular fluctuation in the forecast year.

A trend times seasonal forecast. Another way that a seasonal index can be used in short-range forecasting is to combine the seasonal forecast with a trend forecast. In Chapter 16, the monthly least squares trend equation for the sales of the Metro Company was found to be $Y_c = 41.8 + 0.19X$. This trend equation may be used to calculate monthly trend values for 1977. The monthly trend values are multiplied by the seasonal index of the sales of the Metro Company to get a combined trend and seasonal forecast. The results appear in Table 17-9.

Although the trend projection is a straight line in this illustration, it need not be in every case. The trend equation chosen should be the one that best describes the trend of the series to be projected. This method of forecasting should be valuable for a series where the cyclical and irregular fluctuations have been relatively small and are expected to remain small for the forecast period.

TABLE 17-9. Calculating a Monthly Trend and Seasonal Forecast.

MONTH	*1977 PROJECTED TREND*	*SEASONAL INDEX*	*1977 TREND × SEASONAL FORECAST*
Jan.	52.2	0.842	44.0
Feb.	52.4	0.939	49.2
Mar.	52.6	0.972	51.1
Apr.	52.8	1.093	57.7
May	53.0	1.031	54.6
June	53.2	0.996	53.0
July	53.3	0.928	49.5
Aug.	53.5	0.989	52.9
Sept.	53.7	1.011	54.3
Oct.	53.9	1.040	56.1
Nov.	54.1	1.089	58.9
Dec.	54.3	1.072	58.2

Thirty-day forecasting. A seasonal index is useful for making 30-day forecasts. This can be done when the data to be forecasted are available a day or two after the end of a month. For example, assume that it is January 2, 1977, and that a forecast of the Metro Company's sales in January is desired. If the December 1976 sales volume is known, then the forecast can be based on it. Table 17-1 shows that December 1976 sales amounted to $60.1 million. Using the seasonal index numbers from the two previous illustrations, we can find the January forecast by dividing the December index number into the January index number and multiplying this ratio times the December sales:

$$\frac{84.2}{107.2} \times 60.1 = 47.2$$

(When 107.2 is divided into 84.2, the quotient is 0.785, which means that the Metro Company's January sales typically have been 78.5% of its December sales. This percentage relationship is assumed to exist for the period to be forecasted.) When using this method, the analyst should be reasonably sure that the base figure in the forecast, in this case December 1976 sales, is a normal figure, that is, that no unusual event such as a strike or extreme weather affected the base figure.

When the actual January sales figures are available, the February sales can be predicted using

$$\frac{\text{Feb. index no.}}{\text{Jan. index no.}} \times \text{ actual January sales}$$

Predictions for other months can be made in a like manner.

It is not the intent of this discussion to compare the merits of the three forecasting methods illustrated. None of the three is the best method. The best method for forecasting is the one that is logical and gives the least error.

Deseasonalizing Data with a Stable Seasonal Index

If you look at the tables in any monthly issue of *The Survey of Current Business*, you will find a large number of economic indicators. Many of these have been adjusted for seasonal variation to enable users of the index to see trends that are independent of seasonal variations. The removal of seasonal variations more clearly reveals basic strengths or weaknesses in the data. For example, employment might drop 5% from December to January, but is this an indication that the economy is weakening and perhaps heading for a recession? This question can be answered more accurately if we know the seasonal fluctuations in employment. If there is a sharp seasonal drop in employment from December to January every year, then the 5% drop in employment might be misleading. Perhaps an adjustment for seasonal decline would show that all of the decline is seasonal. If so, then we would conclude that the employment level is constant and that employment figures do not indicate a weakening economy.

Listed in Table 17-10 is the U.S. Index of Industrial Production (1967 = 100) for the first six months of 1976 on both adjusted and unadjusted bases. A comparison reveals the effects of seasonal influences on industrial production in the United States. For example, the unadjusted index shows an increase of 3.5 points from May to June, but the adjusted index shows only a 0.4-point increase; therefore, the increase in production was mostly seasonal. If these seasonal variations in U.S. production were not known and measured, an economic analyst might easily misinterpret changes in the index and come to wrong conclusions about what is happening to the economy.

TABLE 17-10. United States Index of Industrial Production, Jan.—June, 1976 (1967=100).

MONTH	*UNADJUSTED*	*SEASONALLY ADJUSTED*
January	122.1	125.7
February	127.9	127.3
March	128.6	128.1
April	128.7	128.4
May	129.9	129.6
June	133.4	130.0

Source: U.S. Department of Commerce, *Survey of Current Business*, September, 1976.

Because most monthly time series are considered to be a product of trend, cyclical, seasonal, and irregular forces, that is, $T \times C \times S \times I$, time series usually are adjusted for seasonal variation by dividing out the seasonal. Symbolically,

$$\frac{T \times C \times S \times I}{S} = T \times C \times I$$

Table 17-11 illustrates the deseasonalization of the Metro Company's 1976 sales. Notice that the seasonally adjusted figures are higher than the adjusted figures when the seasonal index numbers are less than 100 and lower when the seasonal index numbers are above 100. For a specific example of what seasonal adjustments do, note that the unadjusted figures rose from March to April but declined after seasonal adjustment.

TABLE 17-11. Adjusting Metro Company's 1976 Sales for Seasonal Variation.

MONTH	(1) 1976 SALES UNADJUSTED (MILLIONS OF DOLLARS)	(2) SEASONAL INDEX	(3) 1976 SALES SEASONALLY ADJUSTED (MILLIONS OF DOLLARS) (COL. (1) ÷ COL. (2))
Jan.	41.8	0.842	49.6
Feb.	47.8	0.939	50.9
Mar.	48.8	0.972	50.2
Apr.	50.1	1.093	45.8
May	49.7	1.031	48.2
June	49.2	0.996	49.4
July	47.6	0.928	51.2
Aug.	53.4	0.989	54.0
Sept.	55.9	1.011	55.3
Oct.	57.5	1.040	55.3
Nov.	59.6	1.089	54.7
Dec.	60.1	1.072	56.1

Table 17-12 shows the deseasonalized sales of the Metro Company for the 1968–1976, and Chart 17-4 pictures the company's actual and deseasonalized sales for that period. The deseasonalized data still show much variation because of the heavy influence of irregular fluctuations in the data. So that you can get a better picture of the results of deseasonalizing data, Chart 17-6 shows department store sales in the United States for several years. These data are not affected by irregular fluctuations like the sales of the Metro Company, partly because adjustments were made also for trading days and holidays.

Deseasonalizing with a Moving Seasonal Index

Table 17-13 shows the Metro Company's sales seasonally adjusted with the moving seasonal index presented in Table 17-7. Chart 17-5 pictures the unadjusted and adjusted sales. Although the deseasonalized data show much variation due to irregularities, a better job of removing the seasonal variation has been done because the gradual changes in the seasonal patterns have been accounted for. (You might want to compare Charts 17-4 and 17-6 to see the differences in the results of seasonal adjustments with the stable seasonal index and the moving seasonal index.)

TABLE 17-12. Sales of the Metro Company, Seasonally Adjusted[1], 1968—1976 (Millions of Dollars).

YEAR	*JAN.*	*FEB.*	*MAR.*	*APR.*	*MAY*	*JUNE*	*JULY*	*AUG.*	*SEPT.*	*OCT.*	*NOV.*	*DEC.*
1968	31.7	29.1	27.1	27.3	28.1	30.0	29.4	28.4	31.9	30.9	31.2	31.7
1969	35.7	37.4	33.3	34.6	37.2	37.2	35.5	38.0	42.4	40.2	39.8	39.2
1970	39.1	39.9	46.0	45.3	44.1	39.6	36.1	36.9	34.6	37.6	37.0	38.2
1971	37.4	38.8	40.7	34.2	34.8	34.4	36.9	39.0	36.7	37.8	40.8	40.1
1972	44.9	38.2	43.0	48.5	46.4	44.2	45.7	42.8	42.4	44.1	43.9	45.7
1973	40.6	38.8	36.8	43.4	40.0	42.8	44.7	46.0	43.9	43.7	41.0	41.2
1974	42.9	43.3	42.1	41.2	42.2	47.4	45.3	44.3	43.5	44.5	46.7	47.0
1975	43.3	48.7	45.8	47.0	49.5	50.1	49.4	52.1	52.5	51.6	50.6	50.3
1976	49.6	50.9	50.3	45.8	48.2	49.4	51.2	54.0	55.3	55.3	54.7	56.1

[1]These data were adjusted using the stable seasonal index in Column B of Table 17-5.

Chart 17-4. Sales of the Metro Company, by months, 1968–1976 (millions of dollars).

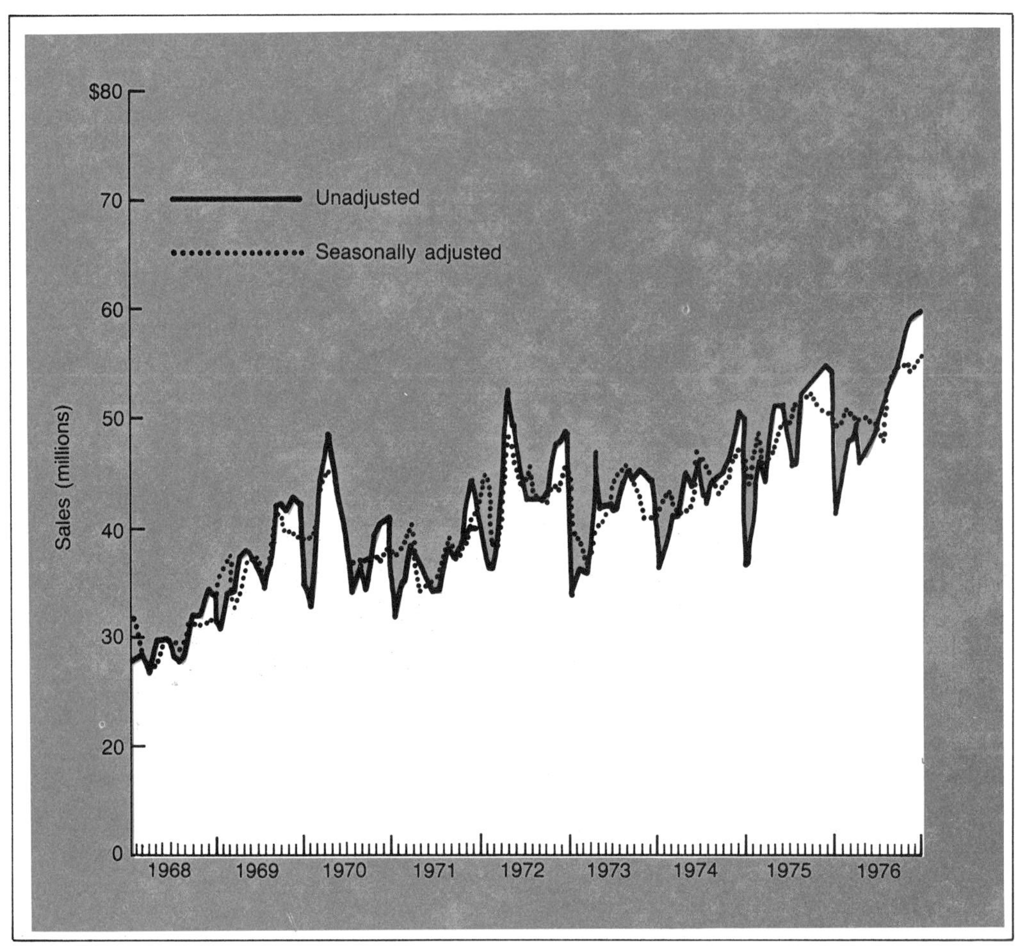

SEASONAL INDEXES OF QUARTERLY DATA

Although only monthly data were used in the foregoing discussion of seasonal indexes, quarterly data could have been used. The same concepts and methods of computation apply, except that when a stable seasonal index is computed from quarterly data, there

Chart 17-5. Monthly sales of department stores in the United States.

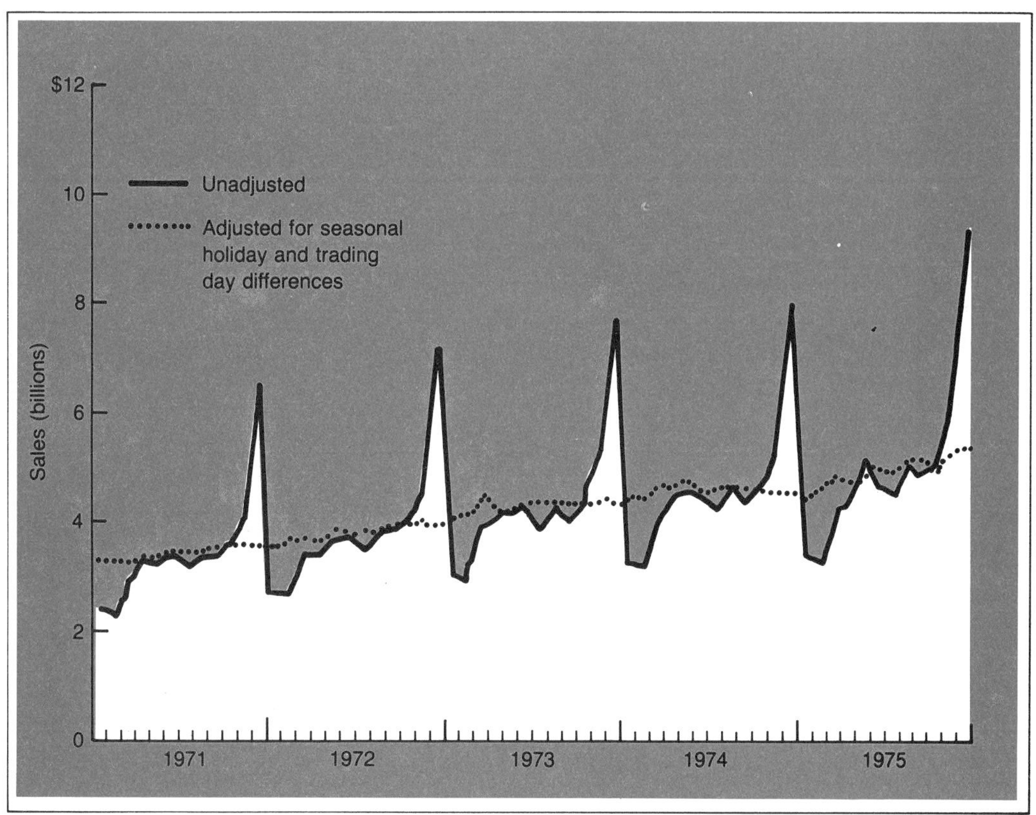

Source: U.S. Department of Commerce

TABLE 17-13. Sales of the Metro Company, by Months Seasonally Adjusted with a Moving Seasonal Index (Millions of Dollars).

MONTH	*1968*	*1969*	*1970*	*1971*	*1972*	*1973*	*1974*	*1975*	*1976*
Jan.	$30.7	$34.9	$38.4	$37.1	$44.8	$40.9	$43.5	$44.3	51.2
Feb.	27.6	35.9	38.8	38.2	38.1	39.1	44.3	50.4	53.5
Mar.	25.9	32.1	45.0	40.1	42.9	37.1	43.0	47.2	52.4
Apr.	25.9	33.2	44.1	33.7	48.4	43.8	42.1	48.7	48.2
May	27.8	36.1	43.2	34.5	46.3	40.4	42.5	50.9	49.4
June	30.9	38.1	40.4	34.9	44.4	42.8	47.2	49.6	48.6
July	30.7	39.0	36.9	37.3	45.7	44.1	44.4	47.9	49.1
Aug.	30.2	39.7	38.0	39.4	42.6	42.0	42.8	49.6	50.7
Sept.	32.4	42.9	34.3	36.9	42.6	44.0	44.2	52.3	54.0
Oct.	31.8	41.1	38.1	38.1	44.2	43.5	42.8	50.8	54.0
Nov.	32.6	40.7	37.5	41.1	44.0	41.0	46.4	50.0	53.8
Dec.	32.7	40.1	38.7	40.5	45.7	40.9	46.4	49.4	54.0

Chart 17-6. Sales of the Metro Company, by months, 1968–1976 (millions of dollars).

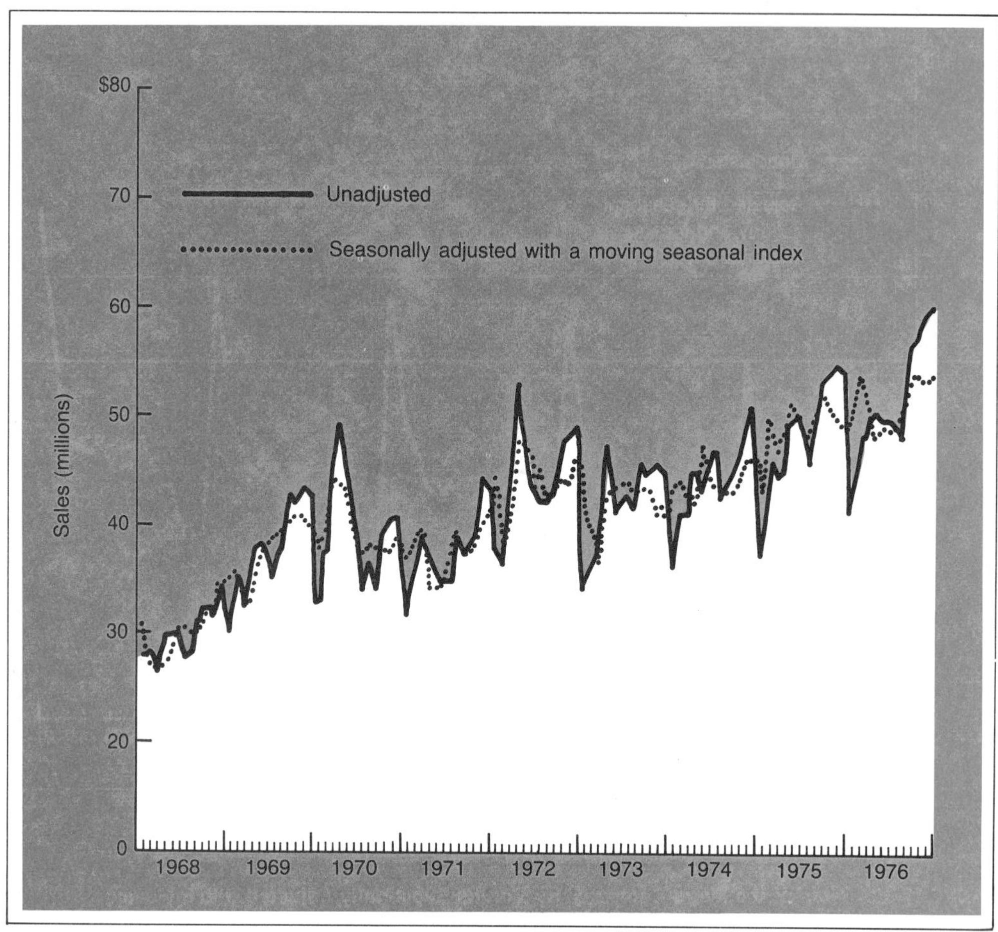

are only four index numbers—one for each quarter. A moving seasonal index for quarterly data has as many index numbers as there are quarterly figures in the original data.

Tables 17-14 and 17-15 show the computation of a stable seasonal index for the quarterly sales of the Metro Company for the years 1968–1976 using a four-quarter-moving-averages method. The indexes, which are shown at the bottom of Table 17-15, can be used to forecast sales and to deseasonalize the original quarterly sales figures. The methods of calculation would be identical to those used for monthly data.

TABLE 17-14. Computation of Percentages of Four-Quarter Moving Averages of Sales of the Metro Company, 1968—1976.

		(1) SALES (MILLIONS)	(2) 4-QUARTER MOVING TOTAL	(3) 2-QUARTER MOVING TOTAL OF COL. (2)	(4) COL. (3) ÷ 8 (4-QUARTER MOVING AVERAGE)	(5) (COL. (1) ÷ COL. (4)) × 100 PERCENT OF 4-QUARTER MOVING AVERAGE
1968	I	80.3				
	II	89.5				
			358.4			
	III	87.7		734.0	91.8	95.5
			375.6			
	IV	100.9		775.0	96.9	104.1
			399.4			
1969	I	97.5		826.6	103.3	94.4
			427.2			
	II	113.3		880.6	110.1	102.9
			453.4*			
	III	115.5		924.4	115.6	99.9
			471.0			
	IV	127.1		963.2	120.4	105.6
			492.2			
1970	I	115.1		973.3	121.7	94.6
			481.1			
	II	134.5		955.4	119.4	112.6
			474.3*			
	III	104.4		940.9	117.6	88.8
			466.6			
	IV	120.3		906.3	113.3	106.2
			439.7			
1971	I	107.4		884.9	110.6	97.1
			445.2			
	II	107.6		896.8	112.1	96.0
			451.6*			
	III	109.9		911.3	113.9	96.5
			459.7			
	IV	126.7		956.6	119.6	105.9
			496.9			
1972	I	115.5		1011.6	126.4	91.4
			514.7			
	II	144.8		1045.3	130.7	110.8
			530.6*			
	III	127.7		1052.0	131.5	97.1
			521.4			
	IV	142.6		1029.2	128.6	110.9
			507.8			
1973	I	106.3		1019.2	127.4	83.4
			511.4			
	II	131.2		1014.4	126.8	103.5
			503.0*			
	III	131.3		1017.4	127.2	103.2
			514.1			
	IV	134.2		1033.3	129.2	103.9
			518.9			
1974	I	117.7		1037.1	129.6	90.8
			518.2			
	II	135.7		1049.7	131.2	103.4
			531.5*			
	III	130.6		1072.0	134.0	97.5
			540.5			
	IV	147.5		1097.6	137.2	107.5
			557.1			
1975	I	126.7		1134.1	141.8	89.4
			577.0			
	II	152.3		1169.2	146.2	104.2
			592.2*			
	III	150.5		1196.1	149.5	100.7
			603.9			
	IV	162.7		1204.5	150.6	107.7
			600.6			
1976	I	138.4		1207.6	151.0	91.7
			607.0			
	II	149.0		122.85	153.6	97.0
			621.5*			
	III	156.9				
	IV	177.2				

*Checkpoints for accuracy of the moving totals.

Tables 17-16 and 17-17 illustrate both of these operations. The method described in Chapter 16 was used to compute the quarterly trend values in Table 17-16. Chart 17-7 shows the quarterly seasonal index. Chart 17-8 shows the original data, the deseasonalized data, the trend, and the $T \times S$ projection to 1977.

TABLE 17-15. Arrayed Percentages of Four-Quarter Moving Averages of Sales of the Metro Company, 1968—1976.

	I	*II*	*III*	*IV*
	83.4	96.0	88.8	103.9
	89.4	97.0	95.5	104.1
	90.8	102.9	96.5	105.6
	91.4	103.4	97.1	105.9
	91.7	103.5	97.5	106.5
	94.4	104.2	99.9	107.5
	94.6	110.8	100.7	107.7
	97.1	112.6	103.2	110.9
Mean*	91.6	103.8	97.4	106.5
Seasonal Index†	91.7	104.0	97.6	106.7

*Mean of the eight figures.

†Mean of the eight figures after adjustment to make them total 400.0

TABLE 17-16. Calculation of a 1977 Quarterly Forecast of Trend Times Seasonal for the Sales of the Metro Company.

1977 QUARTER	T TREND ($Y_c = a+bX$)	S SEASONAL INDEX	$T \times S$
I	156.8	0.917	143.8
II	158.5	1.040	164.8
III	160.2	0.976	156.3
IV	162.0	1.067	172.8

TABLE 17-17. Adjusting the Metro Company's 1976 Quarterly Sales for Seasonal Variation.

QUARTER	(1) 1976 SALES UNADJUSTED (MILLIONS OF DOLLARS) $T \times C \times S \times I$	(2) SEASONAL INDEX S	(3) 1976 SALES SEASONAL ADJUSTED COL. (1) ÷ COL. (2) $T \times C \times I$
I	138.4	0.917	150.9
II	149.0	1.040	143.3
III	156.9	0.976	160.8
IV	177.2	1.067	166.1

Chart 17-7. Seasonal index of sales of the Metro Company.

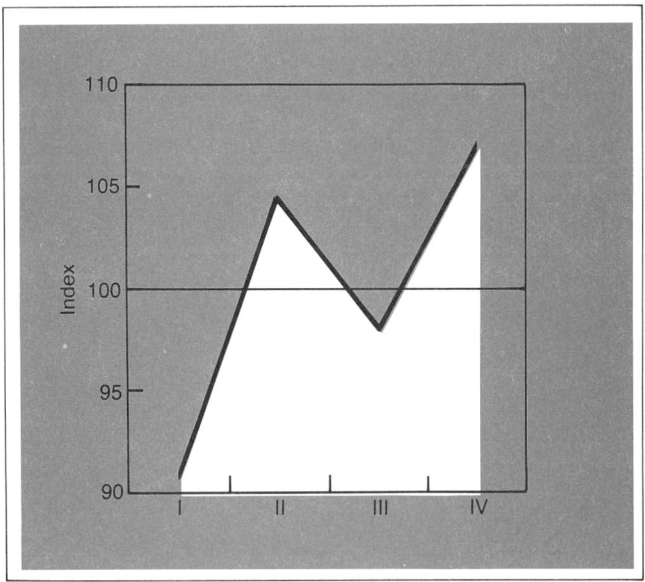

Chart 17-8. Sales of the Metro Company, by quarter, 1968 to 1976 with projection to 1977.

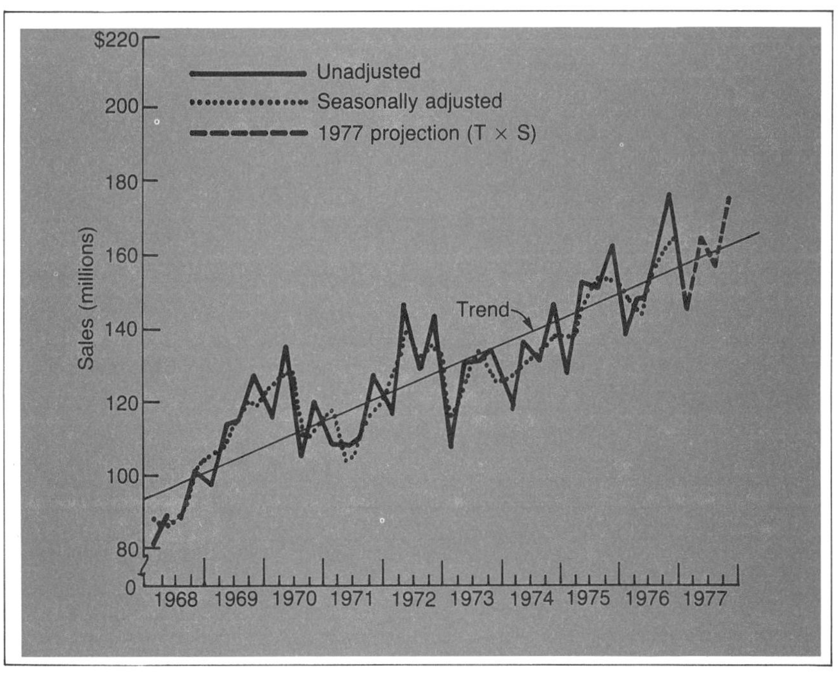

GRAPHIC MEASUREMENT OF SEASONAL VARIATION

If a computer or computer program for a seasonal index is not readily available semi-log paper can be used to quickly measure seasonal variation in a time series. The procedure outlined below will give a seasonal index by the percent of 4-quarter moving-averages-method. The steps are:

Chart 17-9. Value of new construction in the United States, 1970–1975, with a freehand $T \times C$ line.

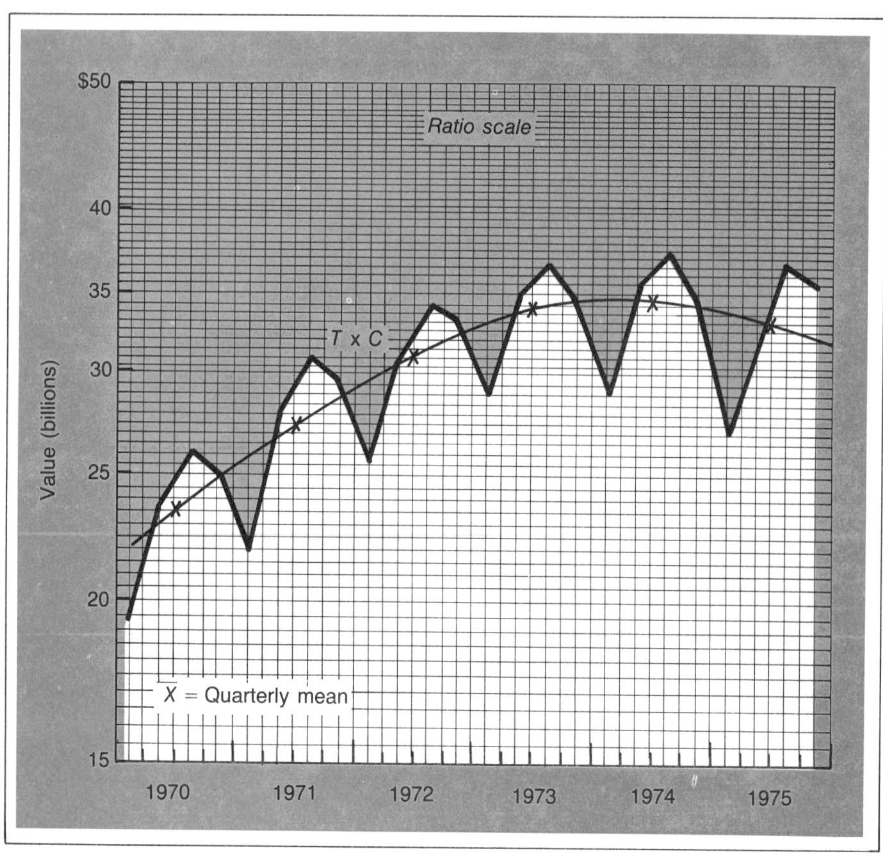

1) Chart the quarterly time series on semi-log paper. Compute the quarterly mean for each year and plot these values at the middle of the years, and draw in, freehand, the trend times cycle ($T \times C$) line through the plotted means. This is your graphic estimate of the 4-quarter moving averages. As an illustration, the data in Table 17-18 have been plotted on Chart 17-9 and the $T \times C$ line has been drawn in.

TABLE 17-18. Value of New Construction in the United States by Quarter, 1970—1975 (Billions of Dollars).

YEAR	I	II	III	IV	TOTAL	MEAN
1970	$19.3	$23.6	$26.0	$25.2	94.1	23.5
1971	21.8	27.9	30.7	29.5	109.9	27.5
1972	25.7	31.3	34.0	33.3	124.3	31.1
1973	28.9	34.5	37.6	35.1	136.1	34.0
1974	28.9	35.2	37.2	34.1	135.4	33.9
1975	27.0	31.9	36.6	35.1	130.6	32.7

Source: U.S. Department of Commerce, *Business Statistics*, 1975; and *Construction Review*, Jan./Feb., 1976.

2) Secure four slips of paper or cards with a straight edge (e.g., 3-by-5 cards), one for each quarter, and label them as shown on Figure 17-1. These will be used to take readings of percentages of 4-quarter moving averages from the semi-log chart. Draw a line in the middle of each card perpendicular to the right edge, and label the line $T \times C$.

3) Place the $T \times C$ line on a card on the $T \times C$ line on the chart for each year and the quarter of concern, and mark on the card the place where the actual value falls, then draw a line that represents an estimate of the average of the values that the several marks represent. For example, the several marks on the card labeled Quarter I were obtained by placing the $T \times C$ line on the card on the $T \times C$ line on Chart 17-9 at the first quarter of each year, and making a mark where the actual value fell. The estimate of the mean of values that the lines represent was made and is labeled $\overline{X}$. This estimate is made by judgment, giving consideration to the bunching (or scatter) of the lines which indicates the degree of homogeneity of the values which the lines represent.

4) Set up values on another log scale so there is a 100 line, place the $T \times C$ line on a card on the 100 line on the log scale, and take a reading for the $\overline{X}$ line from the scale. For example, when the $T \times C$ line on the card for the first quarter was placed on the 100 line, as shown in the Figure 2 the reading for the $\overline{X}$ line was 85%, which is the unadjusted estimate of the seasonal index number for the first quarter. This same procedure, followed for each quarter, produces the readings for the mean lines shown on the card display. These values are the first estimate

Figure 17-1. Graphic readings for a seasonal index of the value of new construction in the United States, 1970–1975.

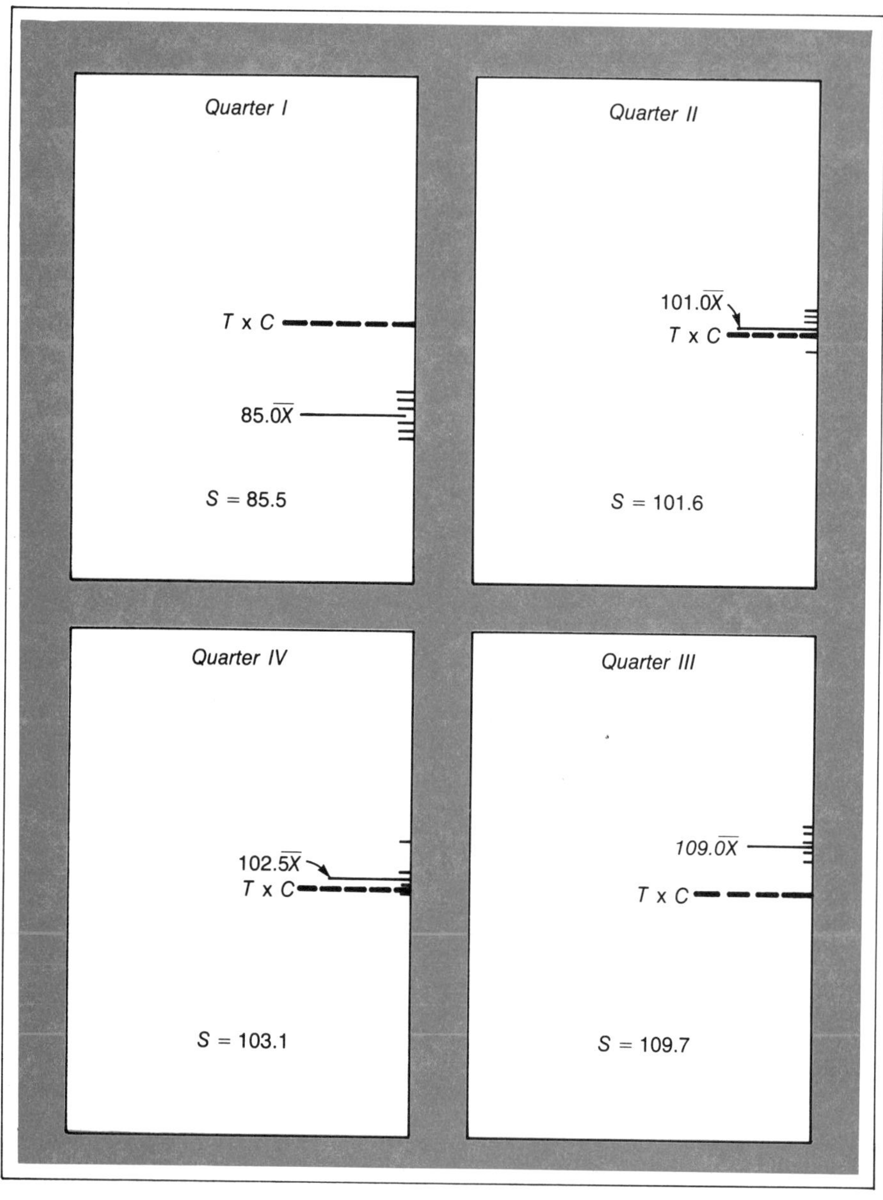

Figure 17-2. How to get the percentage for the mean line on the readings card.

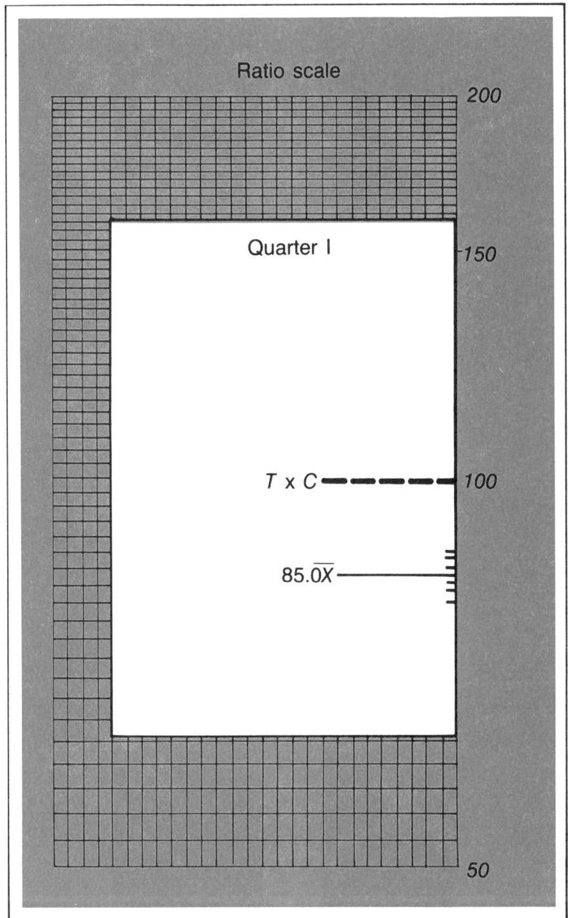

of the quarterly seasonal index. The total of the four values is 397.5, therefore they were adjusted to total 400%. The adjustment was made by multiplying each $\overline{X}$ line reading by

$$\frac{400}{397.5}$$

The adjusted numbers are the final seasonal index numbers, and are labeled S.

Advantages. An advantage of this method, which can be used for calculating monthly seasonal indexes, is that it is quick and helps the analyst get a "feel" for the data. It also helps the student understand what happens when he computes a seasonal index by the moving average method or when a computer computes the index.

When an experienced analyst uses this method on data with which he is familiar, he may get a better measure of the seasonal than that produced by arithmetic, since his freehand drawing of the $T \times C$ line, which does not have to go through the averages for each year, may be a better description of the combined trend and cyclical fluctuation, because the peaks and troughs of the cycles may not be reached when arithmetic is used.

Moving Seasonal by the Graphic Method

If readings from the log scale are recorded on a card for each of the marks on the card and are plotted on a graph, a freehand trend can be drawn through the values and the trend values for each year read from the graph. When this has been done for each of the four quarters the four readings for each year can be adjusted to total 400%.

REVIEW QUESTIONS

1. What are seasonal variations?
2. Why do seasonal variations show a high degree of regularity in timing and in amplitude?
3. What preliminary adjustment should sometimes be made in data before measuring the typical seasonal pattern? Why?
4. What are the two basic purposes for computing a seasonal index?
5. What is the difference between a stable seasonal index and a moving seasonal index?
6. Why might a seasonal pattern change over a long period of time?
7. What is the chief advantage of using the percent-of-12-month-moving-averages method to compute a seasonal index?
8. Show, symbolically, how data are deseasonalized.
9. For what types of business decisions is a seasonal index of sales useful?
10. Why are most important monthly economic indicators adjusted for seasonal variation?

PROBLEMS

1. Chart the retail sales data in Exercise Table 16-1. Leave space on the chart for 1976 and 1977. Compute a stable seasonal index using the percent-of-12-month-moving-averages method. Deseasonalize the data and plot the deseasonalized data on the same chart. Also, make a separate chart of your seasonal index.
2. Using the calculated trend value from Problem 16-1, convert your annual trend equation to a monthly equation and compute the monthly trend values for 1976 and 1977. Multiply these monthly trend values by the seasonal index computed for Problem 1 to get a projection of trend × seasonal for 1976 and 1977. Show these projected values on the chart of the original monthly values that you constructed for Problem 1.

EXERCISE TABLE 17-1. Seasonal Index of Credit Reports.

MONTH	*INDEX*	*MONTH*	*INDEX*
Jan.	83.8	July	86.9
Feb.	91.9	Aug.	92.0
Mar.	87.8	Sept.	105.6
Apr.	102.9	Oct.	111.0
May	101.7	Nov.	119.1
June	98.8	Dec.	118.2

3. A stable seasonal index of the credit reports of a credit bureau is given in Exercise Table 17-1. If the number of credit reports issued in August 1976 was 400,000, use the seasonal index to estimate the number of credit reports that were issued in September 1976. Also, assume that 3,960,000 reports were issued in the entire year of 1976 and break down this figure into estimated monthly figures.

EXERCISE TABLE 17-2. New Plant and Equipment Expenditures by Quarter, United States, 1968—1975 (Billions of Dollars).

YEAR	*I*	*II*	*III*	*IV*	*TOTAL*
1968	15.1	16.8	16.8	19.0	67.7
1969	16.0	18.8	19.2	21.5	75.5
1970	17.5	20.3	20.3	21.7	79.8
1971	17.7	20.6	20.1	22.8	81.2
1972	19.4	22.0	21.9	25.2	88.5
1973	21.5	24.7	25.0	28.5	99.7
1974	24.1	28.2	28.2	31.9	112.4
1975	25.8	28.4	27.8	30.7	112.7

Source: U.S. Department of Commerce, *Business Statistics*, 1975, p. 10; and *Survey of Current Business*, April, 1977.

4. Go to Exercise Table 16-5 and calculate the total shipments of mobile homes for each calendar quarter. Then compute a stable seasonal index of the quarterly data using the four-quarter-moving-averages method. Using the seasonal index, deseasonalize the original quarterly totals. Plot the unadjusted and adjusted data on the same chart.

5. Use the quarterly data on shipments of mobile homes you compiled for Problem 4 and compute a quarterly seasonal index by the graphic method. Compare your answers to those you computed in Problem 4. Are they close?

6. Using the graphic method, compute a quarterly seasonal index of the expenditures data in Exercise Table 17-2. Total expenditures for 1976 were $120.5 billion. Find the quarterly estimates for that year with the seasonal index. How close do they come to the actual quarterly expenditures (which can be found in the *Survey of Current Business*, April, 1977.)

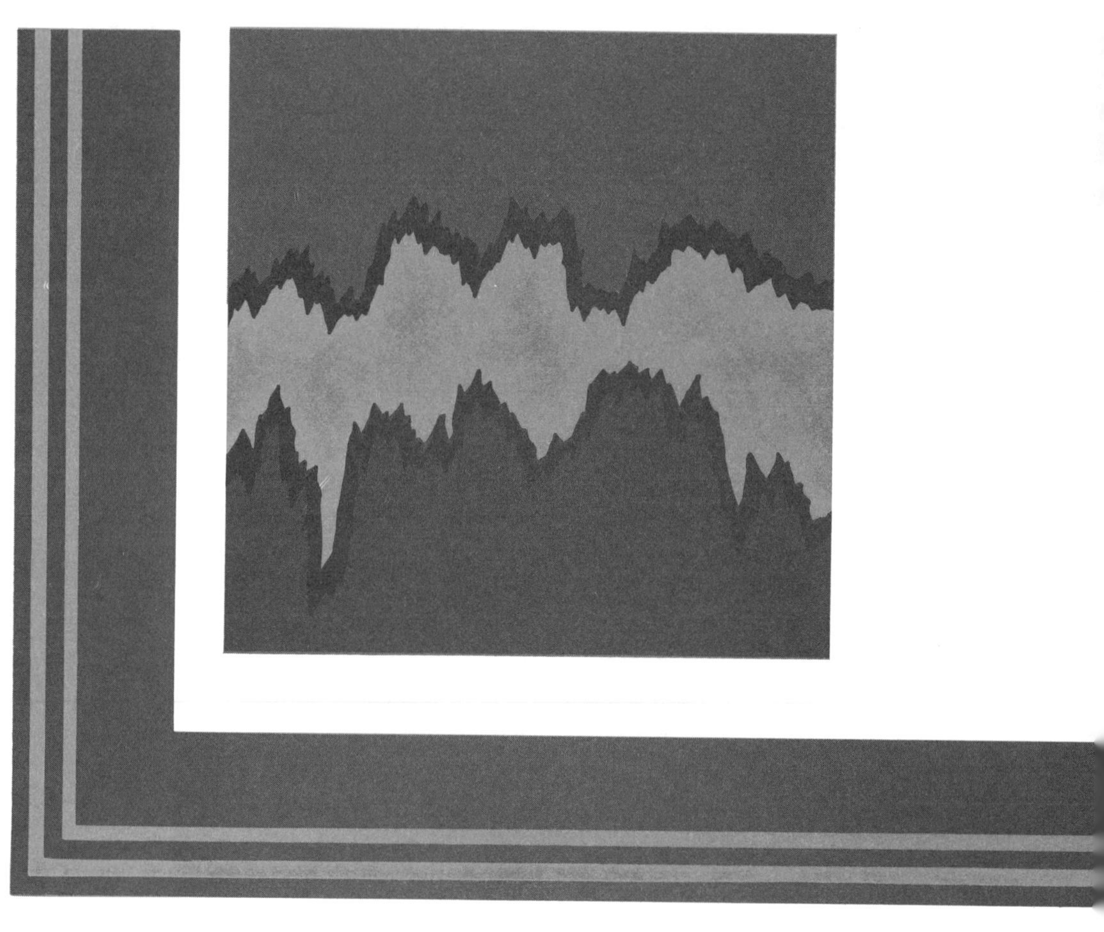

18

Cycles In Time Series

In Chapter 15 we described cyclical variations in time series as those recurrent, but nonperiodic, movements from prosperity to depression* that are caused by maladjustments in the economic forces that affect business activity. Because of the irregularity of the timing and magnitude of upturns and downturns in these fluctuations, measurements of the "average" cycle are of little or no value in forecasting the turning points and magnitudes of future cycles.

Cycles may be used as a forecasting tool, however, if a *lag-lead relationship* is found between the cycles of two series. The hypothetical situation for such forecasting is illustrated on Chart 18-1. Series A shows an upturn four months before Series B and a downturn three months before. If this lag-lead relationship can be rationally explained, then we can use it to predict future cyclical turns for Series B.

Close correlations of the cycles of two series are rare. However, lag-lead relationships may be useful for general forecasting of an economic time series, even though exact timing cannot be predicted. For example, a study of a particular geographic area might show that, historically, a drop in the average weekly hours of production workers in manufacturing has preceded a drop in the number of production workers. This being the case, an analyst would watch the figures on

Chart 18-1. Illustration of a lag-lead relationship between the cycles of two time series, A and B.

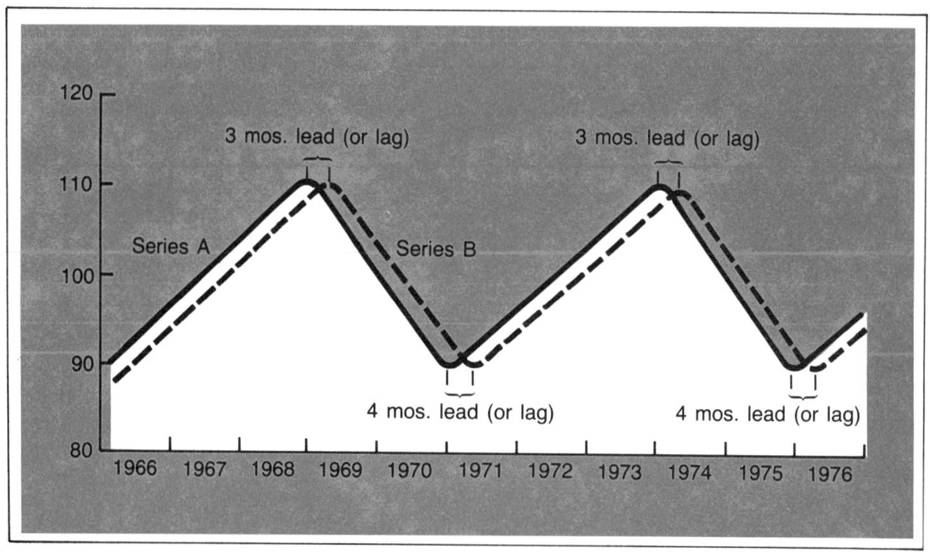

*Depression, as used here, merely means the trough, or low point, in a cycle, not economic conditions as they were in the early 1930's.

weekly hours worked for the area and use them as a guide to predict the number employed at a given time.

FORECASTING GENERAL BUSINESS CONDITIONS

The *general concept* of the lag-lead relationship in economic time series is used widely today to forecast general business conditions. For example, the *Business Conditions Digest*, which is published monthly by the U.S. Department of Commerce, contains economic time series data that were developed by the National Bureau of Economic Research. This publication compares the turning points of several economic time series called "leading" indicators, "roughly coincident" indicators, and "lagging" indicators to the turning points of aggregate economic activity in the United States. These indicators are defined as follows:

Indicators

Leading indicators are those which usually reach peaks or troughs before the corresponding turns in aggregate economic activity; roughly coincident indicators are direct measures of aggregate economic activity or move roughly together with it; lagging indicators usually reach their turning points after the turns in aggregate economic activity.*

The methods used to determine these lag-lead relationships is not as simple as that depicted in Chart 18-1.

Chart 18-2, redrawn from *Business Conditions Digest*, shows five of the forty leading indicators. The shaded areas represent the peak-to-trough period of aggregate economic activity. (Consult the latest issue of this publication to see the other series.)

Businessmen are interested chiefly in watching the leading indicators. For example, if most of them were to fall for three consecutive months, he might conclude that a business recession is imminent, if not already in progress.

*U.S. Department of Commerce, Bureau of the Census, *Business Conditions Digest*, July 1976, p.2.

ISOLATION OF CYCLES

Cycles, of course, must be measured before they can be compared. Most cyclical variations are not regular enough in timing and amplitude for an average to be useful in forecasting. Useful measurements of the cycles of many time series can be made, however, by the residual method, which isolates the cycles by eliminating other components.

Chart 18-2. Cyclical indicators, economic process, and cyclical timing.

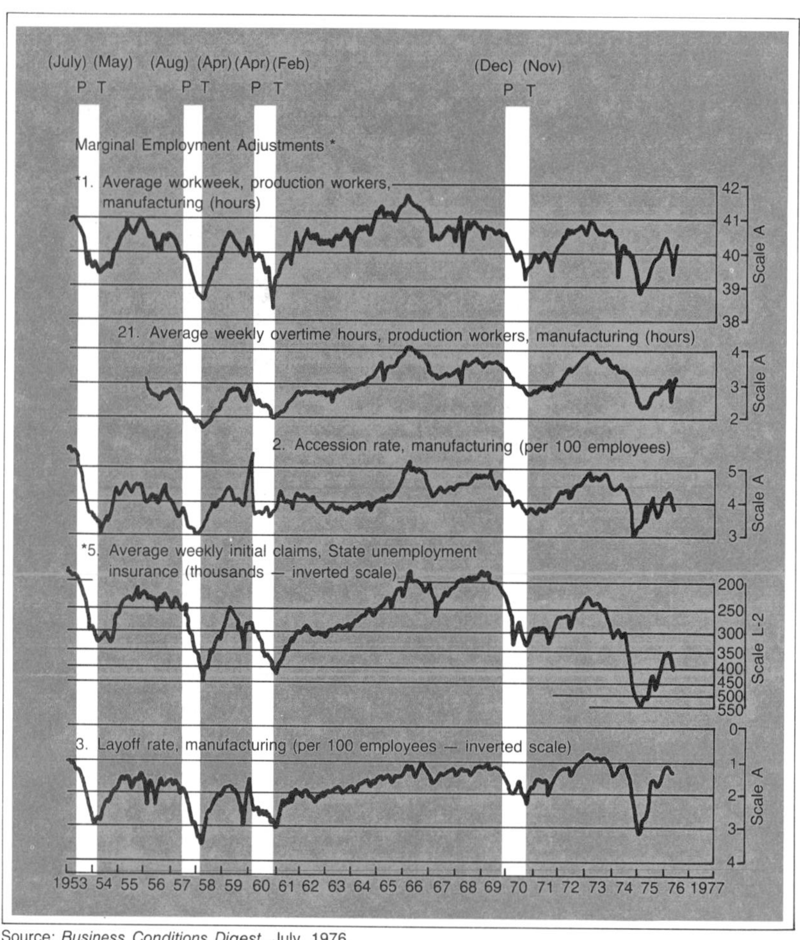

Source: *Business Conditions Digest*, July, 1976.

Chart 18-3 shows the cycles of the annual sales of the Metro Company with irregular fluctuations. These measurements were computed by dividing the original sales data by the least squares trend values computed in Table 18-1. The computations are shown in Table 18-1.

Perhaps a better illustration of the isolation of cyclical fluctuations is found in Chart 18-4. This chart pictures both the cycles of the monthly sales of the Metro Company affected by irregular fluctuations and the same cycles after much of the irregularity has been removed by a five-month moving average. Table 18-2 illustrates the method used to measure these cycles.

What was done in the first five columns can be explained symbolically as

$$\frac{T \times C \times S \times I}{T \times S} = C \times I$$

The $C \times I$ values were smoothed with a five-month moving average to remove much of the I component.

The original data ($T \times C \times S \times I$) are listed in Column (1). Columns (2) and (3) list a trend (T) and a seasonal index (S) computed in the chapters on trend and seasonal variations. Column (4) shows $T \times S$, the product of the figures in Columns (2) and (3). The $C \times I$ figures in Column (5) were obtained by dividing the original sales figures in Column (1) by the $T \times S$ figures in Column (4) and multiplying by

Chart 18-3. Sales of the Metro Company as percent of trend, 1968—1976.

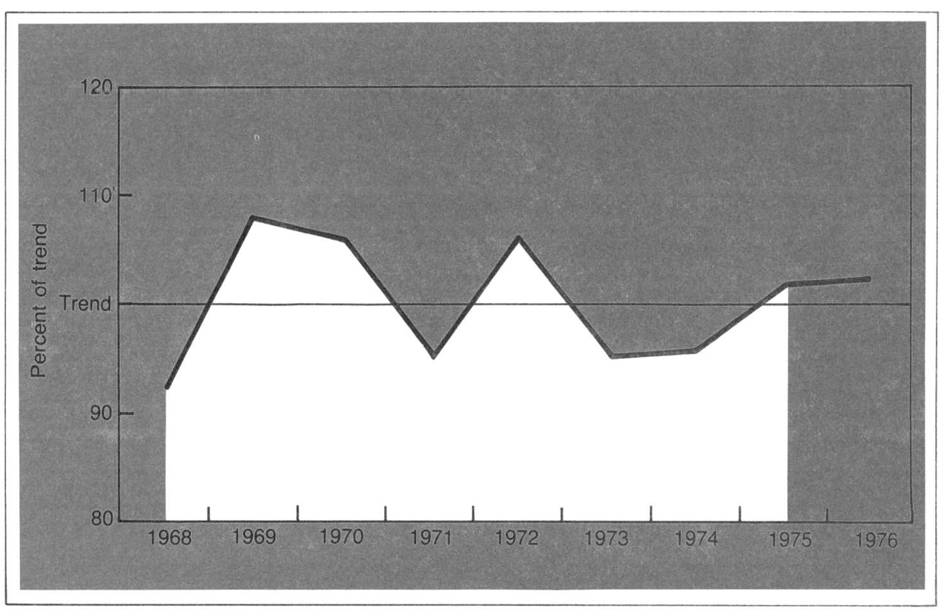

Chart 18-4. Cyclical fluctuations of the sales of the Metro Company, 1968—1976.

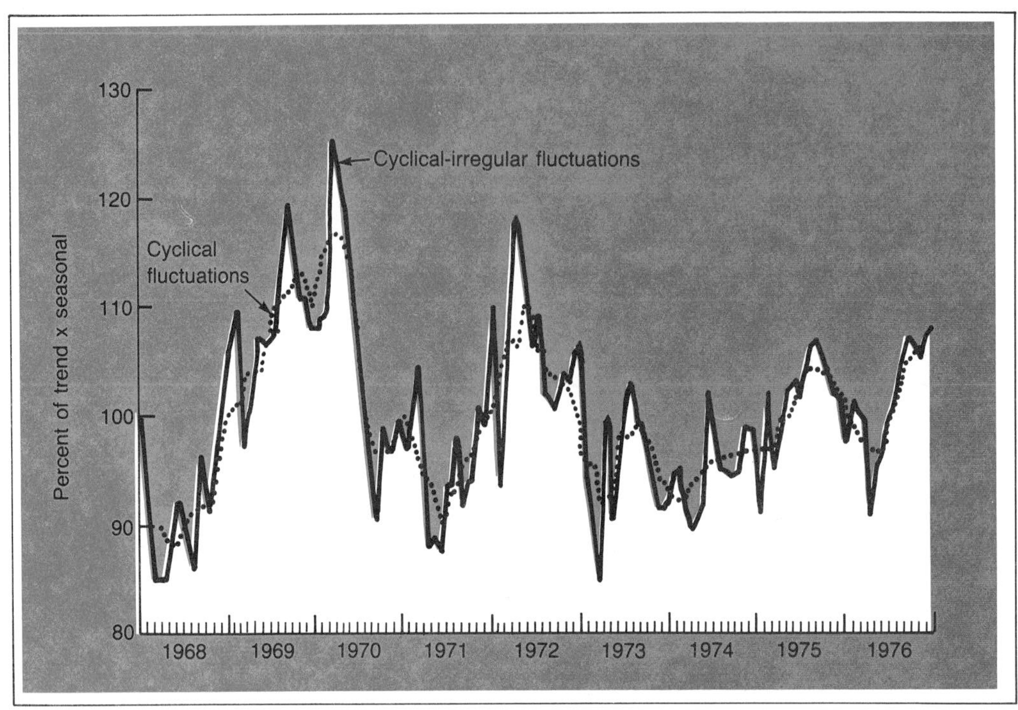

TABLE 18-1. Computation of the Percent of Trend Values of the Sales of the Metro Company, 1968—1976.

YEAR	SALES ($000,000) Y	TREND ($000,000) Y_c	PERCENT OF TREND (Y/Y_c)
1968	385.4	393.0	91.2
1969	453.4	420.2	107.9
1970	474.3	447.4	106.0
1971	451.6	474.6	95.2
1972	530.6	501.8	105.7
1973	503.0	529.0	95.1
1974	531.5	556.0	95.6
1975	592.2	583.4	101.5
1976	621.5	610.6	101.8

100. Column (6) shows the five-month moving totals, which were divided by 5 to get the five-month moving means in Column (7). The data in Column (5) are shown as a solid line on Chart 18-4 and the data in Column (7) are pictured with a dashed line.

A five-month moving mean was used only to illustrate how to remove much of the irregular component. More of this component could have been removed by increasing the term of the moving average to, say, seven or eight months. The choice of the term of the moving average is mostly a subjective one. If we wanted to experiment with several moving averages, we could then choose the one that did the best job of eliminating the irregular fluctuations. Such experimentation, however, is time-consuming and, therefore, expensive.

CORRELATION OF CYCLICAL FLUCTUATIONS

In Chapter 12, we learned that a correlation analysis of two variables classified by time tells whether the two moved in the same or opposite directions and whether the closeness of their association was high or low. The time series that were correlated had not been adjusted for trend or any other of their components. This is often justified, and when it is done, the resulting coefficient of correlation reflects both the relationships between the trends and the relationships between the fluctuations around the trends. If the trends of two time series move in a positive direction with approximately the same slopes and if the other fluctuations are closely and positively related, then a high positive coefficient of correlation will be found. However, if the trends move in opposite directions (negative association) and the other fluctuations move together (positive association), a low coefficient of correlation might result. Also, if there is a positive relationship between the trends and a negative relationship between the other fluctuations of two time series, the closeness of association between the unadjusted data may be low. Under such conditions, it is often advisable to remove the trends and correlate the residual fluctuations. The following example calls for a correlation analysis of the cycles of two annual time series, rather than for the unadjusted time series.

The indexes of value added by manufacture and manufacturing employees shown in Table 18-3 are plotted as a scatter diagram in Chart 18-5. It is obvious that the degree of the closeness of the movements of the two variables is low. In fact, a coefficient of correlation based on a linear relationship between the two variables was computed and found to be −0.234. This low negative coefficient resulted because the trends of the two series are in opposite directions even though the fluctuations around the trends move together in the same directions. Chart 18-6 shows the two times series on a line chart with their least squares trends. We can see that the relationship between the trends counterbalances the relationship between the fluctuations.

TABLE 18-2. Computations for the Measurement of Cycles of the Sales of the Metro Company, 1968—1976.

	(1) SALES ($000,000)	(2) TREND	(3) SEASONAL INDEX	(4) TREND X SEASONAL [COL. (2) × COL. (3)]	(5) CYCLICAL IRREGULAR PERCENTAGE [COL. (1) ÷ COL. (4) × 100]	(6) FIVE-MONTH MOVING TOTAL OF COL. (5)	(7) FIVE-MONTH MOVING MEAN OF COL. (5) [COL. (6) ÷ 5]
Jan. 1968	26.7	31.6	0.842	26.6	100.4		
Feb.	27.3	31.8	0.939	29.9	91.3		
Mar.	26.3	32.0	0.972	31.0	84.8	450.5	90.1
Apr.	29.8	32.2	1.093	35.2	84.7	442.5	88.4
May	29.8	32.4	1.031	33.4	89.2	440.5	88.1
June	29.9	32.6	0.996	32.5	92.0	441.9	88.4
July	27.3	32.8	0.928	30.4	89.8	453.6	90.7
Aug.	28.1	33.0	0.989	32.6	86.2	457.2	91.4
Sept.	32.3	33.1	1.011	33.5	96.4	460.0	92.0
Oct.	32.1	33.3	1.040	34.6	92.8	464.4	92.9
Nov.	34.6	33.5	1.089	36.5	94.8	483.8	96.5
Dec.	34.0	33.7	1.072	36.1	94.2	497.1	99.4
Jan. 1969	30.1	33.9	0.842	28.5	105.6	501.3	100.3
Feb.	35.1	34.1	0.939	32.0	109.7	506.8	101.4
Mar.	32.3	34.3	0.972	33.3	97.0	519.9	104.0
Apr.	37.8	34.5	1.093	37.7	100.3	521.2	104.2
May	38.4	34.7	1.031	35.8	107.3	519.5	103.9
June	37.1	34.8	0.996	34.7	106.9	530.3	106.1
July	35.1	35.0	0.928	32.5	108.0	549.8	110.0
Aug.	37.5	35.2	0.989	34.8	107.8	555.5	111.1
Sept.	42.9	35.4	1.011	35.8	119.8	559.6	111.9
Oct.	41.8	35.6	1.040	37.0	113.0	560.4	112.0
Nov.	43.3	35.8	1.089	39.0	111.0	560.5	112.1
Dec.	42.0	36.0	1.072	38.6	108.8	550.3	110.1
Jan. 1974	36.1	45.3	0.842	38.1	94.8	464.9	92.8
Feb.	40.7	45.5	0.939	42.7	95.3	463.1	92.6

TABLE 18-2. Computations for the Measurement of Cycles of the Sales of the Metro Company, 1968—1976. (Continued)

	(1) SALES ($000,000)	(2) TREND	(3) SEASONAL INDEX	(4) TREND X SEASONAL [COL. (2) × COL. (3)]	(5) CYCLICAL IRREGULAR PERCENTAGE [COL. (1) ÷ COL. (4) × 100]	(6) FIVE-MONTH MOVING TOTAL OF COL. (5)	(7) FIVE-MONTH MOVING MEAN OF COL. (5) [COL. (6) ÷ 5]
Mar.	40.9	45.7	0.972	44.4	92.1	463.4	92.7
Apr.	45.0	45.9	1.093	50.2	89.6	471.0	94.2
May	43.5	46.1	1.031	47.5	91.6	473.4	94.7
June	47.2	46.3	0.996	46.1	102.4	476.3	95.3
July	42.1	46.5	0.928	43.1	97.7	481.2	96.2
Aug.	43.8	46.6	0.989	46.1	95.0	484.3	96.9
Sept.	44.7	46.8	1.011	47.3	94.5	480.9	96.2
Oct.	46.3	47.0	1.040	48.9	94.7	482.2	96.4
Nov.	50.9	47.2	1.089	51.4	99.0	478.2	95.6
Dec.	50.3	47.4	1.072	50.8	99.0	485.5	97.1
Jan. 1975	36.5	47.6	0.842	40.1	91.0	486.1	97.3
Feb.	45.7	47.8	0.939	44.9	101.8	484.6	96.9
Mar.	44.5	48.0	0.972	46.7	95.3	487.8	97.6
Apr.	51.4	48.2	1.093	52.7	97.5	500.1	100.0
May	51.0	48.4	1.031	49.9	102.2	499.8	100.0
June	49.9	48.5	0.996	48.3	103.3	510.9	102.2
July	45.9	48.7	0.928	45.2	101.5	520.5	104.1
Aug.	51.5	48.9	0.989	48.4	106.4	523.0	104.6
Sept.	53.1	49.1	1.011	49.6	107.1	521.9	104.4
Oct.	53.7	49.3	1.040	51.3	104.7	521.7	104.3
Nov.	55.1	49.5	1.089	53.9	102.2	514.8	103.0
Dec.	53.9	49.7	1.072	53.2	101.3	507.2	101.6
Jan. 1976	41.8	49.9	0.842	42.0	99.5	501.8	100.4
Feb.	47.8	50.1	0.939	47.0	101.7	493.2	98.6
Mar.	48.8	50.3	0.972	48.9	99.8	487.1	97.4
Apr.	50.1	50.4	1.093	55.1	90.9	848.4	96.9
May	49.7	50.6	1.031	52.2	95.2	483.7	96.7
June	49.2	50.8	0.996	50.6	97.2	489.4	97.9
July	47.6	51.0	0.928	47.3	100.6	506.0	101.2
Aug.	53.4	51.2	0.989	50.6	105.5	517.9	103.6
Sept.	55.9	51.4	1.011	52.0	107.5	526.2	105.2
Oct.	57.5	51.6	1.040	53.7	107.1	533.5	106.7
Nov.	59.6	51.9	1.089	56.5	105.5		
Dec.	60.1	52.0	1.072	55.7	107.9		

TABLE 18-3. Indexes of Real Value Added by Manufacture and Number of Manufacturing Production Workers Employed, Milwaukee Metropolitan Area, 1951—1975.

	INDEXES (1951=100)			INDEXES (1951=100)	
YEAR	REAL VALUE ADDED BY MANUFACTURE	PRODUCTION WORKERS EMPLOYED	YEAR	REAL VALUE ADDED BY MANUFACTURE	PRODUCTION WORKERS EMPLOYED
1951	100	100	1963	115	83
1952	107	99	1964	121	84
1953	96	98	1965	129	87
1954	86	87	1966	139	90
1955	93	90	1967	140	90
1956	105	94	1968	141	88
1957	101	92	1969	146	88
1958	91	81	1970	144	84
1959	103	87	1971	140	78
1960	106	87	1972	148	81
1961	100	80	1973	156	89
1962	112	78	1974	149	90
			1975	135	81

Source: Metropolitan Milwaukee Association of Commerce.

TABLE 18-4. Percentages of Trend of Indexes of Real Value Added by Manufacture and Number of Manufacturing Production Workers Employed, Milwaukee Metropolitan Area, 1951—1975.

	PERCENT OF TREND			PERCENT OF TREND	
YEAR	REAL VALUE ADDED BY MANUFACTURE	PRODUCTION WORKERS EMPLOYED	YEAR	REAL VALUE ADDED BY MANUFACTURE	PRODUCTION WORKERS EMPLOYED
1951	114	108	1963	96	95
1952	118	107	1964	99	97
1953	103	107	1965	103	101
1954	90	95	1966	108	105
1955	95	99	1967	107	105
1956	104	104	1968	106	103
1957	97	102	1969	107	104
1958	85	90	1970	104	100
1959	94	98	1971	99	93
1960	95	98	1972	102	97
1961	87	91	1973	106	107
1962	95	88	1974	99	109
			1975	88	99

Source: Computed from data in Table 16-3.

Chart 18-5. Scatter diagram of indexes of real value added by manufacture and manufacturing production workers, Milwaukee metropolitan area, 1951—1975.

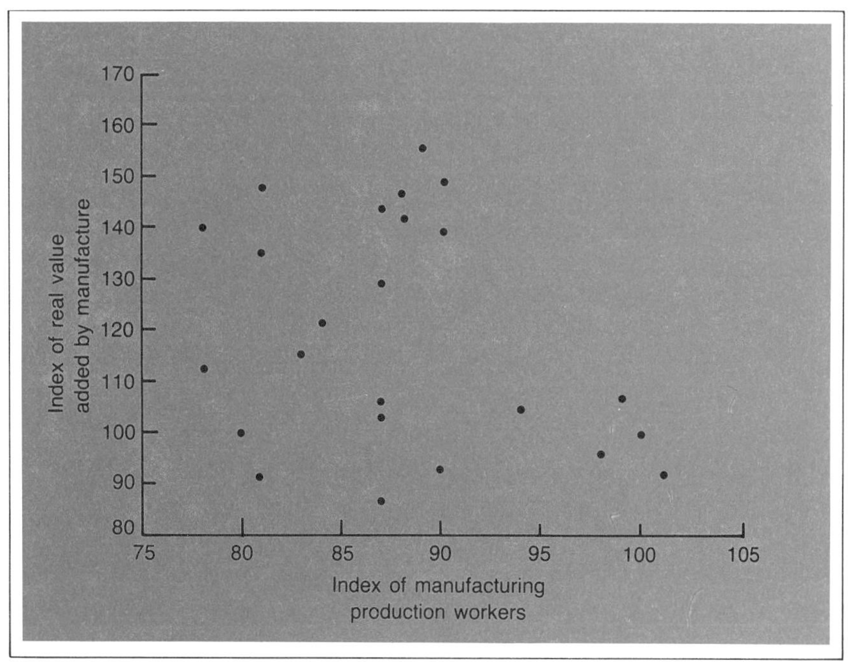

The trends of the two series were computed and removed by dividing the trend values into the original values. The resulting percentages (see Table 18-4) are shown in Chart 18-7 as a scatter diagram and in Chart 18-8 as a line chart. Both charts reveal a reasonably close relationship between the percentages, which are a measure of the combined cyclical and irregular fluctuation ($C \times I$). Since no large irregular fluctuations are identifiable, they can be considered to be primarily cyclical.

To determine the degree of the closeness of the relationship of these cycles, a coefficient of correlation, based on a linear relationship, was computed and found to be +0.753. This coefficient is reasonably high, suggesting that estimates of the cyclical values for one series could be based on given cyclical values of the other.

The preceding illustration used annual data. If monthly or quarterly data are to be correlated, we may desire to remove both trend and seasonal influences from the two series before analyzing them. Also, it is possible, and sometimes important, to remove the effect of the irregular fluctuations with a moving average before correlating the percentages of trend.

Chart 18-6. Indexes of real value added by manufacture and number of manufacturing production workers employed, Milwaukee metropolitan area, 1951—1975.

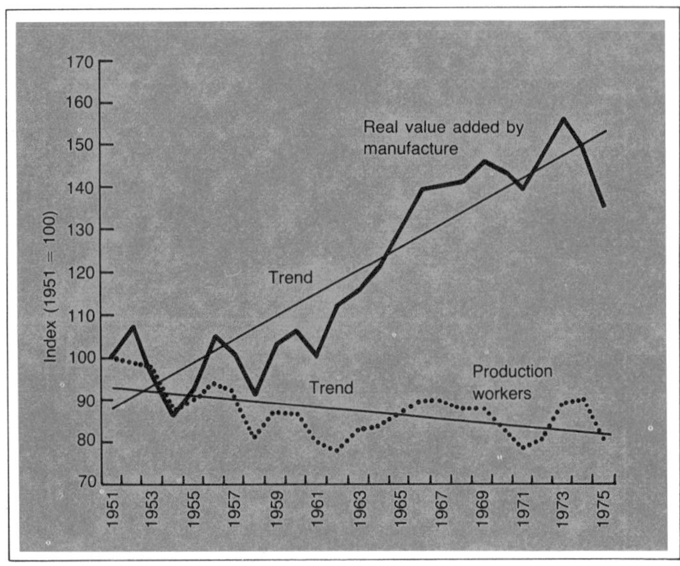

Source of data: Table 18-3.

Chart 18-7. Scatter diagram of the percentages of the trends of indexes of real value added by manufacture and manufacturing production workers, Milwaukee metropolitan area, 1951—1975.

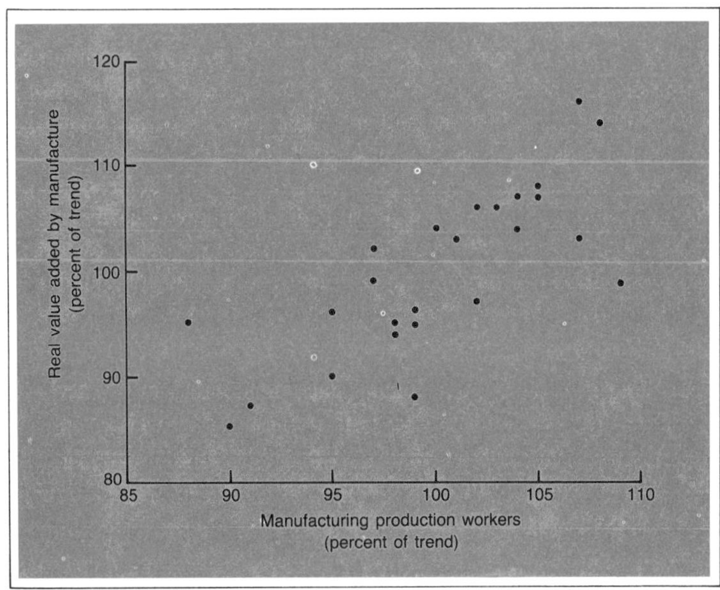

Chart 18-8. Percentages of trends of indexes of real value added by manufacture and number of manufacturing production workers employed, Milwaukee metropolitan area, 1951—1975.

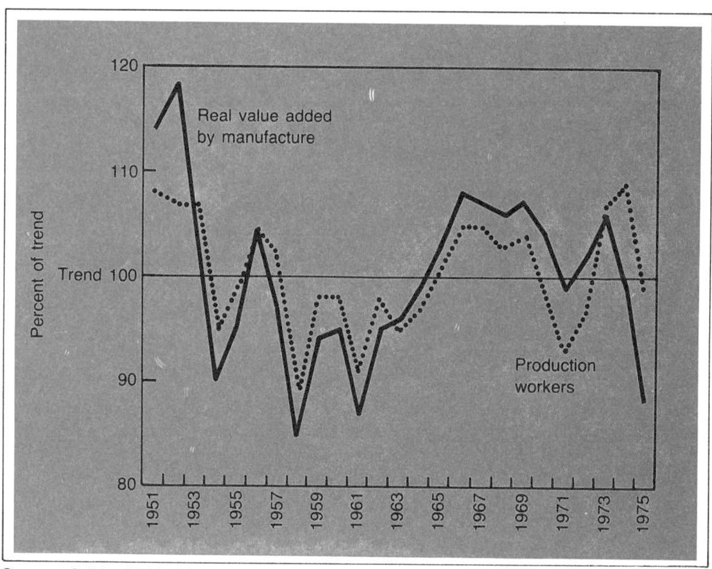

Source of data: Table 18-4.

REVIEW QUESTIONS

1. What is the purpose of measuring cycles of a time series?

2. Why are turning points of business cycles difficult to predict?

3. How are lag-lead relationships used?

4. Why is it difficult to measure, by direct methods, the typical business cycle?

5. How are cycles isolated from the other components of a time series?

PROBLEMS

1. Plot the two indexes in Exercise Table 18-1 on the same arithmetic scale to determine if the changes in the United States dwelling unit permit are closely correlated with the changes in dwelling unit permits in the Milwaukee metropolitan area. What further analysis of these data might be necessary to determine if the United States and Milwaukee data are closely correlated?

EXERCISE TABLE 18-1. Indexes of New Dwelling Unit Permits in the United States and the Milwaukee Metropolitan Area, 1962—1974.

	INDEX (1962=100)	
YEAR	*UNITED STATES*	*MILWAUKEE*
1962	100	100
1963	112	133
1964	108	145
1965	104	151
1966	82	112
1967	96	144
1968	114	133
1969	112	103
1970	114	106
1971	162	161
1972	187	165
1973	153	150
1974	90	88

Source: Computed from data from the U.S. Department of Commerce and the Metropolitan Milwaukee Association of Commerce.

2. Using the calculations from Problem 16-1, measure the cyclical-irregular fluctions in the annual retail sales in the United States for the 1969-1975 period. Construct a line chart showing these fluctuations.

3. With the values you determined in Problems 17-1 and 17-2, compute the trend times seasonal values of retail sales for each month in the United States. Divide the trend times seasonal values out of the original monthly retail sales figures given in Exercise Table 16-1. Compute a five-month moving mean of the resulting quotients (cyclical irregular percentages). Chart these moving averages, which are a measure of the cyclical irregular fluctuations in retail sales.

4. Chart the two time series in Exercise Table 18-2 to get a picture of the association between their values. Make the unemployment rate the dependent variable and determine the degree of correlation between them by computing

$$r = \frac{N\Sigma XY - (\Sigma X)(\Sigma Y)}{\left[N\Sigma X^2 - (\Sigma X)^2\right]\left[N\Sigma Y^2 - (\Sigma Y)^2\right]}$$

Calculate a least squares straight line trend for each time series and remove the trends from the original data by division. Chart the resulting percent of trend values to show the relationship between the two series. Use the formula above to measure the degree of closeness of the changes in the percent of trend values, and compare this coefficient to the one computed for the unadjusted data. Explain why the two coefficients differ.

EXERCISE TABLE 18-2. Expenditures for New Plant and Equipment and the Rate of Unemployment, United States, 1952—1975.

YEAR	*NEW PLANT AND EQUIP. EXP. (BILLIONS)*	*UNEMPLOYMENT RATE* (PERCENT)*	*YEAR*	*NEW PLANT AND EQUIP. EXP. (BILLIONS)*	*UNEMPLOYMENT RATE* (PERCENT)*
1952	$26.4	2.4	1963	$40.8	4.5
1953	28.2	2.5	1964	47.0	3.9
1954	27.2	4.9	1965	54.4	3.2
1955	29.5	3.8	1966	63.5	2.5
1956	35.7	3.4	1967	65.5	2.3
1957	37.9	3.6	1968	67.8	2.2
1958	31.9	6.2	1969	75.6	2.1
1959	33.0	4.7	1970	79.7	3.5
1960	36.8	4.7	1971	81.2	4.4
1961	35.9	5.7	1972	88.4	4.0
1962	38.4	4.6	1973	99.7	3.2
			1974	112.4	3.8

*For men.

Source: U.S. Department of Commerce, *Business Statistics*, 1975.

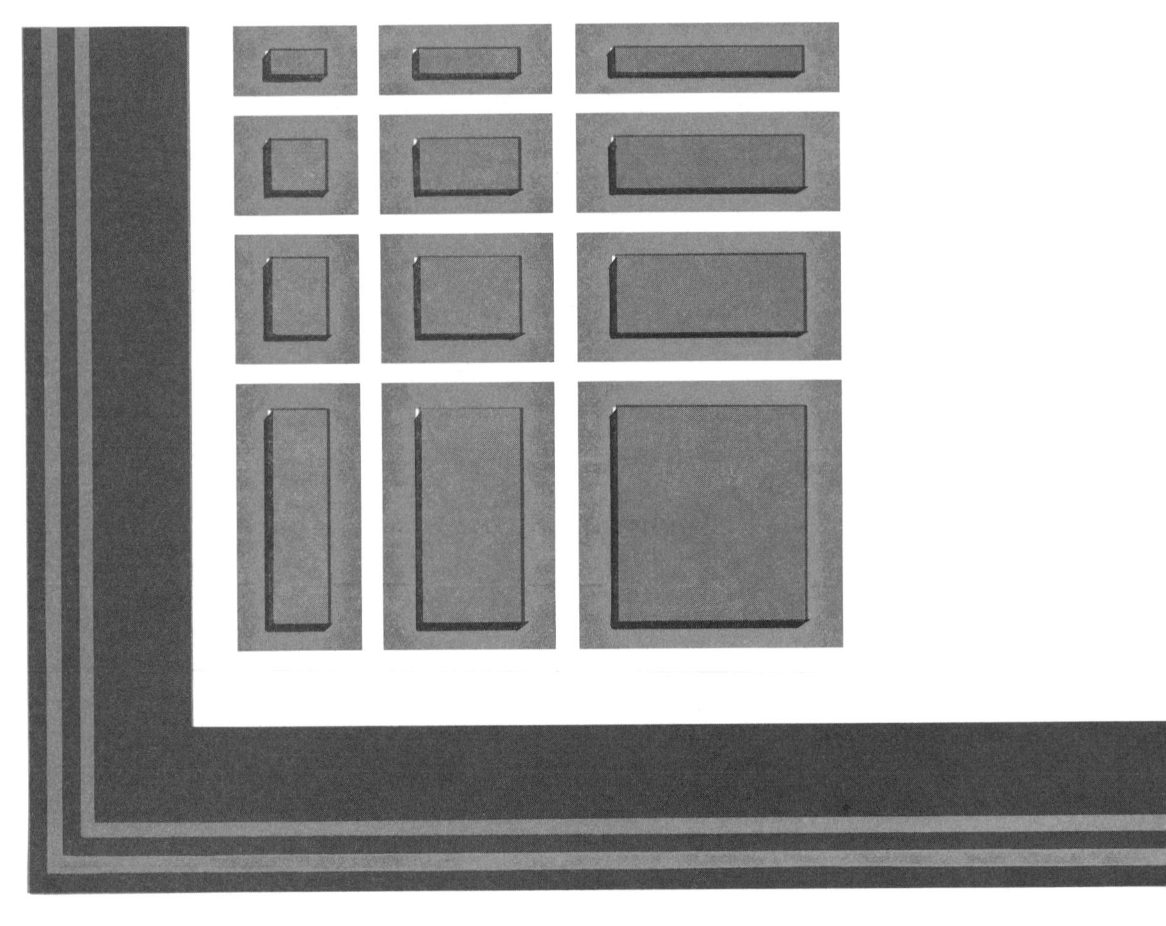

Appendices

APPENDIX A: ROUNDING NUMBERS

When a number is rounded, whether or not the last digit carried is raised or lowered one unit depends on the magnitude of the digits to be eliminated and the "even digits" rule. For example, in a census of population the actual populations counts for four cities given below would be rounded to the nearest thousands as shown.

	ACTUAL FIGURE	ROUNDED TO NEAREST THOUSAND
A	31,499	31,000
B	36,501	37,000
C	22,500	22,000
D	37,500	38,000

It is obvious why A and B were given their respective rounded values. It will be noted, however, that the actual population of city C is as near to 23,000 as 22,000, yet it was rounded *down* to 22,000. Similarly, the population of city D is as near 37,000 as 38,000 yet it was rounded *up* to the latter figure. The rounding of C and D made use of the "even digits" rule, which is used by analysts when the value of the digits to be changed by rounding is exactly one half of the unit of measurement of the last digit retained. This rule permits no change in the value of the last digit to be carried if it is even and requires the raising of the value of the last digit to be carried if it is odd. Therefore, the last digit in a number rounded by the "even digits" rule will always be even. Another example: 27.65 and 27.75 rounded to one decimal place are 27.6 and 27.8, respectively.

Significant Digits

When statistical measures are computed, they are usually rounded to the accuracy desired by the analyst or to the accuracy required by the nature of the data. In either case the results of multiplication and division should have no more significant digits than the number with the fewest significant digits that is used in the calculation.

Dividing. A *significant digit* is one that gives the precise magnitude of the measurement at its place of location. If there are exactly 12,132 students in XY University, then each digit in the number is significant. However, if we round the figure to the nearest thousand, we would say that there are 12,000 students. In this rounded number, there are only two significant digits. The three zeros tell us only that the "12" in the number is measured in thousands rather than some other unit. Now, if we want to compute the number of students per fulltime faculty with the rounded number and there were exactly 488 faculty members the calculation is

$$\frac{12,000}{488} = 24.59016$$

However, the figure should be rounded to 25, two significant digits, because there are only two in the dividend.

Another example: A person who gets 18 miles per gallon of gasoline wants to know how many gallons will be needed to travel 1190 miles. To determine this he divides 18 into 1190 and gets 66.11 gallons. However, this should be rounded to 66 gallons, a two-significant-digit number, because the divisor, 18, has only two significant digits. The reasoning is based on the fact that 18 probably is a number that has been rounded to the nearest whole gallon, so that the actual miles per gallon might be as low as 17.5 or as high as 18.5. Using each of these numbers for the calculation we get:

$$\frac{1190}{17.5} = 68.00$$

$$\frac{1190}{18.5} = 64.32$$

which means the actual number of gallons required will be somewhere between 64.32 and 68.00 gallons. The figure 66.11 gallons computed above indicates a spurious degree of accuracy.

Multiplying. The principle illustrated with division applies also to multiplication. Suppose a manufacturer sold 581 items at an average price of $65. Assuming that the 65 is rounded to the nearest dollar, the total sales volume would be 65 × 581 = $37,765, but the result must be rounded to two significant digits, $38,000, to show its (lack of) accuracy.

Adding and subtracting. Sums and differences should be carried to no more decimal places than the least accurate of the figures used in the calculations. For example, suppose the weights in pounds of three items are reported as 103.15, 160.2, and 188. Assuming that each weight was rounded—the first to the nearest hundredth, the second to the nearest tenth, and the third to the nearest whole pound—the total of these three, which is 451.35 pounds, should be reported as only 451 pounds because 188 is the least precise weight and is expressed in whole pounds.

Exact integers. Numbers that are discrete and exact, such as the number of people in an office or the number of tomatoes in a box, are considered to have an infinite number of significant digits. For example, if 12 people divide $14,952 equally among themselves, each get

$$\frac{14,952}{12} = \$1246$$

It would be incorrect to say \$1200 per person.

If 6 items cost \$15.50 each, the total cost is $6 \times 15.50 = 93.00$. It would be incorrect to give \$90.00 as the answer.

APPENDIX B: THE BINOMIAL EXPANSION

The general formula for expanding a binomial distribution is:

$$(P + q)^n = p^n + np^{n-1}q + \frac{n(n-1)}{1 \times 2}p^{n-2}q^2 + \cdots + q^n$$

This formula shows:

1) In the first term, the exponent of p is n and that of q is zero.
2) In each of the other terms, the exponent of p is 1 less than in the preceding term.
3) In each of the terms, the exponent of q is 1 more than in the preceding term.
4) The first term has a coefficient of 1.
5) The coefficient of the second term is n.
6) The coefficient of each term is equal to the exponent of p for the preceding term times the coefficient of the preceding term divided by the number of the preceding term.
7) The expanded binomial has $n + 1$ terms. As an example, the expansion of $(p + q)^4$ is

$$p^4 + 4p^3q + \frac{4\,(4-1)}{1 \times 2}p^2q^2 + \frac{4\,(3)\,(2)}{1 \times 2 \times 3}pq^3 + q^4 = p^4 + 4p^3q + 6p^2q^2 + 4pq^3 + q^4$$

APPENDIX C: REVIEW OF LOGARITHMS

The logarithm of a number to the base 10 is the power to which 10 must be raised to equal the number. Thus the logarithm of 1000 is 3 because $10^3 = 1000$, and the logarithm of 100 is 2 because $10^2 = 100$. This being true, the logarithm of a number between 100 and 1000 is between 2 and 3 or 2 plus a decimal. For example the logarithm of 500 is 2 + 0.6990 or 2.6990 (Thus, $500 = 10^{2.6990}$). The decimal part of the logarithm, called the *mantissa* was read from Table A-1 (see Appendix E). The 2 in the logarithm is called the *characteristic*.

The logarithm of 0.01 is −2 because

$$0.01 = \frac{1}{100} = \frac{1}{10^2} = 10^{-2}$$

The logarithm of 0.001 = −3 because

$$0.001 = \frac{1}{1000} = \frac{1}{10^3} = 10^{-3}$$

The log of a number between 0.01 and 0.001 is between −2 and −3 or is equal to −3 plus a decimal. To illustrate: the log of 0.005 is equal to −3 + 0.6990 which may be conveniently written as 7.6990 − 10. The characteristic of this log is −3 and the mantissa is +0.6990.

Determining Characteristics

Mantissas are always read from a table, but characteristics are determined by observation of the numbers. The characteristic of the logarithm of a number larger than 1 is one less in value than the number of digits to the left of the decimal point.

The characteristic of the logarithm of a number less than 1 is one more in value than the number of zeros between the decimal point and the first significant digit. The following list gives examples of characteristics determined by this rule.

NUMBER	*CHARACTERISTIC*	*MANTISSA*	*LOGARITHM*
377	2	.5763	2.5763
37.7	1	.5763	1.5763
3.77	0	.5763	.5763
.377	−1	.5763	9.5763 − 10
.0377	−2	.5763	8.5763 − 10
.00377	−3	.5763	7.5763 − 10

Finding Mantissas

The mantissa is the same for all of the numbers in the preceding example because the digits are the same in the same order. The mantissa of 377 was looked up in Table A-1 by going to the column labeled "*n*" and finding 37 and moving across to column 7. At this location the mantissa, .5763, was found.

Determining n, the Antilog

To determine a number from its logarithm, the mantissa is looked up in the body of the table, the digits are copied, and the decimal place is located by noting the characteristic. Thus, to find n = antilog 1.8802, the mantissa, .8802 is found in the body of the table where the digits for n are 759; a decimal point is placed between the 5 and 9 because the characteristic of the logarithm is 1. Therefore, n is 75.9.

Calculating with Logarithms

Sometimes calculations can be made easier by using logarithms. The following laws apply:

1) The logarithm of the product of two or more numbers is equal to the sum of the logarithms of the numbers.
2) The logarithm of a common fraction is equal to the logarithm of the numerator minus the logarithm of the denominator.
3) The logarithm of a number raised to a power is equal to the product of the exponent and the logarithm of the number.

The following exemplifies the use of these laws:

Multiplying:

$$
\begin{aligned}
n &= 2.7 \times 16 \times 10.3 \\
\log n &= \log (2.7 \times 16 \times 10.3) \\
&= \log 2.7 + \log 16 + \log 10.3 \\
&= 0.4314 + 1.2041 + 1.0128 \\
&= 2.6483 \\
\text{so that} \quad n &= 445 \text{ (reading the closest mantissa, .6483)}
\end{aligned}
$$

Dividing:

$$
\begin{aligned}
n &= 72.6 \div 3 \\
\log n &= \log 72.6 - \log 3 \\
&= 1.8609 - 0.4771 \\
&= 1.3838 \\
\text{so that} \quad n &= 24.2 \text{ (reading the closest mantissa, .3838)}
\end{aligned}
$$

Raising a number to a power:

$$
\begin{aligned}
n &= (1.5)^3 \\
\log n &= \log (1.5)^3 = 3 \log 1.5 \\
&= 3 \times 0.1761 \\
&= 0.5283 \\
\text{so that} \quad n &= 3.38 \text{ (reading the closest mantissa, .5283)}
\end{aligned}
$$

Extracting roots: (using the law relating to powers)

$$n = \sqrt[3]{3.38}$$

$$\log n = \log \sqrt[3]{3.38} = \log (3.38)^{1/3}$$

$$= \frac{1}{3}\log 3.38$$

$$= \frac{\log 3.38}{3}$$

$$= \frac{0.5289}{3} = 0.1763$$

so that $n = 1.50$ (reading from the closest mantissa, .1763)

APPENDIX D: USING A SQUARE ROOT TABLE

Table A-6 gives squares and square roots of the numbers 1 through 99. The square root of 10 times each of these numbers is also shown.

This table can be used to get the square and square root of any number with one or two significant digits by properly shifting the decimal places in the printed values. For example, the square of 13, shown in the n^2 column is 169. Therefore, the square of 1.3 would be 1.69 and the square of 0.13 would be 0.0169. The square root of 13 is 3.605551 and the square root of 130 is 11.40175. Therefore the square roots of 0.13 and 1.3 would be 0.360551 and 1.140175, respectively. Interpolations can be made into this table to get close estimates of the square roots of numbers with three significant digits. The difference between 130 and 135 is one half the difference between 130 and 140; therefore the interpolated square root of 135 is

$$\sqrt{130} + ½(\sqrt{140} - \sqrt{130}) = 11.40175 + ½(11.83210 - 11.40175)$$

$$= 11.40175 + \frac{0.43035}{2}$$

$$= 11.616925$$

APPENDIX E: STATISTICAL TABLES

TABLE A-1. Four-Place Logarithms.

n	*0*	*1*	*2*	*3*	*4*	*5*	*6*	*7*	*8*	*9*
10	0000	0043	0086	0128	0170	0212	0253	0294	0334	0374
11	0414	0453	0492	0531	0569	0607	0645	0682	0719	0755
12	0792	0828	0864	0899	0934	0969	1004	1038	1072	1106
13	1139	1173	1206	1239	1271	1303	1335	1367	1399	1430
14	1461	1492	1523	1553	1584	1614	1644	1673	1703	1732
15	1761	1790	1818	1847	1875	1903	1931	1959	1987	2014
16	2041	2068	2095	2122	2148	2175	2201	2227	2253	2279
17	2304	2330	2355	2380	2405	2430	2455	2480	2504	2529
18	2553	2577	2601	2625	2648	2672	2695	2718	2742	2765
19	2788	2810	2833	2856	2878	2900	2923	2945	2967	2989
20	3010	3032	3054	3075	3096	3118	3139	3160	3181	3201
21	3222	3243	3263	3284	3304	3324	3345	3365	3385	3404
22	3424	3444	3464	3483	3502	3522	3541	3560	3579	3598
23	3617	3636	3655	3674	3692	3711	3729	3747	3766	3784
24	3802	3820	3838	3856	3874	3892	3909	3927	3945	3962
25	3979	3997	4014	4031	4048	4065	4082	4099	4116	4133
26	4150	4166	4183	4200	4216	4232	4249	4265	4281	4298
27	4314	4330	4346	4362	4378	4393	4409	4425	4440	4456
28	4472	4487	4502	4518	4533	4548	4564	4579	4594	4609
29	4624	4639	4654	4669	4683	4698	4713	4728	4742	4757
30	4771	4786	4800	4814	4829	4843	4857	4871	4886	4900
31	4914	4928	4942	4955	4969	4983	4997	5011	5024	5038
32	5051	5065	5079	5092	5105	5119	5132	5145	5159	5172
33	5185	5198	5211	5224	5237	5250	5263	5276	5289	5302
34	5315	5328	5340	5353	5366	5378	5391	5403	5416	5428
35	5441	5453	5465	5478	5490	5502	5514	5527	5539	5551
36	5563	5575	5587	5599	5611	5623	5635	5647	5658	5670
37	5682	5694	5705	5717	5729	5740	5752	5763	5775	5786
38	5798	5809	5821	5832	5843	5855	5866	5877	5888	5899
39	5911	5922	5933	5944	5955	5966	5977	5988	5999	6010
40	6021	6031	6042	6053	6064	6075	6085	6096	6107	6117
41	6128	6138	6149	6160	6170	6180	6191	6201	6212	6222
42	6232	6243	6253	6263	6274	6284	6294	6304	6314	6325
43	6336	6345	6355	6365	6375	6385	6395	6405	6415	6425
44	6435	6444	6454	6464	6474	6484	6493	6503	6513	6522
45	6532	6542	6551	6561	6571	6580	6590	6599	6609	6618
46	6628	6637	6646	6656	6665	6675	6684	6693	6702	6712

TABLE A-1. Four-Place Logarithms. (Continued)

n	*0*	*1*	*2*	*3*	*4*	*5*	*6*	*7*	*8*	*9*
47	6721	6730	6739	6749	6758	6767	6776	6785	6794	6803
48	6812	6821	6830	6839	6848	6857	6866	6875	6884	6893
49	6902	6911	6920	6928	6937	6946	6955	6964	6972	6981
50	6990	6998	7007	7016	7024	7033	7042	7050	7059	7067
51	7076	7084	7093	7101	7110	7118	7126	7135	7143	7152
52	7160	7168	7177	7185	7193	7202	7210	7218	7226	7235
53	7243	7251	7259	7267	7275	7284	7292	7300	7308	7316
54	7324	7332	7340	7348	7356	7364	7372	7380	7388	7396
55	7404	7412	7419	7427	7435	7443	7451	7459	7466	7474
56	7482	7490	7497	7505	7513	7520	7528	7536	7543	7551
57	7559	7566	7574	7582	7589	7597	7604	7612	7619	7627
58	7634	7642	7649	7657	7664	7672	7679	7686	7694	7701
59	7709	7716	7723	7731	7738	7745	7752	7760	7767	7774
60	7782	7789	7796	7803	7810	7818	7825	7832	7839	7846
61	7853	7860	7868	7875	7882	7889	7896	7903	7910	7917
62	7924	7931	7938	7945	7952	7959	7966	7973	7980	7987
63	7993	8000	8007	8014	8021	8028	8035	8041	8048	8055
64	8062	8069	8075	8082	8089	8096	8102	8109	8116	8122
65	8129	8136	8142	8149	8156	8162	8169	8176	8182	8189
66	8195	8202	8209	8215	8222	8228	8235	8241	8248	8254
67	8261	8267	8274	8280	8287	8293	8299	8306	8312	8319
68	8325	8331	8338	8344	8351	8357	8363	8370	8376	8382
69	8388	8395	8401	8407	8414	8420	8426	8432	8439	8445
70	8451	8457	8463	8470	8476	8482	8488	8494	8500	8506
71	8513	8519	8525	8531	8537	8543	8549	8555	8561	8567
72	8573	8579	8585	8591	8597	8603	8609	8615	8621	8627
73	8633	8639	8645	8651	8657	8663	8669	8675	8681	8686
74	8692	8698	8704	8710	8716	8722	8727	8733	8739	8745
75	8751	8756	8762	8768	8774	8779	8785	8791	8797	8802
76	8808	8814	8820	8825	8831	8837	8842	8848	8854	8859
77	8865	8871	8876	8882	8887	8893	8899	8904	8910	8915
78	8921	8927	8932	8938	8943	8949	8954	8960	8965	8971
79	8976	8982	8987	8993	8998	9004	9009	9015	9020	9025
80	9031	9036	9042	9047	9053	9058	9063	9069	9074	9079
81	9085	9090	9096	9101	9106	9112	9117	9122	9128	9133
82	9138	9143	9149	9154	9159	9165	9170	9175	9180	9186
83	9191	9196	9201	9206	9212	9217	9222	9227	9232	9238
84	9243	9248	9253	9258	9263	9269	9274	9279	9284	9289
85	9294	9299	9304	9309	9315	9320	9325	9330	9335	9340
86	9345	9350	9355	9360	9365	9370	9375	9380	9385	9390
87	9395	9400	9405	9410	9415	9420	9425	9430	9435	9440
88	9445	9450	9455	9460	9465	9469	9474	9479	9484	9489
89	9494	9499	9504	9509	9513	9518	9523	9528	9533	9538

TABLE A-1. Four-Place Logarithms. (Continued)

n	*0*	*1*	*2*	*3*	*4*	*5*	*6*	*7*	*8*	*9*
90	9542	9547	9552	9557	9562	9566	9571	9576	9581	9586
91	9590	9595	9600	9605	9609	9614	9619	9624	9628	9633
92	9638	9643	9647	9652	9657	9661	9666	9671	9675	9680
93	9685	9689	9694	9699	9703	9708	9713	9717	9722	9727
94	9731	9736	9741	9745	9750	9754	9759	9763	9768	9773
95	9777	9782	9786	9791	9795	9800	9805	9809	9814	9818
96	9823	9827	9832	9836	9841	9845	9850	9854	9859	9863
97	9868	9872	9877	9881	9886	9890	9894	9899	9903	9908
98	9912	9917	9921	9926	9930	9934	9939	9943	9948	9952
99	9956	9961	9965	9969	9974	9978	9983	9987	9991	9996

Source: Reprinted with permission from Leabo, *Basic Statistics for Business and Economics*. Third Ed. Homewood, Ill.: Richard D. Irwin, 1968.

TABLE A-2. Ordinates of the Normal Distribution (Erected at Selected x/σ Distances from the Arithmetic Mean, Expressed as Decimal Fractions of the Ordinate at the Arithmetic Mean).

x/σ	*ORDINATE*	x/σ	*ORDINATE*
.0	1.00000	2.0	.13534
.1	.99501	2.1	.11025
.2	.98019	2.2	.08892
.3	.95601	2.3	.07100
.4	.92312	2.4	.05614
.5	.88250	2.5	.04394
.6	.83527	2.6	.03405
.7	.78270	2.7	.02612
.8	.72615	2.8	.01984
.9	.66698	2.9	.01492
1.0	.60653	3.0	.01111
1.1	.54607	3.1	.00820
1.2	.48675	3.2	.00597
1.3	.42956	3.3	.00431
1.4	.37531	3.4	.00308
1.5	.32465	3.5	.00218
1.6	.27804	3.6	.00153
1.7	.23575	3.7	.00106
1.8	.19790	3.8	.00073
1.9	.16448	3.9	.00050
		4.0	.00035

TABLE A-3. Table of Areas for Standard Normal Probability Distribution.

x/σ	.00	.01	.02	.03	.04	.05	.06	.07	.08	.09
0.0	.0000	.0040	.0080	.0120	.0160	.0199	.0239	.0279	.0319	.0359
0.1	.0398	.0438	.0478	.0517	.0557	.0596	.0636	.0675	.0714	.0753
0.2	.0793	.0832	.0871	.0910	.0948	.0987	.1026	.1064	.1103	.1141
0.3	.1179	.1217	.1255	.1293	.1331	.1368	.1406	.1443	.1480	.1517
0.4	.1554	.1591	.1628	.1664	.1700	.1736	.1772	.1808	.1844	.1879
0.5	.1915	.1950	.1985	.2019	.2054	.2088	.2123	.2157	.2190	.2224
0.6	.2257	.2291	.2324	.2357	.2389	.2422	.2454	.2486	.2518	.2549
0.7	.2580	.2612	.2642	.2673	.2704	.2734	.2764	.2794	.2823	.2852
0.8	.2881	.2910	.2939	.2967	.2995	.3023	.3051	.3078	.3106	.3133
0.9	.3159	.3186	.3212	.3238	.3264	.3289	.3315	.3340	.3365	.3389
1.0	.3413	.3438	.3461	.3485	.3508	.3531	.3554	.3577	.3599	.3621
1.1	.3643	.3665	.3686	.3708	.3729	.3749	.3770	.3790	.3810	.3830
1.2	.3849	.3869	.3888	.3907	.3925	.3944	.3962	.3980	.3997	.4014
1.3	.4032	.4049	.4066	.4082	.4099	.4115	.4131	.4147	.4162	.4177
1.4	.4192	.4207	.4222	.4236	.4251	.4265	.4279	.4292	.4306	.4319
1.5	.4332	.4345	.4357	.4370	.4382	.4394	.4406	.4418	.4429	.4441
1.6	.4452	.4463	.4474	.4484	.4495	.4505	.4515	.4525	.4535	.4545
1.7	.4554	.4564	.4573	.4582	.4591	.4599	.4608	.4616	.4625	.4633
1.8	.4641	.4649	.4656	.4664	.4671	.4678	.4686	.4693	.4699	.4706
1.9	.4713	.4719	.4726	.4732	.4738	.4744	.4750	.4756	.4761	.4767
2.0	.4772	.4778	.4783	.4788	.4793	.4798	.4803	.4808	.4812	.4817
2.1	.4821	.4826	.4830	.4834	.4838	.4842	.4846	.4850	.4854	.4857
2.2	.4861	.4864	.4868	.4871	.4875	.4878	.4881	.4884	.4887	.4890
2.3	.4893	.4896	.4898	.4901	.4904	.4906	.4909	.4911	.4913	.4916
2.4	.4918	.4920	.4922	.4925	.4927	.4929	.4931	.4932	.4934	.4936
2.5	.4938	.4940	.4941	.4943	.4945	.4946	.4948	.4949	.4951	.4952
2.6	.4953	.4955	.4956	.4957	.4959	.4960	.4961	.4962	.4963	.4964
2.7	.4965	.4966	.4967	.4968	.4969	.4970	.4971	.4972	.4973	.4974
2.8	.4974	.4975	.4976	.4977	.4977	.4978	.4979	.4979	.4980	.4981
2.9	.4981	.4982	.4982	.4983	.4984	.4984	.4985	.4985	.4986	.4986
3.0	.49865	.4987	.4987	.4988	.4988	.4989	.4989	.4989	.4990	.4990
3.5	.49977									
4.0	.4999683									

Source: This table is from Neter and Wasserman, *Fundamental Statistics for Business and Economics*. It is used by permission of Allyn and Bacon.

TABLE A-4. Distribution of t.

DEGREES OF FREEDOM	PROBABILITY .50	.30	.20	.10	.05	.02	.01
1	1.000	1.963	3.078	6.314	12.706	31.821	63.657
2	.816	1.386	1.886	2.920	4.303	6.965	9.925
3	.765	1.250	1.638	2.353	3.182	4.541	5.841
4	.741	1.190	1.533	2.132	2.776	3.747	4.604
5	.727	1.156	1.476	2.015	2.571	3.365	4.032
6	.718	1.134	1.440	1.943	2.447	3.143	3.707
7	.711	1.119	1.415	1.895	2.365	2.998	3.499
8	.706	1.108	1.397	1.860	2.306	2.896	3.355
9	.703	1.100	1.383	1.833	2.262	2.821	3.250
10	.700	1.093	1.372	1.812	2.228	2.764	3.169
11	.697	1.088	1.363	1.796	2.201	2.718	3.106
12	.695	1.083	1.356	1.782	2.179	2.681	3.055
13	.694	1.079	1.350	1.771	2.160	2.650	3.012
14	.692	1.076	1.345	1.761	2.145	2.624	2.977
15	.691	1.074	1.341	1.753	2.131	2.602	2.947
16	.690	1.071	1.337	1.746	2.120	2.583	2.921
17	.689	1.069	1.333	1.740	2.110	2.567	2.898
18	.688	1.067	1.330	1.734	2.101	2.552	2.878
19	.688	1.066	1.328	1.729	2.093	2.539	2.861
20	.687	1.064	1.325	1.725	2.086	2.528	2.845
21	.686	1.063	1.323	1.721	2.080	2.518	2.831
22	.686	1.061	1.321	1.717	2.074	2.508	2.819
23	.685	1.060	1.319	1.714	2.069	2.500	2.807
24	.685	1.059	1.318	1.711	2.064	2.492	2.797
25	.684	1.058	1.316	1.708	2.060	2.485	2.787
26	.684	1.058	1.315	1.706	2.056	2.479	2.779
27	.684	1.057	1.314	1.703	2.052	2.473	2.771
28	.683	1.056	1.313	1.701	2.048	2.467	2.763
29	.683	1.055	1.311	1.699	2.045	2.462	2.751
30	.683	1.055	1.310	1.697	2.042	2.457	2.750
40	.681	1.050	1.303	1.684	2.021	2.423	2.704
60	.679	1.046	1.296	1.671	2.000	2.390	2.660
130	.677	1.041	1.289	1.658	1.980	2.358	2.617
∞	.674	1.036	1.282	1.645	1.960	2.326	2.576

Source: Fisher and Yates, *Statistical Tables for Biological, Agricultural and Medical Research,* Edinburgh: Oliver and Boyd, by permission of the authors and publishers.

TABLE A-5. Distribution of χ^2.

DEGREES OF FREEDOM	PROBABILITY .50	.30	.20	.10	.05	.02	.01
1	.445	1.074	1.642	2.706	3.841	5.412	6.635
2	1.386	2.408	3.219	4.605	5.991	7.824	9.210
3	2.366	3.665	2.642	6.251	7.815	9.837	11.345
4	3.357	4.878	5.989	7.779	9.488	11.668	13.277
5	4.351	6.064	7.289	9.236	11.070	13.388	15.086
6	5.348	7.231	8.558	10.645	12.592	15.033	16.812
7	6.346	8.383	9.803	12.017	14.067	16.622	18.475
8	7.344	9.524	11.030	13.362	15.507	18.168	20.090
9	8.343	10.656	12.242	14.684	16.919	19.679	21.666
10	9.342	11.781	13.442	15.987	18.307	21.161	23.209
11	10.341	12.899	14.631	17.275	19.675	22.618	24.725
12	11.340	14.011	15.812	18.549	21.026	24.054	26.217
13	12.340	15.119	16.985	19.812	22.362	25.472	27.688
14	13.339	16.222	18.151	21.064	23.685	26.873	29.141
15	14.339	17.322	19.311	22.307	24.996	28.259	30.578
16	15.338	18.418	20.465	23.542	26.296	29.633	32.000
17	16.338	19.511	21.615	24.769	27.587	30.995	33.409
18	17.338	20.601	22.760	25.989	28.869	33.346	34.805
19	18.338	21.689	23.900	27.204	30.144	33.687	36.191
20	19.337	22.775	25.038	28.412	31.410	35.020	37.566
21	20.337	23.858	26.171	29.615	32.671	36.343	38.932
22	21.337	24.939	27.301	30.813	33.924	37.659	40.289
23	22.337	26.018	28.429	32.007	35.172	38.968	41.638
24	23.337	27.096	29.553	33.196	36.415	40.270	42.980
25	24.337	28.172	30.675	34.382	37.652	41.566	44.314
26	25.336	29.246	31.795	35.563	38.885	42.856	45.642
27	26.336	30.319	32.912	36.741	40.113	44.140	46.963
28	27.336	31.391	34.027	37.916	41.337	45.419	48.278
29	28.336	32.461	35.139	39.087	42.557	46.693	49.588
30	29.336	33.530	36.250	40.256	43.773	47.962	50.892

Source: Fisher and Yates, *Statistical Tables for Biological, Agricultural and Medical Research,* Edinburgh: Oliver and Boyd, by permission of the authors and publishers.

TABLE A-6. Squares and Square Roots.

n	n^2	$\sqrt{n}$	$\sqrt{10n}$	n	n^2	$\sqrt{n}$	$\sqrt{10n}$
1	1	1.000 000	3.162 278	50	2 500	2.071 068	22.36068
2	4	1.414 214	4.472 136	51	2 601	7.141 428	22.58318
3	9	1.732 051	5.477 226	52	2 704	7.211 103	22.80351
4	16	2.000 000	6.324 555	53	2 809	7.280 110	23.02173
5	25	2.236 068	7.071 068	54	2 916	7.348 469	23.23790
6	36	2.449 490	7.745 967	55	3 025	7.416 198	23.45208
7	49	2.645 751	8.366 600	56	3 136	7.483 315	23.66432
8	64	2.828 427	8.944 272	57	3 249	7.549 834	23.87467
9	81	3.000 000	9.486 833	58	3 364	7.615 773	24.08319
10	100	3.162 278	10.00000	59	3 481	7.681 146	24.28992
11	121	3.316 625	10.48809	60	3 600	7.745 967	24.49490
12	144	3.464 102	10.95445	61	3 721	7.810 250	24.69818
13	169	3.605 551	11.40175	62	3 844	7.874 008	24.89980
14	196	3.741 657	11.83216	63	3 969	7.937 254	25.09980
15	225	3.872 983	12.24745	64	4 096	8.000 000	25.29822
16	256	4.000 000	12.64911	65	4 225	8.062 258	25.49510
17	289	4.123 106	13.03840	66	4 356	8.124 038	25.69047
18	324	4.242 641	13.41641	67	4 489	8.185 353	25.88436
19	361	4.358 899	13.78405	68	4 624	8.246 211	26.07681
20	400	4.472 136	14.14214	69	4 761	8.306 024	26.26785
21	441	4.582 576	14.49138	70	4 900	8.366 600	26.45751
22	484	4.690 416	14.83240	71	5 041	8.426 150	26.64583
23	529	4.795 832	15.16575	72	5 184	8.485 281	26.83282
24	576	4.898 979	15.49193	73	5 329	8.544 004	27.01851
25	625	5.000 000	15.81139	74	5 476	8.602 325	27.20294
26	676	5.099 020	16.12452	75	5 625	8.660 254	27.38613
27	729	5.196 152	16.43168	76	5 776	8.717 798	27.56810
28	784	5.291 503	16.73320	77	5 929	8.774 964	27.74887
29	841	5.385 165	17.02939	78	6 084	8.831 761	27.92848
30	900	5.477 226	17.32051	79	6 241	8.888 194	28.10694
31	961	5.567 764	17.60682	80	6 400	8.944 272	28.28427
32	1 024	5.656 854	17.88854	81	6 561	9.000 000	28.46050
33	1 089	5.744 563	18.16590	82	6 724	9.055 385	28.63564
34	1 156	5.830 952	18.43909	83	6 889	9.110 434	28.80972
35	1 225	5.916 080	18.70829	84	7 056	9.165 151	28.98275
36	1 296	6.000 000	18.97367	85	7 225	9.219 544	29.15476
37	1 369	6.082 763	19.23538	86	7 396	9.273 618	29.32576
38	1 444	6.164 414	19.49359	87	7 569	9.327 379	29.49565
39	1 521	6.244 998	19.74842	88	7 744	9.380 832	29.66479
				89	7 921	9.433 981	29.83287

TABLE A-6. Squares and Square Roots. (Continued)

n	n^2	$\sqrt{n}$	$\sqrt{10n}$	n	n^2	$\sqrt{n}$	$\sqrt{10n}$
40	1 600	6.324 555	20.00000	90	8 100	9.486 833	30.00000
41	1 681	6.403 124	20.24846	91	8 281	9.539 392	30.16621
42	1 764	6.480 741	20.49390	92	8 464	9.591 663	30.33150
43	1 849	6.557 439	20.73644	93	8 649	9.643 651	30.49590
44	1 936	6.633 250	20.97618	94	8 836	9.695 360	30.65942
45	2 025	6.708 204	21.21320	95	9 025	9.746 794	30.82207
46	2 116	6.782 330	21.44761	96	9 216	9.797 959	20.98387
47	2 209	2.855 655	21.67948	97	9 409	9.848 858	31.14482
48	2 304	6.928 203	21.90890	98	9 604	9.899 495	31.30495
49	2 401	7.000 000	22.13594	99	9 801	9.949 874	31.46427

TABLE A-7. Table of Random Digits.

10097 32533	76520 13586	34673 54876	80959 09117	39292 74945
37542 04805	64894 74296	24805 24037	20636 10402	00822 91665
08422 68953	19645 09303	23209 02560	15953 34764	35080 33606
99019 02529	09376 70715	38311 31165	88676 74397	04436 27659
12807 99970	80157 36147	64032 36653	98951 16877	12171 76833
66065 74717	34072 76850	36697 36170	65813 39885	11199 29170
31060 10805	45571 82406	35303 42614	86799 07439	23403 09732
85269 77602	02051 65692	68665 74818	73053 85247	18623 88579
63573 32135	05325 47048	90553 57548	28468 28709	83491 25624
73796 45753	03529 64778	35808 34282	60935 20344	35273 88435
98520 17767	14905 68607	22109 40558	60970 93433	50500 73998
11805 05431	39808 27732	50725 68248	29405 24201	52775 67851
83452 99634	06288 98083	13746 70078	18475 40610	68711 77817
88685 40200	86507 58401	36766 67951	90364 76493	26909 11062
99594 67348	87517 64969	91826 08928	93785 61368	23478 34113
65481 17674	17468 50950	58047 76974	73039 57186	40218 16544
80124 35635	17727 08015	45318 22374	21115 78253	14385 53763
74350 99817	77402 77214	43236 00210	45521 64237	96286 02655
69916 26803	66252 29148	36936 87203	76621 13990	94400 56418
09893 20505	14225 68514	46427 56788	96297 78822	54382 14598
91499 14523	68479 27686	46162 83554	94750 89923	37089 20048
80336 94598	26940 36858	70297 34135	53140 33340	42050 82341
44104 81949	85157 47954	32979 26575	57600 40881	22222 06413
12550 73742	11100 02040	12860 74697	96644 89439	28707 25815
63606 49329	16505 34484	40219 52563	43651 77082	07207 31790

TABLE A-7. Table of Random Digits. (Continued)

61196 90446	26457 47774	51924 33729	65394 59593	42582 60527
15474 45266	95270 79953	59367 83848	82396 10118	33211 59466
94557 28573	67897 54387	54622 44431	91190 42592	92927 45973
42481 16213	97344 08721	16868 48767	03071 12059	25701 46670
23523 78317	73208 89837	68935 91416	26252 29663	05522 82562
04493 52494	75246 33824	45862 51025	61962 79335	65337 12472
00549 97654	64051 88159	96119 63896	54692 82391	23287 29529
35963 15307	26898 09354	33351 35462	77974 50024	90103 39333
59808 08391	45427 26842	83609 49700	13021 24892	78565 20106
46058 85236	01390 92286	77281 44077	93910 83647	70617 42941
32179 00597	87379 25241	05567 07007	86743 17157	85394 11838
69234 61406	20117 45204	15956 60000	18743 92423	97118 96338
19565 41430	01758 75379	40419 21585	66674 36806	84962 85207
45155 14938	19476 07246	43667 94543	59047 90033	20826 69541
94864 31994	36168 10851	34888 81553	01540 35456	05014 51176
98086 24826	45240 28404	44999 08896	39094 73407	35441 31880
33185 16232	41941 50949	89435 48581	88695 41994	37548 73043
80951 00406	96382 70774	20151 23387	25016 25298	94624 61171
79752 49140	71961 28296	69861 02591	74852 20539	00387 59579
18633 32537	98145 06571	31010 24674	05455 61427	77938 91936
74029 43902	77557 32270	97790 17119	52527 58021	80814 51748
54178 45611	80993 37143	05335 12969	56127 19255	36040 90324
11664 49883	52079 84827	59381 71539	09973 33440	88461 23356
48324 77928	31249 64710	02295 36870	32307 57546	15020 09994
69074 94138	87637 91976	35584 04401	10518 21615	01848 76938
09188 20097	32825 39527	04220 86304	83389 87374	64278 58044
90045 85497	51981 50654	94938 81997	91870 76150	68476 64659
73189 50207	47677 26269	62290 64464	27124 67018	41361 82760
75768 76490	20971 87749	90429 12272	95375 05871	93823 43178
54016 44056	66281 31003	00682 27398	20714 53295	07706 17813
08358 69910	78542 42785	13661 58873	04618 97553	31223 08420
28306 03264	81333 10591	40510 07893	32604 60475	94119 01840
53840 86233	81594 13628	51215 90290	28466 68795	77762 20791
91757 53741	61613 62269	50263 90212	55781 76514	83483 47055
89415 92694	00397 58391	12607 17646	48949 72306	94541 37408
77513 03820	86864 29901	68414 82774	51908 13980	72893 55507
19502 37174	69979 20288	55210 29773	74287 75251	65344 67415
21818 59313	93278 81757	05686 73156	07082 85046	31853 38452
51474 66499	68107 23621	94049 91345	42836 09191	08007 45449
99559 68331	62535 24170	69777 12830	74819 78142	43860 72834

TABLE A-7. Table of Random Digits. (Continued)

33713 48007	93584 72869	51926 64721	58303 29822	93174 93972
85274 86893	11303 22970	28834 34137	73515 90400	71148 43643
84133 89640	44035 52166	73852 70091	61222 60561	62327 18423
56732 16234	17395 96131	10123 91622	85496 57560	81604 18880
65138 56806	87648 85261	34313 65861	45875 21069	85644 47277
38001 02176	81719 11711	71602 92937	74219 64049	65584 49698
37402 96397	01304 77586	56271 10086	47324 62605	40030 37438
97125 40348	87083 31417	21815 39250	75237 62047	15501 29578
21826 41134	47143 34072	64638 85902	49139 06441	03856 54552
73135 42742	95719 09035	85794 74296	08789 88156	64691 19202
07638 77929	03061 18072	96207 44156	23821 99538	04713 66994
60528 83441	07954 19814	59175 20695	05533 52139	61212 06455
83596 35655	06958 92983	05128 09719	77433 53783	92301 50498
10850 62746	99599 10507	13499 06319	53075 71839	06410 19362
39820 98952	43622 63147	64421 80814	43800 09351	31024 73167
59580 06478	75569 78800	88835 54486	23768 06156	04111 08408
38508 07341	23793 48763	90822 97022	17719 04207	95954 49953
30692 70668	94688 16127	56196 80091	82067 63400	05462 69200
65443 95659	18288 27437	49632 24041	08337 65676	96299 90836
27267 50264	13192 72294	07477 44606	17985 48911	97341 30358
91307 06991	19072 24210	36699 53728	28825 35793	28976 66252
68434 94688	84473 13622	62126 98408	12843 82590	09815 93146
48908 15877	54745 24591	35700 04754	83824 52692	54130 55160
06913 45197	42672 78601	11883 09528	63011 98901	14974 40344
10455 16019	14210 33712	91342 37821	88325 80851	43667 70883
12883 97343	65027 61184	04285 01392	17974 15077	90712 26769
21778 30976	38807 36961	31649 42096	63281 02023	08816 47449
19523 59515	65122 59659	86283 68258	69572 13798	16435 91529
67245 52670	35583 16563	79246 86686	76463 34222	26655 90802
60584 47377	07500 37992	45134 26529	26760 83637	41326 44344
53853 41377	36066 94850	58838 73859	49364 73331	92640 43642
24637 38736	74384 89342	52623 07992	12369 18601	03742 83873
83080 12451	38992 22815	07759 51777	97377 27585	51972 37867
16444 24334	36151 99073	27493 70939	85130 32552	54846 54759
60790 18157	57178 65762	11161 78576	45819 52979	65130 04860

Source: Reprinted by permission from *A Million Random Digits with 100,000 Normal Deviaties* by the Rand Corp., Santa Monica, Calif.

Table A-8. Binomial Distribution For Selected Values of p and n. (Continued)

$$P(r) = \frac{n!}{r!(n-r)!}\, p^r q^{n-r}$$

n	r	.01	.02	.04	.05	.06	.08	.10	.12	.14	.15	.16	.18	.20	.22	.24	.25	.30	.35	.40	.45	.50	r
2	0	980	960	922	902	884	846	810	774	740	722	706	672	640	608	578	562	490	422	360	302	250	0
	1	020	039	077	095	113	147	180	211	241	255	269	295	320	343	365	375	420	455	480	495	500	1
	2	0+	0+	002	002	004	006	010	014	020	022	026	032	040	048	058	062	090	122	160	202	250	2
3	0	970	941	885	857	831	779	729	681	636	614	593	551	512	475	439	422	343	275	216	166	125	0
	1	029	058	111	135	159	203	243	279	311	325	339	363	384	402	416	422	441	444	432	408	375	1
	2	0+	001	005	007	010	018	027	038	051	057	065	080	096	113	131	141	189	239	288	334	375	2
	3	0+	0+	0+	0+	0+	001	001	002	003	003	004	006	008	011	014	016	027	043	064	091	125	3
4	0	961	922	849	815	781	716	656	600	547	522	498	452	410	370	334	316	240	179	130	092	063	0
	1	039	075	142	171	199	249	292	327	356	368	379	397	410	418	421	422	412	384	346	299	250	1
	2	001	002	009	014	019	033	049	067	087	098	108	131	154	177	200	211	265	311	346	368	375	2
	3	0+	0+	0+	0+	001	002	004	006	009	011	014	019	026	033	042	047	076	111	154	200	250	3
	4	0+	0+	0+	0+	0+	0+	0+	0+	0+	001	001	001	002	002	003	004	008	015	026	041	062	4
5	0	951	904	815	774	734	659	590	528	470	444	418	371	328	289	254	237	168	116	078	050	031	0
	1	048	092	170	204	234	287	328	360	383	392	398	407	410	407	400	396	360	312	259	206	156	1
	2	001	004	014	021	030	050	073	098	125	138	152	179	205	230	253	264	309	336	346	337	312	2
	3	0+	0+	001	001	002	004	008	013	020	024	029	039	051	065	080	088	132	181	230	276	312	3
	4	0+	0+	0+	0+	0+	0+	0+	001	002	002	003	004	006	009	013	015	028	049	077	113	156	4
	5	0+	0+	0+	0+	0+	0+	0+	0+	0+	0+	0+	0+	0+	001	001	001	002	005	010	018	031	5
6	0	941	886	783	735	690	606	531	464	405	377	351	304	262	225	193	178	118	075	047	028	016	0
	1	057	108	196	232	264	316	354	380	395	399	401	400	393	381	365	356	303	244	187	136	094	1
	2	001	006	020	031	042	069	098	130	161	176	191	220	246	269	288	297	324	328	311	278	234	2
	3	0+	0+	001	002	004	008	015	024	035	041	049	064	082	101	121	132	185	235	276	303	312	3
	4	0+	0+	0+	0+	0+	001	001	002	004	005	007	011	015	021	029	033	060	095	138	186	234	4
	5	0+	0+	0+	0+	0+	0+	0+	0+	0+	0+	001	001	002	002	004	004	010	020	037	061	094	5
	6	0+	0+	0+	0+	0+	0+	0+	0+	0+	0+	0+	0+	0+	0+	0+	0+	001	002	004	008	016	6
7	0	932	868	751	698	648	558	478	409	348	321	295	249	210	176	146	133	082	049	028	015	008	0
	1	066	124	219	257	290	340	372	390	396	396	393	383	367	347	324	311	247	185	131	087	055	1
	2	002	008	027	041	055	089	124	160	194	210	225	252	275	293	307	311	318	298	261	214	164	2
	3	0+	0+	002	004	006	013	023	036	053	062	071	092	115	138	161	173	227	268	290	292	273	3
	4	0+	0+	0+	0+	0+	001	003	005	009	011	014	020	029	039	051	058	097	144	194	239	273	4
	5	0+	0+	0+	0+	0+	0+	0+	0+	001	001	002	003	004	007	010	012	025	047	077	117	164	5
	6	0+	0+	0+	0+	0+	0+	0+	0+	0+	0+	0+	0+	0+	001	001	001	004	008	017	032	055	6
	7	0+	0+	0+	0+	0+	0+	0+	0+	0+	0+	0+	0+	0+	0+	0+	0+	0+	001	002	004	008	7
8	0	923	851	721	663	610	513	430	360	299	272	248	204	168	137	111	100	058	032	017	008	004	0
	1	075	139	240	279	311	357	383	392	390	385	378	359	336	309	281	267	198	137	090	055	031	1
	2	003	010	035	051	070	109	149	187	222	238	252	276	294	305	311	311	296	259	209	157	109	2
	3	0+	0+	003	005	009	019	033	051	072	084	096	121	147	172	196	208	254	279	279	257	219	3
	4	0+	0+	0+	0+	001	002	005	009	015	018	023	033	046	061	077	087	136	188	232	263	273	4

Table A-8. Binomial Distribution For Selected Values of p and n. (Continued)

$$P(r) = \frac{n!}{r!(n-r)!}\, p^r q^{n-r}$$

n	r	.01	.02	.04	.05	.06	.08	.10	.12	.14	.15	.16	.18	.20	.22	.24	.25	.30	.35	.40	.45	.50	r
	5	0+	0+	0+	0+	0+	0+	0+	001	002	003	003	006	009	014	020	023	047	081	124	172	219	5
	6	0+	0+	0+	0+	0+	0+	0+	0+	0+	0+	0+	001	001	002	003	004	010	022	041	070	109	6
	7	0+	0+	0+	0+	0+	0+	0+	0+	0+	0+	0+	0+	0+	0+	0+	0+	001	003	008	016	031	7
	8	0+	0+	0+	0+	0+	0+	0+	0+	0+	0+	0+	0+	0+	0+	0+	0+	0+	0+	001	002	004	8
9	0	914	834	693	630	573	472	387	316	257	232	208	168	134	107	085	075	040	021	010	005	002	0
	1	083	153	260	299	329	370	387	388	377	368	357	331	302	271	240	225	156	100	060	034	018	1
	2	003	013	043	063	084	129	172	212	245	260	272	291	302	306	304	300	267	216	161	111	070	2
	3	0+	001	004	008	013	026	045	067	093	107	121	149	176	201	224	234	267	272	251	212	164	3
	4	0+	0+	0+	001	001	003	007	014	023	028	035	049	066	085	106	117	172	219	251	260	246	4
	5	0+	0+	0+	0+	0+	0+	001	002	004	005	007	011	017	024	033	039	074	118	167	213	246	5
	6	0+	0+	0+	0+	0+	0+	0+	0+	0+	001	001	002	003	005	007	009	021	042	074	116	164	6
	7	0+	0+	0+	0+	0+	0+	0+	0+	0+	0+	0+	0+	0+	001	001	001	004	010	021	041	070	7
	8	0+	0+	0+	0+	0+	0+	0+	0+	0+	0+	0+	0+	0+	0+	0+	0+	0+	001	004	009	018	8
	9	0+	0+	0+	0+	0+	0+	0+	0+	0+	0+	0+	0+	0+	0+	0+	0+	0+	0+	0+	001	002	9
10	0	904	817	665	599	539	434	349	279	221	197	175	137	107	083	064	056	028	013	006	003	001	0
	1	091	167	277	315	344	378	387	380	360	347	333	302	268	235	203	188	121	072	040	021	010	1
	2	004	015	052	075	099	148	194	233	264	276	286	298	302	298	288	282	233	176	121	076	044	2
	3	0+	001	006	010	017	034	057	085	115	130	145	174	201	224	243	250	267	252	215	166	117	3
	4	0+	0+	0+	001	002	005	011	020	033	040	048	067	088	111	134	146	200	238	251	238	205	4
	5	0+	0+	0+	0+	0+	001	001	003	006	008	011	018	026	037	051	058	103	154	201	234	246	5
	6	0+	0+	0+	0+	0+	0+	0+	0+	001	001	002	003	006	009	013	016	037	069	111	160	205	6
	7	0+	0+	0+	0+	0+	0+	0+	0+	0+	0+	0+	0+	001	001	002	003	009	021	042	075	117	7
	8	0+	0+	0+	0+	0+	0+	0+	0+	0+	0+	0+	0+	0+	0+	0+	0+	001	004	011	023	044	8
	9	0+	0+	0+	0+	0+	0+	0+	0+	0+	0+	0+	0+	0+	0+	0+	0+	0+	001	002	004	010	9
	10	0+	0+	0+	0+	0+	0+	0+	0+	0+	0+	0+	0+	0+	0+	0+	0+	0+	0+	0+	0+	001	10
11	0	895	801	638	569	506	400	314	245	190	167	147	113	086	065	049	042	020	009	004	001	0+	0
	1	099	180	293	329	355	382	384	368	341	325	308	272	236	202	170	155	093	052	027	013	005	1
	2	005	018	061	087	113	166	213	251	277	287	293	299	295	284	268	258	200	140	089	051	027	2
	3	0+	001	008	014	022	043	071	103	135	152	168	197	221	241	254	258	257	225	177	126	081	3
	4	0+	0+	001	001	003	008	016	028	044	054	064	086	111	136	160	172	220	243	236	206	161	4
	5	0+	0+	0+	0+	0+	001	002	005	010	013	017	027	039	054	071	080	132	183	221	236	226	5
	6	0+	0+	0+	0+	0+	0+	0+	001	002	002	003	006	010	015	022	027	057	099	147	193	226	6
	7	0+	0+	0+	0+	0+	0+	0+	0+	0+	0+	0+	001	002	003	005	006	017	038	070	113	161	7
	8	0+	0+	0+	0+	0+	0+	0+	0+	0+	0+	0+	0+	0+	0+	001	001	004	010	023	046	081	8
	9	0+	0+	0+	0+	0+	0+	0+	0+	0+	0+	0+	0+	0+	0+	0+	0+	001	002	005	013	027	9
	10	0+	0+	0+	0+	0+	0+	0+	0+	0+	0+	0+	0+	0+	0+	0+	0+	0+	0+	001	002	005	10
	11	0+	0+	0+	0+	0+	0+	0+	0+	0+	0+	0+	0+	0+	0+	0+	0+	0+	0+	0+	0+	0+	11
12	0	886	785	613	540	476	368	282	216	164	142	123	092	069	051	037	032	014	006	002	001	0+	0
	1	107	192	306	341	365	384	377	353	320	301	282	243	206	172	141	127	071	037	017	008	003	1

Table A-8. Binomial Distribution For Selected Values of p and n. (Continued)

$$P(r) = \frac{n!}{r!(n-r)!}\, p^r q^{n-r}$$

n	r	.01	.02	.04	.05	.06	.08	.10	.12	.14	.15	.16	.18	.20	.22	.24	.25	.30	.35	.40	.45	.50	r
	2	006	022	070	099	128	183	230	265	286	292	296	294	283	266	244	232	168	109	064	034	016	2
	3	0+	001	010	017	027	053	085	120	155	172	188	215	236	250	257	258	240	195	142	092	054	3
	4	0+	0+	001	002	004	010	021	037	057	068	080	106	133	159	183	194	231	237	213	170	121	4
	5	0+	0+	0+	0+	0+	001	004	008	015	019	025	037	053	072	092	103	158	204	227	222	193	5
	6	0+	0+	0+	0+	0+	0+	0+	001	003	004	005	010	016	024	034	040	079	128	177	212	226	6
	7	0+	0+	0+	0+	0+	0+	0+	0+	0+	001	001	002	003	006	009	011	029	059	101	149	193	7
	8	0+	0+	0+	0+	0+	0+	0+	0+	0+	0+	0+	0+	001	001	002	002	008	020	042	076	121	8
	9	0+	0+	0+	0+	0+	0+	0+	0+	0+	0+	0+	0+	0+	0+	0+	0+	001	005	012	028	054	9
	10	0+	0+	0+	0+	0+	0+	0+	0+	0+	0+	0+	0+	0+	0+	0+	0+	0+	001	002	007	016	10
	11	0+	0+	0+	0+	0+	0+	0+	0+	0+	0+	0+	0+	0+	0+	0+	0+	0+	0+	0+	001	003	11
	12	0+	0+	0+	0+	0+	0+	0+	0+	0+	0+	0+	0+	0+	0+	0+	0+	0+	0+	0+	0+	0+	12
13	0	878	769	588	513	447	338	254	190	141	121	104	076	055	040	028	024	010	004	001	0+	0+	0
	1	115	204	319	351	371	382	367	336	298	277	257	216	179	145	116	103	054	026	011	004	002	1
	2	007	025	080	111	142	199	245	275	291	294	293	285	268	245	110	206	139	084	045	022	010	2
	3	0+	002	012	021	033	064	100	138	174	190	205	229	246	254	254	252	218	165	111	066	035	3
	4	0+	0+	001	003	005	014	028	047	071	084	098	126	154	179	201	210	234	222	184	135	087	4
	5	0+	0+	0+	0+	001	002	006	012	021	027	033	050	069	091	114	126	180	215	221	199	157	5
	6	0+	0+	0+	0+	0+	0+	001	002	004	006	008	015	023	034	048	056	103	155	197	217	209	6
	7	0+	0+	0+	0+	0+	0+	0+	0+	001	001	002	003	006	010	015	019	044	083	131	177	209	7
	8	0+	0+	0+	0+	0+	0+	0+	0+	0+	0+	0+	001	001	002	004	005	014	034	066	109	157	8
	9	0+	0+	0+	0+	0+	0+	0+	0+	0+	0+	0+	0+	0+	0+	001	001	003	010	024	050	087	9
	10	0+	0+	0+	0+	0+	0+	0+	0+	0+	0+	0+	0+	0+	0+	0+	0+	001	002	006	016	035	10
	11	0+	0+	0+	0+	0+	0+	0+	0+	0+	0+	0+	0+	0+	0+	0+	0+	0+	0+	001	004	010	11
	12	0+	0+	0+	0+	0+	0+	0+	0+	0+	0+	0+	0+	0+	0+	0+	0+	0+	0+	0+	0+	002	12
	13	0+	0+	0+	0+	0+	0+	0+	0+	0+	0+	0+	0+	0+	0+	0+	0+	0+	0+	0+	0+	0+	13
14	0	869	754	565	488	421	311	229	167	121	103	087	062	044	031	021	018	007	002	001	0+	0+	0
	1	123	215	329	359	376	379	356	319	276	254	232	191	154	122	095	083	041	018	007	003	001	1
	2	008	029	089	123	156	217	257	283	292	291	287	272	250	223	195	180	113	063	032	014	006	2
	3	0+	002	015	026	040	074	114	154	190	206	219	239	250	252	246	240	194	137	085	046	022	3
	4	0+	0+	002	004	007	018	035	058	085	100	115	144	172	195	214	220	229	202	155	104	061	4
	5	0+	0+	0+	0+	001	003	008	016	028	035	044	063	086	110	135	147	196	218	207	170	122	5
	6	0+	0+	0+	0+	0+	0+	001	003	007	009	012	021	032	047	064	073	126	176	207	209	183	6
	7	0+	0+	0+	0+	0+	0+	0+	001	001	002	003	005	009	015	023	028	062	108	157	195	209	7
	8	0+	0+	0+	0+	0+	0+	0+	0+	0+	0+	0+	001	002	004	006	008	023	051	092	140	183	8
	9	0+	0+	0+	0+	0+	0+	0+	0+	0+	0+	0+	0+	0+	001	001	002	007	018	041	076	122	9
	10	0+	0+	0+	0+	0+	0+	0+	0+	0+	0+	0+	0+	0+	0+	0+	0+	001	005	014	031	061	10
	11	0+	0+	0+	0+	0+	0+	0+	0+	0+	0+	0+	0+	0+	0+	0+	0+	0+	001	003	009	022	11
	12	0+	0+	0+	0+	0+	0+	0+	0+	0+	0+	0+	0+	0+	0+	0+	0+	0+	0+	001	002	006	12
	13	0+	0+	0+	0+	0+	0+	0+	0+	0+	0+	0+	0+	0+	0+	0+	0+	0+	0+	0+	0+	001	13
	14	0+	0+	0+	0+	0+	0+	0+	0+	0+	0+	0+	0+	0+	0+	0+	0+	0+	0+	0+	0+	0+	14

Table A-8. Binomial Distribution For Selected Values of p and n. (Continued)

$$P(r) = \frac{n!}{r!(n-r)!}\, p^r q^{n-r}$$

												p											
n	*r*	.01	.02	.04	.05	.06	.08	.10	.12	.14	.15	.16	.18	.20	.22	.24	.25	.30	.35	.40	.45	.50	*r*
15	0	860	739	542	463	395	286	206	147	104	087	073	051	035	024	016	013	005	002	0+	0+	0+	0
	1	130	226	339	366	378	373	343	301	254	231	209	168	132	102	077	067	031	013	005	002	0+	1
	2	009	032	099	135	169	227	267	287	290	286	279	258	231	201	171	156	092	048	022	009	003	2
	3	0+	003	018	031	047	086	129	170	204	218	230	245	250	246	234	225	170	111	063	032	014	3
	4	0+	0+	002	005	009	022	043	069	100	116	131	162	188	208	221	225	219	179	127	078	042	4
	5	0+	0+	0+	001	001	004	010	021	036	045	055	078	103	129	154	165	206	212	186	140	092	5
	6	0+	0+	0+	0+	0+	001	002	005	010	013	017	029	043	061	081	092	147	191	207	191	153	6
	7	0+	0+	0+	0+	0+	0+	0+	001	002	003	004	008	014	022	033	039	081	132	177	201	196	7
	8	0+	0+	0+	0+	0+	0+	0+	0+	0+	001	001	002	003	006	010	013	035	071	118	165	196	8
	9	0+	0+	0+	0+	0+	0+	0+	0+	0+	0+	0+	0+	001	001	003	003	012	030	061	105	153	9
	10	0+	0+	0+	0+	0+	0+	0+	0+	0+	0+	0+	0+	0+	0+	0+	001	003	010	024	051	092	10
	11	0+	0+	0+	0+	0+	0+	0+	0+	0+	0+	0+	0+	0+	0+	0+	0+	001	002	007	019	042	11
	12	0+	0+	0+	0+	0+	0+	0+	0+	0+	0+	0+	0+	0+	0+	0+	0+	0+	0+	002	005	014	12
	13	0+	0+	0+	0+	0+	0+	0+	0+	0+	0+	0+	0+	0+	0+	0+	0+	0+	0+	0+	001	003	13
	14	0+	0+	0+	0+	0+	0+	0+	0+	0+	0+	0+	0+	0+	0+	0+	0+	0+	0+	0+	0+	0+	14
	15	0+	0+	0+	0+	0+	0+	0+	0+	0+	0+	0+	0+	0+	0+	0+	0+	0+	0+	0+	0+	0+	15
16	0	851	724	520	440	372	263	185	129	090	074	061	042	028	019	012	010	003	001	0+	0+	0+	0
	1	138	236	347	371	379	366	329	282	233	210	187	147	113	085	063	053	023	009	003	001	0+	1
	2	010	036	108	146	182	239	275	289	285	277	268	242	211	179	148	134	073	035	015	006	002	2
	3	0+	003	021	036	054	097	142	184	216	229	238	248	246	236	218	208	146	089	047	022	009	3
	4	0+	0+	003	006	011	027	051	081	114	131	147	177	200	216	224	225	204	155	101	057	028	4
	5	0+	0+	0+	001	002	006	014	027	045	056	067	093	120	146	170	180	210	201	162	112	067	5
	6	0+	0+	0+	0+	0+	001	003	007	013	018	023	037	055	076	098	110	165	198	198	168	122	6
	7	0+	0+	0+	0+	0+	0+	0+	001	003	005	006	012	020	030	044	052	101	152	189	197	175	7
	8	0+	0+	0+	0+	0+	0+	0+	0+	001	001	001	003	006	010	016	020	049	092	142	181	196	8
	9	0+	0+	0+	0+	0+	0+	0+	0+	0+	0+	0+	001	001	002	004	006	019	044	084	132	175	9
	10	0+	0+	0+	0+	0+	0+	0+	0+	0+	0+	0+	0+	0+	0+	001	001	006	017	039	075	122	10
	11	0+	0+	0+	0+	0+	0+	0+	0+	0+	0+	0+	0+	0+	0+	0+	0+	001	005	014	034	067	11
	12	0+	0+	0+	0+	0+	0+	0+	0+	0+	0+	0+	0+	0+	0+	0+	0+	0+	001	004	011	028	12
	13	0+	0+	0+	0+	0+	0+	0+	0+	0+	0+	0+	0+	0+	0+	0+	0+	0+	0+	001	003	009	13
	14	0+	0+	0+	0+	0+	0+	0+	0+	0+	0+	0+	0+	0+	0+	0+	0+	0+	0+	0+	001	002	14
	15	0+	0+	0+	0+	0+	0+	0+	0+	0+	0+	0+	0+	0+	0+	0+	0+	0+	0+	0+	0+	0+	15
	16	0+	0+	0+	0+	0+	0+	0+	0+	0+	0+	0+	0+	0+	0+	0+	0+	0+	0+	0+	0+	0+	16
17	0	843	709	500	418	349	242	167	114	077	063	052	034	023	015	009	008	002	001	0+	0+	0+	0
	1	145	246	354	374	379	358	315	264	213	189	167	128	096	070	051	043	017	006	002	001	0+	1
	2	012	040	118	158	194	249	280	288	278	267	255	225	191	158	128	114	058	026	010	004	001	2
	3	001	004	025	041	062	108	156	196	226	236	243	246	239	223	202	189	125	070	034	014	005	3
	4	0+	0+	004	008	014	033	060	094	129	146	162	189	209	221	223	221	187	132	080	041	018	4

Table A-8. Binomial Distribution For Selected Values of p and n. (Continued)

$$P(r) = \frac{n!}{r!(n-r)!}\, p^r q^{n-r}$$

n	r	.01	.02	.04	.05	.06	.08	.10	.12	.14	.15	.16	.18	.20	.22	.24	.25	.30	.35	.40	.45	.50	r
	5	0+	0+	0+	001	002	007	017	033	054	067	080	108	136	162	183	191	208	185	138	087	047	5
	6	0+	0+	0+	0+	0+	001	004	009	018	024	031	047	068	091	116	128	178	199	184	143	094	6
	7	0+	0+	0+	0+	0+	0+	001	002	005	007	009	016	027	040	057	067	120	168	193	184	148	7
	8	0+	0+	0+	0+	0+	0+	0+	0+	001	001	002	004	008	014	023	028	064	113	161	188	185	8
	9	0+	0+	0+	0+	0+	0+	0+	0+	0+	0+	0+	001	002	004	007	009	028	061	107	154	185	9
	10	0+	0+	0+	0+	0+	0+	0+	0+	0+	0+	0+	0+	0+	001	002	002	009	026	057	101	148	10
	11	0+	0+	0+	0+	0+	0+	0+	0+	0+	0+	0+	0+	0+	0+	0+	001	003	009	024	052	094	11
	12	0+	0+	0+	0+	0+	0+	0+	0+	0+	0+	0+	0+	0+	0+	0+	0+	001	002	008	021	047	12
	13	0+	0+	0+	0+	0+	0+	0+	0+	0+	0+	0+	0+	0+	0+	0+	0+	0+	001	002	007	018	13
	14	0+	0+	0+	0+	0+	0+	0+	0+	0+	0+	0+	0+	0+	0+	0+	0+	0+	0+	0+	002	005	14
	15	0+	0+	0+	0+	0+	0+	0+	0+	0+	0+	0+	0+	0+	0+	0+	0+	0+	0+	0+	0+	001	15
	16	0+	0+	0+	0+	0+	0+	0+	0+	0+	0+	0+	0+	0+	0+	0+	0+	0+	0+	0+	0+	0+	16
	17	0+	0+	0+	0+	0+	0+	0+	0+	0+	0+	0+	0+	0+	0+	0+	0+	0+	0+	0+	0+	0+	17
18	0	835	695	480	397	328	223	150	100	066	054	043	028	018	011	007	006	002	0+	0+	0+	0+	0
	1	152	255	360	376	377	349	300	246	194	170	149	111	081	058	041	034	013	004	001	0+	0+	1
	2	013	044	127	168	205	258	284	285	268	256	241	207	172	139	109	096	046	019	007	002	001	2
	3	001	005	028	047	070	120	168	207	233	241	244	243	230	209	184	170	105	055	025	009	003	3
	4	0+	0+	004	009	017	039	070	106	142	159	175	200	215	221	218	213	168	110	061	029	012	4
	5	0+	0+	001	001	003	009	022	040	065	079	093	123	151	175	193	199	202	166	115	067	033	5
	6	0+	0+	0+	0+	0+	002	005	012	023	030	038	058	082	107	132	144	187	194	166	118	071	6
	7	0+	0+	0+	0+	0+	0+	001	003	006	009	013	022	035	052	071	082	138	179	189	166	121	7
	8	0+	0+	0+	0+	0+	0+	0+	001	001	002	003	007	012	020	031	038	081	133	173	186	167	8
	9	0+	0+	0+	0+	0+	0+	0+	0+	0+	0+	001	002	003	006	011	014	039	079	128	169	185	9
	10	0+	0+	0+	0+	0+	0+	0+	0+	0+	0+	0+	0+	001	002	003	004	015	038	077	125	167	10
	11	0+	0+	0+	0+	0+	0+	0+	0+	0+	0+	0+	0+	0+	0+	001	001	005	015	037	074	121	11
	12	0+	0+	0+	0+	0+	0+	0+	0+	0+	0+	0+	0+	0+	0+	0+	0+	001	005	015	035	071	12
	13	0+	0+	0+	0+	0+	0+	0+	0+	0+	0+	0+	0+	0+	0+	0+	0+	0+	001	004	013	033	13
	14	0+	0+	0+	0+	0+	0+	0+	0+	0+	0+	0+	0+	0+	0+	0+	0+	0+	0+	001	004	012	14
	15	0+	0+	0+	0+	0+	0+	0+	0+	0+	0+	0+	0+	0+	0+	0+	0+	0+	0+	0+	001	003	15
	16	0+	0+	0+	0+	0+	0+	0+	0+	0+	0+	0+	0+	0+	0+	0+	0+	0+	0+	0+	0+	001	16
	17	0+	0+	0+	0+	0+	0+	0+	0+	0+	0+	0+	0+	0+	0+	0+	0+	0+	0+	0+	0+	0+	17
	18	0+	0+	0+	0+	0+	0+	0+	0+	0+	0+	0+	0+	0+	0+	0+	0+	0+	0+	0+	0+	0+	18
19	0	826	681	460	377	309	205	135	088	057	046	036	023	014	009	005	004	001	0+	0+	0+	0+	0
	1	159	264	364	377	374	339	285	228	176	153	132	096	068	048	033	027	009	003	001	0+	0+	1
	2	014	049	137	179	215	265	285	280	258	243	226	190	154	121	093	080	036	014	005	001	0+	2
	3	001	006	032	053	078	131	180	217	238	243	244	236	218	194	166	152	087	042	017	006	002	3
	4	0+	0+	005	011	020	045	080	118	155	171	186	207	218	219	210	202	149	091	047	020	007	4

Table A-8. Binomial Distribution For Selected Values of p and n. (Continued)

$$P(r) = \frac{n!}{r!(n-r)!}\, p^r q^{n-r}$$

n	r	.01	.02	.04	.05	.06	.08	.10	.12	.14	.15	.16	.18	.20	.22	.24	.25	.30	.35	.40	.45	.50	r
	5	0+	0+	001	002	004	012	027	048	076	091	106	137	164	185	199	202	192	147	093	050	022	5
	6	0+	0+	0+	0+	001	002	007	015	029	037	047	070	095	122	146	157	192	184	145	095	052	6
	7	0+	0+	0+	0+	0+	0+	001	004	009	012	017	029	044	064	086	097	153	184	180	144	096	7
	8	0+	0+	0+	0+	0+	0+	0+	001	002	003	005	009	017	027	041	049	098	149	180	177	144	8
	9	0+	0+	0+	0+	0+	0+	0+	0+	0+	001	001	003	005	009	016	020	051	098	146	177	176	9
	10	0+	0+	0+	0+	0+	0+	0+	0+	0+	0+	0+	001	001	003	005	007	022	053	098	145	176	10
	11	0+	0+	0+	0+	0+	0+	0+	0+	0+	0+	0+	0+	0+	001	001	002	008	023	053	097	144	11
	12	0+	0+	0+	0+	0+	0+	0+	0+	0+	0+	0+	0+	0+	0+	0+	0+	002	008	024	053	096	12
	13	0+	0+	0+	0+	0+	0+	0+	0+	0+	0+	0+	0+	0+	0+	0+	0+	001	002	008	023	052	13
	14	0+	0+	0+	0+	0+	0+	0+	0+	0+	0+	0+	0+	0+	0+	0+	0+	0+	001	002	008	022	14
	15	0+	0+	0+	0+	0+	0+	0+	0+	0+	0+	0+	0+	0+	0+	0+	0+	0+	0+	001	002	007	15
	16	0+	0+	0+	0+	0+	0+	0+	0+	0+	0+	0+	0+	0+	0+	0+	0+	0+	0+	0+	0+	002	16
	17	0+	0+	0+	0+	0+	0+	0+	0+	0+	0+	0+	0+	0+	0+	0+	0+	0+	0+	0+	0+	0+	17
	18	0+	0+	0+	0+	0+	0+	0+	0+	0+	0+	0+	0+	0+	0+	0+	0+	0+	0+	0+	0+	0+	18
	19	0+	0+	0+	0+	0+	0+	0+	0+	0+	0+	0+	0+	0+	0+	0+	0+	0+	0+	0+	0+	0+	19
20	0	818	668	442	358	290	189	122	078	049	039	031	019	012	007	004	003	001	0+	0+	0+	0+	0
	1	165	272	368	377	370	328	270	212	159	137	117	083	058	039	026	021	007	002	0+	0+	0+	1
	2	016	053	146	189	225	271	285	274	247	229	211	173	137	105	078	067	028	010	003	001	0+	2
	3	001	006	036	060	086	141	190	224	241	243	241	228	205	178	148	134	072	032	012	004	001	3
	4	0+	001	006	013	023	052	090	130	167	182	195	213	218	213	199	190	130	074	035	014	005	4
	5	0+	0+	001	002	005	015	032	057	087	103	119	149	175	192	201	202	179	127	075	036	015	5
	6	0+	0+	0+	0+	001	003	009	019	035	045	057	082	109	136	159	169	192	171	124	075	037	6
	7	0+	0+	0+	0+	0+	001	002	005	012	016	022	036	055	076	100	112	164	184	166	122	074	7
	8	0+	0+	0+	0+	0+	0+	0+	001	003	005	007	013	022	035	051	061	114	161	180	162	120	8
	9	0+	0+	0+	0+	0+	0+	0+	0+	001	001	002	004	007	013	022	027	065	116	160	177	160	9
	10	0+	0+	0+	0+	0+	0+	0+	0+	0+	0+	0+	001	002	004	008	010	031	069	117	159	176	10
	11	0+	0+	0+	0+	0+	0+	0+	0+	0+	0+	0+	0+	0+	001	002	003	012	034	071	119	160	11
	12	0+	0+	0+	0+	0+	0+	0+	0+	0+	0+	0+	0+	0+	0+	001	001	004	014	035	073	120	12
	13	0+	0+	0+	0+	0+	0+	0+	0+	0+	0+	0+	0+	0+	0+	0+	0+	001	004	015	037	074	13
	14	0+	0+	0+	0+	0+	0+	0+	0+	0+	0+	0+	0+	0+	0+	0+	0+	0+	001	005	015	037	14
	15	0+	0+	0+	0+	0+	0+	0+	0+	0+	0+	0+	0+	0+	0+	0+	0+	0+	0+	001	005	015	15
	16	0+	0+	0+	0+	0+	0+	0+	0+	0+	0+	0+	0+	0+	0+	0+	0+	0+	0+	0+	001	005	16
	17	0+	0+	0+	0+	0+	0+	0+	0+	0+	0+	0+	0+	0+	0+	0+	0+	0+	0+	0+	0+	001	17
	18	0+	0+	0+	0+	0+	0+	0+	0+	0+	0+	0+	0+	0+	0+	0+	0+	0+	0+	0+	0+	0+	18
	19	0+	0+	0+	0+	0+	0+	0+	0+	0+	0+	0+	0+	0+	0+	0+	0+	0+	0+	0+	0+	0+	19
	20	0+	0+	0+	0+	0+	0+	0+	0+	0+	0+	0+	0+	0+	0+	0+	0+	0+	0+	0+	0+	0+	20

Table A-8. Binomial Distribution For Selected Values of p and n. (Continued)

$$P(r) = \frac{n!}{r!(n-r)!}\, p^r q^{n-r}$$

n	r	.01	.02	.04	.05	.06	.08	.10	.12	.14	.15	.16	.18	.20	.22	.24	.25	.30	.35	.40	.45	.50	r
21	0	810	654	424	341	273	174	109	068	042	033	026	015	010	005	003	002	001	0+	0+	0+	0+	0
	1	172	280	371	376	366	317	255	195	144	122	103	071	048	032	021	017	005	001	0+	0+	0+	1
	2	017	057	155	198	233	276	284	267	234	215	196	157	121	091	066	055	022	007	002	0+	0+	2
	3	001	007	041	066	094	152	200	230	242	241	236	218	192	162	132	117	058	024	009	003	001	3
	4	0+	001	008	016	027	059	100	141	177	191	202	215	216	205	187	176	113	059	026	009	003	4
	5	0+	0+	001	003	006	018	038	065	098	115	131	161	183	197	201	199	164	109	059	026	010	5
	6	0+	0+	0+	0+	001	004	011	024	043	054	067	094	122	148	169	177	188	156	105	057	026	6
	7	0+	0+	0+	0+	0+	001	003	007	015	020	027	044	065	089	114	126	172	180	149	101	055	7
	8	0+	0+	0+	0+	0+	0+	001	002	004	006	009	017	029	044	063	074	129	169	174	144	097	8
	9	0+	0+	0+	0+	0+	0+	0+	0+	001	002	002	005	010	018	029	036	080	132	168	170	140	9
	10	0+	0+	0+	0+	0+	0+	0+	0+	0+	0+	001	001	003	006	011	014	041	085	134	167	168	10
	11	0+	0+	0+	0+	0+	0+	0+	0+	0+	0+	0+	0+	001	002	003	005	018	046	089	137	168	11
	12	0+	0+	0+	0+	0+	0+	0+	0+	0+	0+	0+	0+	0+	0+	001	001	006	021	050	093	140	12
	13	0+	0+	0+	0+	0+	0+	0+	0+	0+	0+	0+	0+	0+	0+	0+	0+	002	008	023	053	097	13
	14	0+	0+	0+	0+	0+	0+	0+	0+	0+	0+	0+	0+	0+	0+	0+	0+	0+	002	009	025	055	14
	15	0+	0+	0+	0+	0+	0+	0+	0+	0+	0+	0+	0+	0+	0+	0+	0+	0+	001	003	009	026	15
	16	0+	0+	0+	0+	0+	0+	0+	0+	0+	0+	0+	0+	0+	0+	0+	0+	0+	0+	001	003	010	16
	17	0+	0+	0+	0+	0+	0+	0+	0+	0+	0+	0+	0+	0+	0+	0+	0+	0+	0+	0+	001	003	17
	18	0+	0+	0+	0+	0+	0+	0+	0+	0+	0+	0+	0+	0+	0+	0+	0+	0+	0+	0+	0+	001	18
	19	0+	0+	0+	0+	0+	0+	0+	0+	0+	0+	0+	0+	0+	0+	0+	0+	0+	0+	0+	0+	0+	19
	20	0+	0+	0+	0+	0+	0+	0+	0+	0+	0+	0+	0+	0+	0+	0+	0+	0+	0+	0+	0+	0+	20
	21	0+	0+	0+	0+	0+	0+	0+	0+	0+	0+	0+	0+	0+	0+	0+	0+	0+	0+	0+	0+	0+	21

Source: Reproduced with permission from Spurr and Bonini, *Statistical Analysis for Business Decisions* Rev. Ed. Homewood, IL: Richard D. Irwin, Inc., 1973 pp 683–88.

TABLE A-9. Poisson Distribution For Selected Values of m
(r values less than .0005 are left blank)

$$P(r) = (e^{-m}m^r)/r!$$

r	.001	.002	.003	.004	.005	.006	.007	.008	.009	.01	.02	.03	.04	.05	.06	.07	.08	.09	.10	.15	r
0	999	998	997	996	995	994	993	992	991	990	980	970	961	951	942	932	923	914	905	861	0
1	001	002	003	004	005	006	007	008	009	010	020	030	038	048	057	065	074	082	090	129	1
2													001	001	002	002	003	004	005	010	2

r	.20	.25	.30	.40	.50	.60	.70	.80	.90	1.0	1.1	1.2	1.3	1.4	1.5	1.6	1.7	1.8	1.9	2.0	r
0	819	779	741	670	607	549	497	449	407	368	333	301	273	247	223	202	183	165	150	135	0
1	164	195	222	268	303	329	348	359	366	368	366	361	354	345	335	323	311	298	284	271	1
2	016	024	033	054	076	099	122	144	165	184	201	217	230	242	251	258	264	268	270	271	2
3	001	002	003	007	013	020	028	038	049	061	074	087	100	113	126	138	150	161	171	180	3
4				001	002	003	005	008	011	015	020	026	032	039	047	055	063	072	081	090	4
5							001	001	002	003	004	006	008	011	014	018	022	026	031	036	5
6										001	001	001	002	003	004	005	006	008	010	012	6
7														001	001	001	001	002	003	003	7
8																			001	001	8

r	2.1	2.2	2.3	2.4	2.5	2.6	2.7	2.8	2.9	3.0	3.1	3.2	3.3	3.4	3.5	3.6	3.7	3.8	3.9	4.0	r
0	122	111	100	091	082	074	067	061	055	050	045	041	037	033	030	027	025	022	020	018	0
1	257	244	231	218	205	193	181	170	160	149	140	130	122	113	106	098	091	085	079	073	1
2	270	268	265	261	257	251	245	238	231	224	216	209	201	193	185	177	169	162	154	147	2
3	189	197	203	209	214	218	220	222	224	224	224	223	221	219	216	212	209	205	200	195	3
4	099	108	117	125	134	141	149	156	162	168	173	178	182	186	189	191	193	194	195	195	4
5	042	048	054	060	067	074	080	087	094	101	107	114	120	126	132	138	143	148	152	156	5
6	015	017	021	024	028	032	036	041	045	050	056	061	066	072	077	083	088	094	099	104	6
7	004	005	007	008	010	012	014	016	019	022	025	028	031	035	039	042	047	051	055	060	7
8	001	002	002	002	003	004	005	006	007	008	010	011	013	015	017	019	022	024	027	030	8
9				001	001	001	001	002	002	003	003	004	005	006	007	008	009	010	012	013	9
10									001	001	001	001	002	002	002	003	003	004	005	005	10
11														001	001	001	001	001	002	002	11
12																			001	001	12

TABLE A-9. Poisson Distribution For Selected Values of m
(r values less than .0005 are left blank)

$$P(r) = (e^{-m}m^r)/r!$$

r \ m	4.1	4.2	4.3	4.4	4.5	4.6	4.7	4.8	4.9	5.0	5.1	5.2	5.3	5.4	5.5	5.6	5.7	5.8	5.9	6.0	r
0	017	015	014	012	011	010	009	008	007	007	006	006	005	005	004	004	003	003	003	002	0
1	068	063	058	054	050	046	043	040	036	034	031	029	026	024	022	021	019	018	016	015	1
2	139	132	125	119	112	106	100	095	089	084	079	075	070	066	062	058	054	051	048	045	2
3	190	185	180	174	169	163	157	152	146	140	135	129	124	119	113	108	103	098	094	089	3
4	195	194	193	192	190	188	185	182	179	175	172	168	164	160	156	152	147	143	138	134	4
5	160	163	166	169	171	173	174	175	175	175	175	175	174	173	171	170	168	166	163	161	5
6	109	114	119	124	128	132	136	140	143	146	149	151	154	156	157	158	159	160	160	161	6
7	064	069	073	078	082	087	091	096	100	104	109	113	116	120	123	127	130	133	135	138	7
8	033	036	039	043	046	050	054	058	061	065	069	073	077	081	085	089	092	096	100	103	8
9	015	017	019	021	023	026	028	031	033	036	039	042	045	049	052	055	059	062	065	069	9
10	006	007	008	009	010	012	013	015	016	018	020	022	024	026	029	031	033	036	039	041	10
11	002	003	003	004	004	005	006	006	007	008	009	010	012	013	014	016	017	019	021	023	11
12	001	001	001	001	002	002	002	003	003	003	004	005	005	006	007	007	008	009	010	011	12
13					001	001	001	001	001	001	002	002	002	002	003	003	004	004	005	005	13
14											001	001	001	001	001	001	001	002	002	002	14
15																	001	001	001	001	15

r \ m	6.1	6.2	6.3	6.4	6.5	6.6	6.7	6.8	6.9	7.0	7.1	7.2	7.3	7.4	7.5	8.0	8.5	9.0	9.5	10.0	r
0	002	002	002	002	002	001	001	001	001	001	001	001	001	001	001						0
1	014	013	012	011	010	009	008	008	007	006	006	005	005	005	004	003	002	001	001		1
2	042	039	036	034	032	030	028	026	024	022	021	019	018	017	016	011	007	005	003	002	2
3	085	081	077	073	069	065	062	058	055	052	049	046	044	041	039	029	021	015	011	008	3
4	129	125	121	116	112	108	103	099	095	091	087	084	080	076	073	057	044	034	025	019	4
5	158	155	152	149	145	142	138	135	131	128	124	120	117	113	109	092	075	061	048	038	5
6	160	160	159	159	157	156	155	153	151	149	147	144	142	139	137	122	107	091	076	063	6
7	140	142	144	145	146	147	148	149	149	149	149	149	148	147	146	140	129	117	104	090	7
8	107	110	113	116	119	121	124	126	128	130	132	134	135	136	137	140	138	132	123	113	8
9	072	076	079	082	086	089	092	095	098	101	104	107	110	112	114	124	130	132	130	125	9
10	044	047	050	053	056	059	062	065	068	071	074	077	080	083	086	099	110	119	124	125	10
11	024	026	029	031	033	035	038	040	043	045	048	050	053	056	059	072	085	097	107	114	11
12	012	014	015	016	018	019	021	023	025	026	028	030	032	034	037	048	060	073	084	095	12
13	006	007	007	008	009	010	011	012	013	014	015	017	018	020	021	030	040	050	062	073	13
14	003	003	003	004	004	005	005	006	006	007	008	009	009	010	011	017	024	032	042	052	14
15	001	001	001	002	002	002	002	003	003	003	004	004	005	005	006	009	014	019	027	035	15
16			001	001	001	001	001	001	001	001	002	002	002	002	003	005	007	011	016	022	16
17									001	001	001	001	001	001	001	002	004	006	009	013	17
18																001	002	003	005	007	18
19																	001	001	002	004	19
20																		001	001	002	20
21																				001	21

Source: Reproduced with permission from Spurr and Bonini, *Statistical Analysis for Business Decisions* (Rev. Ed. Homewood, IL: Richard D. Irwin, Inc., 1973) pp 696–7.

TABLE A-10 The F Distribution
(5% (Roman Type) and 1% (Bold Face Type) Points for the Distribution of *F*)

d_1 = Degrees of freedom for numerator

d_2 = Degrees of freedom for denominator

d_2	1	2	3	4	5	6	7	8	9	10	11	12	14	16	20	24	30	40	50	75	100	200	500	∞	d_2
1	161	200	216	225	230	234	237	239	241	242	243	244	245	246	248	249	250	251	252	253	253	254	254	254	1
	4,052	**4,999**	**5,403**	**5,625**	**5,764**	**5,859**	**5,928**	**5,981**	**6,022**	**6,056**	**6,082**	**6,106**	**6,142**	**6,169**	**6,208**	**6,234**	**6,261**	**6,286**	**6,302**	**6,323**	**6,334**	**6,352**	**6,361**	**6,366**	
2	18.51	19.00	19.16	19.25	19.30	19.33	19.36	19.37	19.38	19.39	19.40	19.41	19.42	19.43	19.44	19.45	19.46	19.47	19.47	19.48	19.49	19.49	19.50	19.50	2
	98.49	**99.00**	**99.17**	**99.25**	**99.30**	**99.33**	**99.36**	**99.37**	**99.39**	**99.40**	**99.41**	**99.42**	**99.43**	**99.44**	**99.45**	**99.46**	**99.47**	**99.48**	**99.48**	**99.49**	**99.49**	**99.49**	**99.50**	**99.50**	
3	10.13	9.55	9.28	9.12	9.01	8.94	8.88	8.84	8.81	8.78	8.76	8.74	8.71	8.69	8.66	8.64	8.62	8.60	8.58	8.57	8.56	8.54	8.54	8.53	3
	34.12	**30.82**	**29.46**	**28.71**	**28.24**	**27.91**	**27.67**	**27.49**	**27.34**	**27.23**	**27.13**	**27.05**	**26.92**	**26.83**	**26.69**	**26.60**	**26.50**	**26.41**	**26.35**	**26.27**	**26.23**	**26.18**	**26.14**	**26.12**	
4	7.71	6.94	6.59	6.39	6.26	6.16	6.09	6.04	6.00	5.96	5.93	5.91	5.87	5.84	5.80	5.77	5.74	5.71	5.70	5.68	5.66	5.65	5.64	5.63	4
	21.20	**18.00**	**16.69**	**15.98**	**15.52**	**15.21**	**14.98**	**14.80**	**14.66**	**14.54**	**14.45**	**14.37**	**14.24**	**14.15**	**14.02**	**13.93**	**13.83**	**13.74**	**13.69**	**13.61**	**13.57**	**13.52**	**13.48**	**13.46**	
5	6.61	5.79	5.41	5.19	5.05	4.95	4.88	4.82	4.78	4.74	4.70	4.68	4.64	4.60	4.56	4.53	4.50	4.46	4.44	4.42	4.40	4.38	4.37	4.36	5
	16.26	**13.27**	**12.06**	**11.39**	**10.97**	**10.67**	**10.45**	**10.29**	**10.15**	**10.05**	**9.96**	**9.89**	**9.77**	**9.68**	**9.55**	**9.47**	**9.38**	**9.29**	**9.24**	**9.17**	**9.13**	**9.07**	**9.04**	**9.02**	
6	5.99	5.14	4.76	4.53	4.39	4.28	4.21	4.15	4.10	4.06	4.03	4.00	3.96	3.92	3.87	3.84	3.81	3.77	3.75	3.72	3.71	3.69	3.68	3.67	6
	13.74	**10.9**	**9.78**	**9.15**	**8.75**	**8.47**	**8.26**	**8.10**	**7.98**	**7.87**	**7.79**	**7.72**	**7.60**	**7.52**	**7.39**	**7.31**	**7.23**	**7.14**	**7.09**	**7.02**	**6.99**	**6.94**	**6.90**	**6.88**	
7	5.59	4.74	4.35	4.12	3.97	3.87	3.79	3.73	3.68	3.63	3.60	3.57	3.52	3.49	3.44	3.41	3.38	3.34	3.32	3.29	3.28	3.25	3.24	3.23	7
	12.25	**9.55**	**8.45**	**7.85**	**7.46**	**7.19**	**7.00**	**6.84**	**6.71**	**6.62**	**6.54**	**6.47**	**6.35**	**6.27**	**6.15**	**6.07**	**5.98**	**5.90**	**5.85**	**5.78**	**5.75**	**5.70**	**5.67**	**5.65**	
8	5.32	4.46	4.07	3.84	3.69	3.58	3.50	3.44	3.39	3.34	3.31	3.28	3.23	3.20	3.15	3.12	3.08	3.05	3.03	3.00	2.98	2.96	2.94	2.93	8
	11.26	**8.65**	**7.59**	**7.01**	**6.63**	**6.37**	**6.19**	**6.03**	**5.91**	**5.82**	**5.74**	**5.67**	**5.56**	**5.48**	**5.36**	**5.28**	**5.20**	**5.11**	**5.06**	**5.00**	**4.96**	**4.91**	**4.88**	**4.86**	
9	5.12	4.26	3.86	3.63	3.48	3.37	3.29	3.23	3.18	3.13	3.10	3.07	3.02	2.98	2.93	2.90	2.86	2.82	2.80	2.77	2.76	2.73	2.72	2.71	9
	10.56	**8.02**	**6.99**	**6.42**	**6.06**	**5.80**	**5.62**	**5.47**	**5.35**	**5.26**	**5.18**	**5.11**	**5.00**	**4.92**	**4.80**	**4.73**	**4.64**	**4.56**	**4.51**	**4.45**	**4.41**	**4.36**	**4.33**	**4.31**	
10	4.96	4.10	3.71	3.48	3.33	3.22	3.14	3.07	3.02	2.97	2.94	2.91	2.86	2.82	2.77	2.74	2.70	2.67	2.64	2.61	2.59	2.56	2.55	2.54	10
	10.04	**7.56**	**6.55**	**5.99**	**5.64**	**5.39**	**5.21**	**5.06**	**4.95**	**4.85**	**4.78**	**4.71**	**4.60**	**4.52**	**4.41**	**4.33**	**4.25**	**4.17**	**4.12**	**4.05**	**4.01**	**3.96**	**3.93**	**3.91**	
11	4.84	3.98	3.59	3.36	3.20	3.09	3.01	2.95	2.90	2.86	2.82	2.79	2.74	2.70	2.65	2.61	2.57	2.53	2.50	2.47	2.45	2.42	2.41	2.40	11
	9.65	**7.20**	**6.22**	**5.67**	**5.32**	**5.07**	**4.88**	**4.74**	**4.63**	**4.54**	**4.46**	**4.40**	**4.29**	**4.21**	**4.10**	**4.02**	**3.94**	**3.86**	**3.80**	**3.74**	**3.70**	**3.66**	**3.62**	**3.60**	
12	4.75	3.88	3.49	3.26	3.11	3.00	2.92	2.85	2.80	2.76	2.72	2.69	2.64	2.60	2.54	2.50	2.46	2.42	2.40	2.36	2.35	2.32	2.31	2.30	12
	9.33	**6.93**	**5.95**	**5.41**	**5.06**	**4.82**	**4.65**	**4.50**	**4.39**	**4.30**	**4.22**	**4.16**	**4.05**	**3.98**	**3.86**	**3.78**	**3.70**	**3.61**	**3.56**	**3.49**	**3.46**	**3.41**	**3.38**	**3.36**	

TABLE A-10 The F Distribution (Continued)
(5% (Roman Type) and 1% (Bold Face Type) Points for the Distribution of *F*)

d_1 = Degrees of freedom for numerator

d_2 = Degrees of freedom for denominator

d_2	1	2	3	4	5	6	7	8	9	10	11	12	14	16	20	24	30	40	50	75	100	200	500	∞	d_2
13	4.67	3.80	3.41	3.18	3.02	2.92	2.84	2.77	2.72	2.67	2.63	2.60	2.55	2.51	2.46	2.42	2.38	2.34	2.32	2.28	2.26	2.24	2.22	2.21	13
	9.07	**6.70**	**5.74**	**5.20**	**4.86**	**4.62**	**4.44**	**4.30**	**4.19**	**4.10**	**4.02**	**3.96**	**3.85**	**3.78**	**3.67**	**3.59**	**3.51**	**3.42**	**3.37**	**3.30**	**3.27**	**3.21**	**3.18**	**3.16**	
14	4.60	3.74	3.34	3.11	2.96	2.85	2.77	2.70	2.65	2.60	2.56	2.53	2.48	2.44	2.39	2.35	2.31	2.27	2.24	2.21	2.19	2.16	2.14	2.13	14
	8.86	**6.51**	**5.56**	**5.03**	**4.69**	**4.46**	**4.28**	**4.14**	**4.03**	**3.94**	**3.86**	**3.80**	**3.70**	**3.62**	**3.51**	**3.43**	**3.34**	**3.26**	**3.21**	**3.14**	**3.11**	**3.06**	**3.02**	**3.00**	
15	4.54	3.68	3.29	3.06	2.90	2.79	2.70	2.64	2.59	2.55	2.51	2.48	2.43	2.39	2.33	2.29	2.25	2.21	2.18	2.15	2.12	2.10	2.08	2.07	15
	8.68	**6.36**	**5.42**	**4.89**	**4.56**	**4.32**	**4.14**	**4.00**	**3.89**	**3.80**	**3.73**	**3.67**	**3.56**	**3.48**	**3.36**	**3.29**	**3.20**	**3.12**	**3.07**	**3.00**	**2.97**	**2.92**	**2.89**	**2.87**	
16	4.49	3.63	3.24	3.01	2.85	2.74	2.66	2.59	2.54	2.49	2.45	2.42	2.37	2.33	2.28	2.24	2.20	2.16	2.13	2.09	2.07	2.04	2.02	2.01	16
	8.53	**6.23**	**5.29**	**4.77**	**4.44**	**4.20**	**4.03**	**3.89**	**3.78**	**3.69**	**3.61**	**3.55**	**3.45**	**3.37**	**3.25**	**3.18**	**3.10**	**3.01**	**2.96**	**2.98**	**2.86**	**2.80**	**2.77**	**2.75**	
17	4.45	3.59	3.20	2.96	2.81	2.70	2.62	2.55	2.50	2.45	2.41	2.38	2.33	2.29	2.23	2.19	2.15	2.11	2.08	2.04	2.02	1.99	1.97	1.96	17
	8.40	**6.11**	**5.18**	**4.67**	**4.34**	**4.10**	**3.93**	**3.79**	**3.68**	**3.59**	**3.52**	**3.45**	**3.35**	**3.27**	**3.16**	**3.08**	**3.00**	**2.92**	**2.86**	**2.79**	**2.76**	**2.70**	**2.67**	**2.65**	
18	4.41	3.55	3.16	2.93	2.77	3.66	2.58	2.51	2.46	2.41	2.37	2.34	2.29	2.25	2.19	2.15	2.11	2.07	2.04	2.00	1.98	1.95	1.93	1.92	18
	8.28	**6.01**	**5.09**	**4.58**	**4.25**	**4.01**	**3.85**	**3.71**	**3.60**	**3.51**	**3.44**	**3.37**	**3.27**	**3.19**	**3.07**	**3.00**	**2.91**	**2.83**	**2.78**	**2.71**	**2.68**	**2.62**	**2.59**	**2.57**	
19	4.38	3.52	3.13	2.90	2.74	2.63	2.55	2.48	2.43	2.38	2.34	2.31	2.26	2.21	2.15	2.11	2.07	2.02	2.00	1.96	1.94	1.91	1.90	1.88	19
	8.18	**5.93**	**5.01**	**4.50**	**4.17**	**3.94**	**3.77**	**3.63**	**3.52**	**3.43**	**3.36**	**3.30**	**3.19**	**3.12**	**3.00**	**2.92**	**2.84**	**2.76**	**2.70**	**2.63**	**2.60**	**2.54**	**2.51**	**2.49**	
20	4.35	3.49	3.10	2.87	2.71	2.60	2.52	2.45	2.40	2.35	2.31	2.28	2.23	2.18	2.12	2.08	2.04	1.99	1.96	1.92	1.90	1.87	1.85	1.84	20
	8.10	**5.85**	**4.94**	**4.43**	**4.10**	**3.87**	**3.71**	**3.56**	**3.45**	**3.37**	**3.30**	**3.23**	**3.13**	**3.05**	**2.94**	**2.86**	**2.77**	**2.69**	**2.63**	**2.56**	**2.53**	**2.47**	**2.44**	**2.42**	
21	4.32	3.47	3.07	2.84	2.68	2.57	2.49	2.42	2.37	2.32	2.28	2.25	2.20	2.15	2.09	2.05	2.00	1.96	1.93	1.89	1.87	1.84	1.82	1.81	21
	8.02	**5.78**	**4.87**	**4.37**	**4.04**	**3.81**	**3.65**	**3.51**	**3.40**	**3.31**	**3.24**	**3.17**	**3.07**	**2.99**	**2.88**	**2.80**	**2.72**	**2.63**	**2.58**	**2.51**	**2.47**	**2.42**	**2.38**	**2.36**	
22	4.30	3.44	3.05	2.82	2.66	2.55	2.47	2.40	2.35	2.30	2.26	2.23	2.18	2.13	2.07	2.03	1.98	1.93	1.91	1.87	1.84	1.81	1.80	1.78	22
	7.94	**5.72**	**4.82**	**4.31**	**3.99**	**3.76**	**3.59**	**3.45**	**3.35**	**3.26**	**3.18**	**3.12**	**3.02**	**2.94**	**2.83**	**2.75**	**2.67**	**2.58**	**2.53**	**2.46**	**2.42**	**2.37**	**2.33**	**2.31**	
23	4.28	3.42	3.03	2.80	2.64	2.53	2.45	2.38	2.32	2.28	2.24	2.20	2.14	2.10	2.04	2.00	1.96	1.91	1.88	1.84	1.82	1.79	1.77	1.76	23
	7.88	**5.66**	**4.76**	**4.26**	**3.94**	**3.71**	**3.54**	**3.41**	**3.30**	**3.21**	**3.14**	**3.07**	**2.97**	**2.89**	**2.78**	**2.70**	**2.62**	**2.53**	**2.48**	**2.41**	**2.37**	**2.32**	**2.28**	**2.26**	

TABLE A-10 The F Distribution (Continued)
(5% (Roman Type) and 1% (Bold Face Type) Points for the Distribution of *F*)

d_1 = Degrees of freedom for numerator

d_2 = Degrees of freedom for denominator

d_2	1	2	3	4	5	6	7	8	9	10	11	12	14	16	20	24	30	40	50	75	100	200	500	∞	d_2
24	4.26	3.40	3.01	2.78	2.62	2.51	2.43	2.36	2.30	2.26	2.22	2.18	2.13	2.09	2.02	1.98	1.94	1.89	1.86	1.82	1.80	1.76	1.74	1.73	24
	7.82	**5.61**	**4.72**	**4.22**	**3.90**	**3.67**	**3.50**	**3.36**	**3.25**	**3.17**	**3.09**	**3.03**	**2.93**	**2.85**	**2.74**	**2.66**	**2.58**	**2.49**	**2.44**	**2.36**	**2.33**	**2.27**	**2.23**	**2.21**	
25	4.24	3.38	2.99	2.76	2.60	2.49	2.41	2.34	2.28	2.24	2.20	2.16	2.11	2.06	2.00	1.96	192	1.87	1.84	1.80	1.77	1.74	1.72	1.71	25
	7.77	**5.57**	**4.68**	**4.18**	**3.86**	**3.63**	**3.46**	**3.32**	**3.21**	**3.13**	**3.05**	**2.99**	**2.89**	**2.81**	**2.70**	**2.62**	**2.54**	**2.45**	**2.40**	**2.32**	**2.29**	**2.23**	**2.19**	**2.17**	
26	4.22	3.37	2.98	2.74	2.59	2.47	2.39	2.32	2.27	2.22	2.18	2.15	2.10	2.05	1.99	1.95	1.90	1.85	1.82	1.78	1.76	1.72	1.70	1.69	26
	7.72	**5.53**	**4.64**	**4.14**	**3.82**	**3.59**	**3.42**	**3.29**	**3.17**	**3.09**	**3.02**	**2.96**	**2.86**	**2.77**	**2.66**	**2.58**	**2.50**	**2.41**	**2.36**	**2.28**	**2.25**	**2.19**	**2.15**	**2.13**	
27	4.21	3.35	2.96	2.73	2.57	2.46	2.37	2.30	2.25	2.20	2.16	2.13	2.08	2.03	1.97	1.93	1.88	1.84	1.80	1.76	1.74	1.71	1.68	1.67	27
	7.68	**5.49**	**4.60**	**4.11**	**3.79**	**3.56**	**3.39**	**3.26**	**3.14**	**3.06**	**2.98**	**2.93**	**2.83**	**2.74**	**2.63**	**2.55**	**2.47**	**2.38**	**2.33**	**2.25**	**2.21**	**2.16**	**2.12**	**2.10**	
28	4.20	3.34	2.95	2.71	2.56	2.44	2.36	2.29	2.24	2.19	2.15	2.12	2.06	2.02	1.96	1.91	1.87	1.81	1.78	1.75	1.72	1.69	1.67	1.65	28
	7.64	**5.45**	**4.57**	**4.07**	**3.76**	**3.53**	**3.36**	**3.23**	**3.11**	**3.03**	**2.95**	**2.90**	**2.80**	**2.71**	**2.60**	**2.52**	**2.44**	**2.35**	**2.30**	**2.22**	**2.18**	**2.13**	**2.09**	**2.06**	
29	4.18	3.33	2.93	2.70	2.54	2.43	2.35	2.28	2.22	2.18	2.14	2.10	2.05	2.00	1.94	1.90	1.85	1.80	1.77	1.73	1.71	1.68	1.65	1.64	29
	7.60	**5.42**	**4.54**	**4.04**	**3.73**	**3.50**	**3.33**	**3.20**	**3.08**	**3.00**	**2.92**	**2.87**	**2.77**	**2.68**	**2.57**	**2.49**	**2.41**	**2.32**	**2.27**	**2.19**	**2.15**	**2.10**	**2.06**	**2.03**	
30	4.17	3.32	2.92	2.69	2.53	2.42	2.34	2.27	2.21	2.16	2.12	2.09	2.04	1.99	1.93	1.89	1.84	1.79	1.76	1.72	1.69	1.66	1.64	1.62	30
	7.56	**5.39**	**4.51**	**4.02**	**3.70**	**3.47**	**3.30**	**3.17**	**3.06**	**2.98**	**2.90**	**2.84**	**2.74**	**2.66**	**2.55**	**2.47**	**2.38**	**2.29**	**2.24**	**2.16**	**2.13**	**2.07**	**2.03**	**2.01**	
32	4.15	3.30	2.90	2.67	2.51	2.40	2.32	2.25	2.19	2.14	2.10	2.07	2.02	1.97	1.91	1.86	1.82	1.76	1.74	1.69	1.67	1.64	1.61	1.59	32
	7.50	**5.34**	**4.46**	**3.97**	**3.66**	**3.42**	**3.25**	**3.12**	**3.01**	**2.94**	**2.86**	**2.80**	**2.70**	**2.62**	**2.51**	**2.42**	**2.34**	**2.25**	**2.20**	**2.12**	**2.08**	**2.02**	**1.98**	**1.96**	
34	4.13	3.28	2.88	2.65	2.49	2.38	2.30	2.23	2.17	2.12	2.08	2.05	2.00	1.95	1.89	1.84	1.80	1.74	1.71	1.67	1.64	1.61	1.59	1.57	34
	7.44	**5.29**	**4.42**	**3.93**	**3.61**	**3.38**	**3.21**	**3.08**	**2.97**	**2.89**	**2.82**	**2.76**	**2.66**	**2.58**	**2.47**	**2.38**	**2.30**	**2.21**	**2.15**	**2.08**	**2.04**	**1.98**	**1.94**	**1.91**	
36	4.11	3.26	2.86	2.63	2.48	2.36	2.28	2.21	2.15	2.10	2.06	2.03	1.98	1.93	1.87	1.82	1.78	1.72	1.69	1.65	1.62	1.59	1.56	1.55	36
	7.39	**5.25**	**4.38**	**3.89**	**3.58**	**3.35**	**3.18**	**3.04**	**2.94**	**2.86**	**2.78**	**2.72**	**2.62**	**2.54**	**2.43**	**2.35**	**2.26**	**2.17**	**2.12**	**2.04**	**2.00**	**1.94**	**1.90**	**1.87**	
38	4.10	3.25	2.85	2.62	2.46	2.35	2.26	2.19	2.14	2.09	2.05	2.02	1.96	1.92	1.85	1.80	1.76	1.71	1.67	1.63	1.60	1.57	1.54	1.53	38
	7.35	**5.21**	**4.34**	**3.86**	**3.54**	**3.32**	**3.15**	**3.02**	**2.91**	**2.82**	**2.75**	**2.69**	**2.59**	**2.51**	**2.40**	**2.32**	**2.22**	**2.14**	**2.08**	**2.00**	**1.97**	**1.90**	**1.86**	**1.84**	
40	4.08	3.23	2.84	2.61	2.45	2.34	2.25	2.18	2.12	2.07	2.04	2.00	1.95	1.90	1.84	1.79	1.74	1.69	1.66	1.61	1.59	1.55	1.53	1.51	40
	7.31	**5.18**	**4.31**	**3.83**	**3.51**	**3.29**	**3.12**	**2.99**	**2.88**	**2.80**	**2.73**	**2.66**	**2.56**	**2.49**	**2.37**	**2.29**	**2.20**	**2.11**	**2.05**	**1.97**	**1.94**	**1.88**	**1.84**	**1.81**	

TABLE A-10 The F Distribution (Continued)
(5% (Roman Type) and 1% (Bold Face Type) Points for the Distribution of *F*)

d_1 = Degrees of freedom for numerator

d_2 = Degrees of freedom for denominator

d_2	1	2	3	4	5	6	7	8	9	10	11	12	14	16	20	24	30	40	50	75	100	200	500	∞	d_2
42	4.07	3.22	2.83	2.59	2.44	2.32	2.24	2.17	2.11	2.06	2.02	1.99	1.94	1.89	1.82	1.78	1.73	1.68	1.64	1.60	1.57	1.54	1.51	1.49	42
	7.27	**5.15**	**4.29**	**3.80**	**3.49**	**3.26**	**3.10**	**2.96**	**2.86**	**2.77**	**2.70**	**2.64**	**2.54**	**2.46**	**2.35**	**2.26**	**2.17**	**2.08**	**2.02**	**1.94**	**1.91**	**1.85**	**1.80**	**1.78**	
44	4.06	3.21	2.82	2.58	2.43	2.31	2.23	2.16	2.10	2.05	2.01	1.98	1.92	1.88	1.81	1.76	1.72	1.66	1.63	1.58	1.56	1.52	1.50	1.48	44
	7.24	**5.12**	**4.26**	**3.78**	**3.46**	**3.24**	**3.07**	**2.94**	**2.84**	**2.75**	**2.68**	**2.62**	**2.52**	**2.44**	**2.32**	**2.24**	**2.15**	**2.06**	**2.00**	**1.92**	**1.88**	**1.82**	**1.78**	**1.75**	
46	4.05	3.20	2.81	2.57	2.42	2.30	2.22	2.14	2.09	2.04	2.00	1.97	1.91	1.87	1.80	1.75	1.71	1.65	1.62	1.57	1.54	1.51	1.48	1.46	46
	7.21	**5.10**	**4.24**	**3.76**	**3.44**	**3.22**	**3.05**	**2.92**	**2.82**	**2.73**	**2.66**	**2.60**	**2.50**	**2.42**	**2.30**	**2.22**	**2.13**	**2.04**	**1.98**	**1.90**	**1.86**	**1.80**	**1.76**	**1.72**	
48	4.04	3.19	2.80	2.56	2.41	2.30	2.21	2.14	2.08	2.03	1.99	1.96	1.90	1.86	1.79	1.74	1.70	1.64	1.61	1.56	1.53	1.50	1.47	1.45	48
	7.19	**5.08**	**4.22**	**3.74**	**3.42**	**3.20**	**3.04**	**2.90**	**2.80**	**2.71**	**2.64**	**2.58**	**2.48**	**2.40**	**2.28**	**2.20**	**2.11**	**2.02**	**1.96**	**1.88**	**1.84**	**1.78**	**1.73**	**1.70**	
50	4.03	3.18	2.79	2.56	2.40	2.29	2.20	2.13	2.07	2.02	1.98	1.95	1.90	1.85	1.78	1.74	1.69	1.63	1.60	1.55	1.52	1.48	1.46	1.44	50
	7.17	**5.06**	**4.20**	**3.72**	**3.41**	**3.18**	**3.02**	**2.88**	**2.78**	**2.70**	**2.62**	**2.56**	**2.46**	**2.39**	**2.26**	**2.18**	**2.10**	**2.00**	**1.94**	**1.86**	**1.82**	**1.76**	**1.71**	**1.68**	
55	4.02	3.17	2.78	2.54	2.38	2.27	2.18	2.11	2.05	2.00	1.97	1.93	1.88	1.83	1.76	1.72	1.67	1.61	1.58	1.52	1.50	1.46	1.43	1.41	55
	7.12	**5.01**	**4.16**	**3.68**	**3.37**	**3.15**	**2.98**	**2.85**	**2.75**	**2.66**	**2.59**	**2.53**	**2.43**	**2.35**	**2.23**	**2.15**	**2.06**	**1.96**	**1.90**	**1.82**	**1.78**	**1.71**	**1.66**	**1.64**	
60	4.00	3.15	2.76	2.52	2.37	2.25	2.17	2.10	2.04	1.99	1.95	1.92	1.86	1.81	1.75	1.70	1.65	1.59	1.56	1.50	1.48	1.44	1.41	1.39	60
	7.08	**4.98**	**4.13**	**3.65**	**3.34**	**3.12**	**2.95**	**2.82**	**2.72**	**2.63**	**2.56**	**2.50**	**2.40**	**2.32**	**2.20**	**2.12**	**2.03**	**1.93**	**1.87**	**1.79**	**1.74**	**1.68**	**1.63**	**1.60**	
65	3.99	3.14	2.75	2.51	2.36	2.24	2.15	2.08	2.02	1.98	1.94	1.90	1.85	1.80	1.73	1.68	1.63	1.57	1.54	1.49	1.46	1.42	1.39	1.37	65
	7.04	**4.95**	**4.10**	**3.62**	**3.31**	**3.09**	**2.93**	**2.79**	**2.70**	**2.61**	**2.54**	**2.47**	**2.37**	**2.30**	**2.18**	**2.09**	**2.00**	**1.90**	**1.84**	**1.76**	**1.71**	**1.64**	**1.60**	**1.56**	
70	3.98	3.13	2.74	2.50	2.35	2.23	2.14	2.07	2.01	1.97	1.93	1.89	1.84	1.79	1.72	1.67	1.62	1.56	1.53	1.47	1.45	1.40	1.37	1.35	70
	7.01	**4.92**	**4.08**	**3.60**	**3.29**	**3.07**	**2.91**	**2.77**	**2.67**	**2.59**	**2.51**	**2.45**	**2.35**	**2.28**	**2.15**	**2.07**	**1.98**	**1.88**	**1.82**	**1.74**	**1.69**	**1.62**	**1.56**	**1.53**	
80	3.96	3.11	2.72	2.48	2.33	2.21	2.12	2.05	1.99	1.95	1.91	1.88	1.82	1.77	1.70	1.65	1.60	1.54	1.51	1.45	1.42	1.38	1.35	1.32	80
	6.96	**4.88**	**4.04**	**3.56**	**3.25**	**3.04**	**2.87**	**2.74**	**2.64**	**2.55**	**2.48**	**2.41**	**2.32**	**2.24**	**2.11**	**2.03**	**1.94**	**1.84**	**1.78**	**1.70**	**1.65**	**1.57**	**1.52**	**1.49**	
100	3.94	3.09	2.70	2.46	2.30	2.19	2.10	2.03	1.97	1.92	1.88	1.85	1.79	1.75	1.68	1.63	1.57	1.51	1.48	1.42	1.39	1.34	1.30	1.28	100
	6.90	**4.82**	**3.98**	**3.51**	**3.20**	**2.99**	**2.82**	**2.69**	**2.59**	**2.51**	**2.43**	**2.36**	**2.26**	**2.19**	**2.06**	**1.98**	**1.89**	**1.79**	**1.73**	**1.64**	**1.59**	**1.51**	**1.46**	**1.43**	

TABLE A-10 The F Distribution (Continued)
(5% (Roman Type) and 1% (Bold Face Type) Points for the Distribution of *F*)

d_1 = Degrees of freedom for numerator

d_2 = Degrees of freedom for denominator

d_2	1	2	3	4	5	6	7	8	9	10	11	12	14	16	20	24	30	40	50	75	100	200	500	∞	d_2
125	3.92	3.07	2.68	2.44	2.29	2.17	2.08	2.01	1.95	1.90	1.86	1.83	1.77	1.72	1.65	1.60	1.55	1.49	1.45	1.39	1.36	1.31	1.27	1.25	125
	6.84	**4.78**	**3.94**	**3.47**	**3.17**	**2.95**	**2.79**	**2.65**	**2.56**	**2.47**	**2.40**	**2.33**	**2.23**	**2.15**	**2.03**	**1.94**	**1.85**	**1.75**	**1.68**	**1.59**	**1.54**	**1.46**	**1.40**	**1.37**	
150	3.91	3.06	2.67	2.43	2.27	2.16	2.07	2.00	1.94	1.89	1.85	1.82	1.76	1.71	1.64	1.59	1.54	1.47	1.44	1.37	1.34	1.29	1.25	1.22	150
	6.81	**4.75**	**3.91**	**3.44**	**3.14**	**2.92**	**2.76**	**2.62**	**2.53**	**2.44**	**2.37**	**2.30**	**2.20**	**2.12**	**2.00**	**1.91**	**1.83**	**1.72**	**1.66**	**1.56**	**1.51**	**1.43**	**1.37**	**1.33**	
200	3.89	3.04	2.65	2.41	2.26	2.14	2.05	1.98	1.92	1.87	1.83	1.80	1.74	1.69	1.62	1.57	1.52	1.45	1.42	1.35	1.32	1.26	1.22	1.19	200
	6.76	**4.71**	**3.88**	**3.41**	**3.11**	**2.90**	**2.73**	**2.60**	**2.50**	**2.41**	**2.34**	**2.28**	**2.17**	**2.09**	**1.97**	**1.88**	**1.79**	**1.69**	**1.62**	**1.53**	**1.48**	**1.39**	**1.33**	**1.28**	
400	3.86	3.02	2.62	2.39	2.23	2.12	2.03	1.96	1.90	1.85	1.81	1.78	1.72	1.67	1.60	1.54	1.49	1.42	1.38	1.32	1.28	1.22	1.16	1.13	400
	6.70	**4.66**	**3.83**	**3.36**	**3.06**	**2.85**	**2.69**	**2.55**	**2.46**	**2.37**	**2.29**	**2.23**	**2.12**	**2.04**	**1.92**	**1.84**	**1.74**	**1.64**	**1.57**	**1.47**	**1.42**	**1.32**	**1.24**	**1.19**	
1000	3.85	3.00	2.61	2.38	2.22	2.10	2.02	1.95	1.89	1.84	1.80	1.76	1.70	1.65	1.58	1.53	1.47	1.41	1.36	1.30	1.26	1.19	1.13	1.08	1000
	6.66	**4.62**	**3.80**	**3.34**	**3.04**	**2.82**	**2.66**	**2.53**	**2.43**	**2.34**	**2.26**	**2.20**	**2.09**	**2.01**	**1.89**	**1.81**	**1.71**	**1.61**	**1.54**	**1.44**	**1.38**	**1.28**	**1.19**	**1.11**	
∞	3.84	2.99	2.60	2.37	2.21	2.09	2.01	1.94	1.88	1.83	1.79	1.75	1.69	1.64	1.57	1.52	1.46	1.40	1.35	1.28	1.24	1.17	1.11	1.00	∞
	6.64	**4.60**	**3.78**	**3.32**	**3.02**	**2.80**	**2.64**	**2.51**	**2.41**	**2.32**	**2.24**	**2.18**	**2.07**	**1.99**	**1.87**	**1.79**	**1.69**	**1.59**	**1.52**	**1.41**	**1.36**	**1.25**	**1.15**	**1.00**	

d_2 = Degrees of freedom for denominator

Source: Reprinted by permission from *Statistical Methods* by George W. Snedecor and William G. Cochran, (6th ed.). Ames, Iowa, Iowa State University Press, 1967.

APPENDIX F: BIBLIOGRAPHY

1. Bowen, Earl K. *Statistics with Applications in Management and Economics*, Homewood, Ill., Richard D. Irwin, Inc., 1960.
2. Clark, Charles T., and Schkade, Lawrence L. *Statistical Analysis for Administrative Decisions*, 2nd ed. Cincinnati, Ohio, South-Western Publishing Co., 1974.
3. Croxton, Frederick E., Cowden, Dudley J. and Klein, Sidney. *Applied General Statistics*, 3rd ed. Englewood Cliffs, N.J., Prentice-Hall, 1967.
4. Daniel, Wayne W., and Terrell, James C. *Business Statistics*, Boston, Houghton-Mifflin Co., 1975.
5. Dyckman, Thomas R., and Thomas, L. Joseph. *Fundamental Statistics for Business and Economics*, Englewood Cliffs, N.J., Prentice-Hall, 1977.
6. Fruend, John E., and Williams, Frank J. (Revised by Benjamin Perles and Charles Sullivan), *Modern Business Statistics*, Englewood Cliffs, N.J., Prentice-Hall, 1969.
7. Fruend, John E., and Williams, Frank J. *Elementary Business Statistics, The Modern Approach*, 3rd ed. Englewood Cliffs, N.J., Prentice-Hall, 1974.
8. Griffin, John J. *Statistics, Methods and Applications*, New York, Holt, Rinehart and Winston, 1962.
9. Hamburg, Morris, *Statistical Analysis for Decision Making*, 2nd ed. New York, Harcourt, Brace, Jovanovich, Inc., 1977.
10. Hanson, Kermit O. *Managerial Statistics*, New York, Prentice-Hall, Inc., 1955.
11. Harnett, Donald L., and Murphy, James L. *Introductory Statistical Analysis*, Reading, Mass., Addison-Wesley Publishing Company, Inc., 1976.
12. Hoel, Paul G., and Jessen, Raymond J. *Basic Statistics for Business and Economics* 2nd ed. Santa Barbara, John Wiley and Sons, 1977.
13. Lapin, Lawrence, *Statistics for Modern Business Decisions*, 2nd ed. New York, Harcourt, Brace, Jovanovich, Inc., 1978.
14. Leabo, Dick A. *Basic Statistics*, 3rd ed. Homewood, Ill., Richard D. Irwin, Inc., 1968.
15. Lewis, Edward E. *Methods of Statistical Analysis in Economics and Business*, 2nd ed. Boston, Houghton-Mifflin Co., 1963.
16. Mason, Robert D. *Statistical Techniques in Business and Economics*, 4th ed. Homewood, Ill., Richard D. Irwin, 1978.
17. Malik, Henrick, J., and Mullen, Kenneth. *Applied Statistics for Business and Economics*, Reading, Mass., Addison-Wesley Publishing Co., 1975.
18. McAllister, Harry E. *Elements of Business and Economics Statistics*, New York, John Wiley and Sons, Inc., 1975.
19. Mills, Frederick C. *Introduction to Statistics*, New York, Henry Holt and Company, 1956.

20. Neiswanger, William A. *Elementary Statistical Methods* (Rev. ed.). New York, The Macmillan Company, 1956.

21. Nelson, Boyd L. *Elements of Modern Statistics for Students of Economics and Business*, New York, Appleton-Century-Crofts, Inc., 1961.

22. Neter, John, and Wasserman, William. *Fundamental Statistics for Business and Economics*, 3rd ed. Boston, Allyn and Bacon, Inc., 1966.

23. Paden, Donald W., and Linquist, E. F. *Statistics for Economics and Business*, New York, McGraw-Hill Book Company, Inc., 1951.

24. Richmond, Samuel B. *Statistical Analysis*, 2nd ed. New York, The Ronald Press Company, 1964.

25. Shao, Stephen P. *Statistics for Business and Economics*, 3rd ed. Columbus, Ohio, Charles E. Merrill Publ. Co., 1976.

26. Simpson, George, and Kafka, Fritz. *Basic Statistics*, New York, W. W. Norton and Company, Inc., 1957.

27. Spurr, William A., Kellog, Lester S., and Smith, John H. *Business and Economic Statistics*, (Rev. Ed.), Homewood, Ill., Richard D. Irwin, Inc., 1961.

28. Spurr, William A., and Bonini, Charles P. *Statistical Analysis for Business Decision*, (Rev. Ed.), Homewood, Ill., Richard D. Irwin, Inc., 1973.

29. Stockton, John R., and Clark, Charles T. *Introduction to Business and Economic Statistics*, 5th ed. Cincinnati, Ohio, South-Western Publishing Co., 1975.

APPENDIX G: ANSWERS TO EVEN-NUMBERED PROBLEMS

Chapter 4

2. $G - 1 = 1.07 - 1 = 0.07 = 7\%$

4. $\overline{X} = 22{,}625$; $M_e = 22{,}857$; $M_o = 23{,}182$

6. $\overline{X} = 42.7 \qquad H = 42.2$

   Harmonic mean is the best answer to the question.

Chapter 5

2. $$V_1 = \frac{\sigma_1}{\overline{X}_1} = \frac{7.07}{15} = 0.471$$

   $$V_2 = \frac{\sigma_2}{\overline{X}_2} = \frac{7.13}{15} = 0.475$$

   The second list is more varied since V_2 is larger than V_1.

4. (a) $\overline{X} > M_o$, therefore skewed to the right
(b) $M_o = 1018$
(c) $Q_1 = 955$; $Q_2 = 1050$

6. $Q_1 = 410.55$ for Class I
$Q_3 = 668.23$ for Class I
$Q_1 = 585.42$ for Class II
$Q_3 = 763.93$ for Class II

8. For ungrouped data: $\overline{X} = 37.65$; $Q_{\text{Dev}} = 7.75$; M.D. $= 9.48$; $\sigma = 11.48$; $V = 0.30$
For grouped data: $\overline{X} = 37.00$; $Q_{\text{Dev}} = 8.00$; M.D. $= 9.00$ $\sigma = 10.9$; $V = 0.29$
Answers for grouped and ungrouped data differ because measures for grouped data are estimates.

10. $$SK = \frac{M_3^2}{M_2^3} = \frac{(137.29)^2}{(33.14)^3} = 0.52$$

12. $$SK = \frac{M_3^2}{M_2^3} = \frac{(-0.2244)^2}{(1.3244)^3} = 0.0217$$

$$Kur = \frac{M_4}{M_2^2} = \frac{4.0425}{(1.3244)^2} = 2.305$$

Chapter 6

2. 0.05 (assuming the grade made in each course is independent of that of the other).
4. 0.56
6. (a) 12 complete chances
(b) 1/12
8. 0.6
10. 24 displays
12. 1/18
14. 0.1
16. 1/3 or 0.333

Chapter 7

2. $P(3) = 0.0256$

4. $$\begin{aligned}(0.3 + 0.7)^6 &= (0.3)^6 + 6(0.3)^5(0.7) + 15(0.3)^4(0.7)^2 + 20(0.3)^3(0.7)^3 \\ &\quad + 15(0.3)^2(0.7)^4 + 6(0.3)(0.7)^5 + (0.7)^6 \\ &= 0.000729 + 0.010206 + 0.059535 + 0.18522 + 0.324135 \\ &\quad + 0.302525 + 0.117649 = 1\end{aligned}$$

6. $$\left(\frac{1}{4} + \frac{3}{4}\right)^5 = \frac{1}{1024} + \frac{15}{1024} + \frac{90}{1024} + \frac{270}{1024} + \frac{405}{1024} + \frac{243}{1024} = 1$$

8. 0.2304; 0.01024
10. 7/9
12. 7.1

14. 0.88250; 0.48675; 0.19790; 0.02612; 0.01111

16. 0.6827, 0.8664, 0.1359

18. (a) 15.87 and 15.87, (b) 2.5 and 2.5, (c) 5, (d) 0.5 and 0.5, (e) 1, (f) 0.13 and 0.13, (g) 5 and 5, (h) 10, (i) 1 and 1, (j) 2

20. $P(2) = 0.184$ $P(2 \text{ or more}) = 0.264$

Chapter 8

2.
$$z = \frac{\overline{X}_s - \overline{X}_u}{\sigma_{\overline{x}}} = \frac{152 - 150}{2.5} = 0.8$$

A separation of 0.8 standard errors could easily happen by chance. Therefore, it is believable that the sample is random.

4. $17,855 to $19,145 for infinite universe
$17,932 to $19,068 for universe of 1,000

6. 60 for error of $4 or less
240 for error of $2 or less

8. Many answers are possible

10. 930 ± 2.821(87) = 685 to 1,175 customers

12. $z = 1.33$. A z of this size or larger could occur 18.4 times out of 100 as a result of random errors of sampling. Therefore it is reasonable to conclude that the sample is random. The probability that a simple random sample of 1,000 households would show that 70% or more heat with gas is 0.500000 − 0.40824 = 0.092.

14. 53.4% to 66.6%

16. 53.7% to 56.3%

18. 666

20. 24%

Chapter 9

2. Yes, a separation this small could have easily been due to random errors of sampling.

$$z = \frac{X_s - \overline{X}_u}{\sigma_{\overline{x}}} = \frac{13{,}400 - 14{,}000}{481} = -1.25$$

4. Hypothesis is accepted

$$z = \frac{\overline{X}_{s1} - \overline{X}_{s2}}{\sigma_{D_{\overline{x}}}} = \frac{37 - 33}{5.22} = 0.77$$

6. t from t table at 0.05 level for 16 degrees of freedom for one tail is 1.746; therefore the hypothesis is accepted.

$$t = \frac{\overline{X}_s - \overline{X}_h}{\sigma_{\overline{x}}} = \frac{24 - 25}{0.75} = -1.33$$

8. −2.58 is the significance ratio at the 0.01 level; therefore the hypothesis is accepted.

$$z = \frac{p_s - p_h}{\sigma_{\%}} = \frac{41 - 45}{2.5} = -1.6$$

10. 3.125 is larger than the significance ratio at the 0.01 level; therefore, the belief is validated.

$$z = \frac{p_{s_1} - p_{s_2}}{\sigma_{D\%}} = \frac{60 - 50}{3.2} = 3.125$$

12. The difference is significant.

$$z = \frac{p_{s_2} - p_{s_2}}{\sigma_{D\%}} = \frac{45 - 50}{1.06} = 4.7$$

14. Answers will vary.

Chapter 10

2. For columns, $F_{(2,6)} = 19.3$
For rows, $F_{(3,6)} = 0.5$
(1) The hypothesis is rejected.
(2) The hypothesis is accepted.

4. $F_{(2,22)} = 1.07$. Hypothesis is accepted.

Chapter 11

4. $\chi^2 = 9.33$ Which is too large to attribute to chance. The claim is not validated.

6. $\chi^2 = 15.385$. Which is larger than 15.500 the table chi-square value at the 0.05 level. Therefore, the hypothesis is accepted.

8. H(adjusted) = 16.428, Which is significant at the 0.05 level. The null hypothesis is rejected.

10. There is no significant difference in gasoline mileage.

$$z = \frac{X - 0.5 - NPu}{\sigma} = \frac{8 - 0.5 - 15(0.5)}{1.94} = 0$$

12. This separation is greater than −1.96. The hypothesis is rejected. Demand for service was not random.

$$z = \frac{R - E_R}{\sigma_{\%}} = \frac{22 - 30.7}{3.8} = -2.28$$

Chapter 12

2. $Y_c = a + bX = 15.77 - 0.00746X$
when $X = 163$, $Y_c = 15.77 - 0.0075(163) = 14.6$
when $X = 200$, $Y_c = 15.77 - 0.0075(200) = 14.3$
when $X = 220$, $Y_c = 15.77 + 0.0075(220) = 14.1$

4. $Y_c = a + bX = -2.59 + 0.16X$
In County 2, $X = 90$ and $Y_c = -2.59 + 0.16(90) = 11.8$
In County 6, $X = 150$ and $Y_c = -2.59 + 0.16(150) = 21.4$
In County 10, $X = 110$ and $Y_c = -2.59 + 0.16(110) = 15.0$
$r^2 = 0.9542$, which means that 95.42% of the variation in Y has been explained by the variation in X.
$r = \sqrt{0.9542} = +0.98$. r is positive because b is positive. The high coefficient means a close correlation exists.

6. $Y_c = 129.76 + 0.0004X$
$\sigma_{y_u} = 197.86$
$r = +0.97$

8. $r_{rank} = +0.11$. This means there is a very small relationship between the ranked series.

10. $r_{rank} = +0.965$

12. $Y_c = a + bX = -0.952 + 1.174(6.78) = 7.01$

14. $Y_c = a + bX + cX^2 = 21.19 - 1.897X + 0.0344X^2$

16. Answers vary

18. $r = 0.16$. This differs slightly from r computed in Problem 3 because of rounding errors.

Chapter 13

2. $X_{c_1} = -6.6861 + 0.0266(200) + 0.0723(300) = 20.32$
so the estimate is \$20,320. This estimate is quite close because $\sigma_{u_{1.23}} = 0.86$ or about \$860.

4. Answers for a computer program without adjustments for sample data are:
$X_{c_1} = -6.7019167 + 0.026680842\,X_2 + 0.072344959X_3$
$\sigma_{u_{1.23}} = 0.8515$
$R^2_{1.23} = 0.97693$ $\quad R_{1.23} = 0.98840$

6. Answers for a computer program without adjustments for sample data are:
(A) For three variables X_1, X_2, and X_3
$X_{c_{1.23}} = 15.629228 - 0.062152278X_2 + 0.58301979X_2$
$\sigma_{u_{1.23}} = 8.4193$
$r^2_{13.2} = 0.5273517$ $\quad r_{13.2} = 0.7261899$
$r^2_{12.3} = 0.0163866$ $\quad r_{12.3} = -0.1280$
$R^2_{1.23} = 0.55116$ $\quad r_{1.23} = 0.74240$
(B) For Variables X_1, X_2, X_3, and X_4
$X_{c_{1.234}} = -46.612335 + 0.16654766X_2 + 0.86797583X_3 - 0.03062015X_4$
$\sigma_{u_{1.234}} = 5.2668$
$R^2_{1.234} = 0.82435$ $\quad R_{1.234} = 0.9079$

8. $r^2_{13.2} = 0.6317$

10. $r^2_{1.23} = 0.86625$

Chapter 14

2. -0.4%

4. Deflated sales in billions are: 1970 = \$381, 1971 = \$393, 1972 = \$417, 1973 = \$441, 1974 = \$424, 1975 = \$422

6. $I_{1973} = 117.2$ $I_{1974} = 258.5$

8. $I_{1970} = 94.9$ $I_{1974} = 90.5$

10. $I_{1974} = 83.57$ = a 16.43% decline

Chapter 16

2. $Y_c = 83.3 + 8.14X + 3.07X^2$ $Y_c 1976 = 201$
$\log Y_c = 1.9716 + 0.0347X$ $Y_c 1976 = 140$

4. $Y_c = 60.26 + 12.37(5) = 122.1$
$Y_c = 56.6 + 12.37(5) + 0.548(25) = 132.2$

6. $$Y_c = \frac{443}{12} + \frac{18.54}{144}X = 36.92 + 0.129X$$

Three monthly-trend values are:
$Y_{c\ \text{Jan. } 1968} = 36.92 + 0.129(-41.5) = 31.6$
$Y_{c\ \text{July } 1971} = 36.92 + 0.129(0.5) = 37.0$
$Y_{c\ \text{Dec. } 1974} = 36.92 + 0.129(41.5) = 42.3$

8. $Y_c = 10.55 - 0.3582X$
$Y_{c1976} = 10.55 - 0.36(7) = 8.0$
$Y_c = 10.3 - 0.36X + 0.021X^2$
$Y_{c1976} = 10.3 - 0.36(7) + 0.021(49) = 8.8$

10. $Y_c = 89.69 + 3.37X$
$Y_{c1977} = 89.69 + 3.37(11) = 126.8$

Chapter 17

2. $$Y_c = \frac{460.7}{12} + \frac{39.04}{144}X = 384 + 0.27X$$

$Y_{c\text{Jan. } 1976} = 38.4 + .27(42.5) = 49.9$
The other required calculations are:

MONTH	*1976* $T \times S$	*1977* $T \times S$
Jan.	44.3	47.1
Feb.	42.7	45.6
Mar.	49.2	52.5
Apr.	50.1	53.3
May	52.8	56.2
June	52.7	56.1
July	51.9	55.1
Aug.	52.2	55.4
Sept.	50.6	53.9
Oct.	53.6	56.9
Nov.	54.3	57.6
Dec.	62.4	66.3

4. Seasonal Index is: I = 84.6, II = 112.5, III = 108.0, IV = 94.9. Deseasonalized data are:

	I	*II*	*III*	*IV*
1968	76	73	81	91
1969	104	95	105	109
1970	92	97	107	103
1971	106	117	139	132
1972	145	143	138	151
1973	163	153	135	118
1974	102	99	78	51

6. Answers will vary, however, they should be close to the following:
Seasonal Index: I = 90, II = 101, III = 100, IV = 109
1976 Est.: I = 27.1, II = 30.4, III = 30.1, IV = 32.8
1976 Est.: I = 25.9, II 29.7, III 30.4, IV = 34.5

Chapter 18

2. $C \times I$ values are: 1969 = 103.9, 1970 = 99.6, 1971 = 97.2, 1972 = 97.5, 1973 = 112.3, 1974 = 99.9, 1975 = 101.2

4. For data unadjusted for trend:
$r = -0.304$
For data adjusted for trend:
$r = -0.5112$

Index

B

C

D

E

F

G

H

I

J

K

L

M

N

O

P

Q

R

S

W